0121824

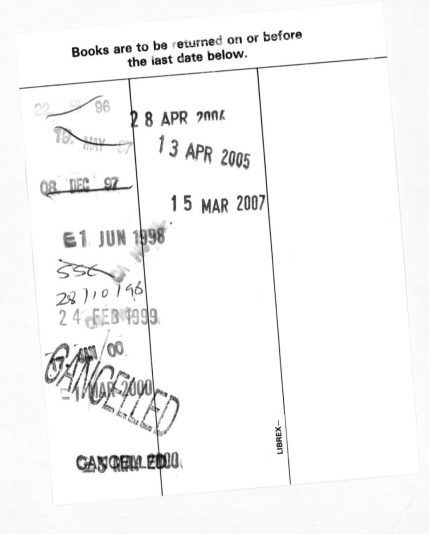

**Books are to be returned on or before
the last date below.**

22 FEB 96	2 8 APR 2004	
19 MAY 97	1 3 APR 2005	
08 DEC 97	1 5 MAR 2007	
E1 JUN 1998		
SSC		
28/10/96		
2 4 FEB 1999		

LIBREX—

CANCELLED

0300065310

Gender, Sex and Subordination
in England 1500–1800

Gender, Sex and Subordination in England 1500–1800

Anthony Fletcher

YALE UNIVERSITY PRESS
NEW HAVEN AND LONDON · 1995

Set in Bembo by Best-set Typesetter Ltd, Hong Kong
Printed and bound in Great Britain by the Bath Press, Avon

Library of Congress Cataloging-in-Publication Data

Fletcher, Anthony.
  Gender, sex, and subordination in England 1500–1800/Anthony Fletcher.
  Includes bibliographical references and index.
  ISBN 0–300–06531–0
  1. Sex role – England – History. 2. Patriarchy – England – History – 16th century. 3. Patriarchy – England – History – 17th century. 4. England – Social conditions – History. 5. Sex role in literature. I. Title.
HQ1075.5.E5F54 1995
305.3'0942 – dc20

95–21565
CIP

A catalogue record for this book is available from the British Library.

Contents

Plates

Readers of this book will find references to the plates, which have been chosen to illustrate some of its main themes and arguments, at appropriate points in the text. At the same time the plates are presented in such a way as to tell their own story. They appear in four distinct and, in each case roughly, chronological sequences. Those between pages 138 and 139 illustrate successively the themes of Dangerous Women (plates 1–11), Cosmological Gender (plates 12–18) and Constructing Gender (plates 19–25). Those between pages 298 and 299 juxtapose a series of images of early modern gender which, besides being informative, have been chosen as contrasting and striking.

Preface and Acknowledgements

A GOOD DEAL of research on gender in early modern England has been published in recent years but this book is the first attempt at a general survey. It will be obvious from the notes that, though I have made selective use of primary sources, I have been enormously dependent upon the work of others. I see the book not so much as a synthesis – it is too early for that – as a first map of a new historical country, a map that is likely quickly to appear primitive as further work is published. My intention has been to provide an initial argument about an aspect of the social landscape that until not long ago was almost entirely neglected. I am concerned with changing attitudes to the meaning of gender over a period of three hundred years from 1500 to 1800. I believe this is an important aspect of the overall agenda of British social history which can be defined as understanding ourselves in time.

In the absence of any extensive historical literature on my subject, I have sought inspiration and help in conceptualising gender in a period two hundred and more years remote from our own time by reading beyond historical works. There are several books I should like to mention here which have been important to me in coming to grips with the subject: Danah Zohar's *The Quantum Self*, an exploration of 'human nature and consciousness rooted in the new physics', brought home to me how important it is for historians to appreciate that Cartesian philosophy and Newtonian physics together created our world view and more particularly our notions about the relationship between mind and body. Working on gender in and before the seventeenth century, I have had to keep reminding myself that the triumph of that world view – and the cultural conditioning it has given us – was not then at all obvious. My thinking about masculinity has been deeply influenced by insights gained from two books, one by a poet and storyteller and the other a profoundly pondered monograph in the field of psychology. Robert Bly based his book *Iron John* around a fairy tale which was first set down by the Grimm brothers around 1820 but which could be, as he says, ten or twenty thousand years old. The book is unclassifiable: besides poetry it is full of anthropology, psychology, mythology and folklore. In his treatment of the Iron John legend, Bly reaches for timeless issues concerning gender and the nature of manhood. Liam Hudson and Bernadine Jacot's *The Way Men Think* is a study of the male mind, men's attitudes to intimacy and their erotic imagination. Its central argument, that infant boys experience a developmental crisis as they distance themselves from their mother's love and establish themselves as male, seems to me highly relevant to much of the historical material I have used about boys' schooling and about male sexuality in the early modern period. In *The Transformation of Intimacy* Anthony Giddens has written a powerful work of modern sociology which is informed by a historical perspective on romantic love and femininity. I have found this very helpful in seeking to understand what may have been beginning to happen to marriage relationships in the eighteenth century. I learnt from Carole Pateman's *The Sexual Contract*, a deeply persuasive feminist reinterpretation of early modern and modern political theory, how crucial it is for the historian to watch for men's silence about women and probe its full meaning as one reads key texts. Finally, I have greatly valued Lisa Jardine's *Still Harping on Daughters*, a book written in the early 1980s by someone who was engaged in research on intellectual history but was at the time thinking about English Renaissance literature. Her particular methodological position, which she described in 1989 in the preface to a new edition of the book, as 'somewhere strategically between history, text criticism and social anthropology', seems to me a most fruitful one. While, as she admits, her position in a literary field which has become something of a battleground was not always comfortable, her focus upon the relation between female characters in Shakespearean and Jacobean drama and beliefs about women who lived in the period is highly illuminating. It has encouraged me to tread interdisciplinary boundaries with, I hope, some of the same boldness.

The personal acknowledgements I must make at the start of this book are just as important as these intellectual ones. Without the support of the Nuffield Foundation, which generously granted me a Research Fellowship for the academic year 1992–3, and of the University of Durham, which granted me periods of research leave in 1989 and 1994, the book would scarcely have been written. When I tried out some of my ideas on audiences in a number of universities on the east coast and in the mid west of the United States in 1992, I was invigorated by the quantities of interest and friendly criticism that I received. Since then I have spoken about early modern gender at seminars in the universities of Cambridge, Durham, Edinburgh, Lancaster, London and Oxford and have been grateful for the many helpful comments and questions that have made me stop and think. I have received much benefit from, and am most grateful for, the detailed comments made by scholars with a particular expertise on certain chapters: Judith Bennett on chapter 12, Jeremy Black and John

Tosh on chapter 16, Ingrid Tague and Sarah Salih on chapter 19. Cynthia Herrup and Lyndal Roper have been generous in the time they have given to reading the whole book. I have made many revisions which arise from their acute critical commentaries. My wife Tresna, Elizabeth Foyster and Claire Harbottle have also commented helpfully on draft chapters. The bibliography was kindly prepared by Elizabeth Foyster and the index by Helen Berry. In Durham, Christopher Brooks, Brian Gibbons and Tim Stretton have been unwearied by numerous conversations about gender. My godmother, Anne Wilson, provided information about the portrait which appears on the cover, an unusual and illuminating statement of patriarchal mastership which no visitor to Parham House in Sussex should miss. Errors which remain in the text which follows of course remain entirely my own responsibility. I am especially grateful to Wendy Duery for her unfailing patience in producing a wordprocessed version of the whole text suitable for the printer.

Durham, October 1994   A.J.F.

Abbreviations

BIHR	*Bulletin of the Institute of Historical Research*
BL	British Library
Capp	B. Capp, *The World of John Taylor the Water-Poet* (Oxford, 1994)
Erickson	A.L. Erickson, *Women and Property in Early Modern England* (London, 1993)
Gibbons	B. Gibbons, 'Gender in British Behmenist Thought', University of Durham PhD thesis, 1993
Gowing	L. Gowing, 'Women, Sex and Honour: The London Church Courts 1572–1640', University of London PhD thesis, 1993
HEH	Henry Huntingdon Library, San Marino, California
HMC	*Historical Manuscripts Commission*
OED	*Oxford English Dictionary*
Pepys	R.C. Latham and W. Matthews, eds, *The Diary of Samuel Pepys*, 11 volumes (London, 1970–83)
PRO	Public Record Office
Roxburghe	W. Chappell, ed., *The Roxburghe Ballads*, vols I–III (London, 1871–80)
Tilley	M.P. Tilley, *A Dictionary of Proverbs in England in the Sixteenth and Seventeenth Centuries* (Ann Arbor, 1950)
TRHS	*Transactions of the Royal Historical Society*
Verney	F.P. Verney, *Memoirs of the Verney Family During the Civil War*, 4 volumes (London, 1970)

You are forced to consider what you feel about love . . . they are in receipt of this great poet with these great truths about human behaviour which I certainly find a great comfort, a great spiritual comfort that this genius from 400 years ago talking about people from 400 years ago makes me feel as though I am not the only stupid prat still kicking about being silly in life and in love.

Kenneth Branagh on the audiences for his film version of *Much Ado about Nothing*[1]

Emma Woodhouse, handsome, clever, and rich, with a comfortable home and happy disposition, seemed to unite some of the best blessings of existence . . . Mr Knightley, a sensible man about seven or eight-and-thirty, was not only a very old and intimate friend of the family but particularly connected with it as the elder brother of Isabella's husband.

Jane Austen, *Emma*[2]

There are times in life when the question of knowing if one can think differently than one thinks, and perceive differently than one sees, is absolutely necessary if one is to go on looking and reflecting at all.

Michel Foucault[3]

1. BBC2, 9 September 1993.
2. J. Austen, *Emma*, ed. R. Blythe (London, 1966), pp. 37, 41.
3. M. Foucault, *The Use of Pleasure* (London, 1987), p. 8.

Introduction

LITTLE MORE THAN two hundred years separates the first performances of *Much Ado about Nothing* and the publication of *Emma*. Yet these two literary works express quite different worlds of gender. Shakespeare's men and women relate to each other, see themselves as males and females, quite differently from Jane Austen's. Something has changed between 1600 and 1800. Gender is both relational and organisational: it 'inhabits social structures, practices and the imagination' while it is also 'an organising principle of social structures, institutions and practices'.[1] In other words, it is about both love and power. Kenneth Branagh spoke of love on television in September 1993 when he told of the comfort he himself found in the 'great truths about human behaviour' of *Much Ado*. His collective project, with those he gathered around him in a Tuscan villa, had been to explore those truths through a contemporary idiom, so he could bring them to an audience many times larger than has ever seen or is likely to see the play. But Branagh's text was historically anchored in the 1590s just as *Emma* belongs to 1812. This does not make the truths people feel from these works less truths. The challenge for the historian, however, is to reveal something of the mental world of the first Beatrice and Benedict, the first Claudio and Hero; and of the mental world in turn of Jane Austen's Emma Woodhouse and Mr Knightley. That is the challenge which this book, in the spirit of Michel Foucault's advice cited above, seeks to answer.

There are problems of terminology at the outset. A crucial term is patriarchy, which is still only on the edge of the discourse of early modern British historians. I mean by the term the institutionalised male dominance over women and children in the family and the subordination of women in society in general. This seems to me to be an outstandingly significant feature of English society between 1500 and 1800 which is crying out for investigation. But we should be clear that this book is

---

1. M. Roper and J. Tosh, *Manful Assertions: Masculinities in Britain since 1800* (London, 1991), p. 11.

about a single historical patriarchy. When socialist and radical feminists took up the notion of patriarchy in the 1960s they were looking for a concept which would help them to theorise as well as historicise male dominance. The trouble with some of this work was that it tended to assume that patriarchy was and is immovable and monumental. It also became, in this reading, a system fired by an undifferentiated and consistent male commitment to domination and control in every sphere of life.[2] In an article reviewing the historiography of patriarchy in 1989, Judith Bennett suggested that the historical study of the subject has since those first days been undercut by an ambivalence about the term, an excessive concern about its origins, and a decision by some feminist historians to concentrate more on women's agency than women's oppression. The term does of course carry powerful resonances of women's oppression and some have found it offensive for this reason. But the case that Bennett makes for the study of patriarchy as a historical phenomenon is nevertheless overwhelming. The core of her argument is that 'patriarchy clearly has existed in many forms and varieties and its history will in fact be a history of many different historical patriarchies'. Patriarchy, in other words, has been shaped and reshaped during the long history of Western Christendom as men have grappled with the effective exercise of social and political power. The structures of domination which sustain patriarchy have never been inert, they have always been adaptable; they were never entirely solid, they always were and still are adjustable. Women have been the agents of, and have often colluded in, patriarchy as well as resisting it; men have shown uncertainties and unease about implementing dominating or exclusive roles. In studying patriarchy's many forms, Bennett advises, 'we must trace not only how the mechanisms of any given patriarchy changed over time but also how those mechanisms affected different women in different ways'.[3] This book is a case study of the kind she proposes that we need. It focuses upon a historical period which seems to exhibit features of crisis in men's control over women. This makes the examination of how patriarchy was adapted and survived between 1500 and 1800 exceptionally interesting.

Whereas at the start of our period gender was not rooted in an understanding of the body, at the end it was becoming so. For gender in Tudor England was still a cosmological principle. It shaped sex rather than the other way round. Woman was seen as a creature distinct from and inferior to man, distinguished by her lesser heat. For heat was the source of strength, and strength, whether of mind, body or moral faculties, was in this formulation what gender was all about. Heat, as the immortal substance of life, was the most crucial element in the humoral physiology.

2. E.g. K. Millet, *Sexual Politics* (London, 1977); for an overview see Roper and Tosh, *Manful Assertions*, pp. 7–11.
3. J.M. Bennett, 'Feminism and History', *Gender and History* 1 (1989), pp. 259–63.

An individual's sexual temperament, in effect gender, was a question of the balance in the body of the hot and cold, dry and moist qualities.[4] This gender system had nothing whatsoever to do with the sexual orientation of men and women. Nor was the visible genital difference, except in so far as it reflected and symbolised someone's place on the continuum between human strength and weakness, of significance. Sex, in other words, was still a sociological and not an ontological category.[5] The point is well made by a passage in *As You Like It*. Rosalind, dressed as a young man Ganymede, and Celia, dressed as his maid Aliena, arrive exhausted in the Forest of Arden. 'I could find it in my heart to disgrace my man's apparel and to cry like a woman,' muses Rosalind, 'but I must comfort the weaker vessel, as doublet and hose ought to show itself courageous to petticoat.' 'Therefore', she declares, turning to her companion, 'courage good Aliena.'[6] The Elizabethan audience, watching a boy in masquerade as a man but actually playing a girl, could identify all the nuances of these lines. Thus the institutions of English patriarchy, inherited from Hebrew and early Christian societies, rested upon twin pillars: the subordination required of women as a punishment for Eve's sin, which was fundamental to biblical teaching, and an understanding of men's and women's bodies, evident among early modern medical writers whose works we will review, in terms of relative strength and weakness. Patriarchy was thus founded upon God's direction and woman's natural physical inferiority. The crucial link was that between the weakness of mind and conscience which caused the first emblematic act of disobedience and the weakness of body which, connected to their reproductive functions, deprived women of a constant public role.

The body was at the centre of Tudor thinking about gender, but not in the sense that we understand the physical aspect of gender identity. People's minds and bodies – the two were not yet disconnected by Cartesian thinking – were seen to be on a continuum from strength to weakness: gender, resting on a single positive principle of manhood, took its meaning from the superior strength of around half the nation. Yet there was not an incommensurable difference between men and women, and exceptional women, as we shall see, could receive praise for showing more strength than many ordinary men. The essence of this gender scheme was overlap. The boundaries could be crossed both ways: manhood, learnt, practised and prized, might always degenerate into effeminacy.[7] This is a wholly different mental world from that of the 1980s and 1990s in which the body has become a contentious academic

4. L. Schiebinger, *The Mind has no Sex?* (Cambridge, Massachusetts, 1989), pp. 161–2.
5. T. Laqueur, *Making Sex: Body and Gender from the Greeks to Freud* (Cambridge, Massachusetts, 1990), p. 8.
6. *As You Like It*, act II, scene iv, 3–7.
7. This theme is explored fully in chapter 6 below.

territory.[8] Some recent writers have tended to empty biological sex of its content to the extent that the body threatens to disappear altogether. The construction of gender has almost entirely taken over. Sherry Ortner and Harriet Whitehead open their introduction to a collection of anthropological papers relating to many parts of the world with an attack upon the bias that they believe underlies studies of sex roles and male dominance: 'an assumption that we know what "men" and "women" are, an assumption that male and female are predominantly natural objects rather than predominantly cultural constructions'. Their volume focuses upon 'gender and sexuality as cultural (symbolic) constructs'.[9] For Joan Scott gender is a 'primary way of signifying relationships of power'.[10] The feminist legal scholar Catherine Mackinnon argues that gender is the division of men and women caused 'by the social requirements of heterosexuality'. Using the terms sex and gender almost interchangeably, she talks of social relations 'organised so that men may dominate and women must submit'.[11] We must take account, on the other side of the balance, of the findings of leading psychologists like Liam Hudson and Bernadine Jacot who, in their account of the origins of modern gender identity, attribute a significant role to genetic make up.[12] However deeply we explore culture we cannot in the end ignore the body. 'It is obvious that sex is something more than what society designates', writes Jeffrey Weeks, 'or what naming makes it.'[13]

The emergence of the history of gender as a serious branch of the discipline owes an enormous amount to the rise of modern feminism and its impact on the redefinition of history's subject matter. The drive to reveal the history of women has led to an intense interest in the private sphere of human activity and a new approach to the public sphere. It has proved just as interesting to explore the strategies of exclusion men have employed in areas where women were given no role at all, such as in political thought, as the particular activities, such as childrearing, which have traditionally been seen as central to their existence. Predictably women's history has broken its own boundaries, leading to investigation

8. L. Segal, *Is the Future Female? Troubled Thoughts on Contemporary Feminism* (London, 1987) and L. Segal *Slow Motion: Changing Masculinities, Changing Men* (London, 1990) provide succinct accounts of recent debates about the body and gender. J. Stoltenberg, *Refusing to be a Man* (London, 1990) is a powerful examination of the issue of male sexual identity.

9. S.B. Ortner and H. Whitehead, eds, *Sexual Meanings: The Cultural Construction of Gender and Sexuality* (Cambridge, 1981), p. 1.

10. J. Scott, 'Gender: A Useful Category of Historical Analysis', *American Historical Review* 91 (1986), p. 1067.

11. C.A. Mackinnon, *Towards a Feminist Theory of the State* (Cambridge, Massachusetts, 1989), cited with further references in Laqueur, *Making Sex*, p. 12.

12. L. Hudson and B. Jacot, *The Way Men Think* (London, 1991), pp. 37–8.

13. J. Weeks, *Sexuality and its Discontents* (London, 1985), p. 122.

of the dynamic of relations between the sexes and the dialectic of power in women's experience.[14] It has become extended to men so it is now 'a way to renew the history of both sexes, to give us a new understanding of the possibilities of the past'.[15] There have been two modes in the writing of women's history over the last twenty years, one which has looked for the universals in female experience, the other for its varieties. It is the latter which provides the more fruitful inspiration for the approach adopted in this book. For the investigation of gender in England between 1500 and 1800 reveals the fluidity of a patriarchal system which was under pressure. The issue facing men seems to have been: could they secure patriarchy more surely by drawing sharper lines between the sexes? Given the huge epistemological shift associated with Descartes and Newton and the beginnings in the seventeenth century of the philosophical world view that has come to be called modernity, men were bound to see that women could be investigated, designated and thus more effectively constructed.[16] Once men saw women as distinct beings, a transformation in the nature of patriarchy, based upon a new reading of gender, became possible.

The sources for the history of gender in early modern England are at the same time multifarious and irritatingly unsatisfactory. For gender shows itself above all in the mind, in the intimacies of personal behaviour and the unspoken and often unrecorded conventions of private and public life. Much of the material used in this book, far too much for comfort, is didactic and prescriptive. It is directly so in the case of conduct and advice literature aimed at husbands and wives and of popular medical tracts. It is less directly but in fact almost as obviously so in popular ballads, dramas and satire, for these genres reflected current preoccupations about male and female behaviour just as strikingly. They may offer escapist or practical solutions to people's dilemmas. The audience for these various forms of literature varied greatly. Serious spiritual guidance about matrimonial conduct, published in a large and expensive tome, cannot have achieved the readership of ephemeral street ballads, which anyway were as much heard as read.

Since the arguments that follow often rest particularly heavily upon citation from contemporary ballads and drama, neither of which is the usual stock in trade of the early modern social historian, something needs to be said about their particular validity as historical sources. Ballads, it has begun to be shown, are one of the great neglected forms of evidence for

14. A. Wilson, ed., *Rethinking Social History: English Society 1570–1920 and its Interpretation* (Manchester, 1993), p. 22.
15. N.Z. Davis, 'What is Women's History?' in J. Gardiner, ed., *What is History Today?* (London, 1988), p. 85.
16. For useful succinct accounts of modernity see D. Zohar, *The Quantum Self* (London, 1990), pp. 74–8 and D. Zohar and I. Marshall, *The Quantum Society* (London, 1993), pp. 107–15.

early modern mentality.[17] We do not need to rely upon Shakespeare's Autolycus for evidence of their authenticity and their importance in popular culture.[18] 'In the shops of artificers and cottages of poor husbandmen', wrote Nicholas Bownde in 1595, 'you shall sooner see one of these new ballads than any of the psalms.'[19] Eager listeners, we are told, gathered in 1634 to hear Thomas Cotton's weekly London newsletter every market day at Colchester 'as people do where ballads are sung'.[20] Dorothy Osborn described in a letter to her husband in the 1650s how she had gone walking on a common 'where a great many young wenches keep sheep and cows and sit in the shade singing of ballads'.[21] The ballad mongers wrote for the market, reflecting current and perennial issues about love and marriage, religion and morality, work and leisure: they tell us about the situations, practices and attitudes that absorbed people. These people were often willing to pay a penny for a broadside with a crude woodcut, or just to stop and listen, and they came from all ranks from the middling sort to the poor.[22]

The drama of the period, we know from research on the Elizabethan and Jacobean theatre, was a collaborative process. The dramatist's text was developed and adapted in production so that what eventually came to be published, following performance, represents collective efforts and debate among the companies of players. The plays, in other words, as Michael Hattaway puts it, derive as much from a 'social milieu' as from an authorial point of view. Drama can thus properly be used as historical evidence, not of realities but of the imaginative and ideological constructions of the period, of its mentality.[23] Probing the opacity of these texts can take us into the meanings which the age attached, for example, to romance, love and marriage, to key elements in the pattern of gender relations. We must have the confidence, while taking full account of the

17. N. Wurzbach, *The Rise of the English Street Ballad 1550–1650* (Cambridge, 1990); T. Watt, *Cheap Print and Popular Piety 1550–1640* (Cambridge, 1991); H. Weinstein, *A Catalogue of the Ballads in the Pepys Collection* (Cambridge, 1993).

18. But for a splendid evocation of how the ballad singer worked see *The Winter's Tale*, act IV, scene iv, 220–327.

19. Cited in M. Spufford, *Small Books and Pleasant Histories: Popular Fiction and its Readership in Seventeenth-Century England* (London, 1981), p. 10.

20. S. Foster, *Notes from the Caroline Underground* (Connecticut, 1978), p. 4.

21. E.A. Parry, ed., *Letters from Dorothy Osborn to Sir William Temple 1652–54* (London, 1903), p. 86.

22. For important recent work on the structure of society in this period see K. Wrightson, 'The Social Order of Early Modern England: Three Approaches', in L. Bonfield, R.M. Smith and K. Wrightson, eds, *The World We Have Gained* (Oxford, 1986), pp. 177–202 and 'Estates, Degrees and Sorts: Changing Perceptions of Society in Tudor and Stuart England', in P.J. Corfield, ed., *Language, History and Class* (Oxford, 1991), pp. 30–52.

23. M. Hattaway in A.R. Braunmuller and M. Hattaway, eds, *The Cambridge Companion to English Renaissance Drama* (Cambridge, 1990), pp. 93–5.

problems of their interpretation, to take literary texts of all kinds seriously as historical source material. I have also argued elsewhere that it may sometimes be appropriate to listen to modern producers.[24] A new production of a play which creatively addresses a text can assist the historian's quest for understanding of past attitudes as fruitfully as the reading of a neglected document. Actors and director, Jonathan Miller argues, can remake 'a work of art that is essentially emergent'.[25] We can learn something, to take an example, from Emma Thompson's playing of Beatrice in the first scene in the film of *Much Ado*, knowing that she and Kenneth Branagh read the previous off-stage relationship between Benedick and Beatrice as a love affair that has gone wrong but left an emotional attachment that then has to be handled in the midst of a crowd of relatives and friends. The dynamic and the tensions of patriarchal authority and youthful passion in this scene would have been immediately apparent to an Elizabethan audience.[26]

The didactic literature was written by men, some of it specifically to instruct women. So were ballads and plays. All these genres tell us how men wanted women to see the gender order, their place in it and themselves. They tell us what women heard, saw, read or were taught. But they tell us nothing about what they thought. Two sections of this book tell the story of men's ideological view of women. It is told from their own point of view and without the contradiction that women of the time, given the chance to speak openly and honestly, might have dared to utter. This is a reflection of the historical record: that this record is partial and that it provides a wholly inadequate basis for assessing women's private feelings and thoughts about early modern patriarchy must be made clear at the outset. In face of the account in part I of men's understanding of the body, sexual activity, pregnancy and conception, the reader might well respond, if so minded, that women who knew about these things did not write and men who wrote did not know. Studies of female visionaries of the seventeenth century show them using a language about their experiences of union with God which is simply incompatible with their having fully adopted the construction of themselves that men sought to impose.[27] Caroline Walker Bynum, who has studied the symbol of Christ as a lactating woman in medieval spirituality, comes close to an essentialist view of women's experience in this respect: 'women's way of using symbols and being religious was different from men's,' she suggests, 'women's sense of religious self seems more continuous with the sense of social and biological self; women's images are most profoundly

24. A.J. Fletcher, 'Men's Dilemma: The Future of Patriarchy in England 1560–1660', *TRHS*, IV (1994), pp. 63–4.
25. Cited in K. McLuskie, *Renaissance Dramatists* (London, 1989), p. 7.
26. *Much Ado about Nothing*, act I, scene i, 35–147.
27. P. Crawford, *Women and Religion in England 1500–1720* (London, 1993), p. 15.

deepenings, not inversions of what "woman" is'.[28] The account in part III of the prescriptive construction of femininity also leaves out women's voices. By the eighteenth century these are much more in evidence: gender is now being contested openly and directly. The book would have become too long if it attempted to explore this issue in detail. As it is it needs to be read throughout with an awareness that the relationship between theory and practice where women are concerned is, as Eileen Power remarked long ago, an 'insidious blend'.[29] There has been a considerable danger of that blend colouring the argument: the reader must judge how far this danger has been avoided.

The structure of the book is based on three substantial sections linked by chapters which outline crucial aspects of the overall argument. It opens with an account, candidly based on literary evidence, of how some men at least saw women as dangerously assertive in the sixteenth and early seventeenth centuries. The problem that the book tackles – adapting patriarchy to secure its foundations more effectively – is thus set out. Chapters 2 to 5 explore the context in men's minds of their view of women in the first part of our period. Chapter 6 argues that gender was created and patriarchy enforced in the sixteenth and seventeenth centuries on the basis of distinct male and female honour codes. A series of literary genres which assisted men in this task are assessed, together with some of women's responses to men's inculcation of prescribed gender roles. Chapters 7 to 13 provide an account, based upon diaries, autobiographies, correspondence, court records and other sources which tell us about real life, of the working of patriarchy. Though this account sometimes strays into the eighteenth century, its focus is upon the period from 1500 to 1700. In many respects this may be regarded as the core of the book and its ultimate test, for, as Amy Erickson reminds us at the end of her study of women and property in this period, 'the ideological view of women readily available in didactic literature instructing them how to behave' was not 'by any stretch of the imagination a reflection of real life'.[30] Chapter 14 introduces the argument that the period between 1660 and 1800 saw the fruition of an ideological construction of gender which, breaking with the simple didacticism of preceding years, built upon its sure foundations in the concepts of manhood and the 'weaker vessel' to create masculinity and femininity in something like a modern sense. Chapters 15 to 19 explore the shape of this ideology in the context of the educational systems of the time. Chapter 20 attempts to draw together the threads of the overall argument of the book.

28. C.W. Bynum, *Jesus as Mother* (Berkeley, 1982); C.W. Bynum, *Holy Feast and Holy Fast: The Religious Significance of Food to Medieval Women* (Berkeley, 1987), pp. 289–90.
29. Erickson, p. 236.
30. Erickson, p. 236.

PART I   BEFORE THE GENDERED
               BODY

1. Prologue: Men's Dilemmas

A NUMBER OF commentators in the sixteenth and seventeenth centuries noted the independence of Englishwomen. They 'have far more liberty than in other lands and know just how to make good use of it', wrote Thomas Platter who travelled the country in 1599, 'for they often stroll out or drive by coach in very gorgeous clothes and the men must put up with such ways and may not punish them for it'.[1] Fynes Moryson's *Itinerary*, published in 1617, contains the following passage comparing English gender relations with German ones:

> May we not then justly marvel that Englishmen having great power over their wives so as they can neither give anything in life nor have power to make a will at death, nor can call anything their own no not so much as their garters, yea the law (I must confess too severely) permitting the husband in some cases to beat his wife and yet the husbands, notwithstanding all their privileges, using their wives with all respect and giving them the chief seats with all honours and preeminences, so as for the most part they would carry burdens, go on foot, fast and suffer anything so their wives might have ease, ride, feast and suffer nothing, notwithstanding no people in the world (that ever I did see) bear more scorns, indignities and injuries from the pampered sort of women than they do.[2]

The well known proverb 'England is a paradise for women' seems to have been based upon the notion that English women enjoyed a peculiar degree of freedom, despite the fact that English marital property law was severe in comparison with the more egalitarian systems of continental countries. One of Thomas Middleton's characters in *A Mad World my Masters* observes that Italians keep their wives 'under lock and key: we Englishmen are careless creatures'. Edward Chamberlayn, in his 1669 tract

1. C. Williams, trans., *Thomas Platter's Travels in England 1599* (London, 1937), pp. 181–2.
2. F. Moryson, *An Itinerary written by Fynes Moryson* (London, 1617), part 3, book 4, p. 221. I am grateful to Tim Stretton for this reference.

on the state of England, said that a wife in England is 'de jure but the best of servants', yet he believed her 'condition de facto is the best in the world; for such is the good nature of Englishmen towards their wives, such is their tenderness and respect, giving them the uppermost place at table and elsewhere ... and putting them upon no drudgery and hardship'. In the eighteenth century, Henry Fielding's Mrs Western told her brother that English women were 'not to be locked up like the Spanish and Italian wives' since they had as much right to liberty as English men.[3] There was a proverb current over a long period in England, and alleged to be current abroad too, which summed up this whole matter. 'If a bridge were made over the narrow seas', it ran as John Ray recorded it in 1670, 'all the women in Europe would come over hither.' As Oliver Goldsmith's Dr Primrose put it in *The Vicar of Wakefield* a hundred years later, 'if a bridge were built across the sea, all the ladies of the continent would come over to take pattern from ours'.[4] It is hard to know what to make of the way Englishmen flattered themselves in this respect. As Amy Erickson remarks, their insistence that English women 'were in practice treated with extraordinary kindness despite their legal disabilities is entirely absent from the writings of women'.[5] What is puzzling, and what made John Ray pause in 1670, is the way the proverbs of the time by contrast suggest an attitude to women which is scathing and caustic. 'It is worth noting', declared Ray, 'that though in no country of the world the men are so fond of, so much governed by, so wedded to their wives yet hath no language so many proverbial invectives against women.'[6] The work of the modern editor of a dictionary of early modern proverbs amply confirms Ray's conclusion: he lists 102 proverbs under 'woman' or 'women', almost every one of which is derogatory.[7] All of them were deeply rooted in an abiding European antifeminist tradition, for the female sex as a whole had long been a target of proverbial utterance.[8]

On the one hand the popular proverb 'better a shrew than a sheep' suggests that the English liked strong women. Ray commented about this proverb that it was held true 'for commonly shrews are good housewives'.[9] On the other hand, there is an extensive literature from this period showing an obsession with the dangers ascribed to womankind and inhabited by fear of women's motives and behaviour. Men's dilemmas were focused upon a stereotype of womankind which left them feeling

3. Citations from Gibbons, p. 60; Erickson, p. 109.
4. O. Goldsmith, *The Vicar of Wakefield* (London, 1766), p. 296.
5. Erickson, p. 109.
6. J. Ray, *A Collection of English Proverbs* (London, 1670), p. 54.
7. Tilley, pp. 741–9.
8. A. Blamires, ed., *Woman Defamed and Woman Defended: An Anthology of Medieval Texts* (Oxford, 1992), p. 8.
9. Ray, *Collection of Proverbs*, p. 50.

intensely vulnerable and unprotected. Women were seen as possessing a powerful and potentially destructive sexuality which made them naturally lascivious, predatory and, most serious of all, once their desire was fully aroused, insatiable. The thinking about the female body, which explained and gave force to this conception of women's sexuality, will be fully explored in chapters 2 and 3.[10] In brief, an important element in male assumptions about women was that they needed sex urgently following the menarche. Wedding nights could thus be portrayed for sober male consideration in terms of fierce female expectancy. Richard Brathwaite told the tale of a bridal night in his satirical *Art Asleep Husband* in terms intended to put his male readers on the alert. The bride, following the initial deflowering, was not pleased when her husband turned on his side and began to pray. She was more interested in 'action' than 'devotion': 'sweetheart why turn you so soon from me? are you so soon weary of me? pray thee, chick, what art doing?' But for the bridegroom that was it. 'What other answer she made to this frump', concluded Brathwaite, 'I have not heard saving only this "Go to husband it seems you are cunning".'[11] A conversation between Beatrice-Joanna and De Flores in *The Changeling*, after she has substituted the virginal maid Diaphanta for herself on her wedding night, strikes the same note. When Diaphanta fails to leave the bed, as Beatrice-Joanna has told her to do immediately after the consummation, she at once assumes her pleasure is the reason. It is her 'greedy appetite', declares Beatrice-Joanna. Women on the occasion of their deflowering, chimes in De Flores, are 'termagents', 'mad whelps': 'you cannot stave 'em off from game royal'.[12] Here, as Lisa Jardine has commented, was the patriarchal imagination pointing 'a threatening eagerness on the part of the bride which common sense tells us can hardly have been matched by any reality'.[13]

The drama of the period makes the most of the fact that the price of women's lasciviousness is often pregnancy and the punishment of painful childbirth that all Eve's daughters risk for the desire expressed in the story of the Fall. Thus, when the Duchess of Malfi becomes pregnant immediately upon her marriage, there is much bawdy play upon her greedy need for apricots, a traditional craving by pregnant women, but no sympathy for her when the fruit makes her sick. Juliet's visible pregnancy in *Measure for Measure* represents the 'sin she carries' in collaboration with Claudio and she makes confession on stage to the Duke: she will 'bear the

---

10. Below, pp. 29–57.
11. R. Brathwaite, *Art Asleep Husband: A Boulster Lecture* (London, 1640), p. 47.
12. *The Changeling*, act V, scene 1, 1–19. For a challenging analysis of the play as a whole see S. Eaton, 'Beatrice-Joanna and the Rhetoric of Love', in D.S. Kastan and P. Stallybrass, eds, *Staging the Renaissance: Reinterpretations of Elizabethan and Jacobean Drama* (London, 1991), pp. 275–89.
13. L. Jardine, *Still Harping on Daughters: Women and Drama in the Age of Shakespeare* (London, 1983), p. 127.

shame most patiently'.[14] In *The Winter's Tale* Shakespeare uses the banter of Hermione's ladies about her figure to activate Leontes' powerful jealousy which is at this point the driving force of the plot:

> You my lords,
> Look on her, mark her well; be but about
> To say she is a goodly lady and
> The justice of your hearts will thereto add
> 'Tis pity she's not honest – honourable

Hermione, he tells them, is an adulteress, a 'bed swerver', for her irrepressible lasciviousness, which he has read into her friendship with Polixenes in the first scenes, has led her astray.[15]

The lascivious woman threatens and challenges manhood; the predatory woman unmasks it. Shakespeare's most powerful women exhibit sexual gluttony. *King Lear* is a play about sexual insubordination and anarchy, for Lear's treatment of Goneril and Regan is a representation of patriarchal misogyny and his humiliation by his two elder daughters is thus indirectly sexual.[16] Hamlet bewails his mother's sensuality and lust, the motives for her overhasty marriage to his father's murderer:

> O shame! where is thy blush?
> . . .
> proclaim no shame
> When the compulsive ardour gives the charge
> Since frost itself as actively doth burn
> And reason panders will.[17]

Lady Macbeth's sexuality is a means of control over her husband whom she taunts and drives into regicide.[18] Again both in *Antony and Cleopatra* and in *Troilus and Cressida* female sexuality is a source of dominion holding man unnaturally in its thrall.[19]

Stories told in popular ballads and narratives, which were sung or read in the market place or tavern, lacked the high-flown dramatisation of performances at the Globe or Swan but they reproduced the same nagging themes of female sexual will and domination. The ballad *Cuck-*

---

14. *The Duchess of Malfi*, act II, scene i, 135–43; *Measure for Measure*, act II, scene iii, 19–20; Jardine, *Still Harping on Daughters*, pp. 132–3.
15. *The Winter's Tale*, act II, scene i, 65–9, 79, 91, 96.
16. K. McLuskie, 'The Patriarchal Bard: Feminist Criticism and Shakespeare: *King Lear* and *Measure for Measure*', in J. Dollimore and A. Sinfield, eds, *Political Shakespeare* (Manchester, 1985), p. 98.
17. *Hamlet*, act III, scene iv, 77, 81–4.
18. J. Adelman, *Suffocating Mothers: Fantasies of Maternal Origin in Shakespeare's Plays, Hamlet to the Tempest* (London, 1992), pp. 137–9.
19. Jardine, *Still Harping on Daughters*, p. 114.

old's Heaven told of 'the married man's misery, who must abide the penalty of being hornified'. Nothing could stop the wilful wife from adultery, the story ran: close surveillance and use of 'lock, bolt and latch' was ineffective, beating her led to infidelity out of spite, placating her failed to make her loyal. She was too clever at circumventing obstacles, too unashamed to respond to direct accusations of misconduct. 'Women, priests and poultry', the saying went, 'have never enough.' Not every single woman was predatory in seeking lovers, the ballad concluded, but 'many do transgress'.[20] There were many cautionary tales about women's wiles when they were set upon sexual adventures. One of them was about a jealous man who had two men oversee all his wife's movements. She fell down in the mire outside her lover's house and made a quick excuse about going inside to wash herself. They simply waited outside while she 'made merry' then 'came forth and went her way'. In another story a woman found in bed with her lover arranged a stratagem to confuse her husband while he was pondering what action he should take. 'An old mother bee of her acquaintance', hearing he had chervil with his supper last night, met him in the street with the salutation 'God save you both'. Challenged by the cuckold, she rubbed her eyes and blamed her mistake on eating chervil 'for ever it maketh me to take one for twain'. So he decided he had been imagining things and 'held his wife excused'.[21] Thomas Deloney's *Jack of Newbury* tells of the entrepreneurial clothier's private life with the lustful widow who seduced him, tricked him into marriage, and then tested him by 'gadding abroad', which was always an indication in such discourses of a search for new lovers. It is only Jack's final threat to leave home himself which turns her into a devoted wife and enables him to confirm himself in his manhood. The popular stereotype of the sexually experienced widow is summarised by the proverb recorded by John Ray:

> He that wives a maid must fain, lie and flatter
> But he that wives a widow must down with his breeches and at
> her.[22]

At the outbreak of the civil war scurrilous pamphleteering, playing upon the spectre of women in the public realm as petitioners, made much of the notion of the female predator. Let men go to the wars, declared the protagonists in *The Resolution of the Women of London to the Parliament*, which was almost certainly a male spoof: they would 'live as merrily as maybe . . . if we have a mind to it, keep and maintain a friend that upon

20. *Roxburghe*, I, pp. 148–53; Anon., *Gnomologia: Adages and Proverbs, Wise Sentences and Witty Sayings* (1732), no. 5809.
21. Twyne, *The Schoolmaster or Teacher of Table Philosophy* (1583), pp. 1–2.
22. Jardine, *Still Harping on Daughters*, pp. 129–30; Ray, *Collection of Proverbs*, p. 49.

occasion may do us pleasure'.[23] Parody of female grievance by making a
connection with insatiable female desire was in fact a common practice in
the seventeenth century and the use of suggestive pseudonym names was
a popular tactic. Thus *The Good Woman's Cryes*, published in 1650,
purported to be by Mary Stiff. It seems men could only read disorderly
female activity in sexual terms and thus constantly sought to nullify
women's taking up a public role by the sexual smear.

In February 1551 Alice Arden of Faversham in Kent procured and
witnessed the murder of her husband, a crime for which she was convicted and burnt alive. The scandal of this crime, which made it notorious, was that Alice's motive was her plan to marry the tailor Mosby, who
was her lover. The case neatly encapsulated the defiance of patriarchal
marriage. There were many allusions to it in chronicles and histories;
the play *Arden of Faversham* can be dated to about 1590; the ballad *The
Complaint and Lamentation of Mistress Arden* was printed about 1633. The
fascination that Alice Arden's crime exercised lay in, as the play's title
page put it, 'the great malice and dissimulation of a wicked woman and
the insatiable desire of filthy lust'. Alice's determined negotiations with a
succession of possible murderers of her husband, the centrepiece of the
play's plot, shows the predatory sexual woman in the strongest possible
light. The ballad recounts the scenes of contracts for murder in detail
within a text of 192 lines, and a number of similar ballads related other
women's killing of their husbands to their adultery. Alice had disrupted
the patriarchal household, keeping her lover in her home with her
husband's knowledge and feeding and clothing him. This aspect of the
case was not unique. A woman at Arundel in Sussex, Susanna Wilson,
was taken to court by her husband James in 1602. It was alleged that she
had effectively replaced him by her lover Thomas Puge. James Wilson
was excluded from his wife's bedchamber and forced to pay for such food
as she prepared or otherwise to provide his own.[24]

If Alice Arden's crime touched one very raw male nerve, the career of
Mary Frith, better known during her long London career as Moll
Cutpurse, touched another. When, in 1611, Thomas Dekker and Thomas
Middleton collaborated in writing a play based on Moll's story, but
presenting her most disarmingly, they chose a titular epithet for her which
was designed as an oxymoron. As *The Roaring Girl* Moll transgressed
boundaries of both class and gender. The roaring boys of the time were
young men of gentry stock known as such for their riotous behaviour as
they tasted the delights of the capital. When the play was first performed
at the Fortune theatre, Moll's appearance in person there was announced

23. *The Resolution of the Women of London to the Parliament* (1642); D. Purkiss, 'Material
    Girls: The Seventeenth-Century Woman Debate', in C. Brant and D. Purkiss, eds,
    Women, Texts and Histories 1575–1760 (London, 1992), pp. 82–3.
24. C. Belsey, *The Subject of Tragedy: Identity and Difference in Renaissance Drama* (London,
    1985), pp. 129–35; Gowing, pp. 146–7.

as forthcoming in the epilogue. The incident formed a principal element in the decision, the following year, to prosecute her for public immorality. Brought before the London consistory court, Mary Frith did not deny that she was a blasphemer, that she got drunk and consorted with bad company in the city's alehouses and tobacco shops and at the playhouses. Nor did she challenge the substance of the account given to the court of her behaviour one day at the Fortune:

> being at a play . . . in man's apparel and in her boots and with a sword by her side, she told the company there present that she thought many of them were of opinion that she was a man but if any of them would come to her lodging they should find that she is a woman and some other immodest and lascivious speeches she also used at that time. And also sat there upon the stage in the public view of all the people there present; in man's apparel, and played upon her lute and sang a song.

So what was it that the authorities found 'immodest and lascivious' about Moll's activities? Obviously, in the first place, it was inflammatory to wear male costume. The transvestite fashion had caught on in London some years previously and had already caused anxious male comment. Masculine dress, besides simply challenging gender boundaries, was seen as empowering and liberating for a woman. Yet, as Stephen Orgel points out, the paradoxical element of the story is that the one charge Moll denied was that she was a whore or had 'drawn other women to lewdness by her persuasions and by carrying herself like a bawd'. She refused the court's attempt to deal with her as a licentious woman seeking to improve her trade by playing the transvestite. Made to do penance at Paul's Cross, she put on a magnificent performance with a feminine display of bitter tears and penitence. This was rumoured to be based upon having drunk a huge amount of sack. John Chamberlain's account referred to her as 'a notorious baggage' who had dressed as a man 'and challenged the field of divers gallants'.[25]

The Roaring Girl was written before all this came to public notice, yet Dekker and Middleton employ the same paradox as the one at the heart of the story in real life. Their Moll, endlessly provocative in her behaviour and outrageous in her costume, is a good girl at heart who helps an innocent young man to achieve the marriage he desires against the patriarchal machinations of his father. At the same time her male persona is taken as representing a powerful and universal sexual prowess. The play takes the male fantasy of female domination and role reversal to its logical and devastating conclusion. Middleton's signed preface to the printed

25. S. Orgel, 'The Subtexts of *The Roaring Girl*', in S. Zimmerman, *Erotic Politics: Desire on the Renaissance Stage* (London, 1992), pp. 12–25; M. Garber, 'The Logic of the Transvestite', in D.S. Kastan and P. Stallybrass, eds, *Staging the Renaissance: Reinterpretations of Elizabethan and Jacobean Drama* (London, 1991), pp. 221–2.

version recommended its sixpence worth of 'venery and laughter' as diversionary reading 'to keep you in an afternoon from dice'.[26] But this is a text that deserves to be treated with the utmost seriousness for the study of gender in this period. For its crux is the sexual inadequacy of men: strip away the clothing in which men prance, its message goes, and you are left with bodies; examine the bodies and you reach the source of male insecurity at a time when men are not quite sure how penises and testicles entitle them to the patriarchal power they claim. If a woman claimed these things, even if only symbolically, might she not be as manly as most men? Where would this leave patriarchy? The broader anxiety is about being and seeming. 'Venus, being a woman, passes through the play in doublet and breeches; a brave disguise and a safe one if the statute untie not her codpiece point,' wrote Middleton in his preface. *The Roaring Girl* is about a woman who defies the Tudor sumptuary laws in a way that is intended to set the patriarchal world upside down. Those on stage always know she is really a woman. In a key scene Sir Alexander Wengrave overhears a tailor fitting Moll, who he believes his son intends to marry, with a pair of breeches or, as the dialogue makes clear, in effect with a phallus.[27] Moll, he declares, with reference to that striking piece of contemporary sartorial manhood, is to be a 'codpiece daughter'. The belittling, which follows soon after, of the randy gallant Laxton is given point by the broad joke at his expense when he first appeared on stage and Sir Alexander greeted him with the words 'furnish Master Laxton with what he wants, a stone'. Laxton is the man without testicles. 'I had rather stand,' the dialogue continues. 'I know you had, good Master Laxton,' quips Sir Alexander. Laxton's potency is in doubt so no wonder Moll, fulfilling her assignation with him in Gray's Inn Fields, can draw her sword and fight him until he pleads for his life.[28] What is crucial here is that Moll the virgin does not want sex, she wants power. *The Roaring Girl* goes to the heart of the patriarchal issue, for her breeches symbolise the phallus and the phallus symbolises male subordination of women. It does not matter if Moll has not in fact got one once she is allowed to behave as if she has one. Men's dilemmas, we can perceive here, are dilemmas for which sexual potency stands as a marker; but they are actually dilemmas of initiative and control which pervade gender relationships from each dawn to each dusk.

Yet the matter of sexual potency is particularly important. It surely underlies much of the male jealousy – the sheer terror of being cuckolded – which is so evident in the dramas and the ballads of the period. The sexual politics of Tudor and Stuart England cannot be properly under-

26. F. Bowers, ed., *The Dramatic Works of Thomas Dekker* (Cambridge, 1958), III, p. 11.
27. For a fuller account of this scene see A.J. Fletcher, 'Men's Dilemma: The Future of Patriarchy in England 1560–1660', *TRHS*, IV (1994), p. 72.
28. Kastan and Stallybrass, eds, *Staging the Renaissance*, p. 224.

stood unless we come to terms with what Lisa Jardine calls the 'taboo aspect' of the literature's emphasis on the voraciousness of female sexual appetite. This is often associated with widowhood. In John Taylor's *A Juniper Lecture* a lusty young widow scornfully refuses an old man whom she cannot believe will satisfy her: 'I will have a husband that shall be always provided like a soldier . . . with his match lighted and cocked bolt upright and ready to do execution, not like a dormouse, always sleeping.'[29] There are English tales at this time, which parallel numerous ones in the *Arabian Nights*, showing how a woman's insistence on equal sexual enjoyment can reduce the boldest lover to impotence. Once a woman was fully aroused sexually, tradition and folklore went, woe betide the lover who failed to satisfy her. In Thomas Nashe's poem 'The Choice of Valentines' a vigorous prostitute made clear her demands to an anxious client:

> "Oh not so fast!" my ravish'd mistress cries
> Lest my content, that on my life relies,
> Be brought too soon from his delightful seat,
> And me unawares of hoped bliss defeat.
> Together let our equal motions stir
> Together let us live and die, my dear.

Die was common parlance for orgasm: this was something women clearly expected to enjoy and providing it was part of the test of male potency. Thus Beatrice, desperate for Benedick in *Much Ado*, 'in despite of all dies for him' and 'shall be buried with her face upwards'.[30] Aphra Behn's poem 'The Disappointment' describes an encounter between Cloris and Lysander that ends disastrously because he fails to satisfy her. The poem describes their lovemaking in graphic detail up to the point of clitoral touch:

> His daring hand that altar seized
> Where Gods of love do sacrifice
> That awful throne, that paradise
> Where rage is calm'd and anger pleas'd
> That fountain where delight still flows
> And gives the universal world repose

Then, as Cloris 'half dead and breathless lay', Lysander's sexual courage failed:

> Ready to taste a thousand joys
> The too transported hapless swain

29. Cited in K.U. Henderson and B.F. McManus, eds, *Half Humankind: Contexts and Texts about Women in England 1540–1640* (Urbana, 1985), p. 48.
30. Jardine, *Still Harping on Daughters*, p. 125; *Much Ado about Nothing*, act 3 scene IV, 50–51. Below, pp. 48–57.

Found the vast pleasure turned to pain

. . .

In vain he toils, in vain commands
The insensible fell weeping in his hand.

His desire turns to fury with himself; his humiliation is increased when
her hand discovers his deflation. Manhood is unmasked.[31] The young
lawyer Arnot Bagot's tribute to women's sexual supremacy in his 1672
tract *Learn to Lye Warm* is so vivid it surely reflects experience:

> Show me Hector himself, the stoutest he that lives, who after a week's
> repose in the bosom of a lusty and youthful beauty, will not say that he
> is become a victim to Venus and a helpless saint under the altar of
> cupid; as his wanted flesh, extenuated eyes, pendant ears, and sneaking
> behaviour may sufficiently demonstrate; whilst she like Aurora looks
> fresh, bucksome, plump and lively; her eyes make bonfires, crowing
> and triumphing for the victory; baffling her castrated cavalier with
> stolen kisses; he mean season only returning a poor and dry salute and
> that more to save his credit than serve his love.

Quoting the proverb 'tis good sheltering under an old hedge', Bagot
advised marriage to older and less demanding women rather than to
younger ones who might prove unfaithful and bring home the pox from
their escapades.[32]

Men's control of women's speech, an aspect of their potency, was at
the heart of the early modern gender system. Speech takes us to the
centre of the issues of patriarchal authority, for it proposes and initiates.
Speech represents personal agency. The woman who speaks neither in
reply to a man nor in submissive request acts as an independent being
who may well, it is assumed, end up with another man than her husband
in her bed. Thus every incident of verbal assertiveness could awake the
spectre of adultery and the dissolution of patriarchal order.

Chaste, silent and obedient: the trilogy of primary female virtues carries
with it a series of logical connections.[33] Men at this time were somewhat
obsessed with a link between shrewish or scolding behaviour and sexual
infidelity. The threat implicit in the bawdy chorus line of the ballad *The
Discontented Married Man*, 'she cannot keep her lips together', went to the
heart of the matter.[34] Proverbs which associated sound and sexuality
hinted at the issue of female mastery which always had adultery as its

---

31. A. Goreau, 'Two English Women in the Seventeenth Century: Notes for an
    Anatomy of Feminine Desire', in P. Aries and A. Bejin, eds, *Western Sexuality*
    (London, 1985), pp. 108–13.
32. A.B., *Learn to Lye Warm* (London, 1672), pp. 8–18.
33. S. Hull, *Chaste, Silent and Obedient: English Books for Women 1435–1640* (San Marino,
    1982).
34. E.A. Foyster, 'A Laughing Matter? Marital Discord and Gender Control in Seven-
    teenth Century England', *Rural History* 4 (1993), p. 17.

ultimate and inherent point of direction: 'she goes as if she cracked nuts with her tail', 'she hath a gad-bee in her tail', 'she is as quiet as a wasp in one's ear', 'she simpers like a frumenty kettle'.[35] Thomas Bentley's vision of the fallen woman was of the woman who lost her speech as the penalty for her adultery: 'the tongue doth not his office; the throat is dammed up; all the senses and instruments are polluted with iniquity'. The whore's permanent loss of sexual control was epitomised by opposite results. Barnaby Rich described her as 'full of words . . . loud and babbling'. The torrent of the whore's speech signified men's total loss of authority over her.[36]

The issue of day-to-day authority connects with the assumptions men made about women's sexual insatiability. It was this which made effective oversight of one's wife's behaviour at every moment essential; yet how could the shrew be dominated or made to submit to male authority? Women were believed to regard bedtime as opportune for guerilla warfare. Thus even Desdemona, hardly the most shrewish of wives, made her promise to further Cassio's suit with Othello:

> I'll watch him, tame and talk him out of patience
> His bed shall seem a school, his board a shrift.[37]

The frontispiece of Richard Brathwaite's lengthy tract *Art Asleep Husband: A Boulster Lecture* shows a loquacious woman hectoring a husband who can get no sleep while the words, as an accompanying rhyme indicates, go in one ear and out of the other[38] (plate 3). A scene in *Much Ado about Nothing* where Beatrice is berated by her uncle Leonato for being 'shrewd of the tongue' explores the relationship between a woman's scolding and her sexuality. If she is too curst, reflects Beatrice, God will not send her a husband and that in turn, quips Leonato, means 'God will send you no horns'. Exactly so, is Beatrice's response, for there was no sort of man that could make an equal relationship with her: either her husband would be emasculated, fit for her to 'dress him in my apparel and make him my waiting gentlewoman' or, if he stood up to her, she would feel bound to cuckold him. Beatrice can be read here as attacking the stereotype of insatiable womanhood in a bantering response to her uncle. Her conclusion is that, if she is really as women are painted, she cannot marry, because she will be bound to shame any husband she is given by exertion of her sexual power against him. What she wants is a real sexual partner: if she cannot have that she will have no husband at all.[39]

35. Anon., *Gnomologia*, nos 4122, 4126, 4130, 4136.
36. Gowing, p. 71.
37. *Othello*, act 3, scene III, 23–4.
38. R. Brathwaite, *Art Asleep Husband* (London, 1640).
39. *Much Ado About Nothing*, act II, scene I, 1–28. I am grateful to Claire Harbottle for discussion of this passage.

Eve's tongue in the mystery play tradition was forked like the serpent's; Adam is undone by female discourse.[40] As Edward Reyner in his 1656 treatise put it, 'original sin came first out at the mouth by speaking before it entered in by eating. The first use we find Eve to have made of her language was to enter parley with the tempter and from that to become a tempter to her husband.'[41] A mass of early modern proverbial wisdom had its roots in this lore: 'a woman's weapon is her tongue', 'a woman's tongue is the last thing about her that dies', 'a woman's tongue, like an aspen leaf, is always in motion', 'a woman's tongue wags like a lamb's tail', 'many women many words, many geese many turds', 'three women and a goose make a market'.[42] The stereotype of the scold was built on these foundations. 'Husbands are in heaven when wives chide not' and 'she will scold the devil out of a haunted house' were further adages recorded in the early eighteenth century.[43] Two couplets from James Howell's 1659 collection of proverbs summarised the scold's offensive unacceptability:

> She is as wholesome a morsel for a man's course
> As a shoulder of mutton is for a sick horse
> The devil with his dam hath more rest in hell
> At every one of her teeth there hangs a great bell.[44]

Leontes makes the same connections in *The Winter's Tale* when he characterises Paulina as a woman of 'boundless tongue who hath late beat her husband'. Paulina, he declares in his jealous rage, is a gross hag and ne'er do well, touched by the devil's art, who deserves to be hanged or better still burnt.[45]

Women's talk always threatens disorder; women's silence thus comes to be prized to an absurd degree. The notion of the mute wife is celebrated in *Epicœne* and various other tales. But it is *King Lear* which treats the theme most dramatically, for Cordelia's aside when asked to speak – 'Love and be silent' – leads to Lear's choice which produces the disorder associated with the misrule of the defiant daughters Goneril and Regan. 'Thou mad'st thy daughters thy mothers', chides the Fool, 'for when thou gav'st them the rod and put'st down thine own breeches'

> Then they for sudden joy did weep
> And I for sorrow sung
> That such a King should play bo-peep
> And go the fools among.

40. Jardine, *Still Harping on Daughters*, pp. 110–11.
41. Cited in J.W. Spargo, *Juridical Folklore in England* (Durham, North Carolina, 1944), p. 113.
42. Tilley, nos 675–8, 686–7, 690.
43. Anon., *Gnomologia*, nos 2579, 4149.
44. J. Howell, *Proverbs or Old Saws and Adages* (London, 1659), p. 23.
45. *The Winter's Tale*, act II, scene iii, 90–2, 109–11, 118.

A recent production showed Lear at this point being ridden and whipped by the Fool, acting the part of the dominant woman in the contemporary woodcuts (plate 1). Goneril and Regan's initial honeyed words hid their independence and deceit. The first scene of the play closes with the evidence that they are ready to do what they will to make Lear's 'unruly waywardness' serve their own turns. The woman on top is first of all the woman who is voluble. Unchecked speech provides the initial training in assertiveness. Men's most primitive fears find expression in the Fool's warning.[46]

George Webb's *The Araignment of an Unruly Tongue*, the printed version of a sermon preached in 1619, was not explicitly an attack on women but there is little doubt that in his condemnation of the malice of an evil tongue which is 'full of guile, dissimulation and evil speaking' and his call for sharp action by magistrates he had women principally in mind.[47] On the title page of Robert Harper's *The Anatomy of a Woman's Tongue* we find a series of discontented men, one stung by a serpent, one whose wife has grown cursed, another turning from the fire 'to show that women's tongues like fire will burn', another sounding a horn to silence a scolding wife. Harper describes the various kinds of good and evil that a woman's tongue may do. To illustrate its poisonous capacity he told of the wife who betrayed a man's faults, with the result that his stomach swelled to burst his doublet buttons at a neighbour's house.[48] This kind of satirical literature illustrated the risk that marriage involved. Young men learnt that choosing a wife was taking a chance, for it involved testing the well known 'grey mare' proverb about women who might come to wear the breeches. James Howell recorded some relevant lines of advice:

> If you are disposed to marry, marry a shrew rather than a sheep for a fool is fulsome yet ye run risk also in the other, for a shrew may so tie your nose to the grindstone that the grey mare will prove the better horse . . . every man knows how to tame a shrew but he who hath her.[49]

A woman of spirit, in other words, promised a good relationship for the man who could cope with her. 'Better a sheep than a shrew' was playing safe, opting for sexual passivity as the price of an easy ride. The dilemma was inescapable.

The proverbial wisdom linked women's love of gossip, the path to independence and infidelity, with the issue of patriarchal control over

---

46. *King Lear*, act 1, scene iv, 169–76; production at the Royal Court Theatre, London, January 1993; Jardine, *Still Harping on Daughters*, pp. 107–10.
47. G. Webb, *The Arraignment of an Unruly Tongue* (London, 1619), pp. 58, 96.
48. R. Harper, *The Anatomy of a Woman's Tongue* (London, 1638) in *Harleian Miscellany II* (1744), pp. 167–78.
49. Howell, *Proverbs or Old Saws and Adages*, preface.

their freedom of movement. 'Women and hens', one proverb ran, 'are lost by gadding.'[50] A late seventeenth-century commonplace book noted the adage 'women are like elm: if kept within doors no timber will last longer, otherways none will corrupt sooner'.[51] 'A rouk-town's seldom a good housewife at home', they said in Yorkshire in the seventeenth century. 'Rouk-town' was dialect for a 'gossiping woman who loved to go from house to house'.[52] Barnaby Rich, in a diatribe against women's imperfections published in 1613, cited Proverbs with regard to the adulterous woman who could not stay in her home but 'must be a ramping and a roysting about to make herself known'.[53]

The issue of gadding went to the heart of the question of the rights and wrongs of male and female behaviour in marriage. The ballad *The Lamentation of a New-Married Man, briefly declaring the Sorrow and Grief that comes by marrying a Young Wanton Wife* sets out the husband's case in the first part and his wife Nan's 'most friendly answer' in the second. The theme is introduced at once with Nan's accusation that he sees it as his right to 'go a gadding', spending the household's purse while she 'must bide at home'. Her demands grow, especially for luxury foods in pregnancy and fine clothes afterwards for her churching. Having brought him a child

> Abroad among her gossips
> Then must she daily go
> Requesting of this favour
> A man must not say no
> Lest that an unkind quarrel
> About this matter grow.

There is no immediate question of infidelity, just fun. She wants to dance with others at village celebrations, coming home late and oversleeping the next day. For the once gay bachelor the new reality is

> Now I must rock the cradle
> And hush the child asleep.

The husband suffers the frustrations of marital responsibility and some budding jealousy of a 'wanton' wife. But what has he to complain about, Nan asks? His respectable married status gives him the chance to rise on the ladder of village offices from headborough to constable and church-warden:

50. Tilley, no. W695.
51. Cited in R.H. Michel, 'English Attitudes towards Women 1640–1700', *Canadian Journal of History*, 8 (1978), p. 48.
52. Ray, *A Collection of English Proverbs*, p. 52.
53. B. Rich, *The Excellency of Good Women* (London, 1613), p. 24.

> If I do blame your gadding
> It is for love, be sure
> Bad company doth always
> Ill counsel still procure.

She deserves a new gown, the pears, apples or cherries he buys for her. In return, besides bringing up the children, 'at night I give you kindly a thousand kisses sweet'. Sexually she is more than compliant. Why should he scorn the cradle? The marital deal, declares loyal Nan, is a fair one: her husband treats her well and he is a man to be reckoned with, so his jealousy is his own problem.[54]

The Lamentation of a New-Married Man is one of a series of ballads which paints marriage negatively in terms of an end to the unallayed pleasures of bachelorhood. Such ballads provide insight into the double standards, both sexual and economic, upon which the household sexual politics of the period were based.[55] The mental world of youthful male expectation turning to soured reality, as living together develops, is well captured by some rhymes recorded by James Howell in his collection of adages:

> Before I was wedded and since I made reckoning
> To make my wife bow at every beckoning
> Bachelors boast how they will teach their wives good
> But many a man speaketh of Robin Hood
> That never shot in his bow, but how I begin to gather
> Every one can rule a shrew save he who hath her
> It is said of old an old dog biteth sore
> But the old bitch biteth sorer and more
> But this is not all, she hath another bliss
> She will lie as fast as a dog will lick a dish
> She is of truth as false as God is true
> She's damnably jealous, for if she chance view
> Me kissing my maids alone but in sport
> That taketh she in earnest after bedlam's sort.[56]

The self-centredness of the standard male attitude to sex is evident in the assumption made here that kissing the maids is venial and does not deserve the storms it can provoke. Just as male sexual adventuring before marriage was popularly seen as 'but a touch of youth', so men's pursuit of extramarital sexual pleasure was regarded in a totally different

---

54. *Roxburghe*, II, pp. 34–41.
55. K.V. Thomas, 'The Double Standard', *Journal of the History of Ideas* XX (1959), pp. 195–216.
56. J. Howell, *Proverbs or Old Saws and Adages* (1659), p. 23.

light from women's.[57] The current proverb 'In the dark Joan is as good as my lady' carried no moral overtones; it merely reflected upon male anxieties that social superiority might bring some kind of special benefits in terms of the quality of sexual pleasure. A countryman, so the story went, who had given a large sum to have sex with a lady was overheard on his way home from behind a hedge moaning about his wasted money with the line that his Joan at home was as good as the lady had turned out.[58]

The same kind of double standard existed with regard to spending money. Men expected to spend in the alehouse; they deplored female extravagance as evidence of shrewishness and a striving for mastery. The battles for economic power and sexual power could easily become intertwined. The unruly wife, Diane Purkiss has argued in her analysis of the seventeenth-century woman debate, was figured in similar terms in the major misogynistic tracts of the period like Joseph Swetman's *Arraignment of Lewd, Idle, Froward and Unconstant Women* as in the ballads. She denies her husband pleasures while at the same time defying him by being sociable herself outside the home. In other words, she challenges the male gender order. Whereas virtue implies silence and obedience, the shrew or scold matches expenditure of words with expenditure of money. Purkiss notes the shrew's 'troubling openness': 'she circulates among her friends instead of remaining stored up at home to signify her husband's ownership of her'. The shrewish wife thus acquires a worldliness which gives her the confidence to question and abuse her husband.[59] The ballad *The Scolding Wife's Vindication* shows how men persistently traced their dilemmas back to the question of sex, for the wife explains her disorderly behaviour as being the result of her husband's sexual inadequacy:

> I am a young buxom dame and fain would my joys renew
> But my poor cuckold is to blame, he nothing at all will do
> He lies like a lump of clay, such husbands there is but few
> 'Twould make a woman run astray, he nothing at all will do.[60]

This is the extreme case: this scolding wife had tried to cure her husband's impotence for two years by feeding him extravagant foods like 'cockbroths'.[61] But, given the assumptions about female desire, the fantasy of sexual failure represented the deepest of all the sources of male anxiety. Manhood consisted in exhibiting the sexual and physical strength which

57. P. Collinson, *The Religion of Protestants: The Church in English Society 1559–1625* (Oxford, 1982), p. 227.
58. Howell, *Proverbs or Old Saws*, p. 13, discussed by J. Swetnam reprinted in K.U. Henderson and B.F. McManus, eds, *Half Humankind*, p. 197.
59. Purkiss in Brant and Purkiss, eds, *Women, Texts and Histories*, p. 79.
60. *Roxburghe*, VII, p. 197.
61. Foyster, 'A Laughing Matter?', *Rural History* 4 (1993), p. 8.

was necessary to keep a wife out of circulation. The real man was able to possess his wife's body through regular sex and her mind through authoritative control of her behaviour and of how she spent her time. Securing the confidence to achieve all this, and the sense that this achievement was more than temporary, the literature suggests, was something many men found hard indeed.

The tensions about issues of this kind were greater and the nervousness of men was certainly more acute in the competitive social world of early modern London than elsewhere. Gadding and its implications are insistent themes in the drama of the period. Coaches and boats on the Thames are the favoured modes of women's gadding from home in those plays which gained their titles from watermen's cries: *Westward Ho, Northward Ho* and *Eastward Ho*. A citizen's wife who demured about going in a coach meets with a predictable sexually coded response: 'yet most of your citizen's wives love jolting'. In Middleton's play *The Family of Love*, a husband outside the orgiastic meeting house where he has followed his wife declares to others 'look to't you that have such gadders to your wives! self-willed they are as children'. The drama makes play with the numerous excuses women found to go abroad, Beaumont and Fletcher's *The Woman Hater*, for example, listing pretended visits to distant churches and to mourning widows.[62]

Boozing groups of female gossips appear often in the ballads and puritan writers were fond of harping on the dangers of excessive gossiping. *Westward for Smelts* is a collection of stories told by a company of fishwives, put together by the waterman who carried them home to Kingston-on-Thames. There, he concludes, they 'went straight to the sign of the Bear, where they found such good liquor that they stayed by it all night'.[63] Male suspicion of such parties accounts no doubt for some exaggeration of the extent to which they were actually subversive of their authority. But Samuel Rowlands wrote two brilliant pieces about this issue which found a sufficient market for them to be reprinted. In the splendidly realised *Well Met Gossip* a widow, a wife who was supposed to be tending the shop in her husband's absence and a maid, whose mother had gone to church, drink and feast in a city tavern while they discuss what men are really like and how they can be managed. This was a piece well designed to send a shiver down male spines. After some reminiscence about the pranks of youthful service, the widow leads the discussion towards sex, insisting that all women learn early they must have it often. The maid is chid for her bashfulness: 'wine and virginity kept stale', she

---

62. L. Woodbridge, *Women and the English Renaissance: Literature and the Nature of Womankind 1540–1620* (Urbana, 1986), pp. 132–3.
63. Cited in R.A. Houlbrooke, 'Women's Social Life and Common Action in England from the Fifteenth Century to the Eve of the Civil War', *Continuity and Change* 2 (1986), p. 173.

is told, 'drinks flat'. The widow is insistent upon female rights to sexual fulfilment in marriage. While the maid dreams romantically of a 'comly man', the widow readily confesses that she would be cuckolding her clownish husband if he were still alive. The wife meanwhile recounts the marital strategies through which she gets the food and drink she best likes and manipulates her husband's humour. The satire is blatantly subversive from start to finish.[64]

A *Crew of Kind Gossips* tells of the unfair abuse men suffer by being wronged behind their backs. Rowlands's satire addresses a severe preface to the maids of London requiring them to refrain from the kind of gossips' feast in which wives are accustomed to indulge. The piece is given dramatic shape by the format of six female declarations by aggrieved wives answered in turn by their offended husbands. The dialogue gives full and colourful rein to the range of men's dilemmas in the course of the marital relationship. Its message is thoroughly patriarchal, laying bare the basic shared assumptions with which men approached the sexual politics of the period and illustrating how women defied them. The men's faults, taking the defences they offer into account, are portrayed as venial. One accused of being a gamester made it up as something to say; another confesses he drinks a lot but swears he is seldom too drunk to stand up; another, seen visiting a bawdy house, explains that he merely wished to see 'a gallant quean in a silk gown loose bodied' rather than try her, to have a smoke and sing a bawdy song. The women, by contrast, are portrayed as universally shrewish and variously spendthrifts, idle and violent. Men's problems with all this are explored in detail. Giving a wife money to spend only encouraged her to demand more and stimulated her pride. Corrective discipline is met blow for blow:

> I valiantly took up a faggot-stick
> For he had given me a blow or twain
> But as he likes it, let him strike again
> The blood ran down about his ears apace
> I brake his head and all bescratch't his face
> Then got him down and with my very fist
> I did bepommell him until he pissed.

Manipulative tricks were shown as hard to combat: one wife charged with extravagance would just 'sit down and cry'; another, not strong enough to answer force with force, thought nothing of putting a stool in her drunken husband's way, then when he had fallen over it setting him to bed in the chair. More seriously, two of the male protagonists fear being cuckolded. One has been told by a friend that a cousin who his wife goes to visit is a whore:

64. S. Rowlands, *Well Met Gossip* (London, 1619), first published as *'Tis Merry When Gossips Meet* (1602), reprinted 1656, 1675.

> To wear a pair of horns I would be loth
> But who can help, the deed once being done
> It is a thread so close with cunning spun.

He plans to give her the rope to hang herself, prove her a whore and then leave her. The other is under suspicion because of her whole pattern of life: sleeping late, pretending illness, playing with her lap dog, beating her maid and gadding with her friends. There is an authentic ring to these tales: they probably take us near some of the realities of the less harmonious marriages among London middling groups. Rowlands knew that his male readers were used to living with women prepared to give as good as they got, either with tongue or fist. He expatiated on real male dilemmas with force and wit:

> And if I speak she answers 'what care I?'
> I'le be maintained gentlewoman like
> Then bends her fist as if she meant to strike
> That sometime I am glad to speak her fair
> For quietness and 'tis an honest care
> To have command only by manly carriage
> For I do know the civil wars of marriage
> Too well, by divers of my neighbours lives,
> That are outmatched in combat with their wives.[65]

There is no way we can authenticate the story told by Thomas Harman in a tract of 1566. He described how a group of women surprised and ambushed the adulterous husband of one of their number at his nocturnal rendezvous, just as he was taking down his hose. They allegedly used them to bind his legs and gave him a severe beating. This is certainly in the spirit of Rowlands's satires.[66]

Women's vanity and pride was seen as the root of much of their challenging and dangerous behaviour. William Heale, in his tract of 1609, identified three aspects of this: 'affected curiosity of apparel, overnice standing on preeminence and womanish dislikings and fond longings'.[67] Richard Brathwaite devoted considerable space to the issue of dress in *The English Gentlewoman*, condemning fashion 'which detracts from the native beauty of the feature'. He had no time for women who spent too long with the looking glass, were too delicate about their clothes, or who spent more energy in the matter 'than decency requires'.[68] Stephen Gosson's verse 'A glass to view the pride of vainglorious women', published in 1596, attacked grave matrons who, he alleged, appeared on the

---

65. S. Rowlands, *A Whole Crew of Kind Gossips* (1609), reprinted 1613. For another subversive gossips' feast, see Capp, p. 117.
66. Houlbrooke, 'Women's Social Life', *Continuity and Change* 2 (1986), p. 173.
67. W. Heale, *An Apology for Women* (London, 1609), p. 37.
68. R. Brathwaite, *The English Gentlewoman* (1641), pp. 275–8.

London streets 'like wanton nags' with their 'painted faces, peacock feathers, periwigs, spangles, lace and naked paps'. 'A woman that paints puts up a bill that she is to be let'; 'the more women look in their glass the less they look to their house'. So the proverbs ran.[69] Barnaby Rich caustically spelt out the implications of excess in apparel:

> Now besides this garishness in apparel what are these paintings of shameless faces, this audacious boldness in company, these impudent gestures without modesty, these wanton looks, these enticing shows, what are these and many other things that might be spoken of but the vaunterers of adultery? . . . as the sin of Adam began at Eve, so the ruin, the confusion, the extortion, the oppression, yea and the sacrilege of many a man begins at the pride of his wife.[70]

William Vaughan argued that rich clothes as 'allurements to spiritual fornication after the pompous gods of the earth be likewise the forerunners of fleshly fornication'.[71] Defenders of women in the debates of the late Elizabethan and Jacobean period attempted to vindicate women's interest in fashion. Esther Sowernam, for example, asked whether a woman should not be commended for having 'as carefully and as curiously as she may set out what she hath received from Almighty God, than to be censured that she doth it to allure wanton and lascivious looks?'[72] But notions about a connection between women's luxury and lustfulness were certainly not easily removed from men's minds. Awareness of the issue is also prominent in the drama of the period. Lisa Jardine notes how Vittoria's love of fine attire in *The White Devil* 'is part of her insidious draining of male strength'. The Duchess of Malfi finds herself accused of both lasciviousness and luxurious living. Petruchio's devices for taming Kate include the denial of her choice of clothes, a scene which audiences will have relished as an issue at the heart of the period's sexual politics.[73]

If matters of dress and cosmetics ultimately always came back to the bedrock issue of sexual fidelity, the proper use of the household purse was always also at stake here. For the body's excesses, declared Rich with some exaggeration, 'hospitality is eaten up and good housekeeping is banished out of the country'.[74] Samuel Rowlands, who had made much of women's demands in this respect in *A Crew of Kind Gossips*, listed avoiding extravagance as the third duty of a wife in his 1617 tract *The Bride*:

69. S. Gosson, *Pleasant Quippes for Upstart Newfangled Gentlewomen* (London, 1596); Tilley, nos W663, W688.
70. Rich, *The Excellency of Good Women*, p. 16.
71. Cited in Gowing, pp. 73–4.
72. Cited in Gibbons, p. 41.
73. Jardine, *Still Harping on Daughters*, pp. 153–4.
74. Rich, *The Excellency of Good Women*, p. 15.

> For many idle housewives, London knows
> Have by their pride been husbands' overthrows.[75]

Besides the cult of extravagant dressing which had become a marked feature of the London social scene by this time, Rowlands may have been thinking of the transvestite fashion, a new kind of female modishness, which had caused a spate of male comment since the 1570s. George Gascoigne was the first to note female transvestism on the streets in a satire on women in 1576.[76] Philip Stubbes, in *The Anatomy of Abuses* published in 1583, produced the first shrill denunciation of women's audacity in public. He quoted Deuteronomy chapter twenty-two which deals with laws concerning sexual purity and insisted:

> Our apparel was given us as a sign distinctive to discern betwixt sex and sex and therefore one to wear the apparel of another sex is to participate with the same and to adulterate the verity of his own kind. Wherefore these women may not improperly be called hermaphrodites, that is monsters of both kinds, half women, half men.[77]

Publications by William Harrison and William Averell made passing references to the fashion later in the same decade. It may have been less virulent during the 1590s, when the critics went silent, but there was more comment by Henry Parrot, Richard Nicols and Thomas Adams between 1606 and 1615. Preachers began to inveigh against the fashion. John Williams, in *A Sermon of Apparel* in 1619, protested that women were even attending church in masculine dress. In a marriage sermon the same year, Thomas Gataker paralleled 'a mankind woman' with a 'masterly wife': both were monsters in nature.[78] Thomas Middleton's play *A Mad World My Masters*, written around 1608, contains a comic scene in which the young gallant Follywit prepares for a prank by having his comrades cover his breeches with the lower part of a gentlewoman's gown, making him half man and half woman. This aped the normal pattern of the transvestite fashion as it had been adopted in the 1570s and continued since then. Follywit laughingly points the moral to his puzzled companions: 'Why the doublet serves as well as the best and is most in fashion. We're all male to th' middle, mankind from the beaver to the bum. 'Tis an Amazonian time; you shall have women shortly tread their husbands.'[79]

---

75. Cited in Henderson and McManus, eds, *Half Humankind*, p. 60.
76. Woodbridge, *Women and the English Renaissance*, p. 139.
77. Deuteronomy, chapter 22, verse 5: 'A woman must not wear men's clothes nor a man put on women's dress; anyone who does this is detestable to Yahweh your God.' P. Stubbes, *The Anatomy of Abuses* (London, 1583), sig F5.
78. Woodbridge, *Women and the English Renaissance*, pp. 141–3; S.C. Shapiro, 'Feminists in Elizabethan England', *History Today*, 1977, p. 704.
79. D.L. Frost, ed., *The Selected Plays of Thomas Middleton* (Cambridge, 1978), pp. 53–4.

Gascoigne's 1576 pamphlet had identified precisely how women transformed the upper part of their bodies: they wore doublets in place of
gowns, the latest styles of ruffs from Spain and France and high 'copt' hats
flaunting a feather in place of coifs or kerchiefs.[80] The account given of
the masculine woman who was to be seen on the London streets more
than forty years later, in pamphlets published in 1620, differs only in a few
details. Short hair had become *de rigueur*; daggers, swords or pistols were
often worn and sometimes boots as well; hats became broad-brimmed and
retained the 'wanton' feather; the long padded doublet of Stubbes's day
was replaced by an indecently short French one; petticoats were abandoned for knee-length skirts. We should note that, although there were
references on the stage at this time which implied that some women wore
breeches as well, they invariably refer to people like tavern hostesses
rather than to the middling sort and gentry.[81] The resonances of all this
are obvious: transvestism of this kind, displayed at the playhouse and on
the London social scene, blatantly challenged the gender order and put
men's patriarchal authority on the line.[82] How many women practised it
is much less important than the fact that it occurred at all and the reaction
that it provoked. The misogynist critics accused the transvestite women of
flaunting their sexuality. The fashion was alleged to include bared breasts
or short doublets 'all unbuttoned to entice'.[83]

Women were credited with an inner weakness that could all too easily
lead them through the assertion of their sexual and emotional power to
defy the patriarchal order and break its boundaries. Two particular categories of such women – the whore and the witch – held special terrors
for men, leading them to develop and propagate stereotypes of these evil
women so that they would be instantly recognisable and susceptible to
control and elimination. The whore – there were plenty in London –
abused the deepest principles of patriarchy, rejecting the household
structure of heterosexual marriage by selling her body, playing upon
men's weak and foolish vulnerability to feminine wiles.[84] John Taylor's
poem 'A whore' emphasised her hold over men:

> She's nimbler than a tumbler as I think
> Lays down and takes up whilst a man can wink
> And though she seems unmeasured in her pleasure
> 'Tis otherwise, a yard's her only measure.

The whore was, in Taylor's portrait, brazen, wholly selfish and totally
unscrupulous:

80. Woodbridge, *Women and the English Renaissance*, p. 139.
81. Henderson and McManus, eds, *Half Humankind*, pp. 266–8, 279–80; Woodbridge,
    Women and the English Renaissance, p. 217.
82. Jardine, *Still Harping on Daughters*, pp. 154–6.
83. Henderson and McManus, eds, *Half Humankind*, pp. 267, 271; Capp, p. 115.
84. For prostitution in Elizabethan London see I. Archer, *The Pursuit of Stability: Social
    Relations in Elizabethan London* (Cambridge, 1991), pp. 211–15.

> She's impudently armed and shameless too
> And never dreads what man to her can do
> Her nether part to stake she'll often lay
> To keep her upper part in fashion gay.

Taylor painted the whore as an ungendered or neuter figure: her abandonment of the rules of scriptural and ordered society left her with no
place in its ranks 'for she's for thee or me or any man'. Sermons and other
descriptions emphasised the deceit involved in prostitution. When the
language of insult touched on alleged whoredom people often used
strategies of exclusion from street and district which played upon deeply
rooted notions of purity and danger. The currency of the word whore
undoubtedly increased during the seventeenth and eighteenth centuries as
both men and women came to use it on the street and in public
altercations by way of general reference to alleged infidelity. The basic
slander remained universally available long after the dilemmas which are
being outlined here had receded. In London consistory court defamation
cases from the period from 1770 to 1810, Anna Clark found that its
implications included charges that 'a woman had no self-respect, that she
did not control herself, that she was loud and sexually promiscuous, that
she roamed the streets or that she did not conform to the control of
husband or father'.[85]

The witch could be seen as the extreme example of the non-conform-
ist, the malignant person who actually sought to bring harm to neighbours
by occult means. Around eighty per cent of those accused of the crime
were women. Merry Weisner has summarised the underlying intellectual concepts which would have supported a link between women and
witchcraft, stressing the importance of a series of generally accepted
dichotomies – between order and disorder, culture and nature, reason
and emotion, mind and body. They were 'all dichotomies in which men
were linked to the first terms and women to the second'.[86] The essence
of English witchcraft, in so far as it can be explored as a series of practices,
was the use of verbal power as a substitute for action. It was very closely
associated with scolding. The helpless old woman who had fallen out
with neighbours had no other resort but to curse them: the 'chief fault'
of witches, wrote Reginald Scot, 'is that they are scolds'.[87] Alexander
Roberts summarised the reasons why most witches were women in his
tract of 1616 *A Treatise of Witchcraft*. They were credulous and thus easily
deceived; having a softer 'complexion' they 'more easily receive the
impression of the devil'; since Eve they had 'a greater facility to fall'; they

85. J. Taylor, *Works* (London, 1630), pp. 106–7; Gowing, pp. 71–2; A. Clark, 'Whores
    and Gossips: Sexual Reputation in London 1770–1825', in A. Angerman, ed., *Current
    Issues in Women's History* (London, 1989), p. 242. See also *OED*: 'whore'.
86. M.E. Weisner, *Women and Gender in Early Modern Europe* (Cambridge, 1993),
    pp. 228–9.
87. K.V. Thomas, *Religion and the Decline of Magic* (London, 1971), pp. 502–12.

tended to anger and had a greater appetite for revenge.[88] Well established patriarchal attitudes, in other words, made a connection in contemporary demonological theory between women and witchcraft predictable. The issue, as in all sexual politics, was one of power. Faced by women who behaved in a way that was suspicious and irrational, men in authority, until at least the late seventeenth century, jumped easily to the conclusion that witchcraft was involved. While a consensus persisted that people could do occult harm to others acting under the devil's auspices, and legislation was available to deal with such people, this was a dilemma more easily solved than most of the others posed by insubordinate women in this period.

Two vignettes from literary sources will suffice to indicate the emotions that witch accusations generated. The examination of Margaret Flower, who was accused of bewitching members of the family of the Earl of Rutland in 1618, is a good example of the extraction of a detailed confession of sexual relations with the devil such as poor women could be persuaded to make when deprived in gaol of sleep and food. She spoke of 'two familiar spirits sucking on her . . . the white sucked under the left breast and the black-spotted within the inward parts of her secrets . . . when she first entertained them she promised them her soul and they covenanted to do all things which she commanded them.' The pamphlet account, following Margaret Flower's execution at Lincoln, makes sober reading about the depths of evil to which women could sink and it drew the moral that the wicked would be punished either in this life, the life to come or both.[89] The case of Anna Trapnell was much less clear. She was accused by some of the Cornish magistrates of being a witch when her trances and prophecies against the Cromwellian government in 1654 attracted large crowds to her bedside. One wanted to use a whip to fetch her out of the bed. What bothered the JPs was the disturbance and potential disorder that Anna Trapnell created. Witchcraft was the obvious charge to throw at a woman who boldly took up so public a role. But after the court hearing, in her own account, 'as I went in the crowd many strangers were very loving and careful . . . and the rude multitude said "sure this woman is no witch, for she speaks many good words, which the witches could not"'. The magistracy saw that it was ill advised to pursue further a public woman with such a following. Yet what was this woman doing in public at all? She had challenged the basic rules of patriarchy, posing another sort of dilemma for men at a time of exceptional political tension.[90]

88. J.A. Sharpe, 'Witchcraft and Women in Seventeenth-century England: Some North-ern Evidence', *Continuity and Change*, 6 (1991), p. 181.
89. Henderson and McManus, eds, *Half Humankind*, p. 378.
90. E. Graham, H. Hinds, E. Hobby and H. Wilcox, eds, *Her Own Life: Autobiographical Writings by Seventeenth-Century Englishwomen* (London, 1989), pp. 71–4.

The antifeminist tradition was deeply rooted in western European society. Exploring the 'wellsprings of medieval misogyny', Alcuin Blamires finds one route leading back to ancient Judaic law and another to the dawn of Greek culture. His anthology of medieval texts on the subject adumbrates all the accusations against women that have been discussed in this chapter.[91] They are accusations that reappear in misogynist tracts of the sixteenth and seventeenth centuries such as *The Schoolhouse of Women* and Joseph Swetman's *The Arraignment of Lewd, Idle, Froward and Unconstant Women*. Swetman's misogynist tirade, first published in 1616, had gone through ten editions by 1634.[92] Composed in line with literary conventions which presented attacks on women in the form of paradoxes and jokes, it was nevertheless open, unabashed and sensational in the hatred of women that it exhibited.

> The lion being bitten with hunger, the bear being robbed of her young ones, the viper being trod on, all these are nothing so terrible as the fury of a woman . . . a froward woman will never be tamed. No spur will make her go, nor no bridle will hold her back, for if a woman will hold an opinion no man can draw her from it . . . At a word, a woman will never forget an injury nor give thanks for a good turn. What wise man then will exchange gold for dross, pleasure for pain, a quiet life for wrangling brawls, from the which the married men are never free?[93]

It is this sensationalism which may account for Swetnam's popularity. It would therefore be highly unwise to take his work seriously as evidence about a sharpening acrimony against women in general. The material used in this chapter by contrast is not all essentially misogynistic; it suggests fears and worries about women's energies and initiative, about their sexual and verbal power, which did not invariably or necessarily amount to a generalised hatred of women.

What seems undeniable is that there was an acutely felt anxiety in Tudor and early Stuart England about how women could best be governed and controlled. It may be that this anxiety was more widespread and deeper in London than in the countryside and it can be suggested that certain social developments go some way towards accounting for it there. It is well established that London developed rapidly in this period as a centre for fashion and conspicuous consumption. The impetus for this process was closely connected with improvements in travel once gentry owned their own coaches and female interest in the delights of the

91. Blamires, *Woman Defamed and Woman Defended*, p. 2.
92. See Henderson and McManus, eds, *Half Humankind* for a full account and for the main texts. See also Hull, *Chaste, Silent and Obedient*, pp. 106–26.
93. M.J.M. Ezell, *The Patriarch's Wife: Literary Evidence and the History of the Family* (Chapel Hill, 1987), pp. 46–7; Henderson and McManus, eds, *Half Humankind*, p. 194.

metropolitan scene burgeoned.[94] James I's campaign to make the gentry return to their estates and perform their customary hospitality and responsibilities there was disliked as much by wives as by husbands. It was 'nothing pleasing to all but least of all to the women', commented John Chamberlain on the latest enquiry into the enforcement of his proclamations in February 1623.[95] He may have wanted scapegoats for general disobedience. But we know that many women were out and about in London, that they went to playhouses, for example.[96] Moreover it is hardly likely that tavern gossiping of the kind satirised by Samuel Rowlands was entirely a figment of male imaginations. Gentry and citizens' wives did not perhaps need to display very much new assertiveness in their actual behaviour in order to arouse men's concern about the gender order. Women's social activities in London were expanding in a manner that seemed to carry a hidden threat. 'The fear of inversion of authority between men and women', Lisa Jardine has remarked, 'has a primitive force.'[97] It is hard to say exactly how it is evoked but that it is easily evoked is not really in question.

The suggestion that the period from around the 1560s to the 1660s saw a general crisis of gender relations in England has been disputed. Based on patchy local material about the prosecution of scolds, the argument seems insecurely based.[98] But, as the wide range of literary evidence cited here shows, there undoubtedly was considerable anxiety about the gender order at this time and this anxiety cannot be seen as simply a London phenomenon (plates 1 and 3). The ballad mongers found a ready market for their scolding tales as they took to the byways of rural England. The satirical literature also undoubtedly circulated beyond the capital. Probing the nature of men's anxiety is difficult since the essence of patriarchy is that men's problems with enforcing it are not talked about. But the literary evidence presented here suggests that its roots lay in turbulence about male sexuality, which was in practice more problematic than men let it appear. We can detect a range of factors which masked men's vulnerability in this respect. In the first place the problematising of women as themselves powerfully sexual as well as

---

94. F.J. Fisher, 'The Development of London as a Centre for Conspicuous Consumption in the Sixteenth and Seventeenth Centuries', *TRHS*, XXX (1948), pp. 37–50.

95. Cited in F. Heal, 'The Crown, the Gentry and London: The Enforcement of Proclamation 1596–1640', in C. Cross, D. Loades and J.J. Scarisbrick, eds, *Law and Government under the Tudors* (Cambridge, 1988), p. 219.

96. A. Gurr, *Playgoing in Shakespeare's London* (Cambridge, 1987), pp. 56–9.

97. Jardine, *Still Harping on Daughters*, p. 162.

98. D.E. Underdown, 'The Taming of the Scold: The Enforcement of Patriarchal Authority in Early Modern England', in Fletcher, A.J. and Stevenson, A., eds, *Order and Disorder, in Early Modern England* (Cambridge, 1985), pp. 137–65; M. Ingram, ' "Scolding Women Cucked or Washed": a Crisis in Gender Relations in Early Modern England?", in J. Kermode and G. Walker, eds, *Women, Crime and the Courts in Early Modern England* (London, 1994), pp. 48–80.

irrational was a solvent to the male sense of responsibility for making relationships endure. Secondly, the division of women into the pure, who were available for marriage and needed to be constantly watched and controlled so they kept within its boundaries, and the impure, the whores and witches who were in one way or another thrown out of society, was temptingly plausible. Thirdly, the double standard may have enabled men to escape some of the need to work at making monogamous relationships succeed over a considerable period of time while expecting women to do so. We are left then with a considerable historical problem. Before exploring how men and women made patriarchy work, however, we need to investigate more fully what conception men had of gender and how they saw the relationship between gender and the body at this time.

2. *Functional Anatomies*

How DID PEOPLE understand and conceptualise their bodies before the medical advances of this period, like Harvey's discovery of the circulation of the blood, became common knowledge? Andrew Wear has emphasised that we have to envisage a largely unregulated medical market place which was characterised by a multiplicity of religious, magical and naturalistic explanations for illness and approaches to treatment. Patients themselves, family, neighbours, clergy, cunning men, midwives, apothecaries and astrologers were all practitioners in this market place, besides surgeons and physicians whose services were beyond the pockets of most people.[1] This is the context of a massive popularisation of medical information for which the conditions were exactly right between 1500 and 1700. There was a body of authorised medicine, even if it was built on the ramshackle edifice of classical learning with later accretions. There were writers eager and willing to spread it. The printed book provided a reasonably inexpensive medium of diffusion. An interested and growing literate audience was ready to purchase.[2]

Variety was its great strength, Paul Slack concluded in an analysis of the vernacular medical literature of sixteenth-century England. This literature ranged from herbals, regimens for health and collections of remedies to heavier tomes like Vicary's *Anatomy of the Body of Man*. At the cheapest end a compendium of recipes for self-treatment like Thomas Moulton's *This is the Mirror or Glass of Health*, which went through seventeen editions by the 1580s, was available for twopence or threepence, making it accessible to a wide public. There were some 392 editions of medical works published between 1486 and 1604, possibly representing, it is suggested, a total of nearly 400,000 printed copies.[3] No parallel study has

1. A. Wear, 'The Popularisation of Medicine in Early Modern England', in R. Porter, ed., *The Popularisation of Medicine 1650–1850* (London, 1992), pp. 17–19.
2. Introduction in Porter, ed., *Popularisation of Medicine*, p. 3.
3. P. Slack, 'Mirrors of Health and Treasures of Poor Men: The Uses of the Vernacular Medical Literature of Tudor England', in C. Webster, ed., *Health, Medicine and Mortality in the Sixteenth Century* (Cambridge, 1979), pp. 237–71. See also H.S. Bennett, *English Books and Readers 1603–1640* (Cambridge, 1970), pp. 140–49.

been done for the seventeenth century but it is evident that this literature went on burgeoning. Many of the textbook writers were not physicians but rather well educated men with a mission to provide people with plain do-it-yourself guides to health. The courtier and humanist Sir Thomas Elyot prefaced his very popular book *The Castle of Health* with an impressive list of the authorities he had consulted.[4] The cleric Andrew Boorde explained at the start of *The Breviary of Health* that his descriptions of diseases included translations of obscure terms in Greek, Latin or Arabic.[5] John Partridge recommended his *Treasury of Commodious Conceits* to good housewives intent on the health of their households.[6] Walter Bruele, in his *The Physicians Practice*, wrote for an audience which he defined as physicians, surgeons, apothecaries and readers who were concerned for their own health.[7] Levinius Lemnius's *The Touchstone of Complexions* was addressed to all who wished 'to know the constitution of the body and affections of the mind'.[8]

The buyers and readers of this medical literature came from the gentry and middling groups; their correspondence and diaries continually remind us about how preoccupied they were with their health.[9] The appeal of the advice books was that they offered the remedy of a coherent, persuasive and plausible structure of information as some kind of defence against fear and anxiety. Women such as Margaret Hoby and Grace Mildmay read their herbals and dispensed physick to their households and neighbourhoods.[10] Diarists like Ralph Josselin, Samuel Pepys and Robert Hooke showed their thirst for explanation and understanding of ill health and a remarkable degree of confidence about diagnosis. Josselin read a treatise by Leonard Lessius on the best course for a healthy old age in 1649 and reflected in his diary upon his need to be more moderate in his diet and take regular exercise. Pepys recorded his experiencing some pain in making water, in 1662, 'having taken cold this morning in staying too long barelegged to pare my corns'. He was always making good resolutions about keeping warm or improving his health by measures such as 'an easy and plentiful going to stool and breaking of wind'. For a while he carried a hare's foot as a charm against colic.[11] Access to crude medical information of some kind was enjoyed by a broader section of the

---

4. Wear in Porter, ed., *Popularisation of Medicine*, pp. 20–21.
5. A. Boorde, *The Breviary of Health* (London, 1547), preface.
6. J. Partridge, *The Treasury of Commodious Conceits* (London, 1584), preface.
7. W. Bruele, *Praxis Medicinae or The Physicians Practice* (London, 1632), preface.
8. L. Lemnius, *The Touchstone of Complexions* (London, 1633), title page.
9. E.g. A.J. Fletcher, *A County Community in Peace and War: Sussex 1600–1660* (London, 1975), pp. 41–2.
10. L.M. Beier, *Sufferers and Healers: The Experience of Illness in Seventeenth Century England* (London, 1987), p. 166.
11. *Pepys*, III, p. 247, X, p. 172; Beier, *Sufferers and Healers*, pp. 164–77, 182–210; A. Macfarlane, ed., *The Diary of Ralph Josselin 1616–1683* (London, 1976), p. 154.

population through almanacs, which usually provided brief herbal sections and sometimes advice on health. By the second half of the seventeenth century as many as 400,000 almanacs may have been sold in some years.[12]

But how did people engage with all these texts? How far did owners actually read the books or almanacs they possessed? How did such reading affect their thinking about gender? In most cases there was little stress on continuity and narrative. The medical textbooks and almanacs were arranged in the expectation that they would be consulted rather than read. Andrew Boorde's and Walter Bruele's compendiums, for example, were set out systematically, in terms of diagnosis, treatment and prognosis, ailment by ailment. The reader could run his eye through the headings to find the entry he required.[13] Mary Fissell's examination of the structure of the *Erra Pater*, a kind of perpetual almanac which went through numerous editions between the 1530s and 1800, reveals the importance of functional repetition. When the *Erra Pater* describes the parts of the body ruled by different signs of the zodiac, it presents the information by means of a woodcut, a discussion in prose and a verse which sums up the basic points.[14] Such devices were normal in a culture devoted to emblems, where no broadside ballad or chapbook appeared without its woodcut frontispiece selling the story.[15]

Sometimes a surviving copy of one of these early medical advice books contains specific evidence, in the form of annotation, about its use and readership. One of the copies of Elyot's *Castle of Health* in the British Library is a good example. On a spare page between the list of contents and the opening of the text someone has noted a 'medicine for the mother', suggesting that the book was used by a woman or by her solicitous husband. There is a strong indication that another reader was especially interested in Elyot's prescriptions about sleep, since directions about this for people of different temperaments are heavily annotated and underlined. A reader has also underlined a section warning against too much use of violent purgations. A further section about the use of urine for self-diagnosis has a long personal commentary written in, apparently consisting of received oral wisdom: 'sperm too much lechery, grains signify rheum and gout, dust the gout or a woman conceived' and so on. Overall there is clear evidence in this volume of multiple use and of an interactive style of reading.[16]

How far this literature, other than the herbals which were little more

12. B. Capp, *Astrology and the Popular Press: English Almanacs 1500–1800* (London, 1979), pp. 44, 204–6.
13. A. Boorde, *The Breviary of Health*; W. Bruele, *Physicians Practice*.
14. M.E. Fissell, 'Readers, Texts and Contexts: Vernacular Medical Works in Early Modern England', in Porter, ed., *The Popularisation of Medicine*, pp. 72–96.
15. T. Watt, *Cheap Print and Popular Piety 1550–1640* (Cambridge, 1991), pp. 131–77.
16. BL, C 54 a 18: Sir T. Elyot, *The Castle of Health* (London, 1534).

than lists of medicines, was read by women as well as men it is hard to say. What is clear is that during the seventeenth century a few books for women did begin to appear which were not just intended for practising midwives. The Norwich doctor John Sadler prefaced his treatise *The Sick Woman's Private Looking Glass*, the first of this genre, with a statement that his work combined his learning from Greek and Latin authors with his experience in practice. He offered medical prescriptions for various conditions of the womb.[17] The translation of the tract *The Woman's Doctor* by Nicholas Fontanus, which appeared in 1652, set out to supply 'an exact and distinct explanation of all such diseases as are peculiar to that sex'.[18] There is implicit recognition here that women were in some sense different from men. Such works, however, were entirely orthodox, that is they were written within the framework of the humoral system, which was the basis for all thinking about the body at this time.

The humoral model presented a common corporeal economy: an all-embracing and coherent scheme of explanation for the functioning of all human bodies which at the same time took account of specific aspects of womanhood, like menstruation and breast feeding, which required explanation. The fluid content of the body in this model was almost entirely made up of the four humours of blood, choler, melancholy and phlegm. Each had two primary qualities: blood is hot and moist, choler is hot and dry, melancholy is cold and dry, phlegm is cold and moist. The analogies in the macrocosm are with air, fire, earth and water. Each humour has its physiological functions: blood warms and moistens the body, choler provokes the expulsion of excrements, melancholy provokes appetite in the stomach, phlegm nourishes the cold and moist members such as the brain and kidneys[19] (plate 12). Every disease in early modern medicine was regarded as explicable in terms of humoral abnormalities. The textbooks considered here set out all their arguments about diagnosis and prognosis within this conceptual framework. The same framework explained gender. With the precise boundary between the heat which made man a man and the cold which predominated to make woman a woman difficult to draw, gender in fact seemed dangerously fluid and indeterminate. Yet sexual temperature was the only way people could look at it. After all, the humoral system explained satisfactorily enough why at some point male ended and female began, just as it explained about diseases and their remedies. This gender scheme blinded people to the sexual significance of differences in reproductive biology. Women were placed on a

17. J. Sadler, *The Sick Woman's Private Looking Glass* (London, 1636). For a bibliography and survey see S.W. Hull, *Chaste, Silent and Obedient: English Books for Women 1435–1640* (San Marino, 1982).
18. N. Fontanus, *The Woman's Doctor* (London, 1652).
19. L. Babb, *The Elizabethan Malady: A Study of Melancholia in English Literature from 1580 to 1642* (Michigan, 1951) contains a good account, pp. 5–20.

vertical hierarchy below men, rather than along a horizontal axis with masculinity and femininity as its two polarities. Understanding the body was how people sought to understand gender and what they learnt was that the one provided no quick and easy line of demarcation for establishing the other.

From the second century AD to the sixteenth the one-sex model of the body invented by Galen of Pergamon proved immensely resilient. It was founded on a structural identity between the male and female reproductive organs. Women, in his reading of human anatomy, were essentially men who through a lack of vital heat had retained inside the body structures that in the male are visible without. The ovaries were female testicles; the penis in this exercise becomes the cervix and vagina; the uterus is an internal scrotum. Nor was the womb anything special in this rendering. The neck of the womb was nothing other than the penis turned inward and the bottom of it nothing but the scrotum inverted in Vesalius's visual account of Galen's conception in his *De Humani Corporis Fabrica* of 1543.[20]

Organs were traditionally associated with purposes. Following the first human dissections around 1400, there was a growing tension between this teleological imperative and the detailed findings of continental anatomists. It is difficult to see a linear progress in knowledge as anatomy at the end of the middle ages became characterised by a jumble of facts which, it has been suggested, 'scholars were hard pressed to harmonise into an orderly synthesis'.[21] The anatomists of the sixteenth century exposed many Aristotelian and Galenic fallacies about the female genitalia, even as they continued to produce representations of the male and female body in terms of structural homology.[22] Major advances in embryology and gynaecology did not come until after 1650 and did not reach England in an accessible form until the 1680s. Meanwhile medical writers in England and Europe struggled to harmonise the basic conceptual framework they inherited from the ancients – one sex, the humoral system and a common corporeal economy – with a growing body of fresh knowledge. They remained Galenists at heart who were often Aristotelian in their thinking. Two questions about woman preoccupied them before 1600: is she an imperfect version of the male, and does she produce fertile semen? By 1600 the vast majority had answered the first question by replacing the notion that woman was less perfect than man with the argument that she was 'equally perfect in her own sex'. Thereby, notes Ian Maclean, 'the late Renaissance Galenists disunite the physiology

20. T. Laqueur, *Making Sex: Body and Gender from the Greeks to Freud*, (Cambridge, Massachusetts, 1990), pp. 4, 25–8; L. Schiebinger, *The Mind has no Sex?* (Cambridge, Massachusetts, 1989), p. 163.

21. D. Jacquart and C. Thomasset, *Sexuality and Medicine in the Middle Ages* (London, 1985), pp. 35–6.

22. For these representations see Laqueur, *Making Sex*, pp. 71–93.

and anatomy of male and female in matters of sex.' They rejected the axiom that a direct comparison can be made between the genitalia of man and woman in function, number and form. In other words they abandoned the one-sex body of antiquity in its full anatomical form.[23]

A good example of a writer taking this stance in England is John Banister whose *The History of Man*, published in 1578, was offered as advice 'to all godly surgeons'. After the customary obeisance to Galen and Hippocrates, he reviewed recent advances in anatomy. When he came to 'the generative parts' he asserted, with a momentary twist towards one-sex thinking, that 'the almighty creator made two men: the male to reach out the effectual beginning of generation, the female aptly to conceive the same and to nourish the infant'. For these respective gifts men and women, said Banister, receive 'fit and peculiar instruments'. He then stopped short at giving an account of the female genitalia, commenting that it would be indecent 'to lift up the veil of nature's secrets in woman's shapes'.[24]

Banister was much more up to date than Thomas Vicary in the second edition of his *The Anatomy of the Body of Man*, originally issued in 1548, which appeared in 1577. Vicary, who was chief surgeon to Henry VIII, lauded Galen as 'the lantern of all surgery'. He began with an account of the 'simple members' of the body – bones, nerves, veins, flesh and so forth – explaining in each case whether they were defined as cold and dry or hot and moist. He then proceeded downwards from top to toe: reaching reproductive anatomies in his ninth chapter, he for the first time showed an awareness of women as well as men. The spermatic vessels, he explained, bring blood to the testicles 'as well in man as in woman, in the which by his further digestion, it is made sperm or nature in men'. The omission at this stage of reference to the female's sperm and the reference to sperm as nature suggest that Vicary supported the Aristotelian principle of generativity. In fact he does not go all the way with Aristotle and deny the existence of female seed. Inside the woman, he states, in what he calls 'the utter mouth of the mouth' are 'two testicles or stones and also two vessels of sperm shorter than man's vessels'. This statement follows an account of 'the matrix in woman' which is wholly Galenic: 'it is an instrument susceptive that is to say a thing receiving or taking ... the likeness of it as it were a yard reversed or turned inward having testicles likewise aforesaid.'[25]

There had been no Latin or Greek words or any in the European vernacular languages for the female sexual organs, for the ovaries, for

23. I. Maclean, *The Renaissance Notion of Woman: A Study in the Fortunes of Scholasticism and Medical Science in European Intellectual Life* (Cambridge, 1980), pp. 28–33.
24. J. Banister, *The History of Man* (London, 1578), fols 85r–88v.
25. T. Vicary, *The Anatomy of the Body of Man* (Early English Text Society, extra series, 53, 1888), p. 11.

example, or the vagina. Thomas Laqueur is surely right to emphasise how this inadequacy of language 'constrained the seeing of opposites and sustained the male body as the canonical human form'.[26] Yet we can trace the efforts of the Tudor and Stuart writers, hampered as they were linguistically, to keep up with advancing medical knowledge. Vicary, writing a few years before Italian authors claimed they had discovered the clitoris, evidently knew something about this female sexual organ. His account sidles up to its purpose for sexual pleasure then shies away. At the mouth of the matrix, he notes the existence of a membrane 'which is called in latin tentigo'. His explanation of its use was that it both contained the bladder and provided a pair of workaday flaps: 'when a woman doth set her thighs abroad it altereth the air that commeth to the matrix for to temper the heat'.[27] Now 'tentigo' is quite clearly a sexual word in the sixteenth century. 'Were you tentiginous?' asks one character of another in Ben Jonson's *The Devil is an Ass*, meaning was he feeling lustful or lecherous.[28] Yet in Vicary's account the point is lost. He seems to have been almost ready to claim the discovery of the clitoris himself but could not quite bring himself to do so. The disturbing implications of there being a female penis, when he had learnt from Galen that the matrix in a woman replicated the penis in a man inside out, was presumably just too much for him. It would be naive to see this kind of confusion as representing actual ignorance of women's sexual sensitivity. Anatomy was simply enslaved to a teleological interpretation in which physiology rather than sexuality reigned supreme.[29]

Anatomical parallelism was replaced, from around 1600, with a physiology that took its stand on specific sexual functions. 'One sex begets in another, the other in itself', as Ian Maclean puts it, 'and each has an appropriately differentiated physiology.' This is the end of bodily homology but it is not the end of two seeds or of sexual oneness. The official discovery of the clitoris in Gabriele Falloppio's *Observationes Anatomicae* of 1561 is the key breakthrough here. This allowed Galen's comparison of uterus and inverted penis to be rejected in favour of a new alignment of clitoris and penis. This was an alignment that anatomists and physicians found they could make sense of in relation to the process of generation. In this new context the uterus, no longer an inferior organ, receives proper recognition and even admiration for its role in reproduction. The new thinking, a step on the way to fully gendered bodies, proposed complementary functional anatomies: much was successfully salvaged from ancient writings and fitted into a modified conceptual scheme and the emphasis on body temperature remained intact. Thus the Galenic

26. Laqueur, *Making Sex*, p. 96; but see E. Partridge, *Shakespeare's Bawdy* (London, 1968), pp. 87, 160–1.
27. Cited in Laqueur, *Making Sex*, p. 98.
28. *OED*: tentiginous.
29. Jacquart and Thomasset, *Sexuality and Medicine*, p. 46.

view that women's semen was colder and less active than men's was commonly adopted in European medical thought at this time.[30]

By the early seventeenth century the clitoris was firmly on the scene in English medical textbooks. 'Properly it is called the woman's yard', declared Helkiah Crooke in *Microcosmographia* published in 1615, with which it 'agrees in situation, substance and composition'.[31] In the standard textbook *Bartholin's Anatomy* which appeared in an English translation in 1668 there was a full description of the anatomy of the clitoris which is described as women's 'chief seat of delight in carnal copulation' and as crucial to orgasm because 'by rubbing thereof the seed is brought away'.[32] For Nicholas Venette, whose *Tableau de L'amour Conjugal* appeared in English in 1703, the clitoris provided 'the fury and rage of love ... the seat of pleasure and lust'. Venette was a medical conservative who nevertheless championed solid knowledge which was recently discovered. He saw the erotic drive as mysterious and sublime, a magical rite the mechanics of which deserved to be as fully explicated as possible so that it could be enjoyed for its procreatory purpose. The most popular sex manual of the eighteenth century, *Aristotle's Master-Piece*, preserved the hoary view that the female genitals are inverted versions of the male:

> For those that have the strictest searchers been
> Find women are but men turned outside in
> And men, if they but cast their eyes about
> May find they're women with their's inside out.

But this apparent dismissal of the clitoris was combined with an acceptance of it as equivalent to the penis elsewhere in the book and a recognition of women's parity in sexual desire.[33] It is strange, notes Brian Gibbons, that 'an anatomical theory which was better suited to underpin the traditional belief in female voluptuousness than the Galenic view rose to dominance in an age that witnessed a growing challenge to the stereotype of the libidinous female'.[34]

Helkiah Crooke was the most distinguished English anatomist of the seventeenth century. His treatise deserves further analysis for it provides the fullest and most influential account of the male and female functional anatomies for much of the seventeenth century, certainly until *Bartholin's Anatomy* reached England in 1668. It was issued in a new edition in 1631 and was clearly much read (plate 18). Crooke drew heavily upon the

30. Maclean, *Renaissance Notion of Woman*, pp. 33–7.
31. H. Crooke, *Microcosmographia: A Description of the Body of Man* (London, 1631 edn), p. 238.
32. N. Culpepper and A. Cole, trans. *Bartholin's Anatomy* (London, 1668), pp. 75–7.
33. R. Porter and L. Hall, *The Facts of Life: The Creation of Sexual Knowledge in Britain 1680–1950* (London, 1995), pp. 52, 65–77.
34. Gibbons, pp. 6–7.

work of two celebrated continental authorities, Gaspard Bauhin, professor of anatomy and botany in Basel, and Andreas Laurentius, professor of medicine at Montpellier and physician to Henry IV. He had imbibed the full legacy of Christian teaching and classical philosophy. He refers often to Galen, Hippocrates and Aristotle, though he is scathing about the efforts of the great Greek philosopher to reach conclusions about the body without experimental knowledge based on the science of dissection: 'he hath very curiously determined of all natural things and their causes but that so darkly and obscurely that he is understood but by few'. Crooke thought Aristotle was talking nonsense when he maintained that women did not produce seed. He is insistently teleological. Thus he is lyrical about the penis, created accurately in size and shape to be a pleasure not a trouble to the other sex. Its secondary use for voiding urine, he explains, is of no interest because this is quite obviously not what it was made for. After all, women 'make water without it'. At this stage of his book, Crooke is prepared to stick with Galenic homology. Men and women have the same reproductive parts: in men 'they appear outward'; in women, 'they are for want of heat retained within'. The teleology again shines through: 'seeing a woman is begotten of a man and perfect also in mankind . . . it is reasonable that the substance yea and the shape of the parts in both sexes should be alike as coming from one and the same set as it were of causes'.[35] In a later section, however, Crooke deals directly and frankly with the problems raised by recent medical advances, including his own discoveries. He knew the stories which are recorded by Michel Montaigne and by Ambroise Paré around this time of girls who during adolescence through some violent movement suddenly sprouted a penis between their legs, stories that made perfect sense for those who could still take Galen's account totally seriously. For in Galen's reading a girl on the edge of masculinity might need just a bit more heat or a swift and decisive action that was manly to cross the narrow gender borderline.[36] Crooke rejected such changes of sex as not credible. Perhaps, he says, the individuals concerned were hermaphrodites or perhaps the ignorant were deceived by a 'woman so hot by nature' that her clitoris 'hangs forth like a man's member'.[37]

The reason for Crooke's sharp critique is that his own professional life was concentrated upon very detailed anatomical observations and his findings constantly, and hardly surprisingly we may say, contradicted the Galenic homologies. The clitoris and penis were quite different, he found, since the former had no passage for seed. This was not too devastating a blow because Crooke persuaded himself that the clitoris was nevertheless

35. Crooke, *Microcosmographia*, pp. 20–4, 211–16.
36. Laqueur, *Making Sex*, pp. 126–8.
37. For a similar argument see A. Ross, *Arcana Microcosmi or The Hidden Secrets of Man's Body Disclosed* (London, 1651), p. 84.

still functional since the motion of it stirred up seed for generation. 'Although by this passage', he wrote, 'their seed is not ejaculated yet by the attrition of it their imagination is wrought to call that out that lieth deeply hidden in the body.' More fundamentally, the vagina could not be a penis inverted, claimed Crooke, because 'three hollow bodies cannot be made of one, but the yard consisteth of three hollow bodies' whereas 'the neck of the womb hath but one cavity'.[38] He had further difficulties about the alleged similitude between the cervix and the male cod or scrotum. He found the skin of the bottom of the womb to be 'very thick and tight membrane, all fleshy within' while 'the cod is a rugous and thin skin'.[39] Crooke makes no comment on what we might think should have been obvious to him, that, if turning the female genitalia into a scrotum and penis is bizarre, the transformation of the male genitals into the repro- ductive anatomy of the female, which was what Galen intended, is manifestly absurd.

For Helkiah Crooke anatomy was not destiny. It was the other way round. Why was woman created, he asked? His answer was functional. He believed woman was a necessary partner in the process of perfect generation, affording 'not only a place wherein to cherish and conceive the seed but also matter for the nourishment and augmentation of the same'. Crooke, in other words, was led to abandon homologous bodies and to restate sexual doubleness, the concept of a single flesh, in philo- sophical terms. The female, no less than the male, represented the 'per- fection of mankind'; her soul was as divine; her body was nature's 'proper and absolute work'. His overall formulation was as follows: 'Both these sexes of male and female do not differ in the kind as we call it or species, that is in the essential form or perfection, but only in some accidents, to wit in temper and in the structure and situation of the parts of gener- ation.' This, it should be noted, both adds to and subtracts from the Galenic model. In their perfection male and female come together on the vertical gender axis. Their sexual temperature separates them. But this is no more than a reiteration of the traditional humoral thinking which pervades Crooke's work. The anatomical differences revealed by early modern research end up becoming incidental to the whole scheme of things. In the opening pages of his book, Crooke expressed his view that the soul carried 'a deep stamp of divinity in the simplicity, invisibility and immortality thereof'; he spoke of its quickening and sustaining the body. In the soul of man he found 'something metaphysical, transcendent above nature'. In his body, abounding with the heat that expressed its perfec- tion, man walked upright unlike other creatures which were too earthy or watery, in order to 'meditate on heavenly things'. The body for Crooke

38. Crooke, *Microcosmographia*, pp. 249–50.
39. Cited from the 1615 edition in Laqueur, *Making Sex*, pp. 90–1. Laqueur has figures which show the anatomical correctness of Crooke's claims.

was 'an epitome or compendium of the whole Creation'.[40] Crooke is
rejecting the Aristotelian tradition which claimed that woman was an
imperfect version of the male, yet he clings to the notion that man is the
standard expression of the human species. He can take the crucial verses
27 and 28 in the first chapter of the Book of Genesis at their face value:
'So God created man in his own image; in the image of God he created
him; male and female he created them.' Yet his understanding of gender
presupposes that man is in some sense superior to woman, that rationality
is more normatively male. For Crooke the brain was the most noble and
divine part of the body, the habitation of wisdom, judgement and understanding: it was the 'prince of the family' to which all other parts were
attendant.[41] Man is still here the microcosm, the little world who has his
place in the Great Chain of Being (plates 14 and 15). The vertical gender
axis leaves women rather less perfect in being, not different in her physical
make-up except in detail, yet definitely in second place.

A few years before Crooke published his *Microcosmographia* a French
doctor, Jacques Duval, had grasped the unusual opportunity presented by
a case before the parlement of Rouen to test his uneasiness with the same
medical tradition that caused Crooke such perplexity. The case concerned
Marie le Marcis, a woman in her early twenties, who, having been
named, dressed and brought up a girl, had changed her clothing, asked to
be called Marin le Marcis, and declared he wished to marry a widow
called Jeane le Febvre. They had been sleeping in the same bed as fellow
servants. The charge against Marie was that, as a lesbian seductress with an
unnaturally enlarged clitoris, she had abused the willing Jeane. Duval's
account of his medical examination of Marie was published in his book
*On Hermaphrodites, Childbirth and the Medical Treatment of Mothers and
Children.* Whereas there had been testimony previously that Marie had
regularly menstruated and a first medical examination had revealed no
sign of a penis, Duval's reaching within the secret fold of her flesh had
enabled him to feel what he described as 'a male organ rather large and
hard'. Furthermore the friction of his touch caused Marie to ejaculate and
the semen, he reported, was thick and white like a man's. Here was a
prodigy, something that confounded the conventional classifications: a
hermaphrodite that, through embodied transvestism, caused astonishment.
What would Crooke have made of such an examination? Very much, one
suspects, what Duval did make of it. The fascination with hermaphrodites
at this time is perfectly intelligible, for it was only through investigation
of the prodigious that men could begin to understand the natural. What
Duval could see and Crooke would have appreciated was that there was
no question of a transformation from woman into man. Marie was both

40. Crooke, *Microcosmographia*, pp. 2–8, 258, 271–3.
41. Schiebinger, *The Mind has no Sex?*, p. 170.

Marie and, in some sense, Marin. His true gender had to be a social decision not a sexual one.[42]

Moving on to Restoration England and to texts like Thomas Bartholin's *Anatomy*, available from 1668, and Thomas Gibson's *The Anatomy of Human Bodies Epitomised*, published in 1682, we enter a new mental world and encounter the beginnings of a new cultural construct: two incommensurable sexes. Bartholin presented a cleaner, more open and more direct account of the differences between the male and female organs than Crooke had done. Separate chapters dealt with each in turn, supported by competent diagrams. He was more scathing about the old homologous conceits than Crooke had been, insisting that they 'fall to the ground by their own weakness'. He dismissed the opinion that women's genitals only differed in their situation, not in their kind as a notion 'hatched by those who accounted a woman to be only an imperfect man'.[43] The drawings which Bartholin produced were an even more emphatic declaration of two sexes than his text: two of them showed the womb without any attempt to liken it to the male organs and another showed the clitoris as a penis. In William Cowper's *The Anatomy of Humane Bodies*, published in 1697, however, the vagina achieved a clearer status of its own, losing the penis-like effect of the sixteenth-century representations[44] (plates 16 and 17). But it is Gibson's work which is more important. He boasted that it contained 'the newest doctrine of the most accurate and learned anatomists'. The book was carefully organised with detailed separate chapters on the male and female genitals. When he came to women's testicles, Gibson noted that, from William Harvey onwards, the most learned experts had denied that women produced seed and maintained that they produced an ovum instead: 'the testicles (so called) are not truly so nor have any such office as those of men.' This was thus one of the first relatively inexpensive works to challenge the concept of functional anatomies sharing a common physiology. Gibson, more decisively than Crooke or Bartholin, presages modern gendered bodies and sexuality.[45]

The mental world with which we are concerned here is a curious transitional world of neither one sex nor two. In his essay dedicated to Mary Griffith describing the 'excellency of the creation of woman' in 1639, William Austin could describe men and women as 'both of one

---

42. S. Greenblatt, *Shakespearean Negotiations: The Circulation of Social Energy in Renaissance England* (Berkeley, 1988), pp. 73–83. See also D. Wilson, *Signs and Portents: Monstrous Births from the Middle Ages to the Enlightenment* (London, 1993), pp. 117–19 and below, p. 84.
43. Culpepper and Cole, trans., *Bartholin's Anatomy*, pp. 53–76.
44. Laqueur, *Making Sex*, pp. 159–60 for diagram and commentary.
45. T. Gibson, *The Anatomy of Human Bodies Epitomised* (London, 1682), pp. 106–63.

figure made by one workman of one substance'. The issue posed by women's reproductive organs was not problematic. Because her function was to carry a child 'the female body hath in it not only all the rooms and divisions in the male body but divers others besides that he has not'. Her extra rooms were intended to 'contain another house within her with an unruly guest'.[46] It could all be made so simple. Yet in terms of anatomy two sexes were being created. The frontispiece to Crooke's *Microcosmographia* (plate 18) in this sense tells us all we need to know. Woman's hands, holding her breasts and covering her pubic area, point to difference as well as sinfulness; man gestures freely with a confidence that woman cannot command. Here are gendered bodies. Laura Gowing has noted that in the sexual speech of the London streets before 1640 references to male and female genitals show an understanding of their incommensurable difference: the penis is described in direct and specific terms, often using the colloquial term 'yard', whereas women's genitalia are called more generally her 'tail' or 'privy parts'.[47] However in a sense this simply confirms the confusion that there was about the nature of women's sexual organs. Those who tried to make some sense of what textbooks were saying found plenty of opportunity for adding to this confusion, as fresh knowledge jostled with an ancient framework of understanding and its limited vocabulary. *The Birth of Mankind*, published by the physician Thomas Raynalde in 1634, was intended for 'the simplest midwife which can read', but it is hard to think that midwives were much helped by the linguistic indeterminacy of this account of the female genitals, cervix and womb:

> The words the matrix, the coffer and the womb do signify but one thing, the place where seed is nourished and augmented . . . the neck of this womb, otherwise called the woman's privity, we will call the womb passage or the privy passage . . . the extreme end or first entrance of this privy or womb passage we shall name the passage port for that it is the port gate or entrance of that passage or way into the womb or matrix.[48]

Jane Sharpe, in her popular treatise of 1671, *The Midwives Book*, harked back to Galenic homologies by describing the vagina as the 'passage for the yard' which resembled it 'turned inward', but two pages later explained that the clitoris would 'stand and fall as the yard doth and makes women lustful'. She wanted the best of both worlds: structural resemblance at the same time as functional complementarity.[49] John Pechy's 1696 treatise was even more confused, declaring implausibly that

46. W. Austin, *Haec Homo* (London 1639), pp. 6, 92.
47. Gowing, p. 44.
48. T. Raynalde, *The Birth of Mankind* (London, 1634), sig C iiii.
49. J. Sharpe, *The Midwives Book* (London, 1671), pp. 40, 42.

the clitoris 'answered' the penis in 'shape, substance and situation'.[50] In the end, though, all this anatomical muddle was much less important than the issue of generation (as it was then called) itself. We must turn to the question of gender roles and of sexual activity, which takes us to the heart of people's experience at the most intimate moments of their lives. This is not an account of that experience as such but simply of the intellectual framework within which men constructed their notions of themselves in their loving and their propagating of the species.

50. J. Pechy, *A General Treatise of the Diseases of Maids, Bigbellied Women, Childbed Women and Widows* (1696), p. 61.

3. *Fungible Fluids, Heat and Concoction*

So FAR, IN this discussion of men's thinking about bodies before a gendered model of them was evolved, we have concentrated upon organs. Yet the core of the humoral model, we have seen, was a common corporeal economy. No sharp distinction between the sexes was possible in a physiological system that worked on the basis of fungible fluids. Blood, semen, milk and the various excrements were the most crucial ingredients of this corporeal economy. It was an economy that had to be held in balance, either by natural or by regulative means. Body and mind were closely related and mutually influential in their effective workings. Air, diet, exercise and sleep, together with the passions of the emotional life, were all relevant to achieving the proper balance that an individual's sexual temperament required. Thus the textbook advice was often set out in terms of treatments suitable for each of the four personal types which were common to both sexes: the sanguine, choleric, melancholic and phlegmatic. Seminal emission, bleeding, purging and sweating, besides the proper functioning of bowels and bladder, were all part of the maintenance regime, so to speak, of this free-trade economy of fluids.[1] The strength of this whole system was that people could, within the limits of their own temperament manage it themselves and feel some control, however illusory it may have been in practice, over their physical lives. At the same time it dovetailed with astrology, was compatible with Christian teaching and related mankind to the macrocosm. The humoral pattern of explanation could be applied to almost any disorder. Thus Pepys, at one point in his recurring accounts of treatment of the abscess which his wife suffered over some years in her vulva, commented on a discussion with a surgeon friend of his visiting to examine the malady. 'It seems', he noted, 'her great conflux of humours heretofore, that used to swell there, did in breaking leave a hollow which hath since gone in further and further, till it is near three inches deep.'[2]

1. T. Laqueur, *Making Sex: Body and Gender from the Greeks to Freud* (Cambridge, Massachusetts, 1990), p. 35.
2. *Pepys*, IV, p. 384.

Good health, many of the medical textbook writers and translators taught, was to quite a large extent in people's own hands. Thomas Phaer, writing around 1630, warned that disease sprang from 'the abuse of things not natural, that is to wit of meat and drink, of sleep and watching, of labour and ease, of fullness and emptiness, of the passions of the mind and of the immoderate use of lechery, for the excess of all these things be almost the chief occasion of all such diseases as do reign among us nowadays'.[3] He was not just being moralistic. Thomas Cogan, an Oxford fellow who directed his work *The Haven of Health* particularly to students, said much the same thing when he set out his treatise under five heads – labour, meat, drink, sleep and 'venus' – and declared that health was preserved 'by a measure used' in all of them. All, insisted Levinius Lemnius, could hope to live a healthy life. The humours were not determinative any more than the stars under which someone was born. Achieving 'a right constitution and state of the body ... whereby every several member dischargeth and orderly executeth his proper function' was a matter of searching out one's own nature and acting accordingly. The choleric man, for example, by the correct diet and amount of sleep and exercise could become milder. Lemnius, like others, was ready to admit that the heat and cold, dry and moist continuums left some people with particular problems. Whereas some women, he thought, simply could not conceive for lack of heat, there were others who, 'rough and thick grown with hair thereabout' in their 'secret privities', gave ample proof of their voracious sexuality. 'The more lecherous,' he opined, 'the more hairy and fruitful.'[4] Cogan saw the sanguine type – hot and moist – in both sexes as especially lustful and offered some advice for those who had real difficulty in subduing the flesh. Citing 1 Corinthians chapter 9 verse 27, where St Paul declares 'I treat my body hard and make it obey me', he suggested earnest study, much labour, often fasting and hard lodging. For males 'also to smell oftentimes to campher is good ... or to sit upon a marble stone or any other very cold stone or cold earth or to plunge the members in cold water or in strong vinegar.'[5]

Evacuation was where males and females were seen to differ because males were hotter and drier. Women menstruated because they were cooler than men; they used up less of their blood and so were left with a surplus of nutriment. Men, on the other hand, were more likely to lose blood from haemorrhoids or nosebleeds.[6] So far as fungibility was concerned, it seemed common sense that what could be converted did not need to be evacuated. Essentially blood was the source of seed in both

---

3. Cited in P. Slack, 'Mirrors of Health and Treasures of Poor Men: The Uses of the Vernacular Medical Literature of Tudor England', in C. Webster, ed., *Health, Medicine and Mortality in the Sixteenth Century* (Cambridge, 1979), p. 268.
4. L. Lemnius, *The Touchstone of Complexions* (London, 1633), pp. 3, 6–9, 67–8.
5. T. Cogan, *The Haven of Health* (London, 1596), pp. 244–6.
6. Laqueur, *Making Sex*, pp. 36–7.

sexes. It was also the source of the milk in women's breasts: 'blood twice concocted' was how Cogan described this milk.[7] Not that, in this single fluid economy, lactating was confined to women. Alexander Ross believed that men who were 'of a cold, moist and feminine complexion' were quite likely to have milk in their breasts.[8] The popularity of the images of Christ's milk nourishing his church and of an infant Jesus with breasts ready to spurt milk in the art and metaphor of medieval Christianity is a reminder not only of Christ's special power but also of the lack of belief in constraints of biological difference.[9]

If blood as seed was the more fully debated topic than blood as milk this is because it went to the core of the issues of reproductive biology that are crucial to an ideology of gender. The sex drive in both men and women was usually seen in teleological terms until the late seventeenth century, yet orgasm was also seen as functional in itself. Thomas Cogan makes the point clearly when he refers to desire as arising from the need for evacuation of 'some part . . . of profitable blood not needful to the parts ordained by nature for procreation'.[10] The diary kept by the scientist Robert Hooke in the 1670s shows a well educated man obsessed with taking medicine and monitoring every aspect of his physical activity, including his orgasms, in the light of their medical effects.[11] There seems little doubt that it was generally believed in Tudor and Stuart England that regular orgasm was good for the health of all adult men and women. Thus it was not until the eighteenth century that masturbation became an openly debated moral issue. Thomas Cogan saw many benefits in 'moderate evacuation' of semen: 'it procureth appetite to meat and helpeth concoction; it maketh the body more light and nimble, it openeth the pores and conduits and purgeth phlegm; it quickeneth the mind, stirreth up the wit, reneweth the senses, driveth away sadness, madness, anger, melancholy, fury.'[12] It was also an article of faith among the puritan clerics who wrote the popular marriage advice manuals of the period from the 1590s to 1640s.[13] At the same time some of these writers, following the medical handbooks, noted the dangers of excessive sex inflaming desire; they warned that too much sex can weaken the body and even shorten life. The popular tract *The Problems*

7. Cogan, *The Haven of Health*, p. 240.
8. Cited in Laqueur, *Making Sex*, p. 106.
9. C.W. Bynum, *Holy Feast and Holy Fast: The Religious Significance of Food to Medieval Women* (Berkeley, 1987), p. 282.
10. Cogan, *The Haven of Health*, p. 240.
11. L.M. Beier, *Sufferers and Healers: The Experience of Illness in Seventeenth Century England* (London, 1987), pp. 167–8.
12. Cogan, *The Haven of Health*, p. 241. For other citations see Gibbons, pp. 13–16.
13. A.J. Fletcher, 'The Protestant Idea of Marriage in Early Modern England', in A.J. Fletcher and P.R. Roberts, eds, *Religion, Culture and Society in Early Modern Britain* (Cambridge, 1994), pp. 175–9.

of Aristotle contained the opinion that immoderate sex was especially hurtful to choleric and melancholic men since 'it dries the bones very much'.[14] Some also worried because they thought that sexual intercourse drew brain tissue down the spine and out of the penis, thus threatening a man's reason as well as his general health.[15]

It was generally believed, following Galen, that once a child was conceived by a mixing of male and female seed it was nourished by menstrual blood in the womb. The surplus which was disposed of monthly was the blood of lower quality unsuitable for this task. This surplus was believed by some to come from veins in the backbone rather than from the womb since, if it did not further generation, what business did it ever have to be there?[16] The early modern notion of menstruation combined the ideas of purification of the blood and of shedding a plethora.[17] 'Some call them purgations', wrote Walter Bruele, 'because that by this flux all a woman's body is purged of superfluous humours.' At the same time Bruele thought that social status affected how much blood needed shedding, for the richer a woman's diet the more blood she would concoct. 'Mean people, where every one must work for a living' escaped the problems of a pampering 'full and dainty fare'. Nicholas Fontanus thought that country women who worked hard in the fields and virgins of a very hot constitution needed little menstrual evacuation.[18]

Reminding his readers that women were 'more moist and cold of constitution', William Whateley, in his conduct book *The Bride Bush*, explained that 'their natural heat not serving to turn their whole nourishment into their own substance yieldeth some overplus for the nourishing and cherishing of their fruit within them' and that this overplus 'must needs find . . . its seasonable evacuations'. A sense of constant mutation inside themselves accepted by those who lived in the humoral body characterises many passages like this one. The fact that Whateley understood and propagated the standard interpretation of menstruation in a widely read marriage advice book strengthens the argument that we are dealing with an immensely resilient model of the body. What Whateley is saying is that menstruation is a local difficulty in women that married couples have to take account of in their sexual lives. He relates his prohibition of intercourse at this time to women's nature, as well as to

---

14. W. Whateley, *The Bride Bush* (London, 1623), pp. 18–19; Anon., *The Problems of Aristotle* (London, 1607), sig E1.
15. M.E. Weiner, *Women and Gender in Early Modern Europe* (Cambridge, 1993), p. 226; see also Gibbons, p. 21.
16. *The Problems of Aristotle*, sig E5.
17. P. Crawford, 'Attitudes to Menstruation in Seventeenth-Century England', *Past and Present* 91 (1981), pp. 49–52.
18. W. Bruele, *Praxis Medicinae or The Physicians Practice* (London, 1632), p. 363; N. Fontanus, *The Woman's Doctor* (London, 1652), p. 9.

scriptural direction; somewhat on the defensive, he claims that, as a minister, he is not immodest in 'speaking these things plainly'.[19] The sheer coherence of the evidence from clinical practice, medical advice literature and popular folklore regarding belief in the physiology of the humoral body is remarkable.[20] Findings in the period between 1500 and 1660 which militated against the economy of fungible fluids were easily ignored.[21]

Women's sexual history was seen as more problematic than men's since there was a tendency, which will be explored below, to attribute all their illnesses to gynaecological problems. The female menarche marked preparation for reproduction, puberty the beginnings of a longing to conceive.[22] John Pechy declared that girls were physically ready for sexual intercourse at fourteen but some writers thought they were not ready for marriage until sixteen.[23] Women were seen as experiencing a growing teenage eroticism which brought them to the readiness to bear children. Ideally this readiness would coincide with marriage and be quickly followed by pregnancy: the fulfilment of a woman's purpose as Adam's helpmeet. A couplet from an anonymous poem expresses the current attitude to this satisfaction of women's natural and voracious sexuality:

> The woman is both wanton and wild
> Till she hath conceived a child.[24]

But things could go less than smoothly. From the menarche onwards, the constant development of seed from a girl's blood made her liable to frustration if she failed to menstruate and lacked orgasmic release. Greensickness, or chlorosis in the contemporary medical jargon, which was the result of this frustration, was a very well known female condition at this time. It crops up regularly in the casebooks of seventeenth-century physicians. Richard Napier, for example, was consulted by eighty-one women in the month of August 1608 and in eight cases he recorded a diagnosis of greensickness: these patients' ages ranged from seventeen to twenty-two, all were unmarried and all had amenorrhea.[25] Dr Barker, practising at Shrewsbury around 1600, prescribed herbal purges for greensickness as well as for other gynaecological disorders such as

19. Whateley, *Bride Bush*, pp. 21–3.
20. Beier, *Sufferers and Healers*, pp. 97–259.
21. Laqueur, *Making Sex*, p. 104.
22. P. Crawford, 'The Construction and Experience of Maternity in Seventeenth-Century England', in V. Fildes, ed., *Women as Mothers in Pre-Industrial England* (London, 1990), p. 6.
23. R.H. Michel, 'English Attitudes Towards Women 1640–1700', *Canadian Journal of History* 8 (1978), p. 42.
24. E. Ashmole, ed., *Theatrum Chemicum Brittanicum* (London, 1652), p. 432. I am grateful to Brian Gibbons for this reference.
25. I. Loudon, 'The Disease called Chlorosis', *Psychological Medicine* 14 (1984), p. 29.

amenorrhea and irregular menstruation. In one case he anointed the patient's side, purged her, ordered that she sit in a bath for three days, then purged her again.[26] A reference in a letter of 1652 to the search for 'a cure for Mrs Ramsdells greensickness' in order that it 'may fall no more into her legs but find an upper vent' shows that the disease was some-times, though much less frequently, diagnosed in married women.[27]

In one of John Taylor's tales a teenager tells her friend how she 'cannot lie any longer alone': 'I do so bite the sheets and toss up and down in the bed like a cat when she is pinched by the tail.' Evidence that the malady was a matter that came up more widely in everyday conversation than merely in medical circles comes from the Shakespearean references to a lovesickness which is virtually indistinguishable from Chlorosis. In *Romeo and Juliet* Shakespeare has Capulet berating his daughter about her refusal gracefully to part with Romeo and marry the gentleman of 'fair demesnes and nobly trained' with whom he has matched her: 'out you greensickness carrion, out you baggage, you tallowface.' His fierce lan-guage, which causes his wife and the nurse to protest, betrays the anger he feels at the state Juliet has got herself into by wanting sex with the man of her choice rather than waiting meekly for the young Count Paris to tame her physical longings.[28] Cesario, describing to Orsino his sister languishing for love, declared:

> She pin'd in thought
> And with a green and yellow melancholy
> She sat like Patience on a monument
> Smiling at grief. Was not this love indeed?[29]

The audience would quickly have grasped the allusion to greensickness here.

Greensickness was known as the virgin's disease. John Lange in the first full account of it, published in 1554, was blunt in his advice that copu-lation was the best cure. Drawing upon his account of the symptoms and upon eighteenth-century descriptions, Irvine Loudon has argued persuas-ively that the disease was a form of chloro-anorexia characterised by amenorrhea, pallor, weakness and appetite disturbance. An additional characteristic was pica: the patient longed for unwholesome foods such as coals, cinders and dirt. This symptom supports Loudon's view that greensickness, besides displaying all the effects of erotic excitement with-out gratification, may have represented an attempt to reduce weight and yet assuage hunger in some kind of act of symbolic regression to early

26. Beier, *Sufferers and Healers*, p. 122.
27. M.H. Nicholson, ed., *Conway Letters: The Correspondence of Anne, Viscountess Conway, Henry More and their Friends 1642–1648* (Oxford, 1930), p. 20.
28. Capp, p. 116; *Romeo and Juliet*, act III, scene v, 157–9. See also L. Jardine, *Still Harping on Daughters: Women and Drama in the Age of Shakespeare* (London, 1983), p. 182.
29. *Twelfth Night*, act II, scene iv, 113–16.

childhood. He has made the interesting suggestion that recently 'chlorosis seems to have been replaced by anorexia nervosa' and that in each generation young females, reacting to the stresses which arise from entry to adult life, are liable to exhibit 'mental and emotional disturbance accompanied by abnormalities of appetite and sometimes by amenorrhea'.[30] What matters for this investigation of gender is that standard early modern texts were in accord about an interpretation of greensickness which fitted humoral theory and provided fertile ground for the development, when the time was ripe, of a construction of women's bodies as different and more problematic than those of men.

A fifteenth-century account which did not actually use the terms greensickness or chlorosis connected amenorrhea with 'thinking too much, being too angry or too sad or eating too little' and mentioned pica. The symptoms described are closely in line with the later accounts of Lazarius Riverius and Levinius Lemnius.[31] Noting symptoms of heaviness of the body, palpitations and difficult breathing, Riverius gave dire warnings of corrupted seed running to the upper parts of the body with oppressive effects. He recommended 'opening medicines' followed by sex 'if it may be legally done . . . for thereby the natural heat is stirred up in parts natural by which the vessels of the womb are much enlarged'. Experience showed, he said, that chlorotic women sometimes menstruated the first night after marriage.[32] Lemnius believed that corruption of unreleased seed was more serious than the corruption of excess blood caused by amenorrhea: 'For the seed grows to be of a venemous quality, hence ariseth that swarth weasel colour in maids when they begin to be in love, hence comes their short breathings, tremblings and pantings of the heart, the expulsive faculty being moved to cast out the swelling humour.'[33]

The popular literature of the period is full of tales of frustrated adolescent heroines.[34] The ballad *The Lonely Lamentation of a Lawyer's Daughter for lack of a Husband*, for example, portrays a pubescent thirteen-year-old ensuring she wears the most fashionable clothes of the moment and attending church every week 'for no devotion sake, but only to spy one I might my true love make'. Doting aged parents hold her back from marriage but her sexuality is ebullient. It is time, she decides, to 'make assay of my virginity'; she pines for a lusty youth 'if I might have my

30. Loudon, 'Disease called Chlorosis', *Psychological Medicine* 14 (1984), pp. 27–36; *OED*: 'greensickness'.
31. B. Rowland, ed., *Medieval Woman's Guide to Health: The First English Gynaecological Handbook* (Kent, Ohio, 1981), pp. 61–3. I am grateful to Tim Stretton for this reference.
32. L. Riverius, *The Practice of Physick* (London 1655), pp. 400–401.
33. L. Lemnius, *The Secret Miracles of Nature* (London, 1658), pp. 18–19.
34. M. Spufford, *Small Books and Pleasant Histories: Popular Fiction and its Readership in Seventeenth-Century England* (London, 1981), p. 63.

will'.[35] In *Constant Fair and Fine Betty* the heroine responds to the lover's poem of praise of her body and character by confessing at once that she is mutually attracted and grown sickly with waiting for him: 'long I cannot carry not my maidenhead.'[36] In his satirical poem *Well Met Gossip*, in which a widow, wife and maid carouse in a tavern, Samuel Rowlands has the other two round on the fifteen-year-old. At her age every girl needs a man:

> They say love creepeth where it cannot go
> Maids must be married, lest they mastered should be
> I will be sworn before I saw fifteen
> I wished that I my wedding day had seen
> I could not for a world have lived a nun
> Oh flesh is frail, we are a sinful sort.[37]

Levinius Lemnius explained that regular sex was vitally important for women:

> if women do not use copulation to cast out their seed they oft times fall into great diseases and cruel symptoms . . . if lusty widows or maids in years happen to be married that their seed by the use of man may be ejected, you shall presently see them look fresh as a rose and to be very amiable and pleasant and not so crabbed and testy, especially if their husbands be men for their turn and can give them their due . . . you shall find that this sex is by no means better won than when the husband often satisfieth them this way.[38]

So it would not have surprised Shakespeare's playgoers to find Desdemona pleading before the Venetian senate to be allowed to accompany Othello to Cyprus in order that her marriage could be consummated: 'if I be left behind . . . the rites for why I love him are bereft me'.[39] Women's desire, once awoken, was seen as unquenchable: their enjoyment of sex was taken for granted. If men found women's insatiability dangerous, it was at the same time seen as a necessary physical outlet. The proverb 'a woman's work is never done' was turned into ballad form. After the chores and care of children

> Perchance my husband wakes and then wakes me
> Then he does that to me which I cannot shun
> Yet I could wish that work were oftener done.[40]

35. A. Clark, ed., *The Shirburn Ballads* (Oxford, 1907), pp. 43–7.
36. *Roxburghe*, I, pp. 207–12.
37. Rowlands, *Well Met Gossip* (London, 1619), sig A3.
38. Lemnius, *Secret Miracles of Nature*, p. 18.
39. *Othello*, act I, scene iii, 250–52.
40. *Roxburghe*, III, pp. 301–06.

In the bawdy tale *The Cooper of Norfolk*, the cooper's wife keeps 'a sheath for another man's knife'. The brewer from down the road visits while the cooper is away on business 'her greensickness to cure'.[41] The same kind of thinking lay behind the dramatists' humorous portrayals of the gyrations of lusty widows like William Congreve's Lady Wishfort.[42] Some of the medical writers faced the problems of sexuality and widowhood squarely. 'If they be young, of a black complexion and hairy . . . and feel within themselves of frequent titillation, their seed being hot and prurient doth irritate and inflame them to venery,' wrote Nicholas Fontanus. He advised a resort to masturbation or to 'the hand of a skilful midwife and a convenient ointment'.[43]

Successive editions of *Aristotle's Master-Piece* reminded parents through the eighteenth century that they should on no account obstruct the marriage of their daughters and risk an attack of greensickness.[44] There was no equivalent male illness linked to unfulfilled lust. In a long technical discussion of chlorosis in his medical textbook of 1762, Jean Astruc took the traditional line that marriage was the only and necessary remedy. Intercourse 'at first used moderately and practised more frequently by degrees' provided the uterus with the 'contractions' and 'oscillations' it needed and produced, through free circulation of the blood, a cure for amenorrhea.[45] Yet views were by then changing, for Henry Manning's textbook of 1771 gave the standard account of the symptoms of chlorosis but dismissed explanations in terms of sexual longing as an old wives' tale. He believed the disease was most common around the age of fourteen and that it was 'generally terminated by the eruption of the menses'.[46]

The story of sexual relating and how it led to the successful conception of a child was seen in terms of the heating of bodies. Early modern England, as Stephen Greenblatt puts it, lived by a 'calorific model of sexuality'.[47] The process of warming can conveniently be discussed in terms of its successive stages, which run from desire to concoction of seeds in the womb. But something needs to be said first about the clash of the pagan and Christian traditions regarding pleasures and the body. In the fifth century AD, St Augustine had attempted to prise people loose from the physical world of their bodies. This was when sex first had guilt

41. E.A. Foyster, 'A Laughing Matter? Marital Discord and Gender Control in Seventeenth-century England', *Rural History* 4 (1993), p. 8.
42. W. Congreve, *The Way of the World* (London, 1701).
43. Fontanus, *The Woman's Doctor*, p. 6.
44. R. Porter and L. Hall, *The Facts of Life: The Creation of Sexual Knowledge in Britain 1680–1950* (London, 1995), p. 43.
45. J. Astruc, *A Treatise on the Diseases of Women* (London, 1762), I, pp. 171–203.
46. H. Manning, *A Treatise on Female Diseases* (London, 1771), pp. 66–92.
47. S. Greenblatt, *Shakespearean Negotiations: The Circulation of Social Energy in Renaissance England* (Berkeley, 1988), pp. 78–93.

written into it. Augustine posited sharply contrasting versions of para-disiacal and postlapsarian sex. Attempting to come to terms with the force of his own sexual desire, he portrayed sexuality in his *Confessions* as a cruel chain which only God could unloose. The hiatus between will and sexual feeling produced by Adam's first act of disobedience and Eve's temptation towards it left all mankind with a punishment suitable to their crime. Peter Brown has explained this catastrophe: 'sexuality and the grave stood one at each end of the life of every human being; like two iron clamps, they delineated inexorably mankind's loss of the primal harmony of body and soul.' Whereas Aristotle had argued that erection was involuntary and thus not susceptible to moral praise or blame, for Augustine the very fact that man's will did not control it was proof that it revealed his fallen state. Impotence, even more tellingly, declared this fallen condition. Augustine had no quarrel with the classical notion that conception depended on a moment of intense and mutual pleasure. But in his dire vision sexual desire became man's ageless adversary, bending him from the undivided act of loving and praising God of which the human soul was capable.[48] The body, in this reading, had to be disciplined. In came the medieval confessor, since the uncontrollable delight of orgasm mocked the will every time it was experienced.[49] Even the act of married intercourse brought back the pang of sin: it was a sad reminder in Augustine's teaching – since orgasm spelt lost control – of the fall. Theology and medical lore had on this point fallen apart.

There is very good reason to think that, powerful as Augustinianism was in the medieval church, the English people never learnt to see sex in his terms. Or if they saw it at all they did not aspire to his standards. The drama and ballad literature of the sixteenth and seventeenth centuries has a consistent vein of bawdy which reflects a spontaneous rather than a guilt-ridden attitude to sexual pleasure. The medical textbooks of the period reflect an approach to reproductive biology which is founded on the teachings of classical medicine and a tradition in which the fire of the sexual act carried with it not guilt but a certain ancient reverence. *Aristotle's Master-Piece* reiterates the same attitudes after 1700. It is a work very much of its time, associating sex, as Lesley Hall and Roy Porter note, neither with danger, nor with recreation nor with 'the unbiddable and mysterious drives of the psyche'. Eighteenth-century readers of the book's numerous editions absorbed a strategy for reproduction which was guided by Aristotelian teleology, sex as 'Nature's way of ensuring generation'.[50] In this biology, a spontaneous, uncomplicated, natural explanation of the creation of new life, libido has no sex: its essence was a common

48. P. Brown, *The Body and Sexuality: Men, Women and Sexual Renunciation in Early Christianity* (London, 1989), pp. 396–447.
49. M. Foucault, *A History of Sexuality*, vol I, *An Introduction* (London, 1987), pp. 58–63.
50. Porter and Hall, *The Facts of Life*, p. 49.

neurology of pleasure, which produced the heating of bodies. A corporeal blaze culminated in orgasm and the concoction of seeds that followed. Sexual union was the realisation of one flesh.[51] This is the biology that provides common ground for the account of sex in marriage given by the puritan conduct writers in the period between 1590 and 1642. They told their readers to enjoy sex and to ensure that neither deprived the other. But their approach was not simply functional. Sex linked the affections of couples ever more firmly, insisted William Gouge; it made 'that house a little heaven where it is carefully observed', declared John Wing; it made spouses 'dearer and dearer to each other's souls', said William Whateley.[52]

Desire in both sexes had its origins in the brain and liver, according to Lemnius, but man acquired his ability to achieve an erection from an additional 'spirit', a mark of his superior heat, which issued from the arteries of the heart.[53] Alexander Ross stressed that males had a hotter heart than females and a larger brain, which between them did 'communicate to all parts the power of generation'.[54] Men lit the blaze. So convinced were these and other textbook writers that desire was natural and spontaneous that they showed little interest in commenting upon it in detail. Shakespeare's great series of comedies from *The Taming of the Shrew* to *Twelfth Night* allow a more fruitful insight into the erotic heat that people were seen to generate in each other. His comic heroes and heroines perform the cosmic dance of love: on stage they dally with words and wit, off stage they are imagined engaged in the bodily pleasures which, through concoction, will produce determinate sexual identity in new beings, the transformation of double nature in men's and women's seeds into single.[55] Helkiah Crooke found the beginnings of sex entirely predictable. Showing traces of Augustinian dualism, he explained that men, with a sense of their divine nature, felt bound to defile themselves 'in such impurities' and women could forget the pains and dangers of childbirth because the sexual act was so intensely pleasurable. 'All these things are forgotten', mused Crooke, 'and we are overtaken with an ecstasy which Hippocrates calleth a little epilepsy or falling sickness.'[56]

The end of pleasure was orgasm and orgasm was the beginning of concoction. What the writers of medical texts were really interested in – and conduct book writers shared their teleology and this interest – was

51. Laqueur, *Making Sex*, pp. 43–4.
52. W. Gouge, *Domestical Duties* (London, 1662), p. 224; J. Wing, *The Crown Conjugal or Spouse Royal* (London, 1620), pp. 132–3; Whateley, *Bride Bush*, p. 25.
53. Lemnius, *Secret Miracles of Nature*, p. 25.
54. A. Ross, *Arcana Microcosmi or the Hidden Secrets of Man's Body Disclosed* (London, 1651), p. 20.
55. Greenblatt, *Shakespearean Negotiations*, pp. 90–91.
56. Crooke, *Microcosmographia*, p. 200.

the efficacy of sexual acts. For them all sex was reproductive. They were concerned with the proper arousal of both partners, with the quality of a couple's lovemaking in mind and spirit as much as body, for generation was a mysterious event linking macrocosm and microcosm, a dramatic blaze of glory, which must in their view of the world express the power of body and imagination in unison. In the first place things should be done in the right order. 'Let motion or exercise precede meat,' wrote Lemnius citing the advice of Galen and Hippocrates, 'after meat use venery, after venus sleep which being done the natural faculties do their parts in forming the child.'[57] Puritan clerics in their advice books emphasised the importance of coming to sex in the right mood. 'Cheerfulness and willingness', declared William Whateley, 'must evermore accompany their meetings.'[58] John Dod and Robert Cleaver told man and wife to 'mark one another and find like heedfulness and buxomness in their duty', which should be performed 'godlily, carefully and cheerfully.'[59] *Aristotle's Master-Piece* said much the same in a more secular tone, encouraging its readers to relax and enjoy some good wine and then ensure that they aroused each other 'with equal ardour': 'for if the spirit flag on either part they will fall short of what nature requires'.[60] So the sexual warmth of this calorific model could be generated by food and wine as well as the power of imagination.

Yet since the objective was mutual orgasm, foreplay was important too. The medical textbook writers, it has been shown, were coy about the clitoris in the sixteenth century and it was not until works like those of Jane Sharp and Nicholas de Venette that advice about its significance was accessible in cheap literature. But many couples no doubt found things out for themselves. A popular ballad, *The Country Lawyer's Maid Joan*, is nearly explicit on this matter. The story opens with a call for bachelors to attend the tale of a girl ready for love, ready to 'sigh and die'. Her sister had a 'sparkish mate', the miller's son had wooed her and then left her. Then:

> At length came lusty Mark
> A country lawyer's clerk
> And tickled her in the dark
> He lit on the very vein
> The place of her grief and pain
> And caused her to laugh amain
> And merrily did reply
> 'O this is the death I die'.[61]

57. Lemnius, *Secret Miracles of Nature*, p. 9.
58. Whateley, *Bride Bush*, p. 24.
59. J. Dod and R. Cleaver, *A Godly Form of Household Government* (London, 1614), sigs K7–8.
60. Porter and Hall, *The Facts of Life*, p. 42.
61. *Roxburghe*, III, pp. 585–7.

Seen in the context of a sound general grasp of the role of the clitoris, a curious reference of Shakespeare's to the gelding of girls suggests some notion of clitoral mutilation. Antigonus, offering dramatic support to his King who fears his sexual honour is betrayed, declares that, if the story is true, he will have all his three daughters 'gelded' before they reach the menarche in case they 'bring false generations'. Antigonus presumably thought mistakenly that, by depriving his daughters of their power to emit seed, he would make them barren.[62]

Each act of intercourse, according to these pronatalist writers, required a considerable emotional commitment on both sides. Men, who enjoyed the self-discipline that women lacked, should be sensible about how often they had sex: 'for to eject immoderately' wrote Lemnius, 'weakens a man and spends his spirits and to forbear longer than it is convenient makes the seed ineffectual.' But, once engaged, much responsibility was believed to rest with them. Lemnius was scathing about husbands who performed their sexual duty 'very faintly and drowsily':

> whence it happens that the child falls short of the parents nature, manners and inbred generosity and hence it is that wise men sometimes beget stupid and slothful children and that are of a feeble mind because they are not much given to these delights. But when the progenitors are hot in venerous actions and do liberally and abundantly apply themselves therein it oft times happens that the children are of the same manners, desires and actions of mind that their parents are.[63]

So what was imagined actually happened at orgasm in these male and female bodies, so similar in their economy of fungible fluids, so well matched in their functional anatomies? Orgasm was nuanced in these still hardly gendered bodies but it was not in any real sense a different experience for the man and the woman. Its paroxysm, like the seeds which it released, reflected hierarchical ordering.[64] The male experience, observably more violent, was seen as producing the greater pang of pleasure; the female, of lesser heat, had to rage less intensely but there was a good reason, it was alleged, why her pleasure was in fact greater and more sustained.[65] She performed a 'double office', as Lemnius put it: 'she draws forth the man's seed and casts her own in with it'.[66] What made her healthy if she had plenty of sex, said Fontanus, was that she was 'refreshed with the man's seed' as well as ejaculating her own.[67] Riverius was rhapsodic about what he believed the other sex experienced: 'her

62. *The Winter's Tale*, act II, scene i, 142–9. For the notion that the clitoris actually produced semen see Laqueur, *Making Sex*, p. 66.
63. Lemnius, *Secret Miracles of Nature*, pp. 12, 28.
64. Crooke, *Microcosmographia*, p. 288.
65. Laqueur, *Making Sex*, pp. 43–50.
66. Lemnius, *Secret Miracles of Nature*, pp. 18–19.
67. Fontanus, *The Woman's Doctor*, p. 4.

genitals ... swell at the instant of generation, that her womb skipping as it were for joy may meet her husband's sperm, graciously and freely receive the same and draw it into its innermost cavity ... and sprinkle it with her own sperm poured forth in that pang of pleasure'.[68] Crooke was emphatic that although these orgasms did not have to be simultaneous for conception to be achieved, with the womb ready 'greedily to draw the seed in' success was the 'sooner and more perfect' if this was so.[69]

The male and female seed were not seen as sexually specific: they were not distinct entities contributed to the embryo. They consisted rather of a hierarchically ordered version of one another according to their supposed power: 'in man it is hot, white and thick', wrote Thomas Vicary, 'the woman's sperm hath contrary qualities, for the woman's sperm is thinner, colder and feebler'.[70] Crooke confirmed Vicary's account, insisting that the 'seed of male and female is of one nature, colour and manner of generation; they have both the same vessels of preparation, concoction and ejaculation only they are distinguished in perfection'. Thus, so far as gender was concerned, concoction really was the crux of the matter. There was some disagreement about how it began. Crooke marvelled at the 'very great and almost incredible' power of the testicles, which he called 'the wellspring of inbred heat', yet he also attributed a 'formative faculty' to the spermatical parts.[71] Ross was quite clear that the 'distinction of the sexes' began with the male's formative power which he placed in the heart 'as being the perfectest member and chief receptacle of heat and blood'. His belief was that, having received its 'special form and essence' in the heart, the male seed was then concocted in the testicles.[72] All writers saw the male role, throughout the process, as the crucial one. When both seeds were shut in the womb, advised the author of *The Problems of Aristotle*, 'the seed of the man doth dispose and prepare the seed of the woman to receive the form, perfection or soul'.[73] If something went wrong it could be assumed that it was the woman's seed that should be blamed. Thus in the tale of a proud merchant's wife in Geneva who had given birth to a monster, the cause of the catastrophe was ascribed to God who in judgement 'grievously scourged me in my seed'. 'In my tender womb of so pure flesh and blood', she relates, God thus created a 'deformed brood' as an example to others.[74]

68. Riverius, *The Practice of Physick*, p. 563.
69. Crooke, *Microcosmographia*, pp. 294–5.
70. Vicary, *Anatomy of the Body of Man*, p. 79; Laqueur, *Making Sex*, p. 38.
71. Crooke, *Microcosmographia*, pp. 45, 52. For a similar account see J. Rueff, *The Expert Midwife* (London, 1637), pp. 4–8.
72. Ross, *Arcana Microcosmi*, p. 21.
73. *Problems of Aristotle*, sigs E3–4.
74. Clark, ed., *Shirburn Ballads*, pp. 133–9. I am grateful to Elizabeth Foyster for this reference.

So why a boy or a girl? 'A woman', answers Crooke, 'is so much less perfect than a man by how much her heat is less and weaker than his.'[75] The issue is seen as one of predominance and during concoction that predominance was not believed to be absolute. The two-seed theory, as Stephen Greenblatt has put it, 'imagines an individual identity emerging from the struggle between conflicting principles'. Before gender, in its modern ontological and eventually genetic sense, was created and discovered, there was seen to be in everyone some trace at birth of gender doubleness. 'By how much more the masculine atoms abound in a female infant', wrote Nathaniel Highmore, 'by so much more the foetus is stronger, healthier and more manlike, a virago. If the female atoms abound in a male infant, then is that issue more weak and effeminate.'[76] Hotter seed came from the right testicle, cooler from the left and this affected the outcome. So did the question whether concoction occurred on the left or right side of the uterus.[77] Lemnius advised women to lie on their right side after intercourse to increase the likelihood of their having a boy.[78] When the power struggle between the male and female elements was too close for it to be decided in the womb the child was born a hermaphrodite. The majority, born on one side or the other of the narrow sexual divide, still had to secure their gender identity in the course of their early life.

The consistent theme of all this prescriptive material is that women are strongly sexual and that it is the man's role to take the lead. He is hotter and stronger; she is less in control of herself. Two proverbs of the time encapsulate the matter. 'All women may be won', or as Demetrius puts it squarely to Chinon in *Titus Andronicus*:

> She is a woman, therefore may be wooed
> She is a woman, therefore may be won.[79]

More roughly there was the proverb 'woo, wed and bed her', which crops up many times in the drama and ballads.[80] There is evidence in the correspondence of the period that men recognised an obligation to satisfy women and believed that this was how they became pregnant. Thus they took credit for both achievements if conception occurred. When the Marquis of Hamilton and his wife decided to try again after a period living apart in 1631 and her pregnancy followed, her sister wrote happily to a brother: 'the good news you will now hear of your sister's great belly will amaze you as it has done all us here but now all our fears is at an

75. Crook, *Microcosmographia*, p. 217.
76. Greenblatt, *Shakespearean Negotiations*, pp. 84–93.
77. I. Maclean, *The Renaissance Notion of Woman: A Study in the Fortunes of Scholasticism and Medical Science in European Intellectual Life* (Cambridge, 1980), pp. 37–8.
78. Lemnius, *Secret Miracles of Nature*, p. 27.
79. *Titus Andronicus*, act II, scene i, 82–3.
80. Tilley, W681, W731.

end'. When Lord Paget wrote teasingly of his own possible intervention in a letter to the wife of his steward, who was still not pregnant, around 1636, he put the blame firmly on her husband. His remark 'I think you very fruitful were you well handled' suggests Paget assumed that arousal and passion were needed to make a young woman conceive.[81]

A letter from Arthur Stanhope to his nephew Theophilus, Earl of Huntingdon, in 1672, advising him when he had been unable to penetrate his bride of two months, is revealing in what it tells us about the combination of down-to-earth resourcefulness and caring concern with which the young man was instructed to tackle his problem. Stanhope assumed that his niece would enjoy sex once the physical problem of lack of elasticity in her vagina was solved. He hoped she would be as patient as her husband was clearly being and would co-operate fully in the measures he suggested for use of medicines and ointments to ease her body and facilitate his entrance. While he sympathised with how 'difficult and troublesome' the whole affair was for Theophilus, he told him that at present 'I am the most concerned for my poor lady when she comes to push a pike with you.' Whereas men tended to take the credit themselves for the birth of a son, the mark of their heat in the sexual act, they were ready to moan and groan about wives who could only produce daughters. When his son was born in 1672, Sir Edward Nicolls boasted to friends 'that he had but two bouts with his wife for it and it came according to the last bout'.[82] The physiology of fungible fluids, heat and concoction carried the message that the woman's seed mattered almost as much as the man's. Their belief in the mingling of her seed with their own in the womb made it impossible for men to think of themselves as wholly gendered male beings until they had struggled free of maternal making and maternal influence. Thus the legacy of the Galenic heritage was the notion of human singleness being achieved out of inherent doubleness. Men found their manhood through their sexual potency and through the act which started the same cycle of twinship and doubleness all over again.

81. Citations from L.A. Pollock, 'Embarking on a Rough Passage: The Experience of Pregnancy in Early Modern Society', in V. Fildes, ed., *Women as Mothers in Pre-Industrial England* (London, 1990), pp. 40–1.
82. Citations from Pollock in Fildes, ed., *Women as Mothers*, pp. 41–2. For examples of moaning about daughters see B.J. Harris, 'Property, Power and Personal Relations: Elite Mothers and Sons in Yorkist and Early Tudor England', *Signs*, XV (1990).

4. *The Weaker Vessel*

THE PHRASE 'the weaker vessel' originated with William Tyndale's translation of the New Testament into English in 1526 and became common usage during the next hundred years or more. Many must have encountered it in the King James version of the Bible. St Peter, founding his admonitions on St Paul's epistle to the Ephesians, urged husbands to 'give honour unto the wife, as unto the weaker vessel, and as being heirs together of the life of grace'.[1] It is hard to think of a single phrase which brings together more aptly the whole Judaeo-Christian tradition of the subjection of women with the humoral physiology of the ancients. 'A woman is the weaker vessel' quickly became an established proverb: it runs through the conduct book literature of the pre-civil war period and recurs in sermons.[2] Preaching at St Paul's Cross in 1601, for example, John Dove discussed why husbands should respect their 'weaker vessel' wives, citing Ephesians, chapter 5.[3] The proverb is also common in Shakespeare. The country girl Jaquenetta, caught with Costard in the King's park at the opening of *Love's Labours Lost*, is characterised by Don Adriano as 'the weaker vessel which I apprehended with the aforesaid swain'. The hostess at the Boar's Head in Eastcheap, ragging Falstaff and Doll Tearsheet about their propensity to quarrel, tells Doll 'one must bear and that must be you, you are the weaker vessel, as they say the emptier vessel'. The notion here of relative emptiness carries all the resonances of the gender order upon which scriptural patriarchy rested, resonances of man's strength, initiative and authority.[4]

1. 1 Peter, chapter 3, verse 7; A. Fraser, *The Weaker Vessel: Woman's Lot in Seventeenth-Century England* (London, 1985), p. 1.
2. E.g. H. Smith, *A Preparative to Marriage* (London, 1591), p. 53; Tilley, p. 743.
3. J. Dove, *Of Divorcement: A Sermon preached at Pauls Cross* (London, 1601), pp. 56–61. I am grateful to Tim Stretton for this reference.
4. *Love's Labours Lost*, act I, scene i, 275; *2 Henry IV*, act II, scene x, 65; see also *Romeo and Juliet*, act I, scene i, 19. For discussion of the sweeping generalisations about women's weak nature in a drama abounding in women of formidable strength see L. Woodbridge, *Women and the English Renaissance: Literature and the Nature of Womankind 1504–1620* (Urbana, 1986), pp. 213–17.

The subordination of women began with the hierarchical ordering of bodies and ended with firmly defined gender roles. Nature imprinted its authority physically. 'Vehement heat', asserted Lemnius, 'maketh men stout of courage, fierce, testy, crafty, subtle, industrious, politic, of which sort of men . . . some . . . in their very entrails and inward parts also have been found rough and hairy.' It made sense, he believed, that women had smooth skin on their bodies but lots of hair on their heads, since 'the vapours do very much and abundantly ascend upward'.[5] William Whateley declared that the print of government appeared in man's 'very face which is more stern and delicate than the woman's' and that they should in their bearing towards their wives 'not suffer this order of nature to be inverted'.[6] Women's protected and conservative role in the household and society was justified by arguments from her naturally preordained function. Indeed her ethical and legal status depended upon this function. It was her frailty, Ian Maclean has shown, which justifies 'her exclusion from public life, responsibility and moral fulfilment'.[7] Thus a doctrine of subordination based upon medical evidence was entirely consonant with the central theological tenets of women's inferiority. The medical foundations on which this whole gender scheme rested were set out with lucidity and confidence in Alexander Ross's textbook of 1651:

> The male is hotter than the female because begot of hotter seed and in a hotter place to wit the right side and because the male hath larger vessels and members, stronger limbs, a more porie skin, a more active body, a stronger concoction, a more courageous mind and for the most part a longer life; all which are effects of heat. . . . the fatness, softness and laxity of the woman's body, besides the abundance of blood which cannot be concocted and exhaled for want of heat argue that she is a colder temper than men. . . . her proneness to anger and venery argue imbecility of mind and strength of imagination not heat.[8]

The conventional roles were often set out in the marriage advice books. Man and wife, said Henry Smith, should see themselves like the cock and the dam: 'the cock flyeth abroad to bring in and the dam sitteth upon the nest to keep all at home'. The 'nature, wit, and strength', of the two sexes, together with God's direction, ordained this. There was a strong consensus that physical capacities made this kind of arrangement ineluctable. Nature had 'forged each part to his office', insisted Sir Thomas Smith, 'the man stern, strong, bold, adventurous, negligent of his beauty

5. L. Lemnius, *The Touchstone of Complexions* (London, 1633), p. 69.
6. W. Whateley, *The Bride Bush* (London, 1623), p. 97.
7. I. Maclean, *The Renaissance Notion of Woman: A Study in the Fortunes of Scholasticism and Medical Science in European Intellectural Life* (Cambridge, 1980), pp. 43–6, 57–8, 68.
8. A. Ross, *Arcana Microcosmi or The Hidden Secrets of Man's Body Disclosed* (London, 1651), p. 86.

and spending; the woman weak, fearful, fair, curious of her beauty and saving'. John Pechy opened his treatise on women's diseases with a forceful statement of the same view: 'kind nature' had bestowed upon women a 'delicate and fine habit of body and designed her only for an easy life and to perform the tender offices of love'. Man, by contrast, was designed more robustly, so he could protect the woman, 'delve and manure the earth and undergo the other toils of life'.[9] William Heale described the two sexes as

> both like and yet dislike, like in specifical nature, their bodies of the like feature. . . . dislike in the individual. . . . the one stronger, the one weaker . . . the one valiant and laborious in the fields, the other mild and diligent within the doors: that what the one had painfully gotten abroad the other might carefully conserve at home. The one fairer and as a delightful picture of beauty: the other more stern and as a perfect mirror of manhood. The one more deeply wise, the other of a pregnant wit.[10]

Menstruation was seen by numerous writers at this time as both a sign and as a cause of women's inferiority and of their predetermined sedentary and domestic roles. For example Fontanus's treatise *The Woman's Doctor* opened with the assertion that women were 'made to stay at home and look after household employments'. Their work was accompanied 'with much ease without any vehement stirrings of the body' therefore 'hath provident nature assigned them their monthly courses'.[11] Patricia Crawford has argued convincingly that 'menstruation served as a reminder of the axiom that women had inferior bodies'.[12] It was an axiom that, so far from being challenged at this time, was reinforced by current notions about blood and purity. Even the quality of blood was gendered. Male blood was treasured, at its hottest and best, as the matter from which the seed of life was created. 'It is to be noted', Thomas Vicary had written in 1577, 'that this sperm that cometh both of man and woman is made and gathered of the most best and purest drops of blood in all the body.'[13] But female blood carried connotations of sexuality and danger. There were those like the Laudian vicar of Great Totham in Essex who found these resonances so powerful they had to act by them. He refused

9. Smith, *A Preparative to Marriage*, p. 43; cited in R.L. Greaves, *Society and Religion in Elizabethan England* (Minneapolis, 1981), p. 255; J. Pechy, *A Geneeal Treatise of the Diseases of Maids, Bigbellied Women, Childbed Women and Widows* (London, 1696), preface.
10. W. Heale, *An Apology for Women* (London, 1609), p. 23.
11. N. Fontanus, *The Woman's Doctor* (London, 1652), p. 1.
12. P. Crawford, 'Attitudes to Menstruation in Seventeenth-Century England', *Past and Present* 91 (1981), p. 73.
13. Cited in M. Hattaway, 'Fleshing his Will in the Spoil of her Honour: Desire, Misogyny and the Perils of Chivalry', *Shakespeare Survey* (1993), p. 126 which has further comment on the contemporary metaphorical language of blood.

communion both to menstruating women and to those who had had sexual intercourse on the previous night.[14] One nonconformist sect at the end of the seventeenth century moved its meeting 'for the present' when a woman polluted their venue by giving birth to a bastard there.[15] Menses in the Galenic corporeal economy were, as we have seen, another kind of blood: a plethora of blood, inferior blood, blood that needed to be cast out. Once again scripture and medical beliefs supported each other and they together supported the patriarchal order. In Isaiah the coverings of images which were defiled were to be cast away 'as a menstrous cloth'. The menstrual simile received emphasis from the marginalia of the Geneva Bible where it was explained that when Isaiah, seeking to discount men's righteousness, declared it was 'as filthy rags' this could be read 'like the menstrous clothes of a woman'. The King James version of the Bible specified that earlier references to the sinful city of Jerusalem as a 'filthy thing' implied that the city was a 'menstrous woman'. Popular superstitions about the venomous quality of menstrual blood were attacked by some textbook writers but given force by new readings.[16] A new translation of Pliny's *History of the World*, for example, went much further than the author had done in the first place, turning the menstruating woman into a dangerous monster:

> If they touch any standing corn in the field it will wither and come to no good. . . . Look they upon a sword, knife or any edged tools, be it never so bright, it waxeth duskish, so doth the lovely hue of ivory. The very bees in the hive die. Iron and steel presently take rust, yea and brass likewise, with a filthy, strong and poisoned stink, if they but lay hand thereupon.[17]

Superstitions about the dangerous powers that menstruating women might exercise remained embedded in English popular culture during the Hanoverian and Victorian periods. Women were excluded from primitive methodist chapels during their periods up to the end of the nineteenth century and as recently as 1974 there was correspondence in the *Lancet* about why flowers handled by a menstruating woman should wilt.[18]

Fontanus cited Hippocrates to the effect that 'the matrix is the cause of all those diseases which happen to women'.[19] The womb gave women something extra but not, by a feat of male legerdemain, something extra which made them more perfect. The less perfect body of woman had to

14. K.V. Thomas, *Religion and the Decline of Magic* (London, 1971), p. 38.
15. P. Crawford, *Women and Religion in England 1500–1720* (London, 1993), p. 56.
16. Crawford, 'Attitudes to Menstruation', *Past and Present* 91 (1981), pp. 57–60.
17. Cited in C. Larner, *Enemies of God: The Witchhunt in Scotland* (Oxford, 1981), p. 93.
18. Crawford 'Attitudes to Menstruation', *Past and present* 91 (1981), p. 61.
19. Fontanus, *Woman's Doctor*, p. 2.

tolerate the womb, an extra item on the physical agenda which, despite all the teleology we have here, was demanding, unpredictable and, in the original Galenic conception, even dangerously mobile in its troublemaking capacities. From the menarche onwards, as has been indicated, it required to be refreshed by regular orgasms which fed it with seed. It also needed to be fortified by being put to the use for which it was intended: women were seen, paradoxically in view of the hazards and pains involved, as becoming healthier by regular pregnancies.[20] Above all it was a vital necessity that the womb was cleared of its excess of poor quality blood through menstruation. Amenorrhea was 'the most usual and universal cause of diseases common to all women' declared Fontanus.[21] That seventeenth-century physicians took all this very seriously is clear from their tendency to take the menstrual and childbearing history of female patients into account for diagnosis and treatment whatever the illness they presented. These casebooks of the midlands practice of John Symcotts and the Shrewsbury practice of Dr Barker provide evidence of this.[22] Their assumption, in dealing with women, was that they shared a particular vulnerability to ill health on account of their reproductive role. They were in a quite literal sense, as well as in other senses that will be discussed, the weaker vessel.

There was still a general consensus in the late eighteenth century that regular and efficient menstruation was the key to women's health. 'So artificially indeed is a woman formed', wrote John Ball in a tract of 1770 about 'disorders to which the fair sex are liable', 'that at some stated seasons that redundancy of blood may be discharged.' But there were 'an infinite number of accidents' which could interrupt 'this salutary work of nature'.[23] Henry Manning emphasised that either too much or too little discharge of blood threatened the crucial 'exact equilibrium in the constitution which guides the scale of health'. His confidence that he was on the right lines in his interpretation of the working of women's bodies sprung from the knowledge that every physician from Hippocrates onwards had shared the conviction that monthly evacuation was 'the great spring and mover in the system'. Manning found traditional plethora theory entirely comprehensible, in the sense that it was necessary, once the menarche was reached, for the uterus to retain a plethora as a reserve for nutrition of the foetus. Thus this nutrition was 'the ultimate and final cause of the plethora itself'. His reading of the female body in terms of its

20. Fontanus, *Woman's Doctor*, pp. 6–7. For pregnancy see L.A. Pollock 'Embarking on a Rough Passage: The Experience of pregnancy in Early Modern Society', in V. Fildes, ed., *Women as Mothers in Pre-Industrial England* (London, 1990), pp. 39–67.
21. Fontanus, *Woman's Doctor*, p. 4.
22. L.M. Beier, *Sufferers and Healers: The Experience of Illness in Seventeenth Century England* (London, 1987), pp. 124–5, 214.
23. J. Ball, *The Female Physician or Every Woman her own Doctress* (London, 1770), p. 21.

reproductive role remained firmly teleological.[24] Manning's treatise is a reminder of the continuing hold of an intense patriarchalism, which coloured English physicians' vision of women's diseases, throughout our period. Imprisoned by a gender stereotype which was founded on the Old Testament and ancient Greek medical texts, they were unable to break free from a notion of women's inferiority and weakness which constrained any positive advance in real understanding of women's bodies. Hilda Smith has characterised seventeenth-century gynaecology as 'a combination of ignorance about internal medicine, bias against women and an almost total reliance on the ancients'.[25] Nevertheless we should note that the system which has been described in the two previous chapters had an internal coherence that gave it resilience. Doctors learnt the supposition that diagnosis began with the fundamental state of the patient being a woman, which might be a sufficient explanation for both the physical and psychological manifestations of certain conditions. Diagnosis became, as Anne Laurence has remarked, 'an attempt by men to supply an explanation for differences in behaviour between men and women'.[26]

The casebooks of the astrologer-physician Richard Napier for the years 1598 to 1632 provide an unusual opportunity to go beyond a body of medical theory which serves as an apologia for male domination and hear some women's voices. More than half his patients were women and what he recorded about their own accounts can be treated seriously since it is clear that he was sexually indifferent towards women and not motivated by any special preoccupation with the mysteries of the feminine heart and body. That women came to him in considerable numbers is not surprising, given their worries about physiological processes of which they had little understanding, their high morbidity rates and their fears about death in childbed. Napier of course always asked them about their menstrual history. What is astonishing is the number who confessed to irregular or painful menstruation. It is evident that they, as much as he, connected bad menstruation in their minds with various broader medical problems. The confusion women suffered about what was happening to them is well illustrated by the case history of a woman who had a pricking, shooting and running of her ear: 'she had no show in ten weeks and then had a show of them almost all this month and feareth they be stricken up into her head or else feareth that by riding they came down yet would know whether she be with child'. Some always wanted a simple answer to the question whether they were pregnant but Ronald Sawyer, who has analysed this material in detail, suggests that nutritional deficiencies and

24. H. Manning, *A Treatise on Female Diseases* (London, 1771), pp. 3–6, 25–6, 51.
25. H. Smith, 'Gynaecology and Ideology in Seventeenth-century England', in B.A. Carroll, ed., *Liberating Women's History* (Urbana, 1976), p. 99.
26. A. Laurence, 'Women's Psychological Disorders in Seventeenth-century Britain', in A. Angerman, ed., *Current Issues in Women's History* (London, 1989), pp. 210–11.

chronic infections may in many cases have disrupted the menstrual cycles of mature women. Many of Napier's female patients suffered 'the whites' as their primary symptom or admitted to it as a secondary symptom. This was a vaginal or uterine discharge, associated by modern commentators with yeast or bacterial infections, which was much discussed by contemporary textbook authors.[27]

Nicholas Fontanus devoted most of his treatise *The Woman's Doctor* to discussion of 'suffocation of the mother'. Like greensickness, this was believed to be caused by retention of fluids that should be excreted, though it was a disease of women of childbearing age not of adolescents. Fontanus gives a traditional account closely in line, for example, with the fifteenth-century treatise on women's diseases which attributed suffocation of the uterus to retaining 'corrupt and venomous humours that should be purged in the same way that men are purged of seed that comes from their testicles'.[28] He described the disease as caused by retention of seed and the menstruum together, in some cases, with 'a cold and moist distemper of the matrix'. The retention, he believed, acted to 'choke and extinguish' the heat of the matrix, breeding 'windy humours' which ascended to other parts of the body. Riverius made the point rather more specifically: 'from the seminal matter so affected, vapours ascend unto the brain which disturb the rational faculty and depose it from its throne'.[29] Medical anthropologists have shown how both physical and mental diseases are defined socially. Rather than attempt retrospective diagnosis of those who were diagnosed as suffering from 'the mother' in early modern England, the historian's task is to make sense of the form that contemporary observations took.[30] The mother represents a classic example of a flexible diagnostic tactic for maladies which presented symptoms that were both emotional and physical. Conventional assumptions about the malfunctioning of women's bodies because of the disturbance of their reproductive role acted as a starting point. Richard Napier concluded that an old woman who complained that 'something hurteth her and inwardly possesseth her' in 1619 was suffering from 'epileptic fits of the mother in

27. M. Macdonald, *Mystical Bedlam: Madness, Anxiety and Healing in Seventeenth-century England* (Cambridge, 1981), pp. 35–40; R.W. Sawyer, 'Patients, Healers and Disease in the South-east Midlands 1597–1634', University of Wisconsin-Madison PhD thesis, 1986, pp. 481–7. I am grateful to Michael Macdonald for supplying me with a copy of these pages from Dr Sawyer's thesis.

28. B. Rowland, ed., *Medieval Women's Guide to Health: The First English Gynaecological Handbook* (Kent, Ohio, 1981), p. 87. I am grateful to Timothy Stretton for this reference.

29. Fontanus, *Woman's Doctor*, pp. 51–112: Riverius *The Practice of Physick* (London, 1655), pp. 417–18; see also L. Lemnius, *The Secret Miracles of Nature* (London 1658), p. 18; H. Crooke, *Microcosmographia: A Description of the Body of Man* (London 1631), p. 231; T. Phaer, *The Regiment of Life* (London, 1550), sig K vi r.

30. M. Macdonald, 'Madness, Suicide and the Computer', in R. Porter and A. Wear, eds, *Problems and Methods in the History of Medicine* (London, 1987), p. 210.

most pitiful manner'.[31] Sir Kenelm Digby connected women's moistness and passivity with the dangers of an 'unpleasing contagion of the imagination'. He knew of one very melancholy woman, subject as he thought 'to the disease called the mother', who 'while she continued in that mood, she thought herself possessed'.[32] Philip Henry described his seventeen-year-old sister's malady as 'fits of the mother' when she lay senseless for eight hours in 1658; these mother-fits were later diagnosed as a 'violent ague' but nearly a year later she was said to be still 'not rid of her mother fits'.[33]

In the first serious treatise on the subject of the mother published in 1603, the circumstances of which have been unravelled by Michael Macdonald, Edward Jorden displayed his command of the classical literature of the subject but was not content simply to repeat the ancient interpretation of hysteria as a disease of the uterus. Jorden was a fellow of the College of Physicians. His learned work accepted that amenorrhea and sexual abstinence were the principal causes of the disease but he did not see them as the only ones. 'Perturbations of the mind are oftentimes to blame,' he declared, insisting that the symptoms of the prepubescent Mary Glover, who others were arguing was bewitched, could be accounted for in natural terms. Jorden was here calling upon the cultural construction of females as the weaker vessel which was at the core of early modern patriarchy. He emphasised women's 'passive condition'. It was the commonplace belief that they were especially vulnerable to psychological stresses which might exhibit themselves in physical symptoms which enabled him to make his case convincing and authoritative. Michael Macdonald has argued that Jorden's work helped a current of scepticism about supernatural causes of illness to gain momentum. Scriptural patriarchy as a whole would need replacing as religious discourse ceased effectively to provide it with adequate foundations. What the politics surrounding the bewitching of Mary Glover shows is that, when men were ready to exploit it, there was potential within the scriptural view of women's bodies to establish a new kind of patriarchy which would be founded on sexual difference rather than homology. With his remark about 'perturbations of the mind', Jorden glimpses that potential but the elaboration of the idea is far from his immediate purpose or intention.[34]

For the present, in the period before 1660, suffocation of the mother was variously regarded and treated. Many medical textbooks mentioned it

---

31. Macdonald, *Mystical Bedlam*, p. 211.
32. Cited in Laurence in Angerman, ed., *Current Issues in Women's History*, p. 211.
33. Crawford, 'Attitudes to Menstruation', *Past and Present* 91 (1981), p. 53.
34. M. Macdonald, ed., *Witchcraft and Hysteria in Elizabethan London* (London, 1991), Introduction, pp. vii–lxiv; E. Jorden, *A Brief Discourse of a Disease Called the Suffocation of the Mother* (London, 1603), fol. 22 v.

in their lists of diseases and gentlewomen included concoctions to remedy
it in their manuals of physick.[35] Elizabeth Grey, for instance, recommended some fern made sodden in Rhennish wine and laid on the
navel in a linen cloth 'as hot as she may suffer it' or sucking in the smoke
produced by powder of white amber burnt in a chafing dish of coals.[36]
For many physicians it was seen as requiring much the same approach as
other menstrual problems and they ordered the standard purges and
vomits. So the Henry girl was let blood in the course of her long period
of mother fits.[37] A Cambridge practitioner around 1620, however, tried
simply to lure the wandering womb in one of his patients back to where
it belonged. She was given sweet applications on her genitals and foul
smells in her nose; he told her to sneeze in order to drive the rising womb
downwards.[38] There is no difficulty in understanding how someone like
this Cambridge healer could view the wandering womb in such literal
terms.[39] The old cosmology was based on principles of metaphysical fixity
and of teleology. Early modern society was obsessed with aberrant movement of one kind or another: suffocation of the mother resonated with
planetary irregularity and vagrants who roamed the state.[40] In a sense it
was simply what men might expect of the weaker vessel. The image of
the wandering womb was a powerful one. A woman's fits or hysteria, the
sad but logical consequence of a failure to remedy amenorrhea or put the
womb to use, was an expression of teleological catastrophe.

In Greek theories of knowledge femaleness was always associated symbolically with what reason was supposed to have left behind, above all
with nature. The Church Fathers explained and elaborated upon a creation story which began with the premise of woman's inferiority. For
Augustine, woman had tempted man into the first disastrous act of the
abandonment of the will and was forever thereafter identified with subjection of mind to body. Her natural subordination to him was a matter
of rational control. For Aquinas woman's meaning was bound up with
reproduction and this fact excluded her from a role in the higher pursuits
of the mind. 'Our trust in a reason that knows no sex', Genevieve Lloyd
has argued, 'has been largely self-deceiving . . . our ideals of reason have
historically incorporated an exclusion of the feminine and that femininity
itself has been partly constituted through such processes of exclusion.'[41] It

35. See citations by P. Slack in C. Webster, ed., *Health, Medicine and Mortality in the
    Sixteenth Century* (Cambridge, 1979), p. 269, n 121.
36. C.F. Otten, ed., *English Women's Voices 1540–1700* (Miami, 1992), p. 185.
37. Crawford, 'Attitudes to Menstruation', *Past and Present* 91 (1981), p. 53.
38. Beier, *Sufferers and Healers*, p. 126.
39. For the Hippocratic account see V.L. Bullough, 'Medieval Medical Views of
    Woman', *Viator* 4 (1973), pp. 493–4.
40. J. Dollimore, *Sexual Dissidence: Augustine to Wilde, Freud to Foucault* (Oxford, 1991),
    pp. 116–17.
41. G. Lloyd, *The Man of Reason: Male and Female in Western Philosophy* (London, 1984),
    pp. x, 2, 33, 36.

had become an axiom by the early modern period that women were much weaker in their minds than men. It was this axiom that Lady Brilliana Harley used playfully when she wrote to Sir Robert in the cold February of 1626 after he had gone to London for the opening of parliament: 'I know you have more wit than a woman and therefore I need not desire you to keep yourself warm.'[42]

The hold of these ideas can be illustrated from a range of sources. In the first place there are the medical writers and those who echo them in attributing female lack of rationality to their humoral constitution. Their extra heat, explained Lemnius, made men 'quick witted and deeper searchers out of matters and more diligent and ripe of judgement than women. . . . a woman in going about affairs and making bargains hath not the like dexterity and seemliness that a man hath'.[43] A mid-seventeenth century author produced the following reasoning in favour of producing male children:

> Those who seek the comfort of having wise children must endeavour that they be born male; for the female, through the cold and moist of their sex, cannot be endowed with so profound a judgement; we find indeed that they take with appearance of knowledge in slight and easy matters but seldom reach any farther than to a slight superficial smattering in any deep science.[44]

Thomas Heywood in his *General History of Women*, generalising from the story of the wandering womb, connected women's restlessness of mind to their 'besettlement by a succession of foul and vain humours'.[45] The Duchess of Newcastle in the preface to one of her works accepted male teaching that the female brain was 'mixed by nature with the coldest and softest elements'. But she herself was described in an elegy on her death as the exception to her sex, 'who have fruitful wombs but barren brains'.[46] The Duchess's devaluation of herself may not be very surprising, seeing that Suzanne Hull concluded from an analysis of books published for a female audience between 1475 and 1640 that 'women were told over and over and over that they were inferior, that they had lesser minds, that they were unable to handle their own affairs'.[47] They also clearly told one another.

Women's supposed lack of reason came easily to hand as an emotive

42. BL, Loan MS 29/72. I am grateful to Jacqueline Eales for this reference.
43. Cited in R.L. Greaves, *Society and Religion in Elizabethan England* (Minneapolis, 1981), p. 256.
44. Cited in Smith in Carroll, ed., *Liberating Women's History*, p. 103.
45. Cited in S. Cahn, *Industry of Devotion: The Transformation of Women's Work in England 1560–1660* (Columbia, 1987), p. 78.
46. Cited in Fraser, *The Weaker Vessel*, p. 5.
47. S.W. Hull, *Chaste, Silent and Obedient: English Books for Women 1435–1640* (San Marino, 1982), pp. 140–2.

point for those who wished to keep them from male preserves. Thus
Gervase Markham protested that women could not possibly grasp the
principles of physic as they would have to do to be allowed to enter the
medical profession.[48] The Northamptonshire physician John Cotta scathingly rebuked ignorant women healers for their audacity in practising
medicine, given that neither God nor nature had 'made them commissioners in the sessions of learned reason and understanding'.[49] He
should charge his wife, Sir William Wentworth advised his son, 'to
abstain from hearing any tenants' suits' since 'flattering tenants will soon
seduce a woman, who neither is like to have a true intelligence of the
matter, nor so sound a judgement as the wiser sort of men have'.[50] The
fiercest denunciations of all came from the church and its ministers. From
1562 onwards the homily on marriage, read regularly in parish churches,
drummed in the message that women were not rational enough to be
trusted: 'the woman is a weak creature not endued with like strength and
constancy of mind; therefore they be the sooner disquieted and they be
the more prone to all weak affections and dispositions of mind, more than
men be, and lighter they be and more vain in their fantasies and opinions'.[51] Richard Hooker justified that deeply characteristic gesture of
patriarchal authority, a bride being given away by her father, by declaring
that it put 'women in mind of a duty whereinto the very imbecility of
their nature and sex doth bind them, namely to be always directed,
guided and ordered by others'.[52] When, in his marriage manual *Matrimonial Honour*, Daniel Rogers stated blankly to his female audience
'remember thy sex is crazy ever since Eve sinned', he was presumably
using the word in the contemporary usage of 'indisposed, ailing . . .
broken down, frail, infirm'.[53] The remark nicely illustrates the conjunction of biblical and philosophical teaching which sustained the notion of
women's mental inferiority.

Oft-repeated proverbs are an especially instructive genre for the study
of mentality and attitudes since they provide some kind of entry into the
oral culture of the time. A coherent group of proverbs from the period
from 1500 to 1660 shows how the notion of women's lack of reason was
seen to need reinforcement and was thus constantly reiterated. Almost
every early modern proverb about women is unthinkingly sexist and
prejudicial. A favourite with the dramatists, which they must have known
would strike a chord of familiarity, was the comparison of women with

48. Cited in Cahn, *Industry of Devotion*, p. 75.
49. Beier, *Sufferers and Healers*, p. 43.
50. J.P. Cooper, ed., *Wentworth Papers 1597–1628* (Camden Fourth Series, 12, 1973),
    pp. 20–1.
51. Cited in L. Jardine, *Still Harping on Daughters: Women and Drama in the Age of
    Shakespeare* (London, 1983), p. 43.
52. Cited in K. Rogers, *The Troublesome Helpmate* (Seattle, 1966), p. 142.
53. D. Rogers, *Matrimonial Honour* (London, 1642), p. 281.

German clocks. 'Their wits (like wheels in Brunswick clocks) being all wound up so far as they could stretch', declared Dekker, 'were all going but not one going truly.' 'Being ready, she consists of an hundred pieces, much like your German clock,' was how Middleton put it. The misogynist Ben Jonson provided a scathing version: 'she takes herself asunder still when she goes to bed into some twenty boxes and about next day noon is put together again, like a great German clock'.[54] But the classic expression of this proverb, which these dramatists probably all knew, was in Berowne's speech in *Love's Labour's Lost* when he was considering how being in love meant he would have to cope with living with a woman:

> What I? I love? I sue? I seek a wife?
> A woman, that is like a German clock,
> Still a-repairing, ever out of frame
> And never going aright, being a watch,
> But being watched that it may still go right.[55]

In its serious yet at the same time laughing tone, Berowne's speech perfectly captures the sense of women's instability of mind which other contemporary proverbs restate: 'a woman is a weathercock'; 'a woman's mind and winter wind change oft'; 'a woman's mind is always mutable'. 'Poor woman', wrote James Clavering to his brother-in-law about his ever anxious wife Ann in 1713 and echoing these proverbs, 'her mind and judgement is as variable and fickle as the weather.' A medieval proverb still current reminded men they should not trust women (which in fact they often did) as the executors of their wills since they were too forgetful. Thus a strong vein of oral tradition painted women as scatty, empty-headed and unreliable, in other words as hopelessly at sea because they lacked the moderating voice of reason. Men should take a woman's first counsel not her second for a woman was 'wise on the sudden and foolish upon deliberation'. Women were 'as wavering as the wind'.[56] This was the very essence of their weakness for all their other characteristics, their emotional unsteadiness and propensity to moral failure, arose from it. 'Frailty thy name is woman': Hamlet's great cry of pain in his first soliloquy, as he muses on his mother's sexual insatiability and over-hasty remarriage, is the heart of the matter.[57]

Men's construction of the female psyche was based upon a relativity which always credited them with less than men: weakness of mind, weakness of will, weakness of moral sense. In the weaker vessel the imagination ran riot. Helkiah Crooke regarded this as an inescapable outcome of the humoral physiology: 'that females are more wanton and

54. Tilley, no. W658.
55. *Love's Labours Lost*, act III, scene i, 191–6.
56. Tilley, nos W653, 668, 673, 674, 698, 700; D. Levine and K. Wrightson, *The Making of an Industrial Society: Whickham 1560–1765* (Oxford, 1991), p. 315.
57. *Hamlet*, act I, scene ii, 146.

petulant than males we think happeneth because of the impotency of
their minds . . . for the imaginations of lustful women are like the imaginations of brute beasts which have no repugnancy or contradiction of
reason to restrain them'.[58] It was a commonplace that women were much
closer to nature and the brute creation than men.[59] Their moral inferiority
was a reflection of their status in Aristotelian theory as imperfect men.
One writer saw them as 'unapt in good things and most prompt in
naughty' because of a natural 'privation'. Women's 'desire to go fine and
deck themselves' represented an attempt 'to supply imperfection by art'.[60]
It was in their sexuality above all that they gave themselves away. Because
they were ruled by their lower parts rather than their upper ones, they
were seen as able to exercise magical powers in the realm of love and
sexual attraction.[61] The vulnerability of their imaginations was another
aspect of their weakness. The face that a woman fixed her mind upon at
the moment of conception, said Lemnius, 'that likeness will the child
represent'.[62] *Aristotle's Master-Piece* endorsed the view that a woman's
imaginative life during pregnancy shaped her child's body and features.[63]
There is evidence about how seriously this was taken at all social levels in
the first part of our period and by some at least after 1700. Alice
Thornton's son had 'a mark of blood upon his heart' because she had
suffered a fright. A man was believed to walk with a staggering gait
because his mother had seen a drunken man during her pregnancy.
Women's fears of the sight of a hare causing a harelip were sufficiently
common for Nicholas Culpepper to record the popular superstition that
a slit smock worn during pregnancy would prevent the disaster expected
from such a misfortune.[64] In 1726, all London was buzzing for several
weeks with the story of Mary Tofts, a poor woman from Godalming who
was alleged to have given birth to a number of rabbits. The strength of
popular belief in the power of a woman to reshape the foetus in her
uterus gave this bizarre tale plausibility. The first newspaper reports played
both upon this belief and upon the notion that a woman's insatiable
sexual desire could produce monsters. Mary Tofts's craving for rabbits to
eat while she was pregnant was described. The broadside *The Doctors in
Labour* was bawdily suggestive:

58. Crooke, *Microcosmographia*, p. 276.
59. K.V. Thomas, *Man and the Natural World* (London, 1983), p. 41.
60. Cited in Gibbons, p. 11.
61. M.E. Weiner, *Women and Gender in Early Modern Europe* (Cambridge, 1993), p. 253.
62. Lemnius, *Secret Miracles of Nature*, p. 11. See also Ross, *Arcana Microcosmi*, p. 49.
63. R. Porter and L. Hall *The Facts of Life: The Creation of Sexual Knowledge in Britain
    1680–1950* (London, 1995), p. 48.
64. P. Crawford, 'The Sucking Child: Adult Attitudes to Child Care in the First
    year of Life in Seventeenth-Century England', *Continuity and Change* 1 (1986), pp.
    27, 46.

> The rabbit all day long ran in my head
> At night I dreamt I had him in my bed
> My husband wak'd me and cried Moll for shame
> Let go – what 'twas he meant I need not name.[65]

A pamphlet controversy about the powers of the imagination of pregnant women among physicians and other scientists following the Tofts case lasted for forty years. Interest in cases of extraordinary childbirth among the English public was at its height during the 1740s, a decade in which *The Gentleman's Magazine* contained no fewer than ninety-two articles on such freaks of nature.[66] In 1746, to take one example, it reported the birth of a monster to a Chelsea woman with a 'nose and eyes like a lion ... claws like a lion instead of fingers, no breastbone ... one foot longer than the other'. She had visited the lions in the Tower 'where she was much terrified with the old lion's noise'.[67]

Women's weakness of will showed in their inability to exercise self-control. So their emotions ran to extremes: as the Senecan proverb, popular in the Elizabethan period, summarised it 'a woman either loves or hates'.[68] 'If she did not hate him deadly she would love him dearly', sighed Don Pedro, only half jokingly, when Beatrice was on the edge of abandoning her scornful and witty stance towards Benedick in *Much Ado about Nothing*.[69] What men found most objectionable in women's emotional nature were their alleged manipulative and devious ways. Tears come easily to them but were not to be trusted as such. Thomas Heywood reminded his male readers in his *Curtain Lecture* that Ovid had made it plain 'there is no heed or regard to be taken of their tears, as commanding them at their will and exposing them at their pleasure'.[70] A succession of proverbs made the same point: 'trust not a woman when she weeps', 'women have tears of dissimulation as well as sorrow', 'women laugh when they can and weep when they will', 'women weep and sicken when they list'. 'Trust not a woman when she cries', declared Dekker in *The Honest Whore*, 'for she will pump water from her eyes.' 'For do but cross a woman, although it be never so little', wrote Joseph Swetnam in his misogynist tract of 1615, 'she will straightway put finger in the eye and cry.' When a man was foolish enough then to flatter her 'she will pour forth the more abundance of deceitful tears', so she should

65. L. Cody, 'The Doctor's in Labour: or a New Whim Wham from Guildford', *Gender and History* 4 (1992), pp. 177–8.
66. G.S. Rousseau, 'Pineapples, Pregnancy, Pica and Peregrine Pickle', pp. 89–93.
67. Cited in R. Porter, 'The Secrets of Generation Display'd: *Aristotle's Master-Piece* in Eighteenth-Century England', in R.P. Maccubbin, ed., *'Tis Nature's Fault: Unauthorised Sexuality during the Enlightenment* (Cambridge, 1987), p. 20.
68. Tilley, no. W651.
69. *Much Ado about Nothing*, act V, scene i, 178–80.
70. T. Heywood, *A Curtain Lecture* (London, 1637), p. 8.

no more be pitied 'than to see a goose go barefoot'.[71] Just as eyes easily watered, so tongues incessantly wagged. 'A woman conceals what she knows not', the proverb ran: she was quite incapable of keeping a secret. 'Give her good counsel how to govern her tongue and to avoid not only base but bad company and guide her therein,' Sir William Wentworth told his son, advising him how he should manage his wife. Making excuses was another female vice. Women did it, men said, by merely looking on their apron strings.[72] 'A kind natured wench', wrote Richard Brathwaite in *Art Asleep Husband*, 'will . . . with twirling of their apron string have as ready an answer if at any time taken napping.'[73] Women were fickle, irresponsible and slippery. Holding on to them was proverbially linked with holding on to a wet eel by the tail. They were also easily tempted by gifts.[74] It was with 'witchcraft of his wits, with traiterous gifts', the Ghost told Hamlet, that his uncle had lured Gertrude to his bed.[75]

Men's reading of women's bodies, it has been made plain, attributed to them a voracious sexuality; their reading of their minds left them without the reason to control it. This situation occasioned much contemporary comment. Robert Burton's rhetorical question in 1621 'of woman's unnatural, insatiable lust what country, what village doth not complain?' was not so much a slur as a statement of conventional wisdom that appeared to make sense in view of the known facts about the limitations of men's sexual performance and about women's capacity for multiple orgasm.[76] The observation by the Elizabethan musician Thomas Wythorne that 'though they be the weaker vessels yet they will overcome two, three or four men in the satisfying of their carnal appetites' reflected these same facts.[77] For those concerned with political obligation this conventional wisdom provided handy evidence of why women had to be ruled. In *The Obedience of a Christian Man* William Tyndale put the matter directly: 'God, which created woman, knoweth what is in that weak vessel (as Peter calleth her) and hath therefore put her under the obedience of her husband to rule her lusts and wanton appetite.[78]

How far men were in fact frightened by women's sexuality is not clear. The English sources have not yet yielded material on this subject which

---

71. K.U. Henderson and B.F. McManus, eds, *Half Humankind: Contexts and Texts of the Controversy about Women in England 1540–1640* (Urbana, 1985), p. 62.
72. Tilley, nos W638, 649, 659, 710, 713, 720; Cooper, ed., *Wentworth papers*, p. 20.
73. R. Brathwaite, *Art Asleep Husband: A Boulster Lecture* (London, 1640), p. 43.
74. Tilley, nos W640, 704.
75. *Hamlet*, act I, scene v, 43.
76. Cited in Thomas, *Religion and the Decline of Magic*, pp. 568–9.
77. Cited in L. Stone, *The Family, Sex and Marriage in England 1500–1800* (London, 1977), p. 495.
78. W. Tyndale, *The Obedience of a Christian Man* (London, 1868 edn), p. 171. I am grateful to Amanda Shepherd for this reference.

provides the same insights as Lyndal Roper's study of weddings in Reformation Augsburg or Emmanuel Le Roy Ladurie's investigation into the real life of a Gascon peasant girl called Francouneto, who was accused of bewitching young men and making them impotent.[79] Learned discourse contains references to women's use of occult powers. James I argued that women were more easily entrapped by the devil because they were frailer than men and he made explicit the connection between this frailty and their sexuality.[80] William Perkins explained that more women than men were witches because men's resolution, in other words their reason, gave them more protection against the devil's temptations.[81] Keith Thomas argues that witchcraft was a genuine temptation as a means of power available to the poor and vulnerable.[82] The unusually well documented case of Margaret Moore of Sutton in Cambridgeshire in 1647 provides insight into how a poor woman, driven by a mixture of experience, emotion and the adoption of the male construction of devilish action, could end up in court telling a story of her own guilt which was not simply invented under interrogation but probably represented genuine belief. The case provides a shaft of light upon the core of her femininity in her love and care as a mother of her children, something which receives no attention in the ideology of womanhood at this time. She had lost three children in infancy and was desperate not to lose her fourth. Her account in court, supported by witnesses, was of a pact with the devil to save this child if she did his bidding. The fantasy is plausible, given her circumstances, Malcolm Gaskill suggests, as either a delusion or a dream. It concerns resisting the domination of death and poverty in a manner that serves constructive personal ends, even if this is at the expense of harm caused to others: 'surrendering her soul for the sake of her child can be equated with a metaphysical extension of the principle of laying down life for love and therefore represents an extension of power, whereby the soul is reified in an imaginary sphere as something with which she is able to bargain'. The important point about the courtroom drama at Ely in 1647 is that it was conducted by participants who on all sides inhabited a common mental universe in which the boundaries between the natural and supernatural worlds were not yet fixed. A key notion in this mentality was a connection between womanhood, sexuality and occult power. This notion made it possible for those who listened to Margaret Moore's story to believe it as fully as she may have done in telling it. With her confession to the magistrate that 'she heard the voice

79. L. Roper, '"Going to Church and Street": Weddings in Reformation Augsburg', Past and Present 106 (1985), pp. 89–92; E. Le Roy Ladurie, Jasmin's Witch (London, 1990).
80. Cited in Larner, Enemies of God, p. 93.
81. Cited in Cahn, Industry of Devotion, p. 77.
82. Thomas, Religion and the Decline of Magic, pp. 502–34.

of her children who had formerly died calling unto her in these words mother, mother, good sweet mother let me in' we perhaps catch a glimpse of her subjectivity.[83]

What was certainly common currency was the notion that the Fall was the proof of women's ultimate flaw and of their ineradicable moral weakness. 'Women receive perfection by men' ran the popular Aristotelian proverb which complemented the assertion of Eve's culpability.[84] For centuries men had imposed a pattern of gendered sinfulness. This remained hugely resilient under protestantism. Elizabeth Josceline, expressing precepts for her unborn child in 1622, believed a girl would face greater danger from pride than a boy: 'thou art weaker and thy temptations to this vice greater'.[85] When, with Augustine and his successors, the guilt was written into sex it was written primarily into women's sexuality. The scapegoating of Eve as the cause of the fall of Adam made all women, as her daughters, guilty for the impotence of man in the face of evil. It was her original seduction which in effect created the Augustinian break between the will and sexual pleasure.[86] The curse laid upon Eve for this deed in the Genesis story inflicted upon woman both the pain of childbirth and the punishment of subjection to her husband.[87] John Wing made the point about subjection with stunning directness in his marriage advice book *The Crown Conjugal* published in 1620: 'the time was when it was natural to your sex to be so excellent but she that first enjoyed it destroyed it, altering the property and losing the prerogative belonging to you all; you must therefore go to that God who made her so good to make you anew because now you are so bad'.[88]

The authors of the conduct books consistently based their case for household patriarchy upon women's inferiority, as evidenced by the Fall, and upon God's direction.[89] But it is important to note that there were times when they sought to modify the harshness of the conventional dismissal of all women as in every respect and always the weaker vessel. The general principle was accepted. Henry Smith told his readers not to expect 'that wisdom, nor that faith, nor that patience, nor that

83. M. Gaskill, 'Witchcraft and Power in Early Modern England: the Case of Margaret Moore', in J. Kermode and G. Walker, eds, *Women, Crime and the Courts in Early Modern England* (London, 1994), pp. 125–45.

84. Tilley, W717.

85. Cited in Fraser, *The Weaker Vessel*, p. 2.

86. R. Radford Ruether, *Sexism and God-Talk* (Boston, Massachusetts, 1983), pp. 165–73. See also A. Shepherd, 'Henry Howard and the Lawful Regiment of Women', *History of Political Thought* XII (1991), pp. 595–8.

87. P. Crawford, 'The Construction and Experience of Maternity in Seventeenth-Century England', in V. Fildes, ed., *Women as Mothers in Pre-Industrial England* (London, 1990), p. 8; Maclean, *The Renaissance Notion of Woman*, pp. 17–18.

88. J. Wing, *The Crown Conjugal or Spouse Royal* (London, 1620), p. 62.

89. For a full account see my essay in A.J. Fletcher and P.R. Roberts, eds, *Religion, Culture and Society in Early Modern Britain* (Cambridge, 1994), pp. 161–75.

strength in the weaker vessel which should be in the stronger'.[90] Yet there could be overlaps in strength and weakness. A woman had to 'learn to know her place and her part and to fashion her mind and her will, her disposition and her practice accordingly', admonished Thomas Gataker, 'yea though she be herself of a greater spirit and in some respects of better parts'.[91] John Dod and Robert Cleaver presented a frontal assault upon the notion of female mental incapacity, insisting 'that women are as men are reasonable creatures'. They possessed 'flexible wits both to good and evil the which with use, discretion and good counsel may be altered and turned'.[92] William Whateley maintained that the wife's duty was always to submit to her husband, even if she had greater gifts such as 'more wit and understanding, more readiness of speech, more dexterity of managing affairs'.[93] These pastors knew enough about the actual behaviour of married men and women to prevent them from putting too literal an argument based on the doctrine of the weaker vessel.

'Wives', wrote William Gouge, 'through the weakness of their sex (for they are the weaker vessels) are much prone to provoke their husbands.'[94] The idea that women's shrewishness related to their weakness of mind and will seems to have been commonly accepted. Attempting to reconcile the Earl of Shrewsbury with the termagent Bess of Hardwick in 1590, Bishop Overton recounted the gossip that she was 'a sharp and bitter shrew' but reminded the Earl of the common jest 'that there is but one shrew in all the world and every man hath her'. 'I doubt not but your great wisdom and experience hath taught you', he concluded, 'to bear some time with a woman as with the weaker vessel.'[95] Thomas Newcome, speaking of troubles with his wife in his autobiography, had no problem in accounting for them in terms of her being difficult because she was weak: 'I must confess I think all women to be thus weak.'[96]

Women were expected to run true to type: they were in bondage to their cold and moist humours. A few might transcend their physical and emotional makeup and such exceptional women gathered generous male tributes. The language of these tributes is worth noting. John Foxe lauded the courage of Agnes Potten and Joan Trunchfield who were burnt at the stake at Ipswich in 1556 with the comment that 'their constancy worthily

90. Smith, *Preparative to Marriage*, p. 53.
91. T. Gataker, *Marriage Duties briefly couched together out of Colossians 3: 18 and 19* (London, 1620), pp. 10–11.
92. J. Dod and R. Cleaver, *A Godly Form of Household Government* (London, 1614), K7.
93. Whateley, *Bride Bush*, p. 191.
94. W. Gouge, *Domestical Duties* (London, 1622), p. 354.
95. Cited in Henderson and McManus, eds, *Half Humankind*, p. 50.
96. H. Newcome, *Autobiography* (ed. R. Parkinson, Chetham Society, XXVI, 1852), pp. 87.

was to be wondered at, who being so simple women so manfully stood to the confession and testimony of God's word'.[97] An admirer of Lady Brilliana Harley's defence of Brampton Bryan castle in the civil war said she had commanded it 'with such a masculine bravery, both for religion, resolution, wisdom and manlike policy that her equal I never saw'.[98] Lucy Hutchinson wrote of the wife of the mayor of Nottingham, who was valiant when the city was under seige, as 'a woman of great zeal and courage and more understanding than woman of her rank usually have'. There is a snobbish note here but Hutchinson, nevertheless, is echoing conventional thinking about women's capacities.[99] On the monument erected by Sir Ralph Bankes to his mother Lady Mary in 1661, he commemorated her defence of Corfe Castle, declaring that she 'had the honour to have born with a constancy and courage above her sex a noble proportion of the late calamities'.[100] On the memorial to Mary Frampton who died in 1698 at Bath Abbey her intellectual capacities were recognised in explicitly masculine terms by the use of John Dryden's phrase a 'female softness in a manly mind'.[101] Conversely the Duke of Buckingham's epigraph on Sir Thomas Fairfax in 1660 recognised the possibility of a man displaying a quality that was positive but specifically female:

> Both the sexes virtues were in him combined
> He had the fierceness of the manliest mind
> And all the meekness too of womankind.[102]

More privately than in these examples Sir William Chaytor confided in a letter to his wife in 1701 his doting feelings for his daughter Anne who had 'a soul above her sex'.[103] The exemplary figures of a long literary tradition which runs from Chaucer's *Legend of Good Women* to Thomas Heywood's *Gynaikeion* often show nobility in adversity in a manner which involves an act of 'manly courage', such as killing themselves to avoid shame and humiliation.[104]

So how in this respect did the nation accommodate itself to the long reign of the Virgin Queen? The conventional solution to the problem of

---

97. J. Foxe, *Acts and Monuments* (ed. G. Townshend, New York, 1965), VIII, p. 101. I am grateful to Martha Yeilding for this reference.

98. Cited in Fraser, *Weaker Vessel*, p. 202.

99. L. Hutchinson, *Memoirs of Colonel John Hutchinson* (ed. J. Sutherland, Oxford, 1973), p. 24.

100. Cited in Fraser, *Weaker Vessel*, p. 196.

101. Cited in R.H. Michel, 'English Attitudes Towards Women 1640–1700', *Canadian Journal of History* 8 (1978), p. 48.

102. Cited in S.R. Gardiner, *History of the Commonwealth and Protectorate* (London, 1903), vol. I, p. 264.

103. North Yorkshire Record Office, Chaytor letters ZQH 9/14/3. I am grateful to Susan Chaytor for this reference.

104. Jardine, *Still Harping on Daughters*, p. 181.

the nation being ruled by a woman was to preserve the model of female subordination by surrounding the monarch with male counsel. This was what Sir Thomas Smith, writing during the reign, said should happen: a queen regnant needed 'the counsel of such able and discreet men as be able to supply all other defaults'. It was what some later believed had happened: writing sixty years or so after Elizabeth's death, Lucy Hutchinson related 'her submission to her masculine and wise councillors'.[105] Such tactics, however, even if practical were not necessary, given the gender scheme we are discussing and its cosmological setting. Elizabeth could allow, and indeed encourage, portrayals of herself as a monarch which stressed how she moved across the uncertain and unstable line of difference between male and female, or, alternatively, portrayals which showed her moving above the realm of gender altogether. No one denied in sixteenth-century England that there were cases in which the weaker vessel could show male attributes, even an extraordinary capacity for strength. In 1590 the Catholic nobleman Henry Howard wrote a detailed account of women's right to inherit and exercise authority, at the request, he maintained, of one of Elizabeth's councillors, in reply to John Knox. Amanda Shepherd shows how Howard argued that aristocratic girls 'should be educated for the possibility of fulfilling a position of authority'. The foundations of his case were notions about inheritance as well as about this gender fluidity. These enable him, by envisaging political circumstances which made female rule appropriate, to suggest an adaptation of patriarchy which might in fact reinforce its overall ideological dominance.[106]

Elizabeth, as Christopher Haigh has argued, was a special woman, never a mere woman: 'she determinedly contrasted herself with the rest of her sex, stressing their frailty but claiming to be an exception' since God's calling made her the Queen. This was her justification when, in 1563, she mused, in a speech to the House of Commons, about whether 'being a woman, wanting both wit and memory' she should be silent. Later the same year, she told a parliamentary delegation 'though I be a woman yet I have as good a courage answerable to my place as ever my father had'. 'I have the heart of a man, not of a woman and I am not afraid of anything,' she claimed in 1581.[107] Whilst she made these bold statements, Elizabeth also encouraged a cult of her monarchy which played with the issue of gender identification. In 1575 she was represented in the royal entertainment at Kenilworth as a questing knight. In the famous Armada portrait the red and gold frogging on the bodice together with the shape of her waist hints, it has been suggested, 'at a softened,

105. Citations in Gibbons, p. 58.
106. A. Shepherd, 'Henry Howard and the Lawful Regiment of Women', *History of Political Thought* XII (1991), pp. 589–603.
107. C. Haigh, *Elizabeth I* (London, 1988), pp. 21–2.

duly feminised, ornamental breastplate, and thus aligns Elizabeth with the armed warrior maidens of the psychomachia, Virtues defeating Vices in armed struggle against evil'.[108] What could be more brilliant in this context than the propagandist device of Elizabeth's Tilbury appearance which challenged the deepest of all the male presumptions against female monarchy that a woman was incapable of leading an army into war?[109] We know that Elizabeth did visit Tilbury while the Armada was in the Channel but the contemporary account says she was simply on horseback and carrying a truncheon. There is no evidence that she ever wore armour and the first depiction of her in armour at Tilbury is by the Caroline engraver Thomas Cecill. Nor did she make the famous speech there which, suggests Stephen Orgel, was subsequently 'approved, if not created, by her and intended for publication'. This showed a manipulation of the current gender scheme and of incipient patriotic loyalty which was skilful and sharply didactic: 'I know I have the body of a weak and feeble woman, but I have the heart and stomach of a king and of a King of England too. . . . Rather than any dishonour shall grow by me, I myself will take up arms, I myself will be your general, judge and rewarder of every one of your virtues in the field.'[110] The gender system allowed Elizabeth to present herself as a man because of its lack of distinction between male and female bodies.

The main drift of Elizabethan portraiture was towards subduing her sexuality and thus placing her outside the realm of nature, beyond the constraints of time and space; towards making her superhuman and transcendent. Nor was this problematic in the way that any similar propagandist campaign would be today. Elizabeth was the chaste maiden who, inviolate and unattainable, gave her knights scope to show their manhood at court or in exploits abroad. In a sense she was still an object of male desire, but it was a sense that was so aloof that it could hardly be called erotic.[111] The comparison with the relationship of Margaret Thatcher with those in her immediate entourage during the 1980s is illuminating. In both cases certainly ascribed gender clashed with assumptions about the exercise of power. Modern patriarchy, characterised by the sexed body and rigid and imprisoning polarities of gendered behaviour, permits no distancing of gender and sexuality. Attempting to cope

108. P. Berry, *Of Chastity and Power: Elizabethan Literature and the Unmarried Queen* (London, 1989), pp. 95–100. A. and C. Belsey, 'Icons of Divinity: Portraits of Elizabeth I', in L. Gent and N. Llewellyn, eds, *Renaissance Bodies: The Human Figure in English Culture 1540–1660* (London, 1990), p. 20.

109. Haigh, *Elizabeth I*, p. 142; A. Shepherd, *Gender and Authority in Sixteenth-Century England* (Keele, 1994), pp. 168–70.

110. S. Orgel, 'The Subtexts of *The Roaring Girl*', in S. Zimmerman, ed., *Erotic Politics: Desire on the Renaissance Stage* (London, 1992), pp. 15–16.

111. Belseys in Gent and Llewellyn, eds, *Renaissance Bodies*, pp. 20, 33; Berry, *Of Chastity and Power*, pp. 36–7.

with the concept of a female prime minister, commentators were forced
to grasp at the bizarre notion, a device for holding modern gender
construction in place, of an 'iron lady'. This would have been nonsense
to the Elizabethans. As their Queen turned into a ragged old woman, they
could happily celebrate her in a portraiture that became increasingly
geometrical, heraldic and iconic.[112] The modern image of Elizabeth I
maintains this stress upon geometry, emphasising the semicircle of those
immense and quite unbelievable sleeves in the Armada portrait. An
advertisement in 1988, proclaiming that 'Elizabeth I enjoyed her Burton
ale', showed her in these very terms.[113] But what we recall is the culmi-
nation of a process of Elizabeth's removal from the human sphere to the
divine which was achieved by stages. In the 'Sieve' portraits, painted
between 1579 and 1583, her chastity was established by reference to the
Vestal Virgin Tuccia, who refuted the slander of fornication by carrying
a sieve full of water from the River Tiber to the Temple of Vesta without
spilling a drop. Her strength as a chaste woman, the first step in the
inversion of the gender hierarchy, was thus demonstrated. The Armada
portrait took the process much further, developing the notion of sexual
self-control with the display of a giant pearl, an emblem of chastity, at the
precise point where the codpiece in the male portraiture of the time gave
such visual effect to the genitals as a signification of manhood.[114] Far the
most original icon of Elizabeth is the woodcut frontispiece to John Case's
Sphaera Civitatis published in the year of the Armada 1588 (plate 13). Here
is an Elizabeth beyond the earth, an Elizabeth indeed in dominion over
both it and the universe. A series of concentric circles moves outwards
from the globe, by way of the planets, each of which is identified with a
particular regal virtue, to the fixed stars and to a final outermost sphere,
which contains an inscription of the official style and title of the Queen.
Only then comes the Queen herself, enfolding and encompassing both
the mundane world and the cosmic one. The resonances of this diagram
with the conventional images of Renaissance cosmology are obvious. But
what is so remarkable is the way the Queen claims the place of God,
mimicking the creator of the universe, who normally in Ptolemaic
astronomy was located well beyond its visible manifestation.[115] Yet Case's
political statement about regal power had done no more than take the
possibilities of the old cosmology to their logical conclusion and it had
demonstrated its ideological vitality. Before the gendered body women, in
men's eyes, were the weaker vessel. Women in this patriarchy, whether
Shakespeare's hostess at the Boar's Head in Eastcheap or the Queen of
England herself, were constrained to play with men's rhetoric and ideol-

---

112. R. Strong, *Gloriana: The Portraits of Queen Elizabeth I* (London, 1987); F.A. Yates,
     Astraea: The Imperial Theme in the Sixteenth Century (London, 1977), pp. 29–120.
113. Cited in Belseys in Gent and Llewellyn, eds, *Renaissance Bodies*, p. 21.
114. Belseys in Gent and Llewellyn, eds, *Renaissance Bodies*, pp. 12–13, 15.
115. Belseys in Gent and Llewellyn, eds, *Renaissance Bodies*, pp. 22–31.

ogy. Men did not see the body, while the old cosmology held sway, as a source of truth about gender that should be investigated and debated as such. On the contrary the body was open to manipulation, to the telling of stories that matched the requirements of God's purposes for the world and men's need to reinvigorate and sustain social order.

5. *Effeminacy and Manhood*

IDEAS ABOUT THE body in early modern England provided shifting sands, it is being argued, for a system of gender order. Allegories of cosmic order remained important to people; there was a belief in a common corporeal economy; there were generally held ideas about orgasm and concoction that pointed to gender singleness emerging from gender doubleness. The need was for a representation of sex that would sustain gender boundaries and ensure successful reproductive mating. While sex was still unstable and indeterminate, it was the more important to ensure that gender provided a respected foundational structure which could make sense of each person's identity and enable society to function without disorder. Out of sexual confusion, friction, the competition of male and female seeds, much was required, much that was necessarily artificial and the subject of social construction. Men were struggling with enforcing patriarchy on the basis of outward gender significations. This meant two things. Firstly that male control had to be seen to rest upon a firm and decisive identification of sexual identity, even where that identification was not actually decisive. Only this could give maleness a sense of privilege and a sense of visible differentiation. Secondly heterosexual mating must remain normative. The structures of patriarchy had to remain in control of expressions of both friendship and of erotic attraction. 'The distinctions of heterosexuality and homosexuality', Randolph Trumbach reminds us, 'though they are so salient for us, did not exist for the seventeenth century man or woman.'[1] Four stories, two from France, one from America, one from Britain, and one Shakespearean play illuminate these issues.

The stories concern a girl from the small French town of Chaumont–

1. R. Trumbach, 'London's Sapphists: From Three Sexes to Four Genders in the Making of Modern Culture', in J. Epstein and K. Straub, eds, *Bodyguards: The Cultural Politics of Gender Ambiguity* (London, 1991), p. 140; see also A. Bray, *Homosexuality in Renaissance England* (London, 1988), pp. 81–114 and A. Bray, 'Homosexuality and the Signs of Male Friendship in Elizabethan England', *History Workshop Journal* 29 (1990), pp. 1–19.

en-Bassigni, a girl from Newcastle-upon-Tyne and the egregious Marie le
Marcis, whom we have already met in these pages. All the stories concern
gender confusion and are well documented; all the individuals concerned
spent the first years of their lives as females; in each case the outcome of
the story is quite different. The Chaumont girl decided in 1580 to dress
as a male; she set herself up as a weaver in a nearby village, fell in love
with a woman, courted her and married her. But the transvestite was
recognised by someone from Chaumont, tried and hanged 'for using
illicit devices to supply her defect in sex'. She was seen as having cheated
the system, claiming a gender to which she was not entitled. In fact, we
may suspect, it was the dildo that mattered. Marie le Marcis, around
twenty years later, was, thanks to Jacques Duval, more fortunate. The
initial reaction to her behaviour was predictably fierce. Her sentence was
to be burned alive with Jeane looking on; Jeane was subsequently, as the
accomplice, to be beaten and banished from Normandy. But this was
moderated, after an appeal for mercy, to strangling to death and a
whipping respectively. Then came Duval's intervention. His physiological
evidence left the court too uncertain about what sex Marie was for it to
act decisively any longer. Marie was simply ordered to wear women's
clothes until she was twenty-five and not to have sexual relations during
that time with either sex. The court seems to have washed its hands about
what should happen thereafter. Marie's case provides fascinating evidence
about the clash of legal and medical discourses, of the demands of society
and respect for empirical evidence, in this fraught area. The clash
produced virtual inertia. Marie had cheated the system but she got away
with it.

The third story concerns Thomasine Hall who, sent to London at
twelve, lived there as a girl until the Cadiz expedition in 1595 when,
cutting her hair and renaming herself Thomas, she enlisted as a soldier.
For more than twenty years sexual metamorphosis became a way of life
for her: she was a needlewoman back in London, sailed as a man to
Virginia and became a chambermaid when she got there. Accused of
going in women's clothes as a transvestite in 1629 by the General Court
of Virginia she gave the unforgettable reply 'I go in women's apparel to
get a bit for my cat'. Thomasine was told by the court, in a remarkable
decision, to freeze herself in acknowledged androgyny, that is she was to
wear man's clothes 'only his head to be attired in a cyse and croscloth
with an apron before him'. Thomasine had perhaps cheated the system
for too long not to get away with it. What these stories tell us is how
vulnerable men in positions of authority felt at this time about someone
who aroused their deepest anxieties regarding gender identity. Marriage
was at the core of patriarchy: both the Chaumont girl and Marie mocked
its function since there was doubt about their capacity for heterosexual
mating. Thomasine's case was less serious because it did not, as such,
involve heterosexual relationship. But in a sense it is the most interesting
of the three, for by making its own decision about how Thomasine

should be dressed in public the Virginia court declared that settling gender clarification was its business. This was enough: the exception here really did prove the rule.[2]

The final story comes almost a century later than the other three and its comparatively tame outcome surely reflects the growing appreciation of the complexities of sexuality in Hanoverian England besides a somewhat less frantic attitude to its less usual manifestations. But the challenge to the fundamental rules of patriarchy remained shocking. England had no laws against men dressing as women or women dressing as men so when Mary Price revealed in 1746 after three months of marriage to Dr Charles Hamilton that her husband was in fact a woman, Mary Hamilton, with whom she had been having lesbian relations, it was hard to find a legal offence she had committed. Henry Fielding wrote a pamphlet denouncing her as *The Female Husband*. The best the courts could think of as a public example was the humiliating as well as painful sentence of public whippings in four Somerset towns followed by six months in Bridewell.[3]

Twelfth Night almost but not quite retells the Chaumont tale that Montaigne heard on his way through that town in 1580. Olivia briefly thinks she has succeeded in marrying Cesario, who is Viola beneath her masculine attire, while in fact she has become contracted to Viola's twin brother Sebastian. It is Sebastian who explains to Olivia what has happened:

> So comes it lady, you have been mistook
> But nature to her bias drew in that
> You would have been contracted to a maid
> Nor are we therein, by my life, deceived
> You are betrothed both to a maid and man.[4]

With these lines, Shakespeare unravels the homosexual coupling Olivia has escaped and replaces the young page she has longed for with a male virgin, whose body to the outside observer is identical to that of the page she desired. As Orsino puts it, marvelling at Sebastian's appearance:

> One face, one voice, one habit and two persons
> A natural perspective, that is and is not.[5]

---

2. These two paragraphs are based upon S. Greenblatt, *Shakespearean Negotiations: The Circulation of Social Energy in Renaissance England* (Berkeley, 1988), pp. 66–93, 178. See also T. Laqueur, *Making Sex: Body and Gender from the Greeks to Freud* (Cambridge, Massachusetts, 1990), pp. 114–15, 136–9. My interpretation differs somewhat from that of Greenblatt.
3. T. Castle, 'Matters Not Fit to be Mentioned: Fielding's *The Female Husband*', *English Literary History* 49 (1982), pp. 602–22. For a summary of the case see A.R. Jones and P. Stallybrass, 'Fetishizing Gender: Constructing the Hermaphrodite in Renaissance Europe', in Epstein and Straub, eds, *Bodyguards*, p. 89.
4. *Twelfth Night*, act V, scene i, 266–70.
5. *Twelfth Night*, act V, scene i, 233–4.

The audience knows at this moment which is a man and which a woman. Olivia, confused, still does not so she looks at the twins uttering the startled phrase 'most wonderful'.[6] Yet, as Stephen Greenblatt nicely puts it, 'only by not getting what she wants has she been able to get what she wants and more important to want what she gets'.[7]

'Nature to her bias drew in that': this is perhaps Shakespeare's outstanding declaration about gender and also his firmest statement in support of patriarchy. For what is he saying? The image is from the game of bowls, the metaphor is a metaphor of swerving. Men and women, Shakespeare concludes, are deflected away from ostensible desires and towards the pairings for which they are destined. In other words, quite starkly stated, here is the attraction of opposites. Behind 'nature' we can see the patriarchal imperative: Olivia, the eligible countess, has to find the partner who will legitimately appropriate her and the estate for which she must provide an heir by her body. She needs the twin with a penis. How else could Shakespeare undo this tangle? What is significant for this discussion is that before the gendered body there is no such thing as an attraction of opposites in a biological sense. Heterosexuality is founded on scripture not on the body. This is explicit in *Twelfth Night* and other crossdressing comedies. The audience has had no problem in seeing Olivia, in love with Viola, going off innocently to marry her male twin Sebastian. But Elizabethan patriarchy requires the outcome that the patriarchal bard provides. 'Nature', in his critical line, actually means culture: nature's triumph in *Twelfth Night* is society's triumph.

Twelfth Night, like Duval's *On Hermaphrodites* and many other texts cited in this section, is a work that helps us to chart the shifts of mentality that underlie a gradual transformation of patriarchy. Single texts are never, of course, decisive; the importance of any particular text is almost impossible to measure. The Shakespearean world of gender was essentially a world in which men's ruling concepts, based on an inherent twinship between male and female principles, were those of effeminacy and manhood. The process of concoction of seeds, it has been shown, was not expected to produce an absolute predominance. The baby penis dangling between the legs of a boy child was not decisive. He came into a woman's world: childbirth and nursing was an entirely female affair. Moreover commentators were unanimous in holding mothers responsible for the early upbringing of children. Robert Burton said it was odd and effeminate for men to play with their children. Sir William Springate's wife noted in a life of her family that when he appeared before the congregation in church with his infant 'in his arms' this was a 'cause of great amazement'. Men continued to abandon

---

6. *Twelfth Night*, act V, scene i, 233.
7. Greenblatt, *Shakespearean Negotiations*, p. 71.

their male offspring to a female regime in their first years throughout the seventeenth century. At the same time there was a growing vein of criticism about women's softness towards their children. Nicholas Culpepper wanted women to wean their babies sooner; Thomas Tryon criticised them for offering the breast too readily when they cried.[8] Women were also thought by some to be much too lenient in disciplining growing toddlers. William Gouge excoriated parental cockering in *Domestical Duties* with especially harsh words for mothers who failed to beat their children because they could not endure hearing their cries: they were 'so far from performing this duty themselves, as they are much offended with their husbands if they do it'.[9]

Men were nervous about whether their boys would acquire the secure manhood to which the inheritance of their hotter seed entitled them. The physical body was seen as vulnerable to the pressures of a blurred gender system. Contemporary usages of the term effeminate refer to unmanly weakness, softness, delicacy and self-indulgence. Adam Martindale was thus reassuring himself when he described his two-year-old son in his diary as 'a beautiful child and very manly and courageous for his age'.[10] So was Mary Verney when, after a period away from home, she wrote hurriedly to her husband Ralph about her first sight for some time of their son: 'As far as I can tell by candlelight, thy boy Jack appears to me to be a brave lusty boy.'[11] Margaret Cavendish recorded that her brothers spent their time in boyhood wrestling, hunting or fencing and that they denounced musical entertainment or dancing as pastimes which were 'too effeminate for masculine spirits'. Lord Thoresby made his sick son travel on horseback from York to Leeds in 1678 because he could not 'endure the effeminacy' of coach travel.[12] In a fictional dialogue of 1633, a young gentleman says that when he was young 'we thought it a kind of solecism, and to savour of effeminacy, for a young gentleman in the flourishing time of his age to creep into a coach and to shroud himself there from wind and weather'.[13] Manhood was thrust upon boys. The ceremonial breeching, at about five or six, represented their release from the nursery into the male world. Grown men could look back and reflect on that effeminate stage of life when they were carefree and without responsibilities. Thus Leontes in *The Winter's Tale* turns from

8. Citations from P. Crawford, 'The Sucking Child: Adult Attitudes to Child Care in the First Year of Life in Seventeenth-Century England', *Continuity and Change* 1 (1986), pp. 41–2.

9. W. Gouge, *Domestical Duties*, (London, 1622), pp. 565–6.

10. R. Parkinson, ed., *Life of Adam Martindale* (Chetham Society, 1845).

11. *Verney*, II, 292.

12. L. A. Pollock, 'Teach her to Live under Obedience: The Making of Women in the Upper Ranks of Early Modern England', *Continuity and Change* 4 (1989), p. 234.

13. Cited in M. Vale, *The Gentleman's Recreations: Accomplishments and Pastimes of the English Gentleman 1580–1630* (Cambridge, 1977), p. 21.

playful chatter with his son Mamillius to musing, as his preoccupation with fears of the boy's mother's infidelity take hold of him, upon his own childhood:

> Looking on the lines
> Of my boy's face, methoughts I did recoil
> Twenty-three years and saw myself unbreeched
> In my green velvet coat
> How like, methought, I then was to this kernel,
> This squash, this gentleman.[14]

Early modern England had no developed concept of adolescence but there was a notion of the rough activities of youth which was an essential part of the making of manhood. There was 'nothing between' ten and twenty-three, reflected the shepherd in *The Winter's Tale*, 'but getting wenches with child, wronging the ancientry, stealing, fighting'.[15] Thomas Elyot recorded the contemporary belief that the child was dominated by the power of imagination and it was only as he grew up 'that reason in him is confirmed with serious living and long experience'. His first inclination was to hear 'things marvellous and exquisite, which hath in it the visage of some things incredible'.[16] The fantasy lives of young men were fed by the popular literature hawked around markets and fairs in the chapmen's packs.[17] 'Give me a ballad, a newsbook, *George on Horseback* or *Bevis of Southampton*, give me some book that teaches curious arts, that tells of old fables,' wrote John Bunyan, recalling his youthful reading.[18] In the chapbook version of *St George*, the noble hero 'never failed of carrying the prize at tilts and tournaments, quelled monsters, overcame giants and slaughtered beasts' (plate 34). The celebrated encounter with the dragon was merely the climax to his adventures, leading to a happy-ever-after-marriage at Coventry with the Egyptian princess he rescued. Another very popular chivalric tale was *Guy of Warwick*, which was available in the middle of the seventeenth century in a twenty-four-page octavo version (plate 33). Guy is the Earl of Warwick's steward who, meanly born, is rejected by the Earl's daughter Phyllis. He performs tremendous feats of arms in Normandy, the Empire and against the Turks, returning to slay a Danish champion who had invaded England. Along the way he defeats giants, dragons and lions. Margaret Spufford has defined Guy's main characteristics as 'superhuman strength, brawn and

14. *The Winter's Tale*, act I, scene ii, 157–60, 163–4.
15. *The Winter's Tale*, act III, scene iii, 159–63.
16. Cited in I.K. Ben-Amos, *Adolescence and Youth in Early Modern England* (London, 1994), pp. 250–1.
17. N. Wurzbach, *The Rise of the English Street Ballad 1550–1650* (Cambridge, 1990), especially pp. 13–23.
18. Cited in M. Spufford, *Small Books and Pleasant Histories: Popular Fiction and its Readership in Seventeenth-Century England* (London, 1981), p. 7.

faithfulness to the lady who inspires his exploits'.[19] Ilana Ben-Amos has noted that such heroes were always very young, whether they were based on the chivalric model, like Guy of Warwick, or were craftsmen and apprentices, like Jack of Newbury and John Hawkwood the protagonists of Thomas Deloney's novels, whose careers also appeared in short chapbook versions. Such stories, once confined to an aristocratic audience, were now transmitted with ease through cheap print, feeding notions of youth as adventurous, vigorous and courageous. There was no cult of youth as such but this literature, Ben-Amos argues, 'nonetheless embodied ideas about what constituted the age of youth, identifying it with the heroes' qualities.[20] Yet this is all, we should note, in male terms: there was no comparable literature for girls who were learning to become women.

'Not all males were men: youths, slaves, eunuchs and sexually passive males were something else.' This remark by Jonathan Walters comes from a study of the shifting construction of masculinity in Greco-Roman civilisation. It is accompanied by the warnings that, if we are to see something of what being a man meant in past societies, we need to loosen the hold of modern concepts of gender over the interpretation of ancient patterns of thought and to appreciate how gender was often cross-cut with other differentials of status.[21] The outstanding fact about early modern youth was its dependency: the vast majority of the adolescent population spent a period in some kind of service or apprenticeship. The official vision of masculinity, stamped upon this society by the protestant church, associated it with marriage and patriarchal control of a household. Lyndal Roper's account of gender relations in Germany at this period is equally applicable to England: 'The real man was a household head, a little patriarch ruling over wife, children, servants, journeymen and apprentices. . . . What gave one access to the world of brothers was one's mastery of a woman which guaranteed one's sexual status.'[22]

The issues of dependency, discipline and upbringing in the patriarchal household will be explored more fully in chapter 11. The present focus must remain on early modern adolescence as a liminal time. Passing into manhood meant separation from the mother, the ending of the sexual twinship which began with conception and the concoction of male and female seeds. Only when this passing was complete could the cycle of generation, which started with male potency and erection, begin again. This is what makes Shakespeare's transvestite theatre, with boys playing all the women's parts, so interesting. 'A conception of gender that is

19. Spufford, *Small Books and Pleasant Histories*, pp. 224–9.
20. Ben-Amos, *Adolescence and Youth*, pp. 23–8.
21. J. Walters, ' "No More than a Boy": The Shifting Construction of Masculinity from Ancient Greece to the Middle Ages', *Gender and History* 5 (1993), p. 30.
22. L. Roper, *Oedipus and the Devil: Witchcraft, Sexuality and Religion in Early Modern Europe* (London, 1994), p. 46.

teleologically male and insists upon a verifiable sign that confirms nature's final cause', argues Stephen Greenblatt, 'finds its supreme literary expression in a transvestite theatre.' The audience understands that there is an open secret of identity, signifying that within differentiated individuals – men and women – there was a single body on the stage which was identifiably but not visibly male. The possibilities for exploring the social realities of gender become enormous.[23]

At a practical level the requirements for playing 'the woman's part' effectively were more easily fulfilled by boys than men. Directing a servant to crossdress in the Induction to *The Taming of the Shrew* the lord is confident:

> I know the boy will well usurp the grace
> Voice, gait and action of a gentlewoman.[24]

Although we know little about the boys who were recruited by the Elizabethan companies of players, it is evident some acquired considerable skills in projecting their treble voices, wearing their costumes persuasively and expressing the requisite body language for their stage roles.[25] Tears might require a technical trick: in this case the lord tells the servant boy to use an onion

> Which in a napkin, being close conveyed
> Shall in despite enforce a watery eye.[26]

But there is more, though, to this use of boy actors than mere contemporary stage convention. The crossdressing pointed up the physical process of gender development which underpinned the whole structure of Tudor and early Stuart patriarchy. As Stephen Greenblatt puts it, male individuation was 'enacted inversely' in *As You Like It* and *Twelfth Night* by its rites: Rosalind and Viola – boys playing women playing men – 'pass through the state of being men in order to become women'.[27] Malvolio's introduction of Viola, dressed as Cesario when he stands at Olivia's door, expresses this notion of a time when males showed the attributes of both genders. He was 'not yet old enough for a man, nor young enough for a boy. As a squash is before 'tis a peascod, or a codling when 'tis almost an apple. 'Tis with him in standing water, between boy and man. He is very well-favoured and he speaks very shrewishly. One would think his mother's milk were scarce out of him.'[28] Rosalind as Ganymede instructs

23. Greenblatt, *Shakespearean Negotiations*, pp. 88, 93.
24. *The Taming of the Shrew*, Induction, scene i, 132–3.
25. A.R. Braunmuller and M. Hattaway, eds, *The Cambridge Companion to English Renaissance Drama* (Cambridge, 1990), pp. 43–5.
26. *The Taming of the Shrew*, Induction, scene i, 127–8; see also K. McLuskie, *Renaissance Dramatists* (London, 1989), pp. 99–122.
27. Greenblatt, *Shakespearean Negotiations*, p. 92.
28. *Twelfth Night*, act I, scene v, 166–72.

Orlando about how he, acting the woman's part, could cure him of love of a woman by playing out the behaviour which boys shared with women. As a moonish youth, the boy playing a girl playing a boy explained, he could: 'grieve, be effeminate, changeable, longing and liking, proud, fantastical, apish, shallow, inconstant, full of tears, full of smiles; for every passion something and for no passion truly anything, as boys and women are for the most part cattle of this colour'.[29]

The Elizabethan theatre allowed the predominantly male audience to explore desire in the safe surroundings of the playhouse. For in this mental world of sexual ambiguity and neutrality, eroticism is not gender-specific. The special interest of *Twelfth Night* is that, as Lisa Jardine's reading shows, it explores eroticism in relation to household order, service and dependency. Viola and Sebastian are shipwrecked in Illyria as young teenagers of good birth with money in their purses. Both exchange their cash assets for the security of household service: Viola, crossdressed as Cesario, is 'bound to the Count Orsino's court'; Sebastian, mistaken for Cesario, enters the service of Olivia, who, unaware that she is meeting identical twins on each side of the gender boundary, can feel desire for them both. The erotic possibilities of the place that the two youngsters occupy in relation to the heads of their adopted households are spelt out in the scenes that follow. Lisa Jardine notes that whereas for a twentieth-century audience the play is about the eroticism of gender confusion, for an Elizabethan audience 'it may be the very clarity of the mistakenness – the very indifference to gendering – which is designed to elicit the pleasurable response from the audience'. Olivia in the end, as we have seen, marries the right twin because 'nature' – or the patriarchal bard's dramatic skill – 'to her bias drew in that'. But the play's resolution is intended to be deeply satisfying, given the context of early modern patriarchy, in other respects as well. Olivia is given a come-uppance – 'patriarchy's retribution' as Jardine puts it – for her socially and sexually transgressive relationship with a young male servant. At the same time the disruptive erotic potential of service is finally constrained by the boundaries of the patriarchal households of Orsino and Olivia, now joined in a kin relationship to each other. Through Sebastian's marriage to Olivia, the dependent boy is elevated into mastership of a household; Viola's marriage to Orsino completes the convenient twinning which brings her too into an appropriate gender relationship.[30]

The Elizabethan and Jacobean theatre, writes Jonathan Dollimore, was 'a model, indeed a sustained exploration, of the role-playing which was so important for social mobility, the appropriation and successful deployment

29. *As You Like It*, act III, scene ii, 129–35.
30. L. Jardine, 'Twins and Transvestites: Gender, Dependency and Sexual Availability in *Twelfth Night*', in S. Zimmerman, ed., *Erotic Politics: Desire on the Renaissance Stage* (London, 1992), pp. 27–38.

of power'.[31] It suggests that gender was role playing by men's rules in this England: nothing more and nothing less. Putting on and taking off clothes could be adopting and abandoning gender itself. They will be too vulnerable if they go to Arden dressed as maids, declares Rosalind: 'beauty provokes the thieves sooner than gold'. Her heart will be full of woman's fear as she goes forth, but she will look the male part, which is all in any case that some men do:

> We'll have a swashing and a martial outside
> As many other mannish cowards have
> That do outface it with their semblances.[32]

Rosalind could never be a figure who threatened gender order because she has real difficulty in being a man. She is a lovesick maid throughout, saucy, imperious and fickle by turns, who faints at the sight of blood and finds it a problem to hold back tears. 'Dost thou think, though I am caparison'd like a man, I have a doublet and hose in my disposition?' she asks Celia, looking for reassurance about her authentic femininity.[33]

Lyndal Roper's examination of masculinity in early modern German towns has led her to emphasise its sheer disruptiveness: 'masculinity and its routine expressions were a serious danger to civic peace rather than a prop to patriarchy'. More research is needed to establish how far this was so in England too.[34] For a boy to establish himself as a man meant engaging fully in a youth culture where manhood was learnt by drinking, fighting and sex. For young unmarried people, especially males, the alehouse was a natural alternative centre to the structured and disciplined household in which they lived and worked.[35] There were certainly strong notions about proper behaviour there. Ballads like *Hang Pinching!*, celebrating the conviviality of the alehouse, condemned those who fought or bred discord and acclaimed the generosity of those who were 'jovial and free' in standing drinks for those too poor to pay.[36] Yet sensitivity to reputation, which meant insults had to be avenged, was always the greater under the influence of strong ale. Most real quarrels that led to violence followed more minor and spontaneous outbursts that left one party or the other feeling his personal standing was on the line. Thomas Pouncey's fight with Richard Paty at Dorchester in 1637 is probably typical.

---

31. J. Dollimore, *Sexual Dissidence: Augustine to Wilde, Freud to Foucault* (Oxford, 1991), p. 291.
32. *As You Like It*, act I, scene iii, 122–4. For commentary on this passage see C. Belsey, 'Disrupting Sexual Difference: Meaning and Gender in the Comedies', in J. Drakakis, *Alternative Shakespeares* (London, 1985), p. 180.
33. *As You Like It*, act III, scene ii, 194–6; J.E. Howard, 'Crossdressing, the Theatre and Gender Struggle in Early Modern England', *Shakespeare Quarterly* 39 (1988), p. 434.
34. Roper, *Oedipus and the Devil*, p. 107.
35. P. Clark, *The English Alehouse* (London, 1983), p. 127.
36. *Roxburghe*, III, 255–60.

Pouncey, characterised by David Underdown as a 'hard-drinking, foul-mouthed thug, always in trouble', exchanged words with Paty at Christopher Edmunds's alehouse. They went outside and fought with their fists then returned to the alehouse, 'all bloody with fighting', and resumed drinking together.[37] 'A man of words and not of deeds', ran the proverb, 'is like a garden full of weeds.'[38] When the Lancashire apprentice Roger Lowe discovered that someone in his neighbourhood had told his sweetheart Em Potter that he had been born a bastard, he obtained assistance from his friends and thrashed the man.[39]

The most telling test of manhood was of course sexual prowess and performance. The imperative of male sexual and physical development underlay the common attitude that simple fornication was hardly a sin but rather 'a pastime, a dalliance and but a touch of youth'. This is illustrated by its own excess in a misogynistic tract like Joseph Swetnam's *Arraignment of Lewd, Idle, Froward and Unconstant Woman* which the author addressed to 'the ordinary wit of giddy-headed young men'. Swetnam himself ran a fencing school and he moved in the circles of young blades of the capital. His tract is concerned with an economy of pleasure which transcends the class boundaries of early Stuart London. All women offer the same pleasure and Swetnam stresses the ease with which this can be obtained: 'women are easily moved and soon won, got with an apple and lost with the paring ... golden gifts easily overcome wanton's desires'.[40] Shakespeare's bawdy offers a huge and rich variety of language for male assertiveness in sexual behaviour. Eric Partridge's classic investigation of the subject reveals 130 terms which portray intercourse as an act of male dominance. There are terms which state assault on a woman's powers of sexual resistance like 'attempt, besiege, entice and try'; terms of seduction like 'corrupt, dishonour and undo'; terms of rape and violation like 'break, deflower, ransack, ravish and sully'. The majority of terms which do not have these brutal implications nevertheless carry an aggressive tone: men in Shakespeare 'board, breach, climb, colt, have, hit, joy, leap, occupy, plough, prickout, revel in, ride, sluice, stuff, throw, thrust to the wall, tread, tumble and vault' their women.[41] Here is the rough sexual culture of Elizabethan London. Brutality is at its most explicit and is used to dramatic effect where Shakespeare treats of excessive sexuality and the search for maidenheads. Bertram, it is reported in *All's Well that Ends Well*, has 'perverted a young gentlewoman here in Florence of a most

---

37. D.E. Underdown, *Fire Under Heaven: The Life of an English Town in the Seventeenth Century* (London, 1992), pp. 163–4.

38. J. Ray, *A Collection of English Proverbs* (London, 1670), p. 211.

39. J.R. Gillis, *For Better, For Worse: British Marriages 1600 to the Present* (Oxford, 1985), p. 41.

40. D. Purkiss, 'Material Girls: The Seventeenth-century Woman Debate', in C. Brant and D. Purkiss, eds, *Women, Texts and Histories* (London, 1992), pp. 71–8.

41. E. Partridge, *Shakespeare's Bawdy* (London, 1968), pp. 16–42.

chaste renown and this night he fleshes his will in the spoil of her honour'.[42] In this image, notes Michael Hattaway, 'losing virginity is an act of sadism and martial pillage'. In Restoration drama wooing is constantly portrayed as a pleasurable activity yet as a means to an end, as a 'hunt' leading to the 'kill' when passion is consummated. In Sir George Etherege's *She Wou'd if She Cou'd* Sir Joslin Jolley claims to be 'a true cock of the game'; another old debauchee Sir Oliver Cockwood describes himself as 'rampant as a lion'. Men are 'aggressive, hunting creatures', notes David Turner, 'lions and greyhounds, while women are described as prey to be hunted, as deers or hares, or to be tamed and used in men's service as horses'.[43] Studies of church court records are revealing reporting male sexual behaviour which is entirely consonant with all this material. Men's speech about sex, Laura Gowing finds, was often bragging and boasting: it was 'characteristically arrogant'.[44] Depositions suggest, notes Tim Meldrum, that, especially in tavern talk, 'some men, far from worrying about their sexual reputation, positively revelled in their notoriety'. William Parker, for example, put it around the neighbourhood that 'he had and could have private conversation and familiarity' with Barbara Dyke when he pleased: he called her husband a cuckold in front of a large group of witnesses who were sympathetic to him.[45]

Effeminacy was avoided by manly activities, by the physical exercise through which men proved to themselves and each other that theirs was the stronger sex. The gentry enjoyed the sport of their deer parks, their bowls and tennis; communal sports tested men's physical prowess and endurance, absorbing competitive vigour. Local tradition was deeply founded in this respect. In Wiltshire football was entrenched in the downlands, while bat-and-ball games like stoolball and trapball flourished in the vales of the north[46] (plate 32). East Anglian villages had their 'camping' grounds with their own indigenous and popular team games.[47] There was something for everyone at the Whitsun Cotswold games, held annually from around 1611 on Dover's Hill, a marvellous green amphitheatre outside Chipping Camden which is now owned by the National Trust. There was hunting and horse-racing for the nobility and gentry and the old sports, like wrestling, singlestick fighting and shin-kicking, for

42. *All's Well that Ends Well*, act IV, scene iii, 12–14.
43. M. Hattaway, 'Fleshing his Will in the Spoil of her Honour: Desire, Misogyny and the Perils of Chivalry', *Shakespeare Survey* (1993), p. 133; D. Turner, 'Rakes, Libertines and Sexual Honour in Restoration England 1660–1700', Durham University MA thesis, 1994, p. 15.
44. Gowing, p. 40.
45. T. Meldrum, 'A Women's Court in London: Defamation at the Bishop of London's Consistory Court 1700–1745', *London Journal* 19 (1994), pp. 10–11.
46. D.E. Underdown, *Revel, Riot and Rebellion* (Oxford, 1985), pp. 75–6.
47. P. Collinson, *The Religion of Protestants: The Church in English Society 1559–1625* (Oxford, 1982), p. 225; D. Dymond, 'A Lost Social Institution: the Camping Close', *Rural History* I (1990), pp. 165–92.

the country populace. The games were a veritable celebration of man-hood which, at least until the 1640s, attracted people of all social ranks from miles around[48] (plate 31).

If the polarity of sexual difference was delineated in men's construction of it by effeminacy and manhood – or conversely strength and weakness – masculinity implied a persistent awareness of the dangers posed by allowing the rule of emotion. Manhood was hot but it was also hard: effeminacy, or femininity, represented dilution and softening. Effeminacy was seen as a condition of instability; men could slip from their gender moorings; their bodies could, as Thomas Laqueur puts it, 'somehow come unglued'.[49] This was the warning that Cassius gave Casca, counterpoint-ing rationality and emotion, early in *Julius Caesar*:

> But, woe the while, our fathers' minds are dead
> And we are govern'd with our mothers' spirits
> Our yoke and sufferance show us womanish.[50]

Shakespearean heroes demonstrate their manhood by showing the will to stifle emotion and move into action. 'Oh I could play the woman with my eyes,' Macduff professes on the news of the slaughter of his wife and children. Mastering himself he takes up his sword in revenge. 'This tune goes manly', replies Malcolm, 'Macbeth is ripe for shaking.'[51] Yet Shake-speare, argues Linda Woodbridge, 'valued tender-heartedness in either sex, looking askance at those who would confuse compassion with effeminacy'.[52] Apart from Friar Laurence's rebuke to Romeo – 'thy tears are womanish' – he limited contempt for male effeminacy to the battle-field.[53] That is he portrayed men showing emotions in circumstances of exceptional stress with sympathy. 'I am yet so near the manners of my mother', declares the young Sebastian to the hardy sea captain Antonio, as he grieves for his sister whom he believes to be drowned, 'that, upon the least occasion more, mine eyes will tell tales of me.'[54] The Duke of Exeter, describing the gory death of the Duke of York in battle to his King, confesses how he had been unable to contain his emotions:

> But I had not so much of man in me
> And all my mother came into my eyes
> And gave me up to tears.[55]

48. C. Whitfield, ed., *Robert Dover and the Cotsworld Games* (London, 1962), pp. 1–57. For the country sports see also R.W. Malcolmson, *Popular Recreations in English Society 1700–1850* (Cambridge, 1973), pp. 34–51.
49. Laqueur, *Making Sex*, p. 123.
50. *Julius Caesar*, act I, scene iii, 82–4.
51. *Macbeth*, act IV, scene iii, 192, 198.
52. L. Woodbridge, *Women and the English Renaissance: Literature and the Nature of Woman-kind 1540–1620* (Urbana, 1986), p. 171.
53. *Romeo and Juliet*, act III, scene iii, 110.
54. *Twelfth Night*, act II, scene i, 42–3.
55. *Henry V*, act IV, scene vi, 30–2.

There was not yet any association of homosexual behaviour with effeminate activity. Sodomy was not yet a vice understood in gendered terms.[56] The effeminate man, lacking virility, lacked all social assertiveness. The ultimate outcome of his ineffectual character was total role reversal. Thus Thomas Heywood in his play *The Brazen Age* portrayed the final horror of the male transvestite: Hercules, turned woman, 'spins, cards and doth charwork' while his mistress sits and makes a cushion of his lion's skin.[57] The obsession about affected dress reflected the fears created by men who appeared to be slipping in this direction and thus undermined the gender order. Philip Stubbes had warned of this danger.[58] Castiglione's *Book of the Courtier*, much read in England from the 1560s, was full of anxiety that men might become soft and womanish through over refinement of looks and dress.[59] Richard Brathwaite excoriated 'that effemination both of youth and age delicacy of apparel'.[60] Barnaby Rich found many of the London gentry in the 1580s 'more new fangled and foolish than any courtesan of Venice'. He was an out-of-work Elizabethan soldier who blamed effeminate fashions on the gentry's insufficient opportunities to engage in war.[61] A hundred years later the fop was a stock figure of Restoration drama. His characteristics were his narcissistic vanity, extravagant dress, delicacy, daintiness and lack of manly sexuality.[62] In William Wycherley's *The Plain Dealer*, the gruff naval type Captain Manly, ashore in fashionable London, is enraged by the fops Novel and Lord Plausible but they are not man enough for him to engage with them: 'Why you impudent, pitiful wretches, you presume sure upon your effeminacy to urge me; for you are in all things so like women that you may think it in me a kind of cowardice to beat you.'[63] In William Congreve's *The Way of the World* the fops Witwoud and Petulant belong to the ladies' gossip circle rather than the male company of the town. But Fainall tells Mirabel he has no jealousy about his wife keeping company with such men since the fops are 'of a kind too contemptible to give scandal'.[64]

A particularly threatening form of effeminacy was the excessive devotion to a woman. 'O sweet Juliet', declares Romeo when he has refused to fight Tybalt,

> Thy beauty has made me effeminate
> And in my temper softened valour's steel.[65]

56. Bray, *Homosexuality in Renaissance England*, pp. 81–114.
57. Woodbridge, *Women and the English Renaissance*, pp. 157–8.
58. Above, p. 23.
59. Laqueur, *Making Sex*, p. 125.
60. R. Brathwaite, *The English Gentleman* (1641), p. 279.
61. Woodbridge, *Women and the English Renaissance*, pp. 159–60.
62. Turner, 'Rakes, Libertines and Sexual Honour', pp. 23–4.
63. W. Wycherley, *The Plain Dealer*, act 2, scene i, 622–5.
64. W. Congreve, *The Way of the World*, act 1, scene ii, 130–31.
65. *Romeo and Juliet*, act III, scene i, 111–13.

In the decade after peace was made with Spain in 1604, Shakespeare wrote three plays which dramatised the conflict between the feminine and masculine values of peace and war. *Troilus and Cressida* opens with Troilus, struck by Cupid's dart, unarming himself within the walls of Troy having lost his military courage:

> I am weaker than a woman's tear
> Tamer than sleep, fonder than ignorance
> Less valiant than the virgin in the night.[66]

In *Antony and Cleopatra* a great military leader leaves the action to follow a woman. In *Coriolanus* the military hero calls off his greatest battle at a woman's behest. In *Much Ado about Nothing* the hero, at first devoted to the values of war, gradually succumbs to the role-playing, with all its dangers of effeminacy, of courtship and then to the reality of love. Beatrice and Benedick come together through the one growing more masculine, the other more feminine.[67] Love in other words can be seen as representing the return to sexual doubleness from which the male emerges in adolescence. What Wycherley in *The Plain Dealer* called 'the effeminating mischief of love' was a perilous journey during which men must court and woo yet retain enough of their manhood intact to reach their destination still glued.[68]

There is plenty of evidence that men felt ambivalent about embarking on this journey, for it was a journey towards responsibility and self-discipline. Full manhood was unattainable without the process of courtship, marriage and household formation, but young men knew that these things implied the abandonment, or at least control, of their drinking, whoring and gorging.[69] Ballads constantly reminded them of the joys of freedom in youth and the perils of matrimony.[70] Once caught in its toils, which were conventionally ascribed to woman's rather than men's doing, it was easy to be nostalgic about the world of masculine friendship. Leontes and Polixenes look back upon it, in *The Winter's Tale*, in the presence of Leontes's wife Hermione. The scene constructs a dream of Eden from which men are expelled by woman as the temptress:

> We were as twinned lambs that did frisk in th'sun
> And bleat the one at th'other. What we changed
> Was innocence for innocence. We knew not
> The doctrine of ill-doing, nor dreamed
> That any did.

66. *Troilus and Cressida*, act I, scene i, 9–11.
67. Woodbridge, *Women and the English Renaissance*, pp. 161, 167.
68. W. Wycherley, *Complete Plays* (ed. G. Weales, New York, 1967), p. 446.
69. For an exploration of this pattern of life in early modern Europe see Roper, *Oedipus and the Devil*, pp. 145–67.
70. *Roxburghe, passim.*

'By this we gather', declares Hermione, 'you have tripped since.'[71] From boyhood to manhood, from mother's milk to the youthful parade in public as a codpiece wearer, was a fraught journey. The kind of misogyny for which Leontes stands as the marker was an explicable defence against its perils and projection of men's fears. Conversely, the codpiece was men's defiant proclamation of their conceptualisation of the gender order: 'it displayed the penis', notes Lyndal Roper, 'to lascivious eyes which would only too easily be incited to lust', given the male reading of women's sexuality. The codpiece casts the male in the role of sexual quarry.[72] But this journey ended, if the moralists had their way, with the sober manhood of the little patriarch ordering his household of wife, children and servants.

So far this book has been presenting an account of the early modern ideological framework of gender. It has traced male ideas and attitudes about the body, relating them to social commentary and seeking to explicate their coherence in relation to a teleological world picture. It is time to turn from ideology to experience, the experience, that is, of men and women who in some way or other absorbed all this ideological instruction, living in the patriarchal society of sixteenth- to eighteenth-century England. The necessary link between ideology and experience or practice is prescription. Much has already emerged about prescription in these chapters. However an account of how prescription was given shape and form by the honour codes of the period is a necessary preliminary to exploring the actual working of patriarchy.

71. *The Winter's Tale*, act I, scene ii, 69–73, 78–9. See the discussion by Hattaway, 'Fleshing his Will in the Spoil of her Honour: Desire, Misogyny and the Perils of Chivalry', *Shakespeare Survey* (1993), 128.
72. Roper, *Oedipus and the Devil*, p. 117.

PART II   THE WORKING OF PATRIARCHY

6. Prologue: Prescription and Honour Codes

THE GENDER SYSTEM in Tudor and early Stuart England was essentially a matter of establishing social roles which were grounded in the physical body and proclaimed by dress and bearing. The enforcement of this system was dependent on honour codes which drew upon the notions of manhood and of women's frailties which have been outlined above. In this chapter we are concerned with the contrast in general terms between the male and female honour codes at a prescriptive level. In the next we shall seek to establish how the Tudor and Stuart gentry elaborated their particular honour code and made it the foundation of their class and gender rule. Sin in this society was inherently gendered; so was honour. The crucial issue was the protection of monogamous marriage as the linchpin of the social order. 'The desire of men for absolute property in women', Keith Thomas has argued, is the likely basis of the insistence on female chastity before and within marriage, for this is 'a desire which cannot be satisfied if the man has reason to believe that the woman has once been possessed by another man, no matter how momentarily and involuntarily and no matter how slight the consequences.'[1] The question of paternity was never far from men's minds, especially but not only among the propertied.[2] But the issue goes deeper than this for, as we have seen, the concept of manhood itself at this time rested upon sexual prowess. A woman's adultery dissolved the household order and thus the social order; cuckolding made nonsense of the gender order: the woman took the blame and was held responsible. Chastity before marriage and fidelity within it was the heart of a code of female honour which was overwhelmingly seen in sexual terms. 'Sexual virtue and scolding speech are the unique definers of women's credit,' writes Laura Gowing on the basis of a detailed study of slander litigation in London between 1560 and 1640. It has been argued above that the two were intimately connected in men's minds.[3]

1. K.V. Thomas, 'The Double Standard', *Journal of the History of Ideas* XX (1959), p. 216.
2. See John Taylor's rhyme, Capp. p. 116.
3. Gowing, p. 82; above, pp. 12–13.

A series of studies of provincial ecclesiastical court business in Norfolk, Yorkshire and Wiltshire, together with an account of the London consistory court between 1700 and 1745, confirms the consistency with which female sexual honour was endlessly discussed, checked and implemented through litigation during our period.[4] But the subject is more complex than it might at first appear. We are not seeing here a simple didactic inculcation of a code based upon certain standards of morality set out by churchmen and lay officials. The prescriptive literature, notes Laura Gowing, did no more than provide 'a set of ideals that could be invoked, adapted or transformed in daily life . . . the enterprise of defamation was as much about defining honesty as repeating predefined prescriptions.'[5] We will explore in chapter 13 how the female honour code acquired abiding strength because cases between and against women served a wide range of personal objectives in tight-knit local communities. For the present the issue is how the code worked as a direct source of gender prescription.

Treatises on defamation discuss its effects on people's livelihood, good name and 'advancement', which for women meant their marriage prospects if they were virgins. This was certainly central to some cases. In London, witnesses for the unmarried sometimes spoke of the discredit suffered by 'a maiden . . . in the way of preferment in marriage'. In a case in the Salisbury court in 1623, the rector of Barford St Martin spoke of a poor girl's 'innocency and credit, the only dowry she hath to work her preferment'. Martin Ingram only found five cases, in a sample of 150 in Wiltshire between 1615 and 1629, which made specific mention of the plaintiff's marriage prospects and five more cases prosecuted by women which suggest that the issue was a prominent motive.[6] This may not give a proper impression of the significance of the general connection men made in their minds between a girl's alleged sexual history, her general moral worth and her material circumstances, all the considerations which weighed in the marriage market. Commentators unthinkingly made these connections. Richard Gough talks of a man who married his servant maid in his Shropshire village, 'a wanton, gadding dame, who had neither goods nor good name'. Adam Martindale described two potential brides he remembered as a youth in terms which suggest that their portions were

4. S.D. Amussen, *An Ordered Society: Gender and Class in Early Modern England* (Oxford, 1988) pp. 98–104, 130–2; J.A. Sharpe, *Defamation and Sexual Slander in Early Modern England: The Church Courts at York* (Borthwick Papers, St Anthony's Hall, York, no. 58, 1981), pp. 9–11, 15–16; M. Ingram, *Church Courts, Sex and Marriage in England 1570–1640* (Cambridge, 1987), pp. 292–319; T. Meldrum. 'A Women's Court in London: Defamation at the Bishop of London's Consistory Court, 1700–1745', *London Journal* 19 (1994), pp. 1–20.

5. L. Gowing, 'Language, Power and the Law: Women's Slander Litigation in Early Modern London', in J. Kermode and G. Walker, eds, *Women, Crime and the Courts in Early Modern England* (London, 1994), p. 40.

6. Ingram, *Church Courts, Sex and Marriage,* p. 311.

tokens of character as much as nest eggs for the future: one with £140 was 'of very suitable years and otherwise likely to make an excellent wife'; the other, with only £40, was 'a young wild airy girl, between fifteen and sixteen years of age, a huge lover and frequenter of wakes, greens and merry nights where music and dancing abounded'.[7]

The precise effects of insult, as of the whole business of gossip, on the operation of the honour codes remain elusive but there is no doubt about rumour's enormous impact on personal reputation. Two cases in 1590, one from Essex the other from Norfolk, indicate how readily defamatory speeches circulated, compounding their damage as they went. At Woodford, Elizabeth Dymsdale was reported to have called Susan Moore 'an arrant whore . . . that lay first with the master and then with the man in Mill Lane'. Two dozen, she said, could witness to it. Susan, previously 'taken by the neighbours hereabouts as a very honest woman', had received great discredit by this scandal. For it had spread 'about all the country thereabouts and she is talked about commonly amongst the neighbours'. Roger Watson brought a series of defamation suits to try to clear his name, when the story that he had been whipped in Norwich for living with a whore spread rapidly from an original allegation at Hethel to the neighbouring villages of Hethersett and Swainsthorpe. Gossip was an effective shaming mechanism, indicating cumulative disapproval by the community as it escalated, but a defamation suit could sometimes limit its impact.[8]

Men's sexual reputations mattered to them as well as women's and their behaviour in this respect was part of their honour code but it was not its centrepiece as it was for women. A key aspect for men was sexual ownership. 'The assumption in both household advice and popular literature', notes Gowing, 'is that female disobedience is a problem caused by male incompetence and that female subjection is natural.' Above everything else, it was a man's business to avoid being made a cuckold. The Elizabethan musician Thomas Whythorne thought that a wife's infidelity was practically inevitable, so argued that her inherent deceitfulness should be exploited to protect a man's reputation. A 'notorious cuckold', he noted in his autobiography, was 'barred of divers functions and callings of estimation in the commonwealth as a man defamed'. 'You may see what a goodly thing it is when a man's honesty and credit doth depend in his wife's toil,' he commented. He thought himself it was best to deal gently with an errant wife, persuading her to future loyalty or at least circumspection: 'it is not good for a man to be too curious and to search too narrowly to know the truth of his wife's folly that way . . . for if he be known to know that his wife is a strumpet and yet doth keep her still, he

7. Citations from Erickson, p. 95.
8. Kermode and Walker, eds, *Women, Crime and the Courts*, p. 39; Amussen, *An Ordered Society*, pp. 130–31.

shall be reputed to be not only a cuckold but also a wittol . . . if he do put her from him yet thereby he denounceth himself to be a cuckold for ever after'.[9] There is a considerable range of references to the contented or complaisant cuckold as a 'wittol' in both ballads and the drama.[10] The condition of his sexual ownership was that he satisfy his wife in bed. 'Women are like soldiers', declared Horner expressing a commonplace in *The Country Wife*, 'made constant and loyal by good pay.'[11] When the wives of those abused as cuckolds bring cases in court we have to be careful not to assume that they are necessarily acting on their own rather than their husband's initiative. There was nothing more disruptive of marital relations than gossip about the cuckold's horns. Anne Fanne's husband would not lie with her, a witness testified, after a neighbour told her in public 'I did see Hopkins and thee together he with his breeches down'.[12] William Burges and his wife fell out so badly that they almost parted, the Salisbury court was told, after Walter Longe had scoffed at Burges with the words 'thou art a wittol and cannot pull on a hose over thy head for the bigness . . . of thy horns'.[13]

It was not that the overriding importance of a man's control of his wife's sexuality meant that he was necessarily insensitive to slanders about his own behaviour. What emerges from the court records is that the language of personal abuse was different because the implications of men and women's sexual behaviour were, as Gowing puts it, 'not only disparate but hardly comparable'.[14] There were cases in which simple fornication was seen as a blot on a bachelor's character, harming his marriage prospects.[15] But, much more commonly, the double standard meant that it was sexual notoriety of one kind or another that lead to defamatory speeches about men. This remained as much so in the early eighteenth century when those who engaged in a prolonged adulterous liaison, who were known 'bastard-getters', spread venereal disease or were suspected of 'whoremongering', still found themselves cited in court.[16] Whereas for a woman sexual reputation was the whole of her reputation, for a man it was merely one part. Honest labour, fair dealing and respect and decency towards others in the local community were the crucial

9. Gowing, p. 153; K. Hodgkin, 'Thomas Whythorne and the Problems of Mastery', *History Workshop Journal* 29 (1990), pp. 35–6.
10. Eg. 'The Catalogue of Contented Cuckolds', *Roxburghe*, III, pp. 481–3; 'The West Country Weaver', *Roxburghe*, VII part I, p. 23; *The Merry Wives of Windsor*, act II, scene 2, 283, 310. I am grateful to Elizabeth Foyster for these references.
11. W. Wycherley, *The Country Wife*, act 1, scene ii, 426–7. I am grateful to David Turner for this reference.
12. Gowing in Kermode and Walker, eds, *Women, Crime and the Courts*, pp. 38–9.
13. Ingram, *Church Courts, Sex and Marriage*, p. 309.
14. L. Gowing, 'Gender and the Language of Insult in Early Modern London', *History Workshop Journal* 35 (1993), p. 3.
15. For an example see Ingram, *Church Courts, Sex and Marriage*, p. 311.
16. T. Meldrum, 'A Women's Court', *London Journal* 19 (1994), p. 11.

mores of country life, besides control of the household.[17] Perjurer, liar, cheat and knave were the commonest slanderous charges from which men sought to clear themselves in the York consistory court.[18] Yet men, just like women, could suffer by people's linking of different kinds of honesty. Thus, when a sexual slander was cast upon his servant Edward Page in 1623, the rector of Barford St Martin in Wiltshire testified that Page, previously commended locally 'for a just dealer in his contracts' and for 'his civil demeanour', was discredited by this 'foul aspersion'.[19]

These, then, in outline are the gendered honour codes of Tudor and Stuart England. Honour took on further and deeper connotations of behaviour and style of life among the gentry which will be explored in the next chapter. First, though, more needs to be said about how men sought to inculcate in their own sex the mores that gave manhood honour and in the other sex the mores which rescued women from all the deficiencies inherent in the weaker vessel. Men learnt their gender role from watching plays and listening to ballads sung in the market place, besides watching and listening to their elders. A few read the weighty and sober tomes produced by puritan clerics about marital and household duties. Many more bought and read ballads. The enforcement of the honour codes is a multi-faceted process largely hidden from us by the loss of unrecorded oral tradition. But something of it can be recaptured and the general framework within which it occurred can be assessed. By naming and displaying the standard female wiles and weaknesses, the literature sought to neutralise the threat that these posed to domestic harmony. The didactic message was always sweetened: there was the pleasure of locating the source of disorder in the household with womankind and expelling the responsibility for its origins from men's own minds.[20] Listening, watching and reading offered the bolstering of men's confidence. Prescriptions provided comfort and support; they also suggested tactics and strategies for the performance of the male gender role. Honour consisted in part in displaying the reason and strength of character attributed to men as the source of discipline for the weaker sex.

The conduct book writers furnished high-flown guidance about choosing a wife which took courtship for granted by assuming female acquiescence. Henry Smith recounted the saying of a godly acquaintance who thanked God 'for he said not that she was the wisest, nor the holiest, nor the humblest nor the modestest wife in the world but the fittest wife

17. A.J. Fletcher, *A County Community in Peace and War: Sussex 1600–1660* (London, 1975), pp. 161–2.
18. Sharpe, *Defamation and Sexual Slander in Early Modern England*, p. 10.
19. Ingram, *Church Courts, Sex and Marriage*, pp. 308–9.
20. D. Purkiss, 'Material Girls: The Seventeenth-Century Woman Debate', in C. Brant and D. Purkiss, eds, *Women, Texts and Histories 1575–1760* (London, 1992) pp. 81–2; see also E. Foyster, 'A Laughing Matter? Marital Discord and Gender Control in Seventeenth-Century England', *Rural History* 4 (1993), pp. 5–21.

for him in the world'. Choosing with interests in common made sense 'so man and wife should be like because they are a pair of friends'. But above all a man needed a wife 'according to his own heart'.[21] It is instructive to compare this view of marriage entry with Shakespeare's treatment of this theme in some of his greatest comedies. When Rosalind finds herself alone in the Forest of Arden with Orlando, the last thing she does is throw herself into his arms. Instead, donning male disguise, she sets the scene for a symbolic testing of his love and for some counsel about the kind of marriage she expects: 'I will speak to him like a saucy lackey and under that habit play the knave with him.'[22] The crossdressing in *As You Like It* and the resonances of forest against court bring into operation the powerful contemporary nuances of inversion and its connections with orderliness. Orlando is being warned that there is a limit to the possession he will have over his wife. That limit is set by her singularity, expressed through her desires, her wit and her tongue: it will be no good his throwing the conventional epithets of scold or shrew at her and expecting compliance. 'The holiday rule of the woman-on-top', as Natalie Zemon Davis puts it, 'confirmed subjection throughout society but it also promoted resistance to it.'[23] Back home from Arden, Rosalind's disguise and freedom from patriarchal precept will vanish but the established dynamic of the couple's relationship will not be easily erased during their subsequent courtship and marriage.

Beatrice and Benedick's desire for each other in *Much Ado about Nothing* is proclaimed at once, hers implicitly by her hectic but derisive talk of him in the first scene when she hears he is back from the wars, his explicitly with a remark about the beauty which might turn him into a lover were the woman concerned not 'possessed with a fury'.[24] Beatrice's loose tongue and unstoppable wit have made her, by the time the play opens, into the kind of difficult girl who, in the eyes of her uncle Leonato, will never get herself a husband. He tells her as much, if she is 'so shrewd of her tongue'. Leonato's brother at once chips in: 'in faith she's too curst'.[25] Whereas Hero submits at her father's command to Claudio's wooing, Beatrice and Benedick play a game of mutual disdain and rebuff throughout the drama. From the start though for Benedick it is the sexual wooing that matters. This is summarised, as the play closes, by the kiss to stop his partner's mouth. 'I will live in thy heart, die in thy lap and be buried in thy eyes,' is his final pronouncement, before he has made the ritual gesture of asking her uncle's agreement to the match.[26] Through this sexual wooing Benedick proves his manhood.

21. H. Smith, *A Preparative to Marriage* (London, 1591), pp. 22–6.
22. *As You Like It*, act 3, scene 2, 95–7.
23. N.Z. Davis, *Society and Culture in Early Modern France* (Stamford, 1975), pp. 135, 151.
24. *Much Ado about Nothing*, act 1, scene 1, 42–88.
25. *Much Ado about Nothing*, act 2, scene 1, 20–22.
26. *Much Ado about Nothing*, act 3, scene 2, 71–2; act 5, scene 2, 102–3.

But, for Beatrice and Benedick to come together as they do, Benedick also needs to prove his honour. Claudio's rejection of his bride at the altar, having been led to believe that she was no virgin through a plot hatched by the malcontent Don John, gave him the opportunity to do so. For the comedy dissolves into serious confrontation as Beatrice, convinced that her cousin is wronged, challenges Benedick, who vows to play the man's part: 'I am engaged . . . by this hand Claudio shall render me a dear account.' Gender roles are sharply etched here for Benedick's response follows a ranting speech from Beatrice, which he cannot effectively interrupt, about the limitations on her action imposed by her sex: 'O that I were a man!' she declares, deriding Claudio's public and slanderous accusation, 'I would eat his heart in the market. . . . Or that I had any friend would be a man for my sake. But manhood is melted into curtsies, valour into compliment and men are only turned into tongue and trim ones too.' Faced with this challenge, Benedick abandons the friends with whom he has returned from the wars and completes his wooing. 'Tarry good Beatrice', he insists as he sees her emotions about how deeply her cousin is wronged, 'by this hand I love thee.'[27]

The Taming of the Shrew is probably the most profound statement about early modern courtship that we have. Its rich and deeply complex exploration of human relationship and patriarchal stringencies makes conduct book stipulations in choosing a wife look simplistic. Although for a good deal of it Petruchio and Kate are married the subject of the whole play is indeed courtship. 'Come Kate we'll to bed', in the closing scene, represents Petruchio's choice of the proper time for sexual consummation.[28] Up to this moment, the play is about the delaying of sexual pleasure until the relationship is right. This is so at two levels. The drunkard Christopher Sly, turned into a great lord, is given a wife in the Induction who is as yet sexually unavailable. His melancholy, the doctors say, must first be cured by seeing a 'pleasant comedy'. He is none too pleased at this denial – 'it stands so that I may hardly tarry so long' – but reluctantly accepts the situation.[29] Sly sees a pleasant comedy, the playgoing audience does so too. Both can appreciate its deeply serious lesson. Petruchio understands that his desire for Kate must wait upon the proof that she has fully accepted what it means to be his wife. Patriarchy has its price for women, a price paid in terms of certain requirements for public behaviour. 'If Kate is changed physically into a wife before she accepts the role on its own purely social terms,' writes Maureen Quilligan, 'the clear separation of social discourse from physical fact would be blurred.'[30] For Petruchio is both a man very much in love and

27. *Much Ado About Nothing*, act 4, scene 1, 289–339.
28. *The Taming of the Shrew*, act V, scene ii, 184.
29. *The Taming of the Shrew*, Induction, scene ii, 124–8.
30. M. Quilligan, 'Staging Gender: William Shakespeare and Elizabeth Cary', in J.G. Turner, ed., *Sexuality and Gender in Early Modern Europe: Institutions, Texts, Images* (Cambridge, 1993), p. 219.

a man of his time, who understands that the only basis for a sound relationship is making Kate accept that his discourse, the discourse of patriarchy, is definitive. Petruchio woos Kate to achieve her love as well as her public obedience to him as master and lord. When he refers to her as his 'goods and chattels' he is telling the world what it wants to hear; when he beats his servants in front of her he is doing what is expected of the master of a patriarchal household; when he calls the sun the moon and insists that Kate should do so too he is saying that it is he who determines reality. But none of this precludes their having a less hierarchical relationship and a richly sexual one in the privacy of their own chamber.

The taming can best be seen, as Jonathan Miller enacted it in a production, as a kind of therapy.[31] There are sound medical reasons, Petruchio declares, for throwing out the meat that his servants have prepared for their homecoming:

> For it engenders choler, planteth anger;
> And better twere that both of us did fast
> Since of ourselves, ourselves are choleric
> Than feed it with such over-roasted flesh.[32]

The taming is physical but not violent: denial of food, sleep, clothes and sex. It is not simply that Kate's humours are imbalanced, though this is part of the story: in the thirteenth-century folk version of the shrew plot the wife submits to her husband's authority at once on being bled by a surgeon.[33] Shakespeare's taming is more sophisticated and more mutual, since Petruchio fasts for company, keeps himself awake with his brawling as well as her and denies himself sex. The play includes an overt statement against wife-beating. She hits him in their initial encounter for his lewd punning on the sexual function of tongues: 'if you strike me,' Kate declares, 'you are no gentleman'.[34] Petruchio always respects this. He begins by redefining Kate against the authority of her father. What choice had she had, unhappy in a household where no one accepted her, but, as a termagent and misfit, to play the shrew? He values her for herself from the start, is interested in her as a person in her own right. His task, once they are back home, is to have her believe that her nature can be transformed. She can unlearn just as she learnt being a shrew. She must unlearn her former behaviour if they are to have the kind of marriage he wants. Kate is tamed, it has been argued, 'by the discovery of her own imagination, for when she learns to recognise the sun for the moon and the moon for the dazzling sun she is discovering the liberating power of

31. K. McLuskie, *Renaissance Dramatists* (London, 1989), p. 7.
32. *The Taming of the Shrew*, act IV, scene ii, 173–8.
33. Quilligan in Turner, ed., *Sexuality and Gender in Early Modern Europe*, p. 213.
34. *The Taming of the Shrew*, act II, scene i, 223.

laughter and play'.[35] By the time it comes to the demand that Kate deliver her stern and celebrated lecture on wifely duty in the last scene, they have an understanding which allows them to put on a performance. Women's submission is natural, declares Kate, in this great final speech; the social roles of husband and wife are written on their bodies. Yet here at the same time, from a woman's mouth, is the creation of gender, men's ideological creation of gender, at its most explicit:

> Thy husband is thy lord, thy life, thy keeper
> Thy head, thy sovereign; one that cares for thee
> And for thy maintenance; commits his body
> To painful labour both by sea and land
> To watch the night in storms, the day in cold
> Whilst thou liest warm at home, secure and safe
> . . .
> Why are our bodies soft and weak and smooth
> Unapt to toil and trouble in the world
> But that our soft conditions and our hearts
> Should well agree with our external parts.[36]

Most men faced the test of establishing their competence as a husband in line with patriarchal precept; only a few faced the test of marriage breakdown signified by a wife's adultery. At a personal level a woman's adultery was the ultimate betrayal; at a social level, men were warned, it sent society as a whole tottering towards dissolution. Two classic statements of these views may be cited, one by Matthew Griffith in his advice book *Bethel*, that represents the clerical view, the other by Thomas Heywood, the playwright, in his prose work *Gunaikeion*, an exploration of womenkind in terms of their virtues and vices. The female adulterer, argued Griffith, committed a greater sin than the male one 'for she at once injures many'. He gave six reasons for this: she injured herself 'because thereby she defiles her body and damns her soul'; her husband as a married man 'from whom she steals away his right which is the sole power over her'; her husband as a father 'upon whom she obtrudes a spurious issue'; her parents who she dishonours by degeneracy and her husband's brothers and sisters by imposing a bastardly brood upon their inheritance. Finally, declares Griffith, the woman's sin is huge 'because take honesty from a woman and all her other virtues are but (like the apples of Sodom) beautiful rottenness'.[37] Heywood follows a panegyric to women's physical beauty, which he sees as equal to the 'excellency of

35. J.C. Bean, 'Comic Structure and the Humanising of Kate in *The Taming of the Shrew*', in C. Lenz, G. Greene and C. Needy, eds, *The Woman's Part: Feminist Criticism of Shakespeare* (Urbana, 1980), p. 72.
36. *The Taming of the Shrew*, act V, scene ii, 146–51, 165–8.
37. M. Griffith, *Bethel* (London, 1633), pp. 299–300.

judgement and wisdom' in which men rightly claim priority, with the following passage:

> If beauty be once branded with impudence or unchastity it makes that which in itself is both laudable and desired rejected and altogether despised. For virtue once violated brings infamy and dishonour not only to the person offending but contaminates the whole progeny, nay more looks back even to the injured ashes of the ancestors be they never so noble: for the mind, as the body, in the act of adultery being both corrupted makes the action infamous and dishonourable, dispensing the poison of the sin ever amongst those from whom she derives her birth, as if with their earthly being they had given her therewith her corruptions and the first occasion of this her infamy. It extends likewise to the posterity which shall arise from so corrupt a seed, generated from unlawful and adulterate copulation.[38]

A man faced with the evidence of his wife's adultery found his honour challenged to the utmost. What action could he and should he take? It was accepted, both by learned commentators and in popular folklore, that a wife's adultery provided good grounds for divorce, or rather for the judicial separation from bed and board which was the only form of divorce available to men at this time through the church courts.[39] But this did not free a husband of all his financial responsibilities to his wife and it was in fact a costly and cumbersome process that men seldom employed.[40] During the 1650s a husband could in theory have his wife indicted for adultery at quarter sessions, where the penalty on conviction was death without benefit of clergy. But the severe 1650 act was virtually unenforceable: there are only two or three cases in which a woman seems to have been hanged.[41] Anyway this made a husband very publicly a cuckold. In these circumstances there was a strong temptation for men to take matters into their own hands, beating their wives for their disloyalty. Those who did so and found themselves before the courts, the London evidence suggests, could expect lenience.[42]

Two plays first performed within three years of each other, *Othello* from 1604 and *A Woman Killed with Kindness* from 1607, treat the issue of how a man sustained his honour in the face of proven adultery. Desdemona, of course, was in fact innocent, whereas Anne Frankford was

38. T. Heywood, *Gunaikeion or Nine Books of Various History concerning Women* (London, 1624), p. 164.
39. W. Heale, *An Apology for Women* (London, 1609) pp. 33, 46; S. Rowlands, *A Crew of Kind Gossips all met to be Merry* (London, 1613), sig B5.
40. L. Stone, *Road to Divorce: England 1530–1987* (Oxford, 1990), p. 193.
41. A.J. Fletcher, *Reform in the Provinces: The Government of Stuart England* (London, 1986), pp. 258–9; Gowing, pp. 145–6, 157, 198–9.
42. L. Jardine, '"Why Should he Call her Whore": Defamation and Desdemona's Case', in M. Tudeau-Clayton and M. Warner, eds, *Addressing Frank Kermode* (Urbana, 1991), pp. 124–53.

guilty. Yet Desdemona is killed by her husband in retribution whereas Anne Frankford starves herself to death out of guilt. It is the substantial defamation of Desdemona brought into public space and unanswered by her which is the crux of the plot of *Othello* in Lisa Jardine's convincing reading of the play. The tragedy lies in Desdemona's failure to understand the need and inability to summon the help necessary to counter the defamatory utterance against her reputation for chastity. For Othello cuckoldry becomes theft when it is public knowledge. He murders Desdemona not out of jealousy but certain of her guilt. For an English audience, there is no question that in law Othello is guilty of murder. Lisa Jardine's examination of church court depositions, however, leads her to argue that 'ostensible verbal incidents between individuals, as they spill over into the community space . . . become recognised as events which generate particular expectations on the part of the audience . . . whatever the audience thought heretofore, the event in question introduces competing versions of fault and blame, which must now be resolved in order that the individuals concerned may be reintegrated into the community.' Alone in Cyprus, Desdemona cannot achieve this end. So, as the hot-tempered Moor sustains his honour, she dies. Some of the male members of the Jacobean audience will surely at least have understood his point.

Did Thomas Heywood see *Othello* and write his play in argument against it? This is a tempting and plausible hypothesis. For *A Woman Killed with Kindness* represents a serious attempt, unique in the drama of the period, by a playwright who, as we have seen, was strongly moved by the stain that adultery left, to tackle the question of what was an appropriate punishment. John Frankford, discovering his wife Anne in bed with his friend Wendoll, to whom he had offered hospitality, and stayed from immediate violence against her by a maid, calms himself sufficiently to retire to his study to consider his course of action. His manhood prompts him to physical retaliation and that is what those around him expect and even approve; his sense of duty as a puritan gentleman and spiritual adviser to his wife makes him pause. Elizabeth Foyster argues that Frankford has to consider both his social honour, what those in his circle expect of a man thus betrayed, and his personal honour based upon emotions of self-worth, which prompts him to seek to give Anne an opportunity to repent for her sin. The course he pursues, sending Anne away to a manor on his estate where it is her decision to starve herself to death, enables him to regain his lost honour in both these senses. For, by asking her husband's forgiveness before she dies, Anne reassumes her proper subordinate role and patriarchal order is restored. At the same time Frankford is true to himself in rejecting violence against her person. Heywood wants men to think about how Christian duty should cause men to modify the impulse to manly vengeance. While it is hard to think that any contemporary husbands are likely to have pursued the kind of course that Frankford adopted, the play is a profound exploration of marital crisis.[43]

The real test for most men was simply everyday living within a marriage partnership. This was where the enforcement of patriarchy rested. The fulfilment of prescribed gender roles was the means to an end and which most men had little time or inclination to contemplate in theoretical terms. When they heard the homily in church which directed them to give their wives honour 'as unto the weaker vessel', they listened to an argument which no man wanted and no woman dared, at least openly, to question.[44] We can compare how two very different genres from the period between the 1580s and 1650s, scripturally inspired conduct books and popular literature, sought to establish in men and women's minds how they ought to behave as husband and wife. The male gender role, the conduct books constantly reiterated, was the exercise of authority tempered by love; the female role was one of submission and obedience. When puritan clerics worked out this pattern of household duties in detail they produced a set of prescriptions which drew upon all the traditional lore about male and female qualities of mind and body. A husband needs to be stored, declared Henry Smith, with 'wisdom and understanding and knowledge and discretion to direct his whole family'.[45] The husband's first duty, announced Daniel Rogers, was 'to be a man of understanding'. His wife's 'reverential love and esteem' of his headship would follow from the guidance for her life that he displayed by his 'gravity, stayedness and prudence of carriage'. The heat which marked his gender superiority showed itself as strength, in a commanding intelligence and a 'cool spirit'. God had given him the 'spirit of cheerfulness, discerning, diligence, dexterity to devise and despatch also, humbleness, courage and patient enduring' that his role required. The virtues a man should use in governing his wife, argued William Whateley in similar vein, were 'justice, wisdom and mildness'.[46]

Above all there was an insistence that a husband must love his wife. Love, in William Gouge's account, was both 'a distinct duty in itself peculiarly appertaining to a husband' and 'a common condition to season every duty'. Love, he argued, prevented a husband from abusing his authority over his wife and enabled him to bear with the provocative behaviour which it was normal for women, as the weaker vessel, to show:

43. I am grateful to Elizabeth Foyster for the use of her unpublished paper, 'Honour, Friendship and Betrayal in Thomas Heywood's *A Woman Killed with Kindness*'.
44. Cited in M. Roberts, 'Sickles and Scythes: Women's Work and Men's Work at Harvest Time', *History Workshop Journal* 7 (1979), p. 11.
45. Smith, *Preparative to Marriage*, p. 48.
46. D. Rogers, *Matrimonial Honour* (London, 1642), pp. 203–8; W. Whateley, *The Bride Bush* (London, 1623), p. 112.

His look, his speech, his carriage and all his actions wherein he hath to do with his wife must be seasoned with love: love must show itself in his commandments, in his reproofs, in his instructions, in his admonitions, in his authority, in his familiarity when they are alone together, when they are in company before others, in civil affairs, in religious matters, at all times, in all things, as salt must be first and last upon the table and eaten with every bit of meat, so must love be first in a husband's heart and last out of it and mixed with everything wherein to hath to do with his wife.[47]

Gouge's kind of love here is not romantic or passionate love; it is rather a devotion based upon measured but constant affection. The passage takes us to the heart of the problem which the conduct book writers sought to tackle. How should a husband enforce his authority, achieve his wife's obedience, play his God given gender role? All these writers, except William Whateley with regard to certain special circumstances, condemned a man's beating his wife. Their conception of marriage was too idealistic to be compatible with this.[48] None of them called for authoritarian husbands: it was accepted that rough or cruel treatment merely produced 'slavish fear and inward contempt'. Husbands were expected to treat their wives as a 'yokefellow and companion' and yet at the same time to rule them.[49] The clerics' high flown discourse set men the severe test of ruling by the example of their own grace and virtue. But it was accepted that this alone would not normally be enough. John Dod and Richard Cleaver advised husbands to reprehend their wives seldom but admonish them often.[50] Whateley saw a role for punishment – withdrawal of kindness and trust – as well as reproof, suggesting that men had to temper their use of authority to an individual's nature. Some women were more pliant than others: tenderness might be appropriate for a 'soft and tender' woman, a severer course with one who was 'rough, boisterous and highspirited'.[51] John Wing agreed with Whateley that it was sometimes proper for a man to humble his wife, when he was justly angry with her, by depriving her for a while of 'some favours and kindness which formerly she hath more freely enjoyed'.[52]

Sharing the consensus of the period about women's abundant sexuality and building upon the wholly traditional notion of 'due benevolence', the puritan writers devoted much attention to the importance of sex in

47. W. Gouge, *Domestical Duties* (London, 1622), pp. 335–6.
48. Whateley, *Bride Bush*, pp. 105–23.
49. Gouge, *Domestical Duties*, pp. 359–61 and below, pp. 174–81. See also my essay 'The Protestant Idea of Marriage', in A.J. Fletcher and P.R. Roberts, eds, *Religion, Culture and Society in Early Modern Britain* (Cambridge, 1994), pp. 168–75.
50. J. Dod and R. Cleaver, *A Godly Form of Household Government* (London, 1614), sig. L4.
51. Whateley, *Bride Bush*, pp. 125–30.
52. J. Wing, *The Crown Conjugal or Spouse Royal* (London, 1620), pp. 47–8.

marriage.[53] At a simple functional level they saw its regularity as a necessary basis for good physical and psychic health. More importantly, so far as the relationship was concerned, they saw it as a crucial ingredient of successful partnership. Through good sex, declared Dod and Cleaver, a couple's life together was 'made more pleasant'; moreover 'they are the more stirred up on both sides to render dutifulness'.[54] If they quarrelled, advised Smith, couples should on no account divide beds for it because then 'their means of reconcilement is taken away'.[55] This positive account can be summarised by a passage from John Wing's marriage sermon *The Crown Conjugal or Spouse Royal*: 'That man knows little in marriage who perceives not that cohabitation is the consolation and contentation of the husband and wife; it carrieth with it all opportunities of good; it cutteth off all occasions of evil; it nourisheth all entire amity and maketh that house a little heaven where it is carefully observed.'[56]

But what does all this mean in terms of prescribed sexual behaviour? There were no modern sex manuals available. Yet it seems clear that the puritan writers, quite conventionally for their period, expected wives to want and seek as much sexual pleasure as their husbands. Gouge indeed spelt out the implications of how scriptural teaching that husband and wife became at marriage part of the same flesh put the sexual relationship on a quite different basis from the social one: 'There may not only be a fellowship but also an equality in some things betwixt those that in other things are one of them inferior and subject as betwixt man and wife in the power of one another's bodies: for the wife (as well as the husband) is therein both a servant and a mistress, a servant to yield her body, a mistress to have the power of his.'[57] The normal rules of patriarchy, in other words, did not apply behind the chamber door. Difficult as it is to judge its impact, this piece of prescriptive advice is of fundamental importance for our understanding of gender in the early modern period. For it seems to mean that the strict and reproving husband was being told to transform himself into a democratic and mutual lover when he and his wife were intimate together. We know a good deal about some aspects of relations between husbands and wives at this time but little in any detail about their sexual relationships. It is at least possible that many married couples, especially those who lived in households full of servants and children, did sustain a kind of public and private separation of the ordering of their married lives such as the fictional Petruchio appears to have had in mind for himself and Kate.

---

53. For 'due benevolence' see K.M. Davies, 'Continuity and Change in Literary Advice on Marriage', in R.B. Outhwaite, ed., *Marriage and Society* (London, 1981), pp. 73–4.
54. Dod and Cleaver, *A Godly Form of Household Government*, sig. K8.
55. Smith, *Preparative to Marriage*, p. 47.
56. Wing, *Crown Conjugal*, pp. 132–3.
57. Gouge, *Domestical Duties*, p. 361.

The puritan clerics catalogued characteristic behaviour of the virtuous wife such as a husband should seek to inculcate and exact. Humility, said Gouge, would help her to yield subjection. Sincerity 'will make her manifest her respect of him before others, behind his back as well as before himself in his presence'. Cheerfulness makes 'subjection pleasing'; constancy 'makes all other virtues perfect'.[58] Rogers made much of the issue of public subservience: 'her very eye, gesture and speech ought also to be aweful and mixed with modesty and blushing, arguing her submission and privity to her weakness'.[59] Wing said that a husband should look for 'all comely behaviour and kingly carriage, a demeanour that keeps good decorum with true greatness'.[60] Several writers excoriated women's misuse of their tongues.[61] Gouge believed that women's pride and gadding were matters which required close attention. He noted that London's 'proud dames' sported their 'silken gowns and beaver hats' when they went out on their own. Thus 'entertaining strangers' and 'ordering a wife's going abroad' were activities that should be firmly under a husband's consent.[62] Rogers established a comprehensive list of pastimes which he characterised as 'fomenters' of adultery: 'haunting of markets, fairs, night-meetings, wakes, dancings and common festivals, needless journeys, gaddings about, intemperate diet, excess of gaming, amorous books, sonnets, stage plays, effeminate disguisings'.[63] Wing had a tirade about the dangers to women's chastity in this 'carnal age'. He maintained that mixed dancing was in itself a kind of adultery, which most of the best divines had sentenced as 'sinful before the Lord'.[64] Robert Horne, in an exposition on the Ten Commandments, distinguished provocations to adultery that belong to the body from those in the body itself. He placed in the former category 'immodesty in apparel and other deckings of the body, intemperance in meats and drinks, wanton pictures and sights with lewd and wanton pastimes, unclean songs and ditties, houses of open whoredom, excessive sleep and idleness'. In the latter category he denounced 'all wanton lookings, whisperings, touchings and other impure behaviour stirring up lust, specially mixed dancing of men and women where all doors are set in for whoredom to come in'.[65] There was no comfort in all this for any wife not content to be a simple household drudge. There was nothing positive she could hold

---

58. Gouge, *Domestical Duties*, pp. 324–38.
59. Rogers, *Matrimonial Honour*, p. 276.
60. Wing, *Crown Conjugal*, pp. 109–10.
61. E.g. Wing, *Crown Conjugal*, pp. 112; Dod and Cleaver, *A Godly Form of Household Government*, sig. G4; Smith, *Preparative to Marriage*, p. 65.
62. Gouge, *Domestical Duties*, pp. 282–3, 292.
63. Rogers, *Matrimonial Honour*, p. 174.
64. Wing, *Crown Conjugal*, pp. 91–9.
65. R. Horne, *Points of Instruction for the Ignorant* (London, 1617), sig. B4. For the issue of dancing and moral reform see below, p. 276.

on to which could make her feel that men valued women for their inherent inner virtues.

The puritan clerics who supplied the market between the 1590s and 1640s with a series of pious advice books were very consciously creating a new genre intended to rival ballads, plays and satirical tracts. John Wing, in his address to the reader at the start of *The Crown Conjugal* in 1620, decried the massive output of these 'prophane, idle and impure' items.[66] The conduct books ranged in length from revised marriage sermons like this one of his – these could reach more than one hundred pages – to the big tomes issued by Gouge and Griffith which were more than five hundred pages in length. Unquestionably these works made heavy reading, yet the best of them, Gouge's well arranged text first published in 1620, went into new editions in 1626 and 1634. Gouge's audience was primarily the earnest substantial householders of London's professional classes and middling sort, men who needed reassurance about the stern and authoritative role their puritan faith made them feel called upon to play in their own households. Nehemiah Wallington bought his copy of Gouge in 1622 and made it the basis for a set of articles for reform and order in his household. Here, unusually, we can trace action following from prescription. Gouge's *Domestical Duties*, in a very practical way, gave shape and purpose to Wallington's energetic fulfilment of a gender role to which he was bidden as much by social pressure as by religious commitment. It was a rather different world by the 1670s when Thomas Shadwell, in *Epsom Wells*, was merciless in his taunting of city merchants who, seen as moral inheritors of puritanism, relied upon anything so old-fashioned as Gouge's kind of patriarchal rhetoric. The cuckold Mr Fribble gets short shrift from his wife when he tells her in a bullying manner 'know your Lord and master and be subject to my government; I though but a haberdasher will be as absolute a monarch over you as the great Turk over his Sultan queens'. 'Know your lady and mistress, sirrah', she tells him, 'I'll order you better you scurvey fellow.'[67]

At the time even we know that Gouge's book proved highly contentious, provoking a group of city dames to visit him and remonstrate about the harshness of some of his prescriptions. It was almost certainly unrealistic for Gouge to tell London citizen wives that they should show proper forms of reverence and obeisance to their husbands 'at suitable partings or sitting or rising from table', just as it was unrealistic to expect these women to show the general degree of submission that the precepts of such works required. Much of the conduct book advice, as an

66. Wing, *Crown Conjugal*, preface; see P. Collinson, *The Birthpangs of Protestant England: Religions and Cultural Change in the Sixteenth and Seventeenth Centuries* (London, 1988), pp. 108–15.

67. T. Shadwell, *Epsom Wells*, act II, scene i, 126; act IV, scene i, 161–2; see also D. Turner, 'Rakes, Libertines and Sexual Honour in Restoration England 1660–1700', Durham University MA thesis, 1994, pp. 36–7.

instrument for creating gender, flew in the face of the established dynamics of London middling-sort households. It simply would not work. Gouge's defensiveness on the whole question of the extent of subordination required of women is a tacit acceptance that in some ways he had gone too far. His final version of *Domestical Duties* set out duties on both sides in a manner that was intended to give visual effect to his belief that, within the ultimate male authoritarianism of the patriarchal system, both parties had their responsibilities. 'I so set down a husband's duties', he declared, 'as if he be wise and conscionable in shewing them, his wife can have no just cause to complain of her subjection.' In view of the tone of Gouge's work as a whole, this might be seen as special pleading.[68]

The popular ballads which the pedlars like Shakespeare's Autolycus in *The Winter's Tale* hawked around the country reached a different audience from the conduct books. This was cheap print – ballads sold at a halfpenny or penny – reaching a wide public from all ranks of society, for the ballads were sung as well as sold and their message was often widely but effectively summarised by a woodcut print.[69] Ballads were popular because they were humorous. They were undoubtedly intended to entertain as well as to release some of the tensions of everyday life. There is little new to add from this material to what has been said already about the contemporary notions of womankind. The creation of female gender here is confined to a familiar catalogue of vices that should be avoided or that men had it in their power to check. In *Have Among You, Good Women*, for instance, a dialogue between two men on the way to Maidstone market reveals a series of local women who get drunk, scold and beat their husbands.[70] Just occasionally a ballad balances the responsibility for marital troubles. Thus *The Countryman's New Care Away* contrasts the situation of the husband who wants comfort because his wife scolds night and day with the plight of the virtuous wife landed with a womaniser 'given unto lewdness, to envy and wrath'.[71] But generally women are entirely the culprits. Elizabeth Foyster argues that a coherent series of ballads treating issues of marital discord which were in circulation in the seventeenth century are an important source for gender control: their humour was didactic, warning readers and listeners that the price of failure to adopt prescribed gender roles could be ridicule. The core of this gender control, these ballads show conclusively, was sexual.[72]

The basic issue the ballad mongers tackled was the same one that faced puritan conduct book writers: how a man could best show his com-

---

68. Gouge, *Domestical Duties*, preface. For a fuller account of this fracas see Fletcher and Roberts, eds, *Religion, Culture and Society in Early Modern Britain*, p. 167.
69. T. Watt, *Cheap Print and Popular Piety 1550–1640* (Cambridge, 1991), pp. 11–12.
70. *Roxburghe*, I, 435–7.
71. *Roxburghe*, I, 114–15.
72. Foyster, 'A Laughing Matter?' *Rural History* 4 (1993), pp. 7, 11.

petence as master of the household. Whereas their highflown discourse emphasised the moral and intellectual qualities of manhood, the ballad stories put much more stress upon physical strength and force of personality. Husbands who withstood verbal and physical abuse from their wives, notes Elizabeth Foyster, were 'only a figure fit for laughter', yet it was also made clear that men should not abuse their physical strength. In *Hold your Hands, Honest Men* the message goes

> Then if you desire to be held men complete
> Whatever you do, your wives do not beat.

And in *The Married Man's Lesson* there was a strong warning against making matters worse:

> If goodness by beating thou seek'st to infuse
> For breaking her flesh, thou all goodness dost bruise.

Dealing with the scolding or adulterous wife, in other words, was a test of character. The message is made explicit in a story told by John Taylor in his tract *Divers Crab-tree Lectures* which was published in 1639. His companions listen intently while a man explains how he tamed his wife by a regimen which included deprivation of sleep, hard labour and a sparse diet of bread and water. 'This is an art you have found out worth all the seven liberal sciences,' one comments and there was talk of setting up a school to spread the good news to men everywhere.[73]

Some of the ballads offered practical strategies for taming a scold; others dealt in fantasy solutions. If men in fact read them to boost their confidence in handling day-to-day authority in the home the denouement may have mattered little, for the point was to drive home the message that men had the strength to rule if only they would apply the will. In several tales, which mix violence with humiliation, wives are treated with bondage. These echo the most brutal of the taming stories of the period which tells of a shrew stripped and beaten and then wrapped in the salted hide of a horse killed for the purpose.[74] The ballad *A Caution for Scolds* is a version of a taming story that also appears in the early sixteenth-century collection *Scoggin's Jests*. A doctor, summoned to 'take the lunacy' out of the scold's brains, begins by shaving her head. In the earlier version he started by letting blood in her arm and foot. It is the threat to cut the woman's tongue that brings her to her senses and makes her plead for forgiveness. In *The Scolding Wife* the husband ties up his wife as one might do a wild animal and, with the help of friends, tears off her clothes and wrings her arms until blood comes out of them.[75] More viciously in *Poor Anthony* a husband, who has himself been endlessly

73. Cited in Foyster, 'A Laughing Matter?', *Rural History* 4 (1993), pp. 15–16.
74. L. Woodbridge, *Women and the English Renaissance: Literature and the Nature of Womankind 1540–1620* (Urbana, 1986), pp. 203–4.
75. A. Boord, *Scoggin's Jests* (London, 1626), p. 33; *Rural History* 4 (1993), pp. 14–15.

humiliated, takes the opportunity of a request to drop a 'sovereign water' in his wife's eyes by replacing the medicine with henbane and mercury steeped in whey which blinds the woman. He gets her a dog and bell to lead her about the market place.[76] Other ballads portray money as the key to power. Thus the husband sums up the lesson he has learnt in *My Wife Will be my Master* as follows:

> But if ever I am a widower and another wife do marry
> I mean to keep her poor and bare and the purse I mean to carry.[77]

The fantasy solutions include a husband who threatens to 'get a soldier's coat and sail beyond the seas', one who dreams of exchanging his wife for the dead wife of an honest friend and another who asks his mother-in-law to take his wife back with double the money he had received as a dowry.[78] The ballad monger who sang the tale of how a scold who rode the devil to hell and deposited her back on earth, when she drew a knife and slit his ear, ended with these comforting lines:

> Then since the world nor hell can well a scold abide
> To make a sail of ships let husbands fall to work
> And give them free consents to send them to the Turk.

The last lines of this ballad, advising that it is not available for purchase by scolds but only by 'honest men and wives', indicate that the text and woodcuts of a ballad like this one had something of the nature of a charm about them. The scolding purchaser would be confirmed in her wicked ways; for the innocent couple the paper itself offered a kind of preservative against discord in the home.[79] It is almost as if some women were seen as unable to help themselves if their blood was too hot. Not even the Devil could hold them.

A song recorded in a collection printed in 1699 told about a pleasant but dumb wife whose husband had her to the doctor to 'cut her chattering string'. He then found himself landed with a scold and complained to the doctor in vain, for, said the doctor, while it was easy to cut a tongue it was 'past the art of man' to make any scold hold her tongue.[80] But we must set against the sense of fateful acquiescence induced by this song the numerous tales which taught men about practical measures to control rather than just punish a shrewish wife. Thomas Heywood told of a husband who first tried to drown his wife's noise with a harsh-tuned pipe,

---

76. T. D'Urfey, *Wit and Mirth or Pills to Purge Melancholy* (1700), II, pp. 152–3.
77. Cited in Foyster, 'A Laughing Matter?', *Rural History* 4 (1993), p. 13.
78. 'The Cruel Shrew', *Roxburghe*, I, 94–8; 'A Merry Jest of John Tomson and Jackaman his Wife', *Roxburghe*, II, 137–42; Foyster, 'A Laughing Matter?', *Rural History* 4 (1993), p. 17.
79. *Roxburghe*, II, 367–71.
80. D'Urfey, *Wit and Mirth or Pills to Purge the Melancholy* (London, 1700), I, p. 293.

then, when she snatched it, tried singing instead. This vexed her so much
that, when her breath ran out, they agreed upon a peace based upon her
not scolding and his not piping and singing.[81] Robert Harper's treatise
included two advisory tales. A man bitten endlessly by his wife's 'serpent'
tongue bound her hands and feet and threatened to cut the tongue itself
but she relented and they lived happily. A countryman was shown the
scriptural phrase in another's pocket book 'the tongue is set upon the fire
of hell', so, on relating he had discovered she carried hell about her when
he got home, his wife hid her face and cried.[82] John Taylor, in his *Juniper
Lecture*, advised slighting the scold by 'singing, dancing, whistling or
clapping thy hands on thy sides' or in the last resort buying a drum
and beating it loudly.[83] All this instruction carried the positive message
that the man who was man enough need not be defeated by a scold
or a shrew.

   The core of all this prescriptive material was a vision of the patriarchal
household. It was conventional, as we have seen, to assume men and
women had clearly defined gender roles indoors and out of doors.[84] The
puritan writers developed the notion of husband and wife as yokefellows
on this basis and used this concept as the context for expounding
gendered honour. The chaste wife, Laura Gowing notes, was not so
much confined as riveted to the home 'which provides her whole power,
status and alignment'.[85] There was 'no honour within the house longer
than a man's wife is honourable,' declared John Dod and Robert
Cleaver.[86] Daniel Rogers provides a classic statement of the case: 'A chaste
wife hath her eyes open, ears watching, heart attending upon the welfare
of the family, husband, children and servants; she thinks that all concern
her: estate, content, posterity; this rivets her into the house; makes her
husband trust to her, commit all to her, heart and all.' In this
conceptualisation of woman as a possession, notes Peter Stallybrass,
surveillance is concentrated upon the mouth, chastity and the threshold of
the home: 'silence and chastity are, in turn, homologous to woman's
enclosure within the house'. The unchaste woman moves abroad: 'now
she is in the home, now in the streets, now she lieth in wait in every
corner', wrote Barnaby Rich quoting Proverbs chapter 7, verse 11, 'she
is still gadding from place to place, from company to company.'[87] 'Many

81. T. Heywood, *A Curtain Lecture* (London, 1637), pp. 164–6.
82. R. Harper, *The Anatomy of a Woman's Tongue* (London, 1638), in *Harleian Miscellany*
    II (1744), pp. 167–78.
83. K.U. Henderson and B.F. McManus, eds, *Half Humankind: Contexts and Texts of the
    Controversy about Women in England 1540–1640* (Urbana, 1985), pp. 303–4.
84. Above, p. 61.
85. Gowing, p. 69.
86. Dod and Cleaver, *A Godly Form of Household Government*, sig L4.
87. Citations from Gowing, pp. 69–70; P. Stallybrass, 'Patriarchal Territories: the Body
    Enclosed', in M.W. Ferguson, M. Quilligan and N.J. Vickers, eds, *Rewriting the
    Renaissance* (Chicago, 1986), pp. 126–7.

evils' come from women's gadding, warned Matthew Griffith. He advised husbands only to let their wives go out to worship, for friendly meetings for charitable purposes with neighbours, for genuine household needs and in their company.[88] The ballads make the same point about the dissolution of the household through the use of humour. The scolding wife begins the subversion of household order by disrespect and violence towards her husband. Making a man do the household chores – 'I humour her in everything because I would be quiet' – establishes inversion of gender roles. Kicking him out of bed to sleep on the floor comes close to the centre of the issue of chastity and male sexual control.[89] The absolute humiliation of cuckolding is the final step. The misogynist literature is also closely in line. Joseph Swetnam's *Arraignment* satirises the moral discourse of the puritan clerics, portraying woman as the keeper or retainer of goods, with woman as the signifier of wastage. Women spend money on their own desires: clothes and feastings that are the harbingers of independence, pride and adultery.[90] We find a remarkable consistency across the genres in the reiteration of the central gender precepts. So far as men are concerned everything comes back to the household, to the display of manhood which, without the easy option of overt violence by beating, kept a woman in her sexual and physical place.

A specific issue which raised the question of men's control over their wives' excessive behaviour in London from the 1580s to the 1620s was the transvestite fashion. When the matter came to a head in 1620, with James I's command to the clergy to preach against the fashion, there was a general recognition that if husbands did not check their wives' dressing no one else could. Pulpits might ring and ballad singers might pronounce, but, as the piece at the centre of the pamphlet debate *Hic Mulier* made clear, it was the householder's responsibility that really mattered. John Chamberlain reported that 'the King threatens to fall upon husbands, parents and friends that have or should have power' and make those who failed in their duty of control pay for it.[91] In this instance, unusually, the implicit chain from royal authority to male gender roles in the privacy of the household came into direct conjunction.

It can be assumed that the prescriptive literature, written in men's interests, was read and fully absorbed more by men than by women, so how far did women absorb and accept the gender role men created for them? Femininity, as we have seen, was presented as no more than a set of negatives. The requirement of chastity was, as we have seen, the overriding measure of female gender. Woman not only had to be chaste

88. Griffith, *Bethel*, pp. 415–16.
89. Foyster, 'A Laughing Matter?', *Rural History* 4 (1993), p. 11.
90. Brant and Purkiss, eds, *Women, Texts and Histories 1575–1760*, p. 74.
91. N.F. McClure, ed., *The Letters of John Chamberlain* (Philadelphia, 1939), II, p. 289; Woodbridge, *Women and the English Renaissance*, pp. 143–4; Henderson and McManus, eds, *Half Humankind*, p. 275.

but had to be seen to be chaste: silence, humility and modesty were the signifiers that she was so. The power of report hung over every married woman's life. This is what made Othello wish to kill Desdemona although she was in fact chaste. The same power that Iago manipulates with such skill in *Othello*, Salome uses in Elizabeth Cary's play *The Tragedy of Marian* to persuade Herod that Marian has been unfaithful.[92] Dorothy Leigh wrote in her book of advice about her children's upbringing, published in 1616, with reference to biblical sources, in favour of the conventional arguments for women's chastity: 'without which we are mere beasts and no women'. She noted how some of the Fathers had declared 'that it is not enough for a woman to be chaste but even so to behave herself that no man may think or deem her unchaste'. Dorothy Leigh had either thoroughly imbibed the ideology of women's sinfulness and inferiority or knew that in public she must appear to have done so: 'Encourage women not to be ashamed to show their infirmities but to give men the first and chief place . . . and because we must needs confess that sin entered by us into our posterity let us show how careful we are to seek to Christ to cast it out of us and our posterity and how fearful we are that our sin should sink any of them to the lowest part of the earth.'[93] Elizabeth Joceline's book of advice, published in 1624, shows her particular preoccupation with the sin of pride, especially in a daughter, for in a girl, she confessed, 'I more fear that vice, pride being now rather accorded a virtue in our sex worthy of praise than a vice fit for reproof.' 'Remember thou art a maid', she insisted, 'and such ought thy modesty to be, that thou shouldest scarce speak but when thou answereth.'[94]

Works like those by Dorothy Leigh and Elizabeth Joceline tempt one to argue that men were very successful in creating gender in Tudor and early Stuart England. In one sense it seems they were but the dangers here are enormous. Lyndal Roper has challenged much that has become almost orthodox about how gender was created at this time in her book *Oedipus and the Devil*, which opens a debate which will not easily be resolved. The early modern world, she reminds us, has come to be seen in terms of an otherness characterised by cultural collectivity and the absence of the concept of the individual self: 'as a result early modern people can threaten to become dancing marionettes, tricked out in ruffs and codpieces, whose subjectivities can neither surprise nor unsettle'. When we work from male prescriptive sources 'gender history threatens to become a reinterpretation of the thought of powerful thinkers', a history of ideas 'which denies individual's capacities to make their own meanings'. It is not apparent, she insists, that people understood their bodies by means of medical theories of the kind that have so far formed

92. Quilligan in Turner, ed., *Sexuality and Gender in Early Modern Europe*, p. 229.
93. D. Leigh, *The Mother's Blessing* (London, 1627), pp. 16, 39–41.
94. E. Joceline, *The Mother's Legacy* (London, 1625), p. 4.

the central ground of this book: this was a culture that 'rested on a very deep apprehension of sexual difference as an organising principle of culture'.[95] In other words, women may have understood in their own consciousness and through their own feelings much about being a woman of which the male ideology took no account. The problem, in considering how the female honour code worked to sustain early modern patriarchy, is that we can only work with women's recorded words and actions. We are deaf to what was really going on in their minds. What is clear is that we can find women corroborating male constructions of them in legal situations in a manner which was often more manipulative than passive. There was nothing women could do in this society to resist the way men insisted upon reading them, but there was much they could do about using those readings to their own advantage.

Tim Stretton's account of women's pleading strategies in the Elizabethan Court of Requests shows litigants and their lawyers drawing upon the common heritage of conventions and stereotypes discussed in this book. He argues that these were 'embedded in the consciousness and culture of literate as well as illiterate society'. He finds the parties were often at one about the duties that each other's role demanded: 'their vehement disagreement was over whether the other party was fulfilling its assigned role'. Thus women often accused men of violence, men accused women of sexual infidelity.[96] Laura Gowing's study of female honour argues that, in defamation cases brought to the London and Chichester consistory courts between 1572 and 1640, we find litigants reiterating a set of images about whoredom drawn from contemporary prescriptive sources and 'redirecting their descriptive powers into insult'. Women were coming to the courts more often during this period as defendants as well as plaintiffs. They were using as evidence reported speech which contravened all the prescriptions about female language but which consistently has the authentic ring of the doorstep and streets. Women, Gowing concludes, are defamed 'almost universally on the grounds of whoredom, either as a general insult or as a carefully specified allegation'. Women accusing other women skilfully built up accusations of fornication with a multiplication of detail which produced a sense of conviction. The degrees of whoredom described in these cases were closely related to a perceived relation of women as male property: once a whore a woman had escaped male control, a common whore was further out of control, becoming the property of the male community. Defiance of male gender indoctrination was thus seen as carefully graduated. The confessional idiom of women's speech in the church court records exemplifies the ecclesiastical language of sinfulness. Women sought to establish their

95. L. Roper, *Oedipus and the Devil: Witchcraft, Sexuality and Religion in Early Modern Europe* (London 1994), pp. 11–19.
96. T. Stretton, Woman Litigants in the Elizabethan Court of Requests, Cambridge University PhD thesis, 1993, pp. 208–54.

sexual honesty competitively, sometimes attempting to prove it by the number of children they had. Moreover, images of dress which focus on breeches as a metaphor show how well women grasped the issue of household patriarchy. After an argument between Alice Baker and Elizabeth Edwards in 1613, Alice's husband pulled a paper off a post near their door 'on which was written that Alice Baker . . . did wear her husband's breeches'.[97] All these tactics point towards the pervasiveness with which the gendered conception of female honour was understood and dramatised in the personal relationships of London people. We can see men and women, but especially women, fighting personal battles that might be largely about other than sexual issues with a language of insult which reflected male hegemony over codes of honour.

The general readiness of both men and women to draw upon the image of woman as the weaker vessel, suggests that, whatever women's private thoughts about their nature, we are talking about a gender system that did have considerable practical strength. There were many possibilities for exploiting orthodox assumptions about feminine weakness. Mary Throckmorton, writing to her father around 1607, explained how she had handled a dispute with a neighbour: 'I have answered his letter like a woman, very submissively, if that will serve, for I perceive that they cannot endure to be told of their faults.' The cause of godliness could prompt a woman to offer political advice. 'Pray take heed of leaving us worse than you found us,' wrote Hannah Brograve to Sir Simonds D'Ewes early in the course of the Long Parliament of 1640, urging him to follow 'the way of Christ'. She added the conventional apology: 'I pray pardon my bold rudeness and take it out of love and the earnest desire of my soul.'[98] In addressing public bodies staffed by men, it was an obvious tactic to play the weaker vessel for all it was worth. Thus Anne Newdegate, opening a petition for the wardship of her sons after the death of her husband, wrote 'pardon this unmannerly presumption of a most unfortunate woman . . . may it please your honour that these scaling womanish lines may bring to your view this my humble suit'.[99] Sir Ralph Verney was of one mind with friends who were advising him in choosing to send his wife Mary to plead the family's case before the Committee for Compounding in 1646, when he did not in any case want to risk returning to England from France himself since he could be imprisoned for debt. His cousin William Denton had told him that 'women were never so useful as now' with the committees. Sir Roger Burgoyne was more directly cynical about the part Lady Verney should play: 'certainly

97. Gowing, pp. 21, 28–9, 33, 35, 40, 43, 47.

98. Cited in P. Crawford, *Women and Religion in England* 1500–1720 (London, 1993), p. 95.

99. Cited in L. Pollock, '"Teach Her to Live under Obedience": The Making of Women in the Upper Ranks of Early Modern England', *Continuity and Change* 4 (1989), pp. 234, 251.

it would not do amiss if she can bring her spirit to a soliciting temper and can tell how to use the juice of an onion sometimes to soften hard hearts'. 'Women are not the worse solicitors', Sir Ralph himself told Lord Devonshire whose help he was seeking, 'their sex entitles them to many privileges'.[100] The times, to Verney's mind, called for a woman ready to use a degree of persuasive deceit. Thus we can see that the strength and resilience of the honour codes lay in the close understanding which people had of them and the flexibility with which they could be interpreted, expressed and manipulated.

100. Citations from A. Fraser, *The Weaker Vessel: Woman's Lot in Seventeenth-Century England* (London, 1985), p. 230; M. Slater, *Family Life in the Seventeenth Century: The Verneys of Claydon House* (London, 1984), p. 66.

7. The Gentry and Honour

THERE WERE SOME aspects of male honour which imposed responsibilities on all men, such as sexual control in marriage and household order. There were others which were specific to the gentry. For them honour in the Tudor and Stuart periods presented a complex and demanding code of living and of behaviour. Richard Brathwaite, himself from a Westmoreland landowning family, assumed in writing his book *The English Gentleman*, published in 1628, that a gentleman would wish his conduct to be guided by the dictates of honour. He wrote that such a man 'may the better understand himself and direct his courses to that bent of honour whereto all generous actions are directed'. In a later work, published in 1652, Brathwaite declared that honour was such a precious odour that it survives man and retains the memory of his actions in a lasting shrine of glory or shame.[1] A gentleman's honour, in other words, was the essence of his reputation in the eyes of his social equals, providing him with his sense of worth and his claim to pride in his own community, contributing to his sense of identity with that community. This was the simple truth of John Cleland's comment in 1607: 'honour is not in his hand who is honoured but in the hearts and opinions of other men'.[2] Honour was accumulative; it was also both a private and a public condition, on display at home in front of family and servants and in need of zealous protection against insult or betrayal on the stage of the world. It provides our point of entry to the working of patriarchy between around 1500 and 1700 since it is the nearest that the gentry came at this time to articulating a concept of masculinity. We need to consider the gentry's honour in terms of lineage, of the physical expression of manhood, and of the virtue and reason which were the guiding precepts that underlay the gentry's leadership of society.

Honour, in the chivalric code, could not be contracted into, nor could

1. Citations from C. Barber, *The Theme of Honour's Tongue: A Study of Social Attitudes in the English Drama from Shakespeare to Dryden* (Goteborg, 1985), pp. 8–9.
2. Cited in M. James, *English Politics and the Concept of Honour* (*Past and Present* supplement, III, 1978), p. 4.

the bond of lineage be broken. Honour belonged to the collectivity; it was a temporary possession for the individual, held in trust. 'For a man's very being as honourable had been transmitted to him with the blood of his ancestors, themselves honourable men,' writes Mervyn James. His decision, the Earl of Westmoreland believed, when he contemplated rising in rebellion against Queen Elizabeth in 1569, was momentous for his lineage: 'I will never blot my house which hath been thus long preserved without staining.' When he did move into action the house of Neville in all its local branches rose with him.[3] These values were changing between 1500 and 1660. Sir Anthony Drury was speaking an old-fashioned language when he wrote to his Norfolk kinsman, Sir William de Grey, describing the speeches of a local adversary in the 1620s. 'To traduce my actions,' he declared, 'stain my blood and dishonour my father, which is long since dead, are three mortal wounds to my soul which can never be cured.'[4] The propaganda of the Tudor and early Stuart state emphasised public service as the gentry's prime obligation rather than loyalty to kin and this propaganda was steadily winning the day. Yet, even as it was doing so, a range of evidence shows how the gentry clung to the notion that honour was expressed as much in loyalty to the lineage as in personal virtue. When Sir Thomas Lucy's wife Alice composed the eulogy which appears on his monument at Charlecote following his death in 1640, she made an emphatic and unusual statement on this issue which presumably reflected her knowledge of her husband's mind. Sir Thomas, the epitaph goes, was 'an extract of a most ancient family but a disesteemer of birth in respect of worth, wherein he out-shone the brightest of his noble ancestors'.[5]

The evidence of the gentry's traditionalism is for the most part visual, though there are also numerous family histories and autobiographical accounts prefaced by weighty references to family ancestry. This evidence – church monuments and domestic decoration – is very much of a piece with the mentality of an age which, as Keith Thomas has shown, sought to shroud political change in a language of ancient prophecies and sleeping heroes.[6] Pride in paternal ancestry led gentry into fiction, invention and a fantasy world of heraldic profusion. The heralds contrived rolls tracing ancestry to the Norman conquerors, the Romans or even the Trojans. The Popham family tree began with Noah in his ark. Lord Lumley removed three medieval effigies from Durham to Chester-le-Street and completed the series with eleven imitations of his own. The Wellesbournes of Buckinghamshire went furthest, establishing a bogus pedigree, manufacturing medieval seals and inventing a certain

3. James, *English Politics and the Concept of Honour*, pp. 15–16.
4. Cited in A.J. Fletcher and A. Stevenson, eds, *Order and Disorder in Early Modern England* (Cambridge, 1985), p. 93.
5. HEH, STT Literature Box (2).
6. K.V. Thomas, *Religion and the Decline of Magic* (London, 1971), pp. 389–432.

Wellesbourne de Montfort who, in the style of effigy appropriate to the thirteenth century, made his appearance in the parish church. Heraldry flourished during the reign of Elizabeth as a demonstration of pride in county connections as well as ancient lineage. At Gilling in the East Riding, the Fairfaxes painted trees for each wapentake with the arms of the gentry as they were listed in the 1584 visitation. The great parlour at Tamworth Castle was decorated by Sir John Ferrers with shields which traced his ancestry back to the Conquest.[7] All these expressions of geographical cohesion and chronological continuity flowed from the same need to demonstrate membership of the community of honour.[8]

It helps to make sense of claims to status of this kind if we look at what commentators were saying about the relationship of virtue to lineage. For it was through lineage, the argument went, that men from ancient families were expected to learn their virtue but the form this virtue took might be adapted to the needs of the Tudor and Stuart state. Elaborate tombs provided manifold opportunities for heraldic display and some tombs indeed comprised hardly anything except heraldry. The heralds and those who wrote about heraldry explained its significance. There was more to it than simply locating the subject on the social scale. Heraldic imagery was actually thought to have the capacity, as Nigel Llewelyn puts it, 'to instil virtue and thereby reinforce the sense of order'. Sir John Ferne in his 1586 tract The Blazon of Gentrie makes the point clearly: 'Much more shall the worthy merits of the ancestor figures, in the secret emblems or sacred sculptures of the coat armour, stir up the son to imitate the same virtues whereby his ancestor obeyed to make them both gentlemen.' In his 1563 treatise on nobility, Laurence Humphrey argued that coats of arms suitably displayed should teach children to 'counterfeit . . . their virtues'. William Bird stressed in his 1642 tract that grants of arms newly made were a reward for virtue, an invitation in fact to enter the community of honour. The herald was in this theory an agent of this lineage community rewarding the deserving: 'for the merits of and certain qualities that he do see in him and for sundry noble acts which he hath performed he . . . giveth him and his heirs there . . . bearings in arms'.

Thus in practice the funeral monuments which were adorned with heraldry can be seen to celebrate virtue as much as blood. Hence their popularity as the new code of public service gradually replaced the old chivalric one. The astonishing wooden triptych erected alongside the high altar at Lydiard Tregoze in Wiltshire in 1615 is an outstanding example of visual propaganda along these lines. The exterior displays an extraordinary range of heraldic data; when the outer doors are opened the viewer finds

7. L. Stone, The Crisis of the Aristocracy (Oxford, 1965), pp. 23–5.
8. For other examples see A. Everitt, The Community of Kent and the Great Rebellion (Leicester, 1966), pp. 45–55.

a simulated architectural space containing life-size figures of the St John family who lived at Lydiard. The triptych's inscriptions allude both to the long ancestry of the St Johns and to their service to the Tudor dynasty. This is just one item in a church stuffed with monuments. In such churches one can sense the tremendous impact of tomb sculpture and its associated heraldry as an exemplification of land and power. All over the English countryside these monuments remain with us, celebrating the civilised ideal of manhood upon which the patriarchal system rested. There are country gentlemen by the score, portrayed in many styles and formats, but alike in their maleness and the authority and command which it entailed. Some lie in effigy in mail or plate armour, some kneel across prayer desks from their wives, some grace church walls as half effigies, a few even prop themselves on an elbow to gaze into eternity. They are bearers of the symbols and signs of power.[9] The common characteristics of these monuments, erected in considerable numbers between the early Tudor period and the Restoration, are their architectural structures and frameworks together with their iconography of classical humanism.[10] The ideals of reason and virtue expressed in service to the commonwealth are sometimes made explicit. The 1620s monument to the first Lord Rich at Felsted in Essex, for example, has panels showing him in action as Speaker of the House of Commons and Lord Chancellor. There are figures of Fortitude, Justice, Hope and Charity.[11] These cardinal virtues also appear on the fine monument to Sir Thomas Gorges, who died in 1635, in Salisbury Cathedral.[12]

Sheer physical courage was central to the chivalric code from which the early modern concept of honour evolved. In Raymond Lull's *Book of the Order of Chivalry*, printed by Caxton in the 1480s, virtue was essentially 'prowess' and the 'nobility of his courage' was the means by which the knight proved his lineage. The very popular *Book of St Albans*, reprinted many times between 1486 and 1610, related all the prime virtues which it recommended men should cultivate – fortitude, prudence, hope, steadfastness – to the conduct of battle. Some Elizabethan writing on honour continued to express this unqualified martial emphasis. Gerald Legh in *The Accedens of Armory*, published in 1562 and reissued in 1597, argued that 'martial prowess' is 'the chief advancer of gentry' and that the virtue which conferred honour on a man was a 'glory got by courage of

9. These two paragraphs are based upon N. Llewellyn, 'Claims to Status through Visual Codes: Heraldry in post-Reformation Funeral Monuments', in S. Anglo, ed., *Chivalry in the Renaissance* (London, 1990), pp. 145–60.

10. The best introduction remains K.A. Esdaile, *English Church Monuments 1560 to 1840* (London, 1946) followed by the *Buildings of England* county by county series edited by N. Pevsner.

11. K.A. Esdaile, 'The Monument to the First Lord Rich at Felsted', *Essex Archaeological Society Transactions* XXII (1940), pp. 59–67.

12. K.A. Esdaile, 'The Gorges Monument in Salisbury Cathedral', *Wiltshire Archaeological Magazine* L (1942–4), pp. 53–62.

manhood'.[13] We have seen how Shakespeare used three plays written in
the decade following peace with Spain in 1604 to reflect upon men's need
to test their manhood in battle and avoid the effeminising influence that
women's love could have upon them. At the level of fantasy literature, we have also seen, manhood remained infused with a residual
prescriptive code of valour well into the seventeenth century: the tales of
Guy of Warwick and St George and the Dragon retained their perennial
popularity.[14]

All this was not just prescription. The Tudor and early Stuart gentry
took war and its opportunities for testing of the courage which their
honour demanded very seriously. The Earl of Northumberland's advice
to his son in 1609, for example, suggested young men should select
physical exercises with regard to usefulness 'for the defence of themselves
or the service of their country', giving particular attention to 'managing
of all sorts of arms'.[15] Henry Slingsby mused in his diary upon his
experience of six weeks' campaigning during the war against the Scots
in 1639:

> I like it as a commendable way of breeding for a young gentleman . . .
> for as idleness is the nurse of all evil, enfeebling the parts both of mind
> and body, this employment of a soldier's is contrary unto it: for it
> greatly improves them, by enabling his body to labour, his mind to
> watchfulness and so, by a contempt of all things but the employment
> he is in, he shall not much care how hard he lyeth nor how meanly
> he fareth.[16]

When it came to civil war there was some conscious revival of the
concepts of chivalry and lineage of blood. Sir John St John erected a tomb
at Lydiard Tregoze for his second son Edward, who died of wounds
received at the battle of Newbury, a wonderful celebration of martial
valour. He used the standing figure motif which had recently been
introduced in a few cases elsewhere, with Edward in a full pose beneath
a baldacchino held back by pages in order to expose his gilded armour
and shields of arms. *Inter homines exemplar* ran the inscription. Another
royalist west country hero celebrated in this way was Colonel William
Rudhall at Ross-on-Wye.[17]

The emergence of the duel in Elizabethan England provided a means
of channelling the traditional disposition of the gentry to avenge disparagement of their virtue or honour by a display of personal courage which
affected no one but themselves. With the duel violence was codified and

13. James, *English Politics and the Concept of Honour*, pp. 2–4.
14. Above, pp. 88–9, 97.
15. Cited in V.G. Kiernan, *The Duel in European History: Honour and the Reign of Aristocracy* (Oxford, 1988), p. 80.
16. D. Parsons, ed., *The Diary of Henry Slingsby* (London, 1836), p. 38.
17. Llewellyn, 'Claims to Status' in Anglo, ed. *Chivalry in the Renaissance*, p. 150.

regulated: it was a highly formal and well-mannered event which contained, by an accepted set of rules, the passions from which it was generated. The opening of the first fashionable fencing school at Blackfriars in 1576, followed by a second one in London in the 1590s, signalled the arrival of the duel with the rapier from Italy and France. The number of duels and challenges mentioned in newsletters and correspondence increased from five in the 1580s to nearly twenty in the 1590s and to thirty-three in the decade from 1610 to 1619. The ritualised test of manhood quickly won favour and respectability. Class and gender came together here in their most compelling form, for the notion that a gentleman's word was his honour went to the heart of a masculinity in which pride and vanity were seen as dominant passions. Joseph Addison made the point well:

> The great violation of the point of honour from man to man is giving the lie. One may tell another he whores, drinks, blasphemes and it may pass unresented, but to say he lies, though but in jest is an affront that nothing but blood can expiate. The reason perhaps may be because no other vice implies a want of courage so much as the making of a lie and therefore telling a man he lies is touching him in the most sensible part of honour and indirectly calling him a coward.[18]

The English nobility and gentry luxuriated in a new code of response to insult and the giving of the lie that, by its insistence upon mortal combat, soon began to take a heavy toll of lives. Many went to the sands of Calais or Ostend to fight it out in order to avoid the penalties of English law. The genuinely pacific James I was horrified. He led a campaign which had considerable success to divert gentry quarrels into the courts, especially the Earl Marshall's court, a moribund institution which now enjoyed a brief revival.[19]

Gentlemen had their own sports the pursuit of which, as an expression of their manhood and source of an endless round of country hospitality, was an important ingredient of their honour code. At Dover's Cotswold games, we have seen, the gentry enjoyed their paradigmatic recreations of hunting and racing whereas the populace was confined to traditional manly sports like wrestling and singlestick fighting (plate 31).[20] The prescriptive literature on this subject gradually changed its tone as martial considerations declined in importance. Roger Ascham's list of exercises which he recommended as 'not only comely and decent but also very necessary' in 1570 included 'running fair at the tilt', shooting well with a

18. Cited in D.T. Andrew, 'The Code of Honour and its Critics: the Opposition to Duelling in England 1700–1850', *Social History* 5 (1980), pp. 411–12.
19. L. Stone, *Crisis of the Aristocracy*, pp. 242–50; Kiernan, *Duel in European History*, pp. 78–88.
20. Above, pp. 94–5.

bow or surely with a gun, leaping, wrestling and swimming as well as hunting, hawking and tennis.[21] John Temple, advising his son later in the century before he set out for Europe, insisted he should 'practice horsemanship and vaulting especially of all bodily exercise and learn of the best teachers whatsoever it cost'.[22] By the 1670s it was still conventional thinking that all boys, whatever their social station, should be tested by physical hardships in their youth for, as Jean Gailhard put it, 'tis well to be fitted to wrestle against what difficulties we shall meet withal'. It was also still generally accepted that the body as well as the mind needed regular exercise. There was nevertheless a lack of the previous emphasis on equestrian skills and more stress was put on riding and hunting as the basis of a gentleman's general physical fitness programme. Gailhard's summary is founded on assumptions about the relationship between this fitness, a man's strength and the inculcation of the manly courage he might need as a resource in adversity:

> It is not only convenient but also necessary to use children to hardships if their strength and constitution will bear it, for thereby not only they will take exercise which is necessary to dissipate bad humours and to use their joints whereby they will be more nimble and stronger and which also will make them grow, but also they will use themselves to labour and make it natural to them; it is a great matter when they are hardened from their childhood for it makes their constitution strong and lusty.[23]

A mass of evidence from gentry correspondence and diaries indicates the enormous appeal that country sports, especially hunting, had for the young. Sir John Bramston recorded how he poached pigeons and fish in his free time as a schoolboy, even getting his master to wink at his activities and allow the baking of a pigeon pie. John Aubrey caught carp in other people's ponds, recalling how Squire White discharged a gun at him to deter his trespassing. Bravado was the essence of such escapades.[24] Thomas Isham's diary entries for 1673, when he was sixteen, list expeditions with his younger brothers to course hares and catch carp and perch as well as to attend the local horse races. Hugh Cholmley later looked back regretfully at the amount of time he spent on such activities on leaving Cambridge at seventeen: 'I was so entered in hunting, hawking and horse races that I could not easily put them out of my mind when,

21. Cited in M. Vale, *The Gentleman's Recreations: Accomplishments and Pastimes of the English Gentleman 1580–1630* (Cambridge, 1977), p. 6.

22. Huntingdon Library, STT 1943.

23. J. Gailhard, *The Compleat Gentleman: or Directions for the Education of Youth as to their Breeding at home and Travelling abroad* (London, 1678), pp. 79–80; R.L., *Letter of Advice to a Young Gentleman leaving the University* (London, 1670), p. 49.

24. R.B. Manning, *Hunters and Poachers: A Social and Cultural History of Unlawful Hunting in England* (Oxford, 1993), p. 15.

by riper years, I saw the vanity of them.'[25] Roger Manning has argued
that hunting was an 'adolescent rite of passage' in the sixteenth and
seventeenth centuries: 'many gentlemen remained perpetual adolescents'
and it is 'sometimes difficult to distinguish' between their rites and
children's games. There were certainly aspects of the widespread poaching
raids on deer parks which were theatrical: the pursuit of prey at night
with vizers or blackened faces, the struggles between gamekeepers and
poachers with one another's dogs regarded as legitimate trophies of battle.
Poaching game was a symbolic substitute for warfare, practised almost
entirely within the gentry class, with rituals of killing, eating and blooding
which signified triumph over the natural world, emotional release and a
sense of male fraternity.[26]

'Unless he was a hunter,' wrote Gilbert White reflecting in 1789 on
what he had known in Hampshire, 'no young person was allowed to be
possessed of manhood and gallantry.' His account struck a note of nostalgia. Around the beginning of the century, he remembered, all his 'country' of southeast England had still been 'wild about deer stealing'. White
believed that most men were 'sportsmen by constitution' for there was
'such an inherent spirit for hunting in human nature as scarcely any
inhibitions can restrain'.[27] His reference is to a tradition in its last days
during his youth in which sport, courage and manliness were seen as
having important connections relevant to the gentry's honour. The
Tudor ideal was that hunting was in a very practical way physical training,
preparing men for the hardships of war. Sir Thomas Elyot's model was a
spare one. The deer should be pursued in spacious forests with the help
of just enough hounds to dislodge them from their cover. Sir Thomas
Cockayne, in his 1591 *Treatise of Hunting*, said hunting taught men to
endure 'continued travail and painful labour'. Henry Peacham related
approvingly how Lord Leonard Guy, while lord deputy of Ireland in the
1530s, had caused his sons to go hunting at midnight in the depths of
winter, returning cold and wet to a breakfast of coarse bread and mouldy
cheese. 'In this manner', Cockayne noted, 'the Spartans and Laconians
dieted and brought up their children till they came into man's estate.'
Two vignettes from this period illustrate how the notion of proving
oneself as a hunter did strongly grip some men. John Selwyn's moment of
audacity in the presence of Queen Elizabeth still remains depicted for us
today on his monumental brass at Walton-on-Thames in Surrey. He leapt
from his horse to the back of a stag during a chase in the royal park at
Oatlands and, guiding it towards the Queen, brought it dead to her feet.
The brass shows him plunging his sword into the stag's throat. Arthur

25. L.A. Pollock, *A Lasting Relationship: Parents and Their Children over Three Centuries*
    (London, 1987), pp. 154-5.
26. Manning, *Hunters and Poachers*, pp. 35-56; for blacking see E.P. Thompson, *Whigs and
    Hunters* (London, 1975), pp. 55-155.
27. Cited in Thompson, *Whigs and Hunters*, p. 58.

Wilson wrote in an autobiographical account of his exploits as a young man in the 1620s about an occasion when, falling from his horse on a slippery bank, he pursued a stag on foot. His reputation in question, because another in the party alleged he had 'fallen for fear', he later jumped from his horse, when the stag was cornered by the dogs, hamstrung its rear legs with his sword and, mounting its back, cut its throat. Wilson was clearly a foolhardy hunter and he confessed he often got himself into dangerous scrapes.[28] But he needed to prove his courage in the approved way a man could do so. The gender content of male honour is at its most striking here. Yet there were Tudor women celebrated for their hunting expertise, such as Lady Berkeley who was proficient with the longbow and also kept merlins in her bedchamber.[29] Some gentlewomen still rode to hounds in the seventeenth century but they were much more likely to be found as spectators of the chase in the park, from the roof-top turrets which became fashionable as banqueting houses on Elizabethan and early Stuart mansions.[30]

The century from the 1560s to the Restoration marked the apogee of the deer-hunting culture. This was the time when the gentry poured their energies into establishing and enjoying their enclosed deer parks, where they could hunt in a leisurely manner with the aid of their dogs and hounds, beaters and nets, trapping the deer for a final slaughter. There were something like a hundred deer parks in Sussex on the eve of the civil war and the gamekeepers there, as elsewhere, were engaged in constant vigilance to protect a privileged sport.[31] Hunting had become, as Roger Manning remarks, 'quite artificial'. It tested skills more than brute strength or sheer physical courage. Together with coursing and hawking, it had become the lifeblood of the gentry's social intercourse. Their correspondence is rich in references to its pleasures. To take just one example, Sir John Lenthall wrote eagerly to his mother-in-law Lady Hester Temple in the 1620s: 'I entreat you that I may see you with Sir Peter Temple, his lady and all the rest of our family here this summer. I reserve a buck which I am promised against your coming and which yourselves shall kill. The rest of your entertainment shall be supplied with a joyful welcome.'[32] A marble panel on the lovely monument to Lord Teynham at Lynsted in Kent by Epiphanias Evesham shows the nobleman's sons kneeling with books in their hands and with a hound and a hawking perch beside them.[33] A gentleman who lacked a deer park could

---

28. Citations from Manning, *Hunters and Poachers*, pp. 6–9; see also K.V. Thomas, *Man and the Natural World* (London, 1983), p. 183.
29. Manning, *Hunters and Poachers*, p. 13.
30. M. Girouard, *Life in the English Country House* (London, 1978), p. 106.
31. A.J. Fletcher, *A County Community in Peace and War: Sussex 1600–1660* (London, 1975), pp. 28–9.
32. Manning, *Hunters and Poachers*, pp. 6–8; HEH, STT 1272.
33. Esdaile, *English Church Monuments*, plate 81.

easily feel at a loss. Sir John Oglander, one such, noted his alternative arrangements for 'sport for my friends': a warren for some rabbits, fishponds and a place to 'breed or keep pheasants and partridges'.[34] Ben Jonson in *Every Man in his Humour* satirised the aspiring country gentleman anxious not to be behind the fashion with the figure of Master Stephen. Having bought the hawk, hood and bells, he asks his London uncle about the treatises on hunting and hawking then on the market offering instruction in the proper manner of following such gentlemen's recreations. 'If man have not skill in the hawking and hunting languages nowadays I'll not give a rush for him', declares Stephen, 'they are more studied than the Greek or the Latin.'[35]

As horses, hawks and dogs became integral to a sporting way of life they became viewed in warmer and more gentle terms than previously. Techniques for training horses were being softened. The hawk was to be cherished: 'there cannot be too much familiarity' between it and its owner, one Jacobean falconer insisted. Gentry tended to treat their hounds with great indulgence.[36] Ambrose Barnes later recalled how in the 1630s and 40s his father would not allow the family to start dinner until he came in from hunting: 'often when the meat lay before the fire to keep warm for them, the hounds which run before would come into the kitchen and snatch it away, whilst none in the home durst mutter a word against it'.[37] This special treatment afforded to the privileged animal species would be taken much further in due course. For the present, though the realities had moved a long way from the prescriptions for roughness and austerity of Elyot or Cockayne, the dominating note for the sporting gentry remained conquest of the prey and the courage this involved. It is an idea of manhood well summarised by the Earl of Shaftesbury's account, written with conscious nostalgia, of the Dorset squire Henry Hastings of Woodland, a man who till past eighty 'rode to the death of a stag as well as any'. Hastings, he noted, was 'an original in our age or rather the copy of our ancient nobility', for he always dressed in hunting green and his home was 'of the old fashion in the midst of a park well stocked with deer'. With his hounds he hunted bucks, foxes, hares, otters and badgers. In his open house his guests were expected to mix with the animals as well as their remains: 'the great hall strewed with marrow bones; full of hawks' perches, hounds, spaniels and terriers; the upper side of the hall hung with fox skins . . . here and there a polecat intermixed; guns and keepers' and hunters' poles in great abundance'.[38]

34. Manning, *Hunters and Poachers*, p. 44.
35. Cited in Vale, *Gentleman's Recreations*, p. 8.
36. Thomas, *Man and the Natural World*, pp. 101–3.
37. W.H.D. Longstaffe, ed., *Memoirs of the Life of Mr Ambrose Barnes* (Surtees Society, L, 1866), p. 33.
38. Cited in Manning, *Hunters and Poachers*, pp. 131–4.

The display of virtue was expected of the honourable man on the public stage as well as on the relatively private one of the household consisting of family and servants. The prescriptive literature constantly makes connections between religious knowledge and conviction and the life of virtue and between the inner virtues and their outward expression in manners, respect and affability.[39] Thus Hugh Rhodes's *Book of Nurture* of 1577 emphasises attendance at sermons and Bible reading, warning against dallying with 'fained fables, vain fantasies and wanton stories'. William Segar's *The School of Virtue* of 1557 ran through the standard vices of dicing, carding, swearing, filthy talk and lying, which once they gained a hold on the youth destined to rule a household were seen as precluding him from any chance of doing so effectively.[40] Pride, anger and envy were regularly inveighed against in such works.[41] Assuming he was first set on the right moral lines, there was then much more to be said about how a gentleman could be schooled in the display of virtue. Tracts published by James Cleland in 1607 and William Martyn in 1613, the latter written for his son Nicholas while a student at Oxford, spell out the pattern of upbringing which was believed, through a combination of learning and moral instruction, to produce an appropriate adult confidence. 'The inward parts of the mind', explained Martyn, had to be 'adorned with splendid virtues and such gentlemanlike qualities as do make a man to be complete.' Religion made a man 'warily and carefully to look unto his ways and wisely to govern and to rule himself'; the offspring of religion was virtue expressed through 'prudence, justice, fortitude and temperance'; study was essential to improve the mind since 'an ignorant man without learning is altogether barren and dry'. The business of tutors, declared Cleland, was to feed their pupils 'with the very marrow and substance of philosophy, to make them truly and firmly honest men'. The young gentleman must learn to love virtue for itself, 'ingeniously like an honest man'. Given this course of training, the educational implications of which we will explore in chapter 15, a young gentleman could be expected to achieve a mode of self-presentation which accorded with the values of honour. His talk would be 'moderate and sparing', not lascivious or voluble. His 'carriage and behaviour' would be 'courteous, affable, gentle and familiar'.[42]

Personal advice to sons that has survived in manuscript form echoes these prescriptions, with an especially strong emphasis among the godly on keeping 'an upright heart with God'. Sir Richard Grovesnor gave his son a library of 'good books' and enjoined him to 'be diligent in reading

---

39. E.g. W. Fiston, *The School of Good Manners* (London, 1609), preface.
40. F.J. Furnivall, ed., *Manners and Meals in Olden Time* (Early English Text Society, XXXII, 1868), pp. 63–5, 337–55.
41. E.g. J. Legrand, *The Book of Good Manners* (London, 1503), sigs A1, C1.
42. J. Cleland, *The Institution of a Young Nobleman* (London, 1607), pp. 62–5; W. Martyn, *Youth's Instruction* (London, 1613), epistle, pp. 13–32.

the scriptures and other godly and commendable authors'.[43] Lady Brilliana Harley wrote lovingly and carefully to her son Edward at Oxford, imploring him to ensure that it was his 'chief care to obey your God in the whole course of your life'. Her letter was stuffed with precepts:

Be courteous to all, but familiar with a few.
Be slow to speak, rather hear others then be hasty to utter your mind.
Believe well of all but trust a few.
Be watchful over yourself that you do not easily speak evil of any.

The overall objective was a style of life which declared godliness and honour to the world: 'show the holiness of your heart by a holy life, let your tongue, eyes, hands and feet be the instruments by which you may express the good affections of your heart'.[44] Lady Brilliana's husband Sir Robert was a paragon of virtue, as a man who was a potential minister in his village was told, 'sweet and humble in his conversation . . . free of his heart and purse'.[45] She expected no less of her son.

The destiny of Edward Harley and hundreds like him who were heirs, whether to great mansions or small manor houses, was the responsibility for and management of a household. It was in his home that a gentleman's enactment of honour found its most consistent daily expression through the standards of behaviour that he set and the leadership that he imposed. The pillars of county society moved in a social world which can be pictured in terms of a series of concentric circles. They are well illustrated by the eulogy which appears on Sir Thomas Lucy's tomb at Charlecote. There was his home: 'his great estate none would better manage or be less servant to: what frugality laid up liberality and magnificence laid out'. There was the immediate neighbourhood: 'his gate was not less propitious to the poor whose valediction to it was always a benediction . . . many neighbour towns he yearly refreshed'. There was the county and district where Lucy was held in esteem as a magistrate, as indeed 'one of the country's greatest glories'. Finally there was Westminster where his wisdom was needed for local as well as national reasons: 'a singular and much honoured patriot, witness the supreme court of this Kingdom whither he was frequently sent by the unanimous and fervent suffrages of his endeared country'.[46]

43. Cited in R. Cust and P.G. Lake, 'Sir Richard Grosvenor and the Rhetoric of Magistracy', *Bulletin of the Institute of Historical Research* LIV (1981), p. 42.
44. BL, Add MS 70118. I am grateful to Margaret Sommez for a transcript of this document.
45. Cited in P. Collinson, *The Religion of Protestants: The Church in English Society 1559–1625* (Oxford, 1982), p. 166.
46. HEH, STT Literature Box 2; for a discussion of the usages of 'country' in this period see Cust and Lake 'Sir Richard Grosvenor', in *BIHR* LIV (1981), pp. 48–9.

Control of a large estate was a demanding and exacting task for which gentry sons were prepared by a rigorous course of education. Some did their own book-keeping; most relied on the assistance of bailiffs and stewards with whom they kept up a close working relationship.[47] Gentry advice to sons made much of careful choice of servants and proper treatment of them. Keep only those that be 'willing, humble, diligent and honest', advised Sir William Wentworth in 1604.[48] Superior understanding, the Earl of Northumberland told his son Algernon in 1609, was essential:

> Both in ancient times and in latter years they have been held in great honour that knew most. Often times they were reputed as Gods, whose understandings did so excel others, that it was believed nothing could lie secret from their knowledges, whether the knowledge grew by inspiration or by act or by deceit or by intelligence or what way soever or in what kind of government soever, yet it did fix in men awe, obedience, reverence, honour.

He should never on any account, Algernon Percy was warned, show himself 'weak or careless by over believing'. Whereas he should consult with chief subordinates, he should always be ready, if their counsels were unsound, to 'show them their errors out of reason'.[49] The size of gentry households varied enormously, from a couple of maids and a few farm labourers in the case of lesser gentry to more than a hundred in the traditional nobleman's great house.[50] But patriarchs held the same obligations in common whatever the numbers in their charge. Servants could expect care and security in sickness. 'His servants' sickness won his sympathy and their recovery his cost,' it was said of Sir Thomas Lucy. The close relationship of trust and dependence that long service to a gentry family involved was often marked by annuities and bequests. One Sussex gentleman, Thomas Jefferay, enumerated legacies in his will to his clerk, bailiff, 'painful servant', dairymaid, cook and brewer, requesting his executors to give them as well 'some of my old coats and worst sort of apparell'. A family estate was seen to be held in trust. In cases where a man was dying without a son of age he might take measures to ensure continuity in the household for an interim period. Thus, in 1633, Sir John Gage directed that, after the customary period of three months' hospitality for all the household servants following his death, some of the older ones should be employed by his executors to keep the mansion and estate at Firle in good order until his son was of age to inherit.[51]

47. See D.R. Hainsworth, *Stewards, Lords and People: The Estate Steward and his World in Late Stuart England* (Cambridge, 1992).
48. J.P. Cooper, ed., *Wentworth Papers 1597–1628* (Camden Society, 12, 1973), p. 15.
49. H. Markland, ed., 'Instructions by Henry Percy Touching the Management of his Estate', *Archaeologia* 27 (1838), pp. 319–20, 327.
50. F. Heal, *Hospitality in Early Modern England* (Oxford, 1990), pp. 44–7.
51. Fletcher, *County Community in Peace and War*, pp. 39–40.

1.   Woman on top. Frontispiece from Anon., *The Deceyte of Women* (1561).

2. *(above)* Skimmington beats her husband. From *English Customs*.

3. The bedtime scold. Title-page from Richard Brathwaite, *Art Asleep Husband: A Boulster Lecture* (1640).

A BOVLSTER LECTVRE.

Dum loquor ista, taces?

Surdo canis

Will: Marshall. sculpsit.

This wife a wondrous racket meanes to keepe,
While th' Husband seemes to sleepe but do'es not sleepe:
But she might full as well her Lecture smother,
For ent'ring one Eare, it goes out at t'other.

4 and 5.   The Montacute Charivari: scenes from the plaster relief (*c.* 1600) in the Great Hall at Montacute House, Somerset.

Who marieth a Wife vppon a Moneday . If she will not be good vppon a Tewesday . Lett him go to y wood vppon a Wensday
And cutt him a cudgell vppon the Thursday. And pay her soundly vppon a Fryday. And she mend not y Diuil take her a Saterday
Then may he eate his meate in peace on the Sonday .

6.   Taming the Shrew. From Thomas Cecil, *A New Yeares Gift for Shrews* (*c.* 1620).

7.   A scold's bridle
and the 'Newcastle
cloak', an illustration
of punishments in
Newcastle-upon-
Tyne (*c.* 1700).

8. Scold's bridle, Newcastle-under-Lyne.

9. Scold's bridle, Doddington Park, Lincolnshire.

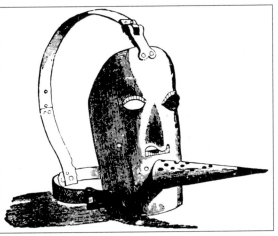

10. Woodcut of a ducking stool, sixteenth-century.

11. William Hogarth's skimmington ride (detail). One of a set of illustrations for Samuel Butler's *Hudibras* (1726).

12. The Four Humours. From L. Thurneisser, *Quinta Essentia* (1574).

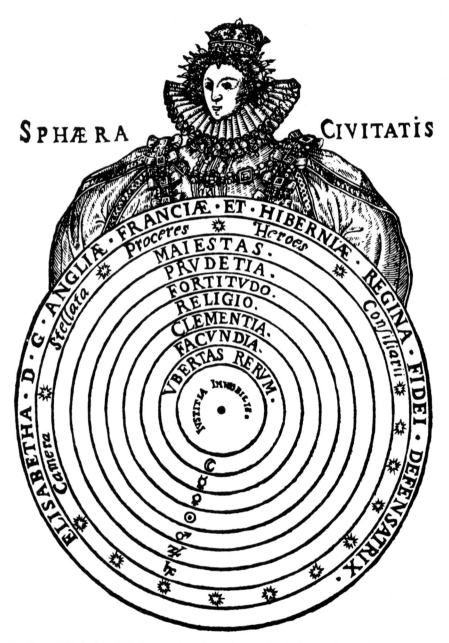

SPHÆRA CIVITATIS

FRANCIÆ · ET · HIBERNIÆ
ANGLIÆ
Proceres
Heroes
MAIESTAS ·
PRVDETIA ·
FORTITVDO ·
RELIGIO ·
CLEMENTIA ·
FACVNDIA ·
VBERTAS RERVM ·
IVSTITIA IMMOBILIS
Stellata
Camera
Consiliarii
REGINA · FIDEI · DEFENSATRIX ·
ELISABETHA · D · G ·

13.   Queen Elizabeth enfolds the cosmic and mundane worlds. Title-page from John Case, *Sphaera Civitatis* (1588).

14. Time unravels the unity of the cosmos. Title-page from Robert Fludd, *Utriusque Cosmi Historia* (1617).

15. The Great Chain of Being: a powerful visual metaphor for a divinely inspired universal hierarchy ranking all forms of higher and lower life; humans are represented by the male alone. From Didacus Valades, *Rhetorica Christiana* (1579).

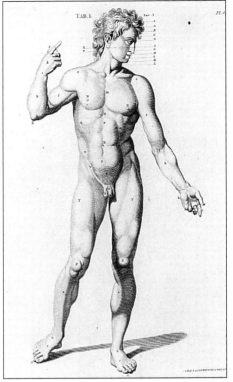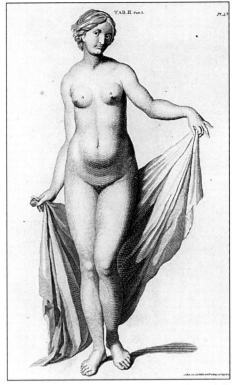

16 and 17. William Cowper's male and female nudes drawn to classical proportions. From Andrew Bell, *Anatomia Britannica: A System of Anatomy* (1798).

18. Title-page from Helkiah Crooke's *Microcosmographia* (1616).

19. Lady Anne Clifford, aged fifteen. From the Great Picture at Appleby
Castle attributed to Jan van Belcamp (1646).

20. *(left)* The attributes of the English gentlewoman. Frontispiece from Richard Brathwaite, *The English Gentlewoman* (1631).

21. The housewife's skills. Detail of frontispiece from Thomas Dawson, *The Good Huswife's Jewell* (1610).

22.   Charles Collyer of Wrexham Hall, Norfolk, aged eleven (1766). By Francis Cotes.

23. Mrs Thrale and her daughter Queenie (1781). By Joshua Reynolds.

24. *Connoisseurs in Rome, c.*1750 (detail).

Most Deare Mother:,

my petition to you is: that you will be pleased to Deliuer this
Enclosed to my father: I haue made bold to send him a
Regester: whereby hee may see my loue: and allso you:
how I haue spent my tyme: not that I haue been all this while
About it: but attgruing to it: I am Entring upon two: or three:
gume of flowers: and A little fruit (if you please) for the basket.
it is bespoken: but not yet made: I am allso Entring upon the
oyall: the which: together with my Dansing: and Sume other
neseßary things take of my tyme from my worke: but all:
Considered: I shall Indeauour to Improue my tyme for
the best: my humble Dutty to your selfe: my Respects
to my sisters: my Joyfull wishes Atending my Sister wooea
my thanks for her fauour: all being done: I beseech you
to beleiue mee:,
                Your most Affectionate: and
                Obedient Daughter:
                Katherine Oxinden:,

My most humble
Service presented:
M: F:

25. A schoolgirl's letter: Katherine Oxenden writes home to her mother (1655).

'Honour and reputation attached to good lordship, generosity and the appearance of an open household,' argues Felicity Heal in her major study of hospitality in this period. With the issue of hospitality, its rhetoric, symbolism and practice, we come to the means by which the gentry's pattern of life came to be invested with honour. The ideal of the open house was often stated and until at least the late seventeenth century, if to a varying extent, it carried weight in most gentry families. His table 'was ever fit to receive three or four besides my family, without any trouble, whatever their fare was they were sure to have a hearty welcome'. So wrote Sir Hugh Cholmley in an account of his own regime at Whitby in the 1630s. Edward Bash of Hertfordshire, as described by Thomas Fuller, is made exemplary: he 'was a hearty gentleman and a good English housekeeper, keeping a full table with solid dishes on it and welcome guests'.[52] Membership of the community of honour at the neighbourhood and county levels required the maintenance of a domestic establishment with the capacity to entertain men and their families from these social circles on both a formal and a spontaneous basis. The manor house should also act as the focus of hospitality for tenantry and the poor of the neighbourhood.

A celebrated quarrel between Sir Thomas Hoby and the Eure clan in the North Riding early in the seventeenth century shows how much shame could be made to attach to the failure to be generous. Hoby, a puritan intruder in a catholic environment, was made to suffer the humiliation of an uninvited hunting party descending on his home at Hackness, where they insulted his wife and damaged property. The case reverberated in Star Chamber and the Privy Council, both sides seeking to reclaim the high ground of honour by their manipulation of the rhetoric of hospitality.[53] A number of gentry household account books, by contrast, show the system working smoothly and illustrate how it did so. We find Sir Thomas Le Strange moving during the 1520s and 30s in a select but county-wide circle of Norfolk kin, friends and associates who often stayed with him at Hunstanton for a week or more. He in turn spent time visiting them in their homes. The pattern appears to have been one of simple conviviality: 'this gentry world', observes Felicity Heal, 'was already one of mutual good cheer, where the honour of the individual depended on a continual accessibility to known men of similar station.' There was some gender differentiation here such as was quite normal in the pattern of gentry sociability. In general we find wives visited Hunstanton with husbands but there were occasions in the Le Strange circle when wives went alone for births or christenings and other occasions, based upon business or hunting, when they were left at

52. Heal, *Hospitality in Early Modern England*, pp. 13, 183.
53. Heal, *Hospitality in Early Modern England*, pp. 13–14; see also G.C.F. Forster, 'Faction and County Government in Stuart Yorkshire', *Northern History* XI (1975), 74–6 and Manning, *Hunters and Poachers*, pp. 228–9.

home.[54] Christenings may more usually have been family affairs because of the involvement of both sexes in godparenthood. Sir Thomas Temple pressed a friend to be godfather to his new-born child in 1619: 'I expect the presence of my Lord Dacres and his lady, Sir Arthur Throckmorton and his lady,' he announced, all of whom together with his own family 'much desired to see you in this place'.[55]

This world of gentry sociability breathes an atmosphere of open and unabashed manhood, of educated but hardly sophisticated or refined men used to action rather than contemplation, who enjoyed everything life had to offer from hunting in their parks to feasting on the range of delicacies that the countryside and its wildlife provided. Two south coast gentry have left unusually intimate personal records which enable us to envisage their style of life and values. The keynote of Sir John Oglander's notebook covering the period from the 1620s to the 1650s is his great pride in the conviction that he kept one of the best houses in the close-knit community of the gentry of the Isle of Wight. Oglander was very much the plain country squire marking every event by sufficient food and drink. His approval of his neighbour and friend Sir Richard Worsley provides a striking insight into where he thought honour lay: he 'kept a very bountiful house and gave great entertainment; lived in great repute in his country and very happily'.[56] The friendships that the Sussex gentleman Sir Thomas Pelham inspired are attested by the record of the rings that some of his colleagues in county affairs gave him in their wills. One of them, Sir Walter Covert, bequeathed him forty pounds to buy 'a piece of plate in token of remembrance of the love I had born him'. Services of all kinds bound Pelham to associates in the neighbourhood of his home at Halland: coastal gentry sent him fish, downland ones ewes and wethers or the wheatears which were a delicacy he especially prized on his table. Correspondence reveals the nuances which preserved a sense of hierarchy within a gentry community such as this Sussex one. Sir Thomas cultivated the friendship of the Earl of Northumberland at Petworth who made available the breeding facilities of his stud. Nicholas Gildredge, a man only beginning to climb his way into the ranks of the county families, could write obsequiously to congratulate Pelham on his second marriage in 1637: 'Be pleased not to disdain this empty appearance of his full joy at this your happy day and choice, whose obligements to you are therefore more than others, because his merits less than any's.' The funeral of such a county figure was a signal moment for the community marked with a spectacular display, as Pelham himself had directed, of 'friends, kinsmen and servants in mourning'. Vast quantities of cloth, ribbon, serge and baize were used; there were black hatbands and livery stockings for servants and tenants; even the coach and horses

54. Heal, *Hospitality in Early Modern England*, pp. 59–62.
55. HEH, STT 2350.
56. Heal, *Hospitality in Early Modern England*, p. 184.

were clothed in black. Pelham's funeral procession expressed by its reverence and respect the neighbourhood and locality's recognition of the virtue and leadership which was seen as inherent in gentry honour.[57]

In some cases religious loyalty or particular intellectual interests pulled against the tradition of open hospitality to all the gentry of the local community. Yet the compromises men adopted in this respect usually gave weight to social solidarity. Gervase Holles records that the Earl of Clare enjoyed civil conversation with all his guests. At the same time, however, he made his table a debating chamber on issues of divinity, philosophy and history. Sir Thomas Lucy was another who fulfilled double objectives:

> To his table, which was always choicely sumptuous, all good men were ever most welcome, especially if professors of either sacred or secular learning, wherein though he were so rare a proficient that he was accounted a living library, yet was he incessantly acted with an impetuous desire after a greater height.

Puritan gentry like Lord Brooke at Warwick Castle were likely to show a strong clerical element in their guest lists, providing as they did a focus for godly ministers to meet in their households. For such men entertaining took the form of maintaining a 'household of faith', as William Hinde put it in his biography of the Cheshire gentleman John Bruen. He kept open house for his Sunday dinners following sermons by invited preachers in his private chapel. His ideal was that all who visited him should do so 'not so much . . . for the ease and refreshing of their bodies, as for the comfort and rejoicing of their hearts, in seeing his face, in hearing his voice, in confessing and advising with him.' Bruen was quite ready to practise a customary kind of hospitality in the hope of making converts. Catholic families had good reason to be exclusive about their social life out of sheer defensiveness with regard to their own exclusion from the inner circles of local and national government. The great catholic families tended to find wives, socialise and support each other across the country as a whole, but this did not preclude some effort to keep a foothold in the county communities of gentry. The Petres at Ingatestone Hall in Essex entertained local protestant gentry like Sir Thomas Mildmay and Sir Gamaliel Capel. Sir Thomas Pelham purchased a goshawk from his catholic neighbour Sir John Gage of Firle and called in the local fiddlers when Lady Gage paid a social call to Halland. The maintenance of their honour demanded gestures by catholic gentry which secured recognition among men of their own kind.[58]

Hospitality and assistance to countrymen and the poor effected the

57. Fletcher, *A County Community in Peace and War*, pp. 49–53.
58. HEH, STT Literature Box 2; Heal, *Hospitality in Early Modern England*, pp. 105, 171, 175–6; Fletcher, *A County Community in Peace and War*, p. 101.

display of virtue in its most direct and practical form. Advice to sons in this regard was highly paternalistic. Sir Richard Grosvenor encouraged his son to be moderate over fines and rents:

> so that they may be diligent to be commanded by you and to be useful to you. Remember they are planted under you not to be tyrannised over but to be protected. . . . Count it your credit to own rich tenants and your glory when they live in plenty and are able with alacrity to call you in and make you drink when you pass by their doors.[59]

Eulogies stressed the performance of charitable roles. At Chipping Camden, where some of his buildings still remain, the monument to Sir Baptist Hicks, who was the town's generous seventeenth-century benefactor, calls upon it to hold him in reverend memory: 'Oh fortunate Camden . . . he adorned your land with spacious buildings and beautiful gardens and did not allow the house of God to be neglected but gave strong support to the poor.' Christopher Wandesford set before his sons in the 1630s the example of their Yorkshire grandfather 'whose neighbourly and friendly behaviour to his equals, mildness and care to perform offices of love and bounty towards his inferiors begot him . . . a singular respect and dependency in the whole country'.[60] 'Many poor labourers he daily employed', it was noted on Sir Thomas Lucy's monument, 'many neighbour towns he yearly refreshed sending them plentiful provision.'[61] The basic ideals remained constant into the eighteenth century, though the form that hospitality took changed considerably during our period. The monument to Sir Robert Atkyns at Sapperton in Gloucestershire summarises a familiar pattern of reputation: 'He was always loyal to his Prince, loving to his wife, faithful to his friends, charitable to the poor, kind and courteous to his neighbours, just to all, sober and serious in his conversation and a peacemaker to the uttermost of his power.'[62]

A central argument of Felicity Heal's study of hospitality in this period is that two dichotomies led to a separation of social experience 'in ways which ultimately sanctioned the marginalization of the notion of hospitality'. The dichotomies were those of the country, which was hospitable, against the city and court which was not, and of the past, which was hospitable, whereas the present was not. The argument relates to the decline of honour as the central motivating concept of gentry manhood and the rise of an alternative concept of civility, which will be discussed in chapter 16 below. In the first place there is the change from a graded hierarchy of sociability to eighteenth-century social polarity. Full commensuality – master, family, guests and servants eating in the hall –

59. Cited in Cust and Lake, 'Sir Richard Grosvenor', in *BIHR* LIV (1981), p. 50.
60. Cited in Heal, *Hospitality in Early Modern England*, p. 184.
61. HEH, STT Literature Box 2.
62. J. Simmons, ed., *English County Historians* (Wakefield, 1978), p. 63.

had vanished in many manor houses by 1500. Yet it was normal throughout the sixteenth and much of the seventeenth century for a good deal of
dining with guests to take place in semi-public great chambers and
parlours. The impulse to privacy made a gradual impact, producing a
widening gulf between employers and employed which came to be
expressed architecturally in various upstairs and downstairs arrangements.
By around 1700 it was becoming common for tenants and visiting
servants on business to be taken into the servants' hall rather than into the
house itself. The related issues were presence and absence and access and
denial. The lure of London made itself strongly felt from the late Elizabethan period onwards and it was strengthened by the increasing
availability of coaches which made travel for wives more comfortable.[63]
With many families purchasing London residences, visits became
longer. Country hospitality declined as households broke up or were
placed on board wages. The formal house, with its linear arrangement of rooms for entertaining, facilitated selectiveness in the squire's
access to guests and the possibility of isolating himself from those he did
not wish to see.

The significance of these changes is indicated by the attitude of
Sir John Reresby to keeping Christmas at home in 1687. 'Hospitality',
he remarked in a letter to the secretary of state, 'being much laid aside of
late in these parts of this time of the year, which dissatisfieth the
common sort of people and makes them apt to despond, I left York
very lately to observe my constant custom of keeping an open Christmas
here.' The note is one of studied attention to political interest and
of active paternalism. Keeping Christmas in lavish and traditional style
had been a contentious issue earlier in the century, when James I
and Charles I sought to drive gentry in London home to their estates
at this time of year. At that stage there was still a consensus that
honour was in some sense at stake. Reresby, by contrast, writes with
calculation and condescension. It was not so much his manly role as a
Yorkshire squire or even social emulation in the circles of the county's
gentry which entered the matter; the issue was more one of social
control.[64]

The household was not a private world. This made it all the more
necessary, many gentry believed, for men in their sector of society to seek
privacy and time to compose themselves. The Earl of Huntingdon's
advice to his son around 1613 concluded with a section on 'the disposing
and due ordering of thine own private affairs'. The Earl of Carberry
recommended his son in 1651 to withdraw 'into your closet or some
private part of your chamber' every night. Sir Henry Slingsby thought
reading from past authors 'in private and retired hours' was the best way

63. Fletcher, *A County Community in Peace and War*, pp. 42–4; above, pp. 27–8.
64. Heal, *Hospitality in Early Modern England*, pp. 40, 147–68, 186–7.

to acquire wisdom.[65] More gentry than previously in the seventeenth century were keeping diaries and commonplace books or composing autobiographical accounts of their lives. This emphasis on serious contemplation and study accords with the dedication to effective oversight of households and estates together with fulfilment of obligations in the conduct of public business which so many gentry displayed. What went with this was an obsession, shared equally by men and women, about privacy. Honour was always in danger from disloyal servants. It was servants over and over again who testified in the adultery and cruelty cases heard in the Court of Arches.[66] The world was seen as infinitely censorious and ready to make the most of gossip.

It is predictable that women should be anxious about the circulation of information regarding such emotionally charged issues as courtship and marriage. 'Let nobody know of these matters though they be but trifling,' wrote Lady Anne Clifford about a proposed marriage her father was negotiating. More commonly it was the possibility of family discord seeping into the public domain that bothered people. A gentleman could not hold up his face against stories that gained currency about his failure to maintain patriarchal household order; a family at variance at once lost credit. When Thomas Elmes and Margaret Verney agreed to part after years of troubled marriage in 1617, Thomas wanted the business to be 'done in a way that nobody may know, certainly guess they will, but know they need not'. When Samuel Pepys found Elizabeth's letter about how unhappy she was in 1663, it was the issue of his 'disgrace and dishonour' if anyone read it that mattered most to him. When they had failed to resolve a family dispute in the 1630s, Sir Simonds D'Ewes pressed his brother-in-law that they should 'continue together ... least the world should imagine we were fallen out'. Their reconciliation, Charles Hatton told his brother Christopher, would 'put a stop to the scandal and disquiet which from an open variance, wheresoever the offence be, must yet equally increase upon them both'. A letter from Lady Philips in 1638, when she and her son were squabbling about payment of her jointure and the debts owed by her late husband, is revealing in what it tells us about how precisely she understood the issue of family honour in such a situation, with its various ingredients of probity, duty and purposiveness over financial obligations: 'Ned do not for your own credit suffer your father's slips to be brought upon the stage to his dishonour by your undutifulness towards me.' Even more interesting, for what it tells us about the dilemma a man faced when his patriarchal imperative clashed with the need to maintain face, is an incident related by Sir John Reresby

65. Citations from L.A. Pollock, 'Living on the Stage of the World: the Concept of Privacy among the Elite of Early Modern England', in A. Wilson, ed., *Rethinking Social History: English Society 1570–1920 and its Interpretation* (Manchester, 1993), p. 85.
66. L. Stone, *Broken Lives: Separation and Divorce in England 1660–1857* (Oxford, 1993).

in his *Memoirs*. In 1686 the Duke of Welbeck had asked him to intervene in a dispute with his wife about who their daughters should marry after he had failed to persuade her to toe his line. One of the suitors then abandoned his courtship. This led Reresby to reflect as follows:

> So fatal to families are those differences occasioned by the folly of husband or wife, or both, and if of the latter, though the man hath spirit (if hath sense with it), he will suffer in some degree the insolency of a woman rather than make it public to the prejudice of his children, especially daughters, who are seldom desired out of such families.[67]

Reresby's assumptions appear to be that the sons of such a house might be under suspicion as men likely to lack manly nerve and command like their father and the daughters, even more seriously, would be suspected of bearing their mother's strain of recalcitrance and disobedience. His words are an acute comment on the current concept of how honour rested in the family as a whole and how the present determined the future. We are reminded just how weighty was the trust that a seventeenth-century gentleman carried.

Throughout the period from 1500 to 1800 local government in England rested on the unpaid services of numerous country gentry who staffed the commissions of the peace, served in the lieutenancy and were pricked annually as sheriffs.[68] Reputation and prestige were the rewards of this service. The language of honour with which it was suffused was part of a common currency in public business understood by all men who became engaged in service to the crown. He always 'esteemed an ounce of honour more than a pound of profit', insisted Lord Hunsdon to Sir Robert Cecil in 1596, seeking the office of justice *en oyer* in the Isle of Wight: it would be 'honour for His Majesty to give and disgrace for me not to receive, being so with a general allowance named to it that none . . . stand competitors with me'.[69] The transactions of honour, such as where men sat on the bench, precedence in public processions and who doffed their caps to whom, were part and parcel of county and urban government, providing constant reiteration through symbolic representations of the differences in social rank and quality on which order rested.[70] Moreover county government emerged as the chief forum for gentry assertiveness, feud and faction fighting absorbing energies which had previously found an outlet in martial and chivalric pursuits. Letters

67. Citations from Wilson, ed., *Rethinking Social History*, pp. 87–9.
68. For a general account see my *Reform in the Provinces: The Government of Stuart England* (London, 1986).
69. *HMC Salisbury MSS*, IV, p. 488; see also Fletcher and Stevenson, eds, *Order and Disorder*, p. 94.
70. For examples see Fletcher and Stevenson, eds, *Order and Disorder*, pp. 96–8.

between Sir Robert Harley and Sir Walter Pye over their election as knights of the shire for Herefordshire in the 1626 parliament illustrate the point. Harley, present at quarter sessions when the matter was discussed, only agreed to serve if named first, reminding the company there that he was a Knight of the Bath whereas Pye was only a Knight Bachelor. 'I understood it would point at my dishonour in this service to have second place,' he wrote subsequently to Pye. An icy correspondence followed, in which both parties vigorously manipulated the concepts of political representation and social solidarity to their own ends. Pye gave way out of good will but reserved his position on the issue of where precedency actually lay: 'I do really and freely desire that you may be first returned and this is done for the love I bear Sir Robert Harley and his house.' In a masterly response Harley insisted with the utmost politeness that he could not let the matter rest, throwing in the argument that precedency besides election depended upon 'a public suffrage of our country': 'If you please not to acknowledge the right precedency to belong to my knighthood before yours, you will then give me leave to justify it in such a way as shall maintain my honour and not impair yours.'[71] What is striking about these exchanges, even if they represent an extreme case, is that gentry could invest themselves and their manhood so deeply in matters of public recognition which signified the importance of their various social roles in the parish, county and nation. Internalising the values of the honour code, they spent their energy on desperate efforts to externalise its effects in a way that becomes almost ritualistic.

Government for huge numbers of country gentry became simply an integral part of a way of life. Recognisances were signed and suspects interviewed in the hall or parlour; petty sessions were held with neighbouring justices who worked in close partnership in the inns of nearby market towns; quarter sessions and assizes in the shire hall were chief occasions of the administrative year when JPs dined and debated in the best hostelries of the county. Magisterial work involved an untiring devotion to the minutiae of local disorder. A letter from Sir Hamon Le Strange to his Norfolk colleague and friend Sir Roger Townshend in 1632 shows how this work was often anchored in the rounds of social intercourse and hospitality: 'I hope your lady is now well recovered again and I desire that you will assist us at Fakenham upon Thursday next in the despatch of common and country business . . . I pray you kiss my pretty godson for me.'[72] Men sought esteem by seeking county offices; the exercise of virtue was a necessary condition to preserve this esteem when they were appointed. Once on the stage a man had to watch every move,

71. BL, Loan MS 29/202. There are accounts in Fletcher and Stevenson, eds, *Order and Disorder*, pp. 98–9 and M.A. Kishlansky, *Parliamentary Selection: Social and Political Choice in Early Modern England* (Cambridge, 1986), p. 69. For parliamentary election procedure in Herefordshire at this time see Kishlansky, p. 26.
72. Norfolk RO, NE 4.

as Edmund Bohun noted in his tract on magisterial office of 1684. 'All men', he was sure, 'will be prying into his most secret retirements and will be as curious to inform themselves of the smallest of his faults as they are negligent of the greatest they are guilty of themselves.'[73] The only possible catastrophe was dismissal from office which could bring mortifying disgrace. This was what Sir Francis Hastings felt he suffered in Somerset when James I deprived him of his places on the bench and in the deputy lieutenancy. 'I might justly think myself a most unhappy man, if after thirty-seven years painful and faithful service . . . I should shut up my last days with disgrace,' he told Sir Robert Cecil in 1605. Later in the year, dismissed from his militia command, he pleaded with the Earl of Hertford to be allowed to appoint his own deputy. Denial of this, he argued, would 'raise great doubts of me in the thoughts of the vulgar sort in my county'. Some, he feared, 'will be found forward enough in willingness to trample upon me if they find even so small stepping stone to lift them up'. There is a palpable feeling that Hastings's sense of identity is slipping from him as his reputation does so. His very manhood, it seems, is under attack and his social position feels equally threatened.[74]

If the correspondence of Sir Francis Hastings shows the vulnerability gentry could suffer once they had taken the public stage, stories of local feuding have an opposite lesson. For if the risks of office were unnerving, the prizes in terms of fame, acclaim and self agrandisment were glittering. The code of gentry honour, as we have seen in the dealings between them of Sir Robert Harley and Sir Walter Pye, required certain routines of courtesy and good manners. These, however, could veil a rank competitiveness which could be prolonged for months and sometimes years. When he was ambushed by his inveterate enemy Sir Arthur Heveningham as he rode along the Wymondham to Norwich highway in 1583, Edward Flowerdew refused to duel, pleading that he was about the Queen's business and unarmed. Heveningham spurred his horse after him and struck him on the head, giving him a grievous wound. The proof of it was showed in court shortly afterwards when one of Flowerdew's servants appeared with his master's bloodstained hat. Flowerdew managed to get Heveningham and his men bound over to keep the peace and later obtained an out of court settlement in a Star Chamber case which involved a payment of six hundred pounds in damages.[75] Another Star Chamber case was fought out between Sir Thomas Hoby, one of the most overbearing and touchy of all Stuart magistrates, and his colleague in

73. E. Bohun, The Justice of Peace his Calling (London, 1684), pp. 19–20; Fletcher, Reform in the Provinces, p. 144.
74. C. Cross, ed., The Letters of Sir Francis Hastings (Somerset Record Society, LXIX, 1969), pp. xxv, 92–7. For a fuller account see Fletcher and Stevenson, eds, Order and Disorder, pp. 95–6.
75. A. Hassell Smith, County and Court (Oxford, 1974), pp. 197–8, 233–4.

the Yorkshire deputy lieutenancy Sir Richard Cholmley. Hoby took Cholmley to court in 1609 alleging that he had twice spoken contemptuously to him at the county musters. He hoped, it seems, to provoke an open quarrel in front of the assembled Yorkshiremen or even perhaps a duel. Cholmley had also, it was said, publicly denounced the validity of warrants issued by Hoby in his capacity as a JP. Hoby kept up a disputatious career with one rival after another in the North Riding for more than thirty years. He was a man who never let go and, despite many local enmities, eventually in the 1630s he became Custos Rotulorum in Yorkshire.[76]

The combination of intransigence and disciplined self-control exhibited by men like Flowerdew and Hoby shows English manhood becoming civil. They showed respect for the rules of the game, kept cool under provocation and channelled anger and resentment into disputations and lengthy legal proceedings. Such men were beginning to embody qualities which came to be seen as part of a peculiarly English set of manly characteristics. By the eighteenth century, notes Keith Thomas with regard to the nation's canine obsession, 'it was above all the bulldog, clinging tenaciously to its much larger opponent, which was singled out for special commendation'. One writer described the British bulldog as 'probably the most courageous creature in the world'. 'The courage of bulldogs', declared David Hume in 1777, 'seems peculiar to England.' In time 'the ancient genuine race of true bred English bulldogs' became, \ with some careful invention of tradition, something of a national emblem.[77] In 1863 the image found its quintessential expression in Charles Kingsley's account of Tom in the *Water Babies*: he 'was always a brave determined little English bulldog who never knew when he was beaten'.[78]

Magistrates varied in their performance from obstinate neglect of duty to indefatigability. Edmund Bohun was scathing about men who 'look to nothing but the credit, honour and reputation' they might obtain through office 'and if they can gain the title of Right Worshipful and have their neighbours stand bare-headed to them they have their designs'.[79] It is easy to sympathise with men's desire as they got older to avoid long days in the saddle and away from home comforts. Henry Wollaston summarised his excuses in a letter to the clerk of the peace at Chelmsford as 'age sixty-four, the length and badness of the ways and culverts'.[80] But there were many whose dedication was remarkable and who worked incredibly hard for long periods of years. The survival of commonplace books, memoranda books and private papers enables us

76. G.C.F. Forster, 'Faction and County Government in Stuart Yorkshire', *Northern History*, XI (1975), pp. 76–82.
77. Thomas, *Man and the Natural World*, p. 108.
78. *OED*: 'bulldog'.
79. Bohun, *The Justice of Peace*, p. 135.
80. A.C. Edwards, *English History from Essex Sources* (Chelmsford, 1952), p. 36.

to appreciate the particular qualities of mind and character which characterised the outstanding magistrates of the age. Men with strong opinions about social order and political authority were well motivated to become engaged. Yet they also needed devotion to methodical and efficient personal record-keeping to perform exceptionally. The Shropshire gentleman Henry Townshend was so singleminded that he spent hours studying the records of administration in his shire, besides central directions, systematically interleaving his copy of the JP's handbook *The Complete Justice* with references. Like the Sussex JP Sir Walter Covert, Townshend intended that his law books should be of use to others who took up the reins of service to the county after him.[81] In this respect Covert's choice of words in his will, made in 1631 at eighty-eight when he had only recently retired from public business, is interesting: his books should remain in his study 'as standards in my house to be and inure to the sole use and benefit of my next heir'. His intention was fulfilled nearly thirty years later when his nephew became a Restoration JP. We can sense how the notions of lineage, virtue and service were mixed in the conception of honour sought and achieved by this notable public man.[82]

The immense correspondence of Sir Daniel Fleming, a JP in Westmoreland from the 1660s to 1701, illustrates the fulfilment that a man of enormous energy and commitment could find in local preeminence. We sense his swelling pride when he reported in 1672 that one of the assize judges had told him he was spoken of in London as 'the most accomplished justice of the peace in the northern counties'.[83] Fleming loved to lead. In 1666 his postbag from London included a declaration by Charles II against the French which had just been proclaimed in London. He used the opportunity of a muster of his foot company at Kendal a few days later for a patriotic ritual against 'a nation which heretofore used to truckle under us':

> I got the mayor of this town – who is my ensign – to appear with all his brethren, the aldermen in their gowns and with their maces etc to be also aiding them . . . together with several justices of the peace for this county and other gentlemen. So soon as the declaration was proclaimed my men gave a volley shot, with a hearty shout to second the same.[84]

81. R.D. Hunt, ed., *Henry Townshend's 'Notes of the Office of Justice of Peace' 1661–3* (Worcestershire Historical Society, IV, 1967, Miscellany, vol. II), pp. 64–75, 80–82, 127–30; Fletcher, *Reform in the Provinces*, pp. 153–4.

82. PRO, Prob 11/161/12; Fletcher, *A County Community in Peace and War*, pp. 121–2. Covert's deputy lieutenancy letter book is in the British Library, Harleian MS 703.

83. *HMC Le Fleming MSS*, p. 91. See also A. Macfarlane, *The Justice and the Mare's Ale* (Oxford, 1981), pp. 39–43.

84. *HMC Le Fleming MSS*, pp. 39–40. For Fleming's activities see also Fletcher, *Reform in the Provinces*, pp. 20, 104, 149–50, 162, 347–8.

For a man like Fleming honour was a matter of example, of studied application and constant performance. The word, as we shall see below in discussion of the ambitions he held for his sons, was one that came easily to his pen.[85]

The godly magistrate, in the full sense of the term, was an untypical figure but one who is important in our consideration of gender and class roles, especially in the Elizabethan and early Stuart period. For such men were exemplars to others. Hassell Smith's research into the memoranda books of Sir Nathaniel Bacon of Stiffkey has revealed how a dynamic and unsparing landlord and JP could create in his own small local corner of Norfolk something that approached his ideal of a godly commonwealth. Bacon was a straitlaced puritan, austere in his housekeeping, scrupulous in his impartiality and exacting in his insistence that public duty always came before private advantage.[86] Men like Sir Nathaniel Barnardiston of Kedington in Suffolk, the Somerset quarter sessions chairman John Harrington, Sir Robert Harley and John Bruen can be considered in the same context. Patrick Collinson's remark about Harley, that in his exemplary and exceptional dedication to religion he was one of 'a very small, special and self-conscious elite', can stand for all these men.[87] Their militant puritanism gave their manhood an extra quality that suffused everything they did. If there was an element of self-fashioning in the puritan's style of life and conduct of public business, his commitment to certain evangelical ideals, to virtue and morality, was at the same time deeply authentic.

'The administration of justice to others should incite us to excel in righteousness ourselves,' Harrington told his colleagues in an address at quarter sessions. There was no boundary between private behaviour and public example for these men. Harrington led campaigns in Somerset against drunkenness, swearing, profaning the sabbath and the practice of usury. His watchword was 'that we have a calling from God to do this work'.[88] Dedicated puritan JPs of this kind often worked in close partnership with a specially chosen and sympathetic cleric who set the tone of the household and parish worship which was the source of strength that sustained their wider efforts for reform. This is the 'magistracy and ministry' which Collinson has explored in his accounts of two particular partnerships: that of Samuel Fairclough and Nathaniel Barnardiston in Suffolk and that of Thomas Pierson and Sir Robert Harley in Herefordshire. Fairclough's funeral elegy for Barnardiston characterises him as 'Thou stately top-bough of a noble stem, one of God's jewels and thy

85. Below, pp. 303–4, 314, 322.
86. A. Hassell Smith, *County and Court*, pp. 169–73; A. Hassell Smith, G.R. Baker and R.W. Kenny, eds, *The Papers of Nathaniel Bacon of Stiffkey*, I and II (Centre of East Anglian Studies, Norwich, 1979, 1983).
87. Collinson, *Religion of Protestants*, p. 168.
88. Cliffe, *Puritan Gentry*, p. 61.

country's gem'. The formulation neatly encapsulates the lineage and
virtue in which his honour consisted and a fluid sense of the local worlds
in which it had been so fruitfully expressed. Barnardiston's 'country' had
been Kedington and Suffolk and East Anglia.[89]

Robert Harley's world, centred upon the remote Welsh borderland
village of Brampton Bryan, is exceptionally well documented. It was
highly exclusive: 'we must be careful of our families, of our parents,
of our kindred, if they be of the household of faith', wrote Lady
Brilliana Harley in her commonplace book, 'our delightest love must only
be to the saints on earth'. At Brampton servants were chosen for their
godliness and godly tenants were treated especially favourably. The house
was a centre of zealous worship with the practice of regular private
fasts. The company at table included the most committed puritan
ministers from around the Welsh Marches. The Harley household lived
intensely.[90] Thomas Froysell maintained in the panegyric at Harley's death
in 1658 that, through his spiritual leadership in the district, 'many
thousand souls' were prevented from the sinful pursuit of Sunday sports
and instead 'sat under the droppings of the word'. Froysell expanded
upon Harley's dedication to moral reform. He was 'a most nimble soul
of zeal against sin. He was full of spirits against all dishonours done to
God, he was a terror to evil works, he knew no respect of persons in
a business wherein God was wronged.'[91] Harley's papers include
correspondence with John Bruen in Cheshire about their joint campaign
for moral and evangelical reform. Bruen used to write to Harley as his
'most dear and Christian cousin'. As Collinson has put it, 'these were
singular men, close and intimate with one another across county boundaries'.[92] When we investigate their minds and enter their society we find
gentry honour so permeated by religion that much of what has been
described in this chapter as its core – the hunting, the good cheer, the
open hospitality – is driven to the periphery. For a select band of gentry
scattered across the country honour virtually became conscience and its
performance could only be viewed in terms of zeal. A puritan, wrote
Harley, formulating his personal definition, was 'one that dares do
nothing in the worship of God or course of his life but what God's word
warrants him . . . his sins are more than other men's, because he
sees them, and greater because he feels them'.[93] Whether we call it
self-fashioning or see it as gender in seventeenth-century terms, the

89. Collinson, *Religion of Protestants*, pp. 164–7.
90. For all this and for the citation see Eales, *Puritans and Roundheads*, pp. 43–69.
91. Cited in J.T. Cliffe, *The Puritan Gentry* (London, 1984), p. 199.
92. Collinson, *Religion of Protestants*, pp. 162–9.
93. Cited in J. Eales, *Puritans and Roundheads: The Harleys of Brampton Bryan and the Outbreak of the English Civil War* (Cambridge, 1990), pp. 46–7. See also J.S. Eales, 'Sir Robert Harley KB (1579–1656) and the "Character" of a Puritan', *British Library Journal* XV (1989).

words bring us as close as we are likely to come to one magistrate's sense of himself and of his purpose and destiny as a man set to lead others.

This chapter has considered honour as a point of entry to male gender in public and private life. Their honour, it is argued, is the concept through which the gentry attempted to live out their manhood in relation to their destined patriarchal role. This amounted to the display, in the various spheres in which they moved, of a set of personal, moral and intellectual qualities learnt and imbibed through the grammar school and university training such men had experienced. William Bellassys, his tomb at Coxwold in Yorkshire announces, had 'lived with honour, both as a youth and an old man'. How far, how deeply and in what sense, all these men really 'lived with honour' is beyond recapture. But we can leave the last word with two wives whose tributes, if hardly objective were certainly not written simply for public consumption. Lady Grace Mildmay's 'meditation upon the corpse' of her husband in the 1620s strikes a note of private grief at the end of almost fifty years as a 'faithful wife'. Her encomium is heartfelt:

> He never carried malice in his heart towards any. He was charitable and of a compassionate mind. . . . He was not covetous nor wordly. He loved hospitality and bounty. He was of a free heart and good nature. He was not treacherous but faithful in all things, nor he never deceived any trust. He was very well instructed from his tender youth in the grounds of his faith in Jesus Christ and in his truth and he was more sincere in his own heart before God than he made show of to the world.[94]

Margaret Cavendish's autobiographical memoir entitled 'a true relation of my birth, breeding and life' was written while she was in exile with her husband the Duke of Newcastle during the 1650s. A passage about his character appears in the midst of a section about the pleasures of their life together. This appeared in print during her lifetime in 1656 appended to her collection of stories entitled *Nature's Pictures*. For Margaret Cavendish her husband's honour was undoubtedly her honour. The core of that honour was his many-sided virtue:

> For the truth is, my lord is a person whose humour is neither extravagantly merry nor unnecessarily sad. His mind is above his fortune, as his generosity is above his purse, his courage above danger, his justice above bribes, his friendship above self-interest, his truth too firm for falsehood, his temperance beyond temptation. His conversation is pleasing and affable; his wit is quick and his judgement is strong, distinguishing clearly without clouds of mistakes, dissecting truth so as

94. L.A. Pollock, *With Faith and Physic: The Life of a Tudor Gentlewoman Lady Grace Mildmay 1552–1620* (London, 1993), p. 41.

it justly admit not of disputes. His discourse is always new upon the occasion, without troubling the hearers with old historical relations, nor stuffed with useless sentences. His behaviour is manly without formality and free without constraint: and his mind hath the same freedom. His nature is noble and his disposition sweet. His loyalty is proved by his public service for his King and country.[95]

Their honour provided the gentry of Tudor and Stuart England with a strongly established and deeply rooted code of behaviour. Universal achievement of the code is not the point. Patriarchy worked because enough men gave themselves to it wholeheartedly to ensure that order in the family, the household and the local community was maintained. We need to explore more fully what kind of a patriarchy this was, how far it actually involved the subordination of women and how far its harsher features were tempered by milder ones.

95. E. Graham, H. Hinds, E. Hoby and H. Wilcox, eds, *Her Own Life: Autobiographical Writings by Seventeenth-Century Englishwomen* (London, 1989), p. 93.

8. *Husbands and Wives: Case Studies*

THIS CHAPTER CONSISTS of nine case studies of well documented gentry marriages between the reigns of Queen Elizabeth and Queen Anne which are intended to open the doors more fully on the sexual politics of intimate relationship at this time. The sources that are used here – letters, diaries and personal memoirs – are private; that is none of those who wrote them can have expected them to reach any kind of public domain. There is no claim, of course, that these case studies have any kind of typicality but they do allow us to make a decisive move from precept to some examples of practice. The series begins with five marriages which seem to exhibit wives, in due course at least, extracting from their more or less willing husbands a considerable degree of real partnership; it continues, by contrast, with two marriages in which the wives remained apparently more basically submissive; and it ends with two cases in which male subordination of wives generated some deep resentment.

The marriage of John Thynne and Joan Hayward in 1575 brought together the heir to Longleat, still then being built, with the merchant wealth of a family that had just invested in land in Shropshire. This was an arranged marriage between a girl of sixteen 'very well brought up both in learning and in all things that do appertain to a gentlewoman' and a youth of twenty-four reported to be 'no roister'. There was no great love or sexual attraction on either side so far as we can tell to start with: rather acquiescence in parental dealings. But Joan was a young woman of spirit who took badly to the way she was treated by her husband's family at Longleat while he enjoyed his young energies in London. Her early letters, signed 'your obedient wife', attempted, probably unsuccessfully, to prompt him to his duty in standing up for her and in pleasing her father with whom he at first lodged. She was spirited enough to call patriarchal obligations into play, urging that her father could reasonably expect John to 'humble yourself and know your duty towards him, as it is the part of a natural son to do to his father as I need not reveal it unto you for you know it very well'.

The maturing relationship between these two young people can be detected behind the rhetoric of submission in Joan's forms of address and parting. Her husband remained throughout their twenty-nine years of marriage simply 'Good Mr Thynne'; she became 'your loving and faithful wife' or more normally his 'ever' or 'assured' 'loving wife'. She was never satisfied with the minimal time he found for her, fretting at the lack of letters from him and urging him to 'heigh ye home'. But, as mistress of Longleat from 1580 onwards, she earned respect from him by her energy and skills in managing the household and estate while he, becoming increasingly cantankerous, built up court contacts from the base of their London home. In her later years, occupying her dowry Caus Castle in Shropshire, Joan Thynne proved herself the master of complex legal affairs as well as of dealing with crops and cattle. The two letters of John Thynne which survive provide explicit evidence that a marriage which began uncertainly had become, more than twenty years later, the mainstay of this couple's lives. John accepted his wife's instructing in how he should handle his legal and political affairs and her criticisms of his inefficient handling of business. He appreciated her wide-ranging competence. She had learnt to give him enough theoretical authority, by her meek phrasings of requests, to satisfy the requirements of his manhood. 'My Good Pug', John Thynne begins his letter of 26 July 1601 excusing his delay in London, 'I must confess that I have been long absent and much longer than my desire.' 'Your ever loving husband during life', he signs himself, declaring at the finish 'God bless you and all my children and send me peace with all the world.'[1]

The letter which Maria Thynne wrote to her mother-in-law Joan on 15 September 1601 must be one of the most touching of all the historical survivals relating to family life in the past in England. It is a plea to be accepted into her husband's family: Maria hopes God will exercise power 'to the turning of your heart towards me' (plate 26). Joan's heart had been turned away since her son Thomas constructed a clandestine marriage with Maria at the Bell Inn in Beaconsfield one night six years previously. Both of them were then sixteen: he was the heir to the Longleat and Caus estates; she was from the house of the Thynne's bitterest enemies in Wiltshire society, the Marvin family. It has been said that, when the marriage was revealed in 1595 and the story was all the rage, Shakespeare was prompted to write *Romeo and Juliet* as a warning against the evil consequences of such gentry feuding. Maria's bid to conciliate her implacable mother-in-law still bears her family's seal with a lock of dark red hair sealed under.

This second Thynne marriage, to which Thomas's parents were never reconciled, was and remained very much a love match. It lasted until

1. For these two paragraphs, see A.D. Wall, 'Elizabethan Precept and Feminine Practice: The Thynne Family of Longleat', *History*, LXX (1990), pp. 27–37; A.D. Wall, ed., *Two Elizabethan Women: Correspondence of Joan and Maria Thynne 1575–1611* (Wiltshire Record Society, vol. XXXVIII, 1983), pp. xvii–xx, 1–31, 54–6.

Maria's death in childbirth at the age of thirty-four. Maria began her letters with phrases like 'My best beloved Thomken' and ended them simply 'Thine'. In one missive of around 1607, in reply to his 'kind wanton letters', the page overflows with desire, as Maria protests at how he has made 'my modest blood flush up into my bashful cheeks'. Her sexual assertiveness is unmistakable: 'thou threatened sound payment', she wrote, 'and I sound repayment, so as when we meet there will be pay and repay, which will pass and repass'. This is followed by a sexual pun in garbled Latin, which refers to Thomas rising up frequently on his return home. What makes a series of letters around this time especially fascinating is the light that they throw upon the tensions of this love match. The fact that they began as adolescent runaways did not mean that the patriarchal issues did not arise in due course. When in 1604, on John Thynne's death, the couple inherited Longleat and the capable and high-spirited Maria took over the role that Joan Thynne had played in the 1580s of managing the estate a new tension came into the marriage. Maria quickly clashed with stewards and retainers of the previous regime, who disliked being beholden to this unconventional young woman. Thomas seems to have come to accept her style but at one point they fell out badly, perhaps because he suddenly felt bound to assert his manhood as the new squire of such a great estate. Maria was hurt and aggrieved. She had been 'a willing compounder and partaker' in his hard fortunes. Now she found he held 'such a contempt of my poor wits' that she was not being given 'discretion to order (according to your appointment) your affairs in your absence'. In this plight, Maria showed an unaccustomed submissiveness which shows how she could adhere, when put to it, to the doctrine of wifely subservience. Others, she declared, could be left to wonder why she was not even allowed to choose her own servants: 'if you be persuaded that it is most for your credit to leave me like an innocent fool here, I will the more contentedly bear the disgrace'. More normally though, confident of her husband's trust, Maria Thynne adopted a faintly derisive tone towards the patriarchal rules of wifely discourse. She began a letter in which she boasted that she would not be inferior to any of her neighbours 'in playing the good housewife' with a conscious dismissal of the kind of writing expected of her as a dutiful wife:

> Mine own sweet Thomken, I have no longer ago than the very last night written such a large volume in praise of thy kindness to me, thy dogs, thy hawks, the horse and the foxes and also in commendation of thy great care of thy businesses in the country that I think I need not amplify any more on that text, for I have crowned thee for an admirable good husband with poetical laurels.

This letter included a request for money for a dependent in trouble with the squire, which she based on the claim that 'this age will not help you to an equal, I mean for a wife', and some chiding about his delay in coming down from London, for which in recompense he must 'make much of thy Mall when thou dost come home'. Maria Thynne's letters show a woman who, except when she was hurt by him into submission, was ready to contradict patriarchy by passion and who expected her husband to soften it by his devotion.[2]

Lady Margaret Hoby's diary is one of the most detailed accounts we have of how a gentlewoman spent her days and what she and her husband did together. What is unusual about it is the insight it provides into the strictness of Lady Margaret's routine of spiritual exercises and the space that she demanded and expected from her equally serious husband to fulfil these on her own. The overall sense is of a couple living contentedly together and enjoying each other's company. On a Sunday afternoon he would read to her from the works of William Perkins. She records how much they talked with each other and hints at the range and diversity of their conversation. Sometimes it was worldly talk, as on a Sunday in August 1599 when they sat over dinner till three o'clock, 'the Lord forgive me, speaking and thinking of many idle matters'. The following Saturday they spent some time in private discussing 'matters concerning conscience and our estates' and on 13 February 1600, Lady Margaret records, she 'talked a good time with Mr Hoby of husbandry and household matters' before they went to bed. The references are always to Mr Hoby: there is none of the skittishness of Maria Thynne here. But Sir Thomas Hoby clearly took his wife seriously and treated her as something like an equal partner in the management of their estate at Hackness which had come to him through his wife's dowry. When they were out and about it was sometimes simply for recreation, as on the August afternoon in 1599 when they 'took the air in the coach'. Often, though, there was business in hand, such as an expedition to 'spy out the best places where cottages might be builded'. At home there were often tenants to be entertained and they did this together.[3] The couple were not popular in the local gentry community, as has been shown by the incident of rough intrusion on their domestic peace, but the diary portrays the security of a routine which apparently underpinned real marital happiness in a secluded Yorkshire valley. A funeral monument recalls their 'mutual entire affection' over a period of thirty-seven years.[4]

Sir Robert Harley was of the same breed of militant puritan gentry as Sir Thomas Hoby. With two marriages behind him and still no heir, now

2. For these two paragraphs, Wall, 'Elizabethan Precept', *History*, LXXXV (1990), pp. 28–37; Wall, ed., *Two Elizabethan Women*, pp. xxv–xxxii, 21–38, 48–9.

3. This account is based upon the extracts in R. Houlbrooke, ed., *English Family Life 1576–1716* (London, 1988), pp. 55–60.

4. D.M. Meads. ed., *The Diary of Lady Margaret Hoby* (London, 1930), p. 39; R.B. Manning, *Hunters and Poachers: A Social and Cultural History of Unlawful Hunting in England* (Oxford, 1993), pp. 228–9; above, p. 139.

in his mid-forties, he was looking in 1623 for a new wife. By choosing
Brilliana Conway, unusually in these circles at twenty-five not yet contracted in marriage, he associated himself with a family that had
formidable court connections and also a puritan tradition to match his
own religious inclinations[5] (plate 28). Harley was in the midst of that
circle of puritan clerics who were publishing forceful statements of
patriarchal doctrine at this time in their marriage advice books. He was a
friend of William Gouge whose *Domestical Duties* was such a best seller
and his wedding day sermon in 1623 was preached and subsequently
published by Thomas Gataker.[6] This could well have been an arranged
marriage, yet there is a hint at least that it was a romantic attachment. Or
so one of his relatives thought who, just before the marriage, told him
that she wanted to know Brilliana better, 'for men in love are always held
not to be their own men and if you be not your own then I would know
whose you are that I might let them know how much I am theirs'. This
teasing may have jolted Sir Robert a little: an aspiring courtier with his
eyes on a parliamentary career, he lived in a competitive male world
where men could not afford any taint of effeminacy. This, as we have
seen, was the problem men were taught to beware about being too much
in love, too much the possession of a woman. There are no surviving
letters from Sir Robert to Brilliana but the epithets he uses about her in
letters to other kin like 'my dear Brill' or 'my dear heart' suggest that his
affection for her was deep. Her immediate and strongly felt devotion to
him is obvious from a mass of correspondence.[7]

Yet a series of her letters in the spring of 1626 perhaps give some
insight into the strains of patriarchal marriage where a thrice married
husband found there were some limits to the emotional commitment he
wished to make and thought wise to show.[8] Alone in the remote Herefordshire countryside while Sir Robert sat in parliament, and at the end
of a second pregnancy, Brilliana was missing her husband dreadfully.
When the child, a second son, was born, Sir Robert told her to have him
christened rather than await his return. Her letter of 21 April began with
a report of this. 'Because you said nothing of the name,' wrote Brilliana
anxiously, 'I chose that name I love the best it being yours.' After a few
lines about Ned, the elder boy, she then let her emotions show in a
breathless passage: 'I would fain tell you that, which I can not, I am sure
not all I can not, how much I long to see you. It is long since you went

5. J. Eales, *Puritans and Roundheads: The Harleys of Brampton Bryan and the Outbreak of the
   English Civil War* (Cambridge, 1990), pp. 20–2; P. Collinson, *The Religion of Protestants:
   The Church in English Society 1559–1625* (Oxford, 1982), pp. 164–8.
6. A.J. Fletcher and P.R. Roberts, eds, *Religion, Culture and Society in Early Modern Britain*
   (Cambridge, 1994), pp. 164, 166–7.
7. Eales, *Puritans and Roundheads*, pp. 22–3.
8. I am grateful to Jacqueline Eales for giving me copies of her transcripts of the letters
   cited here.

and I have no hope given me to look for you shortly.' Catching hold of herself, she latched on to her faith and the teachings in which she had been reared about male and female roles: 'I must yield to the will of the Lord and as the public good is to be preferred before private ends, so at this time I must show that indeed I love that better than my own good.' 'I pray you write to me as often as you can,' she added in an almost pathetic postscript.[9]

Brilliana's stance in this correspondence is every inch that of the submissive wife. She begins her letters 'Dear Sir' and ends 'your most faithful affectionate wife'. She is often anxious when he fails to write back promptly and at times adopts a pleading tone. 'For Ned and Robin I beg your blessing and let me have your prayers and love,' she ended on 3 May. Gentle chiding was the most that Brilliana dared. A fortnight after the christening she let her hurt show about their failure to communicate about the child's name: 'I do not take it well that you do not tell me how you approve of his name.'[10] In due course, during this absence from each other, Brilliana had the courage to challenge Sir Robert about his failure, as she saw it, to 'answer my love with yours'. He seems to have protested at the suggestion that his love was unequal but he went on, showing his emotional defensiveness, to argue that 'to love much was a trouble'. Brilliana's reply to this expresses the dawning recognition of an idealistic young woman that her husband was determined to cling to conventional male reserve whereas she could not help herself: 'I know I love you much, but I find it no trouble, nor cannot think that with all your arguments you can persuade me that to love is a trouble. I desire much to see you, which I think you believe.'[11]

The marriage lasted twenty years. Sir Robert's devotion and trust deepened with time and Brilliana's strength and courage were finally tested to the utmost when she was left to defend the castle at Brampton Bryan against the royalists while he was away sitting in parliament in 1643. She died suddenly of an apoplexy soon after this. Sir Robert heard 'the sad news that the Lord has taken from me my dear wife' in London and submitted himself to the hand of providence 'with a heart of resignation'.[12] Their strong puritan faith had become a durable bond. Indeed such were Brilliana's religious qualities that some saw her as transcending him. Her brother had noted in a letter to Sir Robert in 1637 that their marriage represented the curiosity of 'the order of things inverted': while he wrote to him of cheeses 'my sister writes about a good scholar'.[13] But there had been nothing inverted about their initial relationship and Brilliana, one suspects, never stepped beyond the limits of wifely respect.

9. BL Loan 29/202, also cited in Collinson, *Religion of Protestants*, p. 170.
10. BL Loan 29/72.
11. Eales, *Puritans and Roundheads*, p. 23.
12. Eales, *Puritans and Roundheads*, pp. 174–5.
13. Cited in Collinson, *Religion of Protestants*, p. 169.

Their mature relationship shows how they found the capacity to grow in personal strength together.

The marriage of Sir Ralph Verney and the orphaned heiress Mary Blacknall in 1629 reflected the material considerations so often prominent in finding a suitable match for the heir to a great estate (plate 27). Sir Edmund Verney chose a bride for his son who was only thirteen; Ralph was twenty-six at the time. Mary joined a brood of younger children at Claydon. Her relationship with Sir Ralph, a meticulous, demanding and increasingly irascible man, was necessarily at first submissive. But it became a true partnership. They were separated for more than eighteen months between 1646 and 1648, when Sir Ralph was a royalist in exile, and they then conducted an intense correspondence. This illuminates a marriage which still carried the habitual fussy direction which a husband had learnt to exhibit towards his child bride but which also shows a wife's spirit, her devotion and her considerable capacities. These were the qualities that, taken together, had extracted from Sir Ralph real trust and deep commitment. It has been argued that neither of them ever believed that she was equal in any way, that his order of priorities was different from hers, that she was not the chief focus of his life and that he could not perceive her as a person.[14] Neither their correspondence nor the evidence we have of Sir Ralph's passionate grief at the loss of his wife, aged only thirty-four in 1650, substantiates these assertions.

To be sure, it is ironic and perhaps strange to modern eyes that, when Lady Mary was ill in 1650, his uncle, Doctor Denton, wrote about the new maid he had chosen to send over to Sir Ralph in the terms simply of his sexual requirements. She was a girl, Denton declared, who a Verney servant at home had affirmed 'will match your cock'. Adopting the well known popular simile, the girl, he assured Sir Ralph, would be 'as good as my lady in the dark'. Clearly both men regarded the sexual double standard as a matter of common practice with regard to maidservants.[15] Plainly too what Sir Ralph asked of his wife, in the somewhat cynical tactic of having her plead his case in London, was very demanding. He was endlessly attempting to control her in his letters, showing an attention to detail that made his wife's task doubly difficult. But she was immensely competent and resilient. She had grown into a confident woman able to stand up for herself. So, when he complained about the failure to answer on every point he raised with her, she replied in a tone that was gentle but far from meekly subservient: 'My dear . . . truly I am confident tis by chance if I miss answering of every particular, for I always

14. M. Slater, *Family Life in the Seventeenth Century: The Verneys of Claydon House* (London, 1984), pp. 63–73. See also M. Slater, 'The Weightiest Business: Marriage in an Upper-Class Gentry Family in Seventeenth-Century England', *Past and Present* 72 (1976), pp. 32–8.

15. Slater, *Family Life*, p. 72; Slater, 'The Weightiest Business', *Past and Present* 72 (1976), p. 39.

lay thy letters before me when I write, but however, when thou considerest how much I write and how ill a scribe I am, thou oughtest not to be angry with me for forgetting now and then a little.' His scolding, which earlier may have been more like that of a strict parent with a frivolous adolescent about developing suitable accomplishments, has taken on a half jesting air by 1647: 'For your guitar, if you have forgot any one lesson nay if you have not gotten many more than you had, truly I shall break your fiddle about your pate, therefore look to yourself and follow it hard and expect no mercy in this point.' Lady Mary was run off her feet with making inventories at Claydon, checking the steward's accounts and seeing to the estate, besides prosecuting the case for relief from sequestration which was eventually achieved in December 1647.[16] He knew as well as she did that her guitar was hardly the top priority.

The best evidence we have that the dynamic of their relationship had shifted towards a partnership of minds is the business of their new child's name. Mary returned to England pregnant and raised the issue assertively in a letter shortly before the baby was due: 'If it be a boy I am resolved to have it of thy own name, therefore I charge you do not contradict it. . . . I will be governed by thee in anything but the name if it be a boy, for to tell the truth I must have it have thy name.' Sir Ralph did contradict her but not in an imperious way: 'if it be a boy in earnest you must not deny me, let it be Richard or what you please, except my own name'. In June, writing of the child's safe delivery as 'a most unspeakable blessing to us both', Sir Ralph returned teasingly to the subject: 'If the boy's name is Richard I shall hope he may be a happy man, but if it be otherwise I will not prophecy his ill fortune but rather pray to God to make him an honest man and then he will be happy enough.' He was, after all, not able to be at the christening. Lady Mary got her own way and named their child Ralph.[17] By this time they were at ease with each other, as a lighthearted comment about a shopping expedition Lady Mary made in Paris after she had returned to France in 1649 shows. He blushed, he told a family friend, 'at her boldness but more at my own folly for suffering of her but you know she wears the breeches and will do what she list'.[18]

The Verneys' correspondence includes the usual conventional acknowledgements by Lady Mary of her gender inferiority. When she gives advice about estate matters it is carefully thought out but at the same time prefaced by statements like this one: 'tis only because you bid me do it that I trouble you with my silly advice, for I am sure thy own judgement is much better'. Such rhetoric, as in the Thynne marriages,

16. *Verney*, II, pp. 280, 288.
17. *Verney*, II, pp. 258–9, 265–6.
18. Verney Papers, 13 August 1649.

reassured both parties that their relationship was not stepping too far out of line. But we must set beside it the evidence of deep attachment shown by the desperate emotional longings in the temporary parting these two had to endure after the civil war, and in the final parting that faced Sir Ralph only two years after they were reunited in France. He worried endlessly about her when she was away and confessed, soon after she went, that he found 'the grief of our fatal separation is not to be expressed'. He began his letters affectionately with 'Dear Heart' or 'Dear Budd'. 'My dear heart I must tell you', she wrote to him in November 1646, 'if I had known what it had been to me to have parted so far from thee I should never have done it.' 'I am half wild that I have no letters this week,' she declared the following April, 'my dearest rogue, farewell. I am thine own for ever.'[19]

Lady Mary Verney's death left Sir Ralph inconsolable: he remained a widower for more than forty years. He had her body embalmed and, given all the problems of safe passage to England, it was not until six months after her death that she was laid to rest at Claydon. In the meanwhile, he told his uncle, 'you may put up a great escutcheon; fail not of anything that is fit for so unparalleled a creature'.[20] For three years Sir Ralph was preoccupied with the project of a fine monument to commemorate his loving wife and his brave parents in the little church which still stands, rather awkwardly situated, behind the house at Claydon and only a few feet from its windows. At one point he even thought of demolishing and rebuilding the church, so ambitious were his plans for a work which was to be designed by French and Italian sculptors. The scheme was in due course severely modified but it fully absorbed his energies in the immediacy of Sir Ralph's grief. The bust of Lady Mary now at Claydon remains as a simple reminder of his devotion to her. It is perhaps one of the most telling representations we have of loving marriage at this time.[21] For a letter Sir Ralph wrote to his sister Margaret, with advice about the submissiveness which her husband required of her, indicates that he believed patriarchal expectations carried in turn obligations. He knew he had been a difficult man to live with and he was deeply grateful for his wife's willingness not to divulge his faults and to tolerate his 'pettish humours'. By being such a good wife she had made him, he thought, a better husband:

> You know she brought a far better fortune than my estate deserved and for her gifts of grace and nature I may justly say she was inferior to very few, so that she might well expect all reasonable observance from me, yet such was her goodness that when I was most peevish she would be

19. *Verney*, II, pp. 263, 275; Slater, *Family Life*, p. 67.
20. *Verney*, II, p. 415.
21. L. Stone, 'The Verney Tomb at Middle Claydon', *Records of Bucks*, XVI (1948), pp. 67–82.

most patient and, as if she meant to air my frowardness and frequent follies by the constancy of her forbearance, studied nothing more than a sweet compliance.[22]

When the editors of the manuscript diary kept by Elizabeth Freke between 1671 and her death in 1714 visited just over ninety years ago the manor house at West Bilney where she had lived in her latter years, they discovered a flourishing folklore about this redoubtable lady in a tiny Norfolk community. Until the middle of the previous century, they were told, the old coach in which she travelled to and from London had stood in a barn there keeping her memory alive: strangers had paid a penny to see it. Elizabeth Freke was variously remembered, the stories at West Bilney went, as a local tyrant, a wonderfully clever and learned woman and a witch who roamed the fields at dark. What she herself has left us is a detailed diary of her married life and widowhood, a very conscious piece of female self-fashioning. She fell in love in her teens with an impecunious Irish cousin of much the same age as herself. A long, possibly secret, engagement preceded their marriage which took place without the approval of her father in 1671, when she was twenty-four and he was twenty-six. The marriage, she records, was solemnized on 'a most dreadful rainy day, a presage of all my sorrows and misfortunes to come'. Elizabeth Freke, a woman betrayed in love and seeing the odds against her, apparently gave up the struggle to achieve marital happiness and resigned herself to using her diary as some kind of solace in her unhappiness. Her monument in Westminster Abbey, which was erected by her sister, paints her in quite different colours from the Norfolk folklore. Here we have the standard eulogistic phrases: she was 'of excellent life, frugal to be munificent, a lively Christian pattern of charity and self denial'. So how unhappy was her life? How badly was she treated? What does her story add to this collective portrait of early modern marriages?

The facts appear to be fairly plain. Her husband persistently managed their financial affairs very badly indeed and she was unable to exert any effective influence upon him in this or for that matter anything else. He wasted much of the large dowry she received within two years of their marriage. Her deepest bitterness, though, was about the fact that he seldom had any time for her: she did not have her husband's company at dinner ten times in a period of ten weeks when they were in London in 1684, she recorded, 'which I cannot forget, it was so grievous to me'. She loathed spending time at their home in Ireland where she was often ill. Returning there after an absence of eight years in 1692 she found no furnishings or stock: 'this was the fifth time I came to bare walls and a naked house since I was married'. Percy Freke often left his wife on her

22. *Verney*, II, pp. 423-4.

own for long periods; then he would insist on her return to Ireland. When he did this in 1683, after she had returned to Wiltshire to live with her ageing father, she at first refused to accompany him because of her husband's family's 'unkindness to me whenever I were in their power of command'. She could not forget a row at their parting when he had wished that he might never see her face any more. It took him five months to persuade or bully her into returning home with him; in 1692, when he summoned her from West Bilney where her father had settled an estate on her, it was six months before she 'forced myself to undertake again a journey for Ireland'.

Much of Percy Freke's harassment concerned a trust she held on behalf of herself and her son. Elizabeth was dogged and successful in maintaining some financial independence. She was determined, she wrote, to avoid having to seek 'the charity of my friends' or trust to her husband's or anyone else's kindness. Her private papers reveal that threats of intimidation sometimes turned to force. 'My dear husband borrowed of me not without some force and cruelty £1560', she wrote at one point in 1702. Although, as the record of her estate management at West Bilney and her local reputation shows, she was a formidable woman, in her marriage she was submissive. From 1698 she settled at West Bilney, which relatives helped her to furnish. In the end he came there to her and she nursed him devotedly during the last six months of his life when, as she noted caustically, she felt she had no choice but to 'see my husband murdered by five doctors, two surgeons and three apothecaries'. Her account of his death from a fit of asthma on a Sunday afternoon when the household was at church is full of emotion: 'at the fatal hour . . . no mortal was with him but my wretched self. In my arms . . . which quite distracted me; he bid me not stir from him but my amazed condition was such as my crying out soon filled the house out of the church to be a witness of my unhappy and deplorable fate.' Her arrangements for his burial, in the vault beneath Bilney church that he had had made, were meticulous. The neighbours and gentry 'of my twenty-five years acquaintance' were invited to attend and given wine, cakes and ale. 'I will lay my unhappy and miserable carcass by him when God please to call me,' Elizabeth Freke wrote in her diary on 7 June 1706. Unhappy in her relationship with the man she had fallen in love with as a girl, unhappy in losing him after thirty-five years of marriage, she had tried hard, it would seem, to live up to the demands that her prescribed gender role placed upon her.[23]

23. These three paragraphs are based upon 'Mrs Elizabeth Freke, her Diary 1671–1714', *Journal of the Cork Historical and Archaeological Society*, XVI (1910), pp. 149–67; XVII (1911), pp. 1–16, 45–58, 93–113, 142–155; XVIII (1912), pp. 39–47, 88–97, 151–9, 203–11; XIX (1913), pp. 42–7, 84–90, 134–47. The original diary is BL Add. MSS. 451718-19. See also M. Hunt, 'Wife Beating, Domesticity and Women's Independence in Eighteenth-century London', *Gender and History* 4 (1992), pp. 20, 31.

Assessment of the conduct and attitudes of Lady Grace Mildmay during the fifty years of her marriage with Sir Anthony Mildmay, the eldest son of Queen Elizabeth's Chancellor of the Exchequer, can draw upon a portrait, a monumental inscription, household papers and a personal journal. These representations and sources neatly complement each other. The portrait shows her in old age, with a small prayer book in her hand and with more books, jars, retorts and a workbox beside her. The epitaph, composed by her daughter, was: 'She was most devout, unspottedly chaste maid, wife and widow, compassionate in heart and charitably helpful with physick, clothes, nourishment or counsel to any in misery. She was most careful and wise in managing worldly estate. . . .' Grace was, like Mary Verney, a child bride, married in 1566 at fourteen to the young Anthony Mildmay. His father tried to keep his heir in leading strings by insisting on the match when the young man wished to travel abroad instead, and then by giving the couple a miserably small maintenance. So he went off to court and ambassadorships abroad, running up debts, while she was left in her father-in-law's home during a twenty-year apprenticeship for her eventual role as mistress of the family's Northamptonshire estate. 'My husband was much away', she records, 'and I spent the best part of my youth in solitariness.'

Deeply respectful towards Anthony's austere puritan father, Sir Walter, who had given her a posy in her wedding ring with the words *Maneat inviolata fides*, Grace was dedicated to her marriage. She apparently became resigned to her husband's casual approach towards her. When some tried to entice her to court, she told them that 'God had placed me in the world in this house'. Her account of how she spent her time indicates how she was able, through a secure routine, to remain constant and busy. Her spiritual exercises included readings from scripture, prayer and practising her voice in singing psalms. She played the lute, read herbals and books of physick and created her own designs 'for carpet or cushion work'. The variety of this work, she found, brought recreation to her mind; its loneliness she accepted as God's will. On Sir Walter's death her accomplishments found full rein when she took over full management of the household with its ten servants, but it seems she took no great part in managing the estate while her husband was away from home. Sir Anthony in due course settled down to be a loyal husband who enjoyed his local role in county government and offering hospitality to others. Not that he can have been an easy man to live with. He was known as an irascible man of few words, who took offence easily. He was peeved, for instance, when Lord Burghley asked him for a brace of bucks via his neighbour Lord Boughton rather than directly. Yet his concern for his wife shows in his efforts to provide for her widowhood and his recognition of her capabilities in her appointment as sole executrix. Grace's 'meditation on the corps of my husband', at his death in

1617, acknowledged the devotion which had sustained her submissive behaviour:

> I carried always that reverend respect towards him . . . that I could not find in my heart to challenge him for the worst word or deed which ever he offered me in all his life, as to say Why spake you thus? or why did you that? but in silence passed over all such matters betwixt us; so that we parted in all love and Christian charity until our happy meeting in Heaven.[24]

In the 'great picture' depicting the story of Lady Anne Clifford's long and eventually successful struggle to regain the northern estates to which she was heir the portrait of Richard Sackville, Earl of Dorset, who was her first husband, is almost unnoticeable (plate 19). In the perspective of her life, as it seemed to her in 1646, he was in a sense little more than a trophy of her past.[25] They had married when they were both nineteen, in 1609: he had not yet come into his Kent and Sussex estates and was intent on an extravagant life at James I's court. It did not suit him at all that his wife was already a woman of formidable tenacity and strength of character, who was quite unwilling meekly to accept the arrangement by which her father had left his lands in Westmoreland and elsewhere to her uncle.[26] Lady Anne's diary for the period from 1616 to 1619, which has recently been much anthologised, presents an intimate account of her troubles with her husband over this affair and the effect it had on their marriage. It is a remarkable document, put in the context of this survey of wifely behaviour in early modern England, showing, as one set of editors remark, 'an individual woman holding out against the combined patriarchal forces of father, uncles, husbands, lawyers, churchmen and even the King'.[27] Serious estrangement between husband and wife began in February 1616 when, having refused to sign any documents until she had consulted her mother, Lady Anne travelled north to Brougham Castle. Her husband accompanied her part of the way; when they parted near Lichfield she wrote in her diary that 'I came to my lodgings with a heavy heart, considering how many things stood between my lord and I.' She had not been wholly unhappy as Dorset's wife up till then, believing

---

24. These two paragraphs are based upon R. Weighall, ed., 'An Elizabethan Gentlewoman', *Quarterly Review* CCXV (1911), pp. 119–38 and L.A. Pollock, *With Faith and Physic: The Life of a Tudor Gentlewoman Lady Grace Mildmay 1552–1620* (London, 1993), pp. 8–11, 15.

25. The picture can be seen in the great hall at Appleby Castle. It is reproduced in M. Holmes, *Proud Northern Lady: Lady Anne Clifford 1590–1676* (Chichester, 1975) and in E. Graham, H. Hinds, E. Hoby and H. Wilcox, eds, *Her Own Life: Autobiographical Writings by Seventeenth-Century Englishwomen* (London, 1989), p. 36.

26. Holmes, *Proud Northern Lady*, pp. 23–38.

27. Graham *et al.*, eds, *Her Own Life*, p. 37. For her diaries in full see the new edition edited by D.J.H. Clifford, *The Diary of Lady Anne Clifford* (Stroud, 1990).

him to be a man 'of a just mind, of a sweet disposition and very valiant in his own person'. But the extent of his anger was soon driven into her by a peremptory demand, following intense pressure on her to fall in with his financial arrangements, for Dorset's coach, horses and servants to return from Brougham to London at once without her. Lady Anne, confused, attempted no defiance; within a few days she had decided to balk her husband's plan for a separation by returning south herself. The Countess Pillar is the monument she erected forty years later to mark the spot on that road across the Pennines, two miles from Brougham, where mother and daughter had the 'grievous and heavy parting' which was to prove their last farewell.[28] Back at Knole, Dorset's mansion in Kent, she received 'a cold welcome from my lord'; a few weeks later he made another attempt to separate, sending word he no longer wished her to live at his family homes; this was followed within two days by a demand that their child, Margaret, who was not yet two, should be sent the next day to him in London. Lady Anne met all these slights and insults in the correct and prescribed manner in which a good wife was instructed, that is with obedience and passivity. 'When I considered that it would make my lord more angry with me and be worse for the child,' she noted in her diary, 'I resolved to let her go . . . and wept bitterly.'[29]

May 1616 was a grievous month for Lady Anne. Dorset stayed in London enjoying its leisure pursuits and 'commended', as Lady Anne put it, 'by all the world'. She remained at Knole with her needlework and reading: 'I stayed in the country, having many times a sorrowful and heavy heart and being condemned by most folks because I would not consent to the agreements. So as I may truly say, I am like an owl in the desert.' The image from Psalms came easily to a woman who knew her Old Testament well besides having absorbed Chaucer, historical chronicles and Renaissance literature. On 29 May came the news of her mother's death after a lingering illness and this caused her to spend much of the rest of this year seeing to her funeral, goods and land, in Westmoreland.[30] Things came to a head for Lady Anne in January 1617. The court was buzzing with the story of her wilfulness and the King decided to intervene. He summoned the parties concerned to a public hearing but he first saw the couple privately. In its sheer intensity, this was Lady Anne's greatest trial. It was one thing to disobey her lord and master, another to defy the monarch in person. But this was what she did:

> He put out all that were there, and my lord and I kneeled by his chair sides when he persuaded us both to peace and to put the whole matter wholly into his hands, which my lord consented to, but I beseeched his

28. Holmes, *Proud Northern Lady*, pp. 39–46; N. Pevsner, *Cumberland and Westmoreland* (London, 1967), p. 236.
29. Graham *et al.*, eds, *Her Own Life*, pp. 40–41.
30. Holmes, *Proud Northern Lady*, pp. 50–5; Graham *et al.*, eds, *Her Own Life*, p. 42.

majesty to pardon me, for that I would never part from Westmoreland while I lived upon any condition whatsoever.

When, at the public hearing, Lady Anne maintained this stance the King, she recorded, 'grew in a great chaff' and her husband hastened to have her removed before some kind of public disgrace for his family followed. Dorset's own reputation, after all, was on the line and the gossip that would follow this incident could have blemished his name. He was good to her during this time of public confrontation; she valued his kindness and did everything possible to be the good wife in the next weeks when he was intermittently ill and in need of her care.[31]

The case, of course, went against Lady Anne but it remained financially advantageous to Dorset to get her consent to the contract he himself signed with the Earl of Cumberland in March 1617. In April he was bullying her again and the relationship was tempestuous once more: one day they were dining together and playing barley break on the bowling green at Knole, the next he would not sleep with her after a quarrel. In May he cancelled the jointure he had made on her the previous year and she wrote to let him know how ill she took it, 'but yet told him I was content to bear it with patience whatsoever he thought fit'. In June there was a Sunday when in church 'my eyes were so blubbered with weeping that I could scarce look up'.[32] Lady Anne's sorrow about her husband's total failure to understand just how much her northern estates mattered to her must have hung like a pall over the remaining days of their marriage. At the Earl's death in 1624 she was still only thirty-four: for her the struggle to secure her rightful inheritance had only just begun.[33] What should be noticed about the story of Lady Anne's first marriage was that she had sought to satisfy her husband in everything except in the matter of principle over which she 'referred my cause to God'.[34] Her challenge was not to the honour that lay in the Earl's lineage nor to patriarchy as such. How could any well born woman mount such a challenge in the seventeenth century? It was rather more specifically to a male-dominated legal system which, as she saw it, deprived her of her just rights to her northern estates.[35]

Elizabeth Pepys may seem an unlikely challenger of patriarchy but in her own way this spirited woman, who we learn about through her husband's eyes, was just as brave in standing up for herself as Anne

---

31. Holmes, *Proud Northern Lady*, pp. 73–88; Graham *et al.*, eds, *Her Own Life*, pp. 45–7.
32. Graham *et al.*, eds, *Her Own Life*, pp. 48–51.
33. Holmes, *Proud Northern Lady*, pp. 124–36.
34. Houlbrooke, *English Family Life*, p. 62.
35. See also K. Hodgkin, 'The Diary of Lady Anne Clifford: a Study of Class and Gender in the Seventeenth Century', *History Workshop Journal* 19 (1985), pp. 148–55; M.E. Lamb, 'The Agency of the Split Subject: Lady Anne Clifford and the Uses of Reading', *English Literary Renaissance* 22 (1992), pp. 347–68.

Clifford had been with a domineering king. The celebrated diarist has fixed himself in the mind of posterity with his magnetic charm but there is no question – so candid is he about his personal life – that, though a genuinely affectionate husband, he was also, as his latest editor concludes, 'unfaithful, insensitive and overbearing' (plate 30). Pepys has given us the most intimate record we have of the companionship and emotional dynamics of a seventeenth-century marriage: we learn something about their relationship with each other on almost every day of the nine-year period from 1 January 1660 to 31 May 1669 during which he kept his diary. There was the same kind of discrepancy of age which we have found in other cases. Elizabeth was fifteen, whereas he was twenty-three, at the time of their marriage in 1655.[36] But this was not an arranged marriage like that of Joan Thynne or Mary Verney. Elizabeth Pepys had neither money nor connections: the match brought no material advantages to the rising bureaucrat. He simply fell in love with her. Reflecting on some music which he found had ravished him in 1668, Pepys noted that it 'did wrap up my soul so that it made me really sick, just as I have formerly been when in love with my wife'.[37] Those emotions, which he could refer to after thirteen years of marriage with such casualness, had not sustained a really deep level of devotion. Not that the Pepys's lacked intimacy and companionship. The many times they lay long in bed talking probably meant as much to her as to him. They may indeed have meant more to her, for her commitment was certainly wholehearted and passionate from the start.

We know nothing of what the troubles were in the period before the diary begins which caused the couple to live apart for a time. What is clear is that in 1660, although they were living tolerably happily together in Axe Yard at Westminster, their sexual relationship was not by itself sufficiently rewarding for Pepys. He was already beginning to look elsewhere for sexual excitement.[38] Elizabeth's boredom, as rising status brought a kitchen maid, parlour maid and boy into the home, also put pressures on the relationship. In November 1662 there was a serious quarrel when Samuel was unsympathetic to her suggestion that she should have a companion come to live with her to play cards and music, to set her hair and to go visiting. He disliked the prospect of the expense, burning a letter she wrote to him about her discontent and pondering whether he could find her some work 'to take up her thoughts and time'. His resistance led to their falling out more dramatically the following January, when Elizabeth raised the topic again. She insisted on reading

36. *Pepys*, I, p. xxxv; X, p. 317.
37. *Pepys*, IX, p. 94.
38. *Pepys*, I, pp. 220, 239; L. Stone, *The Family, Sex and Marriage in England 1500–1800* (London, 1977), p. 552. J.H. Wilson, *The Private Life of Mr Pepys* (London, 1959) provides a much fuller chronological account of Pepys's extramarital sexual life between 1660 and 1669 than is possible here.

him a copy of the letter she had written to him, 'most of it true' he notes, about the 'retiredness of her life and how unpleasant it was'. Her recalcitrance about being submissive fired Samuel's anger: she refused to tear up the letter, he forced it from her and tore up before her face not only the letter itself but some of his love letters from previous years and even his will which left her everything. Protecting his reputation was what mattered to Samuel in this episode: the 'disgrace to me and dishonour' if Elizabeth's paper should be found and read. Personal slight, however fair the words she had written, drove him into acting the patriarchal role with a degree of assertiveness that, as he knew well, simply frightened her. Later in the day he sought to buy her off with an expensive new mohair gown. This restored good relations at a price, he confided in the diary, which 'troubles me'. The episode shows well how Pepys operated, and how much or little he cared, how ready he was to bully. Yet he could feel remorse: 'I am sorry for the tearing of so many poor loving letters of mine from sea and elsewhere to her,' he concluded that evening.[39]

The next four years included periods when Samuel's domestic sexual life ceased because of the pain Elizabeth suffered from the abscess that developed in her vaginal area. But it is hard to think it would have been much different even if this had not been so. He had become an inveterate philanderer, enjoying physical contact of one kind or another at this time with around fifty-odd women.[40] Confiding much of the detail of his sexual activities to the privacy of the diary, he managed to keep them entirely secret from his wife. His undoing came when Elizabeth took into their home in 1667 a seventeen-year-old called Deb Willet, whom Pepys at once found 'mighty pretty'. He recognised the dangers the very evening he first set eyes upon her, noting his concern that 'I may be found too much minding her to the discontent of my wife'. The prediction was only too accurate. Deb came on 1 October; within a fortnight Samuel was noting signs of Elizabeth's jealousy of their behaviour to each other. In March a row Deb had with Elizabeth gave him an excuse, as he saw it, to take Deb his knee and fondle her when she came to undress him for bed; on 6 August he managed to reach Deb's genitals with his hand while travelling in the coach with her and Elizabeth; a few days later he persuaded her to handle his penis. Her resistance was diminishing; his desire for her was becoming obsessive. Hence the catastrophic incident, on 25 October 1668, when Elizabeth came suddenly into the room where Deb was combing his head for lice as she usually did and found Samuel's hand right up under her petticoats feeling her vagina. It is doubtful whether the marriage ever fully recovered from this discovery and the loss of trust that it involved; the incident, Pepys recorded, 'occasioned the greatest sorrow to me that ever I knew in this world':

39. *Pepys*, III, pp. 257–8; IV, pp. 9–10.
40. Stone, *Family, Sex and Marriage*, p. 554.

I was at a wonderful loss upon it, and the girl also and I endeavoured to put it off but my wife was struck mute and grew angry and as her voice came to her, grew quite out of order and I do say little but to bed; and my wife said little also, but could not sleep all night but about 2 in the morning waked me and cried . . . till at last it appeared plainly her trouble was at what she saw but yet I did not know how much she saw and therefore said nothing to her.[41]

The diary contains a full account of how, during the next weeks, Elizabeth ranted and stormed at Samuel and he sought to appease her. Their sexual life suddenly blossomed as, between bouts of depression, she became passionate and demanding. Samuel, meanwhile, added devious-ness to deceit. He was ready to play along when, her suspicions falling neither in the right places nor anything like enough places, she accused him of dalliance with Elizabeth Pearce, one of their social circle whom he does not record so much as touching, and with the actress Elizabeth Knepp, whom he had been regularly fondling: 'I did promise her particu-lar demonstrations of my true love to her owning some indiscretion in what I did . . . she at last on these premises was quiet.' So far as Deb was concerned, Elizabeth had her way in due course in having him dismiss her, after making a nonsense of Samuel's protestations that he had never kissed her by extracting a full confession from the girl of everything that had happened. But he continued to see Deb after she had left the Pepys's home and Elizabeth discovered this. Her rage was then so incandescent that he attempted to use the services of Will Hewers, his clerk in the Navy Office, as a go-between to pacify his wife. In the face of threats by Elizabeth that she would find Deb and slit her nose and would publish his infidelity to 'all the world', he agreed to write to the girl saying he would not see her again. He escaped the humiliation of calling Deb a whore in the letter, which Elizabeth demanded, by adopting a form of words which implied that she was not yet his whore but was in danger of becoming so. Thereafter he seems to have as good as abandoned the affair, though with great difficulty. More scenes followed in the next months when Eliza-beth's suspicions were aroused by rumours that reached her. January 1669 was summarised as a month clouded by 'her remembrance of my late unkindness to her with Willet, she not being able to forget it'. Her sorrow at her husband's infidelity was never far from the surface that last year of her life.[42] Elizabeth Pepys died of a fever three weeks after the couple returned from a tour of the Low Countries and Northern France in November 1669.[43] Faced with the evidence of Samuel's philandering in

41. *Pepys*, VIII, pp. 451, 453–4, 458, 468, 477, 481, 585; IX, pp. 143–5, 234, 277, 282, 328, 337–8.
42. *Pepys*, IX, pp. 338–46, 353–4, 356–8, 361–3, 367–71, 384, 387, 395, 422, 413–14, 480–1, 518–21, 534, 546, 564.
43. *Pepys*, X, p. 318.

their own home, she had showed spirit as well as bitterness. Samuel was reduced by the discovery of the affair with Deb Willet, exhibiting a pathetic mixture of remorse and insincerity. The story shows the twistings and turnings of a man who, for all his attempts to keep public and private lives apart, could no longer sustain his patriarchal role once his sexual honour at home was tarnished. The masculinities which sustain patriarchy, in other words, are always relational and always vulnerable. Pepys had lived a double life for a number of years but in the end had betrayed himself. It seems likely that deep inside himself he knew this and suffered about it.

In view of the complexity of the relationships revealed by these case studies it is hard to say anything in general terms about patriarchal marriage. What emerges quite clearly is that these husbands and wives were aware of the public teachings about male authority and female subordination which we find in a whole range of discourses such as homilies and conduct books and which are reflected in the drama of the period, in ballads and satirical literature. But this does not mean that either husbands or wives were able or willing simply to match their behaviour to the rules of prescription. The marriages that have been discussed here were only in certain limited ways patriarchal in practice. In each case there was an internal dynamic to the relationship that intimate historical sources allow us at least to glimpse. The ingredients of this internal dynamic were always particular, consisting of the hopes and desires, the strength of will and the emotional inclinations of the partners concerned. The women in these marriages, and no doubt in thousands of others, were mostly not docile and passive. We can continue this exploration of the nature of early modern marriage, widening the lens by using a fuller range of sources, as we turn to some of the general issues men and women faced when living together.

9. *Living Together*

THE RESTRICTIVE IDEOLOGY of sermons and conduct books, it is suggested, contrasts with a more permissive reality in the way that men and women conducted their married lives. Keith Wrightson makes the point when he argues that the evidence points to 'the private existence of a strong complementary and companionate ethos, side by side with, and often overshadowing theoretical adherence to the doctrine of male authority and public female subordination'.[1] Gentlewomen expounded standard patriarchal doctrine to newly wed daughters in their letters. 'Be careful that whatsoever you do, to love honour and obey your husband in all things that is fitting for a reasonable creature,' Lady Peyton advised her daughter Anne Oxinden. 'In this you shall gain yourself a good repute and show yourself a virtuous wife whose price is not to be valued.' 'You have subjected yourself to him and made him your head', Lady Cotton instructed her daughter Frances Montagu, 'to oppose therefore against what he holdeth fit or spurned against his designs, as it is a thing no wit beseeming a wife so is it a breach of her better to be observed promise'.[2] The irony was that, besides being subordinate, these women were expected to be competent, for the current notion of household order was that it be secured by an active and practical partnership between husband and wife. David Levine and Keith Wrightson have noted the 'fundamental paradox' in this model of marital responsibility: the very considerable personal capacities which women were expected to display represented a 'competence that was both defined and assessed by a spouse whose authority could not be questioned'.[3]

Women, we have seen, were the 'weaker vessel', yet at the same time there was believed to be an overlap in male and female attributes in the

1. K. Wrightson, *English Society 1580–1680* (London, 1982), p. 92.
2. Citations from L.A. Pollock, 'Teach her to Live under Obedience: The Making of Women in the Upper Ranks in Early Modern England', *Continuity and Change* 4 (1989), pp. 247–8.
3. D. Levine and K. Wrightson, *The Making of an Industrial Society: Whickham 1560–1765* (Oxford, 1991), p. 317.

make-up of the human personality. There was a sense in which this notion was something very positive and important in men's conception of how a marital relationship should work in practice. There was something of their manhood which they wanted women to share, while at the same time they wished to see their ultimate authority over women jealously guarded. John Ray's observation that 'commonly shrews are good house-wives' is relevant here.[4] Efficiency in the tasks of running a household, in other words, the kind of efficiency that was displayed by Maria Thynne and Mary Verney, was seen to go with strength of personality. Much here depended on temperament and there were those like Grace Mildmay who could be both very competent and highly deferential. In gentry circles an effective household manager was a prerequisite for the kind of life many men wished to lead, a life involving much time away from home on social and public business.[5] An estate steward could handle lands and rents but a strong woman was needed to deal with the personnel, daily business and financial control of the domestic establishment.[6] Men wanted their wives to be both subordinate and competent. There was bound to be tension about this dual role.[7]

Affection and loving familiarity between spouses shines through many of the collections of the gentry's correspondence. The letters of Thomas Knyvett to his 'sweet heart' Katherine in the 1620s are a celebrated example.[8] The Kentish MP Sir Edward Dering addressed his wife as 'my dear and comfortable numpes'; the Norfolk MP Bassingbourne Gawdy called his wife 'Sweet Bass'.[9] Roger Hill's letter to his pregnant wife Abigail, from a London sliding towards civil war in May 1642, is a classic expression of marital love and concern:

> There is nothing in the world that I can value equal with thee . . . I should be glad to see thee here as soon as thou wilt . . . my dear I thank thee for thy cakes. I never had better nor were any ever better accepted. I wish a happy increase of thy little great belly and that thou mayest be a happy nursing mother shall be the prayer of him that is dearest to thee.[10]

4. J. Ray, *A Collection of English Proverbs* (London, 1670), p. 50.
5. A.J. Fletcher, 'Honour, Reputation and Local Officeholding in Elizabethan and Stuart England', in A.J. Fletcher and J. Stevenson, eds, *Order and Disorder in Early Modern England* (Cambridge, 1985), pp. 92–115; A.J. Fletcher, *A County Community in Peace and War: Sussex 1600–1660* (London, 1975), pp. 22–57.
6. D.R. Hainsworth, *Stewards, Lords and People: The Estate Steward and his World in Late Stuart England* (Cambridge, 1992).
7. For this general argument see Pollock, 'Teach her to Live', *Continuity and Change* 4 (1989), pp. 247–8.
8. Cited in J. Sharpe, *Early Modern England: A Social History 1550–1760* (London, 1987), p. 66.
9. P. Collinson, *The Birthpangs of Protestant England: Religious and Cultural Change in the Sixteenth and Seventeenth Centuries* (London, 1988), pp. 22–3.
10. Cited in V.F. Snow and A.S. Young, eds, *The Private Journals of the Long Parliament* (New Haven, 1992), III, p. 490–91.

A letter to Sir Simonds D'Ewes a few months later from his sister breathes
the same spirit. Such were the distractions of the times that her husband
had 'worn himself lean and denied his health'. 'I have done what I am
able', she reports, 'by persuading and comforting him.'[11] It is only rarely
that we are given testimony from both sides of a marriage to the
fulfilment it brought both partners. Peregrina Chaytor thanked her husband on 14 August 1697 for his long and kind letter from London,
continuing 'though you wrote more like a lover than a husband, yet I
must believe you real having had your affection for above these twenty
years and not in the least lessened by the claims of those who endeavour
to captivate your sex'. She declared that, despite ill health, he could be
confident of 'the like return' till her death. When she died seven years
later, Sir William wrote a 'memorial' about his personal life 'for diverting
my melancholy', which alluded to their partnership. He had run his
family estate at Croft in North Yorkshire from 1666 to 1675 on his own
and then 'I became captivated and calling all the little reasons to account
to induce me to be a captive I found that love, religion and honour were
the great motives, the lady being young, handsome and of an excellent
character.'[12]

Many marriages in this period were broken prematurely by the death
of one of the partners: the documentation associated with such personal
tragedies affords further insight into the depth of emotional attachments.
'I want her at every turn, everywhere and in every work. Methinks
I am but half myself without her,' wrote Oliver Heywood in his diary.
There is a touching entry several years later when he wrote about his
wife as follows: 'Another thing there is which though but small hath
some influence to help my devotion many times, 'tis this, the cushion on
which I sit at my study on which I kneel at prayer hath the two first
letters of my wife's name E.A. which I usually see when going to prayer
alone.'[13] Will-making at all levels of society testifies to marital devotion.
Husbands often made very specific arrangements for a widow's comfort
and well being by setting aside particular rooms in the family home
and pieces of farmland or orchards.[14] The Sussex gentleman Anthony
May, for instance, declared his wife's 'free liberty of the use of the
kitchen', her right to collect firewood and use of facilities for 'dressing
meat and drink'.[15] In view of such provisions, frequent references in wills
to 'my beloved wife' or 'my loving wife' seem to be more than common

11. Cited in J.T. Cliffe, *Puritans in Conflict* (London, 1988), p. 40.
12. S. Chaytor, 'Family Life in the Seventeenth Century: Sir William Chaytor 1639–
    1721', Durham University MA Dissertation, 1992, pp. 14–15.
13. Cited in S. Adams, 'Some Observations of the Religious Life of Family Members
    within the Seventeenth-Century Protestant Household', Durham University BA Dis-
    sertation 1992, p. 41.
14. M. Spufford, *Contrasting Communities: English Villagers in the Sixteenth and Seventeenth
    Centuries* (Cambridge, 1974), pp. 88–90, 111–19, 161–4.
15. Fletcher, *A County Community in Peace and War*, p. 33.

form.[16] Edward Newby, pit overman at Whickham, left a personal testimony, in handing over his smallholding to his wife in his will of 1659: 'that what estate he had together with his wife Jane had got it by their industry and therefore he gave and bequeathed all his whole estate to his loving wife to be at her disposal and that if it were more his said wife deserveth it well.'[17]

Research into seventeenth-century poetry has revealed a few cases of spouses who expressed their devotion in verse. William and Margaret Cavendish, retired from the Restoration court, did this to each other in their rural exile. Gertrude Thimelby celebrated her marriage in several poems, in one of which, written to her husband on New Year's Day in 1657, she wrote of the swiftness with which time passes 'to them that our pure flame can own'. Katharine Philips compared herself and her husband to two watches keeping time. Anne Bradstreet was another woman who wrote poems of, as Mary Prior puts it, 'unclouded wifely devotion'.[18] The death of husbands drew from grieving spouses some heartfelt declarations in verse or prose. 'I had much mercy in my marriage with him,' wrote the widowed Lady Anne Harcourt at the start of her memoir about her life since she married Sir William Waller, 'he being the answer to my prayer, he being a religious, prudent and loving husband.'[19] Lady Ann Fanshaw, in her preface to her son, explained that her prose account of her life was a monument to her husband's memory: 'Glory be to God', she wrote, 'we never had but one mind through our lives, our souls were wrapped up in each other, our aims and designs one, our love one and our resentments one.' 'We so studied one the other that we knew each other's mind by our looks; whatever was real happiness God gave it me in him.'[20] Sir John Lowther concluded a memorandum in his estate book on his wife's death in childbirth in 1647 after 'a most happy, peaceable and loving time together of twenty-two years and ten days' as follows: 'She was a woman both for her person and parts not to be paralleled and in whom I had as much comfort as could be desired, a woman too good for me or this world.'[21] Inscriptions on monuments in many an English church still offer mute testimony to deep and fulfilling marriage

16. Wrightson, *English Society*, pp. 102–3.
17. Cited in K.E. Wrightson, 'Death in Whickham', in J. Walter and R.S. Schofield, eds, *Famine, Disease and Social Order in Early Modern England* (Cambridge, 1989), p. 158.
18. M. Prior, 'Conjugal Love and the Flight from Marriage: Poetry as a Source for the History of Women and the Family', in V. Fildes, ed., *Women as Mothers in Pre-Industrial England* (London, 1990), pp. 189–91; M.J.M. Ezell, *The Patriarch's Wife: Literary Evidence and the History of the Family* (Chapel Hill, 1987), p. 104.
19. C.B. Otten, ed., *English Women's Voices 1540–1700* (Miami, 1992), p. 310.
20. J. Loftis, *The Memoirs of Anne Lady Halkett and Ann Lady Fanshaw* (Oxford, 1979), p. 103.
21. C.B. Phillips, ed., *Lowther Family Estate Books 1617–1675* (Surtees Society, LXLI, for 1976–7, 1979), pp. 62–3.

relationships in this period. Katherine Dyer's words are particularly celebrated but they bear repetition:

> My dearest dust, could not thy hasty day
> Afford thy drowsy patience leave to stay
> One hour longer, so that we might either
> Sat up, or gone to bed together?[22]

Her husband's Hampshire tomb, declared Mary Mills, consecrated her grief and acted 'as a memorial of her imperishable love'.[23] Jean Bakie, records her monument at Chipping Camden of 1674, was 'a great glory of the female sex'. 'She is dead', the inscription continues, 'but her virtue is still fragrant after death, Jean was right dear on earth, Jean is bright clear in heaven.' These are all authentic materials, evidence of the power of human love in bringing just a few of the more intimate of the personal relationships of the time to abundant life. Richard Gough's record of one more marriage that worked in his Shropshire village of Myddle must stand as testimony for the mass of deep human experience of living together lovingly which is lost from our view. He wrote about John and Dorothy Vaughan like this: 'This couple when they were married were so young that they could not make passing thirty years between them and yet neither of them were constrained by parents to marry but they going to school together fell in love with one another and so married. They live lovingly together and have many children.'[24]

Many gentry married girls who had been well trained for the role of household manager in adolescence (plate 20). It was very common to send teenage daughters away to stay with relatives or friends to learn this art with a view to their marriage. Sir Edmund Molineux's purpose in placing his daughters with a cousin and his wife in 1551 was to have them brought up to 'play the gentlewomen and good housewives, to dress meat and oversee their households'.[25] 'She is (as you told me) very fair and well to be liked and I doubt not but as good as fair,' wrote Edward Lord Wotton to John Temple in 1592, reporting the arrival of his daughter Katherine. Wotton explained his hope that the busy routine of their household with his own daughter as Katherine's 'bedfellow and companion' would cure her greensickness.[26] In the 1630s Sir Thomas Pelham's daughter Nan travelled from Sussex to live with cousins of her mother's family the Wilbrahams in Cheshire and she spent much of her time there between the ages of fourteen and eighteen. The Sussex Busbridges and

22. Cited in Ezell, *The Patriarch's Wife*, p. 105.
23. P. Wheeler, 'The Significance of Social and Religious Change in the Development of Funerary Monument Sculpture: Hampshire Parish Churches 1500–1800', Durham University BA Dissertation, 1991, p. 36.
24. R. Gough, *The History of Myddle* (London, 1981), p. 169.
25. R. O'Day, *Education and Society 1500–1800: The Social Foundations of Education in Early Modern Britain* (London, 1982), p. 184.
26. HEH, ST 2583.

the Warwickshire Temples at this time provided reciprocal domestic training for their daughters.[27]

Some of the most heartfelt eulogies of wives probably reflect the performance of women who had undergone this kind of thorough preparation for their wifely role. Sir John Oglander's household account book for the 1640s, for example, contains the following comment on a satisfactory balance: 'I could never have done it without a most careful and thriving wife, who was up before me every day and oversaw all the outhouses, one that would not trust her maid with directions, she would wet her shoe to see all herself acted.'[28] Sir Anthony Ashley Cooper's diary entry on the death of his wife praised her as 'the most sweet, affectionate and observant wife in the world'. She was 'very provident in the least things, exceeding all in anything she undertook, housewifery, preserving, works with the needle, cookery, so that her wit and judgement were expressed in all things, free from any pride or frowardness'.[29] The ninth Earl of Northumberland thought that women exercised more control in the domestic sphere in England than elsewhere because of the demands of English hospitality. She found herself busy, he said, 'entertaining all comers, conducting their guests to their chambers, careful of their breakfasts, keeping them company at cards, with many more complements of this nature'.[30] The typical English gentleman certainly expected his wife to be autonomous and show considerable initiative in day-to-day household management.

There is no question that in this respect marital partnership often worked well. Margaret Hoby kept a household book and paid bills for workmen and for household provisions. 'I took order for things about the house till I went to breakfast' or 'I went about my maids till almost supper time' are typical entries in her diary.[31] Hester Temple's letters to her husband Sir Thomas when he was away on public business show how involved she was in estate affairs at Stowe early in the seventeenth century. In his old age Sir Thomas, as a memorandum of 1631 about the state of certain cases 'for my wife' reveals, handed over to her much of his legal business.[32] The surviving household books from Apethorpe, carefully written in Grace Mildmay's own hand, show the quality of her household management. A letter to 'my good Besse, my housekeeper', on an occasion when she was away from home, gave minute directions about the domestic routine.[33] Mary Pelham did an equally good job at Halland

27. Fletcher, *A County Community in Peace and War*, p. 38.
28. R. Houlbrooke, *English Family Life 1576–1676* (Chichester, 1975), p. 65.
29. Houlbrooke, *English Family Life*, pp. 69–70.
30. Cited in F. Heal, *Hospitality in Early Modern England* (Oxford, 1990), p. 179.
31. Houlbrooke, *English Family Life*, pp. 55–60.
32. HEH, STT 1924; Personal Papers box 8(8).
33. R. Weighall, ed., 'An Elizabethan Gentlewoman', *Quarterly Review* CCXV (1911), p. 134.

in Sussex in the early 1630s when she kept precise accounts for the house and for the children's expenses which Sir Thomas checked with her every few months.[34] It was very usual for such women to combine a managerial role with a practical one, as Sir Anthony Ashley Cooper's remarks indicate. Margaret Hoby baked gingerbread, preserved quinces and plums, made wax lights and spun and dyed cloth.[35] Elizabeth Pepys did less cooking once she had maids to do it for her but she worked with them at her needles, making nightcaps and smocks as well as cushion covers and hangings. This was besides supervising the household, doing much of the shopping and keeping the housekeeping accounts.[36] Sometimes women took on and fulfilled major household responsibilities very young indeed. In a memorandum about his daughter Elinor's marriage in 1651, Sir John Lowther noted how, on her mother's death four years before when the girl was only just fourteen, she had taken charge. During this time, 'both in my presence and absence when we had many soldiers quartered she carried herself with so much temper, sobriety and discretion as was much beyond her years and much to my contentment and her own honour and credit'.[37] Her honour, his contentment; but as a widower, left with no one to manage his large household, his honour had also been much at stake.

So much was conventional. What was more variable was how far wives handled wider responsibilities when their husbands were away from home for considerable periods of time. Some men had no qualms. Joan and Maria Thynne, we have seen, were women trusted to manage things at Longleat for months on end while their husbands stayed in London. Joan's legal expertise was considerable and she developed it further as a widow when she became a force in Shropshire in control of her Caus estate. Maria was strong and independent: she arranged the movement of her husband's livestock, told him what should be done about cutting woods and selling timber and warned him about leases that needed revision.[38] Anthony Bacon's wife managed his whole estate satisfactorily when he was in France in 1582.[39] Some west country women were just as assertive as their husbands might have been over matters of wrecked ships and goods on or close to their estates. Mrs Bassett denied Sir John Arundell his claim to wreck on the Basset manor of Tehidy in a firm letter in 1570. Mrs Edgcombe seized wrecked goods in Plymouth Sound in 1575, ignoring a Privy Council order to give them up. Lady Killigrew organised the seizure and sale of a ship in Falmouth Haven in 1582. Mrs

34. Fletcher, *A County Community in Peace and War*, p. 32.
35. D.M. Meads, ed., *The Diary of Lady Margaret Hoby* (London, 1930), passim.
36. *Pepys*, X, p. 196.
37. Phillips, ed., *Lowther Family Estate Books*, pp. 64–5.
38. A.D. Wall, 'Elizabethan Precept and Feminine Practice: The Thynne Family of Longleat', *History* LXXV (1990), pp. 32–5.
39. Greaves, *Society and Religion in Elizabethan England*, p. 311.

Wilmott Trevelyan, a mother of fourteen children, directed workmen on her husband John's estate while he was away in London in 1574 and 1575, sold farm produce, searched out a lease and visited a landlord to ask him to wait for his rent.[40] Margaret Cavendish recorded that her mother was already so 'skilful in leases and selling of lands and courts, keeping ordering of stewards and the like affairs' that she had no difficulty in taking over entire responsibility for the family estate when she was widowed. In a letter in December 1640, Christian Temple gave her husband Sir Peter firm advice about the action he should take against the Darrell family following an affray over their hunting and coursing in the park at Stowe. He should complain to the Lord Chief Justice: 'pray get his warrant to fetch them up before him'. Sir Peter, she entreated, should also raise the matter in the House of Commons and 'desire order for sending them up to answer this'. Thomas Knyvett could tell his wife during the civil war that she was simply 'the best steward' their estate could have in his absence. 'Dear Heart,' wrote Henry Oxinden to his wife from London in 1649 when he was preoccupied with legal affairs, 'pray be mindful of all my affairs at home, the sole ordering of which I leave to thy providence.'[41] Some husbands fussed from a distance with or without good reason, as we have seen in the case of Sir Ralph Verney. Some again were just not able to extract the competence they wanted their wives to exhibit. Katherine, Lord Henry Berkeley's wife, acted as his receiver-general in Gloucestershire for a time during Elizabeth's reign but, dissatisfied, he then gave her an allowance for her own expenses and deprived her of her responsibilities. Lord Hunsdon's wife found the task of managing a household of forty and dealing with a hundred more who sought food each day beyond her when he was away on state service in 1568. She felt driven to ask William Cecil to intervene with the Queen on her behalf.[42]

How particular partnerships worked depended, of course, upon personality and relationship. There were strong women with great drive who might seem intractable but whose organising abilities persuaded their husbands to tolerate their failure to be submissive. The Earl of Shrewsbury, married to the reputedly shrewish Bess of Hardwick, confessed to Lord Burghley in 1591 that the power his wife had with him was 'very great', though he believed he was not ruled by her 'more than were fit for any man to be by his wife'. Sir Francis Walsingham implored William More, in a letter of 1574, to put himself in his shoes: 'Bear, Sir, with my earnestness in recommending my wife's causes. You are your-

40. J. Chynoweth, The Gentry of Tudor Cornwall, University of Exeter PhD thesis, 1994, p. 101.
41. Pollock, 'Teach her to Live', Continuity and Change, 4 (1989), pp. 234, 236–7; HEH, STT 1913.
42. R.L. Greaves, Society and Religion in Elizabethan England (Minneapolis, 1981), pp. 311–12.

self a married man, You know therefore of what force Mrs More's commandments are to you.'[43] On the other hand, there were sad quiet women who had no stamina for the practical tasks of ordering a household and hardly coped without their husband's presence. Catherine Clavering was one of these, 'my grumbling Dowey' as her husband called her in one of his letters. When she was anxious about moving house, he was irritated at her crying and uneasiness, 'which makes my life not very comfortable and the affairs of the family proceed not with the pleasantness I would wish and desire'. Catherine was deeply dependent. Her kind of submissiveness was probably quite normal in the marriages of gentlewomen who had often not freely chosen their spouse and were significantly younger than their husbands. David Levine and Keith Wrightson see the Claverings' marital difficulties as being as much 'a product of the conventional gender roles of the period as of individual character and circumstances'. James Clavering, a demanding man, saw in his cousin Ann, the wife of Henry Liddell, a sharpness and spirit which he found lacking in his own wife. Ann was her husband's intermediary with Clavering in coal trade matters on Tyneside. There were others, though, who found Ann Liddell's forcefulness unacceptable. The Gateshead coal owner William Cotesworth refused to discuss trading affairs with her when he visited the Liddells' London home: 'I'm a female and consequently not capable of understanding further than some one day betwixt this and Monday morn he leaves the town,'[44] she noted. Such were the tensions which could so easily emerge when a capable woman, confident in her managerial skills, went beyond the purely domestic confines.

Within the home women were always liable to be chided for incompetence or put back in their place when it suited a man to show command. In terms of the didactic advice of the conduct books they were supposed to submit meekly to this. Thus Henry Oxinden, who on another occasion a few years earlier was ready to bewail the 'frailty' of women, could lecture Unton Dering when she professed herself in 1647 'altogether unable and unfit' as a woman to take care of her deceased sister's estate. He attributed her reservations to the 'modesty of your nature', asserting roundly that 'as a woman you are able not only to manage a private estate but also to govern a kingdom if called thereunto'. But when Katherine Knyvett, an efficient estate manager on her husband's behalf during the civil war, sought some say about her son's decision to leave his university education to fight she was told firmly by her husband Thomas to 'meddle not in these masculine affairs'.[45]

A wife's overriding duty was to be fruitful. Moreover in a patrilineal society there was tremendous emphasis on the importance of the birth of sons. When Brilliana Harley's first child was a son in 1624 her father

43. Greaves, *Society and Religion in Elizabethan England*, p. 257.
44. Levine and Wrightson, *Making of an Industrial Society*, pp. 314–17.
45. Pollock, 'Teach her to Live', *Continuity and Change*, 4 (1989), p. 251.

wrote at once to express his joy 'in my Brill's safe delivery and with advantage of the sex'.[46] Failure in this respect was a matter for apology, even, on the husband's part, for indifference. Lady Hutton told her husband in 1678 that she would gladly have laid down her life to procure him a son. Mary Henry, her husband told his father in 1693 on the birth of her third daughter, 'would have been very glad to have brought a namesake for you'. 'The having of another girl I thought so little considerable', related the Earl of Northumberland to the Countess of Leicester in 1636, 'that I made no haste in acquainting you with it.'[47] Many women internalised protestant teaching that they were created for maternity and that a life devoted to endurance of multiple pregnancies and caring for children represented the best way of serving the Lord.[48] So failure to conceive brought anxiety and in some cases anguish. 'We had rather hear of my sister's thickening,' wrote Charles Montagu to his brother Edward in 1613. After two years of marriage Sir Simonds D'Ewes recalled in 1629 'that our hopes . . . were almost turned into despair'.[49] Sarah Savage found she could not reconcile herself to the possibility that she was barren as month followed month in 1687 and she did not become pregnant. Her 'serious thoughts' dwelt upon why God had allowed her sister, who was married after her, to conceive before her.[50] Daughters were very much better than nothing in the sense that they were proof of a woman's fertility. Thomas Chicheley congratulated his daughter on producing a girl in 1671, recalling a saying of her grandfather's about the blessing of a girl including the promise in the future of a boy.[51] She knew a son would have been more welcome, Mary Hutton wrote to her brother Christopher in 1676, but she was 'very well assured' he was glad to have a daughter 'and my sister comes so quick that you have great reason to hope within a year to have a son.'[52] Women were only too aware just how much the sex of their child mattered: the birth of a first son gave them a much stronger position in the family, since the credit of his arrival ensured the family line. John

46. J. Eales, *Puritans and Roundheads: The Harleys of Brampton Bryan and the Outbreak of the English Civil War* (Cambridge, 1990), p. 24.
47. P. Crawford, 'The Construction and Experience of Maternity in Seventeenth-Century England', in Fildes, ed., *Women as Mothers*, pp. 20, 35; P. Crawford, 'Katharine and Philip Henry and their Children: A Case Study in Family Ideology', *Transactions of the Historic Society of Lancashire and Cheshire* 134 (1984), p. 51.
48. E.g. W. Gouge, *Domestical Duties* (London, 1622), pp. 282–94.
49. L. Pollock, 'Embarking on a Rough Passage: The experience of Pregnancy in Early Modern Society', in Fildes, ed., *Women as Mothers*, pp. 39–40, 60.
50. Crawford, 'Katharine and Philip Henry', *Transactions of the Historic Society of Lancashire and Cheshire* 134 (1984), p. 50.
51. Crawford, 'Construction and Experience', in Fildes, ed., *Women as Mothers*, pp. 19–20.
52. L. Pollock, *A Lasting Relationship: Parents and their Children over Three Centuries* (London, 1987), pp. 43–4.

Hutton playfully asked to be recommended to Lady Lisle's 'little boy in your belly', and prayed God that she and her husband would in fact be given a son.[53] 'If it be thy blessed will let it be a boy,' confided Lady Mordaunt to God in her private diary in the 1650s.[54]

Not that one son was enough. In an age of high infant and early mortality there was safety in numbers. Whereas gentlewomen would no doubt have often been happy to have taken advantage of the effects of lactation in delaying the next pregnancy, something well understood at this time, their husbands in most cases insisted upon their employing wetnurses. Women who persuaded their husbands to allow them to breast feed were exceptional in the upper levels of society. One who did so, after her first child was born in 1598, was Anne Newdigate, against the advice of her father and various male friends. When the Countess of Lincoln published her treatise advising women that they should suckle their children themselves in 1622, she had to stand her ground against objections on both moral and physical grounds.[55] Breast feeding and sex were seen as incompatible by clerical moralists and men were in general unwilling to forego sexual pleasure for the sake of the relationship of mother and child.[56] Barbara Harris has argued, furthermore, that in early Tudor England 'the political and social functions of the elite family and household' determined how babies were cared for. They were simply too inconvenient to have around when nurses and gentlewomen to care for them were readily available. For this reason, in marriages among the higher gentry which lasted, very large families were quite common. Harris's sample of 1292 women from the late fifteenth and sixteenth centuries produced 117, or 1 in 11 of them, with 10 or more children.[57] The reliance upon nurses for all aspects of day-to-day care remained popular in the late seventeenth century in marriages that placed a high value on social aspirations. The correspondence of Sir Richard Temple, when he was in London in the 1680s, contains regular reports from his steward rather than from his wife about the children's progress: 'I sent to see how the child did and had the enclosed note from nurse,' wrote William Chaplyn in a letter largely taken up with details on the building of Stowe which was then in progress in 1683.[58]

Yet it is a mistake to adopt too dire a view of men's attitude to

53. B.J. Harris, 'Property, Power and Personal Relations: Elite Mothers and Sons in Yorkist and Early Tudor England', *Signs* XV (1990).
54. S.H. Mendelson, 'Stuart Women's Diaries and Occasional Memoirs', in M. Prior, ed., *Women in English Society 1500–1800* (London, 1985), p. 196.
55. D. McLaren, 'Marital Fertility and Lactation 1570–1720', in M. Prior, ed., *Women in English Society 1500–1800* (London, 1985), pp. 27–8.
56. Crawford, 'The Sucking Child', *Continuity and Change* 1 (1986), p. 30.
57. Harris, 'Property, Power', *Signs* 15 (1990).
58. HEH, STT, boxes 24–5.

their wives' efforts to please them with a healthy family. There is much evidence in diaries and letters of the intense involvement husbands often showed in their wives' pregnancies, in childbirth and in concern about infants, even if the day-to-day management of babies was seen as effeminate and not men's business. Demographic research has suggested that the maternal mortality rate was only about one per cent but childbirth was nevertheless, as Linda Pollock has pointed out, a very conspicuous single cause of mortality.[59] Moreover infant mortality was high. 'Going with child' was indeed, as one textbook writer put it, 'as it were a rough sea on which a big-belly'd woman and her infant floats the space of nine months: and labour, which is the only port, is full of dangerous rocks.'[60] The rough passage was embarked on by husband and wife together and it often proved a test of their partnership, of his care and her patient love and resilience.

The biological and social role of a fertile married woman made her life arduous. 'All the time of their lives is ensnared with troubles,' declared the Duchess of Newcastle, who was herself childless: 'what in breeding and bearing children . . . and if they have children, what troubles and griefs do ensue? Troubled with their frowardness and untowardness, the care for their well being, the fear of their ill doing, their grief for their sickness and their unsufferable sorrow for their death.'[61] Richard Baxter set out the same female synopsis: 'their sickness in breeding, their pain in bringing forth . . . the tedious trouble day and night which they have with their children'.[62] Many women found their pregnancies brought sickness and pain, but worse still was the foreboding and in some cases depression about facing labour. There was also the anxiety that a child would be born deformed, indicating God's punishment for sin. Lady Bridgewater begged in her diary that her baby should be 'without any deformity so that I and its father may not be punished'. 'Notwithstanding all my fears it was free from blemish,' noted Elizabeth Turner in 1670.[63] Women approached pregnancy expecting to be ill and if they were not so at some stage it was regarded as something to worry about. 'I am very well and never was as fat in my life', wrote Frances Hatton in 1678, which 'makes me fear that my child does not thrive I do so much.'[64]

59. Pollock, 'Embarking on a Rough Passage', in Fildes, ed., *Women as Mothers*, p. 47.
60. F. Mauriceau, *The Diseases of Women with Child and in Childbed* (1688), cited in Fildes, ed., *Women as Mothers*, p. 39.
61. Cited in Mendelson, 'Stuart Women's Diaries', in Prior, ed., *Women in English Society*, p. 195.
62. Cited in Pollock, 'Embarking on a Rough Passage', in Fildes, ed., *Women as Mothers*, p. 45.
63. Crawford, 'The Sucking Child', *Continuity and Change* 1 (1986), p. 27. See also A. Laurence, 'Women's Psychological Disorders in Seventeenth-Century Britain', in A. Angerman *et al.*, eds, *Current Issues in Women's History* (London, 1989), pp. 201–10.
64. Cited in Pollock, 'Embarking on a Rough Passage', in Fildes, ed., *Women as Mothers*, p. 46.

Ralph Josselin regularly commended his wife to God's protection during her times of 'sad fears by reason of her approaching travail' during the 1640s and 1650s. When Jane Josselin was very ill during pregnancy she was wont to tell him 'thou and I must part', but it was several of the children who in fact died in infancy not she in childbirth.[65] Alice Thornton's pregnancy went well in 1665 'till about a fortnight before my delivery, when my travail began upon me and then the pangs of child-bearing, often remembering me of that sad estate I was to pass and dangerous perils my soul was to find, even by the gates of death'. When she was again pregnant with her ninth child two years later, she confessed in her diary how she would have rather 'not to have been in this condition', but she submitted herself once again to God's providence. Frances Hatton was advised by the midwife that she had a 'very great child' when she was fretting out her last weeks in 1678. 'But I am apt to think I have two I am so exceeding big,' she wrote to her husband.[66] There is no reason to think that such examples of women's fears and dread of childbirth from among the ranks of gentlewomen were untypical of womankind as a whole at this time. Wives became very dependent: on mothers who issued a stream of cosseting advice, but also on husbands who were desired to be near at hand.

What is striking is the sheer quantity of anecdotal evidence that husbands responded positively to their wives' emotional needs. There were some, of course, who were uncaring or insensitive. Henry Oxinden was warned in 1653 in a letter from a friend that his daughter Margaret, due for her lying in, was not being looked after: 'her husband minds it as much as my cows calving . . . she is as unprovided for as one that walks the highways'.[67] James Clavering was ready to leave his 'big-bellied Dowey' for a shooting trip on the Pennine moors in 1712 as her term was approaching.[68] By and large, though, men faced the fact, in a way that modern husbands cannot imagine, that their whole future – of their marriage, of a healthy brood, of inheritance – was on the line when their wives' confinements came. Sometimes a difficult pregnancy was a pro-longed agony for both partners and men's emotions could be really stirred. Lady Hester Temple made a will in 1606 convinced that her pregnancy that year spelt her end: 'I bequeath my soul to Almighty God whom I believe did shed his precious blood on the cross for me a sinful woman and my body to Stowe worms by my children.' She desired her mother 'to be good' to her poor orphaned brood of twelve while she lay with those who had predeceased her. Sir Thomas Temple has inscribed the will in his own hand: 'Hester I will perform this thy will.' But in fact

65. Houlbrooke, ed., *English Family Life*, pp. 112–18; A. Macfarlane, *The Family Life of Ralph Josselin* (Cambridge, 1970), pp. 84–5.
66. Pollock, *A Lasting Relationship*, pp. 22–8.
67. Cited in Pollock, 'Embarking on a Rough Passage', in Fildes, ed., *Women as Mothers*, p. 53.
68. Levine and Wrightson, *Making of an Industrial Society*, p. 315.

she lived many more years and it was he who died first.[69] Endymion
Porter wrote as follows in heartfelt terms when he found he could not
leave the court in 1620 to be with his wife at the time of her confine-
ment: 'Good sweetheart, show thy love to me now in excusing to thyself
the wrong I do thee to thyself, in not leaving the commands of a master
to see so good a wife at such a time.' Charles Cheyne described the
course of his wife's labour in 1650 in a letter to his brother-in-law. The
letter declares his sense of relief at her safety: 'we were all surprised with
the unexpected coming but I am confident she went her full time . . . the
child is, I thank God, though little and weak born, now well and
thriving'. Ralph Josselin described all Jane's deliveries in terms of his
religious faith, attributing to God when things had been difficult their
happy success despite the deficiencies of the midwife. One of the most
touching of these accounts comes from the pen of Edward Conway,
writing to his brother about his wife Anne in the midst of a very difficult
pregnancy. There had been uncertainty during weeks of illness about
whether she was in fact breeding. Now the baby had quickened and the
couple were advised that Anne 'must expect as hard labour as any woman
in the world ever had'. So he wrote for help in obtaining, in complete
confidence, 'an eagle stone esteemed of great virtue in hard labour' which
she wished to have by her. He concluded the letter with some dismissive
remarks about the male habit of 'gathering together an estate for an heir',
declaring that his current experience confirmed his sealed mind against
'any impetuous desires after children'.[70] The letter forcibly illustrates the
caring and thoughtfulness that could be displayed within the apparently
formal patriarchal structure of seventeenth-century marriage.

Childbirth, and the subsequent lying in which normally lasted for about
a month, was a collective social event in a reserved female space which
has important implications for this account of the practice of patriarchal
relations. It was a time when women expected to offer support to each
other as they witnessed each other's agonies. The Countess of Warwick
recorded in her diary how she went directly when she heard her niece
was in labour: 'I stayed with her all night, she having a most terrible sharp
labour . . . and with much earnestness and many tears begged a safe
delivery of her.'[71] There was much that was ritualistic about the way the
business was conducted. The chamber was darkened, the gossips prepared
the caudle, a nourishing drink to keep up the mother's spirits, the
midwife ruled the room employing her own particular techniques and
experience. She alone touched the mother's vagina and cervix; the gossips
helped with cutting the umbilical cord, washing and swaddling the new-

69. HEH, STT Personal Papers box 5(7), box 6(7).
70. Citations from Pollock, *A Lasting Relationship*, pp. 23, 27, 31–2.
71. Mendelson, 'Stuart Women's Diaries', in Prior, ed., *Women in English Society*, pp.
    196–7.

born child. Husbands, firmly excluded, fretted in another room for release from their waiting. 'My wife was delivered . . . on the 15th of February about 2 of the clock afternoon,' noted John Greene in his diary for 1645, 'my aunt Beresford came in and told me it had a face as big as my boy and that it was a worthy babe'. She clearly understood he needed some consolation for the fact that his second child was a daughter. Samuel Woodforde wrote a moving account of his emotions during his wife's difficult labour in giving birth to his son Heighes in 1664, ending it with the statement that Mrs Ann Norton, one of the six women attending her with 'old goodwife Tailor the midwife', brought him the news.[72]

During the lying in at first only women visited the mother and child but over the four weeks it lasted there was normally a gradual relaxation on the restriction of male visitors. What diarists most often record, indicating its significance, was the churching, another ritual which concluded the event of childbirth, bringing a woman back into the male world with an act of celebration for the ordeal she had survived.[73] Women were strongly attached to churching in this period, Adrian Wilson argues, because it was a woman's ritual which legitimised the whole 'ceremony of childbirth'. What the process of lying in had accomplished, Natalie Zemon Davis has suggested, was a reversal of the normal power relations between a wife and her husband. Temporarily and within generally accepted and understood bounds, the woman was on top. And why not, argued the author of the tract *The Woman's Advocate* published in 1683:

> 'Tis a time of freedom, when women, like parliament men have a privilege to talk petty treason. . . . Women are sociable creatures as well as men and if they can't talk philosophy they must talk of that which they better understand. . . . Men most acknowledge that women have done them a most extraordinary kindness to ease them of that ponderous weight of infant carriage.[74]

Wives enjoyed, as the prize earned at the conclusion of their pregnancies, an opportunity for separateness and the company of her own kind. They withdrew from their husbands two of the fruits of marriage which he most prized: her domestic labour and her sexual services. 'The immersion of the mother in a female collectivity', as Wilson puts it, 'elegantly inverted the central feature of patriarchy, namely its basis in individual

72. Houlbrooke, *English Family Life*, pp. 110–11, 125–6.
73. Macfarlane, ed., *Diary of Ralph Josselin*, pp. 419, 466, 503; Houlbrooke, *English Family Life*, pp. 110–11; see also J. Boulton, *Neighbourhood and Society. A London Suburb in the Seventeenth Century* (Cambridge, 1987), pp. 276–9.
74. Cited in M. Roberts, ' "Words they are Women and Deeds they are Men": Images of Work and Gender in Early Modern England', in L. Charles and L. Duffin, eds., *Women and Work in Pre-Industrial Europe* (London, 1985), pp. 154–5.

male property.'[75] By this very fact it can be argued, just as with other inversions which we will consider later, it contributed to ensuring patriarchy's endurance.

Although, as we have seen, some parents pursued a social life that left them little time for their children, there is plenty of evidence in diaries and letters that most mothers and many fathers were deeply involved with and strongly attached to their children. A mother's pride shines out from the remarkable paper written by Hester Temple in 1602 recording the date and time of the birth of the eleven of her fifteen children born up till then, together with the names of their thirty-three godparents.[76] Mary Woodforde's chronicle covering the years from 1685 to 1690 of the children's doings, comings and goings and progress exhibits this same pride.[77] Elizabeth Freke hurried back to England from dutiful attendance on her husband in Ireland when she heard her baby son had been crippled by a fall.[78] Anne Clifford's diary contains similar records of motherly concern as well as satisfaction at achievements like new teeth and walking without leading strings.[79] Brilliana Harley's letters to her husband when he was away in London are full of the warmth and affection she felt for her children together with her sense that they were shared and precious possessions. 'They all say he is like his father as can be,' she wrote of her second son Robert soon after his birth in 1626. Ned had taken to his weaning well, was beginning to walk and was his grandfather's darling. 'His grandfather will not yield that any should be loved like him, he must be the finest boy in his eyes', she reported on 21 April, before declaring 'now I have done with all my nursery news'. There was more to say about her boys in another letter on 11 May: 'Ned and Robin are well . . . Ned grows like my father or else everyone is much mistaken and Robin like you or else I am.' When Ned eventually went away to Oxford, he received her regular letters showing obsessive and fussy motherly devotion.[80] Katherine Duchess of Buckingham told how she delighted in her baby clapping his hands to music.[81] 'Poor little Susanna

75. A. Wilson, 'The Ceremony of Childbirth and its Interpretation', in Fildes, ed., *Women as Mothers*, pp. 68–107; N.Z. Davis, *Society and Culture in Early Modern France* (Stamford, 1975), p. 145; see also D. Cressy, 'Purification, Thanksgiving and the Churching of Women in Post-Reformation England', *Past and Present* 141 (1993), pp. 106–46.
76. L.L. Peck, *Court Patronage and Corruption in Early Stuart England* (London, 1990), p. 75.
77. D.H. Woodforde, ed., *Woodforde Papers and Diaries* (London, 1932), pp. 12–25.
78. 'Mrs Elizabeth Freke, her Diary', *Journal of the Cork Historical and Archaeological Society* XVII (1911), p. 25.
79. D.J.H. Clifford, ed., *The Diary of Lady Anne Clifford* (Stroud, 1990), pp. 21–82. For an account of infants' progress drawing upon many diaries see L.A. Pollock, *Forgotten Children: Parent-Child Relations from 1500 to 1900* (Cambridge, 1983), pp. 203–61.
80. BL Loan 29/22, 202. I am very grateful to Jacqueline Eales for transcripts of these letters; Eales, *Puritans and Roundheads*, pp. 24–8.
81. Crawford, 'The Sucking Child', *Continuity and Change* 1 (1986), p. 29.

is very ill about her teeth,' wrote Frances Hatton to her husband in 1677. 'Oh my Lord if I should die, show particular kindness to that child for if I have ten thousand sons I can not love them so well.'[82] This heartfelt remark directly challenged the teaching that it was boys who really mattered and deserved particular care in upbringing. Richard Napier, the Bedfordshire astrologer-physician, saw failure to love their children as a sign of abnormality in some female clients. He encountered a number of cases of women whose suicidal feelings included wanting their children to die with them, suggesting the depth of their emotional involvement. Alice Savil, for example, was at one point 'desperate to drown herself' and 'desirous to have her child to go into the water with her'.[83] Here again we catch a glimpse of female subjectivity. None of the prescriptive material of this period yet celebrates motherhood as such but the experience was no less real and consciously significant for this reason.

Men, as we have seen, had to bear in mind the dangers of a return to effeminacy posed by the female world of nurture but plenty of them were far from remote from their children. Henry Newcome wrote about the warm moist kisses of his baby.[84] 'Little Nick hath cast his coat and seemeth metamorphosed into a grasshopper,' reported Nathaniel Bacon to his wife Jane around 1625, with reference to the boy's progress in walking. Next year, showing his pleasure in his daughter's first words, he joked about how he 'should have been glad to have understood some of her new language'. Hugh Cholmley told in his memoirs of his son Richard's bravery as a five-year-old in 1630 when he had to have an incision on a lump in his arm: 'he would say "Father, would you have it done?" and I answered "Yes, sweetheart, the doctor thinks it necessary".'[85] The presents that Sir Thomas Pelham regularly brought home to his Sussex home from London between the 1630s and 1650s attest to his affection for his numerous offspring. It might be a bonnet and drum for Henry, or a muff for Bess or a looking glass for Nan.[86] Ralph Josselin's detailed references to trouble with their children at night contains no suggestion that he took much of the practical responsibility but they indicate how fully the couple shared the stress of 'sudden cryings out'. The Josselins often found the 'little ones a great grief'.[87] The fact that our best evidence about the folklore and natural remedies for childrearing comes from women's commonplace books should not cause us to assume that men entirely failed to involve themselves in these things. Teething

82. Cited in Pollock, *A Lasting Relationship*, p. 73.
83. M. Macdonald, *Mystical Bedlam: Madness, Anxiety and Healing in Seventeenth-Century England* (Cambridge, 1981), pp. 83–4.
84. Crawford, 'The Sucking Child', *Continuity and Change* I (1986), p. 29. For further examples see Wrightson, *English Society*, pp. 114–15.
85. Citations from Pollock, *A Lasting Relationship*, pp. 56, 73.
86. Fletcher, *A County Community in Peace and War*, p. 34.
87. Macfarlane, *Family Life of Ralph Josselin*, p. 89.

was thought to be assisted by a necklace of henbane seed or anointing the child's gums with the brains of a hare or the comb from a cock. There were recipes which invoked moon lore and sympathetic magic. In 1734 Sarah Savage, daughter of a nonconformist minister, passed on to her daughter a recommendation she had heard from an old woman that she should wean her son during the waning of the moon, expressing some scepticism about it as she did so. But she did pass it on.[88] Husbands and wives drew upon this shared and still vibrant mental world of cures and healing in caring together for their children. When they lost them all the available evidence suggests that they felt searing grief. Women like the Countess of Warwick and Alice Thornton used their diaries to pour out this grief.[89] Men like Ralph Josselin, Adam Martindale, Sir Simonds D'Ewes and Nehemiah Wallington are at their most moving in the accounts they have left us of their emotions about the loss of children. Parents, it has been argued convincingly, made a very large emotional investment in their children in early modern England and expected little in return.[90]

Judith Bennett has described marriage at this time as based upon a 'voluntary egalitarianism shadowed by inequality'. Even in sharing, she notes, the husband's greater material resources bespoke inequality; even in sharing, she argues, 'the husband's power remained merely suspended, not fully yielded'. It is clearly the case that the contemporary ideal of conjugal relations was predicated on women's ultimate submission. Bennett is clearly right that the law provided women at this time with little real protection against an abusive marriage and that there was little women could do except tolerate an indifferent husband: a woman could find herself 'a sort of servant to her husband or even cast aside altogether'.[91] Theory, legal precept and the rhetoric of puritan clerics in their conduct literature, despite its lyrical passages about conjugal love, were all stacked against women's being allowed to contemplate the realisation of loving mutuality in their marriages. Yet we cannot dismiss all the anecdotal evidence of wills, monuments, letters, memoirs and diaries which testifies to many people's happiness in the married state at this time. The next

88. Crawford, *Women and Religion in England 1500–1720* (London, 1993), p. 101.
89. Mendelson, 'Stuart Women's Diaries', in Prior, ed., *Women in English Society*, pp. 197–8.
90. L.A. Pollock, *Forgotten Children: Parent–Child Relations from 1500 to 1900* (Cambridge, 1983), pp. 134–7; Macfarlane, ed., *Diary of Ralph Josselin*, pp. 113–14, 202–5, 567–8; Macfarlane, *Family Life of Ralph Josselin*, pp. 165–6; Wrightson, *English Society*, p. 112; Parkinson, ed., *Life of Adam Martindale*, p. 109; examples in Pollock, *A Lasting Relationship*, pp. 123–7; for this issue in a wider social setting see M. Macdonald, *Mystical Bedlam: Madness, Anxiety and Healing in Seventeenth Century England* (Cambridge, 1981), pp. 82–4.
91. J.M. Bennett, 'Medieval Women, Modern Women: Across the Great Divide', in D. Aers, ed., *Culture and History 1350–1600: Essays in English Communities, Identities and Writing* (London, 1992), p. 154.

chapter explores the darker side of early modern marriage. It is appropriate to end this one by noting the relevant findings of Sara Heller
Mendelson's analysis of Stuart women's diaries. Among the 21 marriages
contracted by women who have left sufficient information for our purposes, 15, she finds, were loving and companionable and 6 were unsatisfactory. The happy marriages included 2 love matches which eventually
gained parental consent, 3 marriages made by free choice, 2 arranged ones
where the bride had a clear veto and 1 arranged one in which the bride
was only thirteen. The unhappy marriages included 1 elopement, 2 forced
marriages and the arranged marriage of Lady Anne Clifford. It does seem
that where all parties had the chance of consent there was a better chance
of contentment.[92] Which is to say that the less harshly patriarchy was
enforced to the letter the better the chance of mutual happiness. The
whole success of early modern English patriarchy, it can be argued, lay in
its flexibility and its capacity, as a gender system, to sustain modifications,
cushioning and mitigation.

92. Mendelson, 'Stuart Women's Diaries', in Prior, ed., *Women in English Society*,
    pp. 193–4.

10. *Marital Violence*

WE ARE CONCERNED in this book with a society suffused with personal relationships of dominance and submission, a society in which the use of violence was accepted as a necessary means of maintaining order in hierarchical relationships, both within and outside the household. Wife-beating is an issue at the core of early modern patriarchy and it relates to personal dynamics at the innermost level of marital relationships. We must set beside everything that has been said in the previous two chapters some deeply entrenched beliefs about the relative power of husband and wife. England was no different from other European countries at this time in having a legal code which allowed husbands to inflict what was called 'moderate correction' on their wives, besides beating children and servants when they found it necessary. There were some guidelines, such as that the violence should not draw blood and that if a stick was used it should be no thicker than a man's thumb, the original source of the idea of a rule of thumb. This doctrine was reiterated by a judge as late as 1782. It was assumed that correction meant punishment and the law in this sense did not give men a right to beat their wives at random or on a whim.[1] But such limitations still left the question of what was 'lawful and reasonable correction' wholly open.[2] The old proverbs remained immensely powerful. Probably the most popular one, recorded in Ray's collection of 1670, runs

> A spaniel, a woman and a walnut tree
> The more they're beaten the better they be.

A particularly colourful expression of rough masculinity, which was current in coastal communities, went as follows:

> The crab of the wood is sauce very good
> For the crab of the sea

1. R. Phillips, *Untying the Knot: A Short History of Divorce* (Cambridge, 1991), p. 98; L. Stone, *The Family, Sex and Marriage in England 1500–1800* (London, 1977), p. 326 and plate 19.
2. This occurs in T.E. *The Law's Resolution of Women's Rights* (London, 1632), p. 1281.

> But the wood of a crab is sauce for a drab
> That will not her husband obey.

There was also the punning adage about how 'he that fetches a wife from Shrewsbury must carry her into Staffordshire or else shall live in Cumberland', spelling out the cares which would encumber a man who failed to keep a good stick ready to deal with a scolding wife.[3]

There is good reason in fact to think that wife-beating persisted relentlessly in England from the sixteenth century to the nineteenth century. Historians are unlikely ever to be able to quantify it but there is enough evidence available for us to explore how its occurrence fitted into the pattern of marital relationships. Its persistence was due to a climate of opinion about marriage, evident at least until 1800, which was fairly constant. There was no dishonour for men in the use of moderate violence which, as Laura Gowing puts it, was 'intended to support patriarchal household authority and read as such by its victims, its witnesses and its defenders'. Some men were quite ready to take a stand on this basis, confessing to having administered a beating.[4] Humphrey Stafford declared in the Court of Requests in 1562 that he had beaten his wife Elizabeth 'for the evil government and behaviour of her devilish tongue in uttering many unseemly and quarrelous words' and for 'warning or reformation of her manners and life'.[5] 'Relatively few men or women in early modern England thought wives had an absolute right not to be beaten,' Margaret Hunt concluded.[6] 'Women must have expected to be struck some time by their husbands,' asserts Roderick Phillips, bearing in mind their experience of family life as daughters and as witnesses to other marriages.[7] There is insufficient evidence to judge how far levels of marital violence varied between different social groups. The gentry had their own ways of dealing with the problem when it became serious. Her father moved in when Anne Temple was maltreated by her husband William Andrews in 1625, obtaining a warrant from the Lord Chief Justice for two fellow JPs to investigate and bind Andrews to good behaviour.[8] Similar cases of informal mediation within a particular social circle may have left no record. Marital violence was certainly not confined to the poor.

The absence of systematic records of wife-beating would seem to suggest that it was common and that a moderate level of violence within

3. J. Ray, *A Collection of English Proverbs* (London 1670), pp. 50, 210, 251; Tilley, nos W354, W644, W699.
4. Gowing, p. 136.
5. T. Stretton, 'Women and Litigation in the Elizabethan Court of Requests', in J. Kermode and G. Walker, eds, *Women, Crime and the Courts in Early Modern England* (London, 1994), p. 233.
6. M. Hunt, 'Wife Beating, Domesticity and Women's Independence in Eighteenth-Century London', *Gender and History* 4 (1992), p. 24.
7. Phillips, *Untying the Knot*, p. 102.
8. HEH, STT 40, 1366, 2255, 2273, 2342, 2418, 2420.

marriage was seen as acceptable and not as a matter of public order. What is interesting about the court material, which usually relates to especially severe violence, or otherwise refers to violence incidentally, is that it tells us something about normal expectations both on the part of spouses and of servants and neighbours who may have heard or even seen what was going on. In disastrously unhappy marriages among the gentry, where wives suffered a husband's continuing and brutal cruelty, servants often intervened to the extent of comforting and giving succour to the victim; though they could do nothing to halt her ill-treatment. This could go on for a long time, for it is extraordinary what life-threatening abuse some women managed to endure, as is indicated by the stories of the marriages of Sir Oliver and Lady Anne Butler between 1656 and 1675 and John and Mary Dineley between 1717 and 1741 which have been told in detail by Lawrence Stone.[9] For women living cheek by jowl with other families in towns and villages the best hope of relief from assault lay in assiduous cultivation of sympathy from friends, neighbours and relatives who might be ready, sometimes with the weight of a local magistrate behind them, to mediate. Wives had good reason not to bring in others since they must often have known that it would be likely to exacerbate a difficult relationship with a man who had already shown himself prone to violence. Yet often enough they were sufficiently desperate to do so. The first steps would be to follow a woman suffering some violence in the presence of others. Though it took courage to appeal to relatives or the neighbourhood, in fact they were a woman's main source of power. Margaret Hunt notes that the evidence of the early eighteenth century consistory court cases of legal separation does show women being abused and attacked by their husbands in front of relatives: 'far from being unspeakable, family violence was a dramatic spectacle, played out in the presence of everyone in the immediate vicinity'.[10] It was not invariably the case, though, that women who dared to take their husbands to court, seeking a release from the marriage, did receive wholehearted support from those called as witnesses. A servant's deposition relating to Mary Becke's suit for a separation from her husband William on grounds of cruelty in 1565 is instructive. 'She never heard nor saw Mr Becke use any cruelty', she told the Norwich consistory court, 'but that any woman might well bear at her husband's hands.' This servant thought Mary Becke's earlier action in asking for a bond for William's good behaviour from a JP was a plea for special treatment for he was never 'so cruel or to hate her so much that she should require further security of her life for mutilation of her members than other honest wives have'.[11]

9. L. Stone, *Broken Lives: Separation and Divorce in England 1660–1857* (Oxford, 1993), pp. 27, 33–7, 82–116.

10. Hunt, 'Wife Beating', *Gender and History* 4 (1992), pp. 20–23.

11. S.D. Amussen, *An Ordered Society: Gender and Class in Early Modern England* (Oxford, 1988), p. 129.

The London consistory court evidence for the years from 1711 to 1713 shows that the range of issues that led men to exercise patriarchal rights of correction was very wide. Alleged extravagance, verbal defiance and sexual jealousy are predictably regular items. Control over resources was often at the centre of marital discord. Thomas Hull, a barber and peruke maker, terrorised his wife until she gave him the records of the separate settlement she had brought into the marriage: his dealings included beating her until she miscarried, threatening to confine her to a mad-house, throwing her clothes in the fire and trying to burn her. When Rebecca Hudson was unwilling to sell some of her own estate to pay his debts her husband Garven held a dagger to her neck saying he would cut it if she 'cried out, stirred or spoke'. The butcher Anthony Pitts locked up his wife, beat and kicked her then threw her out in the street because her aunt would not stand as security for him for a loan.[12] Investigating a group of Wiltshire restitution and separation suits from the early seventeenth century, Martin Ingram found all the husbands showed some signs of mental instability, which may have been linked to their decaying economic position and its effect in reinforcing marital tensions. There was ample evidence in each case of blows and unreasonable treatment but these were apparently marriages in dire circumstances rather than cases of gratuitous cruelty.[13] Richard Napier, the early seventeenth-century Bedfordshire astrologer-physician, saw a streak of irrationality and instability in violent husbands, remarking in his notes on one case 'her husband is lightheaded and beateth his wife'.[14]

Refusal of a husband's sexual demands often provoked him into physical and sexual violence. There was of course no legal remedy against marital rape but occasionally a woman attempted to get the help of a JP over other forms of sexual violence. The complaint of Mary Bradshaw, a Middlesex gardener's wife, in 1792 ran that her husband both beat her brutally and committed acts of indecency. References to sexual refusal in a story of the escalating discord which led to a woman's separation suit were quite common. Amelia Brazier, who knew her husband who was a wine vault keeper had been with prostitutes and might be bringing home venereal disease, refused sexual intercourse with him in 1781. He beat her and tried to murder her. In another case in the London consistory court the previous year, Mary Emberson, who declared that her illiterate husband's success as a corn merchant was heavily dependent on her bookkeeping skills, told of how when she sought refuge from him at night with the servants he dragged her from the room and kicked her on the

12. Hunt, 'Wife Beating', *Gender and History* 4 (1992), pp. 17–18.
13. M. Ingram, *Church Courts, Sex and Marriage in England 1570–1640* (Cambridge, 1987), pp. 183–4.
14. M. Macdonald, *Mystical Bedlam: Madness, Anxiety and Healing in Seventeenth-Century England* (Cambridge, 1981), p. 102.

thighs.[15] Sexual dissatisfaction led some men speedily into ill-treatment. Joanne Barrett, looking for a separation from her husband in 1590, explained that he was going elsewhere for sex and was 'so fierce and cruel a man towards her that she dare not dwell with him'.[16]

Wife-beating persisted because of its social acceptability in male circles. The supposed disciplinary function of the practice was never anything more than a fiction, a piece of hypocrisy that reflected the direct and unequivocal power of husbands. Margaret Hunt concludes from her analysis of the London records for 1711 to 1713 that 'in numerous cases there seems to have been no reason at all beyond a man's desire to beat up a woman and not be penalized for it'.[17] The connection between drink and displays of violence evident in popular ballad literature is exceptionally well documented as fact not fiction in the Dorchester offenders book for the 1630s.[18] Methuselah Notting, one of the town's blacksmiths, beat up his wife for questioning his authority when she pleaded with him to stop drinking. When William Miller's wife sent for the constables he declared his patriarchal rights in no uncertain terms: 'in despite of their teeth he would go to the alehouse . . . and have his cup and a pot of sack and a whore, and that his wife should stand by and see it, and that if she would dare to speak he would beat her to pieces'.[19] The wife of Stephen Rawlins told Richard Napier about the beatings she alleged had endured when he went on a drinking spree: he 'thinketh little to gad a-drinking . . . careth not to return until his wife fetch him home'. Another of Napier's clients was Elizabeth Easton, a woman in despair at the treatment she received from her husband and his family. They 'would rate her and slap her as a dog – and a husband ready to beat her'.[20] According to Amelia Brazier's testimony in 1781 her husband had told the magistrate when she first approached him about her sufferings that 'he would beat and pox his wife whenever he thought proper'.[21] It was this notion that a man could do what he liked inside his own home, that his wife was his sexual and physical property, which a man living in Dymchurch in Elizabeth's reign appealed to in an incident which brought him before the archdeacon's court. Hearing that his wife had fallen out with her gossips, he went around saying 'neighbour if you will beat your wife I will beat mine'. This plan for reasserting male supremacy in a Kentish village clearly ran aground due to men's fears that such disciplinary action

15. A. Clark, *Women's Silence, Men's Violence: Sexual Assault in England 1770–1845* (London, 1987), pp. 42–3.
16. Amussen, *An Ordered Society*, p. 128.
17. Hunt, 'Wife Beating', *Gender and History* 4 (1992), p. 16.
18. For a typical ballad reference see *Roxburghe*, II, p. 161.
19. D.E. Underdown, *Fire Under Heaven: The Life of an English Town in the Seventeenth Century* (London, 1992), pp. 71–2.
20. Macdonald, *Mystical Bedlam*, p. 100.
21. Clark, *Women's Silence, Men's Violence*, pp. 42–3.

would not, so far as the women were concerned, be the end of the matter.[22]

A few exceptional women who suffered in silence have left us written testimony of their lot. Elizabeth Freke's story of psychological harassment by her husband we have seen contains some allusions to physical maltreatment.[23] The particular baptist Anne Wentworth, in her *Vindication* of 1677 which justified her decision to leave her husband after living with him for eighteen years, spoke of the 'unspeakable tyrannies of a hard-hearted yokefellow' who, she alleged, had given her 'fierce looks, bitter words, sharp tongue and cruel usage'.[24] When wives did find the courage to seek legal redress we find them employing a conventional language of gender hierarchy which was not seen as inconsistent with a rhetoric of love and affection. They asserted their virtue and acceptance of male supremacy; they protested against their husbands' refusal to fulfil financial obligations and treat a wife according to her merits. In a London consistory court case of 1702, Sarah Sabin, who would not give up her jointure to her husband, declared that she had been 'modest, sober, virtuous and submissive' so he had no cause to abuse her. Yet he had thrown knives at her, taken her clothes and possessions and encouraged his brother to attack her and her maid.[25]

The reluctance of others to intervene sometimes emerged incidentally in court cases. Thus examinations about the death of the Norfolk woman Anne Gosling in 1600 revealed that her family knew her husband John beat her but did nothing to offer help until she was knocked unconscious.[26] A beating which led to death might predictably lead to a court appearance: John Barnes faced the Ely assizes in 1652 because, coming home drunk and being told by his wife that 'he was a rogue and that there was many a truer man hanged', he had beaten and kicked her so severely that she died of her injuries.[27] William Staine found himself in court in 1587 simply because his violence was so excessive. He was charged with 'misusing his wife with stripes contrary to all order and reason'.[28] Moreover the threats of men who were apparently unstable and had a reputation for violence were likely to reach the ears of JPs if they talked of killing. The Essex anti-puritan Richard Bright was reported in 1648 for threatening to drown his wife or burn her 'because she went to sermons'. Essex villagers also petitioned against Thomas Holland in 1676

22. P. Collinson, *The Birthpangs of Protestant England: Religious and Cultural Change in the Sixteenth and Seventeenth Centuries* (London, 1988), p. 72.
23. Above, p. 164.
24. E. Graham, *et al.*, eds, *Her Own Life: Autobiographical Writings by Seventeenth-Century Englishwomen* (London, 1989), pp. 183, 187.
25. Hunt, 'Wife Beating', *Gender and History* 4 (1992), pp. 15–16.
26. Amussen, *An Ordered Society*, p. 129.
27. K. Wrightson, *English Society 1580–1680* (London, 1982), p. 98.
28. Cited in Macdonald, *Mystical Bedlam*, p. 102.

when he told people 'God damn him he would stab his wife and a short life and a merry one was better than a long and sad one.'[29] Villagers were also very sensitive to cases which involved a new charge on the poor rate. Thus a Devon man, reported to quarter sessions in 1618, confessed 'that he had divers and sundry times beaten his wife . . . locking her out of doors in the night season in so much as she was constrained either to live in the street or by the hedges'.[30] But the exceptionally serious nature of these cases makes the point that we cannot expect the court records to tell us much about something which, in its normal manifestations, was accepted as part of the pattern of contemporary marriage.

If men had tried to employ legal action to control wives who offered them violence they would have been a laughing stock. But the satirical literature, as we have seen, suggests that many women could be expected, so far as they had the courage and the physical strength, to give as good as they got in marital quarrels.[31] How many actual marriages matched this kind of dramatised fiction it is impossible to say. But there seems little doubt that the English situation, in general terms, was little different from that in Augsburg in the 1540s where, as Lyndal Roper has shown, the Council treated violence as a regrettable fact of married life. Men's 'chastisement' of their wives, approved by the Council within limits, 'did not proceed in measured, orderly fashion'. Both men and women grabbed objects to hit the other which were nearest to hand.[32] Richard Gough's account of the second marriage of Rowland Muckleston of Myddle in Shropshire around 1700 shows how villagers accepted that there were marriages of this kind. After the death of his first wife who was 'a quiet low spirited woman', Muckleston, he records, married 'a very handsome gentlewoman and of a masculine spirit'. She, we are told, 'would not suffer him to intermeddle with her concerns within doors and she endeavoured to keep a good house, but this caused them to keep an unquiet home and many contests happened between them which ended not without blows'.[33] Such incidental evidence reminds us of a huge untold story of the contestedness of English patriarchy within the early modern home.

In Calvin's Geneva spouse-beating was made a crime.[34] The puritan clerics who condemned wife-beating in England in the conduct books of the period between the 1590s and 1620s would doubtless have supported

29. J.A. Sharpe, 'Domestic Homicide in Early Modern England', *Historical Journal* 24 (1981), p. 31.
30. M. Wolfe, 'The County Government of Devon 1625–1640', Exeter University PhD thesis, 1993, p. 277.
31. Above, pp. 20–21.
32. L. Roper, *The Holy Household: Women and Morals in Reformation Augsburg* (Oxford, 1989), pp. 188–9.
33. D. Hey, *An English Rural Community: Myddle under the Tudors and Stuarts* (Leicester, 1974), p. 214.
34. Phillips, *Untying the Knot*, p. 98.

similar legislation. But their idealistic conception of marriage never pen-
etrated very deeply into the gentry elite as a whole and theirs remained
a distinctly minority view before the civil war. The distinct break they
made with early Tudor advice should nevertheless be noted. Harrington's
Commendations of 1528 simply stated the legal position, that 'the husband
may moderately correct and punish his wife for a lawful cause'. Richard
Whitford's *Work for Householders* of 1530 offered the passing comment that
a 'shrew will sooner be corrected by smiling or laughing than by a staff
or strokes' but issued no prohibition on male violence towards spouses.[35]
Henry Smith, John Wing and William Gouge in their marriage manuals,
by contrast, were emphatic in their rejection of physical correction of
wives. Gouge put the case under three heads: there was no specific
warrant for it in scripture, common sense forbade it and the whole nature
of their relationship, their 'near conjunction and very union', made it
inappropriate. 'Can it be thought reasonable', he asked, 'that she who is
man's perpetual bedfellow, who hath power over his body, who is a joint
parent of the children, a joint governor of the family, should be beaten
by his hands?'[36] The only one of these writers who did advocate wife-
beating in exceptional circumstances of wifely defiance, William
Whateley, tied himself in knots at his unease in recommending a practice
which he knew many saw as 'too imperious in him, too servile in her'.[37]
There was no scriptural precedent for a man to strike his wife, resolved
the Tiverton baptist meeting in 1657. A man was expelled from John
Bunyan's baptist church in the 1670s for beating his wife often 'for very
light matters'.[38]

The puritan notion of marriage as a deep union of bodies and souls lies
behind a tract published by Robert Snawsel in 1610 where the issue is
explored at length in a dialogue between Benezer, husband to the shrewish Xantip and the evangelical Abigail. 'Though he beat her he need not
hate her,' declares Benezer. 'Hath not the man as much power over his
wife's body as the father hath over the child?' he asks. 'He hath power
over the wife's body for procreation and so she hath power over his
and both over the child for correction,' Abigail replies. When Benezer
continues to argue the point, Abigail tells of her own observations:
'the wife would be made more unruly and outrageous by beating. We
are women and have some experience of these things.' Benezer is persuaded to acknowledge that his fighting with Xantip has got him
nowhere and that men, as Abigail teaches, should accept the obligation

35. K.M. Davies, 'Continuity and Change in Literary Advice on Marriage', in R.B.
    Outhwaite, ed., *Marriage and Society* (London 1981), pp. 68, 79.
36. H. Smith, *A Preparative to Marriage* (London, 1591), p. 54; J. Wing, *The Crown
    Conjugal or Spouse Royal* (London, 1620), p. 47; W. Gouge, *Domestical Duties* (London
    1622), pp. 394–7.
37. W. Whateley, *The Bride Bush* (London, 1623) pp. 99–116, 123–5, 210–16.
38. P. Crawford, *Women and Religion in England 1500–1720* (London, 1631), p. 148.

on them as the stronger sex to honour the weaker vessel.[39] It is this pragmatic argument rather than high-flown spiritual ones which is foremost in ballad and other literature. Wife-beating is not only an abuse of superior physical strength and therefore of male honour; it is also counterproductive because it exacerbates rather than resolves marital discord.[40] 'If thou go about to master a woman in hope to bring her to humility', declared the misogynist Joseph Swetnam, 'there is no way to make her good with stripes except thou beat her to death.'[41]

William Heale's *An Apology for Women* is the single tract devoted exclusively to the issue of wife-beating in the seventeenth century. It arose from a public disputation at Oxford in 1609, when Heale answered a fellow academic who took the conventional legal view with a well structured argument intended to prove that this was an 'unnatural and uncivil opinion'. Heale's case, like that of the puritan clerics, was based on the loving intimacy of the marriage bond. He found no 'sweeter taste of friendship than this coupling of souls in this mutuality either of condoling or comforting'. Heale could perceive no proper legal basis for wife-beating, though he was entirely orthodox in his statements of patriarchal authority: 'nature and the God of nature in every kind hath given preeminence unto the male . . . but neither is the one so predominant nor the other so servile as that from them should proceed any other fruits but of a royal protection and loyal subjection'. Besides, he declared, for a man to use violence against his wife was a 'public example dangerous unto the commonwealth'. In practical terms it was a poor way to ensure obedience. Those unable to keep order at home by the force of their personalities and example were evidently unfit for public responsibilities.[42] This was a point on which the conduct book writers were equally emphatic.[43]

In so far as men may have been learning in the period between 1500 and 1660 that force was not the answer, that they had to rely instead upon persuasion and the strength of their personalities to get their way with their wives, outside puritan circles the contribution of the religious message to changing attitudes was probably small. Stories in the satirical literature about beating as a counterproductive tactic may have made much more impact. Thomas Heywood, for example, unravelled the meaning of an old proverb in his *Curtain Lecture* as a story of revenge. The proverb ran: 'If I should be so foolish as to yield unto you where in the meantime can you find a fit tree to which to tie the sow?' A rustic,

39. R. Snawsel, *A Looking Glass for Married Folks* (1631), pp. 109–13.
40. E.A. Foyster, 'A Laughing Matter? Marital Discord and Gender control in Seventeenth-Century England', *Rural History* 4 (1993), pp. 15–16; above, pp. 117–19.
41. K.U. Henderson and B.F. McManus, eds, *Half Humankind: Contexts and Texts of the Controversy about Women in England 1540–1640* (Urbana, 1985), p. 199.
42. W. Heale, *An Apology for Women* (London, 1614), especially pp. 13–19, 31–2.
43. E.g. J. Dod and R. Cleaver, *A Godly Form of Household Government* (London, 1614), cited in Amussen, *An Ordered Society*, pp. 37–8.

he explained, who had beaten his wife 'for reading a lecture to him somewhat too loud' sent her to market next day to sell their sow. Her chance to avenge herself for the beating came on the way when a young man, who had long wooed her unsuccessfully, met her just before she left the path through a thick wood for the open fields ahead.[44]

Margaret Hunt's examination of the London consistory court material for 1711 to 1713 shows that most of the husbands accused of assaulting their wives were from the middling sort or above: they included a gentleman, a physician, a pawnbroker and a wine wholesaler.[45] Yet at this very time a shift in public attitudes towards wife-beating was undoubtedly taking place as part of the discourse of civility which was most clearly expressed in the periodical literature by writers like Richard Addison and Richard Steele. The reissue of Heale's tract shorn of the reference to its origins in 1682 is a significant indication of public interest in the matter. The new extended title of this edition read as follows: '*The great advocate and orator for women, or the arraignment trial and conviction of all such wicked husbands (or monsters) who hold it lawful to beat their wives or to demean themselves severely and tyrannically towards them.*' Wife-beaters, in this version, are condemned in strong language as 'gangreaned members of an unhappy state' who would infect the whole country with a 'fatal distemper'. The writer inserted references to wife-beating as 'detestable to God', 'opposite to the law of nature', and a 'public shame and disgrace'. What is being attempted here with some success, suggests Margaret Hunt, is the demonisation of the wife-beater. What actually happened in respectable families, though, was being veiled in silence. During the eighteenth century there was a deliberate rhetorical displacement of family violence on to the lower classes: wife-beating came to be viewed as a special mark of the inferiority and animality of the poor.[46]

The best evidence we have of profound longer-term changes in attitudes to the use of violence by spouses within the home comes from the patchy but at the same time incontrovertible record of the transformation of charivari. This community shaming ritual – the rough music of pots, pans, effigies and rhymes – was for centuries the authentic voice of the English people about what is tolerable and what intolerable in marital relations[47] (plates 4 and 5). While people's basic assumption remained that patriarchy rested upon force, charivari was directed at wives who beat their husbands. Sixteenth- and seventeenth-century ridings could be perceived by all ranks in society, from the gentry to the poorest

44. T. Heywood, *A Curtain Lecture* (London, 1637), pp. 189–92.
45. Hunt, 'Wife Beating', *Gender and History* 4 (1992), pp. 11–12.
46. [W. Heale], *The Great Advocate and Orator for Women* (1682); Hunt, 'Wife Beating', *Gender and History* 4 (1992), pp. 25–8.
47. The best introduction is M. Ingram, 'Ridings, Rough Music and the "Reform of Popular Culture" in Early Modern England', *Past and Present* 105 (1984), pp. 79–113, see also below, pp. 270–73.

labourer, as a defence of the patriarchal ideal. Henry Oxinden, the squire of Barham in Kent, apparently encouraged a riding in 1643, telling a puritan cleric who objected that it was a 'harmless pastime'. Other gentry families who showed complaisance about the riotous way villagers took matters into their own hands when community mores were offended including the Ishams in Northamptonshire and the Verneys in Bucking-hamshire.[48] But, around 1800, a very significant shift in the function of charivari occurred. While the humiliation of unruly women remained a prominent theme in some regions in the nineteenth century, it was wife-beaters who became the principal target of the ritual. Edward Thompson found it hard to interpret what this meant with regard to the treatment of wives and, surely correctly, warned against easy assumptions about a modernisation of domestic relationships. Victorian rough music against wife-beaters could have been an index of the increasing brutality with which some wives were being treated. But that the shift in targets happened is amply supported by the evidence collected by the Victorian folklorists. They assumed incorrectly from the information they received that inhibiting wife-beating was and always had been the prime objective of charivari.[49]

Thompson emphasised the power in English rural life of these rehearsed and transmitted rites as a means by which people sought to show up manifest wrong and express solidarity against an identified offender. Oral tradition can perhaps communicate that power more force-fully than any written record of a particular incident in the early modern period. Hanson Halstead, who witnessed rough music against a couple living in sin at Siddall in west Yorkshire as a boy early this century, said it was 'like devil's magic'. An inhabitant of the remote north Yorkshire village of Kirkby Malseard recalled in 1931 the emotions that lay behind 'riding the stang' there, a form of rough music still practised at the end of the last century: 'They did that because working class people are more faithful to their wives than are t'nobs. And anyone who beats his wife up or a child is a bad 'un. They really had to feel very, very strongly about this carry on. Then it was a big disgrace, it brought it out in the open. They didn't do it just for a lark.'[50] Patriarchy has always carried the whiff of marital violence because it is a scheme of gender relations based upon dominance and submission. At the same time, it is quite clear that a deeply rooted subversive tradition has persisted in England, sustained by folklore, which has enabled women to keep their heads held high. Bernard Capp notes the recurrence of an episode recorded by John Taylor in early Stuart London in Victorian Oxfordshire. A woman,

48. M. Ingram, 'Ridings, Rough Music and Mocking Rhymes in Early Modern Eng-land', in B. Reay, ed., *Popular Culture in Seventeenth-Century England* (London, 1985), pp. 191–2 and references cited.
49. E.P. Thompson, *Customs in Common* (London, 1991), pp. 505–13.
50. Thompson, *Customs in Common*, pp. 509, 529–33.

beaten by a drunken husband with a rope's end, serves him broth made
with boiled rope instead of eels, adding the quip that she was giving him
what he gave her. Fiona Thompson telling the story in *Lark Rise to
Candleford* called this 'an old country cure for such offences'.[51] How far
there was an actual decline in the employment of violence by men as they
enforced patriarchy in England between 1500 and 1800 is an open
question. What is clear is that charivari remained over these centuries a
legitimate way of saying that violence in the home has real limits and that
during the period after 1700 it became men's violence rather than wom-
en's which was the focus of community attention. Puritan teaching may
have played some part in changing attitudes to domestic violence, but
what we are seeing here is long-term and deep-seated change at the grass
roots of English society. In later chapters of this book, we will explore
men's efforts at an internalising of female subordination, which may have
made the use of violence less needful as a practical instrument of men's
day-to-day control of women in the home.

51. Capp, p. 119.

11. *Household Order*

THE CRUCIAL IMPORTANCE of the patriarchal family as the bedrock of social order in early modern England has long been recognised. It is thirty years since Christopher Hill established an agenda for research into protestantism and family and household relationships that many have since pursued.[1] It is twenty years since Gordon Schochet published the first major study of patriarchalism as an important aspect of the political thought of the seventeenth century.[2] The editor of the most recent edition of Sir Robert Filmer's *Patriarcha*, Johann Sommerville, has argued that Filmer was far from a lone voice and that patriarchalist political thinking was common at the time he wrote.[3] Lawrence Stone is being too schematic when he argues that 'the period from 1530 to 1660 may be regarded as the patriarchal stage in the evolution of the nuclear family'.[4] Yet a number of the country's leading puritan clergy were engaged in a sustained attempt to model the patriarchal family afresh as the basis of authority and obedience between the 1590s and the 1640s.[5] In their circles there was constant talk of the godly household. 'If ever we would have the church of God to continue among us', wrote Richard Greenham, 'we must bring it into our households and nourish it in our families.'[6] John Downame spoke of the family as 'a seminary of the church and

---

1. C. Hill, *Society and Puritanism in Pre-Revolutionary England* (London, 1964), pp. 443–81.
2. G.J. Schochet, *Patriarchalism in Political Thought* (London, 1975).
3. J.P. Sommerville, ed., *Patriarcha and Other Writings* (Cambridge, 1991), p. xviii.
4. L. Stone, *The Family, Sex and Marriage in England 1500–1800* (London, 1977), p. 218.
5. A.J. Fletcher and P.R. Roberts, eds., *Religion, Culture and Society in Early Modern Britain* (Cambridge, 1994), pp. 161–81; see also S.D. Amussen, *An Ordered Society: Gender and Class in Early Modern England* (Oxford, 1988), pp. 34–66; P. Collinson, *The Birthpangs of Protestant England: Religious and Cultural Change in the Sixteenth and Seventeenth Centuries* (London, 1988), pp. 60–93; J. Morgan, *Godly Learning: Puritan Attitudes towards Reason, Learning and Education 1560–1640* (Cambridge, 1986), pp. 142–71; M. Todd, *Christian Humanism and the Puritan Social Order* (Cambridge, 1987), pp. 96–117.
6. R. Greenham, *Works*, p. 799.

commonwealth, and as a private school, wherein children and servants are fitted for public assemblies'.[7] Such writers shared with the social elite as a whole the sense that household order was the foundation of effective government. 'A family', William Gouge insisted, 'is a little commonwealth . . . a school wherein the first principles and grounds of government and subjection are learned.' 'As every man's house is his castle', declared Richard Brathwaite, 'so is his family a private commonwealth, wherein if due government be not observed nothing but confusion is to be expected.'[8]

Everyone who attended church, meanwhile, was receiving the constant reiteration of the principles of husbandly authority over wives and parental authority over children and other subordinates, whether servants or apprentices, through the Homily on Obedience, which was often read on Sundays, and through sermons and catechising. The analogy that Filmer spelt out and upon which he built his political theory came easily: 'as the father over one family so the King, as father over many families, extends his care to preserve, feed, clothe, instruct and defend the whole commonwealth.'[9] There was a coherence about the ideological basis which sustained the church, law and government between the 1560s and 1660s that was powerfully convincing and that left a legacy into the eighteenth century, even if much was then changing. The church, we may say, gave the lead but household discipline made such good sense to all those in authority that it was bound in any case to receive massive public support. The complexities of early modern patriarchy will become more apparent as we explore more fully the issues and practice of a system which set husband and wife beside each other, yet acknowledging the superiority of one over the other, as rulers in their own little kingdom. There were some differences of emphasis among the conduct book writers about how much responsibility wives should be allowed to exercise. Thomas Gataker explained simply that it was a wife's duty to be directed in 'the marshalling and managing of domestic affairs'. William Gouge suggested that husbands should not be too exacting in restraining their spouses over details of furnishing, provisioning and control of maids. They all sought to circumvent the contradiction inherent in making wives subordinate yet responsible by insistence upon a ritual of obedience and deference to the household head. In practice it was the woman who had to do much of the hour-by-hour direction and decision-making about the conduct and activities of young children and of servants under her charge. Issues of their obedience and discipline were bound to be constantly in the forefront in her mind. This was what really tested marital partnership. We must appreciate this context in seeking to understand the response of

7. Cited in Morgan, *Godly Learning*, pp. 142–3.
8. Citations from Amussen, *An Ordered Society*, p. 37.
9. P. Laslett, ed., *Patriarcha and Other Political Writings of Sir Robert Filmer* (Oxford, 1949), p. 63.

Nehemiah Wallington, that quintessential London puritan artisan, when he brought home his copy of William Gouge's *Domestical Duties* soon after it was published in 1622. Wallington was recently married at that time and was, he confesses, feeling the weight of 'the charge of so many souls'. 'Every one of us', he commented, 'may learn and know our duties and honour God every one in his place where God has set them.' He did something about putting the godly household into action, following his reading of Gouge, by drawing up articles 'for the reforming of our lives' which he had his three servants and his apprentice as well as his wife sign. He presumably read them aloud or had each of them read them first.[10] His action was effectively a declaration that household order and harmony was a joint endeavour in which his was simply the leading role.

Gouge's *Domestical Duties* dealt very fully with the issue of the forms of respect that parents should receive from their children, an issue at the very heart of patriarchal order. The way Gouge handles this is defensive and strongly indicative of an attempt to maintain outdated custom. He recommended an elaborate language of obedience by children, according to their sex and age, in the presence of their parents: 'uncovering the head, bending the knee, bowing the body, standing up with the like'. But he confessed he had found some in his congregation who expressed doubts about the specific custom of asking of parental blessings 'both in regard of the thing itself and also of the gesture of kneeling used in the performance thereof'. He cited scriptural references in an attempt to prove the properness and lawfulness of this ritual of deference and obedience.[11] If asking blessings was under question in the households of the godly London gentry and middling sort, it is hardly likely that it was surviving intact as a social practice elsewhere among the religious and well educated, let alone among the poor. This is very difficult territory for the historian to traverse since there are few sources that tell us what actually happened in the practice of parent–child relationships and control. In the case of parental blessings two anecdotes can be cited. Lady Brilliana Harley, writing to Sir Robert in 1626, showed him how she was aware of her duty to school her boys in reverence to the patriarch: 'Ned and Robin, if they could speak, would say something to you, a blessing I am sure they would ask which I pray you give them.'[12] Elizabeth Freke was much distressed when she could not get a ship from Ireland after her ailing father had said he would pay whatever it cost to have her come home 'to give me his last blessing' in 1684.[13] It would be perilous to

---

10. T. Gataker, *Marriage Duties briefly couched together out of Colossians 3:18 and 19* (London, 1620), pp. 14–16; W. Gouge, *Domestical Duties* (London, 1622), pp. 370–2; P.S. Seaver, *Wallington's World* (London, 1985), p. 79.
11. Gouge, *Domestical Duties*, pp. 442–3.
12. BL, Loan MS 29/22. I am grateful to Jacqueline Eales for a transcript of this letter.
13. 'Mrs Elizabeth Freke, her Diary', *Journal of the Cork Historical and Archaeological Society*, XVII (1911), p. 11.

attempt to generalise about puritan gentry families or gentry more widely on the basis of these two cases. All we can say is that the Calvinist emphasis on original sin brought force to the regime of household deference and discipline in some gentry and middling-sort circles where family prayers, catechising and the exposition of scripture, led by the head of the household or in his absence by his wife, set a strong moral tone to daily life.[14] The thinking behind such practice is put starkly by Sir Simonds D'Ewes in a commonplace book entry: 'Parents are especially bound to instruct the children, pray for them and train them up in the fear of God because they drew original corruption from their loins.'[15] Peter Earle argues that London middle-class households at the turn of the eighteenth century preserved much of this atmosphere of formality and distance that is associated with the earlier puritan household. 'They seem', he writes, 'to have been quiet, almost sombre, places where children were seen but not heard.'[16]

Earle's stress on the strong desire of parents in general for respect and obedience is a useful starting point for this discussion. This was a society in which hierarchy was at the very core of every adult householder's thinking about organising his and his wife's life and home. Hierarchy required some body language to express its meaning and importance, even if the demanding precepts that Gouge found in the Bible seemed to some quite excessive expressions of authority and subordination. Patriarchal ritual on the one hand and love and cherishing on the other, we must take it, were not seen by most people to be in contradiction of each other. The necessity of children obeying their parents, however this message was reiterated in homes up and down the country, would not have been disputed by anyone at this time. Those indeed who 'will not be ruled' were classified by Richard Napier as mentally disturbed. Thus Ellen Hixon was reported in a letter written to him to be 'mopish, apish, foolish, untoward'. She would 'not do anything that her parents bid her but at her own mind'. A young gentleman raged at his parents and called them 'all to naught': he was said to suffer from a 'strange melancholy'. Philip Hutley's father complained that he 'useth outrageous words against mother and father' when he was telling Napier about how his son's wits had failed him.[17] Duty and obedience not observed towards a father or that should be observed to a mother in the future was a frequent theme in the wills of middle-class Londoners between 1660 and 1730. Daniel Darrelly was disinherited as a 'very undutiful and disobedient son unto me and his mother'. John Brookes, a wealthy merchant, gave his widow discretion about the distribution of his wealth among his eight children, having regard that those 'most pious, dutiful and diligent may be

14. Hill, *Society and Puritanism*, pp. 443–81.
15. Cited in J.T. Cliffe, *The Puritan Gentry* (London, 1984), p. 69.
16. P. Earle, *The Making of the English Middle Class* (London, 1989), pp. 237–9.
17. M. Macdonald, *Mystical Bedlam: Madness, Anxiety and Healing in Seventeenth-Century England* (Cambridge, 1981), pp. 126–8.

encouraged'.[18] Disinheriting a child altogether was a drastic step that many more exasperated parents probably contemplated than implemented. Ralph Josselin's diary is a rich source of evidence about a stormy father–son relationship which involved at least two severe reprimands before the whole family and threats that his son John would receive nothing more than 'a provision for your life to put bread in your hand'. Josselin's basic line of reasoning was consistent: he should be obeyed as the mediator of God's commands. He assumed he and his wife stood side by side in such matters. A diary entry for 19 December 1676, when he was deeply concerned about John's 'ill husbandry' and his daughter Elizabeth was being courted by a young man from London, ends with a clear statement of parental unity: 'I prayed thrice with them; their mother gave them the same advice, God in mercy give them his blessing.'[19]

Some historians have argued that this was a period of severe parental discipline. The view that he who spares the rod spoils the child was deeply embedded in the traditions of Christian society but in this period, as in the middle ages, direct references to the beating of children in the home are extremely sparse.[20] Keith Wrightson's conclusion that, so far from experiencing a reign of parental terror, children suffered physical punishment only occasionally, that it was administered reluctantly and given in moderation is persuasive.[21] Some of those who wrote accounts of their childhood do mention being beaten. Simon Foman recalled being beaten by his mother when he was eleven and his father had died. Richard Norwood remembered how 'often on a Lord's day at night or Monday morning I prayed to escape beating that week'.[22] The worst thing about his mother's beatings, Roger North recalled, was being made to stop crying and thank 'the good rail which she said was to break our spirits'.[23] The age, like all ages, had its child abusers. In 1563 a man was put in the pillory for beating his son with a leather girdle until his skin was peeled off. The boy was made to stand beside him without his clothes on to show how badly he had been hurt and the father, on the lord mayor's orders, was subsequently whipped until he bled.[24]

There were gentry, like Harbottle Grimston, who advocated severe beating of children but it is not clear that they actually followed their own precepts. There were others, like Sir Nathaniel Barnardiston – and they

18. Earle, *Making of the English Middle Class*, pp. 235–6.
19. A. Macfarlane, *The Family Life of Ralph Josselin* (Cambridge, 1970), pp. 121–3.
20. S. Shahan, *Childhood in the Middle Ages* (London, 1990), p. 111.
21. K. Wrightson, *English Society 1580–1680* (London, 1982), p. 116. For a different view see Stone, *Family, Sex and Marriage*, p. 167 and Earle, *Making of the English Middle Class*, p. 233.
22. L.A. Pollock, *Forgotten Children: Parent-Child Relations from 1500–1900* (Cambridge, 1983), pp. 147–8.
23. Stone, *Family, Sex and Marriage*, p. 168.
24. Cited in R.L. Greaves, *Society and Religion in Elizabethan England* (Minneapolis, 1981), p. 282.

seem to have been a considerable majority – who resisted biblical teaching in this matter both as principle and in practice.[25] That teaching faced them with a real dilemma, for most parents probably found it hard to contemplate subjecting their own flesh and blood to pain, to seeing the marks they made on their bodies and to hearing their cries. The emotional stress of one who brought himself to this act is apparent in Thomas Newcome's diary account of how he beat his twelve-year-old son. 'I discharged my duty of correction to my poor child', he wrote, 'prayed with him after, entreating the Lord that it might be the last correction (if it were his will) that he should need.'[26] The shifts of compromise are evident in the description Sir Thomas More gave his children, in a warm and loving letter of 1517, of how he had treated them when they were younger and why:

> It is not so strange that I love you with my whole heart, for being a father is not a tie which can be ignored . . . you know, for example, how often I kissed you, how seldom I whipped you. My whip was invariably a peacock's tail. Even this I wielded hesitantly and gently so that sorry welts might not disfigure your tender seats. Brutal and unworthy to be called father is he who does not himself weep at the tears of his child.

For More it was almost certainly a symbolic act of submission that mattered, his children's bending of their heads and presenting their buttocks, gestures which we can believe that the austere patriarch of Holbein's drawing of the family at Chelsea thought it proper, if need be, to demand. The curious ritual with the peacock's tail signified, as Richard Marius has put it, 'the offer of love in return for the proper performance of his children'. They were to go forward in the world and 'he would cherish them and be proud of them'.[27]

During the period from the 1560s to the 1640s numerous prescriptive works advocated parental beating, or 'correction' as it was usually called. Robert Snucker's analysis of this material, based upon twenty-two such works, including conduct books, commentaries on scripture, sermons and catechisms, reveals a remarkably consistent pattern of argument. The vigour with which it was being put and certain features of the case these writers made point to a logical inference: that these were men seeking to reinforce and sustain a practice which they believed was being dangerously neglected. The argument was intended to convince men who did not want to beat their children – and there is no distinction made here between boys and girls – that they must do so. It was grievous for the parent to have to correct in this way, Gouge declared, but he should take

25. Cliffe, *The Puritan Gentry*, pp. 73–4; Macfarlane, *Family Life of Ralph Josselin*, pp. 117–25.
26. Cited in Pollock, *Forgotten Children*, p. 149.
27. R. Marius, *Thomas More* (London, 1985), pp. 224–5.

delight in amending a fault. Being beaten was a child's 'great trial of obedience', which he should bear patiently and with profit, remembering it was done in love. There was much agreement between these writers on the conditions which made beating at home acceptable: verbal correction should be tried first, physical as a last resort; children should always be made aware of the fault for which they were being punished; parents should never beat their children in rage or fury; moderation should be used, with severe beating reserved for older children who were 'stout and stubborn' and for sins directly against God's word. It was generally assumed that children would be beaten on their bare buttocks and one puritan writer actually maintained that God's purpose in giving human beings buttocks was so that they could receive the stripes of correction without serious injury to their bodies.[28]

The core of the argument, as it was set out by Gouge, was deeply Calvinist. 'Correction', he insisted, 'is as physick to purge out much corruption which lurketh in children and as a salve to heal many wounds and sores made by their folly.' Beating children was, in his eyes, quite simply a means that God had appointed to help their 'good nurture and education'. Parading one biblical passage after another − Proverbs 20, 22, 23 − he asked defiantly: 'Who can better tell what kind of dealing is fittest for children than God? Who can better nurture children than God? Who doth more truly aim at and procure the good of children than God?' Gouge undoubtedly really believed in 'the inward operation of this physick': it could preserve children, he urged parents, from crime that might later bring them to the gallows as well as from 'eternal death'. He answered his doubters, who said they could not cope with making their own child smart, with the unrelenting insistence that 'the future fruit is more to be considered than the present pain', adding for good measure that he was sure that children learnt much more effectively from blows than words. The most overwrought passages in Gouge's argument concern 'cockering' or coddling of children. He inveighed bitterly against mothers, the chief offenders in this he alleged, who not only refused to beat their children themselves but were offended with their husbands for doing so. The advice books published between 1609 and 1634, it emerges, made much of this issue, which had previously hardly been mentioned. Gouge was not a lone voice. He had even heard it maintained that husbands should give way to the soft words of a spouse, since it was she who had born the travail of bringing the child forth. He answered this point roundly.[29] We know of one marriage that ran into trouble on the issue of the punishment of a child and there may well, as

---

28. R.V. Snucker, 'Puritan Attitudes towards Childhood Discipline 1560–1634', in V. Fildes, ed., *Women as Mothers in Pre-Industrial England* (London, 1988), pp. 108–21; Gouge, *Domestical Duties*, pp. 418, 559–60.
29. Gouge, *Domestical Duties*, pp. 560–7; Fildes, ed., *Women as Mothers*, p. 115.

Gouge hinted, have been others. In 1700 John Richards noted in his diary that he beat his son Jack 'for his bad behaviour in play' and his wife Alice 'showed herself so insolent that I put her out of the room'.[30] But the general significance of the puritan campaign for harsh discipline lies not in anything that it achieved, which was probably minimal, but in what it tells us about anxieties regarding a lapse in household order. The tone may get shriller as the message about severe punishment is seen not to be heeded.

Adolescence, we have seen, was regarded as a liminal time. Boys were seeking to prove themselves as men, to separate finally and decisively from the female world of childhood: their imaginations were fed by the chivalric chapbook literature, they were seen as full of the vigour, passions and the follies of youth. Wisdom, judgement and mastery of the self would come with experience. In the humoral physiology the body gradually dried up with age which meant that while physical strength declined the 'animal spirits' became 'more fixed and the mind more sedate and quiet in its motions'. Girls were blossoming sexually and their greensickness was a portent of disorder if they lacked firm household control. Contemporaries disagreed as to which precisely were youth's most dangerous years. Robert Shelford named fifteen to seventeen, John Aubrey seventeen to twenty; for Roger Ascham seventeen to twenty-seven was 'that most slippery time'. Adult males, those who had come through, were generally agreed that considerable restraint was needed to curb rash and headstrong youths, and moralists and theologians, of course, waxed eloquent on the issue. If teenage offenders escaped the gallows, argued Sir Matthew Hale, 'the kingdom would come to confusion'. For many of the most horrific crimes were committed by youths between fourteen and twenty-one and 'if they should have impunity by the privilege of . . . their minority, no man's life or estate could be safe'.[31] Service was all about getting young people into work in an economy that was labour-intensive. This was a society in which work was seen as a basic form of self-discipline and each youthful masterless life was seen as a portent of disorder. A Buckinghamshire spinster who refused to enter service in 1698 was reported to have offered no proper excuse: she 'only expressed an unwillingness to labour, which may be of ill example to lazy and thriftless people'. JPs were active in enforcing legislation which made young men and women in certain circumstances 'compellable to serve'.[32] All in all it is abundantly clear why the patriarchal household was seen as the key to the disciplining and training of unbridled youth and why

30. R. Houlbrooke, *English Family Life 1576–1716* (London, 1988), p. 93.
31. Citations from K.V. Thomas, 'Age and Authority in Early Modern England', *Proceedings of the British Academy* LXII (1976), pp. 207–8, pp. 219–20.
32. M. Roberts, 'Women and Work in Sixteenth-Century English Towns', in Charles and Duffin, eds, *Women and Work in Pre-Industrial England* (London, 1985), p. 158.

service was such a crucial institution of early modern English society.

Throughout the seventeenth century the age of marriage remained relatively late and a mass of young people spent all or most of the period between puberty and setting up their own household in some form of service or apprenticeship. Local censuses show how the proportions of communities that were servants varied considerably but it could be as high as a quarter as at Coventry in 1523 and Ealing in 1599.[33] The majority of male servants were apprentices, bound by formal indenture, or agricultural servants contracted for the year; young women could be found in both these forms of service but they were more likely to be doing domestic work. For many young people, especially in the middling and upper ranks of society, entry to service was effectively the choice of an occupation and it was navigated and planned with some care and with the help and advice of parents.[34] Many young men from gentry families, especially younger sons, took up apprenticeships, whereas agricultural servants were drawn from the less wealthy and substantial groups. Pauper children were often compulsorily apprenticed in the countryside. Contracts varied as did forms of training and work expectations; the social origins of urban apprentices and rural farm servants overlapped. Yet the relationships between labouring youth and authority can be discussed in terms of their membership of a single multifaceted social institution at the core of patriarchy, the institution of service.

Conduct book writers gave as careful attention to the relationship of master and servant as to that of parent and child.[35] There were close parallels. 'The master oweth to his servant meat, wages, correction, instruction,' wrote the Elizabethan Archbishop of York, Edwin Sandys.[36] The duties of servants – obedience and submission – were no different from those of children. Yet, though both are key elements in the patri-archal scheme of things, there are distinctions to be made between the two kinds of relationship. Service was a childlike and dependent status but it was often short-term and, at most, it usually lasted for the seven years or so of an apprenticeship agreement. Service was at the same time contractual, involving an obligation to work for wages in return for training in a particular craft or trade, in husbandry or in domestic tasks. That training was always seen to have a moral dimension, indeed service as a whole was regarded as the best means available in this society for inculcating good behaviour.[37] Something every apprentice and servant

33. Houlbrooke, *English Family Life*, pp. 172–3.
34. I. Ben-Amos, 'Service and Coming of Age of Young Men in Seventeenth-century England', *Continuity and Change* 3 (1988), pp. 45–52.
35. C.L. Powell, *English Domestic Relations 1487–1653* (New York, 1917), pp. 234–42.
36. Cited in Hill, *Society and Puritanism*, p. 450.
37. For a typical indenture see S. Rappaport, *Worlds within Worlds: Structures of Life in Sixteenth-century London* (Cambridge, 1989), p. 234; Earle, *Making of the English Middle Class*, pp. 85–105 offers a useful general account of the conditions of London apprenticeship.

learnt, which helps us to understand why early modern patriarchy was such a strongly rooted scheme of social order, was the sense of domestic hierarchy. This is well illustrated by a case, which may in itself be quite unusual, in Somerset in 1630. Meredith Davy, an adult servant, had for some while been practising sodomy with his master's apprentice when he had been drinking on Sunday and holiday nights. The boy, John Vicary, was aged about twelve and he slept in the same bed. 'The distinction in status between master and servant', notes Alan Bray, 'was in some respects a model for distinctions between the servants themselves.' Davy no doubt thought he could get away with it but one day the boy cried out and Richard Bryant, another servant who slept in the same room and who had, we might think, been remarkably slow to realise what was going on, took the matter to their dame. She charged Davy with it. But Bryant was now a watchdog for the boy and, some while later, told the quarter sessions court that since that time Davy 'hath lain quietly with him'. What is interesting here is that there was no question of obtaining another bed. John Vicary still shared a bed with the man who in this instance had been assaulting him; he was still in submission to the servant who stood above him in the household hierarchy.[38] Such was normal practice.

Samuel Pepys often shows his concern in the diary about issues of domestic hierarchy: in his case this ran in descending order from Elizabeth's companion through the chambermaid and cookmaid to the under-cookmaid. In April 1663 he recorded that Mary, the new chambermaid employed in February, had left 'she being too high for her though a very good servant'. With two servants in the kitchen it was essential to ensure the relationship between them reflected the same principles of deference and subservience expected elsewhere. He had severe doubts about a prospective new servant to work with the dependable and long-serving Susan in the kitchen in 1664: 'I am afeared she will be over-high for us, she having last been a chambermaid and holds up her head.' He was no happier about another girl sent for interview by a friend whom he did not want to disappoint: 'I am a little dissatisfied that the girl, though young, is taller and bigger than Su and will not I fear be under her command.'[39]

It is important that we should explore actual relationships between masters and their servants in this period because in a sense they provide the most acid test of the kind of patriarchal society this was. Whereas between husbands and wives and parents and children there were blood ties and ties of affection which might soften and modify, even subvert, the harshest prescriptions of men's God-given authority, service was bounded by no such ameliorating circumstances. There was of course the law, which could be used when those outside the household knew and were

38. A. Bray, *Homosexuality in Renaissance England* (London, 1988), pp. 48, 69, 77.
39. *Pepys*, IV, p. 113, V, pp. 158–9, VII, p. 108; Earle, *Making of the English Middle Class*, pp. 226–7.

willing to act, to check brutality or neglect. But it is quite remarkable how wide was the discretion that masters enjoyed, a discretion that would be seen in modern terms as grotesquely inappropriate but which can be accounted for easily enough in a society that lacked adequate means to control the behaviour of ebullient youth. Late medieval gild regulations were explicit about the master's duty to correct servants and apprentices with corporal punishment; Lord Mayors of London reminded masters of their duty in this respect at times of social tension; JPs commonly referred youthful minor offenders to the correction of their masters.[40] Servants and apprentices in their teens and in their early twenties were undoubtedly beaten far more than children. We can understand why this was so if we put household discipline in the context of a system of local government that rested heavily upon whipping and stocking. Yet this is not to say that early modern patriarchy was in this respect generally brutal or deeply repressive. Public records predictably reveal sadists who went far beyond the bounds of what was considered acceptable at the time and the stories such records tell are often disconcerting.[41]

We are faced with the same issue we have encountered before of a lack of concurrence between prescriptive advice which favoured formality and severity and other sources which suggest that practice was often quite different. George Herbert's declaration that parents should show 'more love than terror' to their children and 'more terror than love' to their servants but take equal pride in them summarises the contemporary rhetoric.[42] Popular ballads paraded the sterotype of strict household control: 'Dost fear they master's heavy hand or mistress nimble tongue?' asks the Leicestershire lad of his lover, seeking to persuade her to meet him 'upon the meadow brow'.[43] So what of the practice? There is one instance recorded in a private journal which perfectly illustrates the kind of show of patriarchal brutality which a gentleman, inviolate in the privacy of his manor-house, could display without challenge. His daughter Grace recorded what happened to one of Sir Henry Sharrington's servants at Lacock around 1560. Sharrington, raising three daughters who were his co-heiresses, was a stickler for his household rules: 'I have seen him with his own hands (for example's sake) scourge a young man, naked from his girdle upwards, with fresh rods, for making but a show and

40. C.W. Brooks, 'Apprenticeship', in J. Barry and C.W. Brooks, eds., *The Middling Sort* (London, 1994); A.J. Fletcher and A. Stevenson, eds., *Order and Disorder in Early Modern England* (Cambridge, 1985), p. 34, A.J. Fletcher, *Reform in the Provinces: The Government of Stuart England* (London, 1986), p. 280.
41. For examples see S.R. Smith, 'The London Apprentices as Seventeenth-Century Adolescents', *Past and Present* 61 (1973), p. 152; P.J. Seaver, 'Declining Status in an Aspiring Age: The Problem of the Gentle Apprentice in Seventeenth-century London', in B.Y. Kunze and D.D. Brautigam, eds, *Court, Country and Culture* (Rochester, New York, 1992), p. 138.
42. Cited in Macfarlane, *Family Life of Ralph Josselin*, p. 145.
43. *Roxburghe*, II, 599: 'The Two Leicestershire Lovers'.

countenance of a saucy and unreverent behaviour towards us his children and put him from his service.'[44] Others have left very different kinds of account of how servants fared. Reluctantly seeing one of his cooks off to marry a maid at York in 1638, Sir Henry Slingsby mused about the trouble he had suffered over his less adequate predecessors who had all spent too much time in the alehouse. He had always persevered with them and 'never grew passionate nor threatened them much' but in the end found himself bound, when they did not reform, to dismiss them.[45] Ralph Josselin's references to his servants in his diary are affectionate but also paternalistic, as his choice of words in an entry of 1658 shows: 'I married Mary Potter late my maid to John Penhacke and it grieved me not to deal bountifully with her, my heart sad to see her match to a person that minds not God, nor likely to be a good husband.' It is not of course surprising that as a minister his concern with his servants was spiritual as well as material: twice, in 1645 and again in 1650, he referred to blessing servants when they arrived in his household.[46] He never referred to himself or his wife punishing them which, given his harsh conscience, he would almost certainly have done had he felt beating them to be necessary. A servant's courtships was frequently a source of trouble, especially if it threatened to lose a household a good pair of hands or it was feared a girl would become pregnant. There are cases in early seventeenth-century Durham of women taking the men to whom they were betrothed to court for breach of promise after dames had halted a courtship by banning contact between two young people.[47]

As so often, Pepys is our best source for the actual treatment of servants. He and his wife had to engage at least thirty-eight of them in the nine-year period of the diary in order to keep things running as they wished in their London household. The turnover was much greater than they can have wanted, meaning that there were constantly new servants to be trained, moulded into the household's ways and encouraged to become willing and happy members. For Samuel did care about this: he could forgive unskilfulness; he prized loyalty, modesty and hard work. His use of punishment must be seen in this context. In the first place he was intensely self-conscious about the issue of using violence on the girls. Childless himself, he was genuinely fond of many of those he employed. Hence the remorse and anxiety that he confided to his diary about an incident in 1667 when, arriving home, he found that his 'good drudging'

44. L.A. Pollock, *With Faith and Physic: The Life of a Tudor Gentlewoman Lady Grace Mildmay 1552–1620* (London, 1993), p. 28.
45. D. Parsons, ed., *The Diary of Sir Henry Slingsby of Scriven* (London, 1836), pp. 23–4.
46. Macfarlane, *Family Life of Ralph Josselin*, p. 147.
47. P. Rushton, 'Property, Power and Family Networks in the Problem of Disputed Marriages in Early Modern England', *Journal of Family History* 11 (1986), pp. 213–14.

cookmaid Luce had left his door and window hatch open on the street, an invitation to theft and intrusion. Before he could check himself, he had given her an angry kick, which he at once realised was spotted by Sir William Penn's footboy who was passing by at the time. Although he tried to pass off the incident by some kind words to the boy, he feared the story would be told against him. His insistence that Elizabeth punish the servant girls if need be is of a piece with this sensitivity about kicking Luce. The 19 February 1665 was a relaxing day until Samuel discovered at supper that the kitchen maids had let in a 'rogueing Scotch woman . . . to help them to wash and scour'. Asking someone in without permission, who might steal or carry information to potential thieves of the London underworld, he saw as a serious crime. Elizabeth was told to beat 'our little girl' Susan and she did so sufficiently soundly for the neighbours to be disturbed at the girl's cries before she was shut down in the cellar for the night.[48] Pepys was here following the letter of the household manuals which insisted upon deputing punishment of maids to the dame of the house. Just as 'a man's nature scorneth to be beaten of a woman', declared Henry Smith in 1591, so 'a maid's nature is corrupted with the stripes of a man.'[49]

Most of the Pepys servants, we should note, were never beaten. Those who left usually did so because they had fallen out in one way or another with Elizabeth. But Samuel's attempt to reform the incorrigible rogue Wayneman Birch provides some insight into how his mind worked on the issue of use of his patriarchal authority. Wayneman gave him endless trouble, lying, fighting, stealing and failing quickly to do his errands. Samuel recorded beating the footboy at least eight times in two years. He was reluctant to start on this course, recording on the first occasion that he had some doubts but 'I thought it necessary to do it'. The presence in the house of Jane Birch, the boy's sister, who was Elizabeth's trusted maid, complicated the matter. On one occasion, in 1662, he chose a moment when he had sent the boy to the cellar for some beer to take a cane down there and beat him but Jane heard his cries and came down to remonstrate. Pepys discussed his action with Jane, explaining 'how much I love the boy for her sake and how much it doth concern to correct the boy for his faults or else he would be undone'. Only two months later, Pepys whipped Wayneman even more severely when he knew the boy had lied and he could not extract a confession: 'it is one of the greatest wonders that ever I met with', he reflected after a session which left him with 'my arm very weary', 'that such a little boy could possibly be able to suffer half so much to maintain a lie.' His fears about Wayneman's future were not groundless. Tired of coping with him, Pepys dismissed the footboy in 1663 and the following year he was sent

48. *Pepys*, VI, p. 39, VIII, p. 164; Earle, *Making of the English Middle Class*, pp. 224–6.
49. H. Smith, *A Preparative to Marriage* (London, 1591), p. 25.

as an indentured servant to Barbados. This was a better fate than a life
of crime in England, Pepys believed, considering whether he should
have tried to have had him released. That would probably have brought
Wayneman to the gallows. Pepys had done what he honestly believed was
in the boy's interest, without pleasure and without remorse.[50]

Pepys's willingness hard-heartedly to punish his erring footboy seems to
have rested on the consensual view of youth as wild and irrational that has
been outlined above. Contemporary commentators often adopted the
animal similes of the Old Testament: the young, still in a 'state of nature',
were 'like wild asses and wild heifers'; they were 'like a young colt,
wanton and foolish, till he be broken by education and correction'.[51]
Thus the agencies of control in early modern England – family, household and parish – interlocked in a system of paternalistic control of the
young which was broadly effective and immensely flexible. The authority
of parents, masters and mistresses invariably received magisterial backing
and never more fiercely than when the chain of order was threatened by
open insubordination. A young Dorchester boy, George Hillard, who had
called his mother 'devil', received a warning from the public authorities
that he would be sent to the house of correction if he abused her again.[52]
A London nursemaid, Mary Fawden, was sent by the magistrate to
Bridewell to be whipped after a constable had taken her before him for
abusing her mistress and 'calling her ill names'. Her mistress kissed her at
the whipping post, declaring, 'Mary, God forgive you, I do.'[53]

It is the lack of a distinction between private and public responsibility
in this system that is striking. Exasperated masters regularly sought the
help of a local justice. Thus John Palgrave had his fellow magistrate send
his servant Robert Coo to the Norfolk house of correction in 1664 when
he was in despair about how to secure good service from the roistering
and dishonest lad. 'Coo was out all that night I mentioned to you in my
last letter', Palgrave wrote, 'since which time on Thursday night last he
went again to the same house to a dancing meeting without my leave but
not all night, yet to secure his coming in he took the key of the hall door
with him.'[54] The very detailed early seventeenth-century Dorchester
corporation offenders book reveals children and servants being ordered to
be chastised for minor public misdemeanours. Who did the beating
depended a good deal on the preference of those in authority within the
household. When two brothers got into a fight in Dorchester church

50. *Pepys*, II, p. 207, III, pp. 66, 116, IV, p. 382, X, p. 197; Earle, *Making of the English Middle Class*, pp. 226, 228.
51. Cited in Thomas, 'Age and Authority', *Proceedings of the British Academy* LXII (1976), p. 218.
52. D.E. Underdown, *Fire Under Heaven: The Life of an English Town in the Seventeenth Century* (London, 1992), p. 101.
53. Earle, *Making of the English Middle Class*, p. 226.
54. Fletcher, *Reform in the Provinces*, p. 280.

their father agreed to 'whip them well'. Some parents, it seems, were prepared to give a child a public whipping in the town hall. When John Colliford was sentenced to correction for repeatedly missing church his master preferred to have it done by the beadle.[55] In London masters looked for disciplinary support as necessary from both the courts of their livery companies and from Bridewell. The punishment suffered by the apprentice William Smithe in 1567, left to watch his master's shop, after he had let in a 'harlot' and had had sex with her, was designed to achieve the maximum humiliation for him together with deterrence of others from doing the like. 'In example of other apprentices' he was whipped before an assembly of his mates in Pewterers Hall. Similarly in 1573 Richard Coles, who had stolen cloth from his master's shop and engaged in other practices intended 'to make his master bankrupt', was 'openly punished' in the Clothworkers Hall 'before divers and sundry household-ers and apprentices'.[56]

Gender distinctions, we have seen, had a limited application in all this. There was some sense that infliction of punishment by males on females might pervert the victim but, this aside, there was as yet no developed concept of femininity which precluded girls being beaten. Social distinc-tions are more apparent. Sons of gentry were expected to submit to correction by masters when they were bound apprentices in London: there was a problem of downward mobility here to which young men undoubtedly found it difficult to adjust.[57] This group apart, the gentry as a whole can be seen as fierce defenders of class privilege as well as patriarchal rights in the matter of corporal punishment. They knew the legal textbook references that justified their use of correction on servants. Thus when a JP bound over a Hertfordshire gentleman in 1679, probably in pursuit of a personal vendetta, for 'striking his maidservant two blows with a small switch' a colleague came to his rescue. 'If there be no more in it,' he wrote to the clerk of the peace, 'I conceive 'tis justifiable for a master to correct his servant with a small switch, for that is a lawful weapon in law and of this opinion is Mr Dalton and several other lawyers.'[58] Yet these men's own honour and reputation consisted, as much as in anything else, in their physical inviolability. Very strong emotions lay behind a sharp debate in the House of Commons in 1593 on a proposal to empower justices to stock, whip or imprison parents of bastards at their discretion. Henry Unton's speech against the proviso, which was to be added to the act for continuation and repeal of statutes, is instructive. Whipping was 'slavish and not to be inflicted upon a liberal man'; it 'might chance upon gentlemen or men of quality whom it were

---

55. Underdown, *Fire Under Heaven*, p. 101.
56. Rappaport, *Worlds within Worlds*, pp. 209, 234.
57. Seaver, 'Declining Status', in Kunze and Brautigam, eds, *Court, Country and Culture*, pp. 133–5.
58. Cited in Fletcher and Stevenson, eds, *Order and Disorder*, p. 34.

not fit to put to such a shame'. There was also the fear that powers of summary justice might enable irresponsible or partisan JPs to act out of passion or self-interest. Unton was concerned at the possibility of malice by a magistrate 'that upon ill will might have this correction to one not offending if he were accused by a whore'. The proviso was lost by a majority of twenty-eight. This was despite the fact that the Speaker attempted to calm the House with an amendment that ensured that no offender who agreed to keep and maintain his bastard child could be whipped at the discretion of a justice and an assurance, from an assize judge who was present, that it was already the practice to excuse gentry the whipping allowed by the 1576 statute for punishing parents of bastard children.[59]

What was at stake in this 1593 debate was the gentry's security from any possibility of being whipped themselves. For every member of the House knew perfectly well that it was gentry heads of households who were responsible for a good many of the illegitimate children born at this time. Sexual exploitation of servant girls was an accepted social phenomenon. Its occurrence was inherent in the double exercise of power, as master and man, that characterised master-servant relationships in the patriarchal system. Plenty of cases reached the courts when pregnancy resulted; for every one that did there must have been others that were dealt with privately.[60] A servant who had yielded to her master's advances was always in an extremely vulnerable position. If she told what had happened there was the disgrace of the loss of her honour. By doing so, she risked her master's punishment or ill usage, even the loss of her job. Here was the crux of household patriarchy so far as young women were concerned: the system made rejection of a determined master difficult yet the consequences, if they found themselves to be with child, were dire. A fascinating account of a debate on the matter in 1601 reveals a spectrum of attitudes among MPs who were grappling not only with the question of responsibility for the illicit sexuality of their own kind but with what amounted to a test case in household discipline. The question put by William Wiseman was about where a woman who became pregnant in one house and then left service there for another in a different district should be relieved and where her child should live. At least four quite distinct views emerged in the debate. Sir George More legalistically asserted that the poor law act of 1597, which established the parish of residence as the place of relief, left the matter in no doubt: that parish must also relieve the child. Mr Browne, stating the standard view at the

59. BL, Cotton MS Titus F ii, fols., 800–810; J.R. Kent, 'Attitudes of Members of the House of Commons to the Regulation of Personal Conduct in Late Elizabethan and Early Stuart England', *BIHR* XLV (1972), pp. 44, 49–50.
60. For examples see Fletcher, *Reform in the Provinces*, pp. 255, 261; Macdonald, *Mystical Bedlam*, 87; G.R. Quaife, *Wanton Wenches and Wayward Wives* (London, 1979), pp. 72–3.

time, placed responsibility squarely on the first master: 'Their masters may look better to them than let their servants live for lewdness and therefore, this coming through his negligence and want of care or perhaps by his too much familiarity with his servant, I see no reason but he in whose home the child is gotten should be charged with both.' Mr Fettiplace, drawing on his experience as a London magistrate, explained how this strict view tended to be modified in practice. 'The man of the house', he explained, 'is ever the reputed father till the true father be known or confessed by the woman.' Then, if the servant had become pregnant through a relationship outside the home, the man involved was charged with the child's upkeep if he had means and otherwise the child was sent 'to some hospital or to the parish there to be relieved'. Finally there was another speaker who saw the matter in plainly punitive terms and was apparently little bothered with the social welfare issue. He wanted a 'straight and severe course' for 'her sin and impurity' never mind who, master or fellow servant, had been the sexual partner: 'the sin is so common in short time we shall have nothing more common, especially when we do use such cockering of them as now we do and count it a matter of charity to relieve them'.[61]

So how effective was the patriarchal household in fulfilling its aims? This discussion has taken us some way from the comfortable admonitions of the advice book writers. In the first place much, probably too much, was expected of householders. It is hardly surprising that some MPs objected to a clause in a bill in 1601 concerning absence from church which made husbands responsible for the attendance of their wives and masters for that of their servants. Anthony Dyott picked up the well known proverb to give force to his comment: 'Every man can tame a shrew but he that hath her; perhaps she will not come; and for her wilfulness no reason the husband should be punished.'[62] But members were no doubt just as worried about how they would make their servants attend. When at home they were expected to have an eye to everything servants and apprentices did out of doors: pranks and fun, drinking and courtship. The system prescribed comprehensive personal surveillance. Thus in Elizabethan Winchester, whereas children under twelve were allowed to urinate in public, parents or masters were held responsible if older children or servants did so.[63] Social tension could predictably be expected to lead to new directions for masters to tighten their grip on the young. In August 1553, for example, the London corporation, detecting increased 'vice, sin and stubbornness' among servants and apprentices in

61. BL, Stowe MS 362, fols. 257r–258v; Kent, 'Attitudes of Members', *BIHR* XLV (1972), p. 44; I.W. Archer, *The Pursuit of Stability: Social Relations in Elizabethan London* (Cambridge, 1991), p. 216.
62. Kent, 'Attitudes of Members', *BIHR* XLV (1972), p. 55.
63. M. Pelling, 'Child Health as a Social Value in Early Modern England', *Journal of the Society for the Social History of Medicine*, 1988, p. 140.

the city, instructed masters to improve their discipline and 'suffer them not to run and wander abroad'.[64] At the end of 1659, another moment of potential disorder, the Lord Mayor's reaction in London was to send aldermen and constables from house to house charging heads of families to ensure that sons and servants were kept from unlawful designs. Christopher Hill described the household at this time as 'almost a part of the constitution of the state'.[65] In theory at least its patriarchal head was the linchpin of social order.

There is good reason to take seriously the pessimistic conclusions reached about all this by Ian Archer in his study of social relations in Elizabethan London. It is too easy, he suggests, to take the record of arbitration by craft guilds or City courts as evidence that abuses were kept in check. He is not the only historian of London in our period whose study of the records has led to reflections upon the 'often horrifying severity' of the beatings and ill-treatment that many apprentices and servants endured.[66] And a huge number, as he points out, simply ran away, returning to their homes in the country or disappearing into the City's criminal underworld. Archer stresses the sheer difficulty apprentices had in getting redress unless they could demonstrate vicious brutality and the 'unsuitability of many masters to the demands placed upon them'. Thus there is the strong possibility that the cases of abuse that came to public notice were only a small proportion of those which occurred.[67] The fact is that the power given to masters in the privacy of their homes was so unlimited that it was hard for even the most conscientious magistrate to do more than hold the line against excessive barbarity. The practice of the Suffolk JP Devereux Edgar around 1700 is instructive in this respect. He received many complaints by servants against masters about 'misusage either in diet or beating'. Rather than issue warrants, which put the servant to a charge and gave the master a grudge against him because of the public disgrace of a court appearance, Edgar adopted a personal approach. His notes, which remained effectively private since he did not, as many justices did, employ his own clerk, were earnest remonstrations with the master concerned to do justice to his servant. This scheme was a frank recognition of the weakness of the magisterial position.[68] Between the 1690s and 1800 a spate of new legislation imposing fines on masters and mistresses found guilty of mistreatment of parish apprentices and intended to improve their lot indicates that there was

64. I. Archer, *The Pursuit of Stability: Social Relations in Elizabethan London* (Cambridge, 1991), pp. 243–4.
65. Hill, *Society and Puritanism*, p. 448.
66. See also Earle, *Making of the English Middle Class*, p. 101; Seaver, 'Declining Status', in Kunze and Brautigam, eds, *Court, Country and Culture*, pp. 136–41.
67. Archer, *Pursuit of Stability*, pp. 216–8.
68. W.E. Minchinton, ed., *Wage Regulation in Pre-Industrial England* (Newton Abbot, 1972), pp. 138–9.

considerable awareness among the rural magistracy that the system was deeply flawed.[69] More research is needed into this whole subject. Meanwhile, in terms of humane personal relationships, this review of household discipline must end on a note of cautious disquiet. How many servants and apprentices lived with masters like the kindly Ralph Josselin and how many with men or women who were at least at times brutal and tyrannical? The whole system was open to wide abuse. Early modern government was not constructed to a pattern which allowed oversight of day-to-day standards of care and decency, or of morality and behaviour, within thousands of homes where there were servants and apprentices in residence. It is much less evident that love and devotion counteracted patriarchal licence in men's relations with their servants than in those with their children.

69. K.D.M. Snell, *Annals of the Labouring Poor: Social Change and Agrarian England 1660–1900* (Cambridge, 1985), pp. 284–5.

12. Men's Work, Women's Work

ONE OF THE biggest problems in understanding the mentality of the early modern period is grasping the change since then in people's attitudes about work. Work for most English men and women was then hard and monotonous, dirty and cold. Its realities were marked by various ways in which it was dignified. The protestant reformers made much of the notion of callings. The influential account of these written by William Perkins around 1600 was deeply conservative in its comparison of the range of callings within society to the form of the human body: 'there be sundry parts and members and every one hath his several use and office which it performeth not for itself but for the good of the whole body'. Perkins was explicit about what this meant for women. 'If we compare work to work there is a difference betwixt washing of dishes and preaching the word of God', he declared, 'but as touching to please God none at all.'[1] Protestantism was here providing powerful reinforcement for the prevalent social order and for women's existing occupational subordination. It is important to stress just how ineradicable this was in the structure of early modern patriarchy, even when temporarily wives or widows stood in for their husbands. It followed logically from many of the attitudes to women already mentioned in this book, especially the curse laid on Eve. Men had been given the power to authorise the sexual division of labour as part of their rule over women. In effect, therefore, as Mary Prior has put it, 'whatever a man did was work and what a woman did was her duty'.[2] Yet women were wholly caught up in an ideological formulation which, embracing both what we may call occupations and general social roles, allowed commentators to elevate basic household tasks by giving them a certain vocational dignity.

1. Cited in M. Roberts, 'Words they are Women and Deeds they are Men: Images of Work and Gender in Early Modern England', in L. Charles and L. Duffin, eds, *Women and Work in Pre-Industrial England* (London, 1985), pp. 130–31.
2. M. Prior, 'Women and the Urban Economy: Oxford 1500–1800', in M. Prior, ed., *Women in English Society 1500–1800*, p. 95.

A second approach to work conceived of it, in the words of Michael Roberts, as 'the process whereby mankind interacted with nature by means of art and skill'.[3] Medieval thinking about work was pervaded by ideas about crafts and mysteries, positing a hierarchy of employment which placed artfulness and skills above drudgery. Men's arts, explained Francis Bacon, expanding this argument, could be divided into the liberal and the mechanic: 'grammar, rhetoric and music' were in a different category from mechanic arts like carpentry which required more 'labour of the hand and body than of the mind'.[4] In this hierarchical scheme some quite mundane work could be given respect, as seventeenth-century publications like the *Art of Pruning* and the *Art of Good Husbandry* showed, but many people were condemned to the inferior realm of wage work and service. It was a scheme which was bound to be highly disadvantageous to women, since it rested on the notions of manhood and effeminacy that have been discussed in chapter 5. This was where being literally the weaker vessel counted, and counted catastrophically, against women. Men defined work as requiring physical and mental strength; they defined women as primarily reproductive beings given to idleness and a life of ease. Yet women's strenuous labour, just as much as men's, was actually essential to the early modern economy. The medical textbook writers cleverly adjusted their general theories to observable facts, suggesting, for example, that women who worked long and hard in the fields had so much exercise that they only menstruated briefly.[5]

A third approach to work, which drew upon many of the assumptions discussed here, emphasised the issue of employment as the basis of a thriving economy and a stable social order. Tudor and Stuart governors, from MPs to justices and village officeholders, shared a concern to discourage idleness and prompt honest labour which was intensified by population growth, inflation and commercial difficulties.[6] Men's work had long ago been demarcated into a series of occupations. The whole structure of the medieval guilds was built upon this notion: occupations had long since led to permanent surnames. Occupations, indeed, were solid; they were a continuing means of livelihood in a society in which employment was for many an intermittent experience and work was whatever someone could do at a particular time to scrape a living. So occupations in this society did more than provide a framework for the

3. Roberts, 'Words they are Women', in Charles and Duffin, eds, *Women and Work*, p. 132.
4. Cited in Roberts, 'Words they are Women', in Charles and Duffin, eds, *Women and Work*, pp. 132–3.
5. P. Crawford, 'Attitudes to Menstruation in Seventeenth-Century England', *Past and Present* 91 (1981), p. 68.
6. For the background see K. Wrightson, *English Society 1580–1680* (London, 1982), pp. 121–48; D.C. Coleman, *The Economy of England 1450–1750* (Oxford, 1977); C.G.A. Clay, *Economic Expansion and Social Change: England 1500–1700* (Cambridge, 1984).

discussion of work. They were a cornerstone not only of the class framework but also of the whole patriarchal scheme of things. For what we find, as early modern government became more intensive, is that officeholders grew used to recording and classifying the population in terms which made it possible to identify those who could best fill its requirements. Thus in lists for taxation purposes or for militia training men were 'gentlemen, yeomen, husbandmen and labourers' and 'shoemakers, tailors, wheelwrights and masons'. Men making their own wills, and neighbours drawing up inventories of a man's goods on his death, thought in the same way: they assumed that male social and occupational identity mattered and should be recorded.[7]

But what of women in all this? Their occupational identity, given their gendered role, was simple and threefold: they were spinsters, wives and widows. A woman was almost never identified by her occupation in the ecclesiastical probate records, Amy Erickson found, regardless of the work she undertook.[8] Nor was she in secular court documents. The 1523 census in Coventry never records the name of a wife where her spouse was present in the household. Instead the words 'ex uxor' are used.[9] At Oxford, whereas the earliest in a long series of apprenticeship indentures usually give the names of both husband and wife, as if they were partners in the contract, after 1540 the name of the wife and even 'ex uxor' were normally omitted.[10] Vocabularies identify the exercise of power. For the purposes of government, the state was successfully inculcating a way of looking at social and gender order which reduced the complexities of men's working lifestyles to a straightforward and usually single occupational commitment and left out women altogether. What officeholders were interested in, after all, was heads of households: the active and representative person, male if possible, with whom the state conducted its dealings. Thus if we read these records in a descriptive sense their work identified men; some women did various kinds of work. The 1571 Norwich census of the poor is especially instructive in this respect. There was Thomas Frances 'a smith and boatman' and John Yonges 'cordwainer, journeyman and now a waterman'. Wives were described as women 'that spin white warp', 'that knit and wash and help others' or 'that sew and make bone lace'.[11] Much documentation is therefore available which helps us to expore the legal and fiscal identities of men and women at this time but which is of little help for finding out what

7. For evidence from parish registers, wills and inventories see the citations in Roberts, 'Words they are Women', in Charles and Duffin, eds, *Women and Work*, p. 137.
8. Erickson, p. 39.
9. C. Phythian-Adams, *Desolation of a City: Coventry and the Urban Crisis of the Late Middle Ages* (Cambridge, 1979), p. 87.
10. Prior, ed., *Women in English Society*, p. 104.
11. Cited in Roberts, 'Words they are Women', in Charles and Duffin, eds, *Women and Work*, p. 139.

work men and women actually did. Most of the work that women did was consigned to a residual sphere of activity; it was not graced with labels or anything like the degree of respect in the record keepers' view of the world which male occupations acquired.

There is a problem here which is fundamental to any discussion of work and gender in this period. The contemporary perception of work and labour avoids our comparative devaluation of housework, emphasising instead the crucial contribution of women in, as Michael Roberts has put it, 'the reproduction of social relations through their management of household, kin and community interaction'.[12] The core of this role was housewifery, which was regarded as the quintessentially female skill. This was the measure by which every woman was judged, with the caveat that since sexual reputation had to remain absolutely primary there was a tendency to assume that modesty implied good housewifery and that a spendthrift was likely to be a wanton. The two skills of housewifery in a woman and husbandry in a man, argues Amy Erickson, were 'equally admired by contemporaries and shared the same cardinal virtue – thrift'. We find Richard Gough's highest praise, in reviewing the repute of the inhabitants of Myddle, was for the housewife who was 'prudent, provident and discreet'. The wives of gentry, we have seen, were endlessly busy and active about their homes, managing their servants and taking their own part in household activities and affairs. This was all work, whether it was managerial or otherwise. It was how a woman redeemed herself, achieving stature and repute, as we have seen, in the eyes of her husband. Alice Wandesford, her daughter said, was not 'awanting to make a far greater improvement of my father's estate through her wise and prudential government of his family and by her care was a means to give opportunity of increasing his patrimony'. Grace Mildmay's daughter singled her out in this manner on the epitaph to her parents: 'She was most careful and wise in managing worldly estate, so as her life was a blessing to hers'. That things were still the same in the 1770s is clear from the diaries of Elizabeth Shackleton of Alcincoats in Lancashire. The practice of housekeeping, concludes Amanda Vickery from an analysis of them, provided her with 'an esteemed role' and 'afforded a gratifying means of favourable comparison with other women'. She was not best pleased when, on visiting her new daughter-in-law Betty Parker in 1779, she was put into dirty sheets and a damp bed. Within a year, however, Mrs Parker was redeeming herself. 'My good daughter is a most exceeding good wife,' Elizabeth Shackleton noted, 'she ruffled her husband a shirt and always is industrious and manages with prudent economy'.[13]

12. M. Roberts, 'Women and Work in Sixteenth-century English Towns', in P.J. Corfield and D. Keene, eds, *Work in Towns 850–1850* (Leicester, 1990), pp. 87–90.
13. Citations from Erickson, pp. 53–4; A. Vickery, 'Women and the World of Goods: A Lancashire Consumer and her Possessions 1751–81', in J. Brewer and R. Porter, eds, *Consumption and the World of Goods* (London, 1993), p. 283.

Before assessing how the sexual division of labour actually operated in the period between 1500 and 1800 it is important to review the recent historiography of this subject. In an article published in 1983, Olwen Hufton remarked that feminist writing on the nineteenth century was forcing upon historians of the early modern period the unenviable task 'of locating a *bon vieux temps* when women enjoyed a harmonious, if hard working, domestic role and social responsibility before they were down-graded into social parasites or factory fodder under the corrupting hand of capitalism'. She commented that this *bon vieux temps* was proving elusive.[14] Since 1983 a mass of research, summarised forcibly and effectively in recent articles by Judith Bennett and Amy Erickson, has shown that this golden age never existed. Bennett contends that women's work was generally of low status in the middle ages and that this remained the case from 1300 to 1700.[15] Erickson, taking a perspective from the middle ages to the present day, finds 'more continuity than change in the important features of women's working lives'. The essential features of women's economic position relative to men – the sex ratio of wages, access to training, concentration in the lowest paid sectors of the labour market and the sexual division of labour in the household – all seem, she argues, 'to have been unaffected by either capitalism or industrialisation'.[16]

There are a number of good reasons why historians have been slow to overturn the notion of a great divide between the gender basis of the medieval economy and of the modern one. Anthropological research, which reveals plenty of gendered subsistence agricultural societies, might in fact have led them to have doubts much earlier on. But the main problem has been that an exceptionally authoritative work, Alice Clark's *Working Life of Women in the Seventeenth Century*, which was pioneering in its time, went unchallenged for too long and was given too much credit by many feminist writers, influenced by Marxist thinking, who assumed that women's modern subordination must have been related in some way to the transition from feudalism to capitalism.[17] Some more recent work, which takes an optimistic view, does not bear that stamp.[18] Women's

14. O. Hufton, 'Women in History: Early Modern Europe', *Past and Present* 101 (1983), p. 126.

15. J.M. Bennett, 'Medieval Women, Modern Women: Across the Great Divide', in D. Aers, ed., *Culture and History 1350–1600: Essays in English Communities, Identities and Writings* (London, 1992), p. 151.

16. A. Erikson, Introduction to A. Clark, *Working Life of Women in the Seventeenth Century* (London, 1992 edn), p. xviii–xxii.

17. Clark's work was revised with a critical introduction by M. Chaytor and J. Lewis in 1982. Erikson's 1992 edition takes these criticisms much further. For works in a Marxist mould using Clark see E. Figes, *Patriarchal Attitudes* (London, 1970), R. Hamilton, *The Liberation of Women: A Study of Patriarchy and Capitalism* (London, 1978), and A. Oakley, *Subject Women* (Oxford, 1981).

18. C. Baron, 'The "Golden Age" of Women in Medieval London', in *Medieval Women in Southern England* (Reading Medieval Studies, 15, 1989), pp. 35–58; P.J.P. Goldberg, *Women, Work and Life Cycle in a Medieval Economy* (Oxford, 1992); B.A. Hanawalt,

history, Bennett proposes, has clung to a thesis which 'suits our presumptions about the problems and evils of our own society and our longings for another (in this case, pre-modern) world of a kinder and gentler variety'.[19] Moreover a great transition in the history of women, she notes, fits well with a dominant master narrative of change which only a few have been brave enough to criticise.[20] At a time when male historians were developing aspects of that master narrative in positive terms, there was a strong appeal in the notion of a correspondingly negative transition for women: here was a way of counting the cost of men's alleged triumphs in creating the modern liberal world.[21] Bennett has urged the abandonment of the paradigm of a great divide. Her stress on the need to study the 'mechanisms and operations' of patriarchy, as they affected men's and women's work, is salutory.[22] This is not to abandon an interest in change. Nor must it mean emphasising the politics of gender relations at the expense of short- and long-term economic factors and wider political issues when we try to explain women's varying fortunes in holding on to or losing employment opportunities.

The economy of this period was essentially a family and household one. We have seen how the institutions of service and apprenticeship brought a mass of adolescent and young men and women into households other than their own. There was virtually no place at all for the single man or woman taking up an occupation alone. Following the statute of artificers in 1563, mayors and justices could compel any unmarried woman between twelve and forty into service: adolescent girls who refused this course risked the insinuation that they were whores.[23] Sir Thomas Smith took the view that young men as well as young women could be compelled to get themselves masters.[24] The Coventry court leet forbade single women under forty from setting up house alone, directing them to share a chamber or go into service.[25] A study of the London guilds in the sixteenth century has led to the conclusion that, despite

'Peasant Women's Contribution to the Home Economy in Late Medieval England', in B.A. Hanawalt, ed., *Women and Work in Pre-Industrial Europe* (Bloomington, Indiana, 1986), pp. 3–19; K.E. Lacey, 'Women and Work in Fourteenth and Fifteenth Century London', in Charles and Duffin, eds, *Women and Work*, pp. 24–82.

19. Bennett, 'Medieval Women', in Aers, ed., *Culture and History*, p. 149.

20. E.g. A. Macfarlane, *The Origins of English Individualism: The Family, Property and Social Transition* (Oxford, 1978).

21. Examples include L. Stone, *The Family, Sex and Marriage in England 1500–1800* (London, 1977); L. Stone, *The Road to Divorce: England 1500–1989* (Oxford, 1990); K.V. Thomas, *Religion and the Decline of Magic* (London, 1971) and K.V. Thomas, *Man and the Natural World* (London, 1983).

22. Bennett, 'Medieval Women', in Aers, ed., *Culture and History*, pp. 164–5.

23. W.E. Minchinton, ed., *Wage Regulation in Pre-Industrial England* (Newton Abbot, 1972), p. 237.

24. Cited in M. Macdonald, *Mystical Bedlam: Madness, Anxiety and Healing in Seventeenth-Century England* (Cambridge, 1961), p. 85.

25. Phythian-Adams, *Desolation of a City*, p. 87.

charters and precedents to the contrary, single women had no place in them.[26] The household, we should remember, was a social construction not a natural one. It complemented the marriage patterns of the time and, as we have seen, provided a convenient focus for exacting discipline among the young. It suited the medieval system of guild regulations in towns. Indisputably it was shot through with sexual inequality, for, while the women brought resources to the family economy and worked hard to support it, control of that economy rested firmly in the hands of her husband. Whatever she did her housewifery defined her character whereas his work defined the objectives of family life. What he did was limited and demarcated; what she did was determined by his age, skills, capital resources and occupation.[27] She could get advice about her more obvious tasks from popular manuals like Fitzherbert's *Book of Husbandry* of 1555 and Gervase Markham's *English Housewife* of 1631.[28]

The prescriptive literature of the period contained plenty of rhetoric designed to justify and maintain this state of affairs. Puritan conduct book writers conventionally portrayed husbands and wives as fulfilling complementary roles indoors and out of doors. 'The cock flyeth abroad to bring in and the dam sitteth upon the nest to keep all at home,' declared Henry Smith.[29] The universal assumptions were that women's labour was essential to the household economy and that the partnership in running it was an unequal one. Amy Erickson sees prescriptive representations of domestic roles being complementary as meretricious, since both the division of labour and the division of power within the household was clearly hierarchical.[30] The same prescriptive pattern is taken for granted in the ballad literature but this at least makes no pretence at relating anything but the harsh realities of life. There is no mystification in the frank account, which sounds strangely modern, of a housewife's day provided in the ballad 'A Woman's Work is Never Done', published in the 1650s. While her husband devoted himself singlemindedly to his occupation, she was required to be endlessly adaptable, tireless and patient. The day begins with sweeping and cleaning and making the fire. Children have to be dressed, given breakfast and got off to school. Cooking and preparing more food for a husband, who is quickly back at work with 'scarce a kiss', takes up the morning; knitting, spinning, washing and scouring the afternoon. Then children and husband need further attention. Nights are

---

26. S. Rappaport, *Worlds within Worlds: Structures of Life in Sixteenth-Century London* (Cambridge, 1989), p. 38.
27. Prior, 'Women and the Urban Economy', in Prior, *Women in English Society*, p. 95; Bennett, 'Medieval Women', in Aers, ed., *Culture and History*, pp. 152–5.
28. S.W. Hull, *Chaste, Silent and Obedient: English Books for Women 1435–1640* (San Marino, 1982), pp. 31–70.
29. H. Smith, *A Preparative to Marriage* (London, 1591), p. 43; above, p. 61.
30. Erickson in Clark, *Working Life of Women* (1992 edn), p. xx.

interrupted by a child crying for the breast and sex is about the only consolation.[31] In a ballad which reflects the difficult economic conditions of the 1620s, a 'careful wife' and a 'comfortable husband' debate the deal which they have made with each other and about what they each put in to their marriage. She has the dirtier and more unpleasant jobs:

> In wiving and thriving it is an old song
> More than the bare legs to bed do belong
> What you spend on me, I take for my pain
> For doing such duties as you would disdain.

She is ready to work hard, so they can 'pass this hard year without any strife'. He, in return, accepts their stringencies and will do his best to ease her cares by bringing in the cash:

> I will play the good husband the best that I can
> To live with good credit and pay every man.[32]

'A Merry Dialogue betwixt a Married Man and his Wife', published around the same time, by contrast belies its title and portrays a couple much at odds about which of them has to work the harder, appealing to standard male suspicions about female complaints and shrewishness. The husband sticks to his point that his tasks in the field are more laborious; the wife insists that her 'toiling and moiling' does not end when he returns home to enjoy sitting down on a stool or a chair.[33]

Spouses in this family economy could not separate work and home in practice or in their minds and women were often active in productive capacities that went beyond subsistence. Some kind of effective partnership was essential. Wives helped on the farm, in the shop or in the unskilled or semi-skilled parts of their husband's craft while also carrying out household and childrearing duties. The misogynist streak that shows in a 'Merry Dialogue' may have corroded the mutuality of many partnerships but we should beware of exaggerating its effect or assuming that it necessarily did so. It is impossible to tell what women felt about their lack of independence and control of their own lives. Yet Keith Wrightson is surely right to argue that working together could breed a 'sense of shared endeavour and dogged companionship in facing and surmounting the insecurities of existence'.[34] Unfortunately we only have direct male testimony to this. In 1600, for instance, a Salisbury man, Thomas Reade, left all his property to his loving wife who 'by her joint care, travail and industry hath supported and augmented my estate'. An innkeeper there,

31. *Roxburghe*, III, pp. 302–6; Prior, 'Women and the Urban Economy', in Prior, ed., *Women in English Society*, p. 96.
32. *Roxburghe*, I, pp. 122–5.
33. *Roxburghe*, II, pp. 159–63.
34. D. Levine and K. Wrightson, *The Making of an Industrial Society: Whickham 1560–1765* (Oxford, 1991), p. 318; see also Rappaport, *Worlds within Worlds*, p. 41.

whose will was proved in 1613, made his wife sole beneficiary 'for she hath been married unto me these three and twenty years and worked when I have played'.[35] William Stout recorded in his diary how in his youth his mother was 'not only fully employed in housewifery but in dressing their corn for the market and also in the fields in hay and corn harvests along with our father and servants'. The fruits of his parents' joint labours, he noted, was an improvement in their estate 'to the double what it was when they were married'.[36] Ralph Josselin, clergyman, school-master and working farmer, makes extraordinarily little reference to his wife's activities in his diary but this was presumably because he took it for granted that their marriage was a working partnership. Details of her role emerge quite incidentally and normally because of the personal implica-tions for himself, as when she made him a 'sirup of steeped hissup' for his chest. We only know that they pulled down a tree with a rope together in 1644 because they both fell and Josselin was reminded of the incident in chronicling a series of minor accidents. Very unusually on 31 May 1646 he mentioned a typical housewifely task, stilling roses, probably because it had a calendrical significance.[37] Historians writing in the context of the modern acute sexual division of labour have a problem about entering the mental world of early modern partnership in work. It is a world that Thomas Hardy saw disappearing and he better than anyone, as Keith Snell points out, 'articulated the sense of loss and personal estrangement asso-ciated with the decline of the shared labour and cooperation of the family economy'.[38] There is much in his novels about the search for the condi-tions which, as he saw it, favoured the development of a close working relationship. A passage from *The Woodlanders* makes the point: 'They had planted together and together they had felled; together they had, with the run of the years, mentally collected those remoter signs and symbols which seen in few were of runic obscurity but all together made an alphabet.'[39]

The centrepiece of a patriarchal system of inequality in the workplace has commonly been seen to be a combination of task differentiation within specified areas of work with actual occupational differentiation.[40]

35. S. Wright, '"Churmaids, Huswyfes and Hucksters": The Employment of Women in Tudor and Stuart Salisbury', in Charles and Duffin, eds, *Women and Work*, p. 105.
36. J. Marshall, ed., *The Diary of William Stout of Lancaster* (Chetham Society, XIV, 1967), p. 68.
37. A. Macfarlane, ed., *The Diary of Ralph Josselin 1616–1683*, pp. 17, 61, 218; A. Macfarlane, *The Family Life of Ralph Josselin* (Cambridge, 1970), pp. 33–78, 106–10.
38. K.D.M. Snell, *Annals of the Labouring Poor: Social Change in Agrarian England 1660–1900* (Cambridge, 1985), p. 307.
39. Cited in Snell, *Annals of the Labouring Poor*, p. 308.
40. For a useful conceptualisation see C. Middleton, 'Women's Labour and the Transition to Pre-Industrial Capitalism', in Charles and Duffin, eds, *Women and Work*, pp. 186–8.

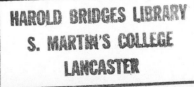

The key issues are those of status, skills and training, security and pay. We can attempt a brief survey, based on the recent secondary literature, of the main categories of women's work between 1500 and 1800. If in fact patriarchy was coming to bear more heavily on women during this three-hundred-year period we would expect to find changes in the numbers of women engaged in jobs which brought status and public standing. One of these was medicine. Womankind's perceived closeness to nature was still in early Tudor England their greatest source of reputation in the world of work, for their arts and skills in relation to the secrets of reproduction and health gave them a special standing that no man – prince, merchant or master craftsman – could match. Women were situated at the intersection of life with death: this put men in awe of them and in many cases probably produced some fear of them. It was a precarious position and one, as it proved, women could not hold as epistemological changes and professional development altered the status of their form of knowledge, the arcane knowledge of experience. A story told by Sir William Wentworth in an account of the providences vouchsafed his family in 1607 perfectly encapsulates the atmosphere of religion, magic and herbal lore which surrounded this female sphere of work. His father, Thomas Wentworth, had recounted a vision he had while desperately ill of a burning fever. It occurred while his mother and the family were out of the room:

> he was not asleep but only lay with closed eyes . . . and when he opened his eyes he saw standing by his bedside a wellfavoured gentle-woman of a middle age in apparel and countenance decent and very demure; and thinking the sight very strange he said to her 'Gentle-woman from whence come you?' She answered 'Wentworth, I come from God'. He said 'what is your name?' She said her name was God's pity and that God had sent her to signify unto him that he had compassion of him and that he should have no more fits of that fever . . . and thereupon she took out of her pocket a box of ointment and dipped some of her fingers therein and offered to put her hand into the bed about the middest thereof. But he, bashfully holding the clothes down, seemed to restrain her hand, but she said 'I must touch thee'. Whereupon he suffering her, she put her hand into the bed and touched his privities and presently took her hand away and then said 'when thou art well go to the well at St Anne of Buxton and there wash thy self and thank God for thy delivery'. He had, as he affirmed, much conference with her, greatly to his contentment.[41]

Women were believed, through their reproductive role and their emotional natures, to be better able than men to activate occult powers.

41. J.P. Cooper, ed., *Wentworth Papers 1597–1628* (Camden Society, XII, 1973), p. 28.

This was double-edged. On the one hand it explains why witchcraft was very largely a gendered crime. On the other, at a time when disease was seen as a foreign presence in the body which needed to be conjured away, it endowed women with great potential for healing. Thomas Wentworth's vision is so instructive because it illustrates the coherence of a mental world which gave women a practical and respected role in the work of healing at all levels of society. A mass of impressionistic evidence indicates that many women were busy, even as the old cosmology was collapsing, as the cunning women, the healers and the gentlewomen benefactors of rural society. What the village charmer and the lady of the manor dispensing physic around her tenants, though of very different social status, had in common was their privileged access to nature.

The practice of these two kinds of healer varied not so much because of any difference in motivation and objectives but because the sources of knowledge and information that each applied were different. Cultivation of healing skills was part of the gentry's tradition of hospitality, which was manifested in offering food and lodging to strangers besides caring for the local poor.[42] Learning something about medicine and cures was a normal element in the upbringing of girls at this social level. It was informed learning since there were practical guidebooks which combined medicinal with other recipes. Women make medicines on the frontispiece of Hannah Wolley's manual *The Acomplisht Lady's Delight* just as they preserve food, cook and beautify themselves.[43] A manual of recipes and cures by Elizabeth Grey, the Countess of Kent, which was first published in 1651, went through nineteen editions over a period of thirty-four years.[44] Many of the manuscript receipt books based on the treatises and manuals that gentlewomen obtained and read have survived in archive collections.[45] Lady Anne Clifford describes how her mother 'was a lover of the study of medicine and the practice of alchemy ... she delighted in distilling waters and getting chemical reactions with her extracts'. Lady Anne followed her mother's example.[46] Margaret Hoby attended to people's wounds in the neighbourhood of Hackness on the north Yorkshire moors. In the year 1600 alone her diary makes thirty-two references to 'dressing patients'.[47] While resident in St Olave's parish in London during the 1620s, Anne Fanshawe recorded, her mother had 'dressed many

42. F. Heal, *Hospitality in Early Modern England* (Oxford, 1990), pp. 1–22.
43. H. Wolley, *The Accomplisht Lady's Delight* (London, 1675); Hull, *Chaste, Silent and Obedient*, pp. 37–45.
44. C.F. Otten, ed., *English Women's Voices 1540–1700* (Miani, 1992), pp. 176, 184–5.
45. D.E. Nagy, *Popular Medicine in Seventeenth-century England* (Bowling Green, Ohio, 1988), p. 67.
46. Cited in H. Bourdillon, *Women as Healers: A History of Women and Medicine* (Cambridge, 1988), p. 17.
47. L.M. Beier, *Sufferers and Healers: The Experience of Illness in Seventeenth Century England* (London, 1987), p. 172.

wounds of miserable people'. Hester Honeywood, lady of the manor at
Earls Colne in Essex, offered Ralph Josselin's family help and advice
in times of illness. His son had a consultation in 1649 when Lady
Honeywood advised an issue 'to which my wife hath no mind'. In 1673,
when the ageing Ralph Josselin was very unwell, Lady Honeywood sent
her coach for him and nursed him for six weeks, during which time she
gave him purges for an ailment 'which they conceived the scurvy'.[48]
Anne, Countess of Arundel, we are told, supplied medicines and salves,
plasters and other remedies to those who came to her because they could
not afford to go to doctors and surgeons. John Evelyn described his
mother's and his sister's work 'in the distillery, the knowledge of plants
and their virtues for the comfort of the poor neighbours'.[49] Elizabeth
Freke's diary contains 446 medicinal and herbal prescriptions.[50]

Grace Mildmay's medical practice was quite exceptional: it was extensive, systematic and at the forefront of contemporary medicine. Linda
Pollock, comparing her treatment with that of professional doctors, found
that 'the range of ailments treated, the medical techniques relied upon and
the ingredients used were similar'. She did not, as others did, dress
wounds among the poor or physically nurse the sick. Her interest was in
treating disease and the manufacture of medications. From the inventory
of her still room one might think she ran an apothecary's shop. Her
extant written remedies make a total of 270 cures. She clearly learnt a
good deal from the work of medical authorities and she corresponded
with other alchemical practitioners. Lady Grace's notes reveal a traditional
understanding of illness in terms of humoral imbalance and an approach
to medical care which was basically Galenic, emphasising alleviation of
symptoms through a regimen which dealt with the patient as a whole
person by taking into account age, sex and physical strength. It was only
a woman with considerable resources of time and money who could
develop such a practice. Grace Mildmay's success in doing so shows how,
as Linda Pollock puts it, the 'flexible structure of early modern medicine supplied a creative and intellectually challenging outlet' for such a
woman's energy and talents.[51]

Throughout the seventeenth century supplying the medicinal needs of
the neighbourhood had become one of the defining characteristics of the
'good woman' and one of the marks of female noblesse oblige which was
most frequently commented upon in published funeral sermons. In 1622
the Cornish Lady Phillipa Ross was praised for making 'her closet as an

48. Cited in Heal, *Hospitality in Early Modern England*, p. 180; Macfarlane, ed., *Diary of Ralph Josselin*, pp. 186, 566.
49. Citations from Bourdillon, *Women as Healers*, pp. 16–17.
50. 'Diary of Elizabeth Freke', *Journal of the Cork Historical and Archaeological Society*, XIX, p. 147.
51. L.A. Pollock, *With Faith and Physic: The Life of a Tudor Gentlewoman Lady Grace Mildmay 1552–1620* (London, 1993), pp. 97–109.

apothecary's shop for the poor neighbours in time of their sickness'.[52] Anthony Walker described his wife Elizabeth's afternoon distributions of 'distilled waters, syrups, oils, ointments and salves', noting that her skill 'both as a physician and surgeon' was based upon learning from doctors of her acquaintance and from authors such as Riverius and Culpepper.[53] Thus gentlewoman healers were conducting an activity that both their husbands and professional doctors approved. George Farquhar's portrait of Lady Bountiful, an 'old civil country gentlewoman', whose repertoire included cures for greensickness and fits of the mother, in *The Beaux Strategem* written in 1707, is thoroughly sympathetic.[54] Such women had no pretensions to be more than amateurs, yet they could offer the best of an established tradition of herbal and alchemical medicine, together with the reassurance and consideration that went with their patriarchal role towards tenants and their families. It was class rather than gender which gave their work standing; at the same time gender, in the sense of current notions about the female constitution and women's occult sensitivity, gave it meaning.

Magical healers overlapped with the orthodox in their prescribing practice, employing the same inherited lore about the properties of plants and minerals. Margaret Hunt in 1528 made reference to her use of herbs for the ague and for sores. Goodwife Veazey's procedure for curing ringworm or tether-worm, as described in 1604, involved application of honey and pepper to the afflicted part. What distinguished these healers from the gentlewomen was their use of rituals which wrapped their healing in mystery. Their prayers were in effect charms, that is they were invocations of occult power rather than requests for God's mercy. The emphasis was on formulas. When Margaret Hunt had prayed for her clients to the Blessed Trinity to heal them from all their wicked enemies she told them how many Paternosters, Aves and Creeds they should say each night and in what order. Goodwife Veazey's ritual began with an admonition to the worm causing disease to be gone 'in the name of the Father, of the Son and of the Holy Ghost'. Curious and bizarre procedures, as these healers surely knew, added to their reputation with a credulous circle of clients. Katherine Thompson and Anne Neselson, presented as 'common charmers of sick folks and their goods' in 1664, used to put the bill of a white duck to the sick person's mouth before they began to mumble. Anne Green's method for charming heartache was to cross a garter over the patient's ears while she repeated nine times an imprecation for the malady to be gone. The essence of the business

52. A. Duffin, 'The Political Allegiance of the Cornish Gentry c. 1600–c. 1642', Exeter University PhD thesis, 1989, p. 237.
53. A. Walker, *The Holy Life of Mrs Elizabeth Walker* (London, 1690), pp. 35, 72, 178. For further examples see A.L. Wyman, 'The Surgeoness: the Female Practitioner of Surgery 1400–1800', *Medical History* 28 (1984), pp. 31–4.
54. G. Farquhar, *The Beaux Strategem*, act 1, 73–4.

was trust and active engagement in whatever strange ceremonies the cunning woman adopted. Yet, authentic as they themselves found their rituals, they were walking a tightrope. For their alleged access to occult power took them into a realm where a narrow line divided benevolence and malevolence: trust could easily collapse. On her first visit to Elizabeth Page in 1555, Elizabeth Wryte could get no more comfort about her sick child than hearing the charmer uttering a rigmarole over the cradle. When she was brave enough to return with a direct request for help 'if it were overlooked or bewitched', she was told the child would recover that night which, as it happens, it did. But things did not always go so smoothly, as the report of the churchwardens of a Gloucestershire village in 1563 shows. Alice Prabury's secrecy about her methods of work had aroused suspicion: she 'useth herself suspiciously in the likelihood of a witch . . . she taketh upon her to help by way of charming and in such ways that she will have nobody privy of her sayings'.[55]

In the course of the seventeenth century the healing remedies of the charmer were losing the respect of the social elite as the taint of dabbling in magic destroyed their reputation for sound herbal lore. It was easy for those with vested interests in professionalisation, like the Northampton-shire physician John Cotta, to deride ignorant practisers of medicine, whether astrologers, cunning men or cunning women.[56] The proverbial wisdom that women were scatty and irrational could be turned to account in denouncing any female healer. Robert Heath advised the Norfolk assize jury in 1633 that Alice Mays, 'a doctor woman' accused of murder by killing some of her patients, could not as a 'silly woman' have had the skill to administer 'inward physic' even if she had had some knowledge about 'outward applictions'.[57] Gentry who wished to cling to their trust in the old lore took precautions in doing so. Thus when Sir Ralph Verney told his wife in 1647 to give their child physick 'such as midwives and old women' prescribed 'for assure yourself they by experience know better than physicians', he directed this was to be done with the advice of their close friend Dr Denton.[58]

The female surgeon was an acknowledged figure of the health care scene in England between 1400 and 1800 but she was being gradually eliminated from the more prestigious aspects of the profession. In a number of cities we can trace specific measures to exclude competition from women. In Norwich, in 1561, the physicians and barber-surgeons complained about 'sundry women practitioners' whom they regarded as

55. Thomas, *Religion and the Decline of Magic*, pp. 178–87.
56. J. Cotta, *A Short Discourse of the Unobserved Dangers of several sorts on Ignorant Practices of Physick in England* (London, 1622).
57. C. Brooks, 'Professions, Ideology and the Middling Sort in the Late Sixteenth and Seventeenth Centuries', in J. Barry and C. Brooks, eds, *The Middling Sort*, (London, 1984), p. 120.
58. *Verney*, II, 270.

quacks. A charter given to the Salisbury barber-surgeons in 1614 inveighed against women 'unskilful in the art of surgery who oftentimes take cures on them to the great danger of the patient'. Women surgeons flourished longest in areas of the profession where ancient lore as much as empirical knowledge held sway, like cures for ringworm of the scalp, bonesetting and leg ulcers.[59] They could make a decent living in country areas where they were unchallenged by incorporated male practitioners and where, before the late eighteenth century, little alternative medical assistance was available. Thus Ralph Josselin turned to two local married women with a reputation for their skill in bonesetting to deal with a limp and an arm out of joint in his family.[60] Richard Gough recalled Elinor Mansell of Myddle, a woman 'very useful and indeed famous for her skill in surgery . . . and in that way she did much good in the country'.[61] In the early eighteenth century Nicholas Blundell, squire of Crosby Hall in Lancashire, several times consulted Mrs Bootle of the nearby village of Peel. Family ailments which she attempted to cure included a burnt finger and a leg sore. Later, dissatisfied with Mrs Bootle, Blundell turned to Betty Bolton, a widow living in Liverpool who is styled in their accounts the 'surgeoness'. She dealt with an ulcer in his wife's leg over a con-siderable period and was well paid for her efforts.[62]

James Primrose's 1651 publication *Popular Errors or the Errors of the People in Physick* put the standard male case against women meddling in physick and surgery. He derided their efforts to cure ulcers and wounds, which 'doth require very much art', by taking remedies from popular manuals or information handed down to them. The exclusively male Royal College of Physicians was gradually succeeding in persuading the educated that scientific knowledge was the only proper basis for all medicine. During the eighteenth century the woman surgeon was more and more a figure of fun in gentry and middle-class circles. Hogarth caricatured the highly successful London bonesetter Mrs Mapp. Apoth-ecaries were becoming more numerous and better organised: their respect as regular medical advisers among those who could not afford the fees of surgeons and physicians rose as that of women practitioners fell. In the same period gentlewomen were beginning to forget their obligation to be healers to the neighbourhood. Richard Steele, in his conduct book *The Ladies Library* of 1714, specifically excused them: 'how far it is convenient for them to be the physician and surgeoness of the village I shall not meddle with reckoning such accomplishments as casual only and not of absolute necessity to the forming a complete gentlewoman'.[63] The 1841

59. Wyman, 'The Surgeoness', *Medical History* (1984), pp. 28, 36–40.
60. Macfarlane, ed., *Diary of Ralph Josselin*, pp. 314, 460.
61. R. Gough, *The History of Myddle* (London, 1981), p. 152.
62. M. Blundell, ed., *Blundell's Diary and Letter Book, 1702–1708* (Liverpool, 1952), pp. 51, 65.
63. R. Steele, *The Ladies Library* (London, 1714), I, p. 20.

census returns listed not a single woman as an apothecary, surgeon or physician.[64] These developments mark a significant narrowing of women's employment opportunities and of their chance to contribute constructively to society.

The exclusion of midwives from professional standing as the medical profession extended its expertise in the fields of gynaecology and obstetrics is a classic example of how women were swept aside by male assertiveness. Traditionally babies were delivered by women of mature age who had themselves borne children. Midwifery was an art not a science. It lacked theoretical underpinning but midwives were often deeply respected for their practical skill and experience. Thus we find a Southampton man being admitted to the freedom in 1601 since his wife was 'of very good opinion amongst the whole inhabitants' because as the town's chief midwife she had 'taken great pains and honest care in her function'.[65] Throughout the seventeenth century midwives maintained their grip on the business of childbirth despite debate about their competence. A sample of the occupations of married couples in London around 1700 reveals a gentleman and a feltmaker whose wives were practising as midwives.[66] But from around the 1720s more men were coming into the field. The term 'man-midwife' is first recorded in 1625; by the middle of the eighteenth century it was fashionable to employ a male 'accoucheur'. The birth chamber had been invaded and was being taken over. The traditional ceremony of childbirth, argues Adrian Wilson, was 'transformed under the impact of the male practitioner'.[67]

The English midwives were degraded into mere assistants. They had been put in an impossible situation. They were attacked for being scientifically ignorant, but they were denied the training they needed. In 1634 Peter Chamberlen, whose family had invented and was reputed for the successful use of the forceps, attempted to organise the midwives of London into a college. The proposal was highly self-interested and the midwives who opposed it were probably right to be suspicious that Chamberlen's intention was to downgrade them rather than give them real professional status on the basis of a thorough knowledge of anatomy. In any case the project was balked by the College of Physicians. It is quite clear that what lay behind its reaction to the scheme was defensive self-interest. The College argued that the midwives were mostly 'very

64. Wyman, 'The Surgeoness', Medical History, 28 (1984), pp. 34–5, 38–9.
65. Wright in '"Churmaids"', Charles and Duffin, eds, Women and Work, p. 108.
66. P. Earle, 'The Female Labour Market in London in the Late Seventeenth and Early Eighteenth Centuries', Economic History Review, 42 (1989), p. 349.
67. J. Donnison, Midwives and Medical Men: A History of Inter-Professional Rivalries and Women's Rights (London, 1977), pp. 7–22; A. Wilson, 'Participant or Patient? Seventeenth Century Childbirth from the Mother's Point of View', in R. Porter, ed., Patients and Practitioners: Lay Perceptions of Medicine in Pre-Industrial Society (Cambridge, 1985), p. 141.

ignorant' and needed training, yet they thought it 'neither necessary nor convenient' that they should become 'a corporation to govern within themselves' which was 'a thing not exampled in any commonwealth'.[68] Both positively and negatively, the midwives' own anatomy was their destiny. Superstition delayed the acceptance of a male presence in the birth chamber and then conventional thinking about the capacities of the weaker vessel made their professionalisation unthinkable.[69] Writers and translators of gynaecological texts at this time excused themselves from providing anatomical information which would be indecent for a woman to see. It is unlikely that any practising midwife would be able to afford to buy, or have access to, works like Helkiah Crooke's *Microcosmographia*, which in any case was insufficiently explicit about the things midwives needed to know. Some no doubt did benefit from reading James Rueff's general advice in *The Expert Midwife*. Nicholas Culpepper was the lone male voice sympathetic to them with his *Directory of Midwives*, which not only sought to get across medical information which the physicians wanted kept secret but actually encouraged midwives to carry on themselves rather than call for help from a man-midwife, 'which is a disparagement not only to yourselves but also to your profession'. The fact is that the midwives were simply not in a position to protect their traditional role. It is interesting that Jane Sharp's assertive claim for this role in *The Midwives Book* of 1671 was essentially biblical and it was a claim that made no attempt to confront the gender hierarchy on which patriarchy rested:

> Though we women cannot deny that men in some things may come to a greater perfection of knowledge than women ordinarily can, by reason of the former helps that women want yet the holy scriptures hath recorded midwives to the perpetual honour of the female sex . . . it is commendable for men to employ their spare time in some things of deeper speculation than is required to the female sex but the art of midwifery chiefly concerns us.[70]

Epistemological change was making it hard to take Jane Sharp seriously. Yet we should be careful not simply to take our knowledge of the practice of midwives in the period from 1500 to 1700 from male sources at face value. Surgeons at this time were usually called in emergencies and it was in their interest to present midwives as incompetent. There are serious issues of definition about what in fact constituted good practice, as Ornella Moscucci has pointed out, stressing that the history of obstetrics has mostly been seen through the eyes of medical practitioners

68. H. Smith, 'Gynaecology and Ideology in Seventeenth-Century England', in B.A. Carroll, ed., *Liberating Women's History* (Urbana, 1976), pp. 109–10.
69. Beier, *Sufferers and Healers*, p. 43.
70. Citations from Smith, 'Gynaecology and Ideology', in Carroll, ed., *Liberating Women's History*, pp. 111–12.

who were persuaded that they were 'bringing rational knowledge to an area dominated by ignorance and tradition'. Certain points about the competence of midwives, which provided an adequate basis for professionalisation had men allowed it, can be made with some confidence. They had well established skills of manual intervention, techniques of their own for reviving a newly born baby or a mother following delivery, experience in helping mothers during their lying in and much general expertise in gynaecological matters.[71] George Crabbe's poem *The Parish Register*, written in 1807, tells the story of the battle between an established village midwife and the new Doctor Glibb. He locates the conflict, Ludmilla Jordanova notes, 'not just between two individuals, classes or professions but between modernity and tradition and between their related stances towards nature'. Moreover he uses a vocabulary for the doctor to press his case which was 'full of implied, sexually tinged aggression'.[72] It was quite clearly an ideological struggle that the midwives lost when professionalisation swept them aside.

When a London draper came to enrol a young woman as an apprentice in 1570 the master and wardens of his company turned him away since 'they had not seen the like heretofore'. However William Dummer, a prominent draper who was thrice warden at this time, when asked for his opinion about whether 'a maiden servant willing to be bound . . . might not be presented in our hall and also enrolled in the chamber of London as other apprentices are and thereby also enjoy the freedom of the city', declared that she could be and that there were precedents for more than a hundred years past.[73] Apprenticeship records are the richest form of documentation we have for the subject of women's work in trades and crafts between 1500 and 1800. Many studies that have been made of them show the reality of female apprenticeship in a wide range of businesses during this period. For every century from the fourteenth to the nineteenth this type of evidence offers tantalising insights into the work women actually did. But this extensive documentation is easier to amass than to interpret. Quantification can only establish outline statistics: percentages of males to females, the diversity of occupations involved. The really important issues are the ones that Dummer's legalistic response to the query put to him cannot reveal, questions about participation in trading and craft activities, about independent trading roles, about the acquisition of status as a skilled tradesperson.

The purpose of these apprenticeships was presumably to provide girls, just like boys, with a skill that they could practise as a means of adult subsistence, either within a family economy or as a *femme sole* if they

71. O. Moscucci, *The Science of Woman: Gynaecology and Gender in England 1800–1929* (Cambridge, 1990), pp. 42–50.
72. L. Jordanova, *Sexual Visions: Images of Gender in Science and Medicine between the Eighteenth and Twentieth Centuries* (Hemel Hempstead, 1989), p. 33.
73. Rappaport, *Worlds within Worlds*, p. 36.

never married. What they involved, for a term of years, was training and a subsidiary role in production under adult and normally but not invariably male control. It is very hard to judge what in fact followed that training but there is a strong overall impression that in many cases it did not lead to guild enfranchisement or economic independence. The female apprenticeship system, in other words, was a device for bringing the very considerable resources of female labour into active support for the economy without risking any dislodging of its fundamental patriarchal characteristics. As such it was a system that worked well. It can be seen at its most forceful when, with the compulsory parish apprenticeship which was erratically applied during our period, the proportion of females to males apprenticed in sample parishes through the southern counties reached forty-one per cent and thirty-four per cent respectively in the seventeenth and eighteenth centuries. Whereas there was a small decline in the proportion of females to males after 1700, it was the eighteenth century which saw the heyday of this rural apprenticeship of poor children in terms of the range of occupations involved. This increased in Keith Snell's sample over the two centuries from eighteen to fifty-one, so that in theory at least we find girls after 1700 learning such specialised crafts as blanket-making, gloving, hatting, bricklaying, dyeing, tanning, japanning, rope-making, tobacco pipe-making and watch-gilding. It is very unlikely that many of these girls acquired sufficient expertise, resources or confidence to set up in business themselves or so much as contemplated doing so. They were essentially assistants working under the eye of a master. Most of these crafts involved some relatively mechanical and unskilled tasks which a competent adolescent girl could be taught to undertake. The skills that were learnt, suggests Michael Roberts, were 'primarily deployed and no doubt further refined, within marriage' which tended to diffuse and dilute women's occupational identity.[74] Such craft apprenticeships were, in any case, a small minority of the whole. Female apprenticeships arranged by parish officers were most usually in housewifery and even when a specialised craft was set down it is probable that general domestic work occupied much of the apprentice's time.[75]

When we turn to apprenticeships entered by parental choice, to give their children a start in the world, all the studies so far show a much lower ratio of indentured girls to boys. A survey of thousands of apprenticeship enrolments in Tudor London by Nancy Adamson produced only seventy-three women among them.[76] Michael Roberts has calculated that three sets of urban apprentice records and five sets of county ones between 1500 and 1760 show that female apprentices were normally less

74. Roberts, 'Words they are Women', in Charles and Duffin, eds, *Women and Work*, p. 143.
75. Snell, *Annals of the Labouring Poor*, pp. 278–83.
76. Cited by Bennett, 'Medieval Women', in Aers, ed., *Culture and History 1350–1600*, p. 172.

than ten per cent of the total.[77] Keith Snell has used returns under the 1709 act for payment of duties on apprenticeship indentures to the Board of Inland Revenue to explore the occupations chosen for children of rather higher social status than those whom overseers pushed into indentured service, in the counties of Surrey, Sussex, Bedfordshire, Warwickshire and Wiltshire. The proportion of women as a percentage of his totals varies from 3.6 per cent to 7.4 per cent, averaging out at 4.9 per cent. This informative survey shows girls apprenticed to carpenters, cordwainers and mercers, to ironmongers, goldsmiths and watch-makers, to a toy-maker, a spectacle-maker and a candlestick-maker. Again we can only speculate about how much they contributed to the business and how far they were trained in these specialised crafts.[78] The pioneering work of O.J. Dunlop and Ivy Pinchbeck established long ago that females were apprenticed to a very wide range of trades in the eighteenth century.[79]

So what came of all this training of young women in such diverse crafts and trades? Despite the obstacles they faced a few did become full guild members, practising their skills in their own right, following their apprenticeship. More research is needed to establish how common this was. Snell's analysis of property rentals mentioned in settlement examinations shows a number of single women practising their own trades. He has also found examples of women active as coopers, glaziers, butchers, soap-makers, wheelwrights and clock-makers, among other occupations, who took apprentices in their own right.[80] Evidence of this kind leads one to beware the narrowness of the misleading descriptive materials which have been discussed above. Officially men's trades were not regarded as equally available to women. Conversely Thomas Powell advised men to avoid certain trades such as brewing, baking and cooking which he called 'housewives' trades but which both men and women were seen as equally capable to undertake.[81] The patriarchal imperative to maintain the argument that women's work was peripheral and inferior is evident in the habit of fusing occupational status with marital standing. Thus a London Common Council act of 1631 about abuses in retailing made reference to 'butchers, bakers and chandlers' together with 'oyster wives, herb wives and tripe wives'.[82]

This is the public face of a patriarchal economy. But the fact is that the seventeenth- and eighteenth-century economy was not one characterised,

77. Roberts, 'Words they are Women', in Charles and Duffin, eds, *Women and Work*, pp. 142, 171.
78. Snell, *Annals of the Labouring Poor*, pp. 291–4.
79. I. Pinchbeck, *Women Workers and the Industrial Revolution 1750–1850* (London, 1969), pp. 284–6, 292–3; O.J. Dunlop and R.D. Denman, *English Apprenticeship and Child Labour* (London, 1912), p. 150.
80. Snell, *Annals of the Labouring Poor*, pp. 299–300.
81. Cited in Roberts, 'Words they are Women', in Charles and Duffin, eds, *Women and Work*, p. 141.
82. Cited in Clark, *Working Life of Women*, p. 202.

except in the highest social circles, by a husband alone working and maintaining his wife. What the family economy meant, in the vast majority of cases, was an economic partnership. There were plenty of cases where this partnership consisted of a wife working as unpaid assistant in the shop or business, but Peter Earle's survey of the London female labour market around 1700 shows that this was not the most common pattern: seventy-two per cent of his sample were doing paid work outside the home. Much of this work was largely unskilled, low in esteem and poorly paid.[83] Towns like Norwich, Salisbury and Portsmouth had a fluctuating group of casual servants who acted as charwomen or nurses and often depended in part on parish relief.[84] Many London women were in domestic service, were washing and scouring, nursing children, and working in the food and drink trades as barmaids. Three areas of female work – brewing, retailing and the clothing trades – deserve further attention in relation to contemporary attitudes to women and their appointed roles. The contrasts in economic opportunity which they present are instructive. During the period between 1500 to 1800 women were excluded from the first of these trades, they maintained a very active role in the second and they flourished in the third.

In fourteenth-century England many women were commercial brewers in town and countryside, both brewing ale and selling it. The slow masculinisation of the brewing trade and of alehouse-keeping between 1300 and 1700 deprived them of work that had been manageable and marketable. There were good practical reasons for women's loss of this economic role, including the change from ale to beer, capitalisation of brewing and the development of a government scheme of regulation of brewing and ale-selling which encouraged local authorities to place responsibility in men rather than women. This process transformed a home-based, female-dominated trade into a factory-based, male-dominated one. Misogyny, Judith Bennett has argued persuasively, also contributed to the process. Drawing upon the abundant evidence of dislike of alewives in late medieval and early modern England, an aspect of a general antipathy to victuallers, she identifies misogyny as the 'crucial element' in this antipathy. The misogynistic themes that Bennett relates draw deeply upon the image of womankind that has been outlined above in chapters 1 and 4: poems, ballads, carvings and drama relating to alewives emphasise their fickleness, capacity for dishonesty, dangerous sexuality and propensity towards evil. Alewives, in other words, threatened patriarchal order: 'in flirting with customers they undermined the authority of their husbands; in handling money, goods and debts they challenged the economic power of men; in bargaining with

83. Earle, 'Female, Labour Market', *Economic History Review*, 42 (1989), pp. 338–9, 348–52; P. Earle, *The Making of the English Middle Class* (London, 1989), pp. 160–66.
84. Wright, '"Churmaids"', in Charles and Duffin, eds, *Women and Work*, pp. 104–8.

male customers they achieved a seemingly unnatural power over men; in avoiding effective regulation of their trade they insulted the power of male officers and magistrates and, perhaps most importantly, in simply pursuing their trade they often worked independently of men.'[85]

In Elizabethan and early Stuart England alehouses were regulated with steadily increasing efficiency. The result was that such female management of them as was allowed was almost entirely confined to widows and they usually had their behaviour assured by male recognisances; men were generally favoured as licensees. Only just over nine per cent of alehouse-keepers in Kent between 1590 and 1619 were women. Similar proportions are found at Northampton in 1577 and at Norwich between 1587 and 1596.[86] In some Salisbury lists of alehouse-keepers between 1627 and 1635, exceptionally, women formed between a third and a half of the total.[87] By this time male power was being exercised to ensure that women at the height of their sexuality were not available behind the alehouse counter. In 1541 the mayor of Chester, declaring that alewives promoted 'wantonness and brawls, affrays and other inconveniences', ordered that no woman between the ages of fourteen and forty should keep an alehouse in the city. The Earl of Bridgewater's anxious enquiry to his constable at Ludlow castle about a rumour that beer was being sold in the town by a 'wench' is redolent of this suspicion of alewives' sexual availibility. In fact, he was informed, the supposed wench was an elderly widow. So we can perceive direct male action as a factor in the exit of women from the trade. But, more subtly and at a level we cannot document, it seems certain that the negative representations of alewives, which were so widespread throughout this period, discouraged women from pursuing the business. Persistent depiction of them as cheating tradeswomen must have aroused anxieties and harmed trust among potential customers, just as it influenced those with the power to regulate the brewing trade. Misogyny undermined women's desire and ability to compete with men in a business that should have been an obvious option for them because it was fundamental to the economy of every village and town in the kingdom.[88]

It was in the market place, Michael Roberts argues, that women's activities 'most clearly contradicted male assumptions about what the scope of female work should be'.[89] Women who kept shops, sold goods in the street or around people's houses, hired a market stall or were long-distance pedlars all alike offended patriarchal sensibilities about their restriction to the world of hearth and home. Much of this work was

85. J.M. Bennett, 'Misogyny, Popular Culture and Women's Work', *History Workshop Journal* 31 (1991), pp. 168–88.
86. P. Clark, *The English Alehouse* (London, 1983), p. 79.
87. Wright, '"Churmaids"', in Charles and Duffin, eds, *Women and Work*, p. 110.
88. Bennett, 'Misogyny', *History Workshop Journal* 31 (1991), pp. 169–83.
89. Roberts in Charles and Duffin, eds, *Women and Work*, p. 153.

tainted with the popular distrust of every kind of dealer, especially the middle person who bought and resold. Yet a massive amount of such activity was tolerated because otherwise the English economy might have collapsed. Tolerance was suffused with disparagement. Women retailers were too obviously visible, talkative and competent: they were knowledgeable about prices and market conditions and they knew how to bargain. So what they were doing chimed in with much proverbial wisdom of the kind discussed in chapter 4, wisdom that denigrated womankind's propensity to noise and gossip. When women scolded, as one expression ran, it was 'like so many butter-whores or oyster-women at Billingsgate'.[90] Men were fond of linking women proverbially with the poultry that traditionally filled their yards. 'Where many geese be, be many turds and where be women are many words,' wrote Stephen Gosinill in *The Schoolhouse of Women* around 1550. 'A straggling hen and a wandering wife', went a 1591 comment, 'deserve small commendation of their life.' It was often said that 'women and hens are lost by gadding.' The Italian proverb 'three women and a goose make a market' was also popular throughout the seventeenth century.[91] It was a cruel jest for some men to respond when women endured the harder labour of childbirth that 'my wife cries five loaves a penny.'[92] Women's role in retailing, poorly rewarded, of no status, unproductive and uninstitutionalised, was thus derided.

Much more research is needed before we can quantify women's involvement in marketing during the whole period from 1500 to 1800. It may well be that demographic and economic factors created a growth in female opportunities in the urban retailing and provisioning trades.[93] At present we have to rely on a few local studies which confirm Peter Earle's survey of the London labour market and Alice Clark's impressionistic account of women everywhere busy peddling and huckstering. Earle found women selling, among other things, linen, earthenware, tea and chocolate, pies in the street, fruit from a cellar, coal and wood, trunks and boxes, fine quiltings and brandy, sugar and calicoes.[94] It is clear that their best opportunities, despite the fact that they never owned or had any purchase on the regulation of markets themselves, lay in selling food and small wares. Early Tudor Coventry, for example, had its fishwives, some women candle-makers and a cake-baker.[95] In early Stuart Salisbury, some

90. Cited in Roberts, 'Words they are Women', in Charles and Duffin, eds, *Women and Work*, p. 154.
91. Tilley, nos W687, W690, W695.
92. Cited in Roberts, 'Words they are Women', in Charles and Duffin, eds, *Women and Work*, p. 154.
93. J. Barry, *The Tudor and Stuart Town: A Reader in English Urban History 1530–1699* (London, 1990), p. 23.
94. Clark, *Working Life of Women*, pp. 197–209; Earle, 'Female Labour Market', *Economic History Review* 42 (1989), pp. 350–1.
95. Phythian-Adams, *Desolation of a City*, p. 88.

poor women, known as 'pudding wives', bought offal from the butchers and resold it around the town; others bought faggots in the market and sold them again 'by the penny'.[96]

A study of marketing in Oxfordshire between 1690 and 1800 reveals that women retained a very small hold on the livestock and corn businesses until the middle of the eighteenth century but a rather stronger one, as we might expect, on the poultry, butter, fruit and vegetable markets. The author of a history of Bicester, published in 1816, recounted the tales he had heard from 'many of the aged inhabitants' about the avenues to the market hill being 'crowded by the farmers' wives with their baskets of butter, eggs and poultry'. The obvious nostalgia of this account points to the eighteenth century as the time when the retailing options for women were decisively reduced. Whereas for the greater part of the century the rural housewife could legitimately run the hen house and dairy and sell her surplus produce in the market place at Oxford, Bicester, Henley or Chipping Norton, a series of developments towards its end combined to destroy this traditional role. Among the changes were engrossing of farms, increasing agricultural specialisation, the emergence of new figures like the butter contractor and the growth of private trading in the male world of the inn parlour. Women lost out in this case, not simply through misogyny, but as victims of a process of economic development.[97]

An illuminating study by Deborah Valenze shows how, between around 1740 and 1840, 'dairying as a science slowly overtook dairying as nature and art', effectively obliterating women's role as producers and managers of the trade. In the early eighteenth-century rural world dairying, as an extension of a woman's good husbandry in the household and yard, was everywhere still women's work. The mistress of the dairy, whether the farmer's wife or a hired manager, worked by experience and lore. This was an occult form of husbandry. 'A superior dairywoman', reported William Marshall from Gloucestershire in 1789, 'is so highly spoken of, and so highly valued, in this district that one is led to imagine everything depends upon management.' Dairymaids also were praised for their expertise. 'The typical dairy at this time', notes Valenze, 'presented a world of labour unto itself, topsy-turvy in its assignment of gender roles.' A largely female workforce was often supported by one or two unskilled men or boys. It was generally accepted that dairying required, as Marshall put it, 'much thought' besides 'much labour', a combination of talents that men simply did not expect to find in labouring women. Yet here were women managing the business very successfully. What changed all this was the growing market for dairy products, especially cheese,

96. Wright, '"Churmaids"', in Charles and Duffin, eds, *Women and Work*, pp. 108–9.
97. W. Thwaites, 'Women in the Market Place: Oxfordshire c. 1690–1800', *Midland History* IX (1984), pp. 23–42.

among the burgeoning working classes of London and the provincial cities. The pressure for profit coincided with intervention by men with an interest in rationalisation and improvement through the application of natural science and empirical methods. Scientific discourses infiltrated the world of dairying in tracts which directly challenged the old style of working and derided its practitioners as stubborn and obtuse, although it was they who provided much of the background information. The emphasis was on uniform standards and techniques: 'through the writing and dissemination of these texts', explains Valenze, 'male practitioners redefined the art of women and appropriated it as their own.' The male manager emerged, working closely with factors who served the urban markets. The agriculturalists, although they saw women turning the heaviest rounds of cheese with their own eyes during the 1780s, did not want to believe that women could perform such a demanding physical task. They blenched and condemned traditional practice, motivated by their secure gender ideology. Improvements in labour-saving machinery followed and combined with a new structure of authority from above to obviate the managerial role of the farmer's wife.[98] At the bottom of the hierarchy, however, there was still the country milkmaid. In Hanoverian May Day rituals she was coming to represent pure female sexuality in the form, as Charles Phythian-Adams describes it, of 'chastity, modesty and clean, but hard, country living'.[99] In the landscape paintings of the period the milkmaid often replaced the shepherdess, notes John Barrell, providing a female presence on the pastoral scene which, in contrast to male capability and strength, had clear resonances of the home and motherhood.[100]

Carole Shammas has made a study of the activities of around 185 women who transacted business with the household of Thomas and Margaret Fell at Swarthmoor in the Furness district of Lancashire between 1673 and 1678. Her account reiterates the crucial importance of gentry households as centres of employment in early modern England.[101] Some women bought cheese from the Fells which they peddled in the surrounding area. Others, a rather larger number, sold goods and services to the household. Shammas found less job segregation in retailing than in craftwork and agricultural labour. It was men, not surprisingly, who owned the shops where the Fell family bought their luxury items from

---

98. D. Valenze, 'The Art of Women and the Business of Men: Women's Work and the Dairy Industry c. 1740–1840', *Past and Present* 130 (1991), pp. 142–69.
99. C. Phythian-Adams, 'Milk and Soot: The Changing Vocabulary of a Popular Ritual in Stuart and Hanoverian London', in D. Fraser and A. Sutcliffe, eds, *The Pursuit of Urban History* (London, 1983), p. 99.
100. J. Barrell, *The Dark Side of the Landscape: The Rural Poor in English Painting 1730–1840* (Cambridge, 1983), p. 51.
101. For this aspect of Sussex gentry life earlier in the century see Anthony Fletcher *A County Community in Peace and War: Sussex 1600–1660* (London, 1975), p. 40.

abroad and also their best fabrics. But local men and women alike supplied them with small wares, meat, butter and cheese and with some of their needs for the farm such as hay and manure. Only women provided the household with bread and only men with livestock and coal. Outside the control of borough authorities, who always had an eye to preserving male economic privilege, we can perceive women – single, married and widowed – inserting themselves into the complex economy of this rural backwater wherever the opportunity arose.[102]

The textile industry had always been the family industry par excellence. Without the city's female thread-makers, spinners and knitters, declares Charles Phythian-Adams, Coventry's textile and clothing industries would have collapsed.[103] In the eighteenth century the male weaver still performed the core craft operation, but he needed his wife and daughters to help with the many subsidiary aspects of his business.[104] There is plenty of evidence that slump and dislocation in the textile industry in the Tudor and early Stuart periods brought restrictive practices to exclude women's participation except where their labour was really needed.[105] But in the second half of our period this became the most significant area of expanding opportunity for women in the English economy. If we add a proportion of Earle's milliners, who were undoubtedly women making clothes, to those engaged in textile manufacture of one kind of another in his statistical snapshot of the London labour market between 1695 and 1725, we find that the clothing trades at that time employed more women for pay than either domestic service or any other category of work. Moreover this leaves aside all the unpaid helpmeet labour provided by women to husbands and fathers in the trade. The range of this work was enormous: there were the silkwinders of the East End, the sempstresses who did plainwork or sewing, the burgeoning numbers of dress-makers and a multitude of specialists. These included women who made bodices, caps, gloves, buttons, scarves, riding hoods, children's coats, fringes and tassels for upholsterers as well as embroiderers, lace-makers and quilters.[106]

The way that women grasped the employment chances made available by a consumer revolution in the clothing trade between 1660 and 1800 is a story of the pursuit of social aspirations. Daniel Defoe's *Moll Flanders* gives a colourful account of what it meant to a young girl to learn the skills of a needlewoman. It was the way to a certain dignity and self-reliance. Moll and those who advised her saw a major distinction between

102. C. Shammas, 'The World Women Knew: Women Workers in the North of England During the Late Seventeenth Century', in R.S. Dunn and M.M. Dunn, eds, *The World of William Penn* (Philadelphia, 1986), pp. 103, 105–9.
103. Phythian-Adams, *Desolation of a City*, p. 88.
104. J. Rule, *The Expeience of Labour in Eighteenth-Century Industry* (London, 1981), p. 41; Earle, *Making of the English Middle Class*, p. 163.
105. Clark, *Working Life of Women*, p. 103.
106. Earle, 'Female Labour Market', *Economic History Review* 42 (1989), pp. 339–41.

this form of employment which they called 'living by her fingers' ends' and the sheer drudgery of housework. Moll feared a servant's discipline too: 'if I can't do it they will beat me and the maids will beat me to do great work and I am but a little girl'.[107] In his *Parents Directory* of 1761 Joseph Collyer listed a series of occupations which were suitable for the daughters of families who wished to avoid their child ending up in the dependence of household service. They included glover and petti-coatmaker, ribbon-weaver and bodice-maker. The trade of child's coatmaker was 'very proper . . . for those a little above the vulgar'. Surrey apprenticeship indentures for 1710 to 1731 show how popular this trade was with young girls in the London suburbs.[108] It was not that women could expect high wages from work of this kind or especially favourable working conditons. They had to tolerate long hours and seasonal unem-ployment. Their wages, if we take those quoted in the 1747 publication *The London Tradesman* as some guide, were well below those of most men.[109] Yet there was some status about their work, graded as it was above the unskilled labouring tasks of domestic service and above the disparaged street selling of the marketing woman. The needlework occu-pations were a godsend for those females who wanted to make something of themselves within the stringencies and limitations of a patriarchally ordered economy. They dominated the female job market in London from the mid-eighteenth century to the mid-nineteenth, as three contem-porary lists of jobs available to women, compiled in 1747, 1761 and 1806 respectively, indicate. New additions included ribbon-weaving, button-making and shoe-binding in 1761 and pin-making and hat-binding appeared in 1806.[110]

The female apprenticeship records from five counties between 1710 and 1760 show that there were two aspects of the fruition of the clothing trades which aspiring families grasped most firmly: the rise of the dress-maker and of the associated milliner's shop.[111] The springboard for the former development was the arrival in the 1670s of the fashion of wearing the mantua, a loose fitting over-garment worn with stays which did not require the expertise of a tailor to cut and stitch it. Mary Prior has traced the long struggle between women determined to make their way in this trade and the Taylors' and Mercers' Companies in Oxford. At one point in 1702 the tailors were so desperate that they prepared to consult widely about getting an act of parliament passed to suppress the mantua-makers. Both companies fought a losing battle, for the rage of fashion ran ahead

107. Roberts, 'Words they are Women', in Charles and Duffin, eds, *Women and Work*, pp. 122–4.
108. Snell, *Annals of the Labouring Poor*, pp. 292–4.
109. Earle, 'Female Labour Market', *Economic History Review* 42 (1989), p. 343.
110. L.D. Schwarz, *London in the Age of Industrialisation: Entrepreneurs, Labour Force and Living Conditions 1700–1851* (Cambridge, 1992), pp. 18–19.
111. Snell, *Annals of the Labouring Poor*, p. 292.

of them. In the 1780s a dress-maker, who had worked in a London establishment which supplied the Queen, advertised that she had returned to Oxford with many new fashions, leaving the local Mercers' Company nonplussed by her energy and enterprise.[112] The milliners' shops, run by women, which proliferated in London and provincial towns in the period between 1750 and 1800 catered for a huge range of women's clothing and accessory needs. Millinery had become a prestigious as well as a genteel trade. In Colchester at this time the milliners took apprentices and made out bills in their own names, even when married, trading from some of the largest shops in the town's best streets. Success, it has been suggested, depended on a good eye for changing fashion, an appropriate manner with customers, social credit, and a network of local connections.[113] But for every woman who reached the peak of this business there were of course many more who laboured long and hard in its lower reaches.

So far this account has concentrated upon a number of specialised areas of the economy. In broader terms we are discussing a society that was overwhelmingly agricultural throughout these centuries, that was massively dependent on manual labour and in which chronic underemployment was pervasive.[114] For a great many people – men as well as women – work was always casual and intermittent. Family survival, beyond the safety net of the poor laws, was for them a matter of grasping whatever paid work became available. Men came first and female unemployment was therefore always bound to be much higher than male. What local studies illustrate is women's determination about inserting themselves into the interstices of the economies of their neighbourhoods as best they could in order to supplement the family wage. David Levine and Keith Wrightson, for example, show that in the Durham coal-mining parish of Whickham the most that women could expect were periods of day labour in wailing of coal at the pithead or staithes. A 1764 listing includes three of these female coal wailers who were over sixty and one of them, Phyllis Denman, said to be eighty. The case of the twenty-seven-year-old Elizabeth Barren, who shovelled coal for thirty-five days in 1752, provides an instance of how this kind of work could assist the domestic economy: each week she boosted it by forty-five per cent, bringing home 17s 6d to set beside the 39s that her father earned at that time. But, as Levine and Wrightson point out, such bonuses from a second earner were wholly unpredictable, since they must be related to short-term economic fluctuations and a long-term cycle.[115]

112. Prior, 'Women and the Urban Economy', in Prior, ed., *Women and English Society*, pp. 111–13.
113. S. D'Cruze, 'To Acquaint the Ladies: Women Traders in Colchester c. 1750–c. 1800', *Local Historian* 17 (1986), pp. 158–61.
114. D.C. Coleman, 'Labour in the English Economy of the Seventeenth Century', *Economic History Review* 8 (1955–6), pp. 280–95.
115. Levine and Wrightson, *Making of an Industrial Society*, pp. 249, 264–7.

With regard to work in the fields, the demand for female harvesters undoubtedly waned in the course of the period from 1600 to 1800 and this was reflected in an increased differential between male and female agricultural wage rates. This was gradual at first but became very sharp in eastern England during the period between 1750 and 1800.[116] The crucial factor here is the increased use of the long-handled scythe which, in its basic form, was first developed in the Roman Empire. Whereas there is evidence of women reaping with the sickle in the late middle ages, the scythe was always handled by men who could cover the ground a good deal more quickly. The sickle cut more accurately and produced a higher quality of harvest. It was still normally used for wheat and rye until the late seventeenth century, whereas oats and barley were already coming under the scythe. When in the late seventeenth century a corn surplus lowered prices and labour costs did not fall, the more general adoption of the corn scythe was predictable. Alice George, an Oxford woman claiming to be over 100 years old, boasted to John Locke in 1681 that in her youth 'she was able to have reaped as much in a day as any man and had as much wages'.[117] Certainly with the sickle a woman could be as efficient a worker as a man. Women were not deprived of exercising this skill in the north of England, where change came more slowly, until well into the nineteenth century. The fact that there was considerable skill involved in effective reaping was recognised in this region's rates for the job remaining the same for women as for men.[118]

Women's wages for harvest work by the day were consistently lower than men's, just as women hired by the year as servants in husbandry were paid a lower wage than men.[119] This was simply a matter of evaluating labour capacity. Henry Best's description of his farming practice in Yorkshire in 1641 provides exceptionally detailed evidence about the care with which a farmer estimated the strength required for various harvest tasks, managed his labour force and paid men, women and boys accordingly. 'Binding and staking of winter corn is a man's labour', he noted, because 'it requireth as much and rather more ability and toil than did reaping.' Trailing the large sweathrake, which brought together the mower's whole swathe at once, could be done by women but he preferred to use boys from the north Yorkshire moors who he found of 'a good ability and strength' for this task. He was willing to have some of his ablest women

116. K.D.M. Snell, 'Agricultural Seasonal Unemployment, the Standard of Living, and Women's Work in the South and East 1690–1860', *Economic History Review* 34 (1981), p. 414.
117. M. Roberts, 'Sickles and Scythes: Women's Work and Men's Work at Harvest Time', *History Workshop* 7 (1979), pp. 3–19.
118. B. Hill, *Women, Work and Sexual Politics in Eighteenth-Century England* (Oxford, 1989), pp. 57–8.
119. Minchinton, ed., *Wage Regulation in Pre-Industrial England*, pp. 160–1; A. Kussmaul, *Servants in Husbandry in Early Modern England* (Cambridge, 1981), p. 37.

gatherers pull peas but his differential payments to men and women for this task, eightpence and sixpence a day respectively, reflected his observations about their typical performance. All this was good economic sense, no more and no less, just as was his advice about bringing home the crops: 'the usual manner is to send out with every wain three folks viz two men and a woman; whereof the one of the men is a loader, the other a forker and the woman to rake after the wain'.[120] Best's realism can be judged from estimates that this century, in the heaviest tasks on pre-war British farms, female productivity was estimated to be less than half that of men. In Mao's China, less strikingly, women's agricultural productivity was reckoned to be only seventy per cent of the male equivalent.[121]

Much more research is needed on the microeconomies of early modern England, but two recent studies of this kind provide some insight into the sophistication of the economies of local communities. Hassell Smith has studied the pattern of work on the estates at Stiffkey in Norfolk of the Elizabethan landlord Nathaniel Bacon, who, as an arable farmer, was simply not able to provide all his tenants with regular day-labouring. He shows how labouring families there adopted a strategy for survival in the difficult decade of the 1590s which meant exploiting to the utmost the multifaceted opportunities of a district with a tradition of spinning and knitting and bounded by salt marsh and the sea. The keys were keeping young unmarried women at home rather than sending them into service, intergenerational co-operation and sometimes a sharing of household premises. Extracting the basic necessities of life from land and water was the driving force behind an exceptionally flexible work strategy among the labouring population. How far this meant that in the family economies of husbandmen, craftsmen and yeomen, whose wives were not employed in the fields and gardens, tasks were interchangeable the study cannot reveal. What it does demonstrate quite clearly is that wives in day-labouring specialised in work that was different from but complemented that of their husbands. The yeoman John Baker's wife did needlework and his stepdaughter stocking knitting; Robert Gye was a weaver and his wife did nursing; William Hill was a sawyer and his two daughters were general labourers; William Lukin was a servant in Bacon's household while his wife made stockings; John Page, the owner of a small fishing boat which he also used to carry cargoes coastwise, had a wife and two daughters in general labouring; John Speller's wife and daughter-in-law ran a flourishing village bakery while he and his son cultivated a holding of thirty-six acres and shared some inshore fishing.

So how far did the conventional wisdom and the pragmatic thinking that Henry Best displayed about differences in physical strength apply

120. Roberts, 'Sickles and Scythes', *History Workshop* 7 (1979), pp. 9–10.
121. Cited in Roberts, 'Sickles and Scythes', *History Workshop* 7 (1979), p. 26.

to the job segregation of this Norfolk community? Assumptions about capacities of mind and body are extremely evident. Men handled the work in building and agriculture, which was heavy and required some learnt skills: in Hassell Smith's summary, they 'built houses, heaved timber, ploughed, harrowed, threshed, carted hay and corn, dug ditches or cut hedges'. They were the wildfowlers and bird-catchers of the marshland. The women did not need the same athletic prowess to cut the marram grass there and collect cockles and mussels from the shore. Women also weeded, picked over corn, made hay, harvested saffron, picked hops and sorted wool. These were back-breaking and exhausting tasks, but not ones requiring as much initiative or sheer strength as those which the men undertook. Deep inside the mentality of this community there was clearly some notion that this segregation of tasks was right and proper as well as convenient. There was a social aspect to it as well. The women liked to work in gangs of around seven to fifteen and they could gossip as they did so. Men needed their contribution to a basic standard of living far too earnestly for them to question this degree of independence from their eye and control.[122]

We have already encountered the women who bought and sold at the Hall in Carole Shammas's study of the Fell household. She also tells us something about day labouring in Furness during the 1670s and her findings match those of Hassell Smith. There were four kinds of work – haywork, harrowing, manuring and peat work – in which both sexes engaged, but it is likely that task specification within those activities gave the women a lighter role. Yet there were twelve kinds of work which only men did and four that only women did. The male jobs were ploughing, weeding in the fields, hedging, reaping, mowing, threshing, garden work, rippling, setting toppins and braking in the flax and hemp grounds, salving and clipping sheep and veterinary work with the livestock. The female jobs were weeding in the garden and the flax and hemp grounds, pulling hemp and pikeing, swingling and hatchelling flax and hemp.[123] The same general considerations about muscle and toughness clearly applied in Lancashire as in Yorkshire and Norfolk.

The exclusion everywhere of women from the most laboursome work, in the sense of tasks requiring brute strength, was pragmatic but it also carried strong ideological overtones. It was a daily manifestation of the doctrine of the weaker vessel and of the fundamental principles of the patriarchal system. There was a sense of masculinity and competition about the kinds of work categorised as the hard jobs. When he was a boy in the 1780s, William Johnson observed an accident that his mother

---

122. These two paragraphs are based upon A. Hassell Smith, 'Labourers in Late Sixteenth-century England: a Case Study from North Norfolk', *Continuity and Change* 4 (1989), pp. 367–94.
123. Shammas, 'World Women Knew', in Dunns, ed., *World of William Penn*, p. 109.

sustained, which he later recalled: she was working in the fields at the time trying to catch up with 'the young men and lasses who were each more anxious to excel another in forking up the hay'. On such occasions this competitiveness could be productive and not divisive in gender terms.[124] But it was male work which was persistently given a heroic tinge through the pastoral tradition in literature and art while women, subsidiary and subservient, were seen as helpmeets. Class romanticism and gender assumptions come together in Robert Herrick's *The Hock Cart* which celebrates the strenuous labour of the harvest swains: they end the day drinking to their lord, to their tools and then 'to the maids with wheaten hats'. Stephen Duck's *The Thresher's Labour*, published in 1736, virtually forgets the part women played in the harvest, relegating them to the chief actors in the ensuing domestic idyll:

> Our good expecting wives, who think we stay,
> Got to the door, soon eye us in the way
> Then from the pot the dumplings catched in haste
> And homely by its side the bacon placed.

Mary's Collier's long poem *The Woman's Labour* was a pointed rejoinder to Duck, emphasising the endless routine tasks and the sheer hardship of being a farmer's wife. She stressed women's role in raking and turning the hay, gleaning and gathering cut corn and cutting peas. The argument was that women scorn no labour, however lowly and harsh, yet there is an acceptance about a boundary line between men's work and 'our proper share' in this poem which shows that Mary Collier was no early feminist.[125]

This survey of the work that men and women actually did and the rewards, financial and otherwise, that it produced in early modern England suggests that in this area prescription and practice were closely, but not evenly, matched. The overall scheme of patriarchal thinking had enormously powerful resonances throughout the working pattern of both urban and rural communities. A broad series of distinctions connected largely segregated jobs to a conception of gender in terms of human strength and weakness. Thinking about what was appropriate as men's work or women's work can be constantly referred to the standard of manhood, a standard which reflected mental capacities as much as physical ones. Women's work comprised everything that was left after men had had their say: as well as bearing the major burden inside the home, women were endlessly inventive about finding ways of going out and bringing in more pennies. In this sense we can reiterate the point made earlier that, so far as women's work is concerned, there was not a

124. Cited in I.K. Ben-Amos, *Adolescence and Youth in Early Modern England* (New Haven and London, 1994), p. 76.
125. Citations from Roberts, 'Words they are Women', in Charles and Duffin, eds, *Women and Work*, pp. 145–7.

transformation from a pre-industrial family economy to a modern industrialised one which had a catastrophic impact on their role. What we can detect over three hundred years is change. In areas such as medicine and brewing women were progressively excluded from active participation by male assertion and by initiatives which they found themselves unable to challenge effectively. But this is not quite straightforward, for occupations that had previously been low-skilled were themselves changing in their very nature. Against these developments we must set the clear evidence outlined here of new occupations, above all the needlework and dressmaking trades, which were opening up for women during the later seventeenth and eighteenth centuries. In the world of work patriarchy was no less dominant in 1800 than in 1500, but this is not to say that the gendered pattern of occupations had remained in any way static.

13. *Beyond the Household*

WE HAVE TRACED women's multifarious involvement in the world of work and established their visibility outside the home. Itinerant chapwomen plied the country lanes. Women everywhere went to market: in Berkshire, where Robert Loder lists his maid's activities; in Lancashire, where the Fell family made a woman servant responsible for marketing and dairy produce; in Sussex, where Giles Moore paid his maidservants for their fetching and carrying trips.[1] Women also travelled for pleasure, a few like Celia Fiennes as resilient tourists, many in order to visit local friends and relatives. They were fully engaged in the social life of their local community, whether this was the round of manor house hospitality or the culture of the local alehouse.[2] They were involved in a broader range of criminal activities than might appear at first sight, and they went to law in large numbers. In times of local or national economic strains or political crisis they claimed a role, sometimes a leading one, as petitioners, rioters, prophetesses and visionaries.[3] Some of course were themselves heads of households. In the Boroughside district of south London fifteen per cent of household heads were female in 1631.[4] So the static, prescriptive and essentially biblical pattern of acceptable behaviour for women breaks down all along the line, which is why it had to be continually re-emphasised. It was a wholly and totally impractical notion in this economy and society. There could be no rigid division in gender

1. Examples cited in Erickson, p. 10.
2. P. Clark, *The English Alehouse* (London, 1983), pp. 126–7, 131–2; above, pp. 139–40.
3. The subject is a large one. It will not be treated fully here since such activities were exceptional in the context of the period from 1500 to 1800 as a whole. See e.g. R.A. Houlbrooke, 'Women's Social Life and Common Action in England from the Fifteenth Century to the Eve of the Civil War', *Continuity and Change* 1 (1986), pp. 171–89; P. Crawford, *Women and Religion in England 1500–1720* (London, 1993), pp. 119–82; P. Crawford, 'The Challenges to Patriarchalism: How did the Revolution affect Women?' in J.S. Morrill, ed., *Revolution and Restoration: England in the 1650s* (London, 1992), pp. 112–28.
4. J. Boulton, *Neighbourhood and Society: A London Suburb in the Seventeenth Century* (Cambridge, 1987), p. 127.

terms between public and private worlds. This chapter will assess the findings of recent research about women's involvement in the community and in legal action. It will also consider the various ways in which, as actors on a public stage, men and women carried the requirements of their honour codes into practice through the sanctions of gossip and ritual. Public action intended to reform personal behaviour sought to remedy the deficiencies of household order and discipline. Patriarchy rested quite as much on what was said and done in the street and market place as behind the closed doors of the home. It is in these areas above all that it was most continually tested, reiterated, consolidated and challenged.

The parish communities of the period were ones in which, within some broad gender boundaries, women were almost as fully involved as men. They did not fill the local village offices but it was they who undertook ancilliary communal tasks. Churchwardens' accounts show it was they who did the sweeping of the church building and washing the linen. They prepared for church ales, the feasts which drew from men's pockets the necessary finance for church expenses.[5] There were also the charity ales, or 'help-ales' as they were often called, at which, in return for some food and drink, villagers provided cash to feed, house and clothe poor neighbours. These charity ales affirmed relationships across the middling range of parishioners from yeomen to the respectable poor. They were hardly noticed by the rich and vagrants and beggars were excluded from the relief they offered. Women were, it seems, very active in these important hospitable events: as organisers, guests, hosts. The charity ales, Judith Bennett has argued, were a resource that 'entertained, sustained and maintained' women as members of their communities, offering them a genuinely reciprocal relationship.[6] Provision of support for others in this way was just one of a number of sources of women's power within their neighbourhood.

Childbirth, as we have seen, immersed a woman in a female collectivity, bringing midwife and gossips into the household.[7] This ritual, taken as a pattern time and again over the years, gave groups of women a sense of their authority and responsibility in the local community which was hallowed by tradition. It is not surprising therefore that women, especially the midwives themselves who had acquired access to the intimate female experience of bringing new life into the world, enjoyed respect as a result. Men were probably not averse to showing this respect. Hence the boldness some women showed in such matters. In a kitchen of the Inns of Court in 1624, Anne Pomeroy objected when she heard Elizabeth Maskall called a maid. 'For she hath had a child,' Anne claimed. 'I can tell upon the sight

5. Crawford, *Women and Religion*, p. 56.
6. J.M. Bennett, 'Conviviality and Charity in Medieval and Early Modern England', *Past and Present* 134 (1992), p. 40, note 53.
7. Above, p. 186.

of one whether she be a maid or no.' Women had their own ideas about how to be sure whether another woman was pregnant, including squeezing her breasts to check for milk. They were quick to examine features and comment in cases of dubious paternity.[8] Churching, we have seen, brought a woman back into the male world with a public thanksgiving for the ordeal which she had survived. For her this was a reintegration that really mattered. There were women who were intent upon making their public thanksgiving even against the objections of their husbands. There was so much in it for a woman: the community's involvement in her recovery, affirmation, confirmation of her status as a breeding woman, a public reappearance which made the mother a centre of attention sitting there in the most prominent seat near the altar.[9]

The first published treatise which dealt with the legal rights and status of women in England was published anonymously in 1632. Women are presented as legally underprivileged, discriminated against in some respects and vulnerable to exploitation. W.R. Prest has argued that *The Lawes Resolutions of Women's Rights* derives from an old established tradition of didactic legal scholarship which provides a narrow viewpoint on women's actual role at law in the sixteenth and seventeenth centuries. Although the courts were staffed and run by men, women were actively involved in the legal process at all levels. Research is revealing more fully their role in crime, in processes of physical examination, in the ecclesiastical probate courts and as litigants in the central courts of the land. It seems that as many as forty per cent of the bills in Chancery during the reign of James I were either on behalf of or directed by women. Although they often appeared in conjunction with their husbands, in about a quarter of these cases they were acting by themselves or together with other women. A broadly similar situation existed in the Court of Requests. Lord Keeper Egerton's moves to exclude females from Westminster Hall are a testimony to the assertive presence of women like Bess of Hardwick, Joan Thynne and Lady Anne Clifford at the heart of the legal system. In 1597 he ordered that no women should be seen in a room overlooking the Court of Star Chamber; in 1603, giving judgement in a case regarding a 'clamorous and impudent woman', he is reported to have 'moved . . . that no woman should be a suitor in any court in her own person'. By 1676, when Wycherley's *The Plain Dealer* was first performed, the knowledgeable and litigious woman, exemplified by Widow Blackacre, was an obvious target for the playwright's satire.[10]

8. L. Gowing, 'Language, Power and the Law: Women's Slander Litigation in Early Modern London', in J. Kermode and G. Walker, eds, *Women, Crime and the Courts in Early Modern England* (London, 1994), p. 31.

9. D. Cressy, 'Purification, Thanksgiving and the Churching of Women in Post-Reformation England', *Past and Present* 141 (1993), pp. 131, 145.

10. W.R. Prest, 'Law and Women's Rights in Early Modern England', *The Seventeenth Century* VI (1991), pp. 177–82. For a petition of 1682 to the London Court of Alderman which is an example of this confidence see C.F. Otten, ed., *English Women's Voices 1540–1700* (Miami, 1992), pp. 122–4.

Garthine Walker's study of female thieves in seventeenth-century Cheshire reveals a flourishing culture of dishonest activity, illustrating how fully women were involved in the criminal world outside the home. It shows, she suggests, activity which was in no way simply a subsidiary aspect of male criminality. Women were just as bold as men in stealing items of worth. They tended to concentrate upon clothes and household linens and also on dishes and utensils, cloth, wool and yarn, all items which concerned them in the normal run of their lives and in which they were wont to make an emotional investment. It was common for women to be involved in pawnbroking and in receiving and selling stolen goods. When one turns to the detection of this kind of crime, women are likewise in the forefront, deposing, searching and passing on information. This pattern reflects the high degree of female economic activity in towns and the countryside which has already been noted. Women did not step into men's public and official roles but they did form their own networks.[11]

Women's special knowledge and accepted wisdom in certain areas led men to invite and obtain their regular participation in the legal process. Their supply of crucial evidence in certain cases, notes Jim Sharpe, was a 'dramatic reversal of their generally powerless role as petitioners, witnesses or parties to legislation'. They were frequently witnesses, for example, in defamation and witchcraft cases. As discovery of the witch's mark, some kind of teat-like growth in the pudenda, became central to proof in witchcraft trials, women, sometimes midwives who were seen as specially qualified in such matters, began to be employed to search suspects. The practice is documented in trials before the leet jury of Southampton in 1579 and in Essex in 1582. It became normal in the seventeenth century for JPs, or sometimes even a constable, to order such searches. At the trial of Elizabeth Sawyer, executed for witchcraft in Middlesex in 1621, the JP driving forward the case had the officers of the court fetch in three women to conduct a search. Two of them, we are told, were 'grave matrons brought in by the officer out of the street, passing there by chance'. Each of the women deposed separately and their findings were decisive in swinging the jury against Sawyer. Women mostly accepted being searched by other women and often had plausible explanations for physical peculiarities that were revealed on their bodies. An Oxfordshire woman actually requested the bench in 1687 to confirm her good reputation when she was rumoured to be a witch by a search of her body by twenty-four 'honest, sober, judicious matrons'. It is not simply that it was

11. G. Walker, 'Women, Theft and the World of Stolen Goods', in Kermode and Walker, eds, *Women, Crime and the Courts*, pp. 81–105. For other studies of female criminality see J.M. Beattie, 'The Criminality of Women in Eighteenth-century England', *Journal of Social History* VIII (1974–5), pp. 80–116 and C.Z. Weiner, 'Sex Roles and Crime in Late Elizabethan Hertfordshire', *Journal of Social History* VIII (1974–5), pp. 38–60.

considered improper for men to view and pronounce upon these things. There was a strong notion of a separate sphere of women's sexuality marked by exclusive knowledge and understanding. If, as has been argued in this book, men feared this they were also, when it came to legal matters, prepared to show it respect. Thus it was usual for female juries to examine women who claimed to be pregnant after conviction for felony. Courts and officers also took it for granted that women should be appointed to examine the alleged victims of incest or rape. When an Essex man was presented for incest with his daughter in 1595, the allegation was said to be founded 'upon the assertion of honest women who have had the examination of the young wench'.[12] John Lamb, who died at the hands of the London mob following conviction for rape of the eleven-year-old Joan Segar in 1628, at one point had attempted to seek refuge in this kind of examination procedure. 'I will have her searched to see if she be torn,' he told the bricklayer's wife Mabel Swinnerton, a friend of her mother's who had already found Joan to be 'very sore'. Lamb wanted the search to be conducted by twelve women in an official manner.[13]

'All of them are understood either married or to be married and their desires are subject to their husband,' wrote the author of *The Lawes Resolution of Women's Rights*, yet 'some women can shift it well enough.'[14] Studies of women's legal agency in certain courts at certain times and places indicate what he meant. Three studies based upon depositions in the London consistory court between 1600 and 1800 enable us to assess its continuing significance as a women's court over a long period. Sexual slander was the largest item in its business, Laura Gowing found, between 1600 and 1640. In the last years of this period eighty-five per cent of these cases were sued by women.[15] By the period from 1700 to 1745 women made up around ninety-five per cent of slander litigants. As the court declined men withdrew from it: a majority of women, Tim Meldrum argues, might be seen as both a symptom and a cause of its decline. Not that men had abandoned slander as part of their armoury and there were still women prepared to take them to court for its use. By the period from 1770 to 1820, studied by Anna Clark, men had simply ceased to bring cases altogether.[16] This slander litigation is a good example of the fictional

12. J. Sharpe, 'Women, Witchcraft and the Legal Process', in Kermode and Walker, eds, *Women, Crime and the Courts*, pp. 108–12; C. Homes, 'Women, Witnesses and Witches', *Past and Present* 140 (1993), pp. 45–78.
13. Otten, ed., *English Women's Voices*, pp. 29–32.
14. Prest, 'Law and Women's Rights', *The Seventeenth Century* VI (1991), p. 179.
15. Gowing, 'Language, Power and the Law', in Kermode and Walker, eds, *Women, Crime and the Courts*, p. 27.
16. T. Meldrum, 'A Women's Court in London: Defamation at the Bishop of London's Consistory Court, 1700–1745', *London Journal* 19 (1994), pp. 5–6, 15; A. Clark, 'Whores and Gossips: Sexual Reputation in London 1700–1825', in A. Angerman, ed., *Current Issues in Women's History* (London, 1989), p. 240.

legal process explored by Natalie Davis in her work on French royal letters of pardon. What we have to analyse and interpret is women's 'forming, shaping and moulding' of elements in the street life of the capital, 'the crafting of a narrative'.[17] Women, we have seen, adopted a language of insult in this litigation which men had imposed upon them through their definition of female honour.[18] It was a language which was the very stuff of street gossip and altercation. Gowing and Meldrum's work shows explicitly that the slanders reported in court had seldom, except where a group of witnesses was deliberately summoned, occurred within households. Women slandered each other from their doorways or by shouting up at each other's windows, in a shop, market place or alehouse. Theatricality was the essence of the business as it was in going to court.[19] Eighty per cent of the slander cases studied by Gowing were settled or abandoned before a formal conclusion; very few of Clark's cases were concluded by the ritual penance in a white sheet but more usually there was a private apology.[20] The litigant's point was not so much to win as to pursue personal grievance and confrontation by every means at her disposal. Whereas in the neighbourhood she could gossip and shout, at court she could shift a semi-public dispute into the official sphere. There was satisfaction, quite apart from the process and outcome, in doing this.

So what was all this slander actually about? Gowing traces women's vigorous litigation to the specific social and demographic conditions of early-seventeenth century London and the kind of gender relations which manifested themselves in the crowded life of the capital: 'conflicts over property boundaries and shared resources were frequently at the root of defamation'.[21] Meldrum and Clark put more emphasis on the eighteenth-century intersection with gender of issues of class, respectability and social identity. It is clear that slander cases in the consistory court very often represented, as Meldrum puts it, 'a single skirmish in an ongoing dispute or the pitched battle that had been brewing for weeks, months or even years'. What was usually at stake, in one form or another, was neighbourhood credit. This was crucial for shopkeeping and artisan women in work. A quarter of the depositions analysed by Anna Clark related to cases brought by women who had their own businesses or were involved

17. N.Z. Davis, *Fiction in the Archives: Pardon Tales and their Tellers in Sixteenth-century France* (Cambridge, 1988), p. 3.
18. Above, pp. 101–3.
19. Gowing, 'Language, Power and the Law', in Kermode and Walker, eds, *Women, Crime and the Courts*, pp. 33–4; Meldrum, 'A Women's Court,' *London Journal*, p. 14.
20. Gowing, 'Language, Power and the Law', in Kermode and Walker, eds, *Women, Crime and the Courts*, p. 41; Clark, 'Whores and Gossips', in Angerman, ed., *Current Issues in Women's History*, p. 239.
21. Gowing, 'Gender and the Language of Insult in Early Modern London', *History Workshop Journal* 35 (1993), p. 18.

in those of their husbands. When Widow Dolling, who kept a poultry shop, for example, was slandered in the street and in the hearing of customers, she felt bound to bring a defamation case to clear herself of the charge that she frequented taverns, which carried a sexual smear. She only drank there, she told the court, 'as her business requires'. For both widows and spinsters marital chances were always an important source of anxiety. It was alleged that, when Jane Adams derided the widow Elizabeth Dodge as a 'common whore, hot-ars't bitch and as common as the highway', she put off a number of suitors. In some cases sheer resentment at class pretensions exacerbated a quarrel. 'You infernal bawd you have reared all your children to be whores from their cradles,' Louisa Vanderpump was reported to have told her sister-in-law in 1789, 'if I was to tell you all that I know of your daughter Betty she would not wear such a high bonnet as she does.' By the later eighteenth century, preserving middle-class respectability and retaining some kind of public role was fraught with difficulty since men were quite ready to use sexual innuendo against economic rivals. When she refused to refer a customer to him in 1793, Alexander Ross gave his rival broker Mary Nowlan this colourful language: 'you're a common whore and all your neighbours know it – there goes the Irish bitch with a feather stuck up her arse.'[22] Polly Morris concluded, on the basis of defamation cases in Somerset between 1733 and 1850, that men took their chances to discipline women who challenged their supremacy, exploiting 'emerging definitions of femininity that denied the contemporary variety of female roles'.[23]

Tim Stretton's examination of litigation regarding the custom of widow's estate in Elizabethan Somerset shows women turning to a central court when local rivals threatened their interests and finding it responsive to their claims. Around 290 of the 350 Somerset Requests actions during the reign involved at least one woman litigant and of these around 80 involved a widow's copyhold estate. This was a contentious area for a whole series of reasons. While all agreed in principle that widows had a right to their husband's lands under custom, customary law was uncertain because it was intensely local. It was essentially unwritten as well as changeable. Moreover copyhold for lives was a form of customary tenure that was changing markedly at this time. Stretton finds that women's participation in the customary process was limited. There are no references to women serving in person on homages and only 9 out of 211 deponents before commissioners from Requests in 50 sampled cases were female. Yet if the 'custody of custom was apparently seen as a male preserve', Stretton concludes nevertheless that the Masters of Requests investigated the rights of widows with diligence 'and occasionally made

22. Meldrum, 'A Women's Court', London Journal 19 (1994), pp. 12–14; Clark, 'Whores and Gossips', in Angerman, ed., Current Issues in Women's History, p. 240.

23. Cited in Clark, 'Whores and Gossips', in Angerman, ed., Current Issues in Women's History, p. 240.

equitable orders imbued with a considerable spirit of charity, showing sympathy to the poor, the aged, the intimidated and the voiceless'. There must have been some local sense of this for women like Joan Ellis, whose suit in 1558 is examined in detail by Stretton, to take the trouble to approach the court in the first place.[24]

The court that a woman was most likely to appear in was the ecclesiastical probate court. Amy Erickson suggests that 'the majority – probably three quarters – of all those coming before the court to exhibit inventories, prove wills and file accounts were women'. Erickson's detailed analysis reveals that, in distributing their real and personal property, fathers normally gave daughters shares which compared in value with those received by sons. Her most important finding is that, despite the legal fiction of coverture which made husband and wife one person, 'in practice wives maintained during marriage substantial property interests of their own' and that this did not just apply to rich families. Marriage settlements were very generally used by ordinary women as well as gentlewomen to circumvent incapacitating aspects of coverture and to protect the bride's property. Neither primogeniture in inheritance nor coverture in marriage, Erickson claims, were 'workable on an everyday level'. Thus probate was a crucial issue in realising women's property rights. Probate accounts show that the ecclesiastical courts, like husbands in general, were much more generous to widows than the letter of the law demanded. The only caveat that must be made here is that men in neither of these capacities intended to make women independently wealthy but simply to provide them with adequate and ample maintenance. Although women exercised more power over property than has been allowed, the legal system at the core of early modern patriarchy, Erickson concludes, 'kept women firmly subordinate'. Individual men ran the system with the dedicated intention of preserving this status quo.[25]

Women in this society had no public role as persons in themselves. The history of local affairs seen through the lens of officeholding and court procedures is thus easily read as an overwhelmingly male one. Civic ritual also deliberately emphasised gender order. The subordination of wives in Tudor Coventry, for example, is exemplified by the fact that they did not usually attend the frequent dinners and drinkings organised by the craft guilds. Although the mayor's wife there wore the civic scarlet, the difference between her status and that of her husband was made plain by her exclusion from the formal inauguration in St Mary's Hall. It was only after this that the retiring mayoress, with a collection of other leading city dames, collected the new mayoress from her home and conducted her to St Michael's church for the service of inauguration. But Coventry did

24. T. Stretton, 'Women, Custom and Equity in the Court of Requests', in J. Kermode and G. Walker, eds, *Women, Crime and the Courts in Early Modern England* (London, 1994), pp. 170–89.
25. Erickson, pp. 19, 223–8.

have in its ceremonial calendar one traditional relaxation of the gender order. In the Hock Tuesday play-cum-mock-battle, which celebrated the overthrow of the Danish yoke by the city's citizens, the drama emphasised 'how valiantly our English women for love of their country behaved themselves'. It is quite clear that some of the Coventry women themselves took part: the local Danes, played by men of course, were 'beaten down, overcome and many led captive for triumph' by the women. Thus female roles, on an occasion of licence from gender order, were nevertheless ritualised by their separateness in the Hock Tuesday performance.[26]

The Coventry Hock Tuesday play indicates how the dynamic of gender was constantly in people's minds. Women's roles and activities outside the household were so multifarious, their contribution to the economy was so necessary, their expectations about contributing actively to the life of the community and even of sometimes going to law to protect their interests were so general that the defence of patriarchy in the public sphere was a demanding task for men. The issue must be considered in its local and social context. The towns and villages of Tudor and Stuart England were moral communities which possessed their own standards of neighbourliness and fair dealing and which sought internal harmony through a great range of sociable activities like drinking, sports and dancing. They were communities in which real inequalities of wealth and living standards were taken for granted and expressed in relationships of paternalism and deference. Moreover they were face-to-face societies, in which individual demeanour in the personal interaction of everyday life was vitally important in maintaining bonds of support and obligation despite social differentiation.[27] The patriarchal relationships of the household could be extended and given additional force in this wider setting. Gender in town and village affairs was a question of status, distinguished and given public representation by people's appearance and by their clothes as well as by their behaviour. In this respect it was very like social rank. Gender and rank were part and parcel of a shared system of meanings.[28] A subtle pattern of gender and social ordering could contain a degree of personal and even communal conflict. It was a system which people understood. Who bought drinks for whom in the alehouse, who doffed his cap for whom, modes of address, respect and sensitivity to the nuances of what others expected and demanded: these were some of the

26. C. Phythian-Adams, *Desolation of a City: Coventry and the Urban Crisis of the Late Middle Ages* (Cambridge, 1979), pp. 90–1.
27. The best general account is K. Wrightson, *English Society 1580–1680* (London, 1982), pp. 37–65.
28. Two important revisionist accounts of the social order are K. Wrightson, 'The Social Order of Early Modern England: Three Approaches', in C. Bonfield, R.M. Smith and K. Wrightson, eds, *The World We Have Gained* (Oxford, 1986), pp. 177–202 and K. Wrightson, 'Estates, Degrees and Sorts: Changing Perceptions of Society in Tudor and Stuart England', in P.J. Corfield, ed., *Language, History and Class* (Oxford, 1991), pp. 30–52.

mechanisms of social and gender order. When the Lancashire gentleman William Blundell was chatting one day with the people in the street of his village, he asked a poor woman how many children she had. He offered sixpence for them when she told him she had six. Her reply was, 'No, sir, I will not sell my children'. The important point was the use of 'sir', as this village woman asserted her proud independence. Blundell too, we should note, was pleased enough with the exchange, for he remembered to write it down.[29]

The single most important weekly demonstration of a community's solidarity and unity was Sunday worship in the parish church. England's magnificent parish churches are still a reminder of how a building erected in the long-distant past can dominate the rural or urban landscape. This was much more the case in the early modern period than today. Churches symbolised continuity with the dead who lay buried within or without the walls. Their naves were usually the parish meeting place for tax assessments or other civil business. Here old and young, male and female, rich and poor came together. Church attendance was not universal, of course, but the protestant evangelisers made much of its importance and most people came if only out of social duty.[30] During the sixteenth century – in some areas such as East Anglia even earlier – church naves began to be filled with pews. What happened at Myddle was typical of many places. The gentry families led the way by installing three rows of seats, the tenant farmers followed and then the cottagers. Seating for the poor was rough benches at the back.[31] By custom seats were commonly assigned to houses, which would have been all very well in a static society. But it meant, in one undergoing economic and social change, that in due course there were many churches where distinctions of wealth and status were no longer being precisely mirrored in seating arrangements. There is much evidence, as Susan Amussen has shown, that people were exercised about where they sat in church. The renting of pews on a yearly or life interest basis, common from the later sixteenth century in some areas, fed this competitiveness.[32]

So how far did church seating reflect gender order? Protestantism emphasised the custom of families sitting together. Gentry who erected magnificent pews of their own did so in order to make a display of their family unit – including children and servants – as a whole. In 1637 the ecclesiastical courts in the diocese of Peterborough ordered 113 gentry

29. Cited in Wrightson, *English Society*, p. 63.
30. K.V. Thomas, *Religion and the Decline of Magic* (London, 1971), pp. 159–66. For the use of tokens to enforce attendance at communion see Boulton, *Neighbourhood and Society*, pp. 280–82.
31. D. Hey, *An English Rural Community: Myddle under the Tudors and Stuarts* (Leicester, 1974), p. 219.
32. S.D. Amussen, *An Ordered Society: Gender and Class in Early Modern England* (Oxford, 1988), pp. 137–44; D. Underdown, *Revel, Riot and Rebellion: Popular Politics and Culture in England 1603–1660* (Oxford, 1985), pp. 30–33.

there to cut down ostentatious pews which obstructed the views others had of the chancel and altar.[33] When churchwardens responded to disputes and dissatisfaction by making reseating plans, they normally took it for granted that they were dealing with families as units. In some places action was only taken when the principle of family togetherness had largely broken down. It was the young and unmarried who often disrupted things. The Temple family, squires of Stowe in Buckinghamshire, sought a commission for their vicar and churchwardens to 'place and displace' the inhabitants there in 1635 'according to their degree and quality.' They explained that 'most of the parishioners do place themselves unreverently and without any order, some young men and servants taking place of married men and some maids sitting above married women, not having any respect unto the quality and condition of the person at all.' The visible print of patriarchy, in other words, as men and women looked around and about them at Stowe, had been catastrophically lacking.[34]

One solution to the problem that had arisen at Stowe was to ensure that everyone sat with their household and to rank households down the church. But in some places there was a tradition that servants did not sit with their masters and dames and, in any case, there was always room for argument about how people's stake in the community determined their correct place in church. Landownership, contribution to parish rates, roles in parish affairs were all seen as relevant. When the churchwardens at Baudeswell in Norfolk attempted to move Margaret Skener to the rear seats for the 'poor and such as took alms', she objected that her husband contributed to the poor rate and other parish charges. But it was the neighbours' view that, since she lived 'as an inmate in the parish within another man's house', she should not 'be ranked and seated with others much her betters'.[35] Similarly, at Tinsbury in Wiltshire in 1637, two widows found themselves displaced in a general reseating organised by the churchwardens. Defiantly declaring 'they would sit in no other seats than what pleased them' got them nowhere.[36]

One way of combining a manifestation of social and gender order that made female inferiority clearly evident, where the building was suitable, was to rank the males backwards in status in the main aisles, seating their wives separately in the side aisles. This provided a parallel display of parish hierarchy. It was the pattern at Holy Trinity, Dorchester, according to a plan of 1617, though several wealthy parishioners did share pews with their wives in the south aisle. The daughters of the respectable parish families in this case sat on benches at the back and

33. A.J. Fielding, 'Conformists, Puritans and the Church Courts: The Diocese of Peterborough 1603–1642', University of Birmingham PhD thesis, 1989, p. 114.
34. HEH, STTM, box 3.
35. Amussen, *An Ordered Society*, p. 140.
36. Underdown, *Revel, Riot and Rebellion*, p. 33.

servants seem to have accommodated themselves on benches where they could.[37] Something similar may have happened at St Michael's Coventry in the later sixteenth century, where women were certainly sitting separately from their husbands.[38] Half-hearted Arminian attempts to return to wholesale segregation of seating by gender, in medieval style, seem not to have got very far.[39] For instance, it is not clear that Clement Corbett's order to the parishioners of West Walton in Norfolk in 1633, that all the men should be on the north side and all the women on the south, was actually enforced. He was shocked at the story reported to him of men and women sitting 'promiscuously together, whereby there is no decency or order observed but mere confusion and disorder'.[40] Archbishop Neile warned Bishop Bridgeman against a scheme to attempt seating the sexes entirely apart in Chester diocese in 1635. It could not succeed: 'your intention for the disposing of the seats . . . will beget more babbles, suits in law and prohibitions than either you or I would be contented to be trouble with'.[41] In general it was the representation of the patriarchal family as a whole, rather than a demonstration of pure gender order, which triumphed in patterns of church seating. But that of course is exactly what we would expect and precisely what made sense in view of the way that the patriarchal system worked inside the household. Family order mirrored public order: public seating symbolised family order.

Whereas Sunday worship was static, a snapshot of gender order, in the day-to-day life of towns and village communities gender had to be constantly negotiated and reputation was constantly at stake. The principal instruments of this negotiation were gossip, slander and ritual. Through these means we find gender relationships expressed in their most dynamic form, since in the moods and actions of groups, sometimes crowds, of men and women each brought their personal values and strong emotions to the issues in hand. We can only expect to recapture this dynamic in a community's relationships at fleeting moments which have reached the historical record. Even then, we need an exceptionally vivid historical source or a probing piece of local research in order to bring to life how men and women made patriarchy actually work, week in and week out. The essence of it all of course was people's credit. Richard Gough's vivid pen portraits of his neighbours in the Shropshire village of

37. D.E. Underdown, *Fire Under Heaven: The Life of an English Town in the Seventeenth Century* (London, 1992), p. 39.
38. C. Phythian-Adams, 'Ceremony and the Citizen: the Communal Year at Coventry 1450–1550', in P. Clark and P. Slack, eds, *Crisis of Order in English Towns 1500–1700* (London, 1972), p. 59.
39. M. Ashton, 'Segregation in Church', in W.J. Sheils and D. Wood, eds, 'Women in the Church', in Studies in Church History 27 (1990), pp. 237–9.
40. Amussen, *An Ordered Society*, pp. 137–8.
41. J. Maltby, 'Approaches to the Study of Religious Conformity in Late Elizabethan and Early Stuart England' University of Cambridge, PhD thesis, 1991, p. 208.

Myddle drew upon a few simple assumptions about what made a man a good husband or a woman a good wife. Manhood consisted in keeping the household fed and the farm going and showing spirit in doing so. Thomas Ash was 'a proper comely person': 'his father gave him a good country education which, with the benefit of a good natural wit, a strong memory, a courteous and mild behaviour, a smooth and affable way of discourse, an honest and religious disposition, made him a complete and hopeful young man'. Thomas Newans was 'unskilled in husbandry, though he would talk much of it'. Michael Chambre was 'wholly addicted to idleness and therefore no marvel that he was lascivious'. Good women were women who were chaste and who kept the house well. Thomas Ash was fortunate to marry 'a lovely proper gentlewoman' and 'therefore they lived a loving and comfortable life together'. Edward Muckleston's wife Anne was 'a good discrete woman and a good house-keeper': the couple had 'many handsome lovely children and do live very plentifully'. Mary Lath 'proving an idle housewife that family which was formerly one of the chiefest in that town came to ruin'. Gough enjoyed being moralistic. His family tales nevertheless have the ring of truth and they show how stories about people's behaviour stamped some kind of image of each of them on those who lived nearby.[42]

As the primary targets of insult, Laura Gowing argues, 'women occu-pied a very particular place in the negotiation of sexual guilt and honour'. She shows how women in early modern London were able to regulate sexuality in the neighbourhood and local community by making them-selves the agents of the definition of sexual honour. They achieved a flexible use in neighbourhood disputes of various kinds of the pejorative accusation of whoredom. By adopting men's account of patriarchy and manipulating it in their own interests, they claimed 'a verbal and legal authority that was at once powerful and fragile'. Each time a London woman defined sexual honesty in a local altercation she in some sense defined womanhood. So this slander was very much about gender. Indeed, adopting Judith Butler's understanding of gender as 'a definition in progress, mobilized through the repetition of particular acts', Gowing suggests that sexual slander can be seen as a set of 'representations and performances' towards defining femininity. There is no clear dividing line here between language and action or between private and public acts of punishment. A range of informal actions was available to women as a means of confronting other women whom they called their husband's whores. In 1632 Mary Sadd went to Horne Alley to find this person. Pointing to the house where Margaret Eadis lodged, a witness testified, she declared that she would 'have the whore out of that house'. Main-taining that her husband had pawned her goods and her children's clothes to maintain Margaret, Mary insisted that 'if she stayed but till tomorrow she would roust her out'.

42. R. Gough, *The History of Myddle* (London, 1981), pp. 10–11, 201–21.

What is important is that rituals were clearly gendered, signifying society's firm attachment to the notion of lapses from specific behaviour appropriate for men and women. Bawdy houses sometimes had their windows broken, so windows in private houses were sometimes broken to show a woman's whoredom. A slit nose represented an injured wife's revenge on a husband's mistress, so we find women threatening this penalty. The exchanges of female insult contained frequent references to the formal institutional penalties, like carting and penance in a white sheet, which were imposed for whoredom and which humiliated the offender in front of the neighbourhood. 'A cart and a basin tyng tyng, a cart and a basin tyng tyng, a cart and a basin if thou wilt not be quiet,' Alice Fulham told Ellen Alsop in 1611. The multiple slander used by Mary Bently against Mary Haviland, but focused upon her daughter, in 1700 is a good example of the process of destruction of reputation intended to produce a ritualistic conclusion. 'Haviland is an old bitch and an old bawd', she allegedly declared, 'and I would have her carted, for she delivered Margaret Haviland of a bastard child at Haviland's house and she pretended Margaret was married to John Spelman, Gent., but she wasn't his wife, but Margaret carried from him one bastard in her arms and one in her belly.'[43] Such women felt themselves to be deeply immersed in, and behaved as active agents of, the male structure of the ordering of other women's personal lives.

The currency of sexual insult against men – 'whoremonger', 'pander' or 'cuckold' – concerned the sexuality of women for whom they were responsible and whom they were expected to control. The general issue was always women's domination and the universal symbol of verbal and ritual humiliation in this respect was the horns. 'Hold it up to thy master his sign', declared Margaret Wigge in 1590 to Joan Drake whose husband kept the Golden Calf in London, 'I will have a pair of horns clapped up to make the calf a bull.' In 1613 Jacob Hunning, coming into Thomas Lambert's shop there, wrote with chalk on the stall that he was 'a fool, a knave and an ass' and 'did also make with his chalk a C'.[44] Gossip was circulating in the village of Stetchworth in Cambridgeshire in 1637 that Robert Bridge's wife had beaten him. Francis Bradford told him he could leave the church by the south door 'if his horns were not too big'. A knowing neighbour asked another in the churchyard 'if he came thither to buy chaff, looking at Bridge and jeering at him'.[45] Men ran the gauntlet in this way time and again in a society where the core of

43. For these two paragraphs see Gowing, 'Language, Power and the Law', in Kermode and Walker, eds, *Women, Crime and the Courts*, pp. 28, 32–3, 36; T. Meldrum, 'A Women's Court in London: Defamation at the Bishop of London's Consistory Court, 1700–1745', *London Journal* 19 (1994), p. 8.
44. Gowing, pp. 60–61.
45. M. Ingram, 'Ridings, Rough Music and Mocking Rhymes in Early Modern England', in B. Reay, ed., *Popular Culture in Seventeenth Century England* (London, 1985), p. 166.

manhood was control of one's wife and everyone saw it as a matter of public order that women should be kept firmly in their place. The essence of the charge was often their stupidity in not watching their wives with sufficient care. 'You are a cuckoldy rogue', Mary Austin told Mary Clements's husband in London in 1700, 'and when your wife was in the country, or at the Bath, then your horns were grafted on.' 'Your husband is a blind cuckold', another Londoner Roger Hart told Jane Whitehead.

Villagers were amazingly ingenious in the pranks they thought of to deride anyone believed to be failing in his gender role. Throwing a pair of ox horns into a shop in Norwich in 1609, a man shouted to its owner 'take that for the key to your bedchamber door'. William Fulbrooke took a countryman to court when he heard about the scandalous words he had used about him in Abingdon market place around 1600: 'Fulbrooke hath longer horns than my cow, dost thou know what I mean by it,' the accuser had gossiped. At Beckington in Somerset, in 1611, a mare was paraded through the village with a pair of horns attached to its head and a mocking rhyme to the stump of its shorn tail summoning William Swarfe to 'a court of cuckolds'. The procession, we are told, involved much 'laughter and derision . . . shouts and outcries'. Thomas Ricketts, discovered in bed with a married woman at Farnham in Berkshire in 1637, found himself greeted by 'a spice mortar, a platter and a candlestick ringing and making a noise' and an attempt to put him in the stocks.[46]

It was not always, although it was more usually, the cuckold rather than the adulterer who suffered. The customary means of humiliation was the charivari (plate 11). We shall never be able to measure the extent and occurrence of charivari, which was essentially an informal community ritual, but the sixty or so cases that are recorded in the seventeenth century come from all over England. We should not infer it was by any means an everyday affair. But it did express a shared culture. Gentry winked at it so long as it did not portend excessive disorder; village constables were sometimes leading figures in its organisation. Charivari, Martin Ingram argues, 'bears witness to a powerful body of shared concepts and symbols elaborated with varying degrees of subtlety at different social and cultural levels'. The village ridings were endemic because, reflecting the patriarchal ideal, 'fundamentally they made conceptual, moral and social sense to the majority of contemporaries of whatever social rank'. We should not make too much of the King's Bench judgements of 1676 and 1693 that riding skimmington constituted

46. Meldrum, 'A Women's Court', *London Journal* 19 (1994), p. 10; D.E. Underdown, 'The Taming of the Scold: The Enforcement of Patriarchal Authority in Early Modern England', in A.J. Fletcher and J. Stevenson, eds, *Order and Disorder in Early Modern England* (Cambridge, 1985), p. 128; M. Ingram, 'Ridings, Rough Music and the Reform of Popular Culture in Early Modern England', *Past and Present* 105 (1984), pp. 87, 90.

a riot and that it was grounds for an action for libel.[47] The ritual was deeply ingrained in local tradition, as Edward Thompson's account of its use until the present century vividly shows.[48]

Charivari was remarkably many-faceted. The core event was processional: 'riding skimmington' in the west of England, 'riding the stang' in the north. The mount might be a real animal or a pole; the victim himself, effigies, or the next-door neighbour who had in some sense failed the community by not acting to quell the gender disorder, might be ridden; the rough music might come from bells or pots and pans or even guns and fireworks. The essence was always mocking laughter and, somewhere in the minds of the organisers, there was normally the immediate or potential issue of cuckolding, the ultimate expression of women on top. All this was in varying degrees festive and penal: the style and atmosphere of a riding could range from mild derision to deeply hostile and tormenting disapproval. At one level the whole affair was a matter of applying sanctions on personal behaviour. Thus one of those who took part in the riding at Haughley and Wetherden in Suffolk in 1604 explained the objective as follows: 'not only the woman which had offended might be shamed for her misdemeanour towards her husband [in beating him] but other women also by her shame might be admonished [not] to offend in like sort'. An account written in 1828 of the riding of Alice Evans at Northenden in Cheshire around 1790 says that the intention of the men involved was to punish her, 'fearing their own spouses might assume the same authority'. Alice Evans, a powerful woman, was alleged to have 'chastised' her lord and master 'for some act of intemperance and neglect of work'. So

> they therefore mounted one of their body, dressed in female apparel on the back of an old donkey, the man holding a spinning wheel in his lap and his back towards the donkey's head. Two men led the animal through the neighbourhood, followed by scores of boys and idle men, tinkling kettles and frying pans, roaring with cows' horns and making a most hideous hullabaloo, stopping every now and then while the exhibitioner on the donkey made the following proclamation:
>
> > Ran a dan, ran a dan, ran a dan
> > Mrs Alice Evans has been beat her good man
> > It was neither with sword, spear, pistol or knife
> > But with a pair of tongs she vowed to take his life.[49]

So the punitive focus could be upon a woman's defiance of patriarchal precept. But there is good reason to think that charivari was always directed primarily, if only implicitly in some cases, against the husband

47. Ingram, 'Ridings', *Past and Present* 105 (1984), pp. 105–12; above, p. 201.
48. E.P. Thompson, *Customs in Common* (London, 1991), pp. 493–505.
49. *Past and Present* 105 (1984), pp. 81–93; Thompson, *Customs in Common*, p. 475.

and that its message was directed at other husbands. The crucial issue was his personal and sexual control over his wife. Charivari could be intended as a warning and no doubt many offenders were subsequently left alone and were terrorised into greater conformity with communal values. But the intention could also be to drum out an offending couple, as happened at Burton-on-Trent in 1618 when William and Margaret Cripple, suspected of living together unmarried, subsequently left the town.[50] At another level charivari was about communities having a reputation to maintain as effective upholders of patriarchy. Notions of rule and misrule, inversion, the world turned upside down are all involved. Riders were often made to ride backwards or two figures were set bum to bum as shown in popular prints. The public drama of a riding was surely the subject of much gossip, not just in the village itself but in the neighbourhood beyond. At the same time, as Martin Ingram has stressed, 'the laughter of charivari bore witness to ambiguities and unresolvable conflicts in the ideal and the actual social system'. For here, more colourfully and more loudly than anywhere else, men's dilemma was acted out. Men knew that women simply could not be dominated to anything like the degree implied by the patriarchal ideal. So drawing some kind of boundaries was all the more important.[51]

In charivari men acted out the same fears from which they found release by reading jests, satires and ballads or watching plays like *The Taming of the Shrew*.[52] What was common to all these experiences was explosive laughter, the cathartic release of tension. Through representations of anarchy the imperative to work constantly for order out of disorder was reinforced. Charivari destroyed the privilege of privacy, a privilege in early modern society which rested on men's willing and energetic conformity in enforcing control at home. We must not underestimate its sheer power to humiliate: 'it announces disgrace', argued Edward Thompson, 'not as a contingent quarrel with neighbours, but as judgement of the community. What had before been gossip or hostile glances becomes common, overt, stripped of the disguises which, however flimsy and artificial, are part of the currency of everyday intercourse . . . rough music is a public naming of what has been named before only in private.'[53] Charivari thus asserted the validity, just as it sought to enforce the strength, of a system of collective values which came above any individual man's wish or inclinations. Without this last resort, it may be suggested, male heads of households as a group would

---

50. J.R. Kent, 'Folk Justice and Royal Justice in Early Seventeenth-Century England: A Charivari in the Midlands', *Midland History* VIII (1983), pp. 70–85.
51. Ingram, 'Ridings', *Past and Present* 105 (1984), pp. 87, 89, 96–7.
52. For this argument with regard to ballads see E.A. Foyster, 'A Laughing Matter? Martial Discord and Gender Control in Seventeenth-Century England', *Rural History* 4 (1993), pp. 5–21. Above, pp. 107–9.
53. Thompson, *Customs in Common*, pp. 487–8.

have felt too vulnerable. Thus, although we think of charivari as integral to popular culture, its social role was recognised as much by gentry as villagers. The huge plasterwork frieze of a skimmington ride that may be seen in the hall at Montacute is an affirmation by Sir Edward Philips, who built the house around 1600, that everyone knew about patriarchy having to have its final sanctions. The story in this case begins with a husband beaten for enjoying a drink while left in charge of the baby. The symbolism of this frieze is striking: decorating the hall of a great manor, where squire and people met and sometimes dined, where servants and retainers gathered, it is at the junction of the household and the local community. So indeed was the ritual of charivari itself.[54]

Another ritual which is equally important to this discussion is the ducking of scolds. The term scold for a turbulent or brawling person was characteristically used of women from the fourteenth century and by about 1700 had become virtually exclusive to them. Martin Ingram's analysis of the court evidence suggests that prosecution of scolds was patchy and selective between 1550 and 1650 and declined thereafter. There was more action in urban than rural areas and crusades against female assertiveness in certain towns can be associated with a puritan impetus. It is clear that the punishment of convicted scolds became more severe than it had been previously in the century after 1550. This was when the cruel brank or scold's bridle, an iron collar with a bit for the mouth to prevent the victim talking, came into use, chiefly in a number of northern towns, for parading offenders through the streets (plates 7, 8 and 9). From 1580 several widely read legal handbooks stressed the duty of manor jurisdictions to keep a ducking stool in good repair. This was the see-saw-like contraption, made in a number of styles depending upon tradition and resources, used to plunge the victim into a pond or river. There is plenty of evidence of the purchase and repair of these elaborate and expensive instruments in the Elizabethan and early Stuart periods, but such evidence tells us little about how often they were actually put to use[55] (plate 10).

The ducking ritual was clearly very similar in its overall objective to the charivari: it was directed against women who had to an exceptional degree offended the community's mores. Prosecutions for scolding arose from the initiative of groups of people, often including some women, who had lost patience with a neighbour. Ingram argues that charges likely to bring women to the ducking stool 'usually involved not merely brawling and abuse but also such offences as indiscriminate slander, tale-bearing, the stirring up of strife, the deliberate sowing of discord between neighbours'. He suggests that in some cases the evidence of irrational, obsessive or violent behaviour by scolds may indicate a degree

54. For charivari and marital violence, see above, pp. 201–3
55. Underdown, 'Taming of the Scold' in Fletcher and Stevenson, eds, *Order and Disorder in Early Modern England*, pp. 123–5.

of mental disturbance. The characteristic of the scold brought to be ducked was her wilful refusal to accommodate herself to the community's expectations of reasonable behaviour. The essence of this intractability, displayed in one way or another, was a verbal assertiveness which was seen as especially unacceptable in a woman.[56] Ducking the scold, in this sense, illustrates how gender permeated English local society. The process of prosecution which produced the punishment is a further reminder of how it was often women who drove forward the patriarchal system. 'Most women will not only conform', wrote Christina Larner, 'but also attack women who by their nonconformity threaten the security of conformist women.'[57] The comment was made in relation to witchcraft prosecutions but it applies to many aspects of community relations beyond the household.

The evangelising campaigns of puritan gentry and clerics between Queen Elizabeth's accession and the civil war involved a drive for moral reform which took some of its impetus from deeply rooted assumptions about the strength and nature of female sexuality. Patrick Collinson's exploration of the combination at this time of magistracy and ministry illustrated such efforts with evidence from Bury St Edmunds and Rye. At Bury fornicators were tied to a post in the market place for twenty-four hours and then given thirty stripes on market day; at Rye they were made to wear a distinctive collar of yellow and green cloth.[58] When there was specific evidence of illicit sexual relations between a young man and woman, magistrates were certainly ready to punish them together. At Norwich, in 1568, Thomas Sparrow's apprentice and servant were whipped and carried through the market place in a cart for their fornication; in a similar case the following year, an incontinent couple were riden at market 'tinkled about with a basin'. But, in towns like this where puritan JPs gave a lead, there was a tendency to punish more female than male offenders, subjecting them to the stocks or whipping. This seems to have been policy, though their 'great bellies' of course often gave them away.[59] The gendered aspect of this drive for moral reform deserves emphasis and a discussion of it will take up the last section of this chapter. The centrepiece was a sustained attack on the sexual laxity of the young female poor. The Elizabethan homily *Against Whoredom and Uncleanness* thundered against the vice of all the nation's young, scathingly rejecting young men's view that fornication should be 'counted no sin at all but

---

56. M. Ingram, ' "Scolding Women Cucked or Washed": A Crisis of Gender Relations in Early Modern England', in Kermode and Walker, eds, *Women, Crime and the Courts*, pp. 48–80.
57. C. Larner, *Witchcraft and Religion: The Politics of Popular Belief* (Oxford, 1984), p. 86.
58. P. Collinson, *The Religion of Protestants: The Church in English Society 1559–1625* (Oxford, 1982), pp. 158–9.
59. M. McClendon, 'The Quiet Reformation: Norwich Magistrates and the Coming of Protestantism', Stanford University PhD thesis, 1990, pp. 230, 235.

rather a pastime, a dalliance and but a touch of youth'.[60] The administrative record however suggests that it was primarily women that new legislation was aimed against and that it was they who bore the brunt of its enforcement.

It is evident that new legislation was put forward by godly magistrates who saw the problem of the poor in terms of reform of behaviour as much as social welfare. Joan Kent, in her investigation of this subject, came up with the names of fourteen MPs associated with this legislation between 1575 and 1628 who can probably be called puritans. Among the most prominent were Sir Robert Wroth, a crucial figure in forwarding the poor law in 1598, Francis Hastings, Sir Francis Barrington, Thomas Hoby and Thomas Crew.[61] More research is needed on the connections and alliances that lay behind efforts in the House of Commons to drive on new legislation. What matters here is the perception of society that underlay the arguments of the promoters of moral reform and the social and moral values and attitudes upon which they drew in debate. Their public objective is readily established by referring to preambles of bills that did actually become law. In the 1576 act 'for setting the poor to work and avoiding idleness' bastard-bearers were to be punished for the effect of their illicit sexual activity, which diverted resources properly due to 'the relief of the impotent and aged true poor of the parish' to the upkeep of their children. Yet the moral impetus of the provision for a commitment to the house of correction is evident in a reference to the women's 'evil example and encouragement of lewd life'.[62]

The work of David Underdown has made us aware of the importance for an understanding of the Elizabethan and early Stuart periods of the attacks on the traditional culture of fellowship and good neighbourhood led by puritan magistrates and clergy.[63] The polarisation that is prominent in much contemporary literature of complaint and is revealed by the records of some local communities at this time is one of moral values: between 'those who gadded to sermons and those who gadded to dances, sports and other pastimes,' as Patrick Collinson has put it, 'those whose speech was seasoned with godly salt and those who used the traditional oaths.'[64] This was a society in which more than half the population may have been under twenty years of age and in which a late age of marriage had become the norm, since economic conditions prevented most young

60. Cited in E.R. Brinkworth, *Shakespeare and the Bawdy Court of Stratford* (Chichester, 1972), p. 73
61. J.R. Kent, 'Attitudes of Members of the House of Commons to the Regulation of Personal Conduct in Late Elizabethan and Early Stuart England', *BIHR*, XLV (1972), pp. 64–71.
62. 18 Elizabeth c3.
63. Underdown, *Revel, Riot and Rebellion*, pp. 44–72.
64. Collinson, *Religion of Protestants*, p. 230.

people from establishing their own household until they had completed a period of service or apprenticeship.[65] A flourishing leisure culture offered fierce competition on Sundays to the parish church. At Nottingham in 1668, for example, thirty-five men were accused of 'being at the football' in time of divine service. The controversy over the Book of Sports between 1618 and 1640 focused attention upon the whole issue of Sunday recreations.[66] Among puritan commentators the greatest anxiety was about dancing. 'Among so many abused exercises', declared Humphrey Roberts in 1572, 'dancing is chief and is so abominably practised in these days that it ought utterly to be rejected and forsaken of all Christians.' He was sure it nourished pride, whoredom and idleness.[67] George Widley was convinced that there were many diversions which distracted people from their proper Sunday observance, including plays, cards, dice and bear-baitings, but none of them 'so much troubleth the ministry of the word' as dancing. It was not that he objected to dancing as such. What horrified him was firstly its new style, secondly that this involved the sexes dancing together. Dancing had 'degenerated so much from that manlike kind of activity and nimbleness into a nice and effeminate wantonness.' Widley rejected the biblical precedents in favour of dancing, asserting that in ancient times it had not been with women: 'we dance promiscuously man and woman together nay good and bad together'.[68]

Christopher Fetherston, John Northbrooke, Humphrey Roberts and Philip Stubbes were among the Elizabethan puritan commentators who made much of an alleged association between dancing and mating, insisting that the maypole not only encouraged young people to base marriage decisions on an immediate sexual attraction but also that it led to many pre-marital pregnancies.[69] Obviously there was a good deal of rhetorical hyperbole in all this and we cannot judge the precise impact of such writings. But they surely contributed, at a time of concern about social and gender order, to an alarm not just about the poor but about youth in general, since the sexuality of youth was seen as so ebullient and vigorous. A small group of militant puritans were able to drive forward moral legislation in the House of Commons on the basis of a groundswell of backbench anxiety and support. If the most dangerous people among the fickle and uneducated multitude of poor were seen to be the youth of the nation, its female youth was seen as doubly dangerous. The

65. Wrightson, *English Society*, pp. 68, 146.
66. Collinson, *Religion of Protestants*, p. 225; Underdown, *Revel Riot and Rebellion*, pp. 65–8.
67. H. Roberts, *An Earnest Complaint of divers Vain Wicked and Abused Exercises* (London, 1572), pp. 53–4.
68. G. Widley, *The Doctrine of the Sabbath* (1604), pp. 102–4.
69. Collinson, *Religion of Protestants*, pp. 224–6.

bastardy legislation of 1576 and 1610 was openly class- and gender-specific. In the first instance JPs were given powers to bind parents to answer for their offence in cases in which the child was or might prove chargeable to the parish: they could make an order for the maintenance of the child by the father if one could be discovered, and, as a matter of discretion, apply corporal punishment. The 1610 statute stated further that 'every lewd woman which shall have any bastard which may be charge-able to the parish, the justices of the peace shall commit such woman to the house of correction, to be punished and set on work during the term of one whole year.' These legislative moves were closely in tune with opinion among the mass of rural justices. Illegitimacy ratios were high in the years following the dearth of the 1590s, especially from 1597 to 1607. JPs found themselves much preoccupied with the laboursome business of establishing paternity and enforcing maintenance orders, either on an individual or on a parish. There was a very practical side to this matter. But the increasing interest on some benches in retribution presaged the harsh 1610 provision for punishing the mother. A steady hardening of gentry opinion brought a shift of emphasis from social welfare to punishment. The Essex bench moved towards severity by stages between the two acts: before 1580 they ordered that mothers should spend a few hours in the stocks; in 1588 came the first order for whipping at the cart's tail but the strokes were to be 'moderately given'; from 1600 women were to be whipped until their backs were bloody. In some counties – Essex, Lancashire and Warwickshire, for example – the new powers regarding the house of correction were applied as soon as the act reached the statute book.[70]

Even before the 1610 policy was established some MPs were turning their attention to what they saw as an even more heinous aspect of female illicit sexuality. The parliaments of 1606–7 and 1610 debated abortive bills against the killing of base children. It was the parliament of 1624 which eventually passed the notorious infanticide act, which, uniquely in this period, abandoned the principle of English justice that the innocent were taken to be so until proved guilty. The act stated that:

> many lewd women that have been delivered of bastard children, to avoid their shame and to escape punishment, do secretly bury or conceal the death of their children and after if the child be found dead the same women do allege that the said child was born dead; whereas it falleth out sometimes (although hardly is it to be proved) that the said child or children were murdered by the said women their lewd mothers or by their assent or procurement.

70. A.J. Fletcher, *Reform in the Provinces: The Government of Stuart England* (London, 1986), pp. 253–7.

According to the act any mother of a bastard who concealed its death was to be presumed guilty of murder unless she could prove by the oath of one witness that the child was born dead.[71]

There undoubtedly were cases of desperate girls killing or disposing of infants in order to save their sexual reputations. The practice was commented upon, connected specifically to bastard-bearers and no doubt much discussed among gentry taken up with their magisterial efforts to combat the intractable common country disorders. William Gouge wrote about 'lewd and unnatural women as leave their new born children under stalls, at men's doors, in church porches, yea many times in open field'.[72] The contemporary obstetrician Percival Willoughby associated infanticide with 'the looser sort'.[73] The enforcement of the 1624 act in the following decades has been investigated by Keith Wrightson using the Essex assize files. Twenty-nine women were hanged for the offence in Essex between 1601 and 1665, and twenty were acquitted.[74] Yet the significance of this extraordinary act has been little emphasised in general accounts of the social and economic dislocation of the period from the 1570s to the 1620s. Its ferociousness indicates an obsessive concern about the problem of uncontrolled female sexuality among the poor. In the infanticide act class and gender came together in a powerfully stark and emotive way.

How did the gentry at Westminster get to the point of legislating in this way? It is not likely that we can establish much more about the facts of the matter than the legal records tell us: how far deaths were the result of natural causes, were related to inadequate care or were the outcome of studied neglect. Keith Wrightson concluded, on the basis of the Essex evidence, that 'many of the accused mothers were innocent of any offence other than concealment'. Even among those who had a strong rational motive and were subject to acute emotional strain, he believes, the actual crime was infrequent. Yet it dramatically focused the gentry's fears. The denunciations of dancing, drinking and May games had alerted them. The church courts were derided by puritans for their laxity and for the inadequacy of their 'toyish censures'.[75] Under this pressure, previous tolerance towards premarital sex and bridal pregnancy collapsed. What we have here, it can be suggested, is the moral panic characteristic of particular historical moments when widespread fears and anxieties can become articulated and concentrated in terms of a moral crisis. With the bastardy and infanticide legislation of 1576, 1610 and 1624 we can see a

---

71. J.R. Kent, 'Attitudes of Members', *BIHR*, XLV (1972), p. 69; 21 James I, c27.
72. W. Gouge, *Domestical Duties* (London, 1622), p. 507.
73. P. Willoughby, *Observations on Midwifery*, ed., H. Blenkinsop (London, 1932), pp. 11–12, 31–4, 273–5.
74. K. Wrightson, 'Infanticide in Earlier Seventeenth Century England', *Local Population Studies* 15 (1975), pp. 10–22.
75. C. Hill, *Society and Puritanism in Pre-Revolutionary England* (London, 1964), pp. 298–351.

particular social group becoming defined as a threat to society's values and interests and thus being made the target for public regulation. The definition of sexuality is often central to these panics, as comparison between this early modern example and the mid-Victorian period shows. News of the Indian mutiny in 1857 created a sense of crisis and loss of control. A critical connection was made between imperial decline and moral laxity at home. Lynda Nead has traced an 'obsessive categorisation of respectable and non-respectable sexual behaviour' over the following months. Prostitution, in this case, became a metaphor for immorality in general, the prostitute representing deviant, dangerous and illicit sex: she was 'the locus for fears concerning public disorder and revolution, she was an agent of chaos bringing with her disruption and social decay'. In both these cases, the early modern village bastard-bearer and the Victorian urban prostitute, class and gender are crucial elements in the process of finding scapegoats. Sexuality was defined across the polarity of the middle-class family home and the teeming city in nineteenth-century England.[76] Less explicitly, but with equal force, it was being defined in Elizabethan and early Stuart England across the polarity of the ordered patriarchal household and the libidinous festive community which was beyond the personal reach of fathers and masters.

The moral panic expressed by the legislation under discussion had the power to bind together men of widely different outlooks. They did not all have to treat unbridled female sexuality with equal vehemence in order to share the sense that new laws were needed. The correspondence between Sir Robert Harley and John Bruen in the Welsh border country in 1624 is a classic example of the militant puritan position. Two 'truly religious' magisterial colleagues had met with an 'impudent affront'. 'I assure you', Bruen wrote to Harley, 'if a strict course be not taken for the punishment of these disorders there will be such a gap opened to profaneness and the devil will get such advantage in these parts as never will be quenched in our time.' Dedicated JPs like Bruen and Harley, the latter famed in his locality as 'a most nimble soul of zeal against sin', might see themselves and their task primarily in evangelical terms. Yet, when family and household could not in themselves more than partially sustain the gender order, they were also the kind of men who acted as patriarchy's most energetic stormtroopers when they took the stage as public men. We began these chapters with prescription: with male honour and officeholding, female honour and chastity. The presence among Harley's papers of an order for the punishment of bastard-bearers testifies to his preoccupation with that matter in his Herefordshire jurisdiction.[77] It neatly relates prescription to magisterial practice. Through a multitude of such individual initiatives early modern patriarchy was made and enforced.

76. L. Nead, *Myths of Sexuality* (Oxford, 1988), pp. 80–118.
77. Collinson, *Religion of Protestants*, p. 167; above, p. 151.

PART III   TOWARDS MODERN
GENDER

14. *Prologue: New Thinking, New Knowledge*

MEN'S POWER IN history has resided in their construction of theology and philosophy, law and custom in their own terms. Their monopoly of these constructions in turn reflected that power. We turn now to their efforts to adapt and transform patriarchy in England by replacing its ancient scriptural and medical basis, which had proved such a potent ideology for many centuries, with a new secular ideology of gender which, in certain respects at least, has proved equally enduring. This process of transformation involved both the organisational and relational aspects of gender.[1] In exploring it we need to give close attention to the interaction of gender and class. The crisis of the English civil war and its radical aftermath was far from simply a political crisis. It shook the confidence of Englishmen in their control of the social and gender order to the roots. The year 1660 marks the beginning of a massive backlash against change which had lasting political, religious and social connotations. In this sense, if there are turning points at all in history, 1660 was the most important in seventeenth-century England. The outcome of the century's upheavals can be described in terms of the triumph of the gentry: their achievement in late Stuart and Hanoverian England was the maintenance of firm government within a framework of social deference and a widely shared respect for the law.[2] By 1700 the gentry had established a sense of class identity, based upon a set of distinct cultural and intellectual assumptions, which differentiated them from the multitude. This class consciousness became the very essence of their way of life. Moreover their view of class henceforth was always gendered, that is, it took its strength from an increasingly rigid and elaborate scheme of gender construction with which they marked themselves off from the masses.[3] The rules were laid down between 1660

1. M. Roper and J. Tosh, eds, *Manful Assertions: Masculinities in Britain since 1800* (London, 1991) p. 11.
2. A.J. Fletcher, *Reform in the Provinces: the Government of Stuart England* (London, 1986), p. 372.
3. K. Wrightson, 'The Social Order of Early Modern England: Three Approaches', in C.

and 1800 in a burgeoning prescriptive literature directed specifically at men and women, but more especially women, in the upper and middling ranks.

The extraordinary resilience of modern English patriarchy can be related to the class system which has given much power in the nation's life until the present day to the Anglican church, riveted to the social scene after 1660 by the new alliance of squire and parson. The English upper class learnt how to root their social hegemony in an effortless display in every sphere of village and town life of gendered behaviour.[4] They set an example to society, which is perfectly captured in the world of Jane Austen's novels, of the proper behaviour to be expected of men and women in their various walks of society. Social distinctions are vital to the whole scheme of upper-class gendered behaviour. 'The yeomanry are precisely the order of people with whom I feel I can have nothing to do,' declares Emma.[5] With this command of social ranking went a powerful and totally assured sense of leadership. The Herefordshire freeholders, announced Viscount Scudamore at the 1661 election, should simply accept the gentry's recommendations for 'it is the order which the wisdom of the creator hath thought good to fix in nature, namely that inferiors are to receive from their superiors that participation of knowledge and light by which their resolutions and actions are to be guided'.[6]

By 1800, the gentry and clergy who ruled English rural communities had acquired a quite remarkable degree of confidence that all was and would remain right with their world. In that year the Somerset parson William Holland paid a visit, which he recorded in his diary, to his second living at Monkton Farley: 'Every one grinned and seemed pleased to see us and the poor seemed very respectful and did not make such dismal complaints of the times as I had expected. We returned to Bath in good time through a land of curtesies and bows and greetings.' John Skinner, another Somerset clergyman, writing as times politically were getting somewhat rougher in 1831, struck a note of nostalgia when he compared his successful domestication of the animals in his care with the proper behaviour to be expected of his social inferiors:

> After dinner this evening there were lying on the rug before the fire my three dogs and a pet lamb of my daughter's, also a large tom cat, and at the window presented itself a tame jackdaw . . . all these

Bonfield, R.M. Smith and K. Wrightson, *The World We Have Gained* (Oxford, 1986), p. 197 and references there.

4. See in general E.P. Thompson, 'Eighteenth-Century English Society: Class Struggle without Class?', *Social History*, III (1978), pp. 133–65; 'Patrician Society, Plebian Culture', *Journal of Social History* VII (1974), pp. 382–405.

5. J. Austen, *Emma* ed., R. Blythe (London, 1966), p. 19.

6. Cited in M. Kishlansky, *Parliamentary Selection: Social and Political Choice in Early Modern England* (Cambridge, 1986), p. 129.

creatures are as happy as creatures can be under our protection, and I may ask, were not my fellow creatures far more happy under the protection of their more powerful superiors years ago when the laws were duly executed than they are now amidst that great diversity of parties in religion and politics.

For such men the political and social hierarchy as a whole possessed a divine sanction.[7] In the Anglican state the church claimed a paramount role in bolstering a coherent vision of an ordered world under the authority, as one commentator suggested, 'of a spiritual commission from Christ himself'.[8]

If we probe the theological assumptions of these Somerset clergy we can appreciate the importance of religion for the strength and coherence of their vision of patriarchal order. Patriarchy was still for them the order of creation. So, to abolish it, one would have to envisage transcending the order of creation, which is the order of the reproduction of the species. 'One had to be able to imagine an original order of nature that was egalitarian,' Rosemary Radford Ruether argues. 'In relation to this egalitarian order patriarchy would then be able to be named as a distortion of nature.' A few radical figures in the sectarian movements of the civil war period did, it seems, come close to seeing such an egalitarian future as a new historical future. But their day was short. Since then it has proved a long road, by way of liberal and socialist thinkers in the nineteenth century who established a universalist language which has since been applied by feminists, to that signal event of 1994: the ordination of women in the English Anglican church. The symbolic significance of this event in overturning the Judaeo-Christian patriarchal tradition is overwhelming, for it gives official denial to the view which has regarded women as less complete expressions of human nature than men. The erastian church affirmed in 1994 that women share equally in the image of God and it follows that God can be imaged equally as male and female.[9]

For men like John Skinner and William Holland patriarchy's scriptural basis, which left all this outside the realm of possibility, still felt intact and sufficient in 1800. Yet for the English upper and middle classes as a whole a transformation in the nature of patriarchy had been taking place in the previous hundred years or so based upon a new reading of gender. It was not in any sense a complete transformation, for men had found it possible to lift much from Christian tradition and integrate it with the new

7. Citations from J.C.D. Clark, 'England's Ancien Regime as a Confessional State', *Albion*, XXI (1989), pp. 473–4.
8. J.C.D. Clark, *English Society 1688–1832* (Cambridge, 1985), p. 275 citing John Bowles's tract *The Claims of the Established Church Considered as an Apostolical Institution* (1815).
9. R.R. Ruether, 'The Liberation of Christology from Patriarchy', in A. Loades, ed., *Feminist Theology: A Reader* (London, 1990), pp. 145–7.

cosmology which was emerging from the scientific revolution. Their adapted mental world could therefore still feel intact when, with the huge epistemological shift associated with Descartes, Newton and others, much about the old way of seeing the world and the universe had collapsed. For instance, the Great Chain of Being, graphically displayed in Valades *Rhetorica Christiana* of 1579, could no longer have the same meaning it once had done. The essence of the Chain was its idealisation of the bonds of order, bonds which linked angels, humans, fowls, fishes, mammals and plants[10] (plate 15). But society was now coming to be seen in terms of polarisation rather than of rank, degree and order.[11] The transition was of course a long one. R.S. Neale has described English society in the period from 1650 to 1750 as 'neither preindustrial nor industrial, neither feudal nor industrial-capitalist, neither classless nor multi-class, neither order based nor class based, neither one thing nor the other'. Keith Wrightson sees elements of two models of social relations beside each other in the sixteenth and seventeenth centuries: 'hierarchy and class can be coexisting dimensions of both individual consciousness and social relations'.[12]

As the Great Chain gradually lost meaning and its social implications began to look irrelevant, an important piece fell out of the cosmological jigsaw which had sustained the old attitudes to gender. For the strong woven chain of Valades's illustration, held in God's right hand and linking him with all creation, encapsulated the crucial tenets of a male creator God and a single standard of humankind which was male. It was a symbolic expression of male generativity and rationality, of in effect one sex. The collapse of the theory of macrocosm and microcosm was even more catastrophic in its effects on traditional views of gender. In Robert Fludd's *Utriusque Cosmi . . . Historia* we are given a visual representation of a way of looking at the cosmos which the male intellectual elite had clung to tenaciously. Man stands with his arms and legs outstretched inside a series of concentric circles (plate 14). Sixteenth-century ideas about the body are illuminated by Fludd's relating of the four humours to the elements and man's anatomy to the signs of the zodiac. While time steps across the clouds unwinding this pattern of unity, man's genitals, at the very centre of the whole design, represent the last knot in this mythical unravelling. It would be hard to think of a more powerful metaphor of the notion of male perfection expressed as one flesh in relation to the cosmos.[13]

10. A.O. Lovejoy, *The Great Chain of Being* (Cambridge, Massachusetts, 1942); E.M.W. Tillyard, *The Elizabethan World Picture* (London, 1943), pp. 18–28, 37–50.

11. A.J. Fletcher and A. Stevenson, eds, *Order and Disorder in Early Modern England* (Cambridge, 1985), pp. 1–15.

12. Wrightson, 'Social Order', in Bonfield, Smith, Wrightson, eds, *World We Have Gained*, p. 198 citing Neale.

13. For Fludd see K.V. Thomas, *Religion and the Decline of Magic* (London, 1971), p. 225; A.G. Debus, *The English Paracelsians* (1965), chapter 3. For comment on his device see D. Callaghan, *Women and Gender in Renaissance Tragedy* (London, 1989), p. 1; A and C. Belsey, 'Icons of Divinity: Portraits of Elizabeth I', in I. Gent and N. Llewellyn,

The general assumptions of humoral medicine, assumptions, as we have seen, which were at the core of the traditional concept of gender as well as the old cosmology as a whole, are set out clearly in an engraving of 1574 in Thurneysser's *Quinta Essentia* (plate 12). The four elements – earth, air, fire and water – were kept in motion by the heavenly bodies; the various planets circulating the earth transmitted different quantities of the four humoral qualities of heat and cold, dryness and moisture; a person's sexual temperament, in effect their gender, was determined by the balance of these qualities and their personality could display the effects of changes in this humoral balance upon their body. Macrocosm and microcosm, the heavenly and earthly correspondences, held all this in place. How could such a theory possibly survive the triumph of the mechanical philosophy in the seventeenth century? This not only destroyed the intellectual basis of a whole series of ancient sciences like astrology, chiromancy, alchemy and physiognomy but also destroyed the intellectual basis of the traditional view of gender as well.[14]

The well documented decline in the prestige of astrology in the course of the seventeenth century can be paralleled to the fate of traditional gender. Astrology could no longer be taken seriously as a science once the Aristotelian distinction between terrestrial and celestial bodies had been undermined. The earth came to be revealed as a planet like other planets and astronomical discovery robbed the heavens of their former perfection. It was the removal of the very idea of the influence of the one upon the other which was fatal. 'The world', argues Keith Thomas, 'could no longer be envisaged as a compact interlocking organism; it was now a mechanism of infinite dimensions, from which the old hierarchical subordination of earth to heavens had irretrievably disappeared.' Whereas in 1600 astrological medicine was flourishing in England, by 1700, it was said, most readers of the almanacs could not even remember what the picture of Anatomical Man was for. In intellectual circles astrology had become a joke.[15] As the zodiac was taken less seriously in people's day-to-day lives, so were the humours which had been supposed to rule people's bodies. Thus the starting point for all thinking about gender could no longer simply be scripture and the fact of male perfection based upon man's greater heat. The Garden of Eden story and the Christian tradition still provided plenty of ammunition for women's subordination. Yet men's dominance, though the survival of patriarchy needed it to be so, was no longer so obviously and patently the order of creation in both physical and theological terms.

The notion of investigating women in order to reassert their inferiority was a predictable outcome of developments in science and philosophy

eds, *Renaissance Bodies: The Human Figure in English Culture c. 1540–1660* (London, 1990), p. 25.

14. Thomas, *Religion and the Decline of Magic*, p. 643.
15. Thomas, *Religion and the Decline of Magic*, pp. 349–57.

during the seventeenth and eighteenth centuries. Not that those with whom we shall be concerned here – primarily Bacon, Descartes and Locke – had anything much to say directly about questions of gender. They neither repeated well worn views about sexual temperament and the body's humours nor established their own positions on the nature and status of women.[16] Yet the whole tenor of their thinking was destructive in many respects of the traditional gender scheme. Science and philosophy, at this time, Evelyn Fox Keller has observed, 'evolved in conjunction with and helped to shape a particular ideology of gender'.[17] Or rather, we might argue, it had such radical implications that it was bound to prompt the replacement of the scriptural theory of patriarchy with something more secular and very largely different.

Francis Bacon saw knowledge as the subjugation of nature. Abandoning the distinction between forms and matter which had held sway since Plato and Aristotle, in the Baconian programme the experimental enquirer was set up as a man able to take on and debunk all the ancients. His task was to investigate and understand the patterns in which matter is organised in accordance with mechanical laws. 'In this new picture', explains Genevieve Lloyd, 'the material world is seen as devoid of mind. . . . Nature is construed not by analogy with an organism, containing its intelligible principles of motion within it, but rather by analogy with a machine.' Bacon's argument was couched in gendered terms, most forthrightly in the fragmentary work of around 1602 entitled *The Masculine Birth of Time*. Nature was female and knowable as such, he declared: the scientist exercised a distinctly virile kind of power by his male domination over her. The elements in this new account of knowledge are traditional enough. Man's rightful domination over nature can be traced to the Genesis story and the theme of the mind's domination of matter to Plato's picture of knowledge. It was not new to personify nature as female. Nevertheless what Bacon achieved was the establishment of a powerful new model of knowledge.[18] Londa Schiebinger has suggested that too much can be made of his call for an explicitly masculine science. Challenging the ancients, Bacon was bound to compare their philosophy, characterised as passive and weak and therefore effeminate, with his own, drawn from 'the light of nature not from the darkness of ambiguity',

16. L. Schiebinger, *The Mind Has no Sex?* (Cambridge, Massachusetts, 1989), p. 170.
17. E.F. Keller, *Reflections on Gender and Science* (New Haven and London, 1985), p. 43.
18. There are useful summaries of Bacon's programme in Keller *Reflections on Gender and Science*, pp. 33–42; C. Merchant, *The Death of Nature: Women, Ecology and the Scientific Revolution* (San Francisco, 1980), pp. 164–90; G. Lloyd, *The Man of Reason: Male and Female in Western Philosophy* (London, 1984), pp. 10–17. See also, L. Jordanova, *Sexual Visions: Images of Gender in Science and Medicine between the Eighteenth and Twentieth Centuries* (Hemel Hampstead, 1989), pp. 24–5.

which was active and virile.[19] But there is more to this, for the purposes of our consideration of gender, than the use of a provocative language. For, as Genevive Lloyd has argued, the Baconian stress on matter, which was seen as both malleable and tractable, as the proper object of knowledge, is a crucial emphasis. The symbolic antithesis between femaleness and the activity of knowledge was retained. Thus the male scientist set about transcending the feminine, for femaleness was traditionally associated with matter, through the exercise of the pure intellect which he alone possessed.[20] Although Bacon never made the point in so many words, he had opened the way, through his connection of knowledge with power, to the construction of female gender as a proper and indeed necessary male intent.

Briefly in the mid-seventeenth century the Renaissance alchemists, inspired by the works of Paracelsus, challenged the Baconian stance.[21] The Restoration, however, marked a massive conservative reaction in the intellectual life of the nation. The alchemists, tarnished with a reputation as religious radicals, were thrown out of the inner circles of intellectual life and viciously attacked in print for their willingness to root medicine in the heart and to cure by love. Truth had no chance of being declared, wrote Joseph Glanville, one of the chief protagonists of the Royal Society, when 'the affections wear the breeches and the female rules'. The foundation of the Royal Society marked the decision of the natural philosophers of the 1660s to opt for the safe course. Gone were all the Interregnum schemes for reform of education and healing the sick. There was no notion any longer of advancement of science within a reformed society. The heart of the matter was instead a realisation of the Baconian programme, a programme that accorded well with the political and religious ambitions of gentry who wished to make the foundations of social and gender order so impregnable that nothing like what they had experienced in the decades from 1640 to 1660 would ever happen again.[22]

René Descartes advocated the search for useful knowledge because thereby human beings 'make themselves, as it were, masters and possessors of nature'. Ludmilla Jordanova has noted the shared ground between Bacon and Descartes in relation to images of knowledge.[23] Descartes did not intend to exclude women from the acquisition of knowledge. Indeed his abandonment of traditional ideas about the humours and sexual

19. Schiebinger, *The Mind Has no Sex?*, p. 137.
20. Lloyd, *Man of Reason*, p. 16.
21. Keller, *Reflections on Gender and Science*, pp. 43–51; see also B. Easlea, *Witch Hunting, Magic and the New Philosophy* (Brighton, 1980).
22. Keller, *Reflections on Gender and Science*, pp. 51–6. See also B.J. Shapiro, *Probability and Certainty in Seventeenth-Century England: A Study of the Relationships between Natural Science, Religion, History, Law and Literature* (Princeton, 1983), pp. 15–73.
23. Jordanova, *Sexual Visions*, p. 25.

temperament opened the way in theory for women, as rational beings like men, to take an equal part in public life and in scientific discovery. What actually happened, as one result of the seventeenth-century triumph of Cartesianism, was that women, still identified as they had always been with nature, became objects of investigation. Descartes brought Western dualism to its most succinct and forceful expression: 'subsequent philosophers have tried in vain', notes Danah Zohar, 'to argue any viable alternative'. Descartes's method, his thoroughgoing account of reason as methodical thought, has to be understood, if we are to appreciate the development of modern gender, in the context of his doctrine of the radical separateness of mind and body. Despite some trends in recent philosophy and medicine, we are mostly still good Cartesians at heart. That is we experience ourselves as a self which has or is within a body. 'We feel ourselves', as Danah Zohar puts it, 'to be deeply private, tucked away, an intangible something that peeks out at the wider world beyond and which might enjoy all manner of capacities and freedoms but for the body's limitations.' Zohar attributes this to the deep cultural conditioning of 300 years of Western thinking, a conditioning which has been given immense support and conviction by Newtonian physics. Given the Newtonian notion of what matter is, how could bodies be anything like minds?[24]

For Descartes the purpose of reason was the acquisition of valid knowledge, the discovery by a pure cognitive process of new truth. His method was intended to systematise an innate faculty which was supposedly equal in all. It is founded on such a clear alignment between the bodily and the non-rational on the one hand and mind and soul on the other that what had previously been contrasts become polarisations. Reason and its opposites coincide in Cartesianism with the distinction between mind and body. The association between maleness and reason, as we have seen, was already deeply established. The arduous thought required for the exercise of reason could only take up a small part of a person's life. Moreover it had to be learnt and it was best exercised, as in the Baconian scientific programme, collectively. So the realities of women's lives precluded them from making a significant impact on the collective efforts of early modern science. Genevieve Lloyd believes that the sharpness of Descartes's separation 'of the ultimate requirements of truth-seeking from the practical affairs of everyday life reinforced already existing distinctions between male and female roles'. The modern version of the sexual division of mental labour, she argues, thus owes much to the theory of mind which Descartes promulgated:

> Women have been assigned responsibility for that realm of the sensuous which the Cartesian Man of Reason must transcend if he is to have

24. D. Zohar, *The Quantum Self* (London, 1990), pp. 74–5.

true knowledge of things. . . . Woman's task is to preserve the sphere of the intermingling of mind and body, to which the Man of Reason will repair for solace, warmth and relaxation.[25]

Late seventeenth and eighteenth-century biomedical explorations of gender revolved around certain assumed dichotomies: between man and woman, culture and nature, mind and body, public and private. The power of these dichotomies was enormous; their ideological content is unquestionable. 'It was as if', comments Ludmilla Jordanova, 'the maintenance of the social order depended on certain key distinctions whose symbolic meanings spread far beyond their explicit context.'[26] Woman's otherness became a central focus of investigations and discussion. The complementarity of men and women, husbands and wives, became the established premise of such investigations.[27]

Despite Descartes's radical separation of mind and body, the development of the biomedical sciences in the eighteenth century did not lead to their being regarded as wholly and absolutely distinct categories. A new model of gender evolved in which lifestyle and social roles were directly related to health through the expectations of a relationship between one and the other. Women's physiology was understood and explored as a whole and in the context of their reproductive, childminding and domestic responsibilities. By 1800 it had become a basic premise of European medical commentators, notes Jordanova, 'that women were distinct from men by virtue of their total anatomy and physiology'.[28] Jane Rendall, summarising the view of women's nature elaborated by Enlightenment writers, notes that they were seen 'as governed more by feeling than reason, particularly subject to the impact of sensations from the outside world, imaginative rather than analytical and possessed of distinctive moral qualities which could be fulfilled only in the right setting'.[29]

The crucial development which made possible this transformation of gender from a theory of hierarchy to one of opposites was the invention of sensational psychology. The leading anatomist Thomas Willis, working in the 1660s, identified the soul with the brain. In this sense he was simply a good Cartesian. But he went on to argue that it depended 'on the nerves for all its functions'. It was nerve theory which finally swept humoral medicine aside, forming the basis of a new physiological system and at the same time combining biology, psychology and social attitudes into a powerful ideology of gender difference. Willis's best student at Oxford was John Locke: his *Essay Concerning Human Understanding*, a

25. Lloyd, *Man of Reason*, pp. 38–50.
26. Jordanova, *Sexual Visions*, pp. 21–2.
27. This is fully investigated by Londa Schiebinger in the context of the origins of modern science in *The Mind Has no Sex?*, pp. 214–44.
28. Jordanova, *Sexual Visions*, pp. 26–7.
29. J. Rendall, *The Origins of Modern Feminism: Women in Britain, France and the United States 1780–1860* (London, 1985), p. 31.

paradigmatic book which can be seen as one of the two or three most influential works of the eighteenth century, systematised the new sensational psychology. Locke's psychology rested on Newtonian physics and especially upon Newton's *Optics*, which, in its second edition of 1717–18, dealt in detail with the relationship of ethereal vibrations to vision and hearing. Lockean and Newtonian ideas were disseminated through academic lectures, through the pulpit and through the burgeoning periodical literature of the time, which was epitomised by *The Spectator*.[30] This journal found favour with a new middle-class audience that, in the words of J.H. Plumb, 'longed to be modish . . . to participate in the world of the great yet be free from its anxieties, to feel smug and superior to provincial rusticity and old world manners'.[31]

Doctors and medical researchers began to specialise in diseases of the nerves. George Cheyne is a critical figure here. In his *The English Malady*, published in 1737, Cheyne wanted to explain in exact language 'the nature and causes of nervous disorders' and thus to sweep aside interpretations of them which smacked of witchcraft or magic. Cheyne's definition of feeling was as follows: 'Feeling is nothing but the impulse, motion or action of bodies, gently or violently impressing the extremities or sides of the nerves of the skin, or other parts of the body, which by their structure and mechanism convey this motion to the sentient principle in the brain, or the musician.' The essence of this nerve theory was sensibility, something which could be cultivated but was also, in its varying degrees, inborn. Cheyne was a close friend of Samuel Richardson, author of the widely read and influential novels *Pamela* and *Clarissa*. He seems to have been the main source for the version of nerve theory which Richardson injected into these novels. So a language of sensibility entered the mainstream of romantic fiction, a language of 'nerves', 'fibres', 'sensations and impressions', 'spirits' and 'vapours'.[32] It is the gendering of this new nerve theory which is at the core of an evolving new model of gender difference, a model which Thomas Lacqueur identified as making possible the confused beginnings of modern gender by establishing 'an anatomy and physiology of incommensurability in the representation of women in relation to men'.[33] Sensibility, argues G.J. Barker-Benfield, came to mean a particular kind of well-developed consciousness invested with spiritual and moral values and largely identified with women. Sensibility, in other words, polarised men and women in a way that the theory of hot and cold and dry and moist had never done: its very essence was difference.

30. G.J. Barker-Benfield. *The Culture of Sensibility: Sex and Society in Eighteenth-Century Britain* (Chicago, 1992), pp. 3–9.
31. For the commercialisation of leisure see N. McKendrick, J. Brewer, J.H. Plumb, *The Birth of a Consumer Society* (London, 1983), especially p. 269.
32. Barker-Benfield, *Culture of Sensibility*, pp. 15–23.
33. T. Lacqueur, *Making Sex: Body and Gender from the Greeks to Freud* (Cambridge, Massachusetts, 1990), pp. 149–54.

The connection between gender and the senses can be traced backwards. Castiglione in *The Book of the Courtier*, available in England from 1561, had declared that the 'timidity of women, though it betrays a degree of imperfection, has a noble origin in the subtlety and readiness of their senses, which conveys images very speedily to the mind, because they are easily moved by external things'. This comment was read in the sixteenth or early seventeenth centuries in terms of current thinking about women's emotionality, an aspect of their constitution as the weaker vessel. There is a world of difference, however, between the mentality of Castiglione and that of the early eighteenth century, exemplified in the reply to a reader of *The British Apollo* who wanted to know if women were as capable of learning as men: women 'are cast in too soft a mould, are made of too fine, too delicate composure to endure the severity of study, the drudgery of contemplation, the fatigue of profound speculation'.[34] In the course of the period from 1660 to 1800 women's subordination in England was naturalised on the basis of their finer sensibility. Yet this radically new construction of female gender bore sufficient linkages with all the traditional thinking about women as simply the weaker vessel for it to be achieved without people having experienced, so far as one can detect, any strong notion that a very important change in the way they ordered the world was occurring.

The master theme of seventeenth-century political theory, the great battle between patriarchalists and social contract theorists, is well known and has been much explored.[35] How is this relevant to our investigation of gender? In traditional patriarchal thought, which assimilates all power relations to paternal rule, the family, with the authority of the father as its head, provides the sole model of authority. Sir Robert Filmer, in his *Patriarcha*, broke with this traditional analogous version of the theory, claiming that paternal and political power were identical. His fully developed argument about political right and obligation was both original and shortlived: by the 1690s, with the defeat of Filmer at the hands of Locke, it can be said to be dead. Filmer's patriarchalism fitted precisely into a mental world which was dissolving even as he wrote his book.[36] In his thinking, patriarchy, whether in the home or the state, was 'a natural institution dependent immediately on God's providence'.[37] Political right becomes, in a sense, simply an aspect of men's scriptural superiority. Locke, by contrast, is famed for his articulation of the separation of the

---

34. Cited in Barker-Benfield, *Culture and Sensibility*, p. 23.
35. G.J. Schochet, *Patriarchalism in Political Thought* (London, 1975); J. Dunn, *The Political Thought of John Locke* (Cambridge, 1969); J.P. Sommerville, *Thomas Hobbes: Political Ideas in Historical Context* (London, 1992); J. Daly, *Sir Robert Filmer and English Political Thought* (Toronto, 1979).
36. For the controversy over the dating of *Patriarcha* see the authoritative survey in the most recent edition: J.P. Sommerville, ed., *Patriarcha and Other Writings* (Cambridge, 1991), pp. xxxii–xxxiv.
37. G. Burgess, *The Politics of the Ancient Constitution: An Introduction to English Political Thought 1603–1642* (London, 1992), p. 135.

familial and the political, the private and public spheres. There is no question that his *Two Treatises of Government* is of fundamental importance as a theoretical contribution to the construction of modern patriarchy. To understand why this is so we need to follow the convincing argument established by Carole Pateman that Locke's political contract contained within it a prior and hidden sexual contract.

At first sight it may appear that Locke went some way towards freeing women from traditional patriarchal subjection. He stresses that a mother exercises authority over her children as much as a father. He suggests that a wife can own property in her own right and even, well ahead of his time, envisages the possibility of divorce. In his treatment of the general patterns of marriage relationships, however, Locke is emphatic that wives should be subject. We know this, he declares, because 'generally the laws of mankind and customs of nations have ordered it so and there is, I grant, a foundation in nature for it'. The foundation to which he refers is that the will of the husband prevails in nature because he is 'the abler and stronger'.[38] Locke's assumption was that in the natural state, before the political contract which is the origin of the state was agreed upon by men, marriage and the family had already existed and men and women were already differentiated in that only men naturally had the characteristics of free and equal beings. Patriarchy, in other words, was still the order of creation, or, in Locke's terminology, the order of nature: the structure of conjugal relations proved it to be so. This puts the marriage contract in the forefront of the argument. On the one hand, according to Locke, women are naturally subject to men; on the other they are expected to enter a marriage contract which secures their subordination. This is where the full theoretical significance of the separation of what Locke calls paternal power from political power becomes apparent. For it was during the genesis of civil society that the sphere of natural subjection was separated out as non-political. Thus, as Carole Pateman argues, sex right or conjugal right, the original political right, becomes completely hidden:

> The concealment was so beautifully executed that contemporary politi-
> cal theorists and activists can forget the private sphere also contains –
> and has its genesis in – a contractual relationship between two adults.
> They have found nothing surprising in the fact that, in modern patri-
> archy, women, unlike sons, never emerge from their 'nonage' and the
> 'protection' of men.[39]

Exploring the issue more deeply, we find that 'the original political right is a man's right to have sexual access to a woman's body so that he could become a father'.[40] Yet Pateman notes that it is very hard actually to discern the sexual contract because it is displaced on to the marriage

38. C. Pateman, *The Sexual Contract* (Oxford, 1988), pp. 52–3.
39. Pateman, *Sexual Contract*, pp. 54, 93–4.
40. Pateman, *Sexual Contract*, p. 95.

contract. Marriage and family life are seen as somehow part of the natural condition. This is the myth that provides the missing half of Locke's story. It is not a story of a sexual contract and a social contract creating two spheres. In a more complex manner, the two spheres of civil society are, as Pateman puts it 'both separate and interwoven'. That women are subject to men in both the private and public spheres is the conclusion that emerges: 'men's patriarchal right is the major structural support binding the two spheres into a social whole'.[41] As we shall see in chapter 19, eighteenth-century prescriptive writers could confidently portray conjugal relations as part of a natural sexual division of labour and structure of female subordination. The transition from the world of Filmer's political theory to that of Locke thus summarises the general drift of the changes in thinking and knowledge that underlay changing attitudes with regard to early modern English gender. The secularisation of gender is central to all these changes: an ideology of ancient scriptural patriarchy is being gradually displaced, between 1660 and 1800, by one of modern secular patriarchy.

The rest of this book is concerned with how this new patriarchy emerged and took root. It may be helpful to explain at this stage why we shall attempt to unravel this highly complex process in the sequence provided by the remaining chapters of the book. Chapter 15 begins the exploration of an early modern masculinity that was essentially artificial and had to be learnt if men were going to act their parts effectively as the subordinators of women. This is a masculinity distinct from, though obviously based upon, the raw manhood which was outlined above in chapter 5. It was not in itself what caused a change in ideology. The major steps towards its inculcation through the grammar school system had in any case occurred before 1660. But in due course, developed and refined, this particularly English form of masculinity provided the power-house of modern patriarchy. Elaborated, it became above all a social training: breaking with motherly apron-strings, schooling and further education at university and sometimes abroad were the key elements. Thus chapter 15 sets the scene for the further discussion in chapter 16 of upper- and middle-class masculinity as a form of gender construction in England between 1660 and 1800.

In chapters 17 to 19 we turn to women, starting with material on their religious experience in the seventeenth century. There is clear chronological overlap here between the old patriarchy upon which our analysis has focused so far and the new one which was arriving. But chapter 17 is placed at this point deliberately because examples of exceptional female spiritual lives provide our first systematic entry to the more positive image of woman, signalling the end of open and general misogyny, which characterises modern patriarchy. The stories of such women were drawn

41. Pateman, *Sexual Contract*, pp. 113–15.

upon, we shall see, with specific didactic intent. Chapter 18 traces the reaction against the intellectual training of girls after 1600 and the emergence during the century of the first girls' finishing schools. While the schools are important in what they tell us about the fashioning of feminine graces and behaviour, their popularity from around the 1620s should not mislead us into missing the striking contrast between the social nature of boys education and the much more individual and personal upbringing of girls to fit them for a domestic role. With women as with men, there is no neat and schematic pattern into which we can mesh the changes in knowledge and thinking that have been described in this chapter and the gradual elaboration of systems of gender construction between 1660 and 1800. But chapter 19, which relates girls' schooling and training at home to the construction of femininity over the long period from the reign of Elizabeth to 1800, argues that prescription and practice in this case show continuity and did move in some kind of harmony. Even if the account in the chapters which follow sometimes appears static, the intention from this point in the book is to trace change. We are concerned with the process through which, by halting steps, men's dilemmas were solved and modern patriarchy, a new system of gender relations, began to be created. If men led the way in all this, women also participated vigorously in providing the ideology for this new patriarchy for, much more than the previous model had done, its requirements told them something positive about themselves. In modern patriarchy women have at least been offered a deal that they can accept or reject, whereas previously their subordination was based upon misogynistic assumptions about them that were entirely negative.

15. Educating Boys

BOYHOOD PROPER BEGAN with the ceremony of the first pair of breeches, usually in the seventeenth century at around six years old.[1] Henry Slingsby was self-conscious about jumping the gun when his wife persuaded him to order a suit of clothes – breeches and doublet – for his son Thomas in 1641: the boy was still only five, he noted in his diary, 'but that his mother had a desire to see him in them, how proper a man he would be'. Anne North's account of the breeching of her grandson Frank in 1639 shows how seriously the event was taken:

> You cannot believe the great concern that was in the whole family here last Wednesday, it being the day the tailor was to help dress little Frank in his breeches. . . . Never had any bride that was to be dressed upon her wedding night more hands about her. . . . When he was quite dressed he acted his part as well as any of them.[2]

The act was symbolic of the first step on the road to manhood, a road that took boys from gentry families away from the care and cosseting of their mothers into the moulding hands of tutors and schoolmasters. These boys were usually accountable more to fathers than mothers, fathers intent upon ensuring that sons, and especially heirs, learnt fully their gender role and destiny. The Marquis of Halifax was doing no more than echo conventional wisdom when he declared in his advice to a daughter that 'the first part of our life is a good deal subjected to you in the nursery, where you reign without competition'.[3] Because there were doubts and worries about the permissiveness and fondness of mothers it was seen as necessary that before too long their reign be decisively terminated. One of the reasons that most gentry opted for early schooling was that this

1. John Josselin, for example, A. Macfarlane, *The Family Life of Ralph Josselin* (Cambridge, 1970), pp. 90–91.
2. L.A. Pollock, *A Lasting Relationship: Parents and their Children over Three Centuries* (London, 1987), pp. 81–2.
3. Cited in P. Crawford, 'The Sucking Child: Adult Attitudes to Child Care in the First Year of Life in the Seventeenth Century', *Continuity and Change* 1 (1986), p. 42.

effect was achieved more easily this way than by bringing in tutors, who might find it difficult to get boys tied to the apron strings entirely to themselves.

The substance as well as the nature and framework of boys' education in the upper and middling ranks was ineluctably gendered, even if some girls also went to school. Essentially his education was academic, hers was not. Claver Morris's references to the education of his son and daughter in the late seventeenth century provide illustration of the point. Betty went to school from seven to thirteen, learning first violin and singing lessons and later writing, French, dancing and violin. William by contrast was at grammar school from eight to eighteen, first by the day and then, from thirteen, as a boarder. In his teens his father paid for extra tuition that he received outside the classical curriculum in writing, arithmetic and drawing.[4] Some fathers insisted upon academic work in advance of breeching. Henry Slingsby made this record in his diary:

> I also committed my son Thomas into the charge and tuition of Mr Cheney whom I intend shall be his schoolmaster and now he doth begin to teach him his primer; I intend he shall begin to spell, and read Latin together with his English, and to learn to speak it more by practice of speaking than by rule; he could the last year, before he was four years old, tell the Latin words for the parts of his body and of his clothes.

Choosing the right schoolmaster was seen by many as a matter of great import. Sydney Smith, writing just after 1800, enquired of a friend about a possible school for his twelve-year-old son Douglas. He had heard good reports of Mr Pillar: 'can they', he asked, 'during the last two years of their stay construe . . . any of the plays of Sophocles and Euripides? Can they construe Homer, Herodotus and the narrative part of Thucydides?'[5]

Their schooling and further education at university, the Inns of Court and through the Grand Tour, was the foundation of the gentry's patriarchal command of English society. The opportunities for boys to go to school increased enormously between 1500 and 1800. At the same time there were important developments and changes in the curriculum and in policies and attitudes towards school discipline which bear upon our investigation of gender. A good deal of research has been published on these topics, but its implications have not been considered in relation to how schooling contributed to the formation of manhood or the establishment of codes of masculine behaviour.

Local educational provision was already being improved by the founding of new elementary and grammar schools before protestantism gave the process an enormous boost in the middle of the sixteenth century. This brought a change in the regimes which founding statutes

---

4. L.A. Pollock, *Forgotten Children: Parent–Child Relations from 1500 to 1900* (Cambridge, 1983), pp. 242–3.
5. Pollock, *Lasting Relationship*, pp. 223, 238.

26. Maria Thynne of Longleat, Wiltshire, *c.* 1587–1611.

27. *(left)* Lady Mary Verney, aged twenty-four (*c*. 1640). By Anthony Van Dyck.

28. Lady Brilliana Harley, *c*. 1625, aged twenty-five.

29. *(right)* Susanna Perwick, died 1661, aged twenty-four. Frontispiece from J. Batchiler, *The Virgin's Pattern*.

30. Samuel Pepys, 1666, aged thirty-three by John Hayls. In his hand is the manuscript of his song *Beauty Retive*.

Her's all that's left. Reader, untimely Death
Hath Snatcht the rest: hee needs would stop the breath
Of this our sweet harmonious Queene of loue
And by her lifeles picture plainly proue
Nor Goodnes, Beauty, Breeding, finest parts
Where sin is found can Shend from his feirce darts
But what th' Effigies wants, the Booke will tell
Her Inward Splendors, looke and View them well.

Chapbook tales

The Famous History
of G v y Earle of *Warwicke*.
By SAMVEL ROWLANDS.

Printed at London by *Elizabeth All-de.* 1607.

33. *(left)* Title-page from Samuel Rowlands, *The Famous History of Guy Earle of Warwick* (1632).

34. Title-page from *The Life and Death of the Famous Champion of England St George* (c. 1685).

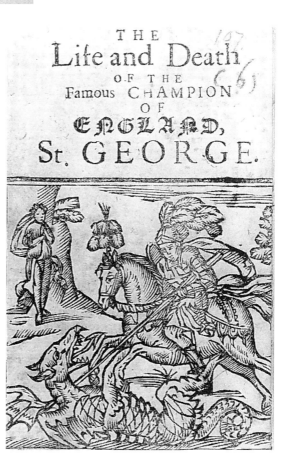

THE
Life and Death
OF THE
Famous CHAMPION
OF
ENGLAND,
St. GEORGE.

35. Fanny Hill beats Mr Barville. From John Cleland, *Memoirs of a Woman of Pleasure* (1766 edn).

36. The mistress of the household beats a servant girl. From the *Newgate Chronicle*.

37. An early eighteenth-century flagellant brothel. Frontispiece from J. H. Meibom, *De flagrorum Usu in Re Medica Venerea et Lumborum Renumque Officio* (1718 edn, translated from the Latin).

38. *Robert Gwillym of Atherton and his Family* (*c.* 1749) by Arthur Devis. The family group includes Robert's heir, Robert Vernon, and his sisters Jane and Elizabeth. The youngest child William is on his mother, Elizabeth's, lap.

39. *George Rogers with his Wife, Margaret, and Sister Margaret Rogers* (*c.* 1750) by Francis Hayman.

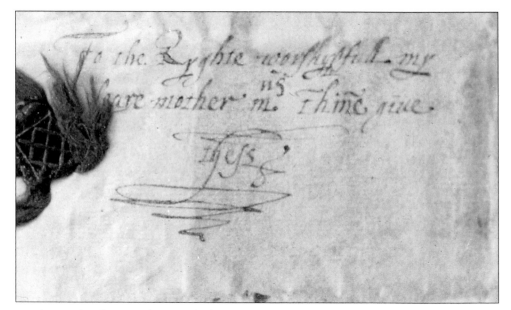

40. Letter written by Maria Thynne, with a lock of hair in the seal, to her mother, Joan Thynne, 15 September 1601.

established. William Fettiplace's free school attached to a chantry at Childrey in Berkshire in 1526 was run by a master who, instructing his pupils in English, was to 'teach the children the alphabet, the Lord's Prayer, the Salutation of the Angel and the Apostles creed . . . the fourteen articles of the faith, the ten commandments, the Seven Deadly Sins, the seven sacraments of the church'. The new grammar schools, which burgeoned across the country between 1560 and 1660, were quickly confined to boys and their curriculum was based firmly on the classics. These schools were founded and endowed by successful merchants and gentry in numerous market towns. Corporations often took an initiative and they were much involved in control, management and the appointment of schoolmasters. The impetus for all this activity came from a mixture of local pride, evangelising zeal and concern for good order. The new grammar schools were decisively religious foundations: statutes insisted upon daily prayers and often upon attendance of the scholars at church under the eye of the master. The issue of regular church attendance was sometimes, at Gloucester in 1612 and Oxford in 1619 for example, followed up in diocesan visitation articles which often placed stress upon schoolmasters' duties in catechising their pupils.[6] Because many of these schools were open free to children of the town and neighbouring villages, they usually attracted a mixed social clientele. They were everywhere at the same time strongly patronised by the gentry, who were quite prepared for their boys to lodge in the town – the 'tabling out' system as it was called – or even board as was possible in some cases within the school. Certain schools with a high reputation, like those at Repton and Shrewsbury, grew rapidly, attracting boys of gentry families from some distance away.[7]

In the long run the particular conditions laid down in the foundation statutes of the Elizabethan and early Stuart grammar schools proved a straightjacket for, following the Restoration, there was a sharp reaction against the classical curriculum. It was dry, arid and unrealistic for most country boys and in no satisfactory way prepared them for earning a living. Thus, between 1660 and 1800, the number of schools which offered an exclusively classical curriculum contracted. In the new schools set up in this period the traditional stress on Latin and Greek was normally combined with English and began to include other subjects in

6. A.J. Fletcher, 'The Expansion of Education in Berkshire and Oxfordshire 1500–1700', *British Journal of Educational Studies*, XV (1967), pp. 51–9. For examples of statutes requiring church attendance see F. Watson, *The English Grammar Schools to 1600* (London, 1968), pp. 45–9; K. Fincham, *Visitation Articles and Injunctions of the Early Stuart Church* (Church of England Record Society, I, 1994), pp. 104, 192 and index sub 'catechising'.
7. R. O'Day, *Education and Society: 1500–1800: The Social Foundations of Education in Early Modern Britain* (London, 1982), pp. 27–38; for examples of boarding arrangements see I.K. Ben-Amos, *Adolescence and Youth in Early Modern England* (London and New Haven, 1994), pp. 54–5, 258.

the curriculum.[8] In Cheshire, for example, new foundations at Audlem, Frodsham, Mottram-in-Longdendale and Sandbach made provision for instruction in English. The founder of Macclesfield school, Sir John Percival, directed that gentlemen's sons and other good men's children from the district 'might be taught grammar', but in the middle of the eighteenth century the governors of his school secured an act of parliament which specified important curriculum changes. This act gave them scope to organise the teaching of 'writing, arithmetic, geography, navigation, mathematics, the modern languages and other such branches of literature and education as shall from time to time be proper and necessary'. By the end of the century, some French was being taught to those not intended for higher education in place of Greek. We find the subjects introduced at Macclesfield appearing in various combinations in the curricula of a number of other Cheshire schools before 1800. While in the old free grammar schools there was no problem about using endowments to continue teaching the classics at no cost to parents, the costs involved in the teaching of the modern subjects had to be covered. For this reason the grammar schools were moving away from being places that catered to a broad social range without payment of fees. There was a very strong market for their facilities, however, among those of the middling and professional ranks who were sufficiently wealthy to give their sons a good start in the world. Thus the grammar schools, after flourishing for decades in a single mould, were becoming during the eighteenth century very much more diversified institutions in terms of their curriculum.[9]

So what, more precisely, can we say about the connection between a boy's experience of schooling and his gender training? The grammar school was formative for a large number of boys, lifting them from the home into a future male world of leisured authority or of respected skilled work. It was at the same time an obvious and apparently promising instrument of social control and discipline. The classical curriculum, enforced by the coercion of the birch rod, offered solid and mono- tonous learning, well designed to check youthful high spirits. 'The prevailing grammar school ethic', suggests Keith Thomas, 'was one of instinctual renunciation.' Boys learnt self-control through long hours of study which it was not pretended would have intrinsic interest for them.[10] They did so under rules which were intended to inculcate

---

8. O'Day, *Education and Society*, pp. 196–216; W.A.L. Vincent, *The Grammar Schools: Their Continuing Tradition 1600–1714* (London, 1969), pp. 16–22; R.S. Tompson, *Classics or Charity? The Dilemma of the Eighteenth Century Grammar School* (Manchester, 1971), pp. 36–72.

9. D. Robson, *Some Aspects of Education in Cheshire in the Eighteenth Century* (Manchester, 1966), pp. 44–65; P. Langford, *A Polite and Commercial People: England 1727–83* (Oxford, 1989), pp. 79–88.

10. K.V. Thomas, *Rule and Misrule in the Schools of Early Modern England* (Univeristy of Reading, 1976), pp. 5–10.

decency, respect for others and good manners. An early seventeenth-century ballad *A Table of Good Nurture* details the precepts which masters were conventionally expected to assert: punctuality, care of basic school possessions like inkhorn, pen and book, neat attire, mild behaviour towards schoolfellows, quietness, obedience and steady application.[11] Given these repressive values, it is not surprising that, at least until the late seventeenth century, there was a ritual, widespread in its occurrence across the north and midlands, which was clearly intended to release cumulative tensions and hostility between master and boys. At 'barring-out' time schoolboys shut the schoolroom or schoolhouse against the master, often requesting suspension of punishment and an amnesty for misbehaviour. Keith Thomas has described barring-out as 'a stylised activity occurring regularly at a predetermined point of the school year and following accepted conventions'. Its essence was a reminder to the master of the limits of his authority: the ritual kept alive the possibility of the boys retaliating, yet it never directly challenged the social order.[12]

From the Elizabethan period to the Restoration it was normal for boys from gentry families to go through these grammar school routines alongside schoolfellows from the middling ranks and below. The most striking development of the period from 1660 to 1800 was the insistence of the upper gentry, while the grammar schools diversified their curriculum, on sticking to schools which preserved the classical regime, with its associated values of restraint on boyhood vigour and harsh discipline through corporal punishment. Boys at this social level were not of course being educated so they could enter a profession, trade or craft. They were being trained to rule, whether at Westminster or in their localities, as public men, landlords and squires. A pattern of class and gender training was thus deliberately entrenched which informed and forwarded Hanoverian and later Victorian masculinity. A select group of old grammar schools emerged as the public schools now monopolised by the governing elite. Thus seventy-two per cent of ministers of state between 1775 and 1800 were at either Eton or Winchester and eighty-three per cent of these ministers had attended one of a dozen or so famous endowed foundations. M.V. Wallbank has sought to establish how far this schooling of politicians was typical of their class by investigating a control sample of noblemen: it appears that more than eighty per cent of them were pupils at one of the same select group of schools.[13]

Walter Ong suggested many years ago that the study of Latin became a puberty rite intended to provide a painful initiation into exclusive adult

11. *Roxburghe*, II, 571–2.

12 Thomas, *Rule and Misrule*, pp. 21–33.

13. M.V. Wallbank, 'Eighteenth-Century Public Schools and the Education of the Governing Elite', *History of Education* 8 (1979), pp. 1–2.

society.[14] His argument can be extended, for it is evident that Latin, beaten into boys in country grammar schools or famous public schools, was the crucial foundation of a whole class and gender system that gradually provided a revised basis for English patriarchy. Latin, between 1600 and 1800, became firmly installed as the male elite's secret language, a language all of its own, a language that could be displayed as a mark of learning, of superiority, of class and gender difference at the dinner table, on the quarter sessions bench and in those final bastions of male privilege the Houses of Lords and Commons. *Paroemiologia Anglo-Latina*, published in 1639, lists the English and Latin versions of proverbs side by side so as to be 'most especially profitable for scholars for the attaining elegancy, sublimity and variety of the best expressions'. There are numerous entries under correction and discipline: 'birchen twigs break no ribs', 'an arse beating's but an arse heating', 'a spur and a whip for a dull horse', 'lack of looking to makes cobwebs grow in boys' tails'.[15] A remarkable anonymous poem, printed at Oxford in 1775 and dedicated to Charles Goring esquire, unveils the emotional basis of the particular form of English upper-class masculinity which Latin and the birch taken together had established. It is entitled simply *The Schoolboy* and it begins and ends with the freedom of boyhood – climbing fences, scaling apple trees, plunging in the 'limpid stream'. The unadulterated joys of boyhood, such as fantasies of triumph in heroic single combats 'to surpass Roman or Grecian chief', are described. The poem's substance is the oppressive and tyrannical power of the schoolmaster, the source of terror, guilt and shame. The description of a momentary loss of concentration, the summons, loosening the breeches, the 'impetuous fury' with which the birch descends 'imprinting horrid wounds . . . and convulsive pangs' is all obviously drawn from bitterly felt experience. The schoolboy longs for the holidays and a return to 'parent fondness', but when they come this cannot remove the memories and recurring fantasies of school whippings:

> For what can aught avail to soothe
> Such raging anguish; oft with sudden glaze
> Before my eyes in all its horror glares
> That well known form and oft I seem to hear
> The thundering scourge.[16]

The poem is a searing indictment of the brutality at the heart of the English public school system over the centuries from the Reformation to almost the present day. It provides insight into the dire emotional impact on males who have struggled with the abuse that such physical punishment represents or have suffered its crushing imprint on their

14. Thomas, *Rule and Misrule*, pp. 9–10.
15. J. Clarke, *Paroemiologia Anglo-Latina* (London, 1639), pp. 75–6, 93.
16. BL, 11630 e 2(7): *The Schoolboy.*

personalities. It tells us so much, illuminating as it does one of the darker sides of early modern English patriarchy[17] (plates 35 and 37).

The fierce inculcation of the classical curriculum was the core of an overall process of hardening, of teaching self-control and endurance as the basis of a particular sophisticated form of manhood. The social objective was to impose discipline on the emotions. Since this can counter to the spontaneity and sensitivity of boyhood it needed constant reinforcement to be achieved. In a letter to his son in Latin on the eve of his ninth birthday in 1741, Lord Chesterfield told him he would never write to him again as a 'little boy': 'you must now commence a different course of life, a different course of studies. No more levity in childish toys and playthings must be thrown aside and your mind directed to serious objects.'[18] Teaching boys Latin marked a crucial boundary between the private world of the family, in which the vernacular was used, and the external world of learning and public affairs to which only males had access and which upper-class males were expected to join. There is the cautionary tale of young Mrs Pilkington who, while helping Jonathan Swift sort some letters from Alexander Pope, came across an embarrassingly indecent Latin tag: ' "But Sir", said I, "here is a Latin sentence writ in italics which, I suppose, means something particular; will you be so kind as to explain it?" "No", replied he, smiling: "I will leave that for your husband to do." ' The convention by this time was dinner-time conversation with the ladies without mentioning the classics; Greek and Latin quotations, whether bawdy or otherwise, were in men's company only.[19]

Sir Daniel Fleming of Rydal in Westmoreland discharged the responsibility of seeing a large brood of sons into the world between the 1660s and 1701. At first content with sending his boys to the local grammar schools at Hawkshead and Kendal, he later pinned his hopes for them on the clergyman Posthumous Wharton, master of Sedbergh School, whose reputation in training boys for university was preeminent in north-west England over more than thirty years from 1674 to 1706. George, Richard, Roger, James and Fletcher Fleming all imbibed their Latin in turn from Wharton. In May 1691 Wharton urged Sir Daniel to insist upon constant diligence from Roger and James during a 'short vacation' for which he had assigned them an exercise and some specific reading. That October Roger was in serious trouble for playing football and fighting. In a frantic and terrified letter after Wharton had told him he was expelled, he pleaded with his father to have him home: 'as you find us deserving of

---

17. For this whole subject see I. Gibson, *The English Vice: Beating, Sex and Shame in Victorian England and After* (London, 1978).
18. Pollock, *Lasting Relationship*, p. 149.
19. Cited in V. Rumbold, *Women's Place in Pope's World* (Cambridge, 1989), pp. 6–7; F.A. Childs, 'Prescriptions for Manners in English Courtesy Literature 1690–1760 and their Social Implications', Oxford University DPhil thesis, 1984, p. 215.

punishing so punish us, pray pardon these lines since I am scarce capable of what I write.' The father of another boy involved visited Sir Daniel, at Wharton's request, with the full story of Roger's disobedience. He expected full support: a 'sharp letter' and the injunction to obey his master. Sir Daniel, troubled at his son's incurring such 'displeasure', persuaded Wharton to take Roger back by giving him a free hand to use his birch rod with whatever severity he thought necessary. Kept at their books and beaten harshly for displays of youthful high spirits, the Fleming boys experienced schooldays which must often have felt miserable. In August 1692 Roger was still finding it difficult to get back into Wharton's good books. In a resigned and somewhat pathetic letter, he explained that he was seeking to deny himself pleasures which had tempted him and to be dutiful: 'I am apt to think that the old grudge is not cold and again finding me more submissive than formerly makes him more severer than usual he hath been but I am resolved to endure whatever comes with patience.' The following September, with Roger now at Oxford and Fletcher the newcomer setting an example in assiduousness, it was James's turn to fall out with Wharton. He was the ringleader in making trips to town alehouses and was undoubtedly severely whipped for this. It was 'a fault I could never endure in my boys', wrote Wharton to Fleming, urging a 'sharp letter' to follow up his own disciplinary measures. James's letter home on 21 September hardly attempted to hide his feelings: 'the master hath been very hard upon us long, which makes our time redound much more to our disadvantage than anything of profit'. He asked for some pocket money but what he really longed for, he confessed pathetically, was 'the sight of the horses' on the road from Kendal. Christmas was 'so nigh', he pleaded on 21 November, could they not be sent to bring the two of them home on 1 December, when some others were leaving, even if school did not officially break up till the 7th of the month? There is no reason to think that Sir Daniel was an exceptionally exacting father. He simply took seriously the doctrines of training and renunciation as a basis for virtuous manhood which were at the core of this educational system.[20]

A conversation at the opening of Thomas Shadwell's play *The Virtuoso*, which was first performed in 1676, catches the flavour of the disillusion among old-fashioned gentry at that time about the decline of interest in classical schooling for young boys. 'Gentlemen', one opinion goes, 'care not what strain they get their sons nor how they breed 'em when they have got 'em.' 'Some are first instructed by ignorant young household pedants', comes the reply, 'who dare not whip the dunces, their pupils, for fear of their lady mothers. Then before they can construe and parse they are sent into France with sordid illiterate creatures called dried-nurses

20. J.R. Magrath, ed., *The Flemings at Oxford* (Oxford Historical Society, XLIV 1903), I, p. 559 (LXXIX, 1924), III, pp. 13, 37–8, 84–5, 139–40, 145–6.

or governors.'[21] There is some evidence that mothers disliked the harsh discipline to which their sons were subjected at school but there was of course little they could do about it.[22] It is very likely that their domestic presence was inhibiting to tutors wishing to use the rod. The issue touched upon in Shadwell's play is clearly the collapse of harsh discipline. Here is the age-old complaint that things are getting too soft for young boys. A review of some of the evidence we have about life at the eighteenth-century public school will show how the upper gentry sought to hold the line on this issue.

In the first place, at a school like Eton, the classical curriculum was still pursued in a thorough and demanding manner. Notes left by a master at the school between 1766 and 1771 suggest that boys spent about twenty-one hours a week on their Latin and Greek. There were regular extra lessons in such subjects as geography, algebra, French, drawing, dancing and fencing. Whereas these related to practical and social accomplishments required by the adult gentleman, work in classics was intended to develop rhetorical and histrionic skills together with linguistic adroitness.[23] The centrality of Latin remained common ground in upper gentry circles; it was seen as the foundation of the making of the rational man and a necessary mark of status. 'Latin I look upon as absolutely necessary for a gentleman,' wrote John Locke, though his commentary on how it was often taught shows how much this was a matter of dispute between traditionalists, who favoured whipping, and educationalists like Locke. His thinking about avoiding fear and treating children as individual human beings, it must be said, made little impact on either the fathers who patronised, or the masters who ran, the public schools.[24]

Boys were not just sent away to the public schools to suffer the drudgery of their Latin lessons. Locke was scathing about what these schools did to boys: 'it is preposterous to sacrifice his innocency to the attainment of confidence and some little skill of bustling for himself among others by his conversation with ill-bred and vicious boys'.[25] This was an acute comment on what public school life was seen to be about: the formation of class solidarity based upon competitive striving and rowdy and aggressive masculine pursuits. Lord Chesterfield advised his godson's father to send him to Winchester, declaring that 'it will teach him to shift for himself and bustle in the world and he will get a tolerable share of classical learning'. The stress put on competition as a basis for

21. T. Shadwell, *The Virtuoso* (1676), act I, scene I, 25–31.
22. E.g. Pollock, *Lasting Relationship*, pp. 193, 200.
23. Wallbank, 'Eighteenth-Century Public Schools', *History of Education* 8 (1979), pp. 11–16.
24. J.L. Axtell, ed., *The Educational Writings of John Locke* (Cambridge, 1969), p. 268. See also M.J.M. Ezell, 'John Locke's Images of Childhood', *Eighteenth Century Studies* 17 (1983–4), pp. 139–55.
25. Axtell, ed., *Educational Writings of John Locke*, pp. 166–7.

learning to be a proper man, so evident later in the Victorian public schools, is already evident in parental instructions to young boys in Hanoverian England. Lord Chesterfield made much of the point, writing in 1746 to his ten-year-old son Philip:

> Therefore I expect, from your truth and your honour, that you will do that, which, independently of your promise, your own interest and ambition ought to incline you to do; that is to excel in everything you undertake. When I was your age, I should have been ashamed if any boy of that age had learned his book better, or played at any play better than I did.

Reginald Heber instructed his son Richard in similar terms in 1783: 'I make no doubt you have many clever boys in your class and I doubt not you will feel and be incited by an honest emulation to keep pace with the best of them in running the race of honour and improvement in learning that is set before you.'[26] Edward Young, in a letter to the Duchess of Portland, noted that boarding education offered practice in 'emulation and early experience in the tempers and talents of others'. 'The first', he remarked, 'is the greatest spur to diligence and the last is an absolutely necessary qualification for making a figure in public life.' His grandmother, replying to news from the ten-year-old Marquis of Titchfield at Winchester, wrote that 'your keeping yourself so long captain of the second form is equally a pleasure to your gaining it so early'. The eight-year-old Charles Fox's father wrote to his brother approving of his son's attitude to combative learning: 'There is at present a great vying between Lord Stavordale and Charles. Your son intends, if possible, to recover the place he has lost as to making Latin, in which mine is got before him and mine is determined he shall not.' An Eton master described examinations as trials 'necessary to raise emulation in the boys' and prizes as 'a great help in encouraging diligence and ambition'.[27]

Teaching the sons of upper-class families to be men in the eighteenth-century public schools was seen as a process of eliminating childishness and working, against the grain of youthful indolence, to produce men with a particular style of body, mind and character, men able effectively to head the social and gender order. In a letter to Lord Herbert in 1696, Dr Thomas Knipe, master of Westminster School, described his difficulties in getting young Henry Herbert to buckle down to the school regime. 'Learning is to children', he reflected, 'as tobacco is to some people, it makes them sick at first.' Hitherto, he explained, Henry 'has been so much a child, that when he had been called from his play to his studies, he has stood in the yard crying and blubbering and roaring, as

26. Citations from Pollock, *Lasting Relationship*, pp. 210–11.
27. Citations from Wallbank, 'Eighteenth-Century Public Schools', *History of Education* 8 (1979), pp. 3–4.

your own servants have sometimes heard him, because he might not play longer.' 'If this infirmity of his leaves him', concluded Knipe with resolution, 'I don't doubt but, upon his continuance with me, to finish him.'[28]

Finishing is the key concept. In Dr Knipe's report the reference is to his own role in this process within the classroom. But what happened outside it, the peer group experience, was just as important to finishing. One of the best accounts of this aspect of upper-class gender training comes from John Aubrey's manuscript of thoughts on education which he composed during the 1670s. He recommended that boys should be 'bred carefully at home' till twelve and then sent 'to a public school to be top'd and finished'. He spelled out what he meant:

> It is now that he is entered to be of the world, to come from his innocent life, tender care, and indulgence of his parents, to be beaten by his school fellows, to be falsely accused, to be whipped by the master, to understand his tyranny. . . . 'Tis here he begins to understand the world, the misery, falseness and deceitfulness of it: 'tis here he begins to understand himself, that he finds others to be his equals and superiors in honour, estate, wit and strength.[29]

There was little attempt in the public schools as they developed between 1660 and 1800 to control and organise the boys' lives. Life at school, as Aubrey's account suggests, was learning the harshness of a newly competitive world of men through mixing with others of the same social background in the raw. George Chapman in his *Treatise on Education*, published in 1773, encouraged cockfighting as a means of inculcating bravery among schoolboys. The cock was a preeminent symbol of masculine fortitude and sexual prowess, praised for the courage and resolution with which he fought to the death, however badly wounded.[30] If the Duke of Wellington really did say that Waterloo was won on the playing fields of Eton this was what he meant. The playing fields there were simply the fields by the Thames where the boys fought each other. There were no organised games, there were simply rules about bounds and certain prohibitions such as on drinking and gambling, enforced by the master's regular flogging rituals. Then taking the birch like a man was part of learning to be a man.[31]

It was common ground that men should learn fortitude and courage. We have seen how significant this was in the gentry's honour code. John Locke argued that this should not be achieved by beating boys for their

28. Pollock, *Lasting Relationship*, p. 148.
29. J.E. Stephens, ed., *Aubrey on Education* (London, 1972), p. 60.
30. K.V. Thomas, *Man and the Natural World* (London, 1983), p. 183.
31. R. Ollard, *An English Education: A Perspective of Eton* (London, 1982), pp. 38–9.

faults but rather through gradually accustoming a boy to pain, by, for instance, 'good smart blows of a wand on his back' given in a loving context:

> The great art in this is to begin with what is but very little painful and to proceed by insensible degrees when you are playing ... when he can take a pride in such marks of his manliness and can prefer the reputation of being brave and stout to the avoiding a little pain or the shrinking under it; you need not despair in time and by the assistance of his growing reason to master his timorousness and mend the weakness of his constitution.[32]

This caring approach presented counsels of perfection which few eighteenth-century fathers can have followed with their sons in practice. Besides the social pressure was much too overwhelming in upper gentry circles to subject sons to the alternative rough initiation rites of learning about pain from the fights, scrapes and punishments of boarding school life. The mentality behind this educational system, a world away from that of John Locke's ideals, is well illustrated by parental reactions after the famous Eton rebellion of 1768, when 160 boys threw their books in the river and marched off to Maidenhead. George Grenville, heir to the Temple earldom, was one of those who fled the school on this occasion and he was returned to be flogged before being removed for good. Lord Ross and his brother, it is related, reaching their London home, were asked by their father, the Marquis of Granby, if they would like to visit the theatre that evening, the Marquis adding 'you shall go there tonight for your own pleasure and tomorrow shall return to Mr Foster and be flogged for mine'.[33]

'Fighting', as Richard Ollard puts it in his history of Eton, 'was both the great test of social acceptability and an approved form of physical recreation.' Thomas Grimston wrote home to his father from Harrow in 1772 as follows: 'I have been obliged to stay from school since Saturday evening last as I had a quarrel with one of the boys and we fought and I had the ill luck to be conquered, receiving many blows on the face; it swelled up very much and I have got two black eyes.... The boy I fought was bigger and stronger than I am.'[34] Within a few weeks of entering Eton at the age of seven, William Windham had been involved in three violent encounters. The level of violence tacitly accepted there was extraordinary. The *London Chronicle* of 1784 printed an account of a fight between two Eton boys in which one was killed and the other was seriously hurt. 'All the gentlemen of the school', it was recorded, attended the funeral, following a verdict of accidental death. Eton boys did not

32. Axtell, ed., *Educational Writings of John Locke*, pp. 220–5.
33. Ollard, *An English Education*, p. 37; Wallbank, 'Eighteenth-Century Public Schools', *History of Education* 8 (1979), p. 9.
34. Pollock, *Lasting Relationship*, p. 156.

only endlessly take on each other but they found victims outside the school as well. In 1768, for example, there was a major battle between the boys and the butchers at Windsor. When Horace Walpole was at Westminster, expeditions against the local bargemen were a popular pastime. Thus the peer group's displays of manliness within their own ranks spilled over into nasty demonstrations of superiority through physical hostility to outsiders. Six Westminster boys on one occasion appeared before the London magistrates for an assault on a man in Dean's Yard when 'they beat and wounded him in a most shocking manner' threatening 'to rip him up' if he would not kneel down and ask their pardon.[35]

It was not cheap sending boys to a school like Eton. Sir Thomas Temple listed ninety pounds in his schedule of annual costs about 1680 for boarding two sons there.[36] Hundreds of others like him from the nation's social elite accepted the financial outlay of sending their sons to learn male coolness and endurance in the training ground of the public school. They did it because they believed in it. 'Frederick is a shy, amiable, industrious boy, not wanting in abilities but a little cowed . . . by the superiority of his elder brother', wrote Frances Shelley in her diary, 'which I think a year at Eton will remove and the independence he will acquire there will be of use to him before he goes to sea.' Fathers as well as mothers often found the partings that were involved hard. Sylvester Douglas wrote of his ten-year-old son's display of the stiff upper lip: 'Fred went off with considerable emotion but he kept it under very well . . . though if he had perceived my agitation I doubt if he would have done quite so well. His poor mother . . . saw him leave Burton Street like a heroine.' John Gisborne confided to his diary similar emotions about his boy's departure at the age of nine: 'My dear Frederic is now on his road to school and for the first time in his life. When I reflect on the many hours which we have pleasantly spent together, I cannot refrain from tears at the loss of his company and his empty chair in my study touches me more sensibly than perhaps it ought to do.'[37] Sending boys away to school occasioned tension in some marriages. Lady Peregrina Chaytor wanted to spend time with her boys herself at Richmond when they were at school there. Her husband, imprisoned for debt in London, wrote with exasperation to her in Yorkshire: 'For God sake what do you intend to make of them? I was sent to Danby Wisk school at ten years old and I lived without the pap there and if you make them too fond of you they will be good for nothing . . . you must prepare and encourage them to part with one another for their advantage.' She compromised with the suggestion that Nanny Peacock be sent to lodgings

---

35. Ollard, *An English Education*, pp. 40–41; Wallbank, 'Eighteenth-Century Public Schools', *History of Education* 8 (1979), p. 7.
36. HEH, STTF, box 1.
37. Citations from Pollock, *Forgotten Children*, p. 246.

at Richmond with her boys 'for Harry has declared so much against Richmond unless he have Nanny with him'. Unless granted his wish, she feared they would 'make him too melancholy'.[38] The parental 'it never did me any harm' syndrome was already entrenched in English upper-class life. The gender imperative of moulding sons through a severe regime of schooling had taken a firm hold. The classic boyhood letters home requesting treats were already before 1800 reaching the manor houses of provincial England. John Verney, writing to his father at Claydon in 1723, was grateful for the gingerbread. He continued: 'I beg the favour of you, if it will not be troublesome, that you will desire my dear Mama to send me a little tea and sugar as also a pair of battledores and shuttlecocks.'[39]

The sons of the gentry flooded the universities of Oxford and Cambridge between Elizabeth's reign and the civil war, entering on average at about seventeen and demanding, through the newly established college tutorship system, an education which, while extending their classical studies, also broke out of the scholastic tradition and gave them an introduction to such subjects as history and geography.[40] The statutes laid down by founders of new colleges, such as Sir Walter Mildmay's at Emmanuel Cambridge, show how higher education was being seen in moral and religious terms as much as academic ones. Youths were to be kept busy and under strict supervision, learning 'all piety and good letters and especially holy writ'. The fellow on duty was directed to check students' chambers at night for late meetings and carousing, imposing a whipping or a fine on offenders according to their age.[41] The decline of corporal punishment at the universities during the seventeenth century may be connected with the change to a median age of entry by 1660 of eighteen rather than seventeen.[42] Documentation relating to college tutors who were conscientious with their students, like Joseph Mede at Cambridge in the 1620s, shows how much trouble they took to check behaviour, direct reading and organise a programme of work fitting for a young gentleman about to enter the world of rural society.[43] Mede's records show his lay students buying considerable numbers of books, although they had no intention of taking a degree and in this

38. S. Chaytor, 'Family Life in the Seventeenth Century: Sir William Chaytor 1639–1721', Durham University MA dissertation, 1992, pp. 24–5.
39. Pollock, Lasting Relationship, p. 144.
40. L. Stone, ed., The University in Society (Princeton, 1975), I, pp. 10–27.
41. F. Stubbings, ed., The Statutes of Sir Walter Mildmay for Emmanuel College (Cambridge, 1983), pp. 69–73.
42. Stone, University in Society, I, p. 31. See also K.V. Thomas, 'Age and Authority in Early Modern England', Proceedings of the British Academy LXII (1976), p. 220.
43. For contacts between tutors and the gentry parents of their charges see V.M.H. Morgan, 'Cambridge University and "The Country" 1560–1600', in Stone, ed., University in Society, I, pp. 226–31.

sense were under little pressure to keep up their studies.[44] It seems clear that it was the tutorial system, together with parental expectations, which made these young men stick to their books. Henry Hobart's letter to his father in 1574, though not specific about it, hints at its effectiveness: 'I can not but give you some account of myself after your great love and kindness to me in placing me here where I may learn my duty to God and you. I shall make it my business, as far as I am able, to be in some measure answerable to the charge you have been at in following my studies.'[45]

'His father means not to have him a scholar by profession', wrote Richard Holdsworth to William Sancroft, Master of Emmanuel College, in 1635, asking him to take care of the son of a friend, 'but only to be seasoned with the varnish of learning and piety which is remarkable in many under your government.'[46] This 'seasoning' had become, by the 1630s, a standard element in the formation of the manhood of the heirs to gentry estates. Two years later, Holdsworth, now ensconced himself as Master at Emmanuel, wrote a manuscript of Directions for a Student in the Universities establishing a list of assigned books prominently featuring works of history and geography. His advice, reiterating his view of the matter, was that they would be useful for such as attend 'only to get such learning as may serve for delight and ornament and such as the want whereof would speak a defect of breeding rather than scholarship'.[47]

The correspondence between Lady Katherine Paston and her son William in the 1620s, when he was at Cambridge, affords insights into the motives of a besotted mother in sparing her son from home, where, as she kept telling him, she would much rather have him. This was a special time for him, she urged on his arrival, 'to gain the truest good both for soul and body':

> for your ground is on the tilled earth, if you sow good seed you shall reap a plentiful and comfortable crop . . . I could wish that you would settle yourself to certain hours tasks every day you rise and those hold yourself to without any weariness . . . you must remember that the sons of Adam were born to dig and delve even in the sweat of our brows, likewise wisdom is not found but is an hidden treasure which must be digged for after much search to find it out. This I thought to put thee in mind of verily believing thou will do this for my sake but more chiefly for thine own, that I may receive thee from that place adorned both with divine and human learning to my soul's comfort, for nothing in this life can be so cordial to me as shall be thy virtuous and civil behaviour.

44. J. Looney, 'Undergraduate Education at Early Stuart Cambridge', *History of Education* 10 (1981), pp. 11–19.
45. Folger Library, Washington DC, Hobart MS Xd 490(16).
46. O'Day, *Education and Society*, p. 125.
47. *History of Education* 10 (1981), p. 19.

Lady Katherine's precepts to William, mixed with constant urging to follow the advice of his tutor, always blended moral, social and academic aspects of his training. 'Take heed to yourself good child', she wrote on 11 June 1624, 'that I may hear a good report of your civil and kind behaviour towards all but chiefly have an especial care to fear and serve God.' When he came home, she declared a few weeks later, she hoped to receive him to her 'furnished with graces as a bee comes laden to her hive even with the best abroad'. 'I hold thee better there a thousand times', she confessed on 6 May 1625 sending the news from home, 'until thy mind be furnished with those liberal sciences which that nursery affordeth to the studious and best minds.' Lady Katherine fretted about William's health and sent him liquorice, or a turkey pie pasty of quinces and marmalade, yet she never wavered from her conviction that Corpus Christi College was for the time where her boy had to be. Her high-flown and idealistic account of the objectives of a Cambridge education provides a rounded ideal of manhood which mixed deep religious sincerity with the benefits of a trained rational mind.[48]

It was predictable that the zealous Sir Robert Harley might choose Magdalen Hall at Oxford, which had a high reputation in the 1630s in godly circles, for his son Ned. We find him getting advice about two potential tutors, both reported as 'honest men and good tutors as the times go'. He placed his son with Edward Perkins, a 'very ready and well study'd divine', insisting that he should not let Ned travel anywhere in the vacations unless in his company. The relationship clearly worked well, for his mother informed him in November 1638 of her happiness about Perkins's good testimony and 'that you esteem him so highly'. Lady Brilliana was just as besotted as Lady Katherine, bombarding her son with advice about his spiritual and physical health. The Herefordshire carrier brought him liquorice for colds and eye water for sore eyes as well as presents of turkey and pigeon pies, apples and violet cakes. When Sir Robert wanted Ned to wear plain clothes, she went along with this at first but was easily persuaded to support her son when, with the approval of his tutor, he sought to purchase a more handsome and dashing wardrobe. In a memorandum written in 1650, looking back on his time at Oxford, Ned expressed his gratitude to God for ensuring that 'I was not given up to the evils of that place'.[49]

Sir Daniel Fleming, who we have already encountered as a parent anxious for his boys to be driven on in their learning at school, was more down to earth, more concerned simply about finding a living for his numerous sons than Lady Katherine or Lady Brilliana. Yet he was equally

48. R. Hughey, ed., *The Correspondence of Lady Katherine Paston 1603–1627* (Norfolk Record Society, XIV, 1941), pp. 65, 70–4, 77–103.

49. J. Eales, *Puritans and Roundheads: The Harleys of Brampton Bryan and the Outbreak of the English Civil War* (Cambridge, 1990), pp. 26–8; J.T. Cliffe, *The Puritan Gentry* (London, 1984), pp. 88–90.

committed to their learning how to fulfil standard notions of male honour. Sir Daniel's own time at Queen's College Oxford, where he subsequently sent his sons, made a great impression on him. He had received every encouragement from his parents at a time when, as royalists in the early 1650s, they had considerable financial problems. 'Dear son', wrote his mother on 26 January 1651, 'so long ever as I hear your doing well it is my daily comfort and you may assure yourself there shall be nothing wanting in me to perform the part of a loving mother.' His father wrote warmly in May 1651 in view of the good reports he had heard from Daniel's tutor. Though his own troubles increased daily, he promised constant support 'so long as you deserve well in applying yourself to your studies . . . and in constant endeavouring your own improvement and good'. He would 'with my utmost powers assist you in pursuance of your accomplishments to make you a man and indeed a gentleman'. Sir Daniel Fleming learnt from his parents the rigorous demands which he in turn was to place on four of his sons, Henry, George, Roger and James, all of whom followed him to Queen's College between 1678 and 1694. A spell at Oxford was the time, he came to believe and as his father had put it to him, 'to lay the foundation of all accomplishments hereafter'.[50]

Although he was far away in the Lake District, Sir Daniel Fleming kept his sons on a tight rein at Oxford, demanding regular reports of progress both from them and from their tutors, lists of books purchased and accounts of money spent. A series of Kendal carriers were intermediaries who conveyed letters and cash, the latter always deficient in quantity so far as the young men were concerned. Excessive expenditure was for Sir Daniel a matter of constant concern. Henry and George were both studious. Henry reported regularly on the work his tutor planned for him in logic and ethics. In due course he moved on to geography, requesting from his father 'some geography books with maps in if you have any that you can spare', and to physics. George expressed an inclination to the law, agreed with deference to his father's wish that he should study divinity as his brother Henry had done, and then found himself unable to follow this through. This distressed Sir Daniel, who honestly believed that sons of his who had the application and ability to succeed were well fitted to the church: 'I own it was and yet is my opinion that the study of divinity is the most honourable and that it would in all probability prove the best for your soul, body and estate.'[51]

The correspondence between Sir Daniel and his younger sons Roger and James became steadily more fraught, since neither ever became a serious scholar. This makes it all the more interesting for what it reveals about a north-country gentleman's aspirations in terms of his children's

50. Magrath, ed., *Flemings at Oxford*, I, pp. 13–14, 17–18.
51. Magrath, ed., *Flemings at Oxford*, I, pp. 262, 304, 318, 320, II, pp. 252, 257, 262, 267, 270–71, 288–9, 296, III, pp. 93, 99, 102–3.

breeding. Sir Daniel was shocked when he heard that his training at Sedbergh had not in fact adequately prepared Roger for university work and that his tutor thought him almost a stranger to Latin and Greek. Rather than withdraw Roger, which would not 'be for your credit', he urged him to supply through his character and commitment what he lacked in intellectual capacities. He should, Roger was advised in April 1693, get 'what university learning you can possibly': 'Who knows but that your religious, studious and civil deportment may help you in time to some preferment. . . . Be careful that you do not squander away your time having lost too much thereof already. . . . Difficult things may most of them be overcome by patience and industry.' Roger was full of protestations of good intentions. 'If you shall continue to be civil, sober and studious', Sir Daniel declared in June 1693, emphasising demeanour rather than accomplishment, 'you may be assured that good men will have a respect for you and that it will be for your honour and profit.' In October, in response to Roger's positive accounts about Oxford life, he reiterated the importance of this 'sober and civil' carriage. It was not until the following spring that Roger began overspending. This seems to have been closely connected with the arrival of his brother James who, from the start, saw Oxford life in terms of having a good time. By November 1694, Sir Daniel was telling George, who, as a respectable clergyman back in Oxford was supposed to be overseeing his rapscallion brothers, that he would pay no more alehouse accounts for ale, brandy, pipes or tobacco. Roger was called home in June 1695, but James managed to play his father along for some time with carefully phrased reports of his academic progress. It helped him that he managed to keep on the right side of his tutor, who even agreed to deal with alehouse arrears yet who Sir Daniel depended upon for accurate information about James's deportment. In February 1695 his father was still talking about his son James's 'honour and profit' in studying as his tutor directed, whereas two letters from James to Roger back in Westmoreland that summer indicate a pattern of living which had clearly been habitual well before Roger went home.[52]

The Fleming boys certainly learnt about manhood at Oxford but the unruly, irresponsible and extravagant way of living they adopted was poles apart from the ideal of civilised, upright and learned manhood that their father intended they should be absorbing. If Oxford was a crucible of gender indoctrination it was one in which orthodox patterns of what were expected of an aspiring country gentleman were contested by the young men themselves. James's letters of 16 July and 3 August 1695 reveal a culture of womanising, drink and pleasure. There were races on Port Meadow, 'Eastgate Jinny' was being held responsible for spreading

52. Magrath, ed., *Flemings at Oxford*, III, pp. 116–19, 122, 124, 128, 140, 169, 172–3, 179.

syphilis, a coffeehouse-keeper had been 'brought in bed' of a child. Roger and James – scallywags, as we have seen, at school where they suffered grievously for it – were letting off their repressed spirits in Oxford for just as long as they could keep parental and tutorial displeasure at bay.[53] These two young men were probably near the end of the spectrum which ran from deeply conscientious and dedicated study to indolence and pleasure. There is considerable debate about the general standards of discipline and dedication to academic study at Oxford and Cambridge in this period.[54] Men like Sir Daniel Fleming who poured money into sons' pockets, it is quite clear, took a risk. The important point for our purpose is that, one way or another, the experience of university was deeply formative in gender terms.

It is well established that many sons of gentry attended the universities, that they spent considerable periods of the year in residence, that they bought books as well as socialised and that in varying degrees they were under the effective eye of their tutors. John and Richard Newdigate's account book suggests, says its editor, that the intellectual intentions of these two Warwickshire youths 'should not be dismissed lightly'. Purchase, upon arrival at Oxford in 1618, of works by Horace, Juvenal, Pliny and Ovid hints at a serious attempt to prepare for matriculation. Later entries in the accounts mention both classical authors like Quintillian, Livy and Seneca and authors of more general interest like Mercator, Camden and Jewel. Many such gentry went on to spend a period at one of the Inns of Court. Their purpose in most cases was not serious attendance at law school but the completion of a liberal education, becoming, as Clement Ellis put it in 1661, 'somewhat more a gentleman than before'.[55] There was no tutorial system at the Inns and no attempt to control personal lives or extramural behaviour. All the temptations and vices of the capital were laid out before young men with money in their purses. It was difficult, in any case, to adapt from the classical curriculum to the study of a subject which could be equally frustrating and tedious if in a different way. The areas of the law which would be most relevant for a country gentleman, magisterial procedure and manorial court business, were in any case not much studied or taught at the Inns. It is clear from the records of young men's activities that serious study was a low priority during their time in London. Justinian Pagitt's diversions in the 1630s included preparation for a masque, dancing school, gaming, playing the lute and attending the Lord Mayor's show. The notes kept by John Greene of his activities each day during 1635 include nothing about legal studies except a single reference to drinking wine at a moot, but he found

53. Magrath, ed., *Flemings at Oxford*, III, pp. 217–21, 228–34.
54. J. McConica, ed., *The History of the University of Oxford*, III: *The Collegiate University* (Oxford, 1986); for a summary see O'Day, *Education and Society*, pp. 106–31.
55. Cited in W.R. Prest, *The Inns of Court under Elizabeth I and the Early Stuarts 1590–1640* (London, 1972), p. 137.

time for regular playgoing, dancing and tennis as well as a trip to Greenwich.[56] The Newdigate account book shows John and Richard pursuing a similar pattern of life: their trips on the river took them to London Bridge, Lambeth and Deptford where a sister was at one of the fashionable ladies academies; they dined out with friends and relatives; they enjoyed the races as well as the theatres.[57]

In the later seventeenth and eighteenth centuries Oxford and Cambridge were no longer so generally seen as offering a suitable general education for young gentlemen. Charges of idleness and debauchery were regularly made against both universities. Yet about sixty per cent of peers born in the mid-eighteenth century went there compared with only thirty-five per cent of those born in the years before 1680. Social contacts became the prime consideration as certain colleges at Oxford and Cambridge acquired an increasingly aristocratic complexion. 'To make any acquaintance that may be useful in future life', declared one young man at Christchurch in 1733, was 'the only reason I am sent to this college.'[58] When Charles Weston, the son of a senior government official, arrived there in 1748, his first letter home described the preliminaries for matriculation and his immediate experiences. A commoner in hall had laughed at something he did 'that I knew was not wrong' and had attempted unsuccessfully 'to set the table in a laugh likewise'. John Black, who had escorted young Weston to Oxford, reported that his tutor had arranged an initial meeting with three or four gentlemen students whom he judged 'most proper for his acquaintance'. 'We hold well here', concluded Charles Weston, 'pray give my duty to my mama and proper respect to all.'[59] Richard Cumberland's account to his brother George of a day in his life at Magdalene College, Cambridge in 1772 gives the impression of a fairly relaxed routine. The bedmaker lit the fire and put on the kettle at seven; for breakfast, following chapel, 'we send to the butler for whatever we choose'; Mr Deighton's lecture on Euclid at nine was followed by one from Mr Purkis for about an hour on 'morality'. The afternoon, when the students often drank wine in each other's rooms, would include a walk and some 'preparation for lectures the next day'. 'We generally form parties for tea, either among ourselves, or from other colleges.'[60] Impressionistic as this kind of evidence is, the constant refrain of sociability is inescapable. Higher education, like the experience of public school, was above all about social connection, about

56. Prest, *Inns of Court*, pp. 137–73.
57. V. Larminie, ed., 'The undergraduate Account Book of John and Richard Newdigate', *Camden Misellany* XXX (Camden Society, 39, 1990), pp. 152, 157–9.
58. J. Cannon, *Aristocratic Century* (Cambridge, 1984), p. 47; citation from Stone, *University in Society* I, p. 53.
59. J.M. Black, 'Going up to Oxford: Charles Weston's Account in 1748', *Oxoniensia*, LIV (1989), pp. 414–15.
60. Pollock, *Lasting Relationship*, p. 137.

learning to be at ease in the peer group, learning its codes of masculinity and manners.

The protracted trip to Europe, usually France and Italy, which heirs to aristocratic and large gentry estates usually took conveniently filled the gap before settling down to marriage and landlord responsibilities. The Grand Tour was a crucial formative aspect of English upper-class manhood which in some cases in the eighteenth century replaced attendance at university and otherwise followed afterwards. But why were many boys from the highest social ranks sent off abroad for as long as two to three years in their early or mid teens at this time, often before they were old enough to benefit from the experience? We have seen that concern about mothers spoiling their boys was deeply rooted. The theme continues to emerge strongly among the essayists and educators of the eighteenth century. Locke warned that boys who were 'bred like fondlings at home' could develop a 'sheepish softness'. Jonathan Swift was scathing about mothers who coddled and expected tutors to do the same. There was said to be persistent tension between mothers and tutors. James Fordyce in the 1770s spoke of mothers who 'perverted and ruined' the character of their boys by indulgence in the nursery. The nub of the issue and the rationale of the Grand Tour, argues Michelle Cohen, was that boys had to be got away from their mothers because under their influence and authority, it was believed, they could not achieve masculinity. Travel involved what Richard Lassels in his account in 1870 of *The Voyage of Italy* called 'wholesome hardship'. It brought pleasure and profit, declared François Misson in *A New Voyage to Italy* in 1697, 'but 'tis no less certain that these advantages cannot be obtained without pain'.[61] The hazards of travel – robbery, dangers to health and life – tested masculine spirit and endurance. Cash could soften the hardships. 'Take good care at all time with whom you lie in bed', John Temple was advised in the early seventeenth century, 'and that you be sure the sheets be clean and sweet; let them . . . be well aired with a good fire.'[62] Yet, taken overall, the point of the Grand Tour was not simply becoming a gentleman but becoming a man.

At another level the Grand Tour was an exercise in social finishing which included acquisition of knowledge and artistic taste, learning accomplishments which provided polish and absorbing a political stance which put English institutions and customs in a favourable perspective by comparing them with those of other states. The key notions were improvement and breeding. The chance of acquiring both these things, as the Earl of Strafford advised his son William in 1636, should not on any account be lost by idleness or dissipation:

61. Citations from M.Cohen, 'The Grand Tour: Constructing the English Gentleman in Eighteenth-Century France', *History of Education* 21 (1992), pp. 249–50.
62. HEH, STT 759.

If you lose the opportunity of learning these noble qualities which grace and become a gentleman, in the whole course of your life, now in your youth, you shall hardly recover a leisure to learn them after, both in regard you will be less apt, but also that other affairs of the world will leave you less spare time than must of necessity be then employed in the gaining of them.[63]

The cost of these tours was prodigious, but then the very fact that these young men could afford to pay their way was a constant reminder to them of their class and gender privilege. 'The variety of scenes through which I had lately passed, the society into which I had been introduced, and the manners and information which I had acquired, made me on my return extremely acceptable to all my old friends and procured me the acquaintance of many,' reflected James Bland Burges in his memoirs. The Grand Tour could give a man standing in his local society; it could give his manhood shape and finesse. There was much common ground about its possible benefits. In reply to a letter from John Quicke in 1747, who was then in Geneva, William Graves approved his attention 'to the government and policy of the several states through which you pass', adding:

> Unquestionably every gentleman should likewise acquaint himself with things of virtuoso-kind, though not strictly reducible to any use in society, yet as the marks of gentility and a polite education: besides some knowledge of buildings, paintings, statues and medals creates a very fine amusement and communicates a wonderful air of elegance to the sensible connoisseur.

Peter Beckford was convinced that comparing the laws, customs and manners of other countries with those of England enlarged the understanding. In doing so they developed the patrician sense of noblesse oblige: 'a continual habit of receiving favours will put us in good humour with the rest of the world, remove our prejudices, increase our sensibility and inspire in us that general benevolence which renders mankind so serviceable to one another'. Thomas Pelham informed his father from Spain that 'visiting other countries is the best indeed the only way of learning how to weigh the perfections and imperfections of our own'.

Many of those who travelled abroad took the matter of improving their social accomplishments very seriously. Thomas Pelham, for example, had lessons in dancing and perspective in Turin. Viscount Fane set about persuading his friends the Spencers in 1727 that it would be best to move from the Hague to Paris. There they would find

---

63. Cited in L.A. Pollock, 'Teach her to Live under Obedience: The Making of Women in the Upper Ranks of Early Modern England', *Continuity and Change* 4 (1989), p. 236.

better opportunities of growing perfect in French, better masters for
mathematics . . . and for any exercise of accomplishment that any of us
might have a mind to advance or perfect ourselves in such as dancing,
fencing, drawing, architecture, fortification, music, the knowledge of
medals, painting, sculpture, antiquity, or whatever we would.

There were mixed views about how far these young tourists could benefit
from social mixing in the places they visited. Some were sure this was a
principal potential gain from the Grand Tour. A friend hoped that his
'affability and good breeding' would introduce Lord Dysart 'into the best
of company'. The social experience of Paris was reckoned to have
considerably 'improved' Thomas Worsley in 1739: he 'talketh more, very
cheerful and gay, makes very good remarks and quite agreeable . . . will
make a great figure in whatever situation he is in'. More confidently and
unscrupulously, some thought they could cheat on the whole business.
Thomas Gage decided to spend a month in Paris in 1750, 'which I
imagine will be long enough to get a right cock to my hat and a suit or
two of clothes à la mode'. He imagined this would 'inform the
world . . . I have been travelling': many, seeing he had been away some
while would believe 'that I have done the Grand Tour'. Stress on the
educational aspects of travel abroad declined, Jeremy Black suggests, in
the course of the eighteenth century. Its basic purpose, however,
remained the same from the early seventeenth century to the early
nineteenth century. The animal imagery of Viscount Lewisham's letter to
his father from Paris in 1775 is apposite: 'From this account you will
certainly be very much surprised if you find me in the spring as unlicked
a cub as when I left England.'[64]

There is no lack of such material attesting to the improvements
achieved or expected yet there was also widespread criticism throughout
the eighteenth century of youths been sent abroad to dissipate themselves
frivolously at too young an age and of the perversion of the Grand Tour's
serious aims. There was certainly much drinking, gaming and whoring.
Jeremy Black has found evidence in quite a few cases of correspondence
and journals which boasted of sexual exploits being tampered with,
presumably by descendants. Travel 'signally failed to produce what it was
supposed to', suggests Michelle Cohen, 'most returning youths were
found wanting'. Given these circumstances, we must attribute the lon-
gevity of the Grand Tour to its role as a rite of passage. It perfectly fits
the classic pattern of such a rite: separation to start with, the removal of
the boy from his family and especially its women members; then
liminality, a transitional stage of life of not boy and not man, which

64. Citations from J.M. Black, *The British Abroad: The Grand Tour in the Eighteenth Century*
    (Stroud, 1992), especially pp. 288–303, on which these two paragraphs are based.

involved the absorbing of knowledge and experience which was expected
to change the boy's very being by his acquisition of a standard of
reference for his own society; finally the return home which was supposed to have the young aristocrat or gentleman flushed with appreciation
of his own country and a better judge of moral issues, customs and
constitutions.[65]

Such was the intention, but we only have to look at a painting like
Connoisseurs in Rome, from around 1750, to detect a potential hollowness
behind its display of authority, virility and elegant dilettantism (plate 24).
The fact is that there was increasing fear in the course of the eighteenth
century that young men might return from abroad effeminate rather than
confirmed in their masculinity. In the 1730s one writer complained that
young gentlemen were so corrupted by the Grand Tour that, on their
return, they were obsessed with ostentation wherever they went. Display,
seen as vain rather than manly, became the centre of the concern over
men's effeminacy. The issue came to a head in the 1770s when a group
of young noblemen, who were enthusiastic about their experience of
Italian culture, formed the Macaroni Club in contempt for the sober and
stuffy Englishmen represented by the Beefsteak Club. In fact, as Paul
Langford points out, there was nothing to prevent affectations such as
daring head-dresses and artificial nosegays going with boisterous masculinity.[66] Nevertheless the phenomenon tells us something about an instability
in the gender order which is directly related to the impact of the Grand
Tour. The *Oxford Magazine* in 1770 made reference to a new 'kind of
animal, neither male nor female, a thing of the neuter gender, lately
started up amongst us . . . it talks without meaning, it smiles without
pleasantry, it eats without appetite, it rides without exercise, it wenches
without passion'. The fears being expressed are reminiscent of the transvestite alarms of the early seventeenth century, but the tone of this
comment is much more restrained. The Macaroni Club was not seen to
threaten the gender order in the drastic way that wanton Elizabethan
women on the streets in their short doublets, hats and feathers had done.

In this case a new fashion in London contributed to a broader general
reaction against French and Italian culture which was turning parents
against sending sons on the Grand Tour. A passage in John Moore's tract
of 1797 *A View of Society and Manners* is interesting for the way it
foreshadows the future. The most important consideration, he argued,
was to make a boy an Englishman, which could best be achieved by a
public school education with its emphasis upon 'manliness of character'.[67]
Thus we find some flux in attitudes to the best pattern for educating boys
at the end of our period. Yet, whether it was by sending them to school,
university, the Inns of Court or abroad, the basic insistence on a pro-

65. M. Cohen, *History of Education* 21 (1992), pp. 251–2.
66. Langford, *A Polite and Commercial People*, pp. 576–7.
67. Citations in these two paragrahs from *History of Education* 21 (1992), pp. 252–3.

gramme which achieved a firm break with maternal tenderness and softness had been consistently pursued in the highest social ranks. In this regard the developments of our period looked towards modern class and gender, presaging the path towards masculinity on which upper- and middle-class boys were placed from the Victorian age until the middle of the present century.[68]

68. P.M. Lewis, 'Mummy, Matron and the Maids: Feminine Presence and Absence in Male Institutions 1934–63', in M. Roper and J. Tosh, eds, *Manful Assertions: Masculinities in Britian since 1800* (London, 1991), pp. 168–89.

16. *The Construction of Masculinity*

IN OCTOBER 1694, as was his wont, Sir Daniel Fleming was lecturing his errant son James in a letter to him at Oxford. 'I am glad to hear you have shaken off some of your loose and idle comrades', he wrote, 'that you are grown more civil, provident and studious and that you will be advised by your brother George and follow his example.' 'This will be much', he continued, 'to your honour and help you to preferment.' The following February Sir Daniel was again harping on honour: 'Be a good husband of your money, books and clothes and follow your studies closely and you'll reap the honour and benefit and I the comfort of it.'[1] Honour in Sir Daniel's mind, it seems, was an accumulative possession; it was a matter of developing certain personal qualities and a style of behaviour; it could be learnt with the help of others older and wiser. What it amounted to was reputation in the eyes of others. We explored in chapter 7 how honour became for the gentry of Stuart England a complex and demanding code of living, expressed through notions of lineage, courage, virtue and reason in the various arenas of household, neighbourhood and local community. It was through seeking honour, it has been argued, that such men lived out their manhood. When wives wrote encomiums on men like Sir Anthony Mildmay and the Duke of Newcastle, they were describing their masculinity as much as their honour. Masculinity, as Michael Roper and John Tosh have shown in their edited studies of it since 1800, has been subject to historical change and has varied in its forms.[2] How far among men living in the Victorian period, let alone during the seventeenth or eighteenth centuries, it involved an internalised identity – an interiority of the mind and emotions – as opposed to a sense of role-playing – is very hard for the historian to judge. It may be significant, though, that the word masculinity, meaning 'the quality or condition of being masculine', had its first recorded usage in England in

1. J.R Magrath, ed., *The Flemings at Oxford* (Oxford Historical Society, XLIV, 1903), III, pp. 241–2, 263.
2. M. Roper and J. Tosh, eds, *Manful Assertions: Masculinities in Britain since 1800* (London, 1991), pp. 1–2.

1748.[3] New words enter the language as people feel the insufficiency of current speech to express something they want to encapsulate. It is not so much that masculinity was entirely different from manhood or manly behaviour, rather perhaps that the word attempted to express a more rounded concept of the complete man. The crucial new ingredient in English masculinity between 1660 and 1800 seems to be the notion of civility. This was more a matter of manners and outward behaviour than of inner qualities, though for some it was seen to reflect these. The detailed attention being given by the conduct book literature of this period to a gentleman's dignity, argues Fenella Childs, 'reveals very clearly the power credited to manners as a vital means of expressing and upholding the social hierarchy'.[4] Manners became the centrepiece of both the social and gender hierarchies, as masculinity in the upper ranks was more closely and deliberately defined and constructed than it had ever been previously.

The dissembling society of Restoration London encouraged the dramatists to develop a vein of cynicism about the values inherent in honour. So, even as remote country gentlemen like Sir Daniel Fleming clung to honour, its sway was being corroded. In Wycherley's *The Country Wife* the women mock the sexual honour they are supposed, for the sake of their menfolk's reputation as much as their own, to preserve. Congreve's *The Way of the World* contrasts integrity and fidelity to genuine convictions with cynicism in establishing the contrasting identities of the two principal characters Fainall and Mirabell. Performed in 1700, the play represents a social world in which honour has become a game 'to save that idol reputation'. 'I knew Fainall to be a man lavish of his morals, an interested and professing friend, a false and designing lover,' Mirabell tells Mrs Fainall, explaining his encouragement to her to seek in him a respectable husband. The important point, however, was that Fainall's 'wit and outward fair behaviour have gained a reputation with the town, enough to make that woman stand excused who has suffered herself to be won by his address'.[5] Not that critiques of this kind on the stage are likely to have done more than prompt some gradual questioning. The early eighteenth-century attack on duelling probably provides a clearer insight into the current status of the traditional male code of honour. John Cockburn, in his *History and Examination of Duels*, and others who followed him intended to redefine the concept so that duelling would cease to be an acceptable expression of honour. They decried modern honour as being based on fear of shame, arguing that whereas honour had been a central principle in ancient classical societies, no one had been insane enough to risk death in its name. True honour was based on a

3. *OED*: masculinity.
4. F.A. Childs, 'Prescriptions for Manners in English Courtesy Literature 1690–1760 and their Social Implications', Oxford DPhil thesis, 1984, p. 326.
5. W. Congreve, *The Way of the World*, act II, scene 1, 234, 237–42.

man's performance in his whole life, not upon a single act; it was the birthright of all, not of a social group. Moreover the duel threatened stable government. Yet, despite the dislike such men expressed of the duel, they reaffirmed the importance of men's attachment to honour and had nothing to put in its place.[6]

This devaluation of honour is very plain in Lord Chesterfield's letters to his eight-year-old son. When he starts on a course of civil instruction it is given some prominence at least as rhetoric: 'the strictest and most scrupulous honour and virtue can alone make you esteemed and valued by mankind', he writes in July 1741. But such references quickly become peripheral to Chesterfield's programme of admonition to young Philip Stanhope about enhancing his 'lesser talents'.[7] It was logical that, as aristocratic values came to be derided, gentility was debased and the middle class grew in confidence, honour should be seen as both out-moded and socially discriminatory. So, in the 1760s, the poet Robert Dodsley could set the dictates of nature against honour, describing it as 'a vain phantom rais'd, To fright the weak from tasting those delights, Which nature's voice, that law supreme, allows'.[8] Duelling came under attack again during the last three decades of the century. This time criticism reached to the basic principals which underlay the code of honour and it was based upon constructive thinking and alternative values. In place of the ritual of personal revenge, the critics proposed the universal applicability and enforcement of the rule of law. 'By claiming the rights of individual sovereignty', notes Donna Andrew, the duellist was seen to defy and threaten 'the continuance of both the law and the state'. The code of honour, it was argued, subverted divine law in a similar fashion, since taking life in a duel was a direct interference with God's purpose and design. William Wilberforce lashed out at it as a cause of incivility. The duel, and the code of honour which it exemplified, were seen as inappropriate to modern times, as archaic and intolerable. Thus John Bennett, in a tract of 1783, dismissed the duel as 'a custom which is founded in gothic ignorance and barbarism – originated, princi-pally, in the ridiculous and now justly exploded notions of chivalry and romance and is unworthy of a man, not only as he is a Christian, but as making the most distant claim to elegance and refinement'.[9]

The eighteenth century has been portrayed as an aristocratic century and clearly in many respects it was so. Yet Paul Langford's account,

6. D.T. Andrew, 'The Code of Honour and its Critics: the Opposition to Duelling in England 1700–1850', *Social History* 5 (1980), pp. 416–20.
7. C. Strachey, ed., *The Letters of the Earl of Chesterfield to his Son* (London, 1901), pp. 87, 93, 103, 112.
8. Cited in P. Langford, *A Polite and Commercial People: England 1727–1783* (Oxford, 1989), p. 464.
9. *Social History* 5 (1980), pp. 420–3; see also Langford, *Polite and Commercial People*, pp. 587–90.

which emphasises the growing wealth and importance of the middle class, is an important corrective. Attitudes to titles were changing as the polarisation of society, which had begun a hundred or more years before, reached its inherent conclusion in class terms. Social aspiration was a driving force in Hanoverian England, unifying the middle ranks in an almost obsessive engagement in seeking entry to the ranks of the gentry by aping their style of life, manners and morals. In exploring the origins of masculinity and femininity in this period the premise, first stated clearly by Leonore Davidoff and Catherine Hall, that in England gender and class 'always operate together' is very important. Seeking status in terms of class, the middle section of society – rising tradesmen, merchants and professional men – was bound to develop a consciousness of its gendered forms. The impact of the affluence of the period on behaviour was just as important as its impact on standards of living. Politeness, Paul Langford has argued, affected everything from possession of goods and intellectual and aesthetic tastes to trivial matters of everyday routine and social convention. Politeness was always shot through with gender.[10]

We have seen how during the seventeenth century the gentry increasingly felt the pull of London. By 1700 the role of the capital in setting the tone of upper-class society was thoroughly and permanently embedded. London became, as Langford puts it, 'the hub of polite transformation', giving polite society, so finely graded yet so secure in its structure, its basic unity in fashion and manners, moral values and behaviour.[11] In plays like *She Stoops to Conquer* the clash of sophisticated and country ways provided rich comic fare. The country bumpkin became a figure of fun. Sir John Reresby's studied use of Christmas hospitality at home in Yorkshire in the 1680s prefigured the new attitude of management and exploitation of country people. As the cultural differentiation which confirmed the gentry's command of the social and political order became rooted, the county became a stage. The performances, which replaced the old face-to-face relations of squire and villagers, had, suggested E.P. Thompson, 'much of the studied self-consciousness of public theatre': the segregated pews with late entries and early departures at church, the prize-giving for some village races or sports, the regular dinners for the tenantry at Christmas or at the audit of rents, the celebration of a birth, a wedding, an election or a coming-of-age.[12]

The prescriptive literature of masculinity took its tone and arguments

10. Langford, *Polite and Commercial People*, esp. pp. 61–8, 71; L. Davidoff and C. Hall, *Family Fortunes: Men and Women of the English Middle Class 1780–1850* (London, 1987), p. 13.
11. Langford, *Polite and Commerical People*, p. 71.
12. E.P. Thompson, 'Patrician Society, Plebeian Culture', *Journal of Social History* VII (1974). See also R.W. Malcolmson, *Popular Recreations in English Society 1700–1850* (Cambridge, 1973), pp. 57–71; M. Girouard, *Life in the English Country House* (London, 1978), pp. 182–206.

from the metropolitan social scene but it was read and adopted just as enthusiastically in the provincial worlds of the country mansion, of the balls and assemblies in the county capitals and of the burgeoning spa towns. Manners as a sign of superior rank and of gender had the distinct advantages of an inalienable connection to the person, of portability and of usefulness in one way or another at all times and places. Moreover a series of developments enabled polite society in the provinces to become more integrated and to match in some kind of way the sophistication of the capital. Peter Borsay has shown how between 1660 and 1770 urban centres steadily gained an increased foothold in gentry and middle-class recreations. The emphasis was on skill in performance and on spectator activities pursued in a polite social setting. Bowling greens, for instance, made their appearance in many towns at this time, having previously been largely confined to gentry mansions.[13] Bowls was a relaxed male activity at the height of its popularity in the early eighteenth century. Its appeal faded somewhat thereafter as cricket became a fashionable game, especially in the counties of Hampshire, Sussex and Kent (plate 22). Many towns developed a close relationship with hunting. In some cases towns maintained their own hounds with corporation support. At the same time the wide range of services available in towns made them the obvious venue for sophisticated and fashionable events such as hunt balls which began to be associated with the chase. Above all, though, it was the rapid development and commercial orientation of horse racing which brought towns into the picture. Borsay lists 308 race meetings established at English towns by 1771, while only around thirty of these were fully operative before the civil war. Racing developed on a grand scale from the 1680s onwards, with improved facilities in many places and large donations of prize money. By the early 1700s, attendance at the county races was becoming a normal part of a gentleman's social round. The breeding and training of racehorses became popular in gentry circles. Subscription lists for gentlemen's race prizes became a roll call of county families: three for Warwick races in the 1730s and 40s included fifteen per cent who were aristocratic and thirty per cent who held the title of knight or above. The county races of Hanoverian England thus express much of the essence of its society through the merging of the economic and social interests of town and country, middle class and aristocracy. The manifold opportunities which such an occasion provided for social leaders to set an example by public gendered behaviour are obvious.[14]

This involvement of the urban centres in country recreations reflected fundamental changes in the overall character of field sports which occurred between 1660 and 1800. The game laws of this period hand-

13. E.g. Petworth: A.J. Fletcher, *A County Community in Peace and War: Sussex 1600–1660* (London, 1975), p. 29.
14. This paragraph is based upon P. Borsay, *The English Urban Renaissance: Culture and Society in the Provincial Town 1660–1770* (Oxford, 1989), pp. 173–96.

somely protected the gentry's sporting privileges. At the same time they brought about a discretionary system, through gentry exercise of a patronage system over sporting rights among the tenantry and tradesmen, which bound together the middling and upper groups in rural society.[15] The relationship between sport and masculinity meanwhile was changing. Hunting deer declined from 1660 onwards as the squirearchy failed fully to restock their parks after the depredations of civil war. For many country gentlemen, unable to afford a full deer park, hunting the hare had previously been the supreme test of his skill. Now the gentry as a whole turned to fox hunting, which remained for much of this period, argues Raymond Carr, a staid business with the emphasis more upon long runs than fast ones. It was the aesthetics of the ritual that mattered. Squires bred their hounds not so much for pace as for cry, adding the sound of the huntsman's horn. In the 1730s the Duke of Richmond kept a *maître de musique* to teach his men the correct notes on the curved French horn then in use. Hawking and netting meanwhile lost out to shooting. The ancient sport of coursing hares was transformed from an informal pastime into an organised event with coursing matches before crowds of spectators. All these developments continued the process, begun in Elizabethan times, of taking the risks and danger out of sport and reducing its spontaneity. By the 1780s it was becoming normal for paths to be cut through the woods on some estates in order that sportsmen hunting for game were spared discomfort in hacking their way through undergrowth. While some traditionalists, like Parson Woodforde, continued activities such as informal hare coursing which brought hunter and prey into an immediate contest, the trend was towards sports which pitted one competitor against another. This was most evident in the evolution of shooting, which tested men's skills in marksmanship and put the emphasis on individual performance. The social context was the country house shooting party. The growth of enthusiasm for shooting and the introduction of the battue in the 1790s which, with the efforts of well drilled beaters, brought the game into the air and even into the participants' line of fire had as its predictable conclusion the absurdly obsessive attitude exemplified by the counting of slaughtered birds. Between 1810 and 1830, for example, Lord Malmesbury kept a record of his killing of 6,737 partridges and 4,113 pheasants.[16] This was upper-class manhood, cossetted and protected from the dangers that were believed to inculcate courage and resourcefulness, displaying itself in its most oppressive form.

Between 1500 and 1800 a number of tensions complicated the straight-

15. For this argument see P.B. Munsche, *Gentlemen and Poachers: The English Game Laws 1672–1831* (Cambridge, 1981), pp. 28–32.
16. R. Carr, *English Fox Hunting: A History* (London, 1976), pp. 22–30; Munsche, *Gentlemen and Poachers*, pp. 32–9; R.B. Manning, *Hunters and Poachers: A Social and Cultural History of Unlawful Hunting in England* (Oxford, 1993), p. 234; E.P. Thompson, *Whigs and Hunters* (London, 1975), pp. 230–31.

forward late medieval relationship between sport, courage and aristocratic privilege. The growth in these centuries of compassion for animals and of a series of critiques of field sports has been traced in detail by Keith Thomas. In a first wave of doubt and uneasiness, inspired by puritan thoughtfulness, the godly Cheshire squire John Bruen was persuaded to lay aside his hounds, hawks and dogs and to abandon his game reserve. Thomas Bywater, a tutor in Lord Sheffield's household in 1605, was less successful in challenging current orthodoxy. His argument that hawks and hounds, which, said Sheffield, 'I did then and do now moderately delight in', were not ordained by God for man's recreation but simply to adorn the world cut little ice with him.[17] The issue became one of balance. It is interesting that Richard Allestree, in his 1660 treatise *The Gentleman's Calling*, should have mentioned addiction to sport among the male debaucheries he felt it necessary to castigate: some, he declared, 'make hawking and hunting their callings'.[18] This is an early hint of the way in which prescriptive literature asserted a notion of masculinity which was to triumph as a new orthodoxy in contradistinction to old-fashioned and unacceptable conventions about sport and manhood. The hunting squire in Restoration drama became the boorish squire too fond of drink. Sir Roger de Coverley, as he appeared in the *Spectator* around 1710, was the first fully developed prose version of this stereotype. It was also paraded by Lord Chesterfield who, from a city perspective, characterised fox hunting as rustic and old-fashioned, associating it with 'sottish drinking' and 'indiscriminate gluttony'. It was given its most colourful representation in Henry Fielding's portrait of Squire Western. Misogyny became a crucial ingredient of the stereotype as the contrast was developed between the homosocial world of the uncouth squire who abused women and the heterosexual world of polite eighteenth-century society. For Western, addicted to the slaughter of 'horseloads of game', it was a maxim that at dinner 'women should come in with the first dish and go out after the first glass'. This was a man who spent his mornings 'in his field exercises' and his evenings 'with bottle companions', coming to bed so drunk that he could not see his wife and rising again in the sporting season 'before it was light'. The keynote of this critique of an old style of manhood is brutality; in some later versions the dissipated drunkard is further identified with the brutal rake. Fielding constantly sets Squire Western against Squire Allworthy, the new man of feeling. Similarly, in *Humphry Clinker*, Tobias Smollett sets his hero Charles Dennison against an elder brother who was a 'foxhunter and sot' and who, harking back to Shakespeare's Petruchio, 'insulted and oppressed his servants'. In Goldsmith's *She Stoops to Conquer* the crudity and chaos of the huntsman's domestic space is

17. K.V. Thomas, *Man and the Natural World* (London, 1983), pp. 161–2.
18. R. Allestree, *The Gentleman's Calling* (London, 1660), pp. 104–5.

constantly emphasised.[19] These representations, through their censure of a style of manhood which was characterised as more physical than rational or civilised, are crucially important to the construction of eighteenth-century masculinity.

The novelists should not be accused of excessive dramatisation: there is a genuine clash of cultures here. At one level it can be related to new conditions. Those who grew up and lived in the burgeoning cities, above all in London, found it hard to appreciate the seriousness with which country gentry and their tenants took the whole business of field sports. Pepys was caustic about the crowd of hunters he met at Deptford in 1665: 'a great many silly stories they tell of their sport, which pleases them mightily and me not at all, such is the different sense of pleasure in mankind'.[20] At another level this is a clash between aristocratic and middle-class values. It was no coincidence, notes Keith Thomas, that 'the opponents of animal sports were often the enemies of the aristocratic duel'. He argues that military values associated with hunting were anathema to those seeking to jettison the legacy of the feudal past. Joseph Addison, in the forefront of a new polite culture in which masculinity and femininity were deliberately polarised, saw field sports as representing the bumpkin mentality. Alexander Pope believed knifing the stag's throat, especially when a lady was expected to perform it, was a barbarous custom.[21]

Genevieve Lloyd has argued that 'the obstacles to female cultivation of reason spring to a large extent from the fact that our ideals of reason have historically incorporated an exclusion of the feminine'. The strength of her case has already been indicated in this book. Manhood, we have seen, was constructed round the polarities of reason on the one hand and emotion and sensuality on the other.[22] The rationale of the grammar school system and its being confined to boys was that it hardened them into manhood through the process of inculcating the classical curriculum. The faith of the highest social ranks in that curriculum, we have observed, remained undiminished throughout the period. Their confidence in Latin and Greek was just a somewhat extreme expression of the conventional premise that men held a monopoly of things of the mind, and that men's potential but not women's in this respect should be developed to the full. 'They hold books as their crown by which they rule and govern,' declared Margaret Cavendish, acutely summarising the power and authority which drove forward early modern patriarchy.[23] 'He that is learned',

19. G.J. Barker-Benfield, *The Culture of Sensibility: Sex and Society in Eighteenth-Century Britain* (Chicago, 1992), pp. 96–7, 240–44.
20. *Pepys*, VI, p. 295.
21. Thomas, *Man and the Natural World*, pp. 183–4.
22. G. Lloyd, *The Man of Reason: Male and Female in Western Philosophy* (London, 1984), p. xix; above, p. 68.
23. E. Graham, et al., eds, *Her Own Life: Autobiographical Writings by Seventeenth-Century English Women* (London, 1989), p. 88.

asserted William Martyn in a tract of 1613, 'treasureth up wisdom whereby he affecteth what he listeth.'[24]

Far and away the most influential tract on boys' education between the Restoration and 1800 was John Locke's *Some Thoughts Concerning Education*. The radical aspects of his thinking, especially the concept of the mind as a *tabula rasa*, have often been emphasised. Editions appeared at the rate of one every five years throughout the eighteenth century. Locke's discovery of the humaneness of the child was perfectly timed to convince at the end of a century of vigorous educational dialogue. Although he was critical of public schools, he was read because, in the main, he was highly orthodox. Classics was the centrepiece of his curriculum. Taught humanely, it amounted to a training in submission of the will to reason: 'he that is not used to submit his will to the reason of others when he is young will scarce hearken or submit to his own reason when he is of an age to make use of it'.[25] Sir John Eardley Wilmot was less optimistic than Locke about human nature, but we find him reiterating Locke's basic precepts about submission as a training for the later exercise of authority:

> Though I am very desirous of having young minds impregnated with classical knowledge, from the pleasure I have derived from it, as well as the utility of it in all stations of life, yet it is but a secondary benefit in my estimate of education; for to break the natural ferocity of human nature, to subdue the passions and to impress the principles of religion and morality and give habits of obedience and subordination to paternal as well as political authority, is the first object to be attended to by all schoolmasters who know their duty.[26]

This kind of thinking appears to be fundamental to the formation of eighteenth-century upper-class masculinity.

Before expanding this discussion to take in the whole pattern of gentlemanly civility, we need to put the advice books of the period after 1660 in context. Courtesy literature relating to male manners and behaviour before then was confined to works in the Italian courtly tradition, a little material from France and a few short English works based on these foreign exemplars. Books like Castiglione's *The Book of the Courtier*, Giovanni Della Casa's *Galateo* and Nicholas Faret's *The Honest Man*, available in English from 1561, 1576 and 1632 respectively, made available rules of courtly behaviour with regard to body and speech. The influence of these works can be detected in the attention paid by writers like James Cleland in *The Institution of a Young Nobleman* and Richard Brathwaite in

24. W. Martyn, *Youth's Instruction* (London, 1613), p. 30.
25. J.L. Axtell, ed., *The Educational Writings of John Locke* (Cambridge, 1969), pp. 64–5, 140.
26. Cited in K.V. Thomas, *Rule and Misrule in the Schools of Early Modern England* (University of Reading, 1970), p. 7.

The English Gentleman to matters of care and control of the body. William
Martyn in *Youth's Instruction*, published 1613, drew specific attention to
Castiglione's work.[27] Yet this whole literature, as Anna Bryson has shown,
was cast in a highly traditional mould. It was essentially about ritualising
relationships of lordship, service and hospitality. It had something to
contribute between 1560 and 1660 in this sense. Yet the claim that this
literature was gradually diffused throughout the landed orders may over-
state its significance.[28] The English gentry were starting in the course of
the seventeenth century to seek something which was much more coherent in their own class and gender terms by way of a prescriptive code. In
so far as the foreign and early seventeenth-century English works showed
interest in manners as something more than ceremonial deference it was
through their stress upon self-presentation.[29]

Four key works which helped to found a new genre of male conduct
books, published between 1660 and 1678, will be considered here in
relation to a revised concept of masculinity. The first is Richard
Allestree's *The Gentleman's Calling*. Published early in 1660, this was a
substantial work of 176 pages divided into nine chapters. Its purpose is
made explicit at the start and is summarised by the title. This argues that
the recovery of the nation from 'the miseries under which we now groan'
is principally the responsibility of the gentry, for whom the book is
intended as a manual of instruction.[30] The analysis revolves around the
advantages of education, wealth, time, authority and reputation, all of
which gentlemen possess, enabling them to provide the kind of class and
gender leadership which could secure Restoration England from any
possibility of a return to radicalism and civil disorder. There is something
almost prophetic about this book. Clement Ellis's tract *The Gentle Sinner*,
also published in 1660, has 261 pages divided into four sections, the third
of which, on the characteristics of the 'true gentleman', is especially
relevant to this discussion. The *Letter of Advice to a Young Gentleman leaving
the University*, published under the initials R.L. in 1670, is a shorter work.
Jean Gailhard's *The Compleat Gentleman*, published in 1678, was the work
of one who had conducted several young men on the Grand Tour.
More than half of it is devoted to a treatise on the education of youth
through travel abroad. Gailhard states his design in the preface: 'to show
the necessity, benefit and excellency of a good breeding' to a youth's
becoming a gentleman, since it was by his 'virtue and merit, more

27. Martyn, *Youth's Instruction*, p. 109.
28. F. Heal, *Hospitality in Early Modern England* (Oxford, 1990), p. 102.
29. This paragraph is based upon A. Bryson, 'The Rhetoric of Status: Gesture,
    Demeanour and the Image of the Gentleman in Sixteenth and Seventeenth-
    Century England', in L. Gent and N. Llewellyn, eds, *Renaissance Bodies: The Human
    Figure in English Culture c. 1540–1660* (London, 1990), pp. 136–53.
30. Allestree, *Gentleman's Calling*, preface; for Allestree's background, see below
    p. 384.

than by his extraction', that he would be 'raised above the commonalty'.[31]

These writers are traditional in their obeisances to masculinity's basis in honour and virtue, but they spend little time on such issues. A gentleman's 'outside and apparel', declares Ellis, will proclaim the 'picture of a noble mind'. Similarly, as we have seen, there is passing reference to physical fitness and training in physical courage.[32] But the core of the argument, and they are very consistent about this, is that the civility which they prescribe rests upon an inner self discipline and exhibits itself in a set of acceptable patterns of carriage and demeanour, affability, speech and benevolence to others. A gentleman's reason, Allestree argued, allowed him, given a superior education, to establish his class domination:

> His discerning faculty is more nimble and agile, can suddenly surround a proposition and discover the infirm and feeble parts and so is not to be imposed upon by such slight sophisms as captivate whole herds of the vulgar.

Erudition, his argument continued, made possible his gender superiority, for it could complete the conquest of 'headstrong passion', make a boy 'obedient to the laws of reason', produce behaviour that was 'affable and civil' and speech that was 'temperate and decent, the product of judgement not of rage'.[33] 'His will and affection he makes the instruments and servants not the guides and mistresses of his soul,' wrote Ellis. He thought this was simply a matter of self-discipline, of learning to subjugate the will to reason and this to religion, of not submitting 'in the least to the tyranny of passion'. Thus 'in this moderation and empire over himself where he gives law to his affections and limits the extravagances of appetite and the insatiable cravings of sensuality, the just rule he goes by is not opinion but knowledge'.[34] The writer R.L. stressed that moulded by reason a man could hope by his behaviour to express 'the sincerity of your heart' and to avoid lust and rage: 'your actions must discover you to be your own master for he is a miserable slave that is under the tyranny of his passion'.[35] Gailhard summarised the benefits of learning: 'It doth enrich the mind, rectify the will, regulate affections, quickens and perfects natural parts and is an ornament to the whole man.' Fathers and tutors should not hesitate to beat their children with moderation, argued Gailhard, so crucial was it that this learning achieved its objectives. There was nothing worse than parents who led their children to destruction by

31. J. Gailhard, *The Compleat Gentleman: or Directions for the Education of Youth as to their Breeding at home and Travelling abroad* (London, 1678), epistle and preface.
32. C. Ellis, *The Gentle Sinner or England's Brave Gentlemen* (London, 1660), pp. 105–8; above, p. 132.
33. Allestree, *Gentleman's Calling*, pp. 22–6.
34. Ellis, *Gentle Sinner*, pp. 129–31.
35. R.L., *Letter of Advice to a Young Gentleman Leaving the University* (London, 1670), pp. 18–21.

'unnatural tenderness'.[36]

Matters of dress and diet were important in showing breeding, but even more important was body language that was correct and adapted to each social situation. In general terms Ellis advocated 'such a gravity as becomes a Christian, such a decency as becomes a gentleman'. In his opinion it was easy to overdo the attentions of the dancing school and the fencing master: the body should be 'made straight and the more itself not (as most men's are) new moulded by art'. Balance was the essence: a man's carriage should be 'masculine and noble, such as becomes his heroic spirit and yet always accompanied with a wonderful humility and courtesy'.[37] Gailhard went into all this in considerable detail, exhorting tutors to frame a young man to a 'civil and handsome behaviour', so he showed himself at all times to be 'meek and respectful', forbore disputing or 'contradicting others' or 'being eager or obstinate in his own opinions':

> His gesture ought to be composed, not to turn his eyes to and fro, move his legs too much, play with his hat, bite his nails, scratch his head, blow his nose without turning aside his head or pick it or his ears with his fingers, spit often . . . move his hand too much, whistle or sing when he hath nothing to say or do the like unbecoming things.[38]

Speech could give everything or nothing away. It should be such, contended Ellis, that you will think 'he intends no less than to give you a taste of his soul at every word'. It should be neither affected nor bombastic but 'grave and noble, serious and weighty'. The civil man's discourse, in Ellis's account, was 'neither flashy nor flat, neither boyish nor effeminate, neither rude nor pedantic . . . sober yet ingenious, virile, strong and masculine yet sweet and winning'.[39] The writer R.L. urged the young gentleman to avoid speech that was given 'with heat and violence . . . with reflection upon men's persons . . . with vanity and self praise'.[40] Gailhard warned against the use of 'filthy or dishonest speech' or seeming to approve this in others: a man must 'not speak too fast or too loud, but softly and gently, not brag of himself or anything of his, despise or speak amiss of others'.[41] The cultivation of affability was strongly recommended. This was the key to maintaining class and male superiority without being excessively patronising. Affability was 'a great ornament of behaviour', as the writer R.L. puts it, 'this argues you well within and that you are a lover of mankind'. It should go with a degree of openheartedness, bounded by adequate 'latitude and discretion' and great

36. Gailhard, *Compleat Gentleman*, pp. 14–31.
37. Ellis, *Gentle Sinner*, pp. 109, 122.
38. Gailhard, *Compleat Gentleman*, pp. 88–9.
39. Ellis, *Gentle Sinner*, pp. 114–15.
40. R.L., *Letter of Advice*, p. 13.
41. Gailhard, *Compleat Gentleman*, pp. 89–90.

care in the choice of friends, confidants and dependents, lest a man betray himself to others.[42] Ellis also stressed the importance of 'magnanimity and greatness of soul': 'the gentleman may well be compared with a great book which always lies open to the world that whosoever wants advice or counsel may freely consult him at pleasure'.[43]

We have seen how deeply rooted was the fear of manhood degenerating into effeminacy. All this advice about male demeanour and breeding trod a fine line in this respect. On the one hand a gentleman must learn exemplary self-control; on the other it was necessary for him to assert his social status by some freedom of gesture. Brathwaite advised readers to avoid over-scrupulousness in posture, an 'apish and servile imitation' which 'detracts much from the worth of a man'. James I in his *Basilikon Doron* told his son to 'eat in a manly, round and honest fashion, avoiding both absurd daintiness and grossness'. There was no greater failing than bashfulness.[44] 'Embolden him against a foolish shamefastness', was James Cleland's advice to tutors, 'in hanging down his head and blushing at every light word.'[45] The fear that in learning manners a young man might fall into the trap of effeminacy is very apparent. So the arts of politeness needed to be constantly balanced by the process of hardening: 'some are brought up in so tender and effeminate a way that 'tis a shame to think on't', reflected Gailhard, 'so that if ever they be put upon any inconvenience they are not able to hold out but sink under any hardship and are soon swept away'.[46] Refinement had always to allow for manly courage and independence.

The further paradox is that this whole business of training young men along gender and class lines was supposedly to proclaim his natural virtue yet the end result was quite obviously a matter of effort and artifice. The ambiguity between natural yet self-concealing behaviour goes back to Castiglione. The most disastrous outcome was affectation, contrived words or body language which revealed themselves as hypocritical. The Earl of Bedford warned his sons about this: 'take heed of affectation and singularity if so you act the nobleman instead of being one'.[47] The problem went away if there was a proper concordance between the inner and outer man. John Locke is important here because his *Some Thoughts Concerning Education*, informed by his reading of a collection of some forty conduct books besides much personal experience, stressed this point. The constituent elements in a young gentleman's education, according to

---

42. R.L., *Letter of Advice*, pp. 28, 34–40.
43. Ellis, *Gentle Sinner*, p. 133.
44. Citations from Gent and Llewellyn, eds, *Renaissance Bodies*, pp. 152–3.
45. J. Cleland, *The Institution of a Young Nobleman* (London, 1607), p. 65.
46. Gailhard, *Compleat Gentleman*, p. 79; see also Childs, 'Prescriptions for Manners', pp. 161, 181.
47. Gent and Llewellyn, eds, *Renaissance Bodies*, p. 153.

Locke, were virtue and wisdom, essentially inner qualities, balanced by breeding and learning, the performance of which reflected these inner qualities to the world.[48] In Locke's thinking a proper sense of self-assurance was a reflection of an internal ability of the mind. This would be evident in 'decency and gracefulness of looks, voice, words, motion, gesture and of all the whole outward demeanour' making 'those with whom we may converse easy and well pleased'.[49]

Between 1693, when Locke published his educational treatise, and 1760 courtesy and advice literature for both sexes burgeoned. Fenella Childs, who has surveyed the whole genre, believes that there were at least five hundred separate editions of courtesy works published in this period, with print runs averaging around 1,000 copies. Locke's book went through fourteen editions between 1693 and 1752 and was enormously influential. It is evident that this body of literature was in several respects a consistent genre. Courtesy literature had previously been narrowly conceived. There were, as we have seen, prescriptions for manners in the court and household and there was also more general advice literature written by puritan clerics confined within a tradition of patriarchal household government. But there was no such thing before 1660 as a prescriptive literature directed towards gender construction as such. The stress in this literature on inculcating behaviour according to a person's place in certain predetermined social and gender categories – gentlemen, ladies, servants, apprentices – was entirely new. Its content, format and viewpoint were all common. Its style was universally systematic and didactic. Its context was always a set of assumptions regarding the reader's aspirations and thinking about the overall conduct of his or her life. Finally, whereas the earlier courtesy book genres were essentially works of religion and moral advice, this courtesy literature was firmly secular in its ideological tone.[50] Gender, one cannot escape thinking in reading this material, is here being reconstructed and transformed. The purposefulness of these writers in establishing a world of two sexes is emphatic. David Hume, writing in 1751 about decency, 'a quality immediately agreeable to others', captures the atmosphere:

> An effeminate behaviour in a man, a rough manner in a woman; these are ugly because unsuitable to each character and different from the qualities we expect in the sexes . . . the disproportions hurt the eye and convey a disagreeable sentiment to the spectators, the source of blame and disapprobation.[51]

48. M.J.M. Ezell, 'John Locke's Images of Childhood', *Eighteenth Century Studies* 17 (1983–4), pp. 141–2.
49. Cited in Childs, 'Prescriptions for Manners', p. 105.
50. Childs, 'Prescriptions for Manners', pp. 19–32.
51. Cited in Childs, 'Prescriptions for Manners', p. 98.

Deeply rooted notions of manhood and effeminacy are evident here. But what is new is that a positive femininity, which will be discussed below in chapter 19, is being set against an established masculinity.

So far as the content of the advice literature between 1690 and 1760 is concerned, there is little here that has not been clearly stated already in works such as those by Ellis and Gailhard. Deportment, equanimity and affability remain key elements of civility, the behaviour pattern through which a gentleman proclaimed his claims to superiority. Display of emotion, a number of writers emphasise, is always unmanly and womanish. Bearing pain if need be with manhood and firmness is a crucial aspect of male dignity. Tears, acceptable in women and children, were an unpardonable weakness in a man. There is an important development, though, in the course of this period and this is encapsulated by the gradual substitution, from around the 1730s, of the word 'politeness' for the word 'breeding'. The new term indicates a much stronger focus than previously on external manners alone. The high level of inner commitment and character training which had been so central to didactic literature in England from writers like Sir Thomas Elyot in the early Tudor period to John Locke in the 1690s has disappeared. Manners by the middle of the eighteenth century have become, more blatantly than ever before, a matter of precise calculation and exhaustive cultivation. They are seen as an embodiment of social and gender authority. Social life lived according to these rules should be a constant performance for an audience.[52]

The man who took this attitude to its logical conclusion and sought to pursue it most obsessively by moulding a child in his own image was Lord Chesterfield. The reams and reams of detailed instructions he wrote to his illegitimate son Philip Stanhope are a poignant historical document, since it emerged when he died at the early age of thirty-six in 1768 that Philip, so far from fulfilling his father's hopes, had been clandestinely married to a low-born Irishwoman. The letters, 430 of them in all, began when Philip was very young. His governesses had to ensure that they were punctually answered. They continued, with the governess replaced by a tutor, when from ten to fourteen Philip was at Westminster and when, thereafter, he undertook a prolonged Grand Tour accompanied by another tutor.[53] Lord Chesterfield's extraordinary dedication to his son's academic and social improvement has given us the eighteenth century's most lasting memorial to the attempted construction of masculinity. A brief review of his advice will show how, by the 1740s, politeness was established in the upper-class mind as a highly coherent, convincing and self-validating gender ideology.

52. This paragraph is based on Childs, 'Prescriptions for Manners', especially pp. 95–181, 227–41.
53. P. Mason, *The English Gentleman: The Rise and Fall of an Ideal* (London, 1982), pp. 62–4; Langford, *Polite and Commercial People*, pp. 586–7.

We have already encountered Chesterfield driving his son to grow up before his childhood innocence had left him and to be competitive as a budding schoolboy.[54] His precepts about virtue, when Philip was eight, show him at his most self-regarding. Virtue consists, he declares, 'in doing good and speaking truth'; its effects are advantageous to mankind and 'to oneself in particular'. His snobbishness is egregious here as he announces that pitying others and relieving some of their misfortunes provides 'an inward comfort and satisfaction which nothing else can do and nothing can rob us of'. As a nine-year-old, Philip started to receive the full blast of Chesterfield's admonitions about developing what he called the 'lesser talents'. These, it is evident from the space and detail he gives them, are the talents that really matter: 'civility, affability and an obliging, agreeable address and manner'. A genteel manner 'is of very great consequence towards pleasing in private life, especially the women'; it 'prepossesses people in your favour, bends them towards you and makes them wish to be like you'. Philip was now entered upon an exacting programme of instruction about how to behave in company, as his father took him to his first dinner parties. Increasingly the emphasis was on learning how to please others by well bred behaviour: his reputation and success in the world would 'in a great measure' depend on the degree of good breeding he could master. He should imitate others, watching their every speech and gesture, to acquire 'that *Je ne sais quoi* that everybody feels although nobody can exactly describe'. Once Philip was at Westminster the deeply cynical vein in Chesterfield's character emerged, as he urged him to watch for deceit in others and to beware of giving trust. When he set out for Europe, the fatherly advice turned to handling social relationships with adults in a way that shows him to be 'modest without being bashful and steady without being impudent'. He has absorbed virtue and learning, Philip is told; now he needs 'polish'. There is no substitute for constant attention to the 'art of pleasing'. 'For, as I have often told you', Chesterfield concluded in a letter of 9 October 1747, 'politeness and good breeding are absolutely necessary to adorn any, or all other good qualities or talents.'[55]

Chesterfield's masculinity, as it was expressed in his attempt to create in his son the model of the perfect gentleman, comes across as harshly cerebral and self-centered. It was in the decade during which he was advising young Philip Stanhope to conduct deceitful sexual affairs in high society, if he felt the inclination to do so, rather than consort with prostitutes that Samuel Richardson's *Clarissa* was published.[56] This novel brought before the reading public the totally unsentimental libertine and

54. Above, pp. 303, 306.
55. Strachey, ed., *Letters of the Earl of Chesterfield*, pp. 85–96, 128–30, 137, 142–51, 163, 178–80.
56. Langford, *Polite and Commercial People*, p. 586.

rake Lovelace. 'God forbid', wrote Henry Fielding to Richardson in 1748, having read the book, 'that the man who reads this with dry eyes should be alone with my daughter when she hath no assistance within call.' The rise of sensibility, which was to revise attitudes to masculinity considerably by the 1760s and 1770s, was still at this point only on the horizon. Fielding's novels, however, did much to open up the issue of squaring manliness with male emotions and sympathy without incurring the charge of effeminacy.[57]

The cult of tender-heartedness had its origins in seventeenth-century thinking about the virtue of benevolence.[58] It had been boosted by the publication of the Earl of Shaftesbury's *Characteristics of Men, Manners, Opinions, Times* in 1711, which sought to soften and temper the roughness of the aristocratic male model. In Shaftesbury's notion of masculinity 'a mind subordinate to reason, a temper humanised and fitted to all natural affections . . . a thorough candour, benignity and good nature with constant security, tranquillity' were the guiding ideals.[59] By the time Chesterfield's letters were actually published in 1774, the mood had changed so much that they had a thoroughly critical reception. Their snobbery was not acceptable and their spirit of calculation offended the cult of feeling. Above all, argues Paul Langford, Chesterfield's approval of dissimulation 'simply outraged the moral earnestness of the sentimentalists'. Henry Mackenzie's *Man of Feeling*, which appeared in 1770, was then all the rage. The appeal of this novel, though it may have involved a misreading of its real message, seems to have been its celebration of a hero who relied on his feelings as a guide to virtuous action in his attempts to mitigate the harsh realities of the world around him.[60] A passage in James Fordyce's advice book of 1777 indicates the shape of an emerging new orthodoxy. Masculinity, for much of the century something rather cerebral and bloodless, was coming to be seen in psychic terms which foreshadowed the Victorian return to ethical values.[61] Fordyce looked in young men for

a lively fancy, a ready understanding, a retentive memory, a resolute spirit, a warm temper and tender affections, a quick sense of humour and disgrace, an irresistible love of action and enterprise, an ambition to be admired and praised, especially for their probity, manhood, generosity, friendship, good nature and other virtues.[62]

---

57. Barker-Benfield, *Culture of Sensibility*, p. 141.
58. Thomas, *Man and the Natural World*, pp. 174–5.
59. Barker-Benfield, *Culture of Sensibility*, pp. 105–14.
60. Langford, *Polite and Commercial People*, pp. 481, 586.
61. J. Tosh, 'What Should Historians do with Masculinity?', *History Workshop* 33 (1994), provides a review of the recent historiography.
62. J. Fordyce, *Addresses to Young Men* (London, 1777), p. 16.

Manhood in Shakespearean England, we have seen, was defined as much as by anything else in terms of sexual assertiveness. His bawdy shows the richness of the contemporary language regarding men's taking of their sexual pleasures. The ideologies of civility and sensibility which have been discussed here concealed the private world of the double standard and of men's insistent enjoyment, almost as their birthright in managing patriarchy, of their sexuality. When we turn from courtesy literature to diaries and correspondence, court records and other genres such as the novel, this whole world comes alive. We need to consider the response of the gentry and middle class to the burgeoning facilities and literature between 1660 and 1800 of commercial sex. In large towns, especially London, these facilities became publicly visible, tolerated and open. Brothels were numerous, pornography was easily available. In the mid-century, it was noted in London that every print shop had 'its windows stuck full with indecent prints to inflame desire through the eye'.[63] By around 1720, London's molly houses had become the centre-piece of a flourishing gay subculture.[64] The most flourishing specialised taste was for flagellation, which was catered for by a number of London brothels[65] (plate 37).

A brief diversion into psychodynamic explanations for men's alleged anxiety about their gender identity may be in order at this point. It is argued by sociologists such as Nancy Chodorow and psychologists such as Liam Hudson and Bernadine Jacot that this is universally, and supposedly always has been, more problematic for men than women. Boys face the difficulties of both freeing themselves from infant identification with the mother and finding a satisfactory role model in a father or father substitute.[66] This is the male wound. Robert Bly, although he writes in an entirely different tradition and from another viewpoint, has used the old hearthside and fairy stories to explore how boys can move 'from the mother's house to the father's house', how, that is, they cope with the male wound. Shakespeare's *Hamlet*, he believes, is a play which 'describes with fantastic wit and heartbreaking detail the difficulty of this move'.[67] Modern man's private behaviour, Hudson and Jacot believe, gives a sense in many cases of 'actions controlled and driven': 'the adult heterosexual

---

63. R. Porter, 'Mixed Feelings: the Enlightenment and Sexuality in Eighteenth-century Britain', in P.G. Boucé, ed., *Sexuality in Eighteenth Century Britain* (Manchester, 1982), pp. 11–12.
64. R. Norton, *Mother Clap's Molly Home: The Gay Subculture in England 1700–1830* (London, 1992), p. 54.
65. P. Wagner, *Eros Revised: Erotica of the Enlightenment in England and America* (London, 1988), pp. 21–4.
66. N. Chodorow, *The Reproduction of Mothering: Psychoanalysis and the Sociology of Gender* (Berkeley, 1978); L. Hudson and B. Jacot, *The Way Men Think* (London, 1991), pp. 37–58.
67. R. Bly, *Iron John: A Book about Men* (Shaftesbury, 1991), pp. 86–8.

male must view the intimately personal – and more specifically the intimately sexual – ambivalently'. They attribute a whole series of sexual patterns of violence, promiscuity and deviation to some men's difficulties in dealing with the wound.[68] The outstanding feature of boys' education in the upper and middling ranks during the seventeenth century was, as we have seen, removal from motherly care into the hands of tutors and schoolmasters. Maternal influence was seen as dangerous, even pernicious. The keynote of boys' experience was the enforced repression of emotional spontaneity.[69] The chronological coincidence between the adulthood of the first generations who had experienced this kind of training in large numbers and the demand for commercial sex of one kind or another is temptingly plausible as an historical connection. The double standard remained deeply rooted: as the Marquis of Halifax explained to his daughter 'our sex seemeth to play the tyrant in distinguishing partiality for ourselves, by making that in the utmost degree criminal in the woman, which in a man passeth under a much gentler censure'.[70]

The double standard was in fact an invitation to men to seek consolation and relief from the pressures and responsibilities that their patriarchal role cast upon them by the pursuit of untrammelled sexual pleasure. Or, to put it another way, hedonism and debauchery beckoned men who were minded to seek refuge from the demanding kind of self control and life of virtue set out in the courtesy literature. The rebellious behaviour of Roger and James Fleming at Oxford against their exacting father is a good example.[71] A gentleman's resort to prostitutes is the most straightforward expression of these kinds of needs. The purchase of one of the various items of pornographic literature which went on sale in London from the 1660s onwards may be almost equally explicable. Protestantism, with its emphasis on the individual conscience, together with the growth of the values of 'economic individualism, clear thinking, orderly actions, prudence and responsibility', David Foxon argues, put 'primary emotions under a heavy strain'. Pornography may be seen as an escape from the responsibilities of adult relationship by regression to an infantile sexuality.[72] Nor should interest in sexual stimulation by the birch rod in the flagellant brothels at this time cause any real surprise, since we have seen that its use in school punishment regimes had for some time been deeply rooted. John Cleland, author of the famous erotic novel *Fanny Hill*, published in 1748, knew all about this as an ex-pupil of Westminster and included in the book a beating scene which shows remarkable psychological perception. The sensitive Fanny, no sadist herself,

68. Hudson and Jacot, *The Way Men Think*, pp. 118–35.
69. Above, pp. 302–3.
70. Cited in K.V. Thomas, 'The Double Standard', *Journal of the History of Ideas* XX (1959), p. 196.
71. Above, pp. 313–15.
72. D. Foxon, *Libertine Literature in England 1660–1745* (London 1965), p. 51.

recognises the inner turmoil of her client Mr Barville, who could not achieve sexual pleasure 'till he submitted to these extraordinary means of procuring it at the hands of pain' so she worked hard to satisfy his needs[73] (plate 35).

Samuel Pepys has left us the fullest record we have in this period of one man's sexual activities over a period of years (plate 30). Since it so happens that he was an aspiring professional man who lived life intensely in the capital he may well in fact be a good subject for the assessment of a psychic pattern of male sexuality that has been suggested here. Three aspects of his diary entries are relevant. First there are his regular fondling activities with several of the maids in his home and with other women who were friends and acquaintances in his social circle.[74] This was fairly straightforward and routine low key promiscuity of a kind which for all we know may have been typical of some middle-class London men at this time. Then there is his propensity to masturbatory fantasy, something he was at first somewhat shameful about. In due course it seems to have caused him only passing humiliation, such as on an occasion when it happened in the Queen's chapel. In 1663, with his wife away, one night he fancied himself 'to sport with Mrs Steward with great pleasure' and another he was 'sporting in my fancy with the Queen'. He was tickled at the fact that he learnt to fantasise so effectively that he could bring himself to ejaculation without using his hands and with his eyes open. This shows how unabashed he could be about sex. Pepys's diary entry for 15 August 1665 when, like all those around him, he was in dread of the plague, is a touching account of how his sexual feelings tied in with his emotions. He had remembered the dream he had the previous night, 'which I think is the best that ever was dreamed':

> I had my Lady Castlemayne in my arms and was admitted to use all the dalliance I desired with her . . . since it was a dream and that I took so much real pleasure in it, what a happy thing it would be, if when we are in our graves (as Shakespeare resembles it) we could dream and dream but such dreams as this – that then we should not need to be so fearful of death as we are this plaguetime.[75]

Where Pepys did seem to feel real shame was over his reading in 1668 of the French pornographic tract *L'escholle de Filles* which was much

---

73. I. Gibson, *The English Vice: Beating, Sex and Shame in Victorian England and After* (London, 1978), pp. 13–16; see also A.J. Fletcher, 'Prescription and Practice: Protestantism and the Upbringing of Children 1560–1700', in D. Wood, ed., *The Church and Childhood* (Studies in Church History, XXXI, Oxford, 1994), pp. 345–6.

74. For a short account see L. Stone, *The Family, Sex and Marriage in England 1500–1800* (London, 1977), pp. 552–7; for the maids, Earle, *Making of the English Middle Class* (London, 1989), pp. 224, 337; above, p. 170.

75. *Pepys*, IV, pp. 204, 230, 232, VI, pp. 191, 331; VII, p. 365, VIII, p. 588; IX, p. 184.

talked of in London around that time. Horner in *The Country Wife* denied having brought a copy back from France.[76] Pepys found it at his bookseller on 13 January and resisted the temptation to buy it until 8 February. He then did so with a vow to burn it as soon as it was read. He went through it the next night, after drinking a good deal of wine, telling himself in the diary that it 'doth me no wrong to read for information sake', while admitting that doing so gave him an intensely enjoyable sexual experience.[77] Pepys's discomfort and ambivalence about all this can be attributed to the fact that it was a first-time experience in getting pleasure from pornography. It was one, so far as we know, he did not repeat. Pepys, despite these hesitations, seems to have regarded all aspects of his rich sexual life as an acceptable part of the structure within which he fashioned himself as a man of standing in professional London society. This is not, of course, to say that he would actually have boasted about them all to others. He drew a firm line between his private pleasures and the kind of frolics and debauchery indulged in by some of the libertines of the 1660s. He did not approve, when he heard about it in October 1668, for example, of Sir Charles Sidley and Lord Buckhurst 'running up and down all the night with their arses bare through the streets'.[78] Whereas he was, he believed, always within the gender rules, this was simply licentiousness and obscenity.

The message that upper-class Englishmen of the eighteenth century took from Enlightenment writers was that the pursuit of pleasure was the central purpose of life: 'pleasure is now, and ought to be, your business', Chesterfield told his son. Roy Porter has argued that the period saw a 'hedonistic liberation of the libido', which complemented a whole series of contemporary trends of thought. Nature was good and proper behaviour sought to realise and fulfil it. In the new sensational psychology touch was given special prominence. Yet at the same time an important aspect of traditional humoral medicine which prompted regular sexual activity, the notion that discharge was needed for physical health, found its way into Enlightenment hydraulic physiology.[79] Given the powerful impact of the double standard, it is no surprise that the increased sexual freedom which all this encouraged was confined to males. Parents in upper-class circles expected and intended more openly than ever that sons should prove their manhood by sowing wild oats. This was also an insurance policy to ensure that they were going to be straight not gay. The dowager Lady Saville, according to a report by Henry Harris in 1750, was frantic about her son Sir George's youthful activities. He had, to her

76. W. Wycherley, *The Country Wife*, act I, scene 1.
77. *Pepys*, IX, pp. 21–2, 57–9.
78. *Pepys*, IX, pp. 335–6.
79. Porter, 'Mixed Feelings', in Boucé, ed., *Sexuality in Eighteenth-Century Britain*, pp. 4–6.

knowledge, just begun 'a new score in a stable yard with the waiter at Mount's coffee house':

> His good mother, a most religious lady, is now wringing her hands and bemoaning herself that she kept so strict a hand upon him at home and rather than he should have given way to such abominable impure burnings, she now wishes he had fucked every Abigail about her and had been indulged with the refreshing breeze of all the well twirled mops in her family.

Motherly duty, in this case, prompted a planned programme of sexual redemption. Within three months, Harris was reporting that 'Lady Saville had taken her young twig of Sodom into the country and, by way of weaning him from that unnatural vice, takes great pains to cocker him with every Abigail in her house and all the milk maid cunts in the neighbourhood'.[80]

Beneath the veneer of civility and politeness, virility in gentry circles was established by sexual conquests. These needed to be boasted about and they were the staple of male gossip. The correspondence of the period provides insights into all this. Female servants were fair game as a starting point. Just after 1800 we find Thomas Parry, squire of Llidiadom in Cardiganshire, revelling in his son's sexual precociousness: 'George is a noble fellow . . . he is even at this age a very naughty boy. I am afraid he is often found in bed with little Penelope's nurse.'[81] Henry Fox, the Secretary at War, gave his nineteen-year-old nephew Harry Digby, later a peer, some candid advice in 1750: 'what signifies at your age whether a woman is handsome or ugly? Whenever you can, whomever you can with safety; let that be your maxim.'[82] The diary of the aspiring young cleric John Thomlinson, between 1717 and 1721, includes London gossip regarding his circle of friends and relatives retailed to his brother in the north. In December 1721 he reported, 'Cousin Clarke said that Mr Repington was clap'd and yet he lies with Sarah.' On another occasion he made reference to his own exploits: having 'tried one woman and did not like her', he was 'to try another shortly and if I found her answer the description I intended to attack her very briskly and take her by storm'.[83] Resort to prostitutes always carried the risk of venereal disease. Pepys, though he sometimes could not resist the temptation to go to Fleet Alley

80. Farmington, Lewis Walpole Library, Hanbury Williams papers, vol. 68, fols 110, 146. I am grateful to Jeremy Black for these references, all of which he cites in an unpublished paper 'The Language of Licentiousness' which he kindly lent me.
81. Cited in J. Barker, ' "Stolen Goods": The Sexual Harassment of Female Servants in West Wales during the Nineteenth Century', *Rural History* 4 (1993), p. 132.
82. Farmington, Lewis Walpole Library, Hanbury Williams papers, vol. 68, fol 151. I am grateful to Jeremy Black for this reference.
83. BL, Add. MS 22560, see also J.C. Hodgson, *Six North Country Diaries* (Surtees Society, 64, 1910), p. 64.

'out of an itch to look upon the sluts there', always for this reason turned away. Many were less cautious.[84] In 1749 Thomas Gage related to his friend Charles Hotham how, having found London so 'intolerably stupid and dull' on a recent visit there from his family estate in Sussex, 'the only way I could devise to divert myself was with a wench who has obligingly given me a pretty plaything to divert me in the country, in bestowing a most generous clap upon me'. Its 'copious flowings', he explained, he was 'endeavouring with the assistance of injection and purgations to put a stop to'.[85] At the core of this relaxed and exuberant attitude to sexuality, there was a celebration of priapic power which we must regard as inherent to the private side of Hanoverian masculinity. This, more than anything else, points to the element of hypocrisy that lay behind courtesy book politeness and civility. Chesterfield is the most apt commentator. In 1728, he enquired of his fellow aristocrat and diplomat Lord Waldegrave about his latest sexual exploits:

> . . . your private pleasure; does that manly vigour and that noble contempt of danger still continue? I am informed it distinguished itself at Paris; I hope it does so at Vienna too. As I know that both your rammer and balls are made for a German calibre, you may certainly attack with infinite success and I know your fortitude too well to suppose that you will decline the combat, let the danger be ever so great.[86]

The Grand Tour had a special role to play here. It was his advice to his son that he should seek the company of French women who could offer invaluable sexual experience besides the polish of sprightly conversation which earned Chesterfield Samuel Johnson's famous comment that his letters 'teach the morals of a whore and the manners of a dancing master'. Sex with foreign women preserved the chastity of women at home. Moreover French women were seen as inconstant and ready, in any case, to indulge in short-term liaisons. Wooing a French lady, argued John Andrews in a tract of 1783, was good practice for the much harder task in store later of wooing with an Englishwoman, for it was so easy:

> Any man must be endowed with a very extraordinary share of firmness and constancy, in his preference of the less shining qualities of candour, discretion, modesty and the other countless ornaments of an English woman's character to oppose them effectually . . . to the more splendid though less amiable qualifications of wit, vivacity and sprightliness of humour and deportment that embellish the whole system of so many

84. *Pepys*, IV, pp. 64, 301, V, p. 219.
85. Hull University Library, Hotham papers DDH. 4/3. I am grateful to Jeremy Black for this reference.
86. The letter is printed in full in J. Black, 'Anglo-Dutch Relations 1728–1732: The Chesterfield-Waldegrave Correspondence', *Nederlandse Historische Bronnen* 10 (1992), pp. 140–41.

French ladies and render them completely irresistible in their attempts to subdue the hearts of pliant inexperienced youth.[87]

We have become used to regarding the hallmarks of Hanoverian society as order and elegance: 'the polite world saw themselves as an elite', writes Mark Girouard, 'whose claim to run the country was based on a stake in it as property owners, and was reinforced by the culture, education and *savoir-faire* of which its country houses were an advertisement'.[88] So much of the evidence left behind refers to these notions in one way or another. The flush facades of neat brickwork which still express eighteenth-century proportions and symmetry in numerous streets of country towns conceal, in many cases, the medieval timberwork jetting and plaster which had gone out of fashion.[89] The portraiture of the period speaks of male authority and control. Marcia Pointon has examined how the wig became 'invested with a powerful symbolic significance' which was given widespread currency as a form of upper-class male self-enactment.[90] In this sense the young Tom Pelham, heir to one of the greatest Sussex estates, being shaved and fitted with his first wig at the age of seven in 1659 is a vignette which encapsulates this whole new world of class and gender. Here was a potent new version of the symbolic breeching. Tom's father, Sir John Pelham, knew where the world was going on the eve of Restoration.[91] Yet, beneath this facade of sophistication, as we have seen, there was a deeply selfish set of sexual mores and an unabashed male hedonism. Much more work needs to be done on how the prescriptive material cited here was translated into practice. But it is clear from some of the advice fathers gave to sons that the basic principles of male gender construction that it embodies – principles like discretion, judgement, benevolence and patriotism – were broadly accepted and promulgated.[92] What we have been concerned with in this chapter is the theory of a coherent ideology of masculinity, one that was rounded but demanding, that men in the upper levels of society could not afford to ignore however they adapted themselves to it or sought to adapt it to them. This ideology was necessary because the previous foundations of English patriarchy, in scripture and an outdated reading of the body, were simply inadequate to new social conditions. The problem for historians of gender is that, as John Tosh has put it, 'those aspects of masculinity which bear most directly on the upholding of men's social power are least likely to be

87. M. Cohen, 'The Grand Tour: Constructing the English Gentleman in Eighteenth-Century France', *History of Education* 21 (1992), pp. 255–6.
88. Girouard, *Life in the English Country House*, p. 189.
89. Borsay, *English Urban Renaissance*, pp. 56–9.
90. M. Pointon, *Hanging the Head* (New Haven, 1993), p. 112.
91. A.J. Fletcher, *A County Community in Peace and War: Sussex 1600–1660* (London, 1975), p. 35.
92. E.g. Earl of Warrington, *Advice to his Children* (London, 1696), T. Scott, *A Father's Instructions to his Son*.

made explicit'.[93] We need to investigate fully and deeply the ways in which authority over women sustained men's sense of themselves as men. Civility and politeness on the one hand and sexual power on the other begin to look like two sides of a coin.

93. Tosh, 'What Should Historians do?', *History Workshop* 33 (1994), pp. 179–202.

17.   *Women and Religion*

As THE WEAKER vessel, it was generally taken for granted that women were naturally more religious than men in this period. This was seen as inherent in their physical and temperamental constitution. Men had various explanations for the emotionality which was regarded as the foundation of female piety. Richard Hooker discussed it and attempted to explain it in his *Laws of Ecclesiastical Polity*.[1] Richard Sibbes thought that women's frequent brushes with death in childbirth forced them to 'nearer communion with God'.[2] Sir Henry Slingsby described his wife as 'by nature timorous and compassionate which makes her full of prayer in behalf of others'. More scathingly, Henry Paynter attributed women's piety to their sense 'of their own imbecility and weakness' and the consequent need 'to shroud themselves under the shadow of the Almighty and to be much and often under his wing'.[3] Hence, the protestant doctrine of the patriarchal family provided women with a means to express this religiosity while at the same time it afforded men the chance to channel and order it in ways they found appropriate. The family became, as we have seen, 'a little church, a little commonwealth'. If it was a school in which wives learnt subjection, it was at the same time one in which they could act in partnership with their husbands in the ordering of private worship. Not that the family constituted an entirely private world: it is better seen as a meeting point between the public and private, where husbands and wives worked in a joint command over children and servants to prepare the young for a moral life and dutiful citizenship. The fact that women did not have a public function did not imply they had no public calling, said William Gouge, for 'a conscionable performance of household duties,

1. J. Keble, ed., *Works of Richard Hooker* (London, 1888), I, pp. 152–3.
2. Cited in P. Crawford, *Women and Religion in England 1550–1720* (London, 1993), p. 73.
3. D. Parsons, ed., *Diary of Sir Henry Slingsby* (London, 1838), p. 2; Cited in P. Lake, 'Feminine Piety and Personal Potency: the Emancipation of Mrs Jane Ratcliffe', *The Seventeenth Century*, II (1987), p. 147.

in regard to the end and fruit thereof, may be accounted a public work'.[4]

The issue for men was balancing trust and control. There is little doubt that female spirituality was actually not only more intense than men's but also different from theirs. They might attend the same worship and imbibe the same theology and yet, as Caroline Walker Bynum has put it, experience the gender symbols in religion differently.[5] In fact, for some deeply pious women, their whole experience of gender, their understanding of themselves as women, could become focused upon their spiritual lives. In this case there was no easy dividing line in their minds and emotions between engagement in household religion and their private devotions and meditation. By the middle of the seventeenth century there were ministers who were sufficiently impressed by the piety of some women they knew to challenge the misogynistic Christian tradition. Samuel Torshell saw in the spiritual capacities of women evidence of the nobility of feminine nature; his fellow minister in Cheshire, John Ley, quoted favourable remarks by St Jerome on women's abilities in his panegyric to Mrs Jane Ratcliffe. In dedicating his life of her to two other 'elect ladies', Alice Lucy and Brilliana Harley, Ley was giving respectability to a new kind of sisterhood in Christ among the midlands' gentry. 'There can be little doubt', Peter Lake has argued, 'that the puritan view of godliness could and often did create a more positive image of womankind and allow female believers to claim areas of spiritual and social space for the development and exercise of their personalities.' Godliness, Lake suggests, could provide a spur and sanction for 'an urgent autodidacticism'.[6] This in turn could enlarge the mental world of godly women and enhance their image of themselves. Some women, by this means, gained a sense of control over their lives, a confidence in themselves and a new level of assurance about their gender identity.

The sources that will be used here to investigate women's spiritual experience in the seventeenth century are published funeral sermons for godly women and women's own accounts of their meditations and religious exercises in autobiographies and memoirs. The fashion for reading godly lives seems to have been begun by Philip Stubbs, who published a brief biography of his wife Katherine in 1591, *A Crystal Glass for Christian Women*, when she died in childbirth four years after their marriage. This went through twenty-four editions by 1637. It was followed in 1601 by the more elaborate memorial to Mrs Katherine Brettergh, another wife who died young, which was based on two funeral sermons preached in the Lancashire village of Childnal. The

4. Cited in Crawford, *Women and Religion in England*, pp. 49–50 who develops this argument. See above, pp. 204–6.
5. C. Walker Bynum, S. Hassell and P. Richman, eds., *Gender and Religion: On the Complexity of Symbols* (Boston, 1986), pp. 8–16.
6. Lake, 'Feminine Piety', *The Seventeenth Century*, II (1987), pp. 147–9.

second, by William Leigh, was in fact a free-standing biography, setting a precedent sometimes followed thereafter for a husband or relative to provide a narrative account to accompany the eulogy. This work was reprinted four times before 1617. Funeral sermons had caught on and were becoming a staple item of the book trade: some seventy printed between 1600 and 1640 survive, a good many of them being for women.[7] The genre continued to flourish throughout the period up to 1700. Samuel Clarke's *Lives of Sundry Eminent Persons in this Later Age*, published in 1683, capitalised on the market by lifting biographies in many cases directly from sermons.[8] Around thirty of these sermons for godly women published over the period from 1591 to 1720 will be drawn upon in this survey. They can be seen as formulaic or idealised to an extent that makes them bear little relation to reality, but there are two good reasons for thinking that this is not in fact so.[9] In the first place, as Peter Lake has argued, the whole ideological rationale of these pieces lay 'in there being a basic fit or congruence between the image produced in the pulpit and the recollection of the auditory who had known the subject in life'. If the objective was to provide examples of godly living and behaviour that others would wish to imitate, the preachers were strongly motivated to use vignettes and specific details which fixed a particular godly woman in people's minds. Some idealisation was in order, the preacher could select incidents and omit aspects that did not assist his case, but the individual must shine through. The didactic purpose had to be in synthesis with, and to take account of, the characteristics of the subject.[10] Secondly the personal materials written by, as opposed to written about, godly women in this period paint a picture of female piety very similar to that set out in the published sermons.[11]

Of course in using funeral sermons we are looking through a glass darkly. The clergy who preached them held the general set of attitudes promulgated by their colleagues in the advice literature about what constituted good and dutiful wifely behaviour. The female duties of reverence and obedience were never far from their minds; the standard assumptions about male and female roles indoors and out of doors

7. P. Collinson, ' "A Magazine of Religious Patterns": An Erasmian Topic Transposed in English Protestantism', in D. Baker, ed., *Renaissance and Renewal in Christian History* (Oxford, 1977), pp. 234, 245–7; A.D. Wall, 'Elizabethan Precept and Feminine Practice: The Thynne Family of Longleat', in *History* 75 (1990), pp. 23–5.

8. J. Eales, 'Samuel Clarke and the "Lives" of Godly Women in Seventeenth Century England', in W. Sheils, ed., *Women in the Church* (Studies in Church History, 27, 1990), pp. 365–8.

9. Alison Wall argues this, 'Elizabethan Precept', *History* 75 (1990), pp. 23–5.

10. Lake, 'Feminine Piety', *The Seventeenth Century*, II (1987), pp. 160–1.

11. S.H. Mendelson, 'Stuart Women's Diaries and Occasional Memoirs', in M. Prior, ed., *Women in English Society* (London, 1985), pp. 185–90.

governed their approach to compiling an exemplary portrait.[12] Yet the irony was that the more a godly woman took charge of her own spiritual life and that of her family and household, the more likely it was that her self-confidence and sense of authority would bring her into conflict with her husband. We have to work with asides and vignettes here which may well be the mere tip of an iceberg of conflict and tension.[13] Katherine Brettergh could legitimately, we are told, upbraid her husband for being angry on the sabbath and she also criticised him for trying to collect rent from a poor man in a way that amounted to oppression. We are not told what her husband Arthur, a civil lawyer, thought about Margaret Ducke's refusals of social invitations to them both but they may well have troubled him. William Gouge's sermon about her made much of her determination not to accept them, 'lest she should be tempted to see those vanities which she resolved to condemn and so be unwittingly wrought and brought to desire what she so willingly despised'. Richard Baxter's *Life* of his wife Margaret reveals that they were seriously at odds about the issue of leading family worship. He saw this as a distraction from his writing and something she could perfectly well do for him. Margaret took up a defensive stance which angered her husband: 'When I was at any time from home, she would not pray in the family, though she could not endure to be without it. She would privately talk to the servants and read good books to them. Most of the open speaking part of religion she omitted, through a diseased enmity to ostentation and hypocrisy.' Margaret may well have felt that the deal which Richard Baxter records he insisted upon, that 'she would expect none of my time which my ministerial work should require', was hardly tolerable and so found her own forms of protest. Baxter ended up taking the crusty view that marriage for clerics had 'great inconveniences' and that it was 'to be avoided as far as lawfully one may', citing Corinthians 7, verse 32. 'My conscience', he confessed, 'hath forced me many times to omit secret prayer with my wife when she desired it, for want of time, not daring to omit far greater work.'[14] Yet several of the conduct book writers – Gouge, Rogers and Whateley, for example – emphasised the importance of husbands and wives praying together and helping each other in the growth of grace.[15]

In the case of John Ley's funeral sermon for the widow Jane Ratcliffe, there are a couple of incidents recalled from her married life which hint

---

12. For a full account see A.J. Fletcher, 'The Protestant Idea of Marriage in Early Modern England', in A.J. Fletcher and P.R. Roberts, eds, *Religion, Culture and Society in Early Modern Britain* (Cambridge, 1994), pp. 161–81.

13. Lake, 'Feminine Piety', *The Seventeenth Century*, II (1987), pp. 143–4.

14. My account of these incidents is based on Eales 'Samuel Clarke', in Sheils, ed., *Women in the Church*, pp. 372–3.

15. Fletcher and Roberts, eds, *Religion, Culture and Society in Early Modern Britain*, pp. 179–80.

at tensions that had existed with her husband John, a Chester brewer who was twice mayor and also sat in parliament. Ley had actually been present one day when the alderman came home with a new dress for her. Jane was not keen on fine clothes 'for she would have been clothed with humility':

> She humbly besought with trickling tears on her cheeks that it might not come upon her back. . . . She said little with her tongue (but with her eyes spoke much) because she was loath to contradict him whom she was bound to obey, yet she suffered a contradiction within herself (and that a strong one) where the strife was not betwixt pride and covetousness or two adverse vices as many times it is but betwixt two humilities, whether the humility of prompt obedience without gainsaying or the humility of refusing gay clothes should prevail.

Here were personal godliness and social convention in stark contradiction. His wife's fine clothes proclaimed the alderman's standing in the city. He won because she decided that, since the dress 'was no better than others of her rank did wear', she could submit, displaying 'her own loyal and obsequious subjection' to her husband's will. Yet in a real sense, Jane Ratcliffe won a moral victory through this little scene. There could hardly be a better example, notes Peter Lake, 'of the contrast between the formally patriarchal content of puritan ideology and the subtle ways in which the personal godliness of individual women could be invoked to subvert that patriarchalism'. Ley also told of Jane's scruples over kneeling at communion. Under threat of suspension from communion, she read some of the books on the controversy about kneeling and consulted divines and godly friends before resolving her doubts and conforming. How embarrassing all this must have been for the alderman! What was more public in Chester than how people received communion in the cathedral? We are not told about his role; rather it was the minister, John Ley, who persuaded Jane to conform and then in the funeral sermon sought to quell rumours that on her deathbed she had been 'troubled in conscience' about doing so. Here again Jane performed an act of assent to male authority, but not before she had demonstrated her spiritual potency, this time in a more public arena than her own parlour.[16]

We can observe, with the aid of a rich store of first- and second-hand accounts, how godly women acted and behaved in three separate spheres: the privacy of their closets, the semi-public sphere of the parlour and the public sphere of the parish church. To take the last two first: a Margaret Baxter or Jane Ratcliffe might occasionally kick against the pricks, but, for the most part, women contained the personal potency that their religion gave them within conventional forms and structures of deference and

16. This paragraph is based on Lake, 'Feminine Piety', in *The Seventeenth Century*, II (1987), pp. 150–3.

passivity. With the gathering of children and servants to hear the Bible, pray and be catechised, the holy household of protestant England achieved its most emblematic form. Male leadership was taken for granted but a wife could deputise. Katherine Clarke, for example, 'would pray with her family morning and evening' when her husband was away and also 'in his presence, in case of his sickness and inability to perform the duty himself'.[17] It was said of Dorothy Shaw that, during twenty-five years of marriage, she did not fail to gather her family twice daily for prayer, psalm-singing and a scripture reading when her husband was absent.[18] For the most part women's leadership was ancillary and additional to the central act of household worship. Children were the first and foremost responsibility. Elizabeth Walker's routine included spending much of her afternoons with the children inculcating reading and a straightforward catechism.[19] Alice Lucy's scheme was to have one of the children read a passage to the others before supper, 'frequently taking occasion of instilling into them some sweet and profitable instructions'. Before bedtime they came to her to sing a psalm together.[20] The spiritual education of servants was taken very seriously. Lady Strode repeated the sermons she had heard to her maidservants in her chamber, catechised them and 'laboured to season them with the true fear of the Lord'.[21] Lady Falkland's custom was to spend an hour in the morning praying with and catechising her maids.[22] Lucy Thornton, Elizabeth Walker and Elizabeth Bury were others who were diligent in the regular instruction of the servants of the house.[23]

These women saw attendance at public worship as integral with their household and private devotions. Katherine Clarke, those at her funeral were told, liked to hear 'those who were most plain, practical and powerful preachers, from whose sermons and God's blessing upon them she always sucked some spiritual nourishment'. She was also dedicated in attending days of humiliation and thanksgiving.[24] Lady Strode, like Katherine Clarke, took copious sermon notes for later meditation.[25] Mary Gunter grasped every opportunity to receive communion: 'for many years

17. Cited in Sheils, ed., *Women in the Church*, p. 373.
18. Crawford, *Women and Religion in England*, p. 87.
19. A. Walker, *The Holy Life of Mrs Elizabeth Walker* (London, 1690), p. 35.
20. S. Clarke, *Lives of Sundry Eminent Persons in this Later Age* (1683), p. 141. I am grateful to Jacqueline Eales for this reference.
21. J. Barlow, *The True Guide to Glory* (London, 1619), p. 48.
22. Crawford, *Women and Religion in England*, p. 88.
23. K.U. Henderson and B.F. McManus, eds, *Half Humankind: Contexts and Texts of the Controversy about Women in England 1540–1640* (Urbana, 1985), pp. 336–7; Walker, *Life of Mrs Elizabeth Walker*, pp. 32, 40; W. Tong, *An Account of the Life and Death of Mrs Elizabeth Bury* (London, 1720), p. 28; see also M. Todd, *Christian Humanism and the Puritan Social Order* (Cambridge, 1987), pp. 105–7.
24. Sheils, ed., *Women in the Church*, p. 371.
25. Barlow, *The True Guide to Glory*, p. 48.

she laid a bond upon herself never to receive it but the day before to
sit and examine herself seriously and deeply to humble herself before
the Lord in fasting and prayer all the day long'.[26] Elizabeth Walker,
it is related, had her children answer the catechism publicly, 'that the
meaner sort might be ashamed not to send their children and the poor
children might be quickened and encouraged by their example and
company'.[27] John Ley, like many of these preachers, emphasised Jane
Ratcliffe's intense desire to attend church and receive the sacrament
regularly.[28]

Yet the core of the godly woman's spiritual experience consisted of
private devotions. This commitment, Peter Lake argues in his portrait
of Jane Ratcliffe, could be contained within conventional female virtues.
Mrs Ratcliffe practised 'a sort of displaced patriarchalism': her 'increasingly complete subjection to and possession by her God enabled her,
if not to resist, then to circumvent the usual constraints of female
existence'. Lake sees Jane Ratcliffe as creating for herself 'a persona of
some potency' through a process of sublimation and internalisation of
her religion. He suggests that passivity and internalised zeal to this degree
of intensity was a peculiarly female phenomenon.[29] The argument can be
extended from Lake's single case study, using funeral sermons and
personal materials, into an account of the form of self-fashioning
which, transmitted to others through the mechanism of print, became the
first positive attempt at female gender construction in England. We need
to consider firstly how godly women sought their personal potency and
secondly how a specific literary genre gave that potency didactic
shape and purpose.

The eulogists often stressed that godly women rose at an early hour and
began the day with private prayer.[30] Alice Lucy's 'first employment every
day', so we are told, 'was her humble addresses to Almighty God in
secret; her next was to read some part of God's word and of other good
and profitable books'. A pattern of prayer and reading punctuated these
women's days. Mary Gunter distinguished 'family duties' from 'private
prayers' with her maids, besides which 'she was thrice on her knees every
day before God in secret'. She also spent long hours with her Bible,
reading it from cover to cover every year and noting passages she found
difficult and which she could consult about with ministers or 'other
understanding Christians'.[31] During the hours she spent on her own in her

---

26. Clarke, *Lives of Sundry Eminent Persons*, p. 138.
27. Walker, *Holy Life of Mrs Elizabeth Walker*, p. 71.
28. Lake, 'Feminine Piety', *The Seventeenth Century*, II (1987), p. 162.
29. Lake, 'Feminine Piety', *The Seventeenth Century*, II (1987), p. 158.
30. E.g. J.B. Williams, *Memoirs of the Life of Mrs Sarah Savage* (London, 1829), p. 25;
    Walker, *Holy Life of Mrs Elizabeth Walker*, p. 32. See also M. Prior, ed., *Women in
    English Society 1500–1800* (London, 1985), p. 89.
31. Clarke, *Lives of Sundry Eminent Persons*, pp. 137, 141.

closet each day, Lady Vere 'redeemed much precious time, in reading the holy scriptures and other godly books that might give her further light into them'. Margaret Ducke's private devotions occupied her most of the time she was not ordering the affairs of the household or educating her children: she read so deeply, it was said, that she made her heart 'a library of Christ'.[32]

The steps which women took to conceal their devotional writings indicate the importance to them of the privacy of this sphere of their living. Much of Elizabeth Bury's diary defeated her husband who after her death tried to decipher its 'peculiar characters and abbreviations'. However, using what he could to put together a memoir, he was convinced that it showed 'great sincerity, humility and modesty without any art or affectation'. Elizabeth Dunton used a shorthand of her own invention and, lest she was seen to cultivate the vainglory of a posthumous reputation, wanted her papers burnt. Sarah Savage recorded her endeavours to keep her diary private. Elizabeth Walker, caught red-handed by her husband, made him promise he would not look at her papers during her lifetime. After her death he found among them in her desk spiritual instructions to her two daughters, including six pages of extracts from books about 'meekness of spirit'. There was also a set of memorials of God's providences to him, herself and their children.[33]

Sara Heller Mendelson established in a survey of twenty-three surviving Stuart women's diaries – there must be many more that are lost – that three-quarters of them contain 'considerable devotional content'. Women wrote diaries to enforce their spiritual regime, discipline them-selves, impose order on their experience of life and provide a means of self-examination. The first known example is Lady Margaret Hoby's journal, begun in 1599. Guides to self-examination such as John Featley's *A Fountain of Tears*, published in 1646, undoubtedly prompted more diary-keeping and in 1656 John Beadle published his systematic manual about the practice. Diary-keeping would become the core of a godly woman's life, a source of assurance and catharsis. Sarah Savage hoped her diary might be 'a means to make me the more watchful of the frame of my heart when it must be kept on record'. Elizabeth Bury, it was noted in her funeral sermon, 'would often say that, were it not for her diary, she should neither know what she was or what she did'. Elizabeth Mordaunt found the recording and repudiation of her sins immensely reassuring. She kept her diary from 1656 to her death in 1678: 'Oh how I am filled with love and wonder when I

---

32. Sheils, ed., *Women in the Church*, pp. 374–5.
33. Citations from S.H. Mendelson in 'Stuart Women's Diaries and Occasional Memoirs' in Prior, ed., *Women in English Society*, pp. 183–4. See also Tong, *An Account of the Life and Death of Mrs Elizabeth Bury*, sig. A2, p. 11; Walker, *Holy Life of Mrs Elizabeth Walker*, pp. 6, 73–4.

meditate upon thy mercies to me and mine,' she wrote on 1 March 1664.[34]

It is plain that meditation on passages of scripture was peculiarly likely to raise women's consciousness and the level of their spiritual experience. Recognition of the need for repentance, understanding of the divine gift of God's restoring grace and gratitude for deliverances from sin and death were each of them aspects of the meditative dialogue. As women's hearts were stirred, they experienced personal discovery not only of God but also of themselves, relating what they learnt about God's mercy and truth to their own human condition. Elizabeth Grymeston wrote her collection of meditative writings, published in 1604 with a further three editions by 1618, to instruct her son in meditation. She was a recusant but some of her work, with its emphasis on deliverance by Christ from the miseries of sin, resonates with protestant meditative themes. Elizabeth Richardson's *A Lady's Legacy to her Daughters*, written in 1625, was a book of prayers she had composed, matter, she asserted when it went into print, which 'surely concerns and belongs to women as well as to the best learned men'. She included 'a sorrowful widow's prayer' and a 'prayer to be prepared for a happy death'. Lady Anne Harcourt's prayers and meditations, unpublished in our period, concentrate upon escapes in the civil war with her second husband, Sir William Waller, which were seen in providential terms, and upon deliverances from diseases and death in childbirth. Lady Elizabeth Delaval's meditations include an account of her having worms removed from her gums at the age of seventeen. She was much concerned that the local woman who did this was reputed a witch but concluded that, since the worms were clearly a punishment by which God was testing her, she could not be one because she was the agent through whom God, 'in his good time', mercifully removed her pains.[35] Some produced meditations in verse. Those by An Collins, which were published in 1653, are rich with the imagery of the virgin's female soul, the 'enclosed garden' as an emblem of perfection and her awaiting for God as the 'beloved'.[36]

One of the most interesting of these personal memoirs is the autobiography that Alice Thornton late in her life reworked from a tiny notebook she had started after her husband's death in 1668 chronicling, as a 'Book of Remembrances', the 'deliverances' of herself and her family since 1626. In the preface to the actual autobiography, which filled three large notebooks against the single one used for the original version, she

---

34. Prior, ed., *Women in English Society*, pp. 185–7; C.F. Otten, ed., *English Women's Voices 1540–1700* (Miami, 1992), pp. 285, 324–9.
35. Otten, ed., *English Women's Voices*, pp. 277–346.
36. Graham, et al., eds, *Her Own Life: Autobiographical Writings by Seventeenth-Century Englishwomen* (London, 1989), pp. 53–70.

explained that it was the duty of true Christians to take notice of God's providences:

> I therefore, his creature and unworthy handmaid, who have not tasted only of the droppings of his dew, but has been showered plentifully upon my head with the continued streams of goodness, do most humbly desire to furnish my heart with the deep thoughts and apprehensions and sincere meditations of and thankfulness for his free grace, love, mercy and inconceivable goodness to me.[37]

Alice Thornton's work continually mixes clinical detail with biblical exegesis. The deliverances often read like a catalogue of sufferings; indeed the book has been called 'a work of mourning'. We hear of escapes from measles and smallpox, from wounds and dangers in childbirth, from drowning, fire and shipwreck. Charlotte Otten argues that the autobiography can be seen as creating a 'construct of the female self'.[38] This comment makes sense in view of the unremitting detail about pregnancies, miscarriages and births. Refining this notion of construction, the editors of an anthology of women's writings see Alice as presenting herself as 'an extreme model of feminine passivity'. But they stress that though there is much about the books that suggests a submissive woman constrained in various ways by her class and upbringing, Alice at the same time reveals herself as tenacious and self-possessed. She displays a remarkable emotional articulateness about her griefs as she sets straight the record of her worldly and spiritual life. The argument that her intention was that all versions of the autobiography should circulate in manuscript among her family and be handed down to her children and descendants is persuasive.[39] Alice Thornton's may be the autobiography which, through its intricate mixing of personal experience and spiritual reflections, gives us our deepest and most comprehensive insight into the seventeenth-century female religious mind.

The tension between secularity and spirituality, the corruption of earthly things and divine perfectibility, is a constant underlying theme in this genre of female meditative verse and prose. How this emerges depends very much on the writer's condition: the perspective changes for maid, wife and widow. Yet universally it seems lack of sexual fulfilment contributed something to the power of these women's creative muse. Katherine Austen's diary for 1664 to 1666 records the prayers, thoughts and draft letters to her children of a woman widowed six years before at the age of twenty-nine. Her prayers focus on the needs of her children. Her concern to preserve and increase their fortunes was an important

37. C. Jackson, ed., *The Autobiography of Mrs Alice Thornton* (Surtees Society, LXII, 1873), p. 1 and passim.
38. Otten, ed., *English Women's Voices*, p. 225.
39. Graham, et al., eds, *Her Own Life*, pp. 147–9.

consideration in refusing a suitor at this time. Her attachment to her husband is hinted at by several references to him, his family and posterity. She recorded a dream, for example, about playing a game of cribbage with her husband. In a moving passage, Katherine explained for her own satisfaction why she had decided to remain single. Her denial of sexual pleasure in favour of friendship has explicit spiritual overtones:

> As for my body it can be enjoyed but by one and I hope its the worst part of me and that which every servant maid and country wench may excel mine and can give the same satisfaction as mine. But that which my desire is should far excel my body is my soul and the virtues and qualities of that. And this I think may be useful to more than one and not confined to a single person and if any thing in me is to be loved I hope 'tis my mind. . . . Thus all my friends may partake of me and be married in the dearness and usefulness and benefits of friendship.

Katherine Austen died in 1683 after a widowhood of twenty-five years.[40] It was quite possible for a widow who became deeply immersed in piety to carry her relationship with a heavenly spouse into the experience of mystical visions. This happened to Anne Bathurst whose erotic transference was expressed in recorded incidents such as Christ seeming 'to kiss me with the kisses of his mouth'.[41]

Diaries can be an illuminating source for marital conflict. The Countess of Warwick's diary, kept from 1666 to 1673, records various occasions when she was struggling to repress her strong will. 'I bore it patiently without saying anything to provoke it farther,' she wrote after one time when her husband lost his temper with her. But she did not always manage so well: another time she argued and was 'very passionately affected and wept much and spoke unadvisedly'. In her diary she begged God's pardon for her lapses.[42] Where women have left us a considerable body of devotional material, we can go somewhat deeper into how a woman's private spiritual life could either be a refuge from the inadequacies and lack of fulfilment of wedlock or complement its happiness. We can take three examples here: Grace Mildmay, whose writings between 1566 and 1620 are now available in a modern edition; Elizabeth Egerton, the Countess of Bridgewater, whose occasional meditations and prayers between around 1648 and 1663 are in the British Library; and Lady Elizabeth Delaval, whose autobiographical memoir with prayers and meditations has also recently been edited and published. Grace Mildmay, by her own account, was a submissive wife but the sense runs through all her writings that her attitude to her marriage was one of resigned

40. BL. Add. MS 4454, especially fols 4v–5r, 23r, 25r, 42r, 64, 92r, 94r–95v. See also, B.J. Todd, 'The Remarrying Widow: A Stereotype Reconsidered', in Prior, ed., *Women in English Society*, pp. 76–7.
41. Cited in Prior, ed., *Women in English Society*, p. 195.
42. BL. Add. MS 27351, fol. 11v and cited in Prior, ed., *Women in English Society*, p. 194.

acceptance rather than joy or pleasure. Her description of the process of entry into meditation can probably stand in its essentials for that of many godly women. The reading she chose was usually a chapter from the books of Moses and Prophets, one from the gospels and another from the epistles: 'wherein I found that, as the water pierceth the hard stone by often dropping thereupon, so the continual exercise in the word of God made a deep impression in my stony heart with an aptness to incline unto the will of God and to delight in the meditation thereof upon every occasion of thought arising in my mind, or upon whatsoever mine eye did behold or mine ear did hear, applying the same as I was directed by the spirit of God'. Linda Pollock has commented upon how Grace's meditations 'bring home the sheer exaltation of faith, the joy, awe and wonder of faith, the beauty and majesty of God to her, her passionate engagement and rapturous dwelling on Christ'. In her lyrical accounts, God was a creature of strength with eyes 'as a flame of fire', 'my fortress and my refuge . . . my castle and house of defence, my buckler, my shield and the horn of my salvation'. Christ would protect and love her always. Faith was her 'armour' and her 'balm'.[43]

The Countess of Bridgewater's papers contain a remarkable passage headed 'considerations concerning marriage' which deserves full analysis. In theory, she states, showing her knowledge of the conduct book advice, marriage must be unhappy for women since 'there is an obedience must belong from the wife to the husband and 'tis great reason it should so be, since we are commanded by those that are above our capacity of reason, by God himself'. Women have to accept this: they must be able to feel 'esteem of such a person so as to value his judgement and in matter of consequence to yield to his counsel'. At the same time she should be able to stand up to him, not by showing the awe of a servant to his master but by having 'an affection and love to him as to a friend and so to speak their mind and opinion freely to him yet not value him the less'. If he has the same attitude, she believes, patriarchy can be modified by love, whereas excessive submissiveness on her part makes it an intolerable yoke:

> If he have a reciprocal affection to his wife it makes them both blessed in one another whereas other ways, of the wife be so meek and low in spirit to be in subjection for every word, she makes him fear he is troublesome and that she had rather be alone than in his company; this is far from a companion's way; if high and lofty and wilful then of the other side he is not himself when he is with her, so then rather though he loves her than bring himself into an unquiet disturbed life, he leaves her to go into some other company, caring not how little he is with her and when he sees her in company, doubts she will give him some undigested words and if so, then he is discontented with the sight of

---

43. L.A. Pollock, *With Faith and Physic: The Life of a Tudor Gentlewoman Lady Grace Mildmay 1552–1620* (London, 1993), pp. 34–5, 68, 74; above, pp. 165–6.

her so must give her a reprehension at least in private, thus doth this indiscretion cause a miserable life to them both.

The Countess's somewhat tangled prose reveals a conviction about the personal dynamic of marital partnership. If a woman, she goes on, is 'overawed by her own fancies' this will trouble her husband. She must recognise that he is willing to be a 'friendly companion'. This is what makes a marriage happy, especially if a wife can avoid interpreting small slights as evidence that he 'loves me not' and can give no cause for his anger. She thinks that some husbands who were 'fickle and various', giving their wives little attention, simply drove them into the arms of God whereas others, more sensitively, respected their privacy:

> Then may the wife make her own happiness for then she may give herself up to prayer . . . and thus in his absence she is as much God's as a virgin; and if she have a loving discreet husband and one that fears God he will doubtless not hinder her duty to God, but endeavour the increase of her faith and holiness.

Elizabeth Egerton's belief in marriage was clearly based on experience: 'where both these parties do perfectly agree with passionate and sincere affection but 'tis the happiest condition, a friendship never to be broke'. Among her extensive collection of prayers for her times of labour, for 'resolution against despair', and against 'sluggishness in religious duties' are prayers on the 'happy day' of her husband's twenty-seventh birthday and for his protection when in danger.[44]

Elizabeth Delaval's meditations have been described as the expression of the personal anguish of a powerless young woman regarding friendship, courtship, love and marriage.[45] In 1670, a few months after the man she loved was married to someone else, her father arranged her marriage to Robert Delaval, heir to the important Northumberland estate of Seaton Delaval. Her bitterness against her father was incandescent and she could not keep it to herself, 'which I am sensible is a very great wickedness in me; the Lord in much mercy pardon it'. Her meditative narratives are interspersed with prayers which show her attempting to find serenity by calls on God to help her resolve her conflicts, forgive her enemies whom she holds responsible for sins against her and salve her own deep sense of unworthiness. Prayer for Elizabeth Delaval did not change anything but it offered her catharsis. Attempting to focus her mind on Good Friday in 1671, for instance, she wrote as follows: 'Betwixt vanity and cares my life has hitherto been trifled away, and I have but slightly considered the things which belong unto my eternal peace, so that when I begin to turn my thoughts to the meditations of my Saviour's bitter passion, I find

44. BL Egerton MS, fols 28r, 78v–83v, 88r, 111v–114, see also Prior, ed., *Women in English Society*, p. 194.
45. Otten, ed., *English Women's Voices*, p. 286.

myself lost in a labyrinth'. Her reaction to marriage, she was distressed to find, was to seek diversions and neglect her spiritual devotions. Her confusion is palpable: 'Having quitted my beloved virgin state of life . . . I scarce yet know where I am. That pleasing word of liberty, being now no more to be pronounced by me as what I have a right to. I cannot but at the first putting on of shackles find their weight heavy. So to put off that thought I fly solitude and seek busyness.' Her father had just died and she was racked with guilt at having been peevish even at his deathbed about unkindness to her, 'which I had reason to believe he bitterly repented of '. Elizabeth Delaval was simply unable to be the subservient wife. Her husband quickly broke the vow of temperance he gave her at their marriage, getting into the debauched company of other young men. If only, she regretted in 1671 six months into their marriage, she had been able to be mild in telling him of his faults instead of employing 'proud ill natured words'. These had 'too often tempted him to fall into the fury of a mad and sinful passion' which simply increased both their iniquities. The marriage was deeply unhappy. In 1674 Robert Delaval, declaring to his father his wife's unkindness, wrote 'but I may find a way to be even with her just yet'. In 1681 Elizabeth left Seaton Delaval for Scotland, dismissing her father-in-law with the remark that he was 'fool and knave governed by his sot wife'. Elizabeth Delaval was a woman who could not let herself be so governed. What can be said of her recorded spiritual life is that it undoubtedly gave her some kind of comfort and direction, even if she often found herself 'frozen and benumbed' with sin 'like the decadent time of winter'. She knew well her own words on 12 May 1671 and tried to trust them: 'Our Saviour's blest command, watch and pray, ought to be the constant practice of our lives, for he gave us no precept but what was given with the design of a reward attending our obedience, a glorious reward far above all we can wish for or imagine.'[46]

If women like Elizabeth Delaval have left us the authentic voice of personal experience in this period, writers like John Ley, the eulogist of Jane Ratcliffe, have given us a genre of published works which is of signal importance in a different sense. We have to accept that the construction of gender which the funeral sermons present is an almost accidental by-product of their didactic spiritual purpose. Yet the genre, for the story this book tells, is not the less important for that. The sermons make apparent a crucial link between protestantism and the evolution of modern English gender. Peter Lake has written of the intentions of a man like John Ley in terms of an 'ideology of personal godliness'. This allowed female gender to be portrayed for the first time in wholly positive terms. He sees funeral sermons as works at the heart of the new protestant divinity: each one by its influence on a multitude could help to transform an individual

46. D.G. Greene, ed., *The Meditations of Lady Elizabeth Delaval* (Surtees Society, CXC, 1978), pp. 9–13, 161–212.

life of piety through 'a process of collective growth in grace and increasing spiritual perfection'. How was this achieved? Although the format of the published sermons varies somewhat, the pattern is common, organising a woman's activities and behaviour to exemplify her graces, converting a life lived into a series of exempla for the edification of the godly community, presenting the holy woman almost, Lake suggests, as a holy object in herself, or at least as a touchstone whose 'shining example could only increase the collective unity, purity and strength of godly consciousness'.[47]

A life of moderation was seen as the essence of the female regime of godliness. This could mean a considerable degree of asceticism and self-denial. Katherine Stubbs, it was reported, refused 'to pamper her body with delicate meats, wines or strong drink but refrained from them altogether'. Elizabeth Walker was said to confine herself at dinner to eating a small piece of white bread with some household beer. The tensions between spirit and flesh were constantly in the minds of preachers. Wantonness, as Nicholas Breton put it in his 1626 pamphlet *The Good and the Badde*, was associated with 'the excess of dainties'.[48] John Ley put this ascetic imperative in its most emphatic form in his account of Jane Ratcliffe:

> Though while she lived she could not choose but be in the world, she so loved her Lord Jesus Christ that for his sake she was exceedingly estranged from the world, which was plainly perceived by a threefold freedom. First from desire of sensual delights. Secondly from love of worldly profits. Thirdly from the liking of life itself.[49]

Limiting sleep and self-denial with regard to the pleasures of food and sex were all part of the pattern of godliness which these sermons promulgated.

The same negative prescription applied, predictably enough, to rich clothes, that most snaring invitation to female pride. Lady Strode's dress was so modest 'that a curious eye could not justly pick a quarrel at it'.[50] Elizabeth Machell, who was twenty-three at her death, possessed a 'gravity, sobriety and modesty matching the oldest matrons'. One way she achieved this was by living up to her own ideal that 'apparel is an adjunct that sets out a woman and makes her seem excellent'.[51] Elizabeth Walker always dressed in black to be entirely on the safe side.[52] John Batchiller's account of the short life of Susanna Fenwick, who died in 1661, explained that after the early death of her fiancé she adopted a plain neat garb,

47. Lake, 'Feminine Piety', *The Seventeenth Century*, II (1987), pp. 144–5.
48. Citations from Crawford, *Women and Religion in England*, p. 92.
49. Cited in Lake, 'Feminine Piety', *The Seventeenth Century*, II (1987), p. 146.
50. Barlow, *The True Guide to Glory* (1619), p. 49.
51. S. Geree, *The Ornament of Women* (London, 1639), pp. 40, 64.
52. Walker, *Holy Life of Mrs Elizabeth Walker*, p. 75.

abandoning the black spots and patches which were becoming the rage as facial decoration at that time and insisting that the girls at the fashionable boarding school at Hackney kept by her parents did so too.[53] John Mayer praised Lucy Thornton in his sermon in 1619 for her humility, instancing the way she 'despised the ornaments of vanity which other women so much delight in'. 'Her outward habit', he declared, 'did show the inward lowliness and modesty of her mind.'[54]

The pattern of female virtue invariably had as its keynote characterisations in terms of modesty and humility. Everything the preachers wanted to say could be built upon these notions: devotion to private religious duties, household leadership, public works of charity. Mayer was one of the more schematic in the way he wrote his eulogy for his patron's wife at Little Wratting in Suffolk. The 'epistle consolatory' to Roger Thornton expressed the hope that she would be one of those who act as 'patterns before our eyes'. Five points about Lucy Thornton were made. She was 'anointed with a religious zeal'; her wisdom enabled her to use her time to spiritual advantage; 'she was anointed with true love, causing in her plenty of good works'; she was 'anointed with humility ... the lowly handmaiden of the Lord'; 'she was anointed with due subjection to her husband, as Sarah who reverenced her husband'.[55] At times the individual seems clouded by rhetoric, but at other times the speech, behaviour and carriage of these godly women, the actual ground of this first genre of gender construction, shines through. Katherine Stubbs, we are told, resisted temptation to brawl or scold, whereas she was fond of asking her husband's advice about passages of scripture she had been reading. She was always ready to reprove those around her for scurrilous or blasphemous talk: there was 'never one filthy unclean, indecent or unseemly word heard to come out of her mouth'.[56] Elizabeth Machell, insisted the minister Stephen Geree, sedulously avoided gossip and always spoke 'with grace and fear of God'.[57] Elizabeth Walker's husband remembered how strict she had been in checking 'uncivil or wanton gestures' between men and maidservants, explaining the severe view she took of women's responsibility to preserve their honour: 'Modesty was a woman's ornament and a guard of chastity which would seldom or never be attempted did not some lightness or unwary carriage embolden those who did assault it and the flames which scorched the female honour were mostly kindled by sparks of their own striking.'[58]

This chapter has concentrated on women who sought personal

53. A. Fraser, *The Weaker Vessel: Woman's Lot in Seventeenth-Century England* (London, 1985), pp. 158–60.
54. Henderson and McManus, eds, *Half Humankind*, p. 338.
55. Henderson and McManus, eds, *Half Humankind*, pp. 336–42.
56. P. Stubbes, *A Christal Glass for Christian Women* (London, 1591), sigs A2, A3.
57. Geree, *The Ornament of Women*, pp. 31–2.
58. Walker, *Holy Life of Mrs Elizabeth Walker*, p. 91.

fulfilment through an intense and largely private spiritual life. These godly women lived out their lives within the structure of the patriarchal household; they respected and accepted its values and offered no basic challenge to its survival. Whereas there was a smaller group of women whose religious activities in the 1640s and 1650s did actually challenge patriarchy or sought to surmount it altogether.[59] But the irony is that the women who have been discussed here may be the more important ones for our unravelling of the transformation of English gender in the long term. Religion for these women can be seen as a form of social control, as a means by which a subordinate group sometimes harassed by the griefs of childbirth and of losing children were given solace and taught to bear with life's tragedies. Their household piety, in this reading, becomes functionalist, confining rather than releasing them. Yet the essence of the flight to spiritual experience was personal release, as many of the stories told here confirm. Moreover the use that preachers made of that experience in published funeral sermons was innovatory. The godly woman transcended the negative stereotypes of the weaker vessel.

For the first time, without having to question anything about the orthodox account of women as more emotional than rational, people could read accounts of the good woman based upon contemporary example and in rounded prose. If the good woman was now being socially produced – constructed indeed – this was the direction in which the world of gender was moving. Protestant ministers may have constructed their portraits for conservative didactic effect but they were contributing to a genre which can be seen as the first step, in prescriptive terms, on the road to modern femininity.

59. See the account in Crawford, *Women and Religion in England*, pp. 119–82 and P. Mack, *Visionary Women: Ecstatic Prophecy in Seventeenth Century England* (Berkeley, California, 1992).

18. *Educating Girls*

'THE BREEDING OF men were after a different manner of ways from those of women,' noted Margaret Cavendish around 1630, writing about the upbringing of herself and her brothers.[1] Educational writers paid little attention to a curriculum for girls: it was as if the male experience comprised the whole human experience. Hezekiah Woodward devoted a single chapter of his 1640 tract *A Childes Patrimony Laid Out upon the Good Culture of Tilling over his whole Man* to girls' education. John Milton's educational system in the *Tractate of Education*, published in 1644, entirely ignored girls. Its goal was to produce 'brave men and worthy patriots', scorning all their 'childish and ill-taught qualities'.[2] John Locke said a little more in some asides during the course of his major work on education and in the much-quoted letter he wrote to Mrs Clarke, the mother of children he tutored. His tirade against the vices of boys' public schools, for instance, includes an approving reference to the 'retirement and bashfulness' in which daughters were brought up. This could be modified into a 'becoming assurance' as they later learnt the art of conversation. He was concerned about the effects of too much sun on their tender skins, health and beauty. He stressed the necessity for early training at home by a dancing master to provide girls with 'fashion and easy comely motion'. Fathers should not beat them or even chide them: 'their governing and correcting, I think', he told Mrs Clarke, 'properly belongs to the mother'.[3] Locke, in other words, was thoroughly orthodox.

For the most part it simply did not cross men's minds that girls could be taught to reason as boys could. It was assumed that the developmental

---

1. Cited in L.A. Pollock, 'Teach her to Live under Obedience: The Making of Women in the Upper Ranks of Early Modern England', *Continuity and Change* 4 (1989), p. 238.
2. H.L. Smith, '"All Men and Both Sexes": Concepts of Men's Development, Women's Education and Feminism in the Seventeenth Century', in D.C. Mall, ed., *Man, God and Nature in the Enlightenment* (London, 1989), pp. 75–7.
3. J.L. Axtell, ed., *The Educational Writings of John Locke*, (Cambridge, 1969) pp. 346–8.

stages of the young male provided a basis for a rigorous academic curriculum that was inapplicable to the female mind. These presuppositions emerge clearly in some passages of the instructions that the Earl of Northumberland wrote for his son Algernon Percy. 'Mark but women's education from their cradles', he wrote, 'and then shall we perceive that their bringings up can promise no deep insight into matters of knowledge but such as are soon got and easily learned.' Northumberland regarded girls as uneducable by nature:

> And this you may observe generally, that women at very young years are as grave and well fashioned, as ever after, for their outward carriage, making small progress in any learnings after; saving in love, a little craft and a little thriftiness, if they be so addicted out of disposition, handsomeness and trimness being the idol of their hearts, till time write deep wrinkles in their foreheads.

There were occasionally women, he confessed, some of the most virtuous, who 'will cast their eyes upon the higher arguments of the scriptures', but this was not fundamentally what girls were made for. Their education was social and gender-specific. Northumberland provides a classic statement about parental aspirations in fashioning daughters for marriage: their care is to see them 'modest, neat, graceful, obedient', he declares, 'to draw on the likings of husbands, whereby fathers may put them off and provide them fortunes during the rest of their lives that must be got either when they are young or never, for then are they the prettiest'.[4]

We can compare Northumberland's view, which is undoubtedly characteristic of the English gentry as a whole, with a comment in the satirical pamphlet *The Women's Sharp Revenge* in 1640. This shows glimmerings of an understanding about the connection between male dominance and the male monopoly of education. Men's policy, it was alleged, had been to 'curb us of that benefit, by striving to keep us under and to make us men's mere vassals even unto posterity'.[5] After 1660 a small group of women like Bathsua Makin, Elizabeth Elstob and Mary Astell took up this critique of the English educational system, argued that women had the capacity to benefit from academic training, deplored the social education that was imposed upon them and insisted that they were being denied the possibility of personal development through intellectual enquiry.[6] The incapacity, as Mary Astell put it in 1696, 'if there be any, is acquired not natural'.[7] The attack focused upon the circularity of the

4. H. Markland, 'Instructions by Henry Percy touching the Management of his Estate', *Archaeologia*, XXVII (1838), pp. 330–31.
5. Cited in M.J.M. Ezell, *The Patriarch's Wife: Literary Evidence and the History of the Family* (Chapel Hill, 1987), p. 52. For John Taylor's authorship of *The Women's Sharp Revenge* see Capp, pp. 118–99.
6. See H.L. Smith, *Reason's Disciples* (Urbana, 1982), pp. 117–39, 192–201; H.L. Smith in Mall, ed., *Man, God and Nature in the Enlightenment*, pp. 75–84; J.K. Kinnaird, 'Mary

conservative view. Fenelon's *Treatise on the Education of Daughters*, available in an English translation from 1707, is a good example. 'Women in general', he argued, 'possess a weaker but more inquisitive mind than men . . . their bodies as well as minds are less strong and energetic than those of men but to compensate for their defects nature has bestowed on them a spirit of industry, united with propriety of behaviour, and an economy which renders them at once the ornament and comfort of home.' A programme of learning shorn of everything that was intellectually demanding followed for this standpoint. Yet, as the century wore on, there were even men ready to argue women's case. Thus Vicesimus Knox, writing in 1739, dismissed the view that 'learning belongs not to the female character' as a narrow prejudice. 'The superior advantages of boys' education', he maintained, 'are perhaps the sole reason of their subsequent superiority.'[8]

Richard Mulcaster noted that 'young maidens ordinarily share' the earliest stages of boys' schooling.[9] There is no solid evidence that they ever advanced at sixteenth-century schools beyond the reading and writing stage and entered upon the classical curriculum. Certain schools founded between the 1590s and 1630s, such as those at Bunbury in Cheshire, Thaxted in Essex and West Chiltington in Sussex, that admitted girls were quite specific that they could only attend to learn to read English and that they could stay at the longest till the age of nine or ten. At the same time there were moves in some cases to prevent girls enrolling at all. The 1590 rules at Harrow explicitly excluded them. Other schools that did so about the same time included St Olave's School in Southwark, Felsted in Essex and Tiverton in Devon.[10] Thomas Saunders asserted in his Founder's Rules at Uffington in Berkshire in 1637 that the common practice of sending daughters to learn English 'with and amongst all sorts of youths' was unacceptable, since this course was 'by many conceived very uncomely and not decent'.[11]

A very small group of young women, mainly from noble families, did experience the classical curriculum in the sixteenth and seventeenth centuries through the expertise of tutors at home. The influence of the catholic humanist Juan Luis Vives, who argued that a carefully organised

Astell and the Conservative Contribution to English Feminism', *Journal of British Studies* 19 (1979), pp. 53–75; J. Nadelhaft, 'The Englishwoman's Sexual Civil War: Feminist Attitudes towards Men, Women and Marriage 1650–1740', *Journal of the History of Ideas* 43 (1982), pp. 555–79.

7. Cited in V. Jones, ed., *Women in the Eighteenth Century: Constructions of Femininity* (London, 1990), p. 98.

8. Citations from Jones, ed., *Women in the Eighteenth Century*, pp. 102, 109.

9. Cited in K.U. Henderson and B.F. McManus, eds, *Half Humankind: Contexts and Texts of the Controversy about Women in England 1540–1640* (Urbana, 1985), p. 89.

10. N. McMullen, 'The Education of English Gentlewomen 1540–1640', *History of Education* 6 (1977), pp. 91–2.

11. Cited in Henderson and McManus, eds., *Half Humankind*, p. 89.

educational programme in Latin and Greek could, if taught together with Christian learning, develop virtue in a woman, was paramount behind this short-lived development. Thomas More, inspired by famous learned women in Italy, gave his three daughters the same classical education as his son. The daughters of Sir Anthony Cooke, in similar fashion, were guinea-pigs in a humanist experiment.[12] A few others followed in their footsteps. Lucy Hutchinson, born in 1620, was something of a prodigy: having a Frenchwoman as her dry nurse she learned to speak French and English at the same time and she was reading at four. Aged seven, she later claimed she had eight tutors at one and the same time, teaching her languages besides writing, music, dancing and needlework. She had no time for traditional female accomplishments, however, so her father, accepting her precocity, gave her her head with Latin. He was by this time an exceptional father in daring to do so and his daughter's education caused some tensions:

> I was so apt that I outstript my brothers who were at school, although my father's chaplain that was my tutor was a pitiful dull fellow. My brothers, who had a great deal of wit, had some emulation at the progress I made in my learning, which very well pleased my father, though my mother would have been contented I had not so wholly addicted myself to that as to neglect my other qualities.[13]

There were a number of other families who hired tutors for their girls in the course of the seventeenth century, bucking the increasing trend towards confining their education to social and domestic attributes. There are also occasional cases of women being singled out for praise for their educated minds. Lady Judith Barrington, for example, was described in a funeral sermon by Thomas Goodwin as exceeding 'most of her sex' and being 'in the very upper form of female scholars'.[14] The daughters of Viscount Hatton, it was recorded around 1698, were 'good Latin scholars'.[15] But such girls were very much exceptions.

The dislike of intellectual women seems to have emerged strongly in the first decades of the seventeenth century. The Jacobean dramatists were clearly playing to known prejudice in their biting portraits of learned women.[16] A proper gentlewoman, declared Richard Brathwaite in his

12. Henderson and McManus, eds., *Half Humankind*, pp. 81–6; R. O'Day, *Education and Society 1500–1800: The Social Foundations of Education in Early Modern Britain* (London, 1982), pp. 183–6; A. Shepherd, *Gender and Authority in Sixteenth-Century England* (Keele, 1994), pp. 106–16.

13. Cited in McMullen, 'Education of English Gentlewomen', *History of Education* 6 (1977), p. 99; L.A. Pollock, *A Lasting Relationship: Parents and their Children over Three Centuries* (London, 1987), p. 222.

14. Cited in Ezell, *Patriarch's Wife*, p. 15, who gives other examples.

15. Cited in Pollock, 'Teach her to Live', *Continuity and Change* 4 (1989), p. 240.

16. For the stage attacks see L. Woodbridge, *Women and the English Renaissance: Literature and the Nature of Womankind 1540–1620* (Urbana, 1986), pp. 208–9.

tract of 1642, desired not 'the esteem of any she-clerks; she had rather be approved by her living than learning'.[17] This kind of prejudice was hard for women brought up in more sympathetic days, producing in some cases ambivalence about what was best for their own child. Elizabeth Joceline, losing her mother at six, had been brought up and educated by her godfather, Laurence Chaderton, Bishop of Lincoln. He taught her languages, including Latin and history, as well as how to live piously. The best selling tract under her name, *A Mother's Legacy to her Unborn Child*, was based on a treatise of advice to her husband which she left in her desk and which was found by her husband when she died in childbirth at the age of twenty-seven. An important passage about any daughter she might have, which brings out the confusion in which awareness of the changing attitudes of her lifetime had left her, deserves quotation in full:

> I desire her bringing up to be learning the bible, as my sisters do, good housewifery, writing and good works; other learning a woman needs not, though I admire it in those whom God hath blest with discretion. Yet I desired not so much in my own, having seen that sometimes women have greater portions of learning than wisdom, which is of no better use to them than a mainsail to a flyboat which runs under water. But where learning and wisdom meet in a virtuous disposed woman, she is the fittest closet of all goodness. . . . But, my dear, though she have all this in her, she will hardly make a poor man's wife. Yet I leave it to thy will. If thou desirest a learned daughter, I pray God give her a wise and religious heart, that she may use it to his glory, thy comfort and her own salvation.[18]

Irrelevance was certainly a crucial part of the general case against female schooling. There was a strong and widely held belief that education should be suited to a person's future lifestyle. 'My dear heart', the Earl of Strafford advised his daughter Anne in 1641, 'ply your book and other learnings which will be of use unto you hereafter.'[19] He did not have Latin or Greek authors in mind. Men had a vested interest in not wanting women to develop their minds, for what was eloquence in a male looked like scolding in a woman. Yet this is not quite the full story, for any kind of academic education was seen above all as threatening to a woman's modesty. The central theme, as we shall see, of female gender construction, was humility and obedience. He should bring up his daughters, John Evelyn counselled his grandson in 1704, to be 'humble, modest, moder-

---

17. Cited in S. Cahn, *Industry of Devotion: The Transformation of Women's Work in England 1550–1660* (Columbia, 1987), p. 114.
18. E Jocelyn, *A Mother's Legacy to her Unborn Child* (London, 1624), p. 4.
19. M. Blundell, ed., *Letters of William Blundell to his Friends 1620–1689*, p. 45; cited in *Continuity and Change* 4 (1989), p. 241.

ate, good housewives, discreetly frugal, without high expectations which will otherwise render them discontented'.[20] Sir Ralph Verney's letter to his friend Dr Denton about the education of his godchild Nancy in 1651 exemplifies this attitude: 'Let not your girl learn Latin, nor shorthand; the difficulty of the first may keep her from that vice, for so I must esteem it in a woman; but the easiness of the other may be a prejudice to her; for the pride of taking sermon notes hath made multitudes of women most unfortunate.'[21] Girls, in other words, must expect to contain their expectations of living to the utmost of all their abilities: moulding and repression are the essence of female training. When, for some girls, this came to include schooling, as it did from around the 1620s, a consistent ideological pattern can be found in the teaching of the attributes of femininity at school which complemented men's approach to an upbringing at home.

One of the first girls' boarding schools – about the only one documented, in fact, before 1600 – was run by a gentlewoman of Windsor who charged sixteen pounds a year 'for diet, lodging, washing and teaching them to work, reading, writing and dancing'. 'But for music', an applicant for her daughters was informed, 'you must pay for besides according as you will have them learn.' The school offered instruction in the viol, singing, the virginals and the lute. This was a fairly typical finishing school regime. Between 1617, when the highly reputed Ladies Hall at Deptford was opened, and the 1640s schools of this kind sprung up around the London suburbs and are also recorded in provincial towns like Exeter and Manchester. Queen Anne paid a visit to Deptford in 1617 and was presented with examples of needlework by the pupils there. They were dressed for the occasion, we are told, in loose green garments covered in silver and carnation lace. Mrs Friend's school at Stepney taught writing, needlework and music. There were several schools at Hackney, including the very flourishing one run by Robert Perwick and his wife which was educating more than a hundred girls at a time in the 1640s and 50s (plate 29). After the Restoration, Hackney and Putney seem to have become the fashionable locations for the capital's finishing schools. John Evelyn took a trip by barge to see 'the schools and colleges of the young gentlewomen' in Putney.[22] Pepys recorded a visit to Hackney on 21 April 1667: 'that which we went chiefly to see was the young ladies of the schools, whereof there is great store, very pretty'. Pepys had an acute eye for breeding, which was what this kind of education was all about, when it came to employing new servants. The day the fateful Deb Willet made

20. Cited in Pollock, 'Teach her to Live', *Continuity and Change* 4 (1989), p. 242.
21. Pollock, *Lasting Relationship*, p. 226.
22. O'Day, *Education and Society* pp. 186–7; A. Fraser, *The Weaker Vessel: Woman's Lot in Seventeenth-Century England* (London, 1985), p. 154; D. Gardiner, *English Girlhood at School* (London, 1929), pp. 223–34; Henderson and McManus, eds, *Half Humankind*, pp. 90–91.

her first appearance in the Pepys household for an interview, 27 September 1667, he came home from the office to see her: she was 'mighty pretty'. Besides which, he wrote, 'she seems by her discourse to be grave beyond her bigness and age and exceeding well-bred as to her deportment, having been a scholar in a school at Bow these seven or eight year'.[23] We know nothing of Deb Willet's social background but it is interesting that parental aspirations were drawing some London parents to send girls to the new finishing schools who were not rich enough simply to have them come home and join the marriage market.

Even if they did as teenagers go off to one of the fashionable boarding schools, girls spent much more time than boys being educated at home. That education, especially in the hands of the kind of godly women whose lives we have seen recorded in funeral sermons, was distinctive in that it was moral above all else. In time basic reading and writing and then a range of social and domestic accomplishments came into play (plates 20 and 25). Henry Slingsby, fussing in 1640 about his four-year-old son's progress in Latin, was contented to record that his five-year-old daughter Barbara was already able 'to say all her prayers, answer to her catechism, read and write a little'.[24] Elizabeth Dunton, Thomas Rogers related, favoured good words over the rod in educating her girls: 'she betimes guards them against self will and peevishness and obstinacy and the too great love of play'. Her method was to have one read while the others sewed, suggesting useful sayings for those with their fingers employed. Her catechising was constant and demanding so that her girls should 'think of what is good when they lie down and when they rise'.[25] Elizabeth Walker began her two girls on learning prayers and psalms by heart before they were four years old. She favoured a plain familiar catechism and was watchful that the servants did not lead them astray by telling them foolish stories or teaching them idle songs 'which might tincture their fancies with vain or hurtful imaginations'. To teach them how to be charitable she had her girls themselves give out the farthings or gifts of food offered to travelling people who came to their door. Above all she sought to combat any signs of vanity or pride. The nine-year-old Mall Blundell, it was noted, was often beaten because of her 'rolling untidy gate' and 'wild carriage of the head'. Rather than send her girls to boarding school, Elizabeth Walker in due course brought in a French dancing master and writing and singing masters.[26]

Lady Grace Mildmay's adult recollections of her childhood and upbringing in the 1560s at Lacock in Wiltshire provide a record which may be unique in its intimate portrayal of a young girl's training in virtue

23. *Pepys*, VIII, pp. 174, 451. For Pepys and Deb Willet see above pp. 170–71.
24. Pollock, *Lasting Relationship*, p. 223.
25. T. Rogers, *The Character of a Good Woman* (London, 1697), pp. 24–6.
26. A. Walker, *The Holy Life of Mrs Elizabeth Walker* (London, 1690), pp. 68–70.

and piety. Her governess was a relative – 'very religious, wise and chaste' – whom Grace enormously admired: 'she won my eldest sister and me to be in love with her and to delight in all her speeches and actions, for her mirth was very savoury and full of wit and in her sadness she uttered forth nothing but wisdom and gravity'. Grace's governess used the day-to-day experience of the household as a book to teach her charges. She stressed the need for total honesty and of awareness of the dangers of gossip. 'To hear much and speak little' was her precept: 'she scoffed at all dalliance, idle talk and wanton behaviour.' She and her charges discussed the conduct of visitors to the house – a gentleman who had 'gloried in his own wit' at her father's table, for example, and a couple, each married to someone else, whose behaviour they found 'imprudent' and 'licentious'. Her father Sir Henry Sharrington, Grace records, had 'a very careful eye over us': he

> could not abide to see a woman unstable or light in her carriage, to hold her hand one way and her hands another and her feet a third way, her eyes turning about in every place and the features of her face disfigured by evil countenances. But he liked a woman well graced with a constant and settled countenance and good behaviour through-out her whole parts, which presenteth unto all men a good hope of an established mind and virtuous disposition to be in her.

Grace's mother inculcated her deep piety, instructing her in meditation and prayers by heart and urging her to 'trust in God only and hang upon him alone in all my necessities'. Grace was never allowed to be idle. Her mother had her read the Bible, the *Imitation of Christ* and Foxe's *Book of Martyrs*; her governess imposed a regime which included writing and casting accounts, reading books like Dr Turner's herbal, psalm-singing and needlework. The keynote of this whole course of upbringing was subjugation of the self: her mother 'willed me . . . that I should carry myself silent and humble in mine own conceit, esteeming others better than myself and only seek to find out mine own defaults and endeavour to reform them'.[27] Sir Ralph Verney's basic attitude with regard to Nancy Denton's upbringing in the 1650s was much the same as that of Sir Henry Sharrington towards his daughter Grace in the 1560s. 'Believe me a Bible (with the common prayer) and a good plain catechism in your mother tongue being well read and practised is worth all the rest and much more suitable to your sex.' This was how he chided her when she was straining to learn classical languages. By the middle of the seventeenth century it had become fashionable for young girls to learn French. Sir Ralph was enthusiastic about this, seeing it as entirely different from Latin, because

27. This paragraph is based upon L.A. Pollock, *With Faith and Physic; The Life of a Tudor Gentlewoman Lady Grace Mildmay 1552–1620* (London, 1993), pp. 25–9.

it would extend Nancy's feminine accomplishments: 'that language affords many admirable books fit for you as romances, plays, poetry, stories of illustrious (not learned) women, receipts for preserving, making creams and all sorts of cookery, ordering your gardens and in brief all manner of good housewifery'.[28] The male view of appropriate female training had not changed among the Verneys in the 1680s, when Sir Edmund agreed to his eight-year-old daughter's request to learn the art of japanning boxes: 'I approve of it and so I shall of anything that is good and virtuous . . . for I admire all accomplishments that will render you considerable and lovely in the sight of God and man.'[29]

By the middle of the seventeenth century the pattern of upbringing for girls from gentry families was very firmly established. Whether it was taught at home with the aid of a governess or in one of the new finishing schools was very much a matter of parental preference and of convenience. Mr Bevan at Ashford hit exactly the right note to attract the patronage of Kentish gentry who aspired for their daughters to marry well but there was in fact little he provided which could not be expected from a good governess. Henry Oxinden sent his daughters to Mr Bevan's school at eleven and twelve. It was a family establishment, the staff consisting, besides Mr Bevan, of his wife, recommended as 'an excellent good woman' and his daughter, 'a civil well qualified maid'. The standard ornamental attainments were available, explained Henry's Oxinden's cousin in a letter, besides which 'he will be careful also that their behaviour be modest and such as becomes their quality and that they grow in knowledge and understanding for God and their duty to him which is above all'.[30]

John Evelyn's eulogy on his daughter Susannah at her marriage summarises the completion of a training process and the satisfaction that a father felt about its results:

> She is a good child, religious, discreet, ingenious and qualified with all the ornaments of her sex. She has a peculiar talent in design, as painting in oil and miniature, and an extraordinary genius for whatever hands can do with a needle. She has the French tongue, has read most of the Greek and Roman authors, using her talents with great modesty; exquisitely shaped and of an agreeable countenance.

Any possibility of Susannah thinking too much of her own achievements was checked, Evelyn could reassure himself, by the requisite dose of female humility. The essence of this training of girls from the highest social ranks was keeping them constantly busy. Lady Ann Farnshaw, born in 1625, recorded that her education supplied 'all the advantages that time

28. Pollock, *Lasting Relationship*, p. 226.
29. Cited in Pollock, 'Teach her to Live', *Continuity and Change* 4 (1989), p. 239.
30. Pollock, *Lasting Relationship*, p. 223.

afforded', in other words needlework, French, singing, instruction on the
lute and virginals and dancing. Lady Anne Halketh, born in 1623, recalled
a similar course of tuition. Sir Ralph Verney reflected that his daughter
Peg, who was studying French, singing, dancing and writing in 1647,
though slow, 'will be scholar enough for a woman'.[31] Roger North
considered Anne Barrett-Leonard, who learnt to speak and read French
and Italian in the 1670s, a highly educated woman. What he most
admired was her 'exceeding obliging temper' and 'a more than ordinary
wit and fluency of discourse'.[32] The last word on this exacting pattern of
female training can be left with Katherine Oxinden whose letter home
from school in 1655, inscribed with the utmost care, breathes an atmosphere of duty and attentiveness. 'Most dear mother', she began, and
explained how she was sending a 'register' for her father 'whereby he may
see my love and also you: how I have spent my time'. She mentions her
work with gumflowers, her 'entering upon the viol' and her practise in
dancing. 'I shall endeavour to improve my time for the best,' she concluded, inscribing herself 'your most affectionate and obedient daughter'[33]
(plate 25).

The number and variety of girls' schools expanded enormously during
the eighteenth century. The city of Chester, for example, came to boast
a dozen or so schools, most of which fell into the traditional finishing
school pattern. The core curriculum at Mrs Courtney's boarding school
for young ladies in 1785 was English, French, music, dancing, writing and
accounts. Mrs West's new school in Cross Street in 1780 paid special
attention to the 'health, morals and deportment of young ladies', besides
offering, in addition to the usual subjects, 'embroidery, tambour and
different ornaments of fine needlework'. Mrs Briscoe in Queen Street was
unusual in offering a choice of Latin or English in 1775; Mrs Tapley that
year was providing paints, silks and muslins for pupils ready to pay for
instruction in embroidery.[34] Some girls were being allowed back into
men's intellectual pantheon now that it was more clearly established than
it had been previously that they were a different kind of being and one
that was less threatening than had been assumed to men's hegemony.
Schools with a more academic curriculum were certainly more common
in London and the suburbs than in provincial centres such as Chester and
they became more numerous as the century went on. At Mrs Lorrington's
boarding establishment in Chelsea in the 1760s, girls could learn classical
languages, French, Italian, astronomy and arithmetic. Classics also featured

31. Citations from Pollock, 'Teach her to Live', *Continuity and Change* 4 (1989), pp. 238, 245.
32. L. Stone, *The Family, Sex and Marriage in England 1500–1800* (London, 1977), pp. 346–7.
33. There is a transcription in Pollock, *Lasting Relationship*, pp. 138–9.
34. D. Robson, *Some Aspects of Education in Cheshire in the Eighteenth Century* (Manchester, 1966), p. 79.

prominently at Abbey House School, attended among others by Jane Austen, which opened in Reading in the 1740s and was relocated to Chelsea in the 1790s.[35] Yet it remained the case, despite the revival of intellectual accomplishments, that girls' schools were primarily educating their charges for the marriage market. Bernard Mandeville commented in his tract of 1724 *The Virgin Unmasked* that boarding schools were set up to appeal to middle-class parents wanting to make fine ladies out of their girls.[36] Jane Austen's description in *Emma* of Mrs Goddard's school at Highbury – 'a particularly healthy spot' – neatly captures the atmosphere of such schools and their commitment to what had become traditional notions of female gender training. Austen's fictional establishment was 'a real, honest, old fashioned boarding school, where a reasonable quality of accomplishments were sold at a reasonable price and where girls might be sent to be out of the way and scramble themselves into a little education without any danger of coming back prodigies'.[37]

Improving facilities and the availability of well qualified governesses enabled thoughtful parents to plan flexibly and as they thought most appropriate for their daughters.[38] At Bury St Edmunds, for example, James Oakes's daughters were taught by Miss Routh in the early 1780s, a governess who came from a family of educationalists. Maria also had French lessons from Dr Valpy who had been educated in France and both she and Charlotte had dancing lessons. All the family gathered for their dancing displays. Miss Routh left when Maria completed her education at seventeen and Charlotte, only twelve then, was sent to a London boarding school until she was just over sixteen. Her last summer there James travelled up to London to watch Charlotte perform her dancing with her fellow pupils.[39] Parents had come to take the gendered basis of the educational system for granted. Charlotte Papendick recorded in her journal in 1791 her choice of Mrs Roach's day school, finding her 'a woman of strict principle if not altogether of the ornamental manner of good breeding'. 'I am constantly', she wrote, 'looking after the progress they made, urging them to perseverance and exhorting them against any inclination to indolence, idleness or self will.'[40]

When Sarah Fielding published *The Governess or Little Female Academy*, which was the first girls' school story, in 1749, its prescriptions were entirely traditional. Mrs Teachum's principal aim in her 'little female academy' for nine scholars was to improve her girls 'in all useful knowl-

35. O'Day, *Education and Society*, pp. 188–9.
36. G.J. Barker-Benfield, *The Culture of Sensibility: Sex and Society in Eighteenth-Century Britain* (Chicago, 1992), p. 164.
37. J. Austen, *Emma*, ed. R. Blythe (London, 1966), p. 52.
38. For a survey see A. Browne, *The Eighteenth Century Feminist Mind* (Brighton, 1987), pp. 102–21.
39. J. Fiske, ed., *The Oakes Diaries: Business, Politics and the Family in Bury St Edmunds 1728–1827* (Suffolk Records Society, XXXII, 1989–90), I, pp. 175–6.
40. Pollock, *Lasting Relationship*, pp. 236–7.

edge, to render them obedient to their superiors and gentle, kind and affectionate to each other'. She was also concerned with teaching 'an exact neatness in their persons and dress and a perfect gentility in their whole carriage'. Fielding's heroine, Jenny Peace, was the very epitome of priggish schoolgirl morality.[41] The overwhelming effect of such a book was to secure the system as it stood and to reinforce gender definitions. Much the same can be said of girls' schooling during the eighteenth century as a whole. 'It appears', wrote Fenelon, 'that they have a house and establishment to regulate, a husband to make happy and children to rear.' The qualities demanded for this task, which determined the pattern of a girl's education, were in his view, 'besides their natural assiduity . . . a carefulness, attention to particular industry, and a soft and persuasive manner'. In her *Letters on the Improvement of the Mind addressed to a Young Lady* in 1773, Hester Chapone reiterated the case for the standard female curriculum. Dancing and French could not be dispensed with; music and drawing were useful accomplishments for 'those intervals of time which too often hang heavily on the hands of a woman'. The classics and 'abstruce sciences', on the other hand, should be avoided at all costs because of 'the danger of pedantry and prescription in a woman . . . of her exchanging the graces of imagination for the severity and preciseness of a scholar'.[42] Men's fear of the bluestocking remained strong throughout the century, yet it seems to have gradually become rather more acceptable for a woman to indulge in intellectual interests so long as these were not to the detriment of her domestic pursuits and her ornamental capacities.[43] The discourse of containment dominated men's thinking about the education of girls from 1600 to 1800. Moreover in this case there was a close match between prescription and practice in that the work of the family governess and of the schools that have been discussed here by and large retained a consistent general pattern over two hundred years. Girls, as his friend Dr Denton reminded Sir Ralph Verney with regard to his godchild Nancy in 1651, should be taught above all to 'live under obedience'. Marriage and a domestic role were seen as the ultimate fulfilment and objective. Edward Montagu was reassured in 1632 that his proposed bride's religion was 'very perfect and her education most modest without exception'. Later in the century a correspondent sought to persuade Peregrine Osborne to favour a proposed bride who was 'very modestly bred'.[44] Since marriage was the central institution through which women in the early modern patriarchal system were subordinated, the highest priority in their upbringing and training was their future effectiveness and obedience as wives.

---

41. S. Fielding, *The Governess or Little Female Academy* (Oxford, 1968 edn), pp. 1–2.
42. Jones, ed., *Women in the Eighteenth Century*, pp. 104–6.
43. I am grateful to Sarah Salih for discussion of this point.
44. Citations from Pollock, 'Teach her to Live', *Continuity and Change* 4 (1989), pp. 244–5, 256.

19. *The Construction of Femininity*

MEN'S LIVES FOLLOWED a single charted course through boyhood to maturity and old age; women's lives were regarded by men as passing through three clearly delineated stages or conditions of maid, wife and widow. Girls, as we have seen, were educated for marriage through a moral and social programme rather than an academic one. Those in gentry circles grew up knowing that nothing but a good marriage – that is a prestigious and advantageous one – would fully secure their family's lasting approval. Thus gender differentiation from an early age was rooted in this society's values and universally taken for granted. Sir Richard Temple's steward at Stowe knew the kind of thing his master wanted to hear when he included reports on the children's progress in his weekly bulletins to Sir Richard in London. Mr Arthur, he wrote on 27 May 1683, was 'very well and brisk as ever'; whereas miss 'comes on apace and grows very beautiful as the old women say'.[1] Once well into the teens a girl could not escape the marriage market. 'Our young scholars at Westminster are striving hard who shall get first to the university', wrote Thomas Aldick to Thomas Isham in 1569, 'and our young lasses who shall first get husbands.'[2] Perspectives varied but the subject of choosing a wife or finding a husband was generally preoccupying. Sir Richard Temple received advice from his friend Sir Henry Andrewes in 1673 about one of the daughters of Sir Richard Atkins as a possible spouse: 'I think them fit wives but you had best inform yourself . . . I heard one say they are bred fit for any court and no question 5, 6 or 7000 will be their portions and it may be the last.' Andrewes was confident about their chastity: 'the ladies I believe have never been blown upon'.[3] Let her be 'of a healthful body, of a good complexion, humble and virtuous, some few years younger than yourself and not of a simple wit', Sir William Wentworth

1. HEH, STT Box 25, 291.
2. Cited in Pollock, 'Teach her to Live under Obedience: The Making of Women in the Upper Ranks of Modern England', *Continuity and Change* 4 (1989), p. 244.
3. HEH, STT 1571: Sir Henry Andrewes to Sir Richard Temple, 16 and 27 October 1673.

advised his son.[4] 'And this let me tell you, though a fair fortune and a fair face never want suitors to them', Justinian Isham advised his daughters, 'yet I cannot say whether they have oftener availed or betrayed their owners.' Virtue was the best means to a good husband, Isham insisted: 'I am sure the internal graces of the mind will be your best and surest portion, both unto yourselves, and unto men of such discretions as I believe you would willingly give yourselves unto.'[5] Our discussion of femininity from the historical sources of the sixteenth and seventeenth centuries has so far portrayed it almost entirely in negative terms. But the eulogies of godly women, it has been argued, mark a new beginning. There is of course chronological overlap between the misogynistic tradition and the first flowering of a positive ideology of womanhood. It was only very gradually that men cast aside that tradition and sought to propagate a constructive view of femininity as a counterpart to their strong sense of what they meant by masculinity. Thus modern femininity defined by men in terms of a set of positive values emerged slowly from their set of prohibitions.[6] Concentrating on prescriptive materials over the period from 1550 to 1800, this chapter seeks to explore how this occurred.

The prohibitions were the subject of the first chapter of this book. We saw how a good many men at least were deeply concerned about women's supposed sexual voraciousness, pride, shrewishness and tendency to scold. The exploration of the contemporary conception of women as the weaker vessel in chapter 5 showed how closely this was connected with the humoral notions about men's and women's bodies.[7] The argument that chastity was the overriding measure of female honour set out in chapter 7 followed from these medical assumptions besides the teaching of the Bible. Commentators like the puritan divine Matthew Griffith and the playwright Thomas Heywood were cited to illustrate the point that sexual behaviour was seen as the keystone of patriarchy.[8] Other genres which have not been considered in detail in this book contributed to the sixteenth- and early seventeenth-century debate on women. An extensive literature, including satirical works and the controversial works of the Swetman and Sowernam debate drawn upon briefly in chapter 1, focused upon the broad issues about good and bad women.[9] The

4. J.P. Cooper, ed., *Wentworth Papers 1597–1628* (Camden Fourth Series, 12, 1973), p. 20.
5. L.A. Pollock, *A Lasting Relationship: Parents and their Childrren over Three Centuries* (London, 1987), p. 250.
6. *OED*: 'Femininity'.
7. Above, especially, pp. 61–2.
8. Above, pp. 109–10.
9. For a useful summary see M.J.M Ezell, *The Patriarch's Wife: Literary Evidence and the History of the Family* (Chapel Hill, 1987), pp. 36–61. For texts see K.U. Henderson and B.F. McManus, eds, *Half Humankind: Contexts and Texts of the Controversy about Women in England 1540–1640* (Urbana, 1985), pp. 136–325.

considerable output of clerical puritan advice books on marriage between the 1590s and 1640s stated the scriptural case for obedience which men saw as the basic solution to women's wiles and weakness.[10] Ballad literature, we have seen, echoed the same prescriptions, so did the drama.[11] The stress throughout all this material and these genres was upon men's and women's gender roles, upon acceptable and prohibited behaviour, upon social boundaries like the one between activity indoors and out of doors. The mode of discourse was moralising and didactic and was founded consistently and surely upon the coherent biblical case for women's subordination. The difference between this literature and the one that we shall now turn to considering is that the new writings after the Restoration represent a serious attempt to persuade women to internalise the prescriptions which men seek to impose. Yet we should not attempt to make this important change of tactics too sudden. We need first to look at some pieces of the period from the 1570s to the 1640s, which show that some men were moving in the direction of modern gender construction within the confines of a traditional pattern of patriarchal thinking.

Suzanne Hull, in her survey of educational guidebooks for women between 1475 and 1640, calls Thomas Salter's *The Mirror of Modesty* of 1578 an 'almost viciously strict tract' on the upbringing of young girls.[12] Salter's interest was getting girls on 'the direct and straight path to eternal felicity'. He was scathing about parents whose prudence was blinded by affection, especially those fathers who allowed their daughters to read 'ballads, songs, sonnets and ditties of dalliance'. He recommended finding a governess who was 'grave, prudent, modest and of good counsel', a woman who would inculcate virtue so that it took deep root. She should stress above all the 'goodly ornament of chastity'. The governess should keep her girls from the corrupting influence of kitchen servants and beat them if necessary, in the spirit 'of a good physician who to cure young children of corporal maladies do give them wormwood or such like bitter thing'. She should confine their reading to books written by 'godly fathers' to the 'soul's health', together with the godly deeds of 'virtuous virgins and worthy women' of the past. Humility had to be inculcated as the crucial virtue: 'How foul, filthy, unseemly and disorderly a thing it is for any woman to learn every day of an other woman (being abroad and seeing them that are bravest attired) how to trick and trim up themselves after the newest and gallantest fashion to set out their bodily beauty.' A girl should be taught suitable needlework, the distaff and spindle; not on

10. See A.J. Fletcher, in A.J. Fletcher and P.R. Roberts, eds., *Religion, Culture and Society in Early Modern Britain* (Cambridge, 1994), especially pp. 168–70.
11. For a good example of the standard prescriptions see 'The Virgin's ABC', *Roxburghe*, II, p. 651. See above, pp. 110–20.
12. S.W. Hull, *Chaste, Silent and Obedient: English Books for Women 1435–1640* (San Marino, 1982), p. 201; for commentary and extracts see pp. 58–9.

any account to lie; to be friendly, affable and courteous to all; not to babble or be a great talker but rather keep silent; to avoid shamefastness or fearfulness, though it was acceptable to blush if her virtue was remarked upon 'casting her eyes to the earth'; to avoid banquets and the 'company of light housewives' in favour of the recreation of quiet walks in gardens and pleasant orchards. The prohibitions of this remarkably comprehensive programme of moral and social training anticipate much of the central ground of the new female gender ideology that others would elaborate. Yet it was an isolated piece, available only briefly in a single edition, so it can hardly have acquired a wide readership.

Thomas Bentley's *The Monument of Matrons*, published in 1582, includes many brief lives of biblical and other model women. Colin and Jo Atkinson have investigated how Bentley edited these lives, indulging in considerable textual manipulation in order to reinforce patriarchal values: 'wicked women seem to inspire him . . . the smallest biblical reference can make him sit up and take notice if any kind of sexual activity is present'. Bentley was quite capable of silently folding into biblical narratives text from marginal commentary in the Geneva Bible or from elsewhere, perhaps in some cases from his own mind. Using New Testament women as examples, he argues the imperative for female obedience to husbands, for humility and godliness. Thus in the story of poor Dinah, which concerns the murder of the lord Sechem, who had raped her, by her brothers seeking revenge, the main point becomes a warning about females gadding from home. Time and again Bentley rearranges his material so as to present models of submissive female behaviour. What is striking is the scale of this highly orthodox tract and the length to which Bentley will go in pursuit of his didactic purpose. There is nothing in his view of the world that women can do to redeem themselves but obey and learn the modes of behaviour which signify and symbolise that obedience.[13]

The puritan advice book writers discussed the specific issue of acceptable female characteristics when considering how a man should choose a wife. Thomas Gataker listed 'virtue, wisdom, discretion, godliness' as the crucial personal qualities a man should seek.[14] John Wing advised a suitor to take note of the company a woman kept and the kind of language she used. His standard should be 'all comely behaviour and kingly carriage, a demeanour that keeps good decorum with true greatness'. No girl who was 'prophane, light, irreligious, unsober or vain' deserved his notice.[15] John Dod and Robert Cleaver stressed 'report, name and fame' as the surest indication of a good woman, suggesting men look for one who showed a 'modest countenance' and exhibited her silence, who

13. C. and J.B. Atkinson, 'Subordinating Women: Thomas Bentley's use of Biblical Women in "The Monument of Matrons" (1582)', *Church History*, 60 (1991), pp. 289–300.
14. T. Gataker, *A Good Wife God's Gift* (London, 1624), p. 17.
15. J. Wing, *The Crown Conjugal or Spouse Royal* (London, 1620), pp. 109–12.

dressed in 'honest and sober raiment' and avoided 'wicked and ungodly company'.[16] Such writers, in other words, set out the usual and predictable prohibitions in what amounts to an essentially negative account of womankind.

The interest of two advice books by women which went through multiple editions and attracted a wide readership is that they show how fully men's teaching was taken up by some married women. Dorothy Leigh's posthumous *The Mother's Blessing*, first available in 1616, offered a guide to Christian living for her sons but was in fact as much concerned with the upbringing of girls. Mrs Leigh fully accepted women's subordination on the basis of the Fall: 'because we must needs confess that sin entered by us into our posterity let us show how careful we are to seek to Christ to cut it out of us and our posterity and how fearful we are that our sin should sink any of them to the lowest part of the earth'. Her recipe was that women should take the utmost care to protect their chastity 'without which we are mere beasts and no women'. It was not enough for a woman 'to be chaste but even so to behave herself'.[17] Elizabeth Joceline was deeply concerned lest she left behind a daughter who became proud. 'I am so fearful to bring thee a proud high minded child', she told her husband, 'that though I know thy care will need no spur yet I cannot but desire thee to double thy watchfulness over this vice, it is such a crafty insinuating devil.' The standard prohibitions – profuse clothes, vanity, idleness – followed and the standard remedies – prayer, study, healthy recreation – were enjoined. 'Remember', declared this strictly trained mother, 'thou art a maid and such ought thy modesty to be that thou shouldest scarce speak but when thou answereth'.[18]

Richard Brathwaite's *The English Gentlewoman*, published in 1631, has some claim to be regarded as the first conduct book directed specifically at the female sex. Its format is quite different from Salter or Bentley's works and from the marriage advice manuals. There is an implicit if rudimentary grasp of the principle of gender construction, cast in the traditional mould of the inculcation of virtue and honour and pursued in terms of day-to-day behaviour. 'I have here presented unto your view one of your own sex', writes Brathwaite in the preface, 'one whose improved education will be no blemish but a beauty to her nation.' He starts with dress, arguing predictably that modesty must be a woman's guide, 'virtuous thoughts' her guard. He is particularly concerned about 'delicacy' of apparel, a habit, he believes, which 'begets an effeminacy in the heart'. He condemns women who bolster their greatness by long gowns or their vanity by great sleeves, trains and huge hats. Class as well as gender is explicit in his account of apt body language which should

16. J. Dod and R. Cleaver, *A Godly Form of Household Government* (London, 1614), sigs. G3–4.
17. D. Leigh, *The Mother's Blessing* (London, 1627), pp. 16, 38–41.
18. E. Joceline, *The Mother's Legacy* (London, 1625), p. 69; above, p. 368.

demonstrate self-control: 'For your carriage it should neither be too precise nor too loose. The simpering made faces partake more of chambermaid than gentlewoman. Modesty and mildness hold sweetest correspondence.' Brathwaite ends with a conventional diatribe against painting faces, taking coaches to the playhouses or the Exchange and the 'buzzing and rustling' that women full of pride display in boxes at the theatre.[19]

We can complete this survey by making reference to two unpublished pieces. The first, Sir Justinian Isham's code of conduct for his daughters, written after the death of their mother in 1642, is a predictable expression of male views set out with exceptional clarity and obvious affection. His girls, he explains to Jane, Elizabeth, Judith and Susan, are already half orphaned at nine and downwards and they could lose him too before long. He will attempt no 'general or exact treatise of a complete woman' but rather some brief instruction in female virtues for their benefit. He begins with their spiritual life, which he is emphatic has gender boundaries:

> Prayers, meditations and such like holy treatises I rather commend unto you than knotty disputes, and although your sex is not so capable of those stronger abilities of the intellect, to make you so learned and knowing as men ought to be; yet be sure to keep your hearts upright and your affections towards God unfeigned and there is no doubt but that will be more acceptable unto him than all the wisdom of the whole world besides.

Isham then directs his girls' attention to the many virtuous women 'of exemplary life . . . of our house' whose style of living they should imitate. Finally he lists the 'principal graces and virtues' which, in his reading of scripture, are 'most proper for your sex'. Entirely unsurprising, the list is nevertheless worth quoting in full as one gentleman's overall view of the qualities of a good woman: 'holiness, chastity, obedience, charity, meekness, modesty, sobriety, silence, discretion, frugality and affability' constitute her virtue.[20]

Sir Robert Filmer's essay 'In Praise of the Virtuous Wife' is a manuscript found among his papers and probably composed in the early 1640s. Margaret Ezell describes its tone as scriptural yet up to the minute: a sophisticated blend 'of several types of discourse about women'. Filmer was undoubtedly well read in literature ranging from the classics to satire and jest books; above all he knew his Bible. His argument, based upon Proverbs, the fourth verse of chapter twelve and the tenth of chapter thirty-one, revolves around the nature of a woman's virtue and how it

19. R. Brathwaite, *The English Gentlewoman* (London, 1641), especially pp. 273, 278–83, 285, 293, 297–9. For the frontispiece illustration to the original 1631 edition see Hull, *Chaste, Silent and Obedient*, p. 33.
20. Pollock, *Lasting Relationship*, pp. 249–50.

should be manifested in a wife. Where he is unusual is in his not defining virtue as chastity but rather as courage and strength. It is his definition of courage which is really interesting and the analysis which he develops on this basis: 'That courage is true virtue it appeareth because true virtue is the moderation of the affections by faith and prudence, that one showing what is lawful, the other what is possible and convenient, now this moderation is nothing but courage.' What Filmer seems to be saying is that above all women must learn self discipline. His 'means to attain courage' are instructive: 'first skill in housewifery and religion to prevent bodily and ghostly terrors, secondly labour, thirdly temperance'. What women must avoid is 'lewd company, surfeiting and voluptuousness', all of which undermine their strength and 'disable their minds'. A wife, in other words, has a role to play; she is seen not as corrupted but as full of talents which deserve nurture. 'The trials of a woman's position as the most earnest and loving member of the couple yet still second in authority', notes Margaret Ezell, 'are balanced by the dignity of the theoretical and practical power she does wield.' Filmer also makes much of women's spiritual power. His argument, more than that of other tracts discussed here so far, foreshadows the whole romantic and emotional conception of womanhood which was to emerge as the core of English femininity. The words in Proverbs are the key: 'a virtuous wife is the crown of her husband' and 'who can find a virtuous woman for her price is above rubies?' Where does this virtue lie, asks Filmer? In the courage, strength, support and sustenance, he answers, that a woman brings to the daily life, the trials and tribulations of her spouse.[21]

The agenda set out by these writers is consistent and has much in common. It takes us back to our starting point in the first chapter of this book. Women's weaknesses and susceptibilities require that the biblical case for their subordination, so much in the minds of writers like Bentley, Salter, and even Dorothy Leigh, be enforced. Women must learn a set of behavioural defences to protect themselves against their own sinful ways. Men need constant reminders of how easily women are snared so that they remain fully on the alert about their duty of control and subordination. The stress is still upon men's and women's gender roles and upon what was seen as acceptable and prohibited behaviour for the weaker sex. The bedrock is scripture and the overriding issue is men's authority. But Brathwaite's prose at times is tinged with the secular ideological emphasis that was to characterise the gendered conduct books. His reference to an 'improved education', like the whole tenor of Isham's advice for his daughters, is based upon an implicit belief in gendered training and upbringing. We have seen in the last chapter just how deliberate and widespread in its application this was, even before the Restoration. Filmer's essay, though it can have had no public impact, is crucial for

21. Ezell, *The Patriarch's Wife*, pp. 131–8.

what it tells about the direction gender construction would take. The shift of emphasis from chastity to courage signifies a change of viewpoint from the negative to the positive. The formation of a more fully internalised female personality, a complementary partner with her own particular role in a marriage, is foreshadowed. This internalisation, as we have seen in discussing godly women, could become powerful when conviction and commitment were joined together. Yet in spite of these developments we should note that men had not yet thought, before 1660, of establishing a systematised literature of gender construction based upon an argument about the nature of women. The material considered here, based on a secure awareness of gender boundaries, was nevertheless piecemeal, fragmentary and unsystematic. There was no such thing, in Sir Justinian Isham's words, as a 'general or exact treatise of a complete woman', a full portrait of gender rules and behaviour, before the Restoration. So how did a literature of female gender construction as such emerge?

The new epistemological methods of Bacon and Descartes, we have seen, made possible the systematic investigation of woman. Their fundamental and long term impact can be connected to the rise to a new series of genres which, taken together, comprise the properly established discourse, from around the 1670s onwards, of modern gender construction. A steady stream of conduct books for women was published, reprinted and eagerly absorbed by a burgeoning reading public between 1670 and 1800.[22] An extensive medical literature focused during the eighteenth century on sexual difference in respect of the total physiology and psychology of the individual.[23] The periodical literature of the period was much concerned with the nature and social role of women.[24] The rise of the novel is also crucial to our understanding of modern gender relations.[25] The prescriptive sources for the history of gender, in other words, expand out of all recognition in the last part of our period. The account of their content given here has to be selective.

22. The only general account of this important literature is Fenella Childs's unpublished Oxford DPhil thesis which covers the period from 1690 to 1760. Further work is in progress by Sarah Sahil and Ingrid Tague.

23. L. Jordanova's *Sexual Visions: Images of Gender in Science and Medicine between the Eighteenth and Twentieth Centuries* (Hemel Hempstead, 1989) has much on this theme. See also R. Porter and L. Hall, *The Facts of Life: The Creation of Sexual Knowledge in Britain, 1650–1950* (London, 1994), pp. 65–90.

24. K. Shevelow, *Women and Print Culture: The Construction of Femininity in the Early Periodical* (London, 1989) is an initial survey of much of the popular periodical press for the years from 1690 to 1760. Further work is in progress by Helen Berry.

25. The most important works in an extensive literature on the novel and gender include I. Watt, *The Rise of the Novel* (London, 1957); J. Spencer, *The Rise of the Woman Novelist: from Aphra Behn to Jane Austen* (Oxford, 1987); M. McKeon, *The Origins of the English Novel 1600–1740* (Baltimore, 1987); and J.P. Hunter, *Before Novels: The Cultural Context of Eighteenth-century Fiction* (London, 1990). A.G. Sulloway, *Jane Austen and the Province of Womanhood* (Philadelphia, 1989) is an illuminating discussion of the author's oblique satirical purposes.

It is always dangerous to ascribe considerable influence and significance to a particular text in a discussion of the emergence of an ideology but the publication of Richard Allestree's *The Ladies Calling* in 1673 seems to have a real claim to be a signal moment in the creation of modern English femininity. Allestree was the scion of an ancient Shropshire family fallen on hard times who had made his way as a dedicated royalist fighting for Charles I in his youth and acting for Charles II in the 1650s. His rewards were the Regius chair of divinity at Oxford and the Provostship of Eton. He preached before the King several times during the 1660s. His book *The Gentleman's Calling* successfully captured the mood of Charles II's return from exile. *The Ladies Calling* was sufficiently in demand for it to be reprinted twice by 1675 and seven times between 1693 and 1727. It strongly influenced much conduct literature over the next hundred years or so.[26] The appeal of the book undoubtedly lay partly in its exceptional clarity and its well organised framework of exposition. It discussed what was required of women from the upper ranks of society – the class motive is pervasive – firstly in terms of five 'general qualifications, duties and ornaments of women' and secondly with regard to the 'respective duties' and 'peculiar cautions' of the three stages of a woman's life.[27] Almost everything Allestree says about womankind is highly traditional. This no doubt helped to give the book such a secure readership. What is innovatory is the extent to which his account, taken as a whole, shifts the ground of early modern gender. The book is about moulding the female personality. It is comprehensive in a way no earlier work had been. It rests on a caustic view of the female sex as a whole yet it leaves women with some kind of promise of personal fulfilment, if they obey Allestree's rules. It is powerfully argued and vigorously didactic. It deserves much more notice than it has hitherto received as the first coherent account of female gender construction in largely secular terms to be published in England. A full analysis of the argument, providing a starting point for our consideration of a whole new genre, is required here.

Allestree wrote at a moment when men felt that the need for social and gender order was insistent. The 1640s and 50s had seen women petitioners on the streets, prophetesses commanding public attention, women preachers and tales of women's participation in Ranter orgies. Backlash was the essence of the socially exclusive Anglican culture which he imbibed. Living through the 1660s, he saw how much there was to be done to secure lasting order and settlement. Allestree simply had the inspiration and the skills to put an argument that many may have grasped about how women could be defined and controlled. He drew heavily upon the current educational programmes and upon flourishing pre-

26. *DNB*: Richard Allestree; F.A. Childs, 'Prescriptions for Manners in English Courtesy Literature 1690–1760 and their Social Implications', (Oxford University DPhil thesis, 1984), p. 73.
27. R. Allestree, *The Ladies Calling* (London, 1673), II, p. 1.

existing genres such as funeral sermons for godly women. 'All ages and nations', Allestree began by stating, 'have made some distinction between masculine and feminine virtues.' He went further: nature had 'in their very mould and constitution implanted peculiar aptness and proprieties of mind'.[28] Gone was cosmological hierarchy; here was sexual difference. One is left feeling, as one reads Allestree's tract, that he believed in sex as the foundation of gender, sex as its immovable and intractable basis.

Allestree consistently came back to women's nature. His medical ideas were entirely orthodox but he gave them new ideological force. Meekness, in his view, was a necessary human virtue; nature, creating women with bodies that were 'more smooth and soft' than men's, seemed to teach this. Inside, their 'more cool and temperate constitution' deprived their personalities of fire, inducing in them 'a natural feebleness' so they were 'unable to back and assert their angers with any effective force'. The typical attempt to substitute tongues for fists, Allestree maintained, merely brought contempt upon women. Women, he believed, had a propensity to 'commiseration'. He saw the roots of female compassion as lying in 'a native tenderness' which predisposed women, 'who need but swim with the stream of their own inclinations', to virtue. God now masquerades as nature, just as, in general terms, prescriptions of femininity masquerade in this literature as descriptions. Allestree clearly believed that God created women to be intellectually and physically weaker than men so there was not, in his view, any point in struggling against the divine scheme of things. Nature did not supersede God but simply masked the divine imperative. Thus the section on women's mercy is concluded with the remark that they must preserve and use 'that tenderness and compassion which God and nature do equally enforce and recommend'. Women's affability, however, rests upon their generosity of mind, a quality which can be improved by the noble education available to girls of the 'best extractions'. Their practice of piety engages two passions in which women were eminent, those of fear and love. Its propriety to them seemed obvious to Allestree: it was 'their greatest ornament and advantage' since 'they have somewhat more of a predisposition towards it in their native temper'. The initial survey of women's crucial qualities ends with a trumpeting of women's weakness 'as in this sense their strength': 'God . . . as he brings light out of darkness . . . so converts their natural infirmities into a means of spiritual strength, makes the impotencies and defects of their nature subservient to the operation of grace . . . this gives them an obligation to let their passions run in the channel God has cut for them.'[29] So women's nature is the consistent starting point for their gender training. Allestree's programme has five elements. He starts with

28. Allestree, *Ladies Calling*, I, pp. 3–4.
29. Allestree, *Ladies Calling*, I, pp. 29, 43, 49, 57, 64–5, 81–2.

control of the will. Modesty is the core of self-discipline: 'It is indeed a virtue of general influence, does not only ballast the mind with sober and humble thoughts of one's self but also steers every part of the outward frame.' Modesty, predictably enough, teaches a woman to tune her language, avoid bluster, beware wantonness and rich clothes and choose her company with care. Chastity was the core of the matter. Her modesty will lead her to watch 'all lightness of carriage, wanton glances, obscure discourse, things that show a woman weary of her honour that the next comer may reasonably expect a surrender'. Meekness of will was perhaps women's greatest test, something that they had to acquire through the lesson of reason, weak as they were in this attribute: 'As a will thus resigned to reason and just authority is a felicity all rational natures should aspire to, so especially the feminine sex, whose passions being naturally the more impetuous ought to be more strictly guarded and kept under the severe discipline of reason.'[30]

So much for sheer repression. Through their mercy and compassion, their affability and their piety women were able to turn their natures to good account. Femininity begins to see the light of day as a set of positive virtues. Allestree strikes a note of nostalgia with his call for a revival of the 'primitive charity' of helping the poor, not, as we have seen, that this had by any means collapsed in the 1670s. This, he declared, was where women excelled: gentlewomen 'thought no retinue so desirable, so honourable as a train of almsfolks'. He is equally class-conscious in recommending gentlewomen to keep up their local reputation by a studied affability which will endear them to all: 'a kind look or word from a superior is strangely charming'. Piety was a crucial virtue. Their 'plenty and ease' gave women much time to exercise and develop it in such a way that the snares of pride were always kept at bay. If a woman learns how to order her life in this way at home, Allestree argued, she would know how to behave in public when at church. He was caustic about women who arrived late, missing the confession of sins, and then clapped the pew door, drowning the reader's words. The same message as in the funeral sermons comes across. Religion is seen as the central means to hold women to their gendered role and secure their reputation in the male universe: 'as neither beauty nor wit (the two celebrated accomplishments of women) so will neither greatness and honour give any advantage without piety', Allestree insisted.[31]

The forty pages which Allestree devoted to the role of wives in his tract is the most substantial treatment of the subject, besides being the most positive and systematic, in the seventeenth-century conduct literature. His basic standpoint about wifely obedience — 'the mulct that was laid upon the first woman's disobedience to God' — is totally orthodox. His insistence that women overlook their husband's adultery with patient

30. Allestree, *Ladies Calling*, I, pp. 5–7, 12–13, 16, 25, 39–40.
31. Allestree, *Ladies Calling*, I, pp. 55, 66, 82, 102, 120–1, 141.

submission and even pity but entertain 'no thought or imagination much less any parley or treaty' contrary to their own fidelity is to be expected. What are more interesting as pointers towards a more constructive view of femininity are his precepts about her role as mistress of the household and its servants, about offering hospitality, about guarding her husband's fortune and about motherhood. Not that any of this is unconventional. Much of what Allestree says reiterates thinking and practice that we have already encountered. It is perhaps his words about a wife's responsibility for her husband's reputation, though, that most strikingly begin to carry the overall tone of an emotional involvement of women in their marriages. A wife should set out privately to cure her husband's imperfections by her virtue and example, always setting his reputation in the best and clearest light for public consumption. The same kind of emotional strength is called upon with regard to the upbringing and discipline of children. A mother's love 'by strength of feminine passion', asserts Allestree, usually exceeds a father's, which means that there is danger of doting affection blinding a woman to the need for 'prudent severity'. She must be prepared to beat her children, moulding their will whilst it was 'supple and pliant'. The subject induces all Allestree's reactionary verve: 'the irregularities of youth', he believed, had only reached their present height through 'shelter from the practice of their elders'. The key issue here and the one that goes to the centre of female gender construction is woman's nurturing role and example as wife and mother.[32]

Fenella Childs has traced the influence of Allestree's book in eight of the principal courtesy manuals for women published between 1694 and 1753.[33] In the most blatant case, Richard Steele's *The Ladies Library*, large sections of *The Ladies Calling* are borrowed verbatim.[34] Yet the propagandist case about women's gender formation did not stand still in the substantial literature of the years from the 1670s to 1800. We will survey its development and seek the origins of modern prescriptive femininity on the basis of nine of the most popular items from among the extensive conduct literature. The Marquis of Halifax addressed his daughter in 1688 as a tender plant requiring the pruning and shelter of some fatherly rules written out of kindness rather than authority. The format was cloying and one that was much imitated later. But Halifax's substance was so powerful that demand led to at least fourteen editions during the eighteenth century.[35] Steele was quite unabashed in his preface to *The Ladies Library*, published in three volumes in 1714, about having collected his material following the announcement of his project in *The Spectator* from writings of 'our greatest divines' and other sources. He wished, he stated directly,

32. Allestree, *Ladies Calling*, II, pp. 23–65.
33. Childs, Prescriptions for Manners, p. 267.
34. See e.g. R. Steele, *The Ladies Library* (London, 1714), pp. 179, 184, 240, 254.
35. V. Jones, *Women in the Eighteenth Century: Constructions of Femininity* (London, 1990), pp. 14, 17.

to promote the 'interests of religion and virtue' by providing 'general rules for conduct in all the circumstances of the life of women'.[36] John Essex's *The Young Ladies Conduct* in 1722 was a well organised and written summary in 130 pages of advice especially aimed at young wives. Wetenhall Wilkes's *Letter of Genteel and Moral Advice to a Young Lady*, much the same length and published in 1740, was purported to be based upon a letter of advice to a favourite niece aged sixteen. Its title declared its objective as establishing 'a system of rules and informations to qualify the fair sex to be useful and happy in every state of life'. William Kenrick's *The Whole Duty of Woman*, published in 1753 and reissued in three new editions during the 1790s, is structured in twenty-five short sections dealing with particular female attributes and qualities. A somewhat fanciful introduction entreats the reader to 'walk in the ways of my counsel'. Thomas Marriott's tract of 1759 on *Female Conduct* was subtitled 'an essay on the art of pleasing'.[37] James Fordyce's formula, in his *Sermons to Young Women* of 1766, has been described as 'anodyne prescriptions compatible with a decently undisturbing middle-class form of virtue'. Fordyce was a successful nonconformist minister, much admired for his pulpit performances by female congregations.[38] John Gregory's *A Father's Legacy to his Daughters*, first published in 1774, was instantly successful and for some years effectively swept the board. The preface, explaining that the tract had its origins in letters written in his own declining health for private use after his girls had lost their mother, gave it emotional force. Gregory declared his zeal for the improvement of his daughters 'in whatever can make a woman amiable'. Finally Hester Chapone's *Letter to a New Married Lady* was aimed at an established audience, following the success of her earlier *Letters on the Improvement of the Mind*, with which in one edition it was combined together with Gregory's tract.[39] This was a quite different piece in that it was written by one woman for another. Several of these works were read not only very widely but over a very long period. In the 1790s, when debate about women's education and proper social role was so vigorous, Mary Wollstonecraft found it worthwhile in her *Vindication of the Rights of Women* to ridicule Wilkes, express her disapproval of the anti-intellectual tone of Gregory and Fordyce and champion the rationalist Chapone.[40]

Halifax took up Allestree's notion of sexual difference, using it to develop an adept and forceful argument in defence of patriarchy. This may not have struck those who read it as particularly original since the

36. Steele, *The Ladies Library*, preface.
37. T. Marriott, *Female Conduct* (London, 1759).
38. P. Langford, *A Polite and Commercial People: England 1727–1783* (Oxford, 1989), pp. 606–7.
39. H. Chapone, *Letter to a New Married Lady* (London, 1780).
40. A. Browne, *The Eighteenth Century Feminist Mind* (Brighton, 1987), pp. 43, 106, 114, 159.

ground had been thoroughly prepared, but we can see, from the perspective provided by our earlier discussion of hierarchical bodies, how radical he in fact was. Nature had called the whole patriarchal structure into being. It had to be generally accepted, he insisted, 'that there is inequality in the sexes, and that for the better economy of the world, the men, who were to be the law-givers, had the larger share of reason bestowed upon them'. But women had no cause for complaint, for nature had made 'such large amends by other advantages': 'We are made of differing tempers, that our defects may the better be mutually supplied: your sex wanteth our reason for your conduct and our strength for your protection: ours wanteth your gentleness to soften and to entertain us.' We will take up some of the profoundly important implications of this formulation later in this chapter. For the present, we need to follow Halifax's argument to its conclusion. Some women may plead, he recognises, that nature has in certain instances been 'so kind as to raise them above the level of their own sex'. Nevertheless, he asserts, patriarchy rests upon marriage, an institution 'too sacred to admit a liberty of objecting to it'. To preserve marriage the weaker sex as a whole must accept that it is reasonable for them to be subject to men, even if this involves injustice in a few cases; better this 'than to break into an establishment upon which the order of humane society doth so much depend'. The double standard is defensible, so far as Halifax is concerned, in the same terms: men's adultery does not threaten blemishing the blood of the family whilst women's does. Chastity, in this reading of early modern patriarchy, becomes the overwhelming female imperative and the foundation of all gender construction. Halifax's must have been the most adamant statement of the whole case that achieved wide circulation in the late seventeenth century. It is direct, shorn of all biblical argumentation and wholly secular. Even Allestree's glancing references to God are missing.[41] Steele, by comparison, is much more conventional in tone, echoing Allestree and arguing that it is obvious that one must command the other obey, and that men have a threefold right to sovereignty based upon nature's design, use and custom in addition to the laws of God.[42]

By 1730 any kind of religious influence on the case for the gender training of women had all but disappeared. Nothing more was left behind than occasional sidelong references to subjection and Eve's sin.[43] By then the ambiguity of the doctrine of nature was being exploited with increasing subtlety. Thus we find John Essex making much of the weaknesses and strengths of female nature in setting out his argument. He begins with the softness of girls in their tender years, making them 'unstable and irresolute', together with their natural affectation which

41. K.V Thomas, 'The Double Standard', *Journal of the History of Ideas* XX (1959), 210–14; Jones, ed., *Women in the Eighteenth Century*, pp. 18–20.
42. Steele, *The Ladies Library*, II, pp. 58–60.
43. Childs, *Prescriptions for Manners*, pp. 266–7.

produced vanity. He sees them as prey to their passions and imaginations and vulnerable to a 'depraved fancy pernicious to body and mind'. Yet, when he sets about recommending a course of instruction through reason, he is ready to argue that girls were easier to train than boys as 'favourite works of nature, composed of more soft and delicate passions and so more naturally disposed to modesty and obedience' and 'more susceptible to the impressions of religion and virtue'.[44] Conduct book writers heightened their stress upon men's and women's natures as they sought to give sexual difference increasing ideological force. Wilkes in 1740 was still fairly restrained in this respect, confining himself to linking his argument to nature where it helped him to make an effect. Compassion, for instance, was seen as 'so natural an ornament to your sex whose soft breasts are made and disposed to entertain tenderness and pity'. A woman who lived up to the rules of chastity flourished 'like a rose in June with all her virgin graces about her'. Thomas Marriott in 1759 simply repeated Essex's lines, seeing women's natural docility, for example, as fitting them for social training.[45]

Fordyce and Gregory, by contrast, went much further because they were committed to establishing deeply polarised concepts of masculinity and femininity. When sensibility won the day, the argument from nature remained crucial. Moreover several influential handbooks of female medicine, which were published between 1762 and 1771, explored the issue of women's hysteria in a manner which broke finally and decisively with the old humoral interpretation of it in terms of suffocation of the mother. Thomas Willis had led the way in this regard in his *London Practice of Physick* in 1685, arguing that the source for symptoms of hysteria was the brain rather than the womb, that, in other words, it was a mental not a sexual condition. In the account given by Henry Manning in 1771 which was quite largely based on an earlier one by Jean Astruc, hysteria becomes a classic female disorder of the nervous system characterised by listlessness, languor, breathing difficulties and palpitations. The disease, he insisted, chiefly seized women who were 'delicate and endowed with great sensibility' and its occasions included 'violent passions of the mind'. There was 'no disease so vexatious to the fair sex as this', declared John Ball, and it was 'common to maids, wives and widows'.[46] This kind of writing tended to drive home the point that women's bodies were quite different from men's so they could be expected to differ as well in their

44. J. Essex, *The Young Ladies Conduct* (London, 1722), pp. vii, xxvi, 1–2.

45. W. Wilkes, *A Letter of Genteel and Moral Advice to a Young Lady* (London, 1740), pp. 68, 75; Marriott, *Female Conduct*, p. xvii.

46. H. Smith, 'Gynaecology and Ideology in Seventeenth-Century England', in B.A. Carroll, ed., *Liberating Women's History* (Urbana, 1970), pp. 106–7; J. Astruc, *A Treatise on the Diseases of Women* (London, 1762), pp. 245–85; J. Ball, *The Female Physician or Every Woman her own Doctress* (London, 1770), pp. 1–2; H. Manning, *A Treatise on Female Diseases* (London, 1771), pp. 204–7, 216.

emotional and mental characteristics. In an extended sermon on female reserve, Fordyce stressed how 'necessary and wise' it was for women to show the shamefastness proper to their sex: 'A masculine woman must be naturally an unamiable creature. I confess myself shocked whenever I see the sexes confounded. An effeminate fellow . . . is an object of contempt and aversion at once . . . the transformation on either side must ever be monstrous.' He was emphatic, preaching about female virtue, that nature knew what it was doing in complementing 'the more delicate frame' of women's bodies with less intellectual vigour: 'it is not the argumentative but the sentimental talents which give you that insight and those openings into the human heart that lend to your principal ends as women'. In a series of sermons on female piety he stressed women's propensity to 'tender affection', besides the propitiousness of their domestic circumstances for cultivating private devotions. A degree of fearfulness, he contended, becomes women for 'an intrepid female seems to renounce our aid and in some respect to invade our province'. Meekness, he claimed in this sermon, was a virtue required of all women together with 'a timidity peculiar to your sex and also a degree of complacence, yieldingness and sweetness beyond what we look for in men'.[47]

Nowhere is the construction of femininity expressed in such a thoroughgoing, concrete and concerted form before 1800 than in Gregory's *A Father's Legacy*. The sheer confidence of his prescriptive analysis is remarkable. His approach is wholly secular. His attitude to women is deeply condescending yet entirely unselfconscious in being so. The 'usual severity' of a girl's education receives no more than passing comment. It is as if the natural woman – chaste, silent and obedient – that we have seen men have yearned and striven for is at last taken for granted. The supreme statement of this comes after some pages of the usual advice about the informative but not too learned reading a girl should pursue to perfect her social graces. 'I do not want to make you anything,' declares Gregory, 'I want to know what nature has made you and to perfect you on her plan.' With Gregory we encounter gender at its most constructed, its most artificial, yet at the same time such is his conviction that he can parade its spontaneity. It all shows how nature proves a wonderfully fluid and adaptable concept in the hands of eighteenth-century ideologists intent upon fixing men and women in a framework of polarity. Her duties, he tells his daughter, lie 'where the heart is chiefly concerned'; her 'natural softness and sensibility' of disposition settles it this way, he explains. In just the same way 'the natural warmth of your imagination' is the fount of female piety, a check upon the 'natural vivacity and perhaps the natural vanity of your sex'. He thrills to the idea of a woman's blushing, showing the 'modest reserve' which leaves her disconcerted at

47. J. Fordyce, *Sermons to Young Women* (London, 1766), I, pp. 86, 104, 271–3, II, pp. 62, 111–18, 222–4.

an admiring gaze: 'That extreme sensibility which it indicates may be a weakness and incumbrance in our sex, as I have too often felt; but in yours it is peculiarly engaging. . . . Nature has made you to blush when you are guilty of no fault and has forced us to love you because you do so.' It is constantly impressed upon Miss Gregory that men's expectations are the only rule and precept in how she should employ a sense of what is proper. 'The love of dress is natural to you', but she must remember how much 'we consider your dress expensive of your characters'. In the process of courtship, a girl must expect to be passive. Gregory reassured himself that, though 'nature has not given you that unlimited range in your choice which we enjoy, she has wisely and benevolently assigned to you a greater flexibility of taste on this subject'. A suitor displays 'some agreeable qualities'; the girl is bound to show gratitude; 'this gratitude rises into a preference'; his attachment brings hers in response. Thus a girl shows her 'taste and delicacy' by esteeming and loving the man who chooses her. She does no choosing herself, and it never enters Gregory's mind that she should wish or expect to do so.[48]

Perhaps the most striking shift between Allestree's tract and Gregory's, just over a hundred years apart as they are in publication, is that Gregory takes a very much less dire view of women's nature than his predecessor. This undoubtedly reflects a growth of male assurance about women's ability, given the proper advice and upbringing, to control their passions, above all their sexuality. In very general terms two stages can be identified in this process. Up until the 1740s the conduct book writers invariably built in one way or another upon Allestree's 'outworks' of chastity – the issues of modesty and meekness – in making their case for an internalised female virtue. Thereafter less attention was devoted to the specifics of behaviour. The cumulative impact of bio-medical discourses and the development of a romantic notion of womanhood were combining, it seems, to desexualise women in the eyes of men. This removed the immediacy of the threat, which we began by exploring from Elizabethan and Jacobean material, of female sexual voraciousness.[49]

Women's preservation of their chastity, avowed Steele, represented their triumph over 'fierce and unruly desire' and over 'false hopes and imaginary delights'. Her whole conduct, properly constructed, would declare to her husband that she was void of all suspicion as well as blame: 'A chaste conversation requires not only the purity and cleanness of the heart but such an outward, innocent and decent carriage as may denote that inward purity.'[50] Essex regarded young women as constantly at war with immoderate desires and emotions. The 'itch of novelty' was the 'bane of virtue'. He expanded in considerable detail upon issues of body

48. J. Gregory, *A Father's Legacy to his Daughters* (London, 1774), pp. 10, 54–6, 82–3; see also Jones, ed., *Women in the Eighteenth Century*, pp. 44–53.
49. Above, pp. 4–12.
50. Steele, *The Ladies Library*, I, p. 155, II, pp. 66–8.

language. As in the case of men, presentation becomes critical. Chastity required no hazard of immodesty or intemperance: a 'wanton step' could give away an 'inward disposition of heart'. The display of grace without flirtation in walking, sitting and dancing required thoughtful attention. How she entered a room or left it was important. 'Your air, your shape, your choice in dress' as she walked, the reader was told, could be 'agreeably expressed'. Good sense and regular education would be evident from such nuances as 'the fine turn of the head and neck, the uprightness of the body and the decorum of the feet'.[51] Women should avoid any familiar talk with men, advised Kenrick, since there could be no confidence in their discretion; even a kiss on the cheek could leave a sweetness which 'inflamed him to desire'.[52] Vanity and desire, reflected Wilkes, were so prevalent in men 'that we are apt to interpret every obliging look, gesture, smile or sentence of a female we like on the hopeful side'. It was her responsibility, he insisted, by showing 'genteel distance' to avoid running herself into hazard. A woman must take hold of her sexuality and make its proper direction the rule of her life. There was a dark warning against the 'irregular desires' which produced the voluntary pollution of masturbation. Chastity was 'a kind of quick and delicate feeling in the soul which makes her shrink and withdraw herself from everything that is wanton or has danger in it'.[53]

As chastity became interpreted more and more as an inner virtue based upon lack of sexual desire, the double standard changed from a policing mechanism which required women to repress some aspects of their behaviour to an internalised ideology. Women were taught to perceive themselves as desexualised embodiments of spiritual value.[54] Developments in reproductive theory were interpreted in a way which strengthened the notion of female sexual passivity, absolving women of responsibility for arousing their partners or themselves. By the end of the seventeenth century, the ovum theory had generally replaced the two seed theory. Scientists now argued that the child was preformed in the spermatozoa for which the woman provided a receptacle.[55] There is an echo of Aristotelian thinking about the activity and passivity of the male and female seeds in the formulation of *Aristotle's Master-Piece*: sexual desire 'in men proceeds from a desire for emission and in women from a desire for completion'; 'the active is the man's seed . . . the passive is an ovum or egg'.[56] The implication was that women's sexual pleasure was no longer essential to conception. Women 'take it ill', as one commentator

51. Essex, *The Young Ladies Conduct*, pp. xxvi, 9–17, 46–7, 80–1.
52. W. Kenrick, *The Whole Duty of Woman* (London, 1753), pp. 39–41.
53. Wilkes, *Letter of Genteel and Moral Advice*, pp. 75–7, 108, 114–15.
54. Gibbons, pp. 34–5, Browne, *The Eighteenth-Century Feminist Mind*, pp. 146–7.
55. A. Eccles, *Obstetrics and Gynaecology in Tudor and Stuart England* (London, 1982), p. 32.
56. Cited in Gibbons, pp. 5–6.

put it in 1718, 'to be thought merely passive in those wars wherein they make such vigorous encounters'.[57] Lady Peregrina Chaytor, writing to her husband to announce her pregnancy in 1701, expresses the fact in words which show there was no longer any idea in her mind of heat and concoction. 'I must wish you had not given it me at this time', she declared, 'when I would think of better things.'[58] By 1800 the traditional defence in rape cases, that if pregnancy followed the woman must have enjoyed the sexual act, was no longer seen as valid.[59]

We can trace the gradual transition from chastity as something women had to learn by hard graft against the direction of their whole being to chastity as the essence of natural innocence. Bernard Mandeville, in a pamphlet of 1724, paraded the old story of the female's inherent pleasure in sex, arguing that 'to counterbalance this violent natural desire all young women have strong notions of honour carefully inculcated into them from their infancy'. 'This sense of honour and interest', he explained, 'is what we may call artificial chastity and it is upon this compound of natural and artificial chastity that every woman's real actual chastity depends.'[60] In the same year, we find Eliza Haywood purveying a similar notion of women's sexuality in her novel *Love in Excess* by a scene in which a woman is panting, heaving and confessing her wish to yield yet is given an innocence and irresponsibility of mind which excuses her until someone interrupts just in time. The heroine is still sexual; her sexuality is dangerous; her honour is her only defence. In Richardson's *Clarissa* honour is still the issue at stake but her virtue, the core of her personality, is taken for granted to the extent that she becomes almost superhuman. A scene from Fanny Burney's novel *Camilla*, published in 1796, indicates the progress of ideological repression. It is now the heroine who will check herself. Having indiscreetly fallen in love, her father writes to advise her: 'It is not strength of mind you want but reflection to obtain a strict and unremitting control over your passions.' Then, apologising for the word, which will 'pain' her, he reminds her that 'you have no passions, my innocent girl, at which you need blush, though enough at which I must tremble'. He appears to mean, suggests Patricia Spacks, that Camilla has no clear sexual feelings but only 'less specific desires which could lure her into dangerous situations'.[61]

All this prescriptive material needs to be put into a historiographical context. Three influential books published during the 1970s by Edward

57. Cited in P. Crawford, ed., *Exploring Women's Past* (London, 1983), p. 65.
58. S. Chaytor, 'Family Life in the Seventeenth Century: Sir William Chaytor 1639–1721' (Durham University MA dissertation, 1992), p. 28.
59. Browne, *Eighteenth-Century Feminist Mind*, p. 193.
60. Jones, ed., *Women in the Eighteenth-Century*, p. 65.
61. P. Spacks, 'Ev'ry Woman is at Heart a Rake', *Eighteenth Century Studies*, VIII (1974–5), pp. 28–9, 32–3. For *Clarissa* see the account in Browne, *Eighteenth-Century Feminist Mind*, pp. 59–66.

Shorter, Lawrence Stone and Randolph Trumbach discussed gender relationships as they were allegedly actually lived in eighteenth-century upper-class families. This was the period, these writers claimed, which saw the birth of the affectionate nuclear family. The argument about a process of what we might call emotional modernisation was based on points about economic and pragmatic considerations in selection of partners, formality and distance in relationships and a lack of interest in privacy before the eighteenth century and upon the development of intimacy, between both husbands and wives and parents and children, during that century.[62] The important issue for this book, and for the construction of femininity in particular, is that it was claimed in these works that the so-called companionate marriage of the eighteenth century was less patriarchal than its predecessor. It is argued here that the romantic ideal of companionate marriage was indeed strongly articulated in the eighteenth century and that the conduct books provide a principal source for its expression. However this does not mean that women gained greater equality in practice or that any kind of emancipated notion of femininity was promulgated. On the contrary, the very essence of the companionate marriage, it can be suggested, was the subordination of women (plates 38 and 39). The construction of femininity and woman's imprisonment in an ideological straightjacket went hand in hand. The companionate family is more appropriately termed, as Susan Okin has persuasively argued, the sentimental family. The conduct books support her view, on the basis of contemporary political theory, that during the eighteenth century patriarchal relations between men and women were reinforced by a potent new secular ideology of subordination. Okin makes three points about this new ideology. Two of them the conduct book writers virtually take as read at least so far as the upper classes are concerned that 'women's spheres of dependence and domesticity are divided from the outside world more strictly than before', and that 'the legitimacy of male rule both within and outside the family is reinforced on the grounds that the interests of the family are totally united'. The third point is the one where the conduct book material is peculiarly apposite as a testing ground. Okin argues that 'women increasingly came to be characterised as creatures of sentiment and love rather than of the rationality that was perceived as necessary for citizenship'.[63] The evidence over the centuries seems to suggest that there is an essential continuity about human emotion but that how it is expressed varies from one historical context to another. It is a central contention of this book that

62. E. Shorter, *The Making of the Modern Family* (London, 1975); L. Stone, *The Family, Sex and Marriage in England 1500–1800* (London, 1977); R. Trumbach, *The Rise of the Egalitarian Family* (London, 1978). The phrase 'emotional modernisation' is taken from Erickson, p. 7.

63. S.M. Okin, 'Women and the Making of the Sentimental Family', *Philosophy and Public Affairs* 11 (1982), pp. 72–4.

there was a strong male imperative from the Elizabethan period onwards to reconstruct patriarchy on more effective foundations. In this context the construction of femininity as a prescriptive code of personal characteristics and behaviour between the 1670s and 1800 falls into place.[64]

Fenella Childs concluded from her survey of the prescriptive material from 1690 to 1760 that strict didacticism steadily gave way to sweetly worded and persuasive phrases about women's goodness, softness and tenderness as the domestic cult of womanhood based on complementary spheres gathered strength.[65] The core of the argument about femininity became the question of a wife's emotional support for her husband. Halifax was very important indeed here. He stated a woman's role in this sense more directly than anyone had done hitherto: men needed women's 'gentleness to soften and to entertain us'. This he confessed gave them an influence over men which it behoved them to use responsibly: 'you have more strength in your looks than we have in our laws and more power by your tears than we have by our arguments'.[66] We have seen how the keynote of Allestree's treatment of the role of the wife and mother was the exercise of her emotional strength. Steele's account, which draws so heavily on Allestree, develops the point. It was of course easy to do so since all the conventional precepts about mildness and meekness only needed a small twist in a positive direction for the good wife to become a nurturing as well as a deeply faithful spouse. Keeping a man's secrets, warning him of dangers to his reputation, gentle admonishment for his faults, besides overlooking his infidelities, become central requirements of a woman's love. Her duty above all is emotional support: 'With love, the wife owes her husband all friendliness and kindness of conversation. She is to endeavour to bring him as much assistance, comfort of life as is possible that so she may answer that special end of the woman's creation, the being a help to her husband.'[67] Woman, in this reading, is no longer a lesser form of man, but neither is she a separate person in her own right. She is discrete yet still only real, in a new way now, in her relation to a man.

No longer are women being told simply how to conduct themselves to avoid the snares of their weak nature. Responsibility is heaped upon them as the advice books set out their duties in their own sphere of household management and the care of children. But the centrepiece remains their special responsibility within the marital relationship. Essex takes the argument a bit farther than Steele. The two sexes have 'different qualifications', so each may supply the defects of the other: 'You are generally endowed with a great deal of patience, courtesy and fortitude, to which I would recommend complaisance and gentleness to soften and divert

64. Erickson, p. 7.
65. Childs, 'Prescriptions for Manners', pp. 284–5.
66. Jones, ed., *Women in the Eighteenth Century*, p. 18.
67. Steele, *The Ladies Library*, II, pp. 80–96.

those troubles and cares which ruffle the tempers of mankind and to which they are naturally exposed by their affairs and business in the world.' A wife must expect to correct her own ill habits but when her husband was 'surly and peevish' she must act to allay his mood as well. Rather than engage in curtain lectures, she must allure him 'to your charms'.[68] Wilkes paraphrased Halifax with the formulation 'her looks have more power than his laws and a few sweet words from her can soften all his fury'. He regarded a wife's good nature, tenderness and affection as the instruments which would reclaim an 'ill managing' man from his errors. The wife emerges in his tract of 1740 as the fully fledged moral exemplar.[69] The new ideal is even more fully realised in Marriott's 1759 treatise which praises women's role as mother and homemaker and gives them, through their virtue, the power to reform the morals of society. 'Women', he insists, 'have it very much in their power by their exemplary behaviour to render virtue fashionable and to discountenance vice among men.'[70] Fordyce is emphatic that it is their 'constitutional softness' which makes women virtuous. He sees its basis in 'the original make or specific character of the sex'. Their higher degree of sensibility is proven by 'their strong propensity to a union of hearts, their unutterable fondness . . . their lovely peculiarities in their temperament, their finer tunings of their mind'. Fordyce found it entirely logical, in view of all this, that women should be destined to disarm men's fierceness and appease wrath, to assuage 'the cares' and calm 'the sorrows' of the men in their lives.[71] Gregory took the same things for granted. He was in no doubt, he announced near the start of his tract, that his view of the female sex was an honourable one, seeing them as he did 'not as domestic drudges or the slaves of our pleasures but as companions and equals, as designed to soften our hearts and polish our manners'.[72]

In order to understand the unassuming seriousness with which Gregory refers to wives as 'companions and equals' we need to consider the question of changing attitudes to women's reading and learning. We have seen how facilities for girls' education improved in their range and variety and how there was debate about the stress that should be put upon academic or social accomplishments.[73] As men's confidence grew about the ideology of gender construction, they could afford to take a more liberal attitude than previously to women's learning and intellectual fulfilments. It is a sign of changing attitudes that the published funeral sermon for Elizabeth Bury, a late example of the genre in 1720, empha-

---

68. Essex, *The Young Ladies Conduct*, pp. 69–70.
69. Wilkes, *A Letter of Genteel and Moral Advice*, pp. 116–18.
70. Marriott, *Female Conduct*, pp. xxvii–xxviii; Childs, 'Prescriptions for Manners', p. 285.
71. Fordyce, *Sermons to Young Women*, pp. 225–6.
72. Gregory, *A Father's Legacy*, pp. 6–7.
73. Above, pp. 373–4.

sised her knowledge of philosophy, history, mathematics, French, anatomy and medicine besides divinity. She was reported to have been distressed 'that so many learned men should be so uncharitable to her sex . . . and be so loath to assist their feebler faculties' when they accepted 'that souls were not distinguished by sexes'.[74] The conduct books under review provide a conspectus on the new positive treatment of women's learning that was emerging. Steele called for a broad programme of reading in the histories of Greece, Rome and Britain, accounts of voyages and travels and French and Italian authors, while allowing that there was also a place for poetry, music and painting. He was concerned above all to inculcate serious study and check the excesses of the female imagination. It was men's fault, he opined, that women had not been allowed to develop talents which were as good as men's 'by accustoming them to the practice of vanity and trifles'. Steele looked for a self-fashioning in terms of knowledge as much as virtue: a 'well informed and discerning mind' enabled a woman to see through and scorn the 'silly artifices used to ensnare and deceive them'.[75] Essex was equally convinced that many women's mental endowments and 'good taste of reason' put them on a level with any qualifications 'the provident man can boast'. Improving 'the faculties of sense and reason which God and nature had given them' was much more appropriate than playing cards or drinking tea.[76] Learning, in Wilkes's view, helped a woman to fix in herself her duty. It should include the New Testament and the reasonings of the ancient philosophers to embellish the soul with love of virtue. Such reading, he told his female readers, 'will direct you how to live as closely up to the dignity of your nature as your imperfect state will admit you'.[77] Fordyce argued that the pleasures arising from 'reading, writing, agreeable reflection and rational conversation' were the best way for a woman to form the taste which would enable her to correct her otherwise ungovernable passions. He thought many of the fashionable boarding schools neglected their duty in this respect.[78] The theme which runs through all this advice is that learning is now being advocated as a principal means of female gender construction whereas in the seventeenth century it was thought too dangerous in women's hands. Yet at the same time not all gentlemen in Hanoverian England wanted an accomplished wife. Hence the defensive tone of the fictional correspondent employed by Vicesimus Knox in his tract of 1729, who expects social displacement on account of her range of

74. W. Tong, *An Account of the Life and Death of Mrs Elizabeth Bury* (London, 1720), pp. 5–7.
75. Steele, *The Ladies Library*, I, pp. 21–8, II, pp. 438–41.
76. Essex, *The Young Ladies Conduct*, pp. 39–40.
77. Wilkes, *A Letter of Genteel and Moral Advice*, pp. 96–101.
78. Fordyce, *Sermons to Young Women*, I, p. 288, II, pp. 5–14.

learning but asserts that she is glad of the intellectual satisfaction she has attained for its own sake.[79]

The romantic idea of emotional companionship is more fully set out than anywhere else before 1800 in Hester Chapone's *Letter to a New Married Lady* published in 1780. This took the argument much further than her earlier account of the standard female social and intellectual accomplishments which, as we have seen, simply carried the usual warnings about pedantry and presumption in the learned woman.[80] The letter was addressed to a fictional correspondent, chosen out of affection rather than given in marriage by her parents, who faced the business of proving, as Chapone put it, 'the sincerity of your attachment'. Her task is to build 'the solid foundation of a durable friendship' before his initial passion palls. So she must always prefer his company and that of his special friends to her own diversions: 'By studying his taste rather than your own and making the gratifications of it your highest pleasure you must convince him that his heart is your own.' Ask him, advised Chapone, to read with you, practice music, teach you a language or science. One side of the picture is of the adoring deferential dependent sitting at her master's feet. The other is the loving spouse with an inexhaustible supply of emotional support. A man gets hurt by the world and its affairs, explains Chapone, 'which may sometimes affect his temper': 'But when he returns to his own house, let him there find everything serene and peaceful and let your cheerful complacency restore his good humour and quiet every uneasy passion.'[81] Leonore Davidoff and Catherine Hall have demonstrated how, through the evangelical movement, 'the idea of a privatised home, separate from the world' came to have 'a powerful moral force' in the first decades of the nineteenth century. Home became, in this thinking, the chief focus of women's mission. This was where they could reveal their true nature and aptitude, wielding their moral influence in such a way that they saved 'not only themselves, but men as well, from the fall which they had brought about'.[82] Chapone stands in the forefront of this tradition. She requires of her new married lady the depths of subordination: she must show dignity to an adulterous husband seeking to regain his heart, avoid all disputes and dissension by sour or thwarting behaviour, accept his sentiments regarding friends and relatives. Chapone's wife carries the burden of the marriage by the tone she sets at home of caring attentiveness. If her husband, a wife is advised, is less tender to her than

79. Jones, ed., *Women in the Eighteenth Century*, pp. 100, 106–9. Jones's anthology provides a useful introduction to the debate about women's education.
80. Passages from H. Chapone, *Letters on the Improvement of the Mind* appear in Jones, ed., *Women in the Eighteenth Century*, pp. 104–6.
81. Chapone, *Letter to a New Married Lady*, pp. 213–18.
82. L. Davidoff and C. Hall, *Family Fortunes: Men and Women of the English Middle Class 1780–1850* (London, 1987), pp. 115–16.

he might be, it is her responsibility to 'awaken his passion by displaying some new grace'.[83]

The regularity with which conduct book writers stress the need for women to read serious books testifies to their concern at the impact and influence of the romantic novels which flooded the eighteenth-century market. Yet up to a point this had simply to be condoned because such reading was part of the formation of what we may call the romantic love complex through which men constructed femininity in the advice literature. It was through this complex, it may be suggested, that the negative image of womanhood was eventually vanquished. The ideology of difference made possible the positive and idealised notions of domestic nurturing and emotional warmth which gave the wife and mother her place in society. 'The man bears rule over his wife's person and conduct', an article on marriage in 1839 noted, 'he governs by law, she by persuasion . . . the empire of the woman is an empire of softness . . . her commands are caresses, her menaces are tears.'[84] Halifax had said it all in a single succinct formulation almost 150 years earlier. During the eighteenth century men were working out and promulgating a deal which has shaped modern gender relations until near the present day. The starting point was woman's otherness, the sense that each sex is a mystery to the other. On this was built a domestic ideology and an ideology of motherhood. Its core was the romantic notion that a woman fastened her emotion upon a married partner, idealised him and projected the course of her life in terms of her mission to sustain and care for his needs and salve his every emotional wound. Chapone's young lady was chosen and did not herself choose or fall in love: otherwise all the ingredients are there in her tract. Many of them are apparent in earlier works like Steele's. Thus we can detect the origins of the modern construction of femininity in a set of ideas which allied women's subordination to romantic love and to a high degree of separation from the outside world. As Amy Erickson puts it, 'romantic ideals were simply a means of maintaining male dominance at a time when overt demands of submission were no longer acceptable'.[85] By 1800 the positive qualities which this pattern of life demanded, the prescriptive literature shows, were becoming well defined. For a long time thereafter the subversive aspect of romantic love, that it knows no rules, was to be held in check by an association of this love with marriage and motherhood. Meanwhile romantic love proved to be patriarchy's strongest bulwark.[86]

83. Chapone, *Letter to a New Married Lady*, pp. 220–4.
84. Cited in A. Giddens, *The Transformation of Intimacy: Sexuality, Love and Eroticism in Modern Societies* (London, 1992), p. 43.
85. Erickson, p. 7.
86. This argument is outlined in Giddens, *Transformation of Intimacy*, pp. 41–7. For comment on the work of Giddens as historical sociology see A. Wilson, ed., *Rethinking Social History: English Society 1570–1920 and its Interpretation* (Manchester, 1993), pp. 40–41, 69.

20. Gender, Patriarchy and Early Modern Society

GENDER, IT WAS noted at the start of this book, is both relational and organisational. This account of the period from 1500 to 1800 has concentrated more on the first aspect than on the second. Little has been said about the prominent sites on which masculine relationships worked themselves out in the public sphere – in government and administration, in the court and parliament, in men's fellowships and associations – or about how precisely such institutions affected women. Shifts in the meaning of masculinity and femininity have instead been traced through attitudes to behaviour in the household and the local community and, where the records permit, through the conduct of intimate personal relationships. Our concern has been with the mental world of gender, the experience as people lived their daily lives of being a man or a woman, the expectations that were created around this distinction and the reactions of individuals to the basic sexual division in society. So in what sense was this a period in which gender was transformed?[1] It would be hazardous to put specific dates on aspects of a process that is immensely complex and the various elements of which are hard to disentangle. The intention has been to investigate and outline change in the means by which relations of power between men and women were conducted, recognising that the process may have been marked by many twists and cross-currents. The starting point was men's need to find a more secure basis and future for patriarchy. We must return first to their dilemmas, before considering, in drawing the threads of an argument together, the context of household and social structures in which they were acting, what they were attempting to replace with what, and the impact and success of their prescriptive campaign and efforts.

The dilemmas felt by men about women, it was suggested in the first chapter, were based not so much on simple misogyny as upon anxiety and fears about women's assertiveness and independence in speech and action,

1. For comment on volatility and long term change in gender relations see L. Roper, *Oedipus and the Devil: Witchcraft, Sexuality and Religion in Early Modern Europe* (London, 1994), pp. 37–8.

fears which often came back to their sexuality. The exploration which followed in chapters 2, 3 and 4 of men's reading of women – of their minds, bodies and emotions – makes it apparent why they could have felt like this. For men's long-established and traditional conception of womankind as the weaker vessel, it seems, left them in possession of sources of power which men found mysterious and threatening. Meanwhile men's overall conception of gender, in terms of hierarchy rather than incommensurable difference, gave them an insufficiently competent means of imposing a patriarchal order rooted in nature. Medical writers and puritan clerics could persist in proclaiming women's subordination in terms of a relative weakness which was consonant with theological tenets of women's inferiority and they could demand prescriptive social roles which were fixed accordingly. But, in the end, the uncomfortable fact was that this didacticism rested on nothing but the compulsive strength of men's own manhood.

This manhood in itself was more questionable, it is suggested, than we have realised: more problematic to achieve, more problematic to retain and exercise according to the rules that this society set down. For the core of early modern patriarchy was household order and much was expected of men in that regard. What the patriarchal imperative finally imposed was a test of male confidence and character. The masculine and feminine honour codes prescribed soberness, authority, steady and honest labour on the one hand, and chastity and quiet obedience on the other. A good many men were able to conduct an effective marital relationship, as some of the case studies in chapter 8 showed, within this conceptual framework. They usually did so by a mixture of kindness, persuasion and manipulation rather than by outright oppression.[2] Yet masculinity, as Lyndal Roper shows in her account of sixteenth-century Augsburg, was at best an 'ambivalent commodity' at this time. A man could beat his unruly wife and he controlled the family's material assets. However even the prescriptive writers, we have seen, increasingly questioned the efficacy of wife-beating, and the costly and deleterious effects of men's heavy drinking at the alehouse on marital relations was a refrain of the ballad literature. Men were constantly tempted to drink and fight to show that they were men; they kept having to prove themselves sexually for the same reason. Seeking 'the elusive pulse of masculinity', Lyndal Roper finds herself led back 'to the male body itself conceived as a turbulent cauldron of lusts and energies'.[3] There have been hints throughout the central chapters of this book of the impact that these lusts and energies in English manhood had on the implementation of household and social order. Male culture, in England as in Germany, was far from providing a simple set of functional behaviour patterns which could instate a secure basis for men's enforce-

2. Above, particularly pp. 154–66.
3. Roper, *Oedipus and the Devil*, pp. 109, 117.

ment of patriarchy. Yet such was the importance of this culture in the way men were brought up that they were usually on the watch for each other's inadequacies. Hence the significance of charivari as a final resort in the village community. Hence the significance of the anxiety a man could feel about everything people – both men and women – were saying about him in his own neighbourhood. He 'was in some grief', wrote the Lancashire apprentice Roger Lowe in his diary in 1663, because it was being reported locally 'that I said such things concerning women's natural infirmities which I never did and troubled me extremely'.[4] Lowe was not yet master of a household of his own but he wanted and expected to be; he knew that finding a good wife, let alone achieving effective mastership in his home, depended upon his local repute.

Another trouble was that there was no way that the household could be made consistent with a simple model of gender hierarchy. The hier-archies of age and class continually cut across that of gender. We can imagine, for instance, how the sons of gentry families, coming to London from landed estates, will have felt about the subordination and discipline imposed upon them as London apprentices.[5] Widowhood also posed a particular problem which, so long as there was a son of age, was usually solved by provision of bed and board in her son's house for life. This was often made explicit in wills, Margaret Spufford found, in the Cambridge-shire villages of Chippenham, Orwell and Willingham. When her son inherited the family home in 1585, for example, Grace Meade was left the right to use the little parlour with its furnishings; her son was to plough four acres of land for her and give her a load of hay and her husband gave her some sheep and cows as well.[6] For all this it was she, in very practical ways, who became the subordinate even if the nature of the emotional tie did not make it feel like this. The Sussex gentleman Anthony May of Ticehurst, in his will of 1636, listed the chambers that were to be his wife's and declared that his son should respect her use of the kitchen and right to collect firewood. Where a man had worries that the reversal of roles might bring patriarchal assertion, he occasionally made specific testamentary comments. 'I desire my dear wife and my son George to be aiding and assisting and comforting to each other that her love may appear to him and his duty to her,' wrote another Sussex gentleman, Sir Thomas Parker, in the will that he made in 1653.[7]

Usually among the wealthier gentry there was a dower house available on the estate to which a widow could retire. The Lancashire widow Elizabeth Shackleton recorded the stages of her handing over of the

4. Cited in Erickson, p. 9.
5. Above, pp. 213–14.
6. M. Spufford, *Contrasting Communities: English Villagers in the Sixteenth and Seventeenth Centuries* (Cambridge, 1974), pp. 88–93, 111–14, 161–4.
7. A.J. Fletcher, *A County Community in Peace and War: Sussex 1600–1660* (London 1975), p. 33.

family home to her son Tom on his majority in 1777 when she was fifty-one years old. 'Great alteration in this family', she wrote, 'Tom was whole and sole master of Alkincoats.' First she gave him all her diamonds and valuables. Then, next year, she ritually handed over 'the keys of the bureau where he would find all the keys'. Finally, on Tom's marriage in 1779, she actually moved out to the dower house: 'they all saw me come off bag and baggage. Am happy to leave my once happy home to my dear Tom. . . . Grant them health and long life, prosperity and comfort. May they enjoy domestic peace . . . may good old Alkincoats flourish in every degree. Long may the usual generous hospitality flourish within and without these walls that ever did.' The power of Elizabeth Shackleton's emotion as she completed a transaction that was essential to the patriarchal scheme of things shines through her diary entries. Amanda Vickery notes the resignation and acceptance with which she prepared for a 'spectacular loss of status' on handing over her inheritance by marriage to the next generation.[8]

A number of social customs were designed to mitigate the ambivalence surrounding wifely authority in the household. Boys, it has been shown, were hurried forth and away from debilitating female influences by placing them in the hands of tutors or schoolmasters. Yet there was no avoiding a considerable amount of daily control of servants, both male and female, by their dame. How else could a man devote himself to his bread-winning role or, if his status allowed, pursue the public responsibilities which contributed to his local honour? Discipline though, at least if it came to beating servants, was, as the Pepys household indicates, often clearly gendered. There were inherent difficulties in marital partnership as the basis of household patriarchy. There were also plenty of cases in which there simply was not an adult male available to take up the patriarchal role.[9] A remarkable and quite exceptional example of a woman exercising this role in her own person was Lady Anne Clifford's rule on her northern estates, following her two marriages to southern nobility, from 1644 to her death in 1676. Katherine Hodgkin has contrasted Lady Anne's life of boredom and emotional vulnerability as the Earl of Dorset's wife at Knole with her later experience as the mistress to a hoard of tenants in terms of the centrality in the first case of gender and in the second of class. Lady Anne had always attached huge importance to her family identity. Her intention, in restoring her castles and rebuilding churches, was to secure her patrimony for her descendants. In doing so she proved how this gender system was sufficiently flexible to accommodate a woman as a ruthless but benevolent landlord, who toured

8. A. Vickery, 'Women and the World of Goods: A Lancashire Consumer and her Possessions 1751–81', in J. Brewer and R. Porter, eds, Consumption and the World of Goods (London, 1993), p. 288.
9. Above, pp. 215–17.

her estates in style with her retinue and dispensed alms to the local poor.[10]

Sexual desire was not easily contained within the intricate pattern of class and gender relations represented by the household containing various kinds of dependents and servants. The most notorious way it was disruptive, one which gentry took for granted as something understood and winked at, was men's sexual exploitation of servant girls.[11] The autobiography of the itinerant Elizabethan musician Thomas Whytheorne, who acted variously as a teacher, performer, and accompanist living as a dependent in other people's houses, illustrates the tensions that could arise in relationships between such men and the mistress of a house. Whythorne continually struggled to establish his class location as a gentleman himself with a special craft of his own, his masculinity while he was being summoned or dismissed by women confident of their social position, and his sexuality, which he sought to protect by manipulation and dissimulation. Whythorne, we have seen, believed women were invariably designing themselves as well as voracious. He seems to have lived a tortured life. It had its moments of agony when he thought women who employed him wished to seduce him and his fears of being underneath or mastered became intense. His problem was an intense bashfulness: he enjoyed flirtation but 'if it came to making love by word, sign or deed ... I had no more face to do that than had a sheep'. A seductive mistress, he thought, could 'bring me in such a doting love towards her, whereby I should suffer her to ride and deride me as she lists'. Recalling a widowed employer who had mocked him for his reticence as a 'huddypick', a word which refers to sexual simplicity, he took refuge in the wisdom offered by one of the many current proverbs about lascivious widows: 'he that wooeth a widow must not carry quick eels in his codpiece but show some proof that he is stiff before'. 'Her invitation', notes Katherine Hodgkin, is seen as 'the result of an inability to control her lusts, while he knows how to hold his in check.' Whythorne's experiences are paradigmatic of the nervous manhood which at times made the actual operation of early modern patriarchy so insecure.[12] His self-deprecation and obsession with the misogynistic tradition shows how he lacked sufficient assertiveness to perform his gender role whereas the lack of self-discipline of gentry who got their servants with bastard children illustrates the excessive confidence of unchecked male power. Neither trait assisted in securing a stable society on the basis of household patriarchy.

There is a further respect in which the interaction of class and sexuality became problematic and potentially disruptive in Elizabethan and early

10. K. Hodgkin, 'Thomas Whythorne and the Problems of Mastery', *History Workshop Journal* 19 (1985), pp. 148–61.
11. Above, p. 219.
12. K. Hodgkin, 'Thomas Whythorne and the Problems of Mastery', *History Workshop Journal*, 29 (1990), pp. 20–41.

Stuart England. In this society most people slept with someone else and, since the rooms of manor houses led directly into one another and servants mingled with masters, which men slept in the same bed was public knowledge. Being someone's 'bedfellow' had implications in terms of male friendship and intimacy, often of patronage and influence, but not of sexual activity. Whereas sodomy was associated with treason and heresy, explains Alan Bray, 'the image of the masculine friend was far removed from this, an image of intimacy between men in stark contrast to the forbidden intimacy of homosexuality'. This was fine so long as certain conventions were commonly observed. The assumption had been that masters and their close servants shared a class identity, that as the author of a tract in 1598 put it they were 'made of their own metal, even a loaf of their own dough, which being done . . . the gentleman received even a gentleman into his service'. Another assumption was that the relationship of master and servant was personal and mutually supportive rather than mercenary. This kind of personal service, reminiscent of hordes of retainers, was in decay in Tudor England. Yet whereas the conventions of service were changing, the language of male friendship was not. This gave men a weapon when they wanted to use it: the public signs of male friendship, the body language of kisses and embraces that was then considered normal, could be read in a sodomitical light, especially where there was a clear implication of social disparity in a male relationship. Christopher Marlowe's *Edward II* thus cunningly conjures up the image of the sodomite, an enemy both to nature and social order, in the portrayal of Piers Gaveston, the disruptive figure in a royal household. The account by Simonds D'Ewes in his autobiography of Lord Chancellor Bacon's life in disgrace during James I's reign plays on these notions. He 'would not relinquish the practice of his most horrible and secret sin of sodomy, keeping still one Godrick a very effeminate faced youth to be his catamite and bedfellow, although he had discharged the most of his other household servants'. D'Ewes has no direct evidence of the sodomy of which he accused Francis Bacon. He merely links his sharing a bed with a menial servant and something darker. The ambivalence of intimacy between men, at a time when social convention approved its open expression but its meaning had become less secure, raised the possibility of accusations of replacement of the heterosexual bond which was at the core of household patriarchy.[13] The case of the Earl of Castlehaven, which involved sodomy, conspiracy with servants and the sexual victimisation of the lady of the household, thus raised a spectre of disorder of a frightening magnitude and with unthinkable consequences.[14]

It is not being argued here that household order came to be seen by

13. A. Bray, 'Homosexuality and the Signs of Male Friendship in Elizabethan England', *History Workshop Journal*, 29 (1990), pp. 1–19.
14. Work in progress by Cynthia Herrup will explore the significance of this case in full.

men as providing a wholly inadequate foundation for early modern patriarchy, merely that it was increasingly apparent that it was insufficient in itself. The pattern of intellectual changes which were described and assessed in chapter 14, the very gradual replacement, that is, of one cosmology and mental world by another, has to be seen as both the cause of the collapse of traditional gender and the cue for the search for a new framework of gender relations. The Great Chain of Being, macrocosm and microcosm, humoral medicine and astrology were all going down together, yet much, it was argued, could be preserved and reintegrated into a new world picture which was no longer teleological but was based instead upon ideas of human progress. It was not so much that men abandoned the trust that they had long put upon God's word in scripture or on the tradition which condoned male power and the use of force but that they sought a framework for gender which rested on something more permanent and more secure than either of these things. The central intention was the proper internalisation of gender values. If they could teach both boys and girls, men thought, to see sexual difference as fundamental and intractable, sustaining their superiority and women's subordination would become easier. It was not the programme and content of gender training which changed between 1500 and 1800 but merely its mechanism. The programme itself, men believed, was perfectly satisfactory. As chapters 15 to 19 have tried to show, men's energy and vigour went into ensuring that the programme was fully developed, spelt out, explained and inculcated.

It does seem that the boundaries between male and female became more clearcut between 1500 and 1800, that in Jane Austen's world of gender there was an assurance among men, and apparent acceptance among women, about the stability and security of the social roles and patterns of behaviour expected respectively of men and women. Yet we should beware of treating the span of time which has been adopted for this book in too neat a fashion. If a sense of confidence in the gender order can be detected around 1800, this may only be temporary. By definition a system of ideological subordination produces continuing anxiety in those who are doing the subordinating, together with a constant need for reiteration and for responses to those who are contesting the system. We have been attempting to trace a stage in the evolution of historical patriarchies, not argue for a full stop. Then there is the problem of how successfully gender was in fact being inculcated at this time. Was what we are calling the construction of gender a widespread or even universal reality in 1800? There are large questions which this book cannot hope or claim to answer. The male construction of femininity, as it has been considered in chapter 19, was after all being strongly contested by a first wave of feminists in 1800 and they have not been heard, except in passing, in these pages. What can be offered here is a brief consideration of the whole issue of prescription and internalisation,

a subject which requires much more attention from historians than it has
yet received. At one level it is simply hard to believe in women's
imperviousness, given the kind of views that Ann Clifford or Grace
Mildmay articulated about the duty they felt to their husbands or that
Dorothy Leigh or Elizabeth Joceline set down about the upbringing of
girls.

It is quite evident from much that has been said already that mothers
worried about their daughters' looks and their social accomplishments,
seeing these as the main assets they needed to make the most of in order
to acquire a good husband. The upbringing of girls was certainly based
upon this requirement. 'My daughter Nanny is grown almost as tall as I,
Susanna breeds her teeth apace,' wrote Frances Halton to her husband in
1678, 'little Betty grows a very fine child; she is the most likely to make
a handsomer woman than Susanna.' Proposing that their daughter Nancy
be taught singing in a letter to her husband in 1697, Lady Peregrina
Chaytor declared that it would 'advantage her much if she learn . . . it will
help to make up the want in her face'. Emily Kildare was already looking
to the future in her description of her daughter Caroline at eleven days
old: 'she is in the first place small, but fat and plump, has very fine dark
long eyes which I think a great beauty, don't you? and her nose
and mouth like my mother's, with a peeked chin like me'.[15] An
eighteenth-century gentleman such as James Woodforde, curate at Castle
Cary in Somerset, would compliment himself on his judgement of
women by means of his diary entries after a social evening such as this one
in 1767:

> I dined, supped and spent the evening at Justice Creed's, with him, his
> father, Mrs Betty Baker, her three nieces of Bridgewater, that is, Miss
> Baker rather ordinary, Miss Betsy very pretty and Miss Sukey very
> middling, rather pretty than otherwise, all very sensible and agreeable,
> and quite fine ladies, both in behaviour and dress and fortunes.[16]

These were the realities in gentry and middling circles and it behoved
parents and daughters to respect them. To ignore the gender commandments altogether would be suicidal. Besides there was no reason in
many cases to do so. Life was to be lived. Eugenia Wynne, aged
seventeen, confided to her diary in 1796 her intense excitement on being
invited to a ball. The vicar had twitted her with the idea it should be
abandoned, to 'make a sacrifice of it, take it as a notification, etcetera and
God knows what stuff'. 'I made no answers', she recorded, 'but thought
my friend, if instead of that black robe you had a petticoat on, if instead

15. L.A. Pollock, *A Lasting Relationship: Parents and their Children over Three Centuries*
    (London, 1987), pp. 56–7; cited in S. Chaytor, 'Family Life in the Seventeenth
    Century: Sir William Chaytor 1639–1721' (Durham University MA dissertation,
    1992), p. 20.
16. R. Blythe, ed., *A Country Parson: James Woodforde's Diary 1759–1802* (London, 1985),
    p. 27.

of the weight of fifty years you had only seventeen, you would not speak so.'[17]

The best hope we have of testing the relationship between prescription and practice in the life and conduct of adult women is through the study, which is beginning to be properly undertaken, of writings by women themselves which are personal and reflective. There are some general considerations we should bear in mind. In the first place, almost all of this material relates to the experience of women near the top of the social hierarchy, whose class position and privilege of rank can be expected to have mitigated a sense of patriarchal subordination, so that they accepted and perhaps even furthered the notion of female submission. Upper-class women were, it could be said, coopted into the gender system. Kate Lilley, in a study of women's elegy between 1640 and 1700, has found a common theme of stoicism and muted heroism: such poems 'elegize and eulogise the modest, private, retired, accomplished, well-born woman, and point to the properly circumscribed, domestic character of a woman's life, idealising virtue, quietism, good name and service'.[18] There is also the general argument that conduct books, novels, sermons and periodicals, which advocated a particular pattern of femininity, may have been hegemonic yet their hegemony could never be absolute. We have seen already how much religious contemplation and meditation had to offer women caught in unpropitious or unhappy circumstances. The Christian concept of equality of souls was liberating and empowering, allowing women to exploit prescriptive contradictions, to contest and interpret prescriptive meanings.[19]

The diary kept by Lady Sarah Cowper for the sixteen years from 1700 to 1716, about 2,300 pages in all, is highly instructive in this respect. She is so explicit at various times about her motivation that we can reconstruct the many layers of impulse and intention which lay behind her immense scribbling effort. What makes this an especially fascinating and possibly unique source is Lady Sarah's method, for her diary is 'the product of not just the selection and fashioning of her own personal reflections, but of specific prescriptive texts as well': 'she incorporated the words of other writers seamlessly into her own personal observations', Anne Kugler has discovered, 'in effect she spoke in the voice of others generally without signalling that fact'. This shameless borrowing makes sense when we consider it in the light of the conditions of her life and the needs that diary-keeping fulfilled for her. In the first place, this was a spiritual journal. Her extracts pointed towards improving or admonishing faults and weaknesses, discovered through self-examination, by bringing to bear the authority of others more wise

17. Pollock, *Lasting Relationship*, p. 156.
18. K. Lilley, 'True State Within: Women's Elegy 1640–1700', in I. Grundy and S. Wiseman, eds, *Women, Writing, History 1640–1740* (London, 1992), p. 61.
19. Above, pp. 354–60.

or learned. The diaries also convey, as Kugler puts it, 'a sustained personal effort at tranquillity through subduing passion'. This passage makes the point:

> In these writings may be seen the sentiments of my mind. Sometimes I am cheerful, pleased, sedate and quiet. Other whiles grieved, complaining, struggling with my passions, blaming myself and resolving for the future . . . to support all the uneasiness of life. Then by unexpected unforeseen accidents discomposed and shocked, till I have rallied . . . and by making resistance gained the better of my troubles and restored my mind to peace.

Yet even here, we find, the words are not her own, but rather a paraphrase of the preface to Mary Chudleigh's *Poems upon Several Occasions*, published in 1703. Lady Sarah was recording and monitoring as a woman in middle age the progress she made towards salvation, providing an outlet for the anger and frustration of an unsatisfactory marriage and distracting herself from domestic loneliness. It seems clear she intended that the diary should be read by others but probably only by her husband and descendants. Until her husband's death, its indignant tone shows how important it was to her as a weapon in marital battles. During times of family difficulties it was a means of help in adversity. Overall we can see it, in Kugler's words, as 'an individualised reassuring book of self'.

So how does this unusual source help us to resolve issues of prescription and practice? It shows how subtle and free-wheeling the process of appropriation of texts could be. Its special value is that it bridges a gap, making visible a process of reading, reworking and applying gender ideology. Lady Sarah fashioned herself through her diary as an aggrieved and innocent wife and mother, gentlewoman and pious Christian. 'Reshaping culled precepts', concludes Anne Kugler, she 'subverted a socially approved literary format in order to furnish herself with an emotional outlet, a targeted vindication and self affirming portrayals of her multiple identities.' Sir William Cowper, for example, was an extraordinarily controlling husband in household matters, so Lady Sarah selected material from her wide reading to buttress her claims to domestic authority. Whenever William Gouge or Richard Allestree emphasised mutual duties rather than simply wifely obligation, she seized upon their words in self-righteous justification. In one instance, when she wanted to expose a particular fault of her husband, that of avarice, she detached passages from Halifax's celebrated advice to his daughter and rearranged them in a different context, dramatically subverting his text.[20] This is a good example of the dynamic process which Elaine Hoby has identified

20. These two paragraphs are based upon A. Kugler, Prescription, Culture and Shaping Identity: Lady Sarah Cowper (1644–1720), University of Michigan PhD thesis, 1994, especially pp. 7–24, 39–41, 54–162. I am very grateful to Anne Kugler for making this material available to me and for discussion of the issues which it raises.

as being at the heart of patriarchy. Male domination sets limits against which at least some women persistently struggle; 'the framework is being constantly challenged and to some extent renegotiated by women "making a virtue of necessity"'; in women's writings we find many examples of how they could 'turn constraints into permissions, into little pockets of liberty or autonomy'.[21]

All this can be said, and much more could be said, about how women have contested English patriarchy. But in the end the simple fact is that men revised a scheme of gender relations that served their interests as men so effectively during the three centuries from 1500 to 1800 that it has survived. Some would say it has survived virtually intact; most would admit that it is with us at least in general outline in the last decade of the twentieth century. That this survival has involved the constant application of further revision, the development of new elements in prescriptive codes and much necessary adaptation to changing economic and political circumstances is not the point. Our final question must be to ask what has been the legacy of early modern patriarchy for the society of modern Britain. If we focus our attention upon the constructions of masculinity and femininity that have been traced here, one difference between the two of them is apparent. So far as masculinity is concerned, we have found a good deal of continuity between the ruling concepts of the Elizabethan and Hanoverian periods, concepts elaborated around the polarity of manhood and effeminacy. The essence of prescriptive English masculinity, despite revisions and elaborations, remained throughout these three hundred years some kind of mastery or self-discipline, based upon reason, which conveyed male superiority in control of the emotions.[22] We can find a clear statement of this in terms, including the class overtones, which would have made perfect sense to a gentleman in 1800 as early as the 1530s. Sir Thomas Elyot, advising on the education of boys in the ruling elite, put it like this:

It is to be noted that to him that is a governor of a public weal belongeth a double governance, that is to say, an interior or inward governance, and an exterior or outward governance. The first is of his affects and passions, which do inhabit within his soul, and be subjects to reason. The second is of his children, his servants and other subjects to his authority.[23]

Honour and then civility provided conceptions of manly behaviour and self-expression which built upon this basic image of the man who had first mastered himself. But when we turn to women, although there is

21. E. Hoby, *Virtue of Necessity: English Women's Writings 1649–1688* (London, 1988), p. 8.
22. For a useful discussion see Hodgkin, 'Thomas Whythorne', *History Workshop Journal* 29 (1990), pp. 20–26.
23. T. Elyot, *The Book of the Governor* (1531, reprinted London, 1962), p. 183.

a consistent underlying sense of limited and specific childbearing and domestic purposes, the keynote is discontinuity. The overwhelmingly negative construction of womanhood was replaced between 1500 and 1800 by something less demonised and more positive: women were desexualised by the elaboration of a newly perceived gender construction but, at the same time, their moral, intellectual and spiritual qualities received much more open and evident validation and acknowledgement.

One of the most important and enduring aspects of the early modern legacy of gender must be the distinctive educational regimes which we have seen were so firmly established during the seventeenth and eighteenth centuries. Schooling itself was not new but it had vastly expanded. Thus an increasing number of boys and girls from the gentry and middling sort were experiencing a kind of gendered schooling which seems to be peculiar in certain respects to England at this time. What was customary then became formative in the national educational tradition. Yet it is not schools on their own, but schools seen in conjunction with parents and with parental attitudes and upbringing in the home that we should consider, if we are to understand what was so specifically English about the particular historical patriarchy which this book has explored. Both sets of prescriptions, the male and the female, it can be argued, have been developed in a manner which has been unfortunately, even in some sense grossly, limiting and restricting for the unbounded and free expression of human potential and personality. The indictment is one of English class and gender taken together. For boys, the price has been emotional reticence and inhibition which has tarnished many lives. The protestant church, it has to be said, bears considerable responsibility here, since it became identified with a set of prescriptions for harsh boyhood discipline which, while parents usually refused to follow them, allowed schoolmasters to erect their own petty tyrannies. The church has been slow fully to repudiate this tradition which, fundamentally of course, is the legacy of biblical teachings. For girls, the long-term dissemination and impact of the Enlightenment cult of womanhood has been even more onerous in the extent to which it has deprived them of living full lives. What was so damaging about the tradition of female gender construction, as it was brought to its full and coherent form by writers like James Fordyce, was its insidious undermining of female confidence to achieve anything outside a narrow and restricted sphere of activity. The construction of femininity outlined in chapter 19 was only positive in that at last women were allowed a positive sphere of influence and activity. Deep misogynist assumptions remained concealed in a new admiration for the 'fair sex', assumptions which rested in the last resort on the same rigid and schematic interpretations of female nature which had given such resilience to the notion of women as the 'weaker vessel'. Again the Bible, used and interpreted by the church to condone a restrictive pattern of female gender training, has much to answer for. The femininity described by the conduct book writers, seeking to sweep aside women's sexuality, independence and assertiveness once and for all, has lain like a pall, in so far as it has been successfully inculcated, across many women's lives.

For the coda to this study we will return to some vignettes. The excitement for the empirical historian of painting the big picture, telling the big story, is tempting but along the way the experience can feel precarious. Nowhere more so, perhaps, than in the investigation of something so intangible as gender and of systems of human relations as complex as historical patriarchies. Some things we can be more sure about, though, than others. Where people have given us something about their intimate emotions and relationships, about the feelings of their lived experience as men and women, we can often tell from the nature of the record that they are being authentic. Such feelings are often about love, which enables people to live their manhood or womanhood more securely and deeply than anything else. So we can recall, for the devotion of love, the words of Grace Mildmay, meditating on her husband's corpse, 'that I could not find it in my heart to challenge him . . . but in silence passed over all such matters; so that we parted in all love and Christian charity'. For the emotions love creates, there was that music which Samuel Pepys heard in 1668 causing him to reflect that it 'did wrap up my soul so that it made me really sick, just as I have formerly been when in love with my wife'. For the passion of a love that cannot remain unsatisfied, there is Maria Thynne in 1607, pining at Longleat for 'mine own sweet Thomken', threatening 'sound repayment, so as when we meet there will be pay and repay, which will pass and repass'. This is the woman who had written a courageous letter to her mother-in-law a few years previously, seeking a reconciliation after the estrangement caused by the runaway marriage that she had made to Thomas Thynne. We can hold this letter in our hands and see the lock of Maria's dark red hair, sealed by the Audley seal, still where she placed it on that particular day, 15 September 1601. 'Knowing there is in God both a power and a will', Maria wrote, 'I cannot but hope that he will exercise that power to the turning of your heart towards me . . . give me leave my dear mother to conclude with this assurance that if ever it be my great good fortune to gain your favour there shall never want a will in me to deserve the continuance of it with my greatest affection and best service, with this resolution and infinite well-wishings I rest now and ever your very loving and obedient daughter Maria Thynne.'[24] So we end with the strains of a relationship between two women which was necessitated by their relationships to the same man.

24. A.D. Wall, ed., *Two Elizabethan Women: Correspondence of Joan and Maria Thynne 1575–1611* (*Wiltshire Record Society, XXXVIII, 1982*), pp. xxv–xxvii, 21. The letter is to be found among the Thynne Papers (volume VIII, folio 12) which are at Longleat and can be consulted by appointment with the archivist.

Bibliography

PRIMARY SOURCES

A.B., *Learn to Lye Warm* (London, 1672).

Allestree, R., *The Gentleman's Calling* (London, 1660).

Allestree, R., *The Ladies Calling* (London, 1673).

Anon., *The Institution of a Gentleman* (London, 1568).

Anon., *The Problems of Aristotle* (London, 1607).

Anon., *The Resolution of the Women of London to the Parliament* (London, 1642).

Anon., *Gnomologia: Adages and Proverbs, Wise Sentences and Witty Sayings* (London, 1732).

Ashmole, E., ed., *Theatrum Chemicum Brittanicum* (London, 1652).

Astruc, J., *A Treatise on the Diseases of Women* (London, 1762).

Austen, J., *Emma*, ed., R. Blythe (London, 1966).

Austin, W., *Haec Homo* (London, 1639).

Ball, J., *The Female Physician or Every Woman her own Doctress* (London, 1770).

Banister, J., *The History of Man* (London, 1578).

Barlow, J., *The True Guide to Glory* (London, 1619).

Blundell, M., ed., *Letters of William Blundell to his Friends 1620–1689* (London, 1933).

Blythe, R. ed., *A Country Parson: James Woodforde's Diary 1759–1802* (London, 1985).

Bohun, E., *The Justice of Peace his Calling* (London, 1684).

Boord, A., *Scoggin's Jests* (London, 1626).

Boorde, A., *The Breviary of Health* (London, 1547).

Bowers, F., ed., *The Dramatic Works of Thomas Dekker* (Cambridge, 1958).

Brathwaite, R., *The English Gentleman* (London, 1628).

Brathwaite, R., *The English Gentlewoman* (London, 1631).

Brathwaite, R., *Art Asleep Husband: A Boulster Lecture* (London, 1640).

Bruele, W., *Praxis Medicinae or The Physicians Practice* (London, 1632).

Chapone, H., *Letter to a New Married Lady* (London, 1780).

Chappell, W., ed., *The Roxburghe Ballads* vols I–III (London, 1871–80).

Clark, A., ed., *The Shirburn Ballads* (Oxford, 1907).

Clarke, J., *Paroemiologia Anglo-Latina* (London, 1639).

Clarke, S., *Lives of Sundry Eminent Persons in this Later Age* (London, 1683).

Cleland, J., *The Institution of a Young Nobleman* (London, 1607).

Clifford, D.J.H., ed., *The Diary of Lady Anne Clifford* (Stroud, 1990).

Cogan, T., *The Haven of Health* (London, 1596).

Cooper, J.P., ed., *Wentworth Papers 1597–1628* (Camden Fourth Series, 12, 1973).

Cotta, J., *A Short Discourse of the Unobserved Dangers of several sorts of Ignorant Practices of Physick in England* (London, 1622).

Cowper, W., *The Anatomy of Humane Bodies* (London, 1697).

Crooke, H., *Microcosmographia: A Description of the Body of Man* (London, 1615).

Cross, C., ed., *The Letters of Sir Francis Hastings* (Somerset Record Society, LXIX, 1969).

Culpepper, N. and Cole, A., trans., *Bartholin's Anatomy* (London, 1668).

Dod, J. and Cleaver, R., *A Godly Form of Household Government* (London, 1614).

Dove, J., *Of Divorcement: A Sermon preached at Pauls Cross* (London, 1601).

D'Urfey, T., *Wit and Mirth or Pills to Purge the Melancholy* (London, 1700).

Ellis, C., *The Gentle Sinner or England's Brave Gentleman* (London, 1660).

Elyot, T., *The Book of the Governor* (1531, repr. London, 1962).

Elyot, T., *The Castle of Health* (London, 1534).

Essex, J., *The Young Ladies Conduct* (London, 1722).

Fielding, S., *The Governess or Little Female Academy* (Oxford, 1968 edn).

Fincham, K., *Visitation Articles and Injunctions of the Early Stuart Church* (Church of England Record Society, I, 1994).

Fiske, J., ed., *The Oakes Diaries: Business, Politics and the Family in Bury St Edmunds 1728– 1827* (Suffolk Records Society, XXXII, 1989–90).

Fiston, W., *The School of Good Manners* (London, 1609).

Fontanus, N., *The Woman's Doctor* (London, 1652).

Fordyce, J., *Sermons to Young Women* (London, 1766).

Fordyce, J., *Addresses to Young Men* (London, 1777).

Foxe, J., *Acts and Monuments* (ed. G. Townshend, New York, 1965).

Frost, D.L., ed., *The Selected Plays of Thomas Middleton* (Cambridge, 1978).

Gailhard, J., *The Compleat Gentleman: or Directions for the Education of Youth as to their Breeding at home and Travelling abroad* (London, 1678).

Gataker, T., *Marriage Duties briefly couched together out of Colossians 3:18 and 19* (London, 1620).

Gataker, T., *A Good Wife God's Gift* (London, 1624).

Geree, S., *The Ornament of Women* (London, 1639).

Gibson, T., *The Anatomy of Human Bodies Epitomised* (London, 1682).

Goldsmith, O., *The Vicar of Wakefield* (London, 1766).

Gosson, S., *Pleasant Quippes for Upstart Newfangled Gentlewomen* (London, 1596).

Gouge, W., *Domestical Duties* (London, 1622).

Gough, R., *The History of Myddle* (London, 1981).

Greene, D.G., ed., *The Meditations of Lady Elizabeth Delaval* (Surtees Society, CXC, 1978).

Gregory, J., *A Father's Legacy to his Daughters* (London, 1774).

Griffith, M., *Bethel* (London, 1633).

Harper, R., *The Anatomy of a Woman's Tongue* (London, 1638).

Harper, R., *The Anatomy of a Woman's Tongue* (London, 1638), *Harleian Miscellany* II (1744).

Hassell Smith, A., Baker, G.R., and Kenny, R.W., eds, *The Papers of Nathaniel Bacon of Stiffkey* (Centre of East Anglian Studies, Norwich, 1979, 1983).

Heale, W., *An Apology for Women* (London, 1609).

Heale, W., *The Great Advocate and Orator for Women* (London, 1682).

Heywood, T., *Gunaikeion or Nine Books of Various History concerning Women* (London, 1624).

Heywood, T., *A Curtain Lecture* (London, 1637).

Hodgson, J.C., *Six North Country Diaries* (Surtees Society, 64, 1910).

Horne, R., *Points of Instruction for the Ignorant* (London, 1617).

Howell, J., *Proverbs or Old Saws and Adages* (London, 1659).

Hughey, R., ed., *The Correspondence of Lady Katherine Paston 1603–1627* (Norfolk Record Society, XIV, 1941).

Hunt, R.D., ed., *Henry Townshend's 'Notes of the Office of Justice of Peace' 1661–3* (Worcestershire Historical Society, IV, Miscellany, vol. II, 1967).

Hutchinson, L., *Memoirs of Colonel John Hutchinson* (ed. J. Sutherland, Oxford, 1973).

Jackson, C., ed., *The Autobiography of Mrs Alice Thornton* (Surtees Society, LXII, 1873).

Joceline, E., *A Mother's Legacy to her Unborn Child* (London, 1624).

Jorden, E., *A Brief Discourse of a Disease Called the Suffocation of the Mother* (London, 1603).

Keble, J., ed., *Works of Richard Hooker* (London, 1888).

Kenrick, W., *The Whole Duty of Woman* (London, 1753).

Laslett, P., ed., *Patriarcha and Other Political Works of Sir Robert Filmer* (Oxford, 1949).

Latham, R.C. and Matthew, W., eds, *The Diary of Samuel Pepys*, 11 vols (London, 1970–83).

Legrand, J., *The Book of Good Manners* (London, 1503).

Leigh, D., *The Mother's Blessing* (London, 1627).

Lemnius, L., *The Touchstone of Complexions* (London, 1633).

Lemnius, L., *The Secret Miracles of Nature* (London, 1658).

Longstaffe, W.H.D., ed., *Memoirs of the Life of Mr Ambrose Barnes* (Surtees Society, L, 1866).

Macfarlane, A., ed., *The Diary of Ralph Josselin 1616–1683* (London, 1976).

McClure, N.F., ed., *The Letters of John Chamberlain* (Philadelphia, 1939).

Magrath, J.R., ed., *The Flemings at Oxford* (Oxford Historical Society, XLIV, 1903; LXXIX, 1924).

Manning, H., *A Treatise on Female Diseases* (London, 1771).

Marriott, T., *Female Conduct* (London, 1759).

Marshall, J., ed., *The Diary of William Stout of Lancaster* (Chetham Society, XIV, 1967).

Martyn, W., *Youth's Instruction* (London, 1613).

Meads, D.M., ed., *The Diary of Lady Margaret Hoby* (London, 1930).

Moryson, F., *An Itinerary written by Fynes Moryson* (London, 1617).

Newcome, T., *Autobiography* (ed. R. Parkinson, Chetham Society, XXVI, 1852).

Nicholson, M.H., ed., *Conway Letters: The Correspondence of Anne, Viscountess Conway, Henry More and their Friends 1642–1684* (Oxford, 1930).

Parry, E.A., ed., *Letters from Dorothy Osborne to Sir William Temple 1652–54* (London, 1903).

Parsons, D., ed., *The Diary of Sir Henry Slingsby of Scriven* (London, 1836).

Partridge, J., *The Treasury of Commodious Conceits* (London, 1584).

Pechy, J., *A General Treatise of the Diseases of Maids, Bigbellied Women, Childbed Women and Widows* (London, 1696).

Phaer, T., *The Regiment of Life* (London, 1550).

Phillips, C.B., ed., *Lowther Family Estate Books 1617–1675* (Surteers Society, LXLI, for 1976–7, 1979).

Ray, J., *A Collection of English Proverbs* (London, 1670).

Raynalde, T., *The Birth of Mankind* (London, 1634).

Rich, B., *The Excellency of Good Women* (London, 1613).

Riverius, L., *The Practice of Physick* (London, 1655).

R.L., *Letter of Advice to a Young Gentleman leaving the University* (London, 1670).

Roberts, H., *An Earnest Complaint of divers Vain Wicked and Abused Exercises* (London, 1572).

Rogers, D., *Matrimonial Honour* (London, 1642).

Rogers, T., *The Character of a Good Woman* (London, 1697).

Ross, A., *Arcana Microcosmi or The Hidden Secrets of Man's Body Disclosed* (London, 1651).

Rowlands, S., *A Crew of Kind Gossips all met to be Merry* (London, 1613).

Rowlands, S., *Well Met Gossip* (London, 1619).

Rueff, J., *The Expert Midwife* (London, 1637).

Sadler, J., *The Sick Woman's Private Looking Glass* (London, 1636).

Sharpe, J., *The Midwives Book* (London, 1671).

Smith, H., *A Preparative to Marriage* (London, 1591).

Snawsel, R., *A Looking Glass for Married Folks* (London, 1631).

Snow, V.F. and Young, A.S., *The Private Journals of the Long Parliament* (New Haven, 1992).

Somerville, J.P., ed., *Patriarcha and Other Writings* (Cambridge, 1991).

Steele, R., *The Ladies Library* (London, 1714).

Strachey, C., ed., *The Letters of the Earl of Chesterfield to his Son* (London, 1901).

Stubbes, P., *The Anatomy of Abuses* (London, 1583).

Stubbes, P., *A Christal Glass for Christian Women* (London, 1591).

Stubbings, F., ed., *The Statutes of Sir Walter Mildmay for Emmanuel College* (Cambridge, 1983).

Taylor, J., *Works* (London, 1630).

T.E., *The Law's Resolution of Women's Rights* (London, 1632).

Tilney, E., *The Flower of Friendship* (London, 1568).

Timothy, R., *The Character of a Good Woman* (London, 1697).

Tong, W., *An Account of the Life and Death of Mrs Elizabeth Bury* (London, 1720).

Twyne, *The Schoolmaster or Teacher of Table Philosophy* (London, 1583).

Tyndale, W., *The Obedience of a Christian Man* (London, 1868 edn).

Venette, N., *The Mysteries of Conjugal Love Revealed* (London, 1712).

Verney, F.P., ed., *Memoirs of the Verney Family During the Civil War*, 4 vols (London, 1970).

Vicary, T., *The Anatomy of the Body of Man* (Early English Text Society, extra series, 53, 1888).

Walker, A., *The Holy Life of Mrs Elizabeth Walker* (London, 1690).

Wall, A.D., ed., *Two Elizabethan Women: Correspondence of Joan and Maria Thynne 1575–1611* (Wiltshire Record Society, vol. XXXVIII, 1982).

Warrington, Earl of, *Advice to his Children* (London, 1696).

Webb, G., *The Arraignment of an Unruly Tongue* (London, 1619).

Weighall, R., ed., 'An Elizabethan Gentlewoman: the Journal of Lady Mildmay', *Quarterly Review* CCXV (1911).

Weinstein, H., *A Catalogue of the Ballads in the Pepys Collection* (Cambridge, 1993).

Whateley, W., *The Bride Bush* (London, 1623).

Widley, G., *The Doctrine of the Sabbath* (London, 1604).

Wilkes, W., *A Letter of Genteel and Moral Advice to a Young Lady* (London, 1740).

Williams, C., trans, *Thomas Platter's Travels in England 1599* (London, 1937).

Williams, J.B., *Memoirs of the Life of Mrs Sarah Savage* (London, 1829).

Willoughby, P., *Observations on Midwifery*, ed., H. Blenkinsop (London, 1932).

Wing, J., *The Crown Conjugal or Spouse Royal* (London, 1620).

Wolley, H., *The Accomplisht Lady's Delight* (London, 1675).

Woodforde, D.H., ed., *Woodforde Papers and Diaries* (London, 1932).

BOOKS

Adelman, J., *Suffocating Mothers: Fantasies of Maternal Origin in Shakespeare's Plays, Hamlet to the Tempest* (London, 1992).

Amussen, S.D., *An Ordered Society: Gender and Class in Early Modern England* (Oxford, 1988).

Archer, I., *The Pursuit of Stability: Social Relations in Elizabethan London* (Cambridge, 1991).

Armstrong, N., *Desire and Domestic Fiction* (Oxford, 1987).

Axtell, J.L., ed., *The Educational Writings of John Locke* (Cambridge, 1969).

Babb, L., *The Elizabethan Malady: A Study of Melancholia in English Literature from 1580–1642* (Michigan, 1951).

Barber, C., *The Theme of Honour's Tongue: A Study of Social Attitudes in the English Drama from Shakespeare to Dryden* (Goteborg, 1985).

Barker-Benfield, G.J., *The Culture of Sensibility: Sex and Society in Eighteenth-Century Britain* (Chicago, 1992).

Barrell, J., *The Dark Side of the Landscape: The Rural Poor in English Painting 1730–1840* (Cambridge, 1983).

Barry, J., *The Tudor and Stuart Town: A Reader in English Urban History 1530–1699* (London, 1990).

Beier, L.M., *Sufferers and Healers: The Experience of Illness in Seventeenth Century England* (London, 1987).

Belsey, C., *The Subject of Tragedy: Identity and Difference in Renaissance Drama* (London, 1985).

Ben-Amos, I.K., *Adolescence and Youth in Early Modern England* (London and New Haven, 1994).

Bennett, H.S., *English Books and Readers 1603–1640* (Cambridge, 1970).

Berry, P., *Of Chastity and Power: Elizabethan Literature and the Unmarried Queen* (London, 1989).

Black, J.M., *The British Abroad: The Grand Tour in the Eighteenth Century* (Stroud, 1992).

Blamires, A., ed., *Woman Defamed and Woman Defended: An Anthology of Medieval Texts* (Oxford, 1992).

Bly, R., *Iron John: A Book about Men* (Shaftesbury, 1991).

Borsay, P., *The English Urban Renaissance: Culture and Society in the Provincial Town 1660–1770* (Oxford, 1989).

Boulton, J., *Neighbourhood and Society. A London Suburb in the Seventeenth Century* (Cambridge, 1987).

Bourdillon, H., *Women as Healers: A History of Women and Medicine* (Cambridge, 1988).

Braunmuller, A.R. and Hattaway, M., eds, *The Cambridge Companion to English Renaissance Drama* (Cambridge, 1990).

Bray, A., *Homosexuality in Renaissance England* (London, 1988).

Brinkworth, E.R., *Shakespeare and the Bawdy Court of Stratford* (Chichester, 1972).

Brown, P., *The Body and Sexuality: Men, Women and Sexual Renunciation in Early Christi-anity* (London, 1989).

Browne, A., *The Eighteenth Century Feminist Mind* (Brighton, 1987).

Burgess, G., *The Politics of the Ancient Constitution: An Introduction to English Political Thought 1603–1642* (London, 1992).

Bynum, C.W., *Jesus as Mother* (Berkeley, 1982).

Bynum, C.W., *Holy Feast and Holy Fast: The Religious Significance of Food to Medieval Women* (Berkeley, 1987).

Cahn, S., *Industry of Devotion: The Transformation of Women's Work in England 1560–1660* (Columbia, 1987).

Callaghan, D., *Women and Gender in Renaissance Tragedy* (London, 1989).

Cannon, J., *Aristocratic Century* (Cambridge, 1984).

Capp, B., *Astrology and the Popular Press: English Almanacs 1500–1800* (London, 1979).

Carr, R., *English Fox Hunting: A History* (London, 1976).

Chodorow, N., *The Reproduction of Mothering: Psychoanalysis and the Sociology of Gender* (Berkeley, 1978).

Clark, A., *Women's Silence, Men's Violence: Sexual Assault in England 1770–1845* (London, 1987).

Clark, A., *Working Life of Women in the Seventeenth Century* (London, 1992 edn).

Clark, J.C.D., *English Society 1688–1832* (Cambridge, 1985).

Clark, P., *The English Alehouse* (London, 1983).

Clay, C.G.A., *Economic Expansion and Social Change: England 1500–1700* (Cambridge, 1984).

Cliffe, J.T., *The Puritan Gentry* (London, 1984).

Cliffe, J.T., *Puritans in Conflict* (London, 1988).

Coleman, D.C., *The Economy of England 1450–1750* (Oxford, 1977).

Collinson, P., *The Religion of Protestants: The Church in English Society 1559–1625* (Oxford, 1982).

Collinson, P., *The Birthpangs of Protestant England: Religious and Cultural Change in the Sixteenth and Seventeenth Centuries* (London, 1988).

Coole, D.H., *Women in Political Theory: From Ancient Misogyny to Contemporary Feminism* (London, 1988).

Crawford, P., ed., *Exploring Women's Past* (London, 1983).

Crawford, P., *Women and Religion in England 1500–1720* (London, 1993).

Daly, J., *Sir Robert Filmer and English Political Thought* (Toronto, 1979).

Davidoff, L. and Hall, C., *Family Fortunes: Men and Women of the English Middle Class 1780–1850* (London, 1987).

Davis, N.Z., *Society and Culture in Early Modern France* (Stamford, 1975).

Davis, N.Z., *Fiction in the Archives: Pardon Tales and their Tellers in Sixteenth-Century France* (Cambridge, 1988).

Debus, A.G., *The English Paracelsians* (London, 1965).

Dollimore, J., *Sexual Dissidence: Augustine to Wilde, Freud to Foucault* (Oxford, 1991).

Donnison, J., *Midwives and Medical Men: A History of Inter-Professional Rivalries and Women's Rights* (London, 1977).

Dunlop, O.J. and Denman, R.D., *English Apprenticeship and Child Labour* (London, 1912).

Dunn, J., *The Political Thought of John Locke* (Cambridge, 1969).

Eales, J., *Puritans and Roundheads: The Harleys of Brampton Bryan and the Outbreak of the English Civil War* (Cambridge, 1990).

Earle, P., *The Making of the English Middle Class* (London, 1989).

Easlea, B., *Witch Hunting, Magic and the New Philosophy* (Brighton, 1980).

Eccles, A., *Obstetrics and Gynaecology in Tudor and Stuart England* (London, 1982).

Edwards, A.C., *English History from Essex Sources* (Chelmsford, 1952).

Erickson, A.L., *Women and Property in Early Modern England* (London, 1993).

Esdaile, K.A., *English Church Monuments 1560–1840* (London, 1946).

Everitt, A., *The Community of Kent and the Great Rebellion* (Leicester, 1965).

Ezell, M.J.M., *The Patriarch's Wife: Literary Evidence and the History of the Family* (Chapel Hill, 1987).

Figes, E., *Patriarchal Attitudes* (London, 1970).

Fletcher, A.J., *A County Community in Peace and War: Sussex 1600–1660* (London, 1975).

Fletcher, A.J., *Reform in the Provinces: The Government of Stuart England* (London, 1986).

Fletcher, A.J. and Roberts, P.R., eds, *Religion, Culture and Society in Early Modern Britain* (Cambridge, 1994).

Fletcher, A.J. and Stevenson, J., eds, *Order and Disorder in Early Modern England* (Cambridge, 1985).

Foster, S., *Notes from the Caroline Underground* (Connecticut, 1978).

Foucault, M., *A History of Sexuality*, vol. I, *An Introduction* (London, 1987).

Foucault, M., *The History of Sexuality*, vol, II, *The Use of Pleasure* (London, 1987).

Foxon, D., *Libertine Literature in England 1660–1745* (London, 1965).

Fraser, A., *The Weaker Vessel: Woman's Lot in Seventeenth-Century England* (London, 1985).

Gardiner, D., *English Girlhood at School* (London, 1929).

Gardiner, S.R., *History of the Commonwealth and Protectorate* (London, 1903).

Gibson, I., *The English Vice: Beating, Sex and Shame in Victorian England and After* (London, 1978).

Giddens, A., *The Transformation of Intimacy: Sexuality, Love and Eroticism in Modern Societies* (London, 1992).

Gillis, J.R., *For Better, For Worse: British Marriages 1600 to the Present* (Oxford, 1985).

Ginzburg, C., *The Cheese and the Worms* (London, 1980).

Girouard, M., *Life in the English Country House* (London, 1978).

Goldberg, P.J.P., *Women, Work and the Life Cycle in a Medieval Economy* (Oxford, 1992).

Graham, E., Hinds, H., Hoby, E. and Wilcox, H., eds, *Her Own Life: Autobiographical Writings by Seventeenth-Century Englishwomen* (London, 1989).

Greaves, R.L., *Society and Religion in Elizabethan England* (Minneapolis, 1981).

Greenblatt, S., *Shakespearian Negotiations: The Circulation of Social Energy in Renaissance England* (Berkeley, 1988).

Gurr, A., *Playgoing in Shakespeare's London* (Cambridge, 1987).

Haigh, C., *Elizabeth I* (London, 1988).

Hainsworth, D.R., *Stewards, Lords and People: The Estate Steward and his World in Late Stuart England* (Cambridge, 1992).

Hall, A., *The Revolution in Science* (London, 1983).

Hamilton, R., *The Liberation of Women: A Study of Patriarchy and Capitalism* (London, 1978).

Hassell Smith, A., *County and Court* (Oxford, 1974).

Heal, F., *Hospitality in Early Modern England* (Oxford, 1990).

Henderson, K.U. and McManus, B.F., eds, *Half Humankind: Contexts and Texts of the Controversy about Women in England 1540–1640* (Urbana, 1985).

Hey, D., *An English Rural Community: Myddle under the Tudors and Stuarts* (Leicester, 1974).

Hill, B., *Women, Work and Sexual Politics in Eighteenth-Century England* (Oxford, 1989).

Hill, C., *Society and Puritanism in Pre-Revolutionary England* (London, 1964).

Hoby, E., *Virtue of Necessity: English Women's Writings 1649–1688* (London, 1988).

Holmes, M., *Proud Northern Lady: Lady Anne Clifford 1590–1676* (Chichester, 1975).

Houlbrooke, R., ed., *English Family Life 1576–1716* (London, 1988).

Hudson, L. and Jacot, B., *The Way Men Think* (London, 1991).

Hull, S.W., *Chaste, Silent and Obedient: English Books for Women 1435–1640* (San Marino, 1982).

Hunter, J.P., *Before Novels: The Cultural Context of Eighteenth-Century Fiction* (London, 1990).

Hunter, M., *Science and Society in Restoration England* (Cambridge, 1981).

Ingram, M., *Church Courts, Sex and Marriage in England 1570–1640* (Cambridge, 1987).

Jacquart, D. and Thomasset, C., *Sexuality and Medicine in the Middle Ages* (London, 1985).

James, M., *English Politics and the Concept of Honour* (Past and Present Supplement, III, 1978).

Jardine, L., *Still Harping on Daughters: Women and Drama in the Age of Shakespeare* (London, 1983).

Jones, V., *Women in the Eighteenth Century: Constructions of Femininity* (London, 1990).

Jordanova, L., *Sexual Visions: Images of Gender in Science and Medicine between the Eighteenth and Twentieth Centuries* (Hemel Hempstead, 1989).

Keller, E.F., *Reflections on Gender and Science* (New Haven and London, 1985).

Kermode, J. and Walker, G. eds, *Women, Crime and the Courts in Early Modern England* (London, 1994).

Kiernan, V.G., *The Duel in European History: Honour and the Reign of Aristocracy* (Oxford, 1988).

Kishlansky, M.A., *Parliamentary Selection: Social and Political Choice in Early Modern England* (Cambridge, 1986).

Kuhn, T.S., *The Structure of Scientific Revolutions* (Chicago, 1962).

Kussmaul, A., *Servants in Husbandry in Early Modern England* (Cambridge, 1981).

Langford, P., *A Polite and Commercial People: England 1727–1783* (Oxford, 1989).

Laqueur, T., *Making Sex: Body and Gender from the Greeks to Freud* (Cambridge, Massachusetts, 1990).

Larner, C., *Enemies of God: The Witchhunt in Scotland* (Oxford, 1981).

Larner, C., *Witchcraft and Religion: The Politics of Popular Belief* (Oxford, 1984).

Lerner, G., *The Creation of Patriarchy* (Oxford, 1986).

Le Roy Ladurie, E., *Jasmin's Witch* (London, 1990).

Levack, B.P., *The Witch-Hunt in Early Modern Europe* (London, 1987).

Levine, D. and Wrightson, K., *The Making of an Industrial Society: Whickham 1560–1765* (Oxford, 1991).

Lloyd, G., *The Man of Reason: Male and Female in Western Philosophy* (London, 1984).

Loftis, J., *The Memoirs of Anne Lady Halkett and Ann Lady Fanshaw* (Oxford, 1979).

Lovejoy, A.O., *The Great Chain of Being* (Cambridge, Massachusetts, 1942).

McConica, J., ed., *The History of the University of Oxford III: The Collegiate University* (Oxford, 1986).

Macdonald, M., *Mystical Bedlam: Madness, Anxiety and Healing in Seventeenth Century England* (Cambridge, 1981).

Macdonald, M., ed., *Witchcraft and Hysteria in Elizabethan London* (London, 1991).

Macfarlane, A., *The Family Life of Ralph Josselin* (Cambridge, 1970).

Macfarlane, A., *The Origins of English Individualism: The Family, Property and Social Transition* (Oxford, 1978).

Macfarlane, A., *The Justice and the Mare's Ale* (Oxford, 1981).

Mack, P., *Visionary Women: Ecstatic Prophecy in Seventeenth Century England* (Berkeley, California, 1992).

McKendrick, N., Brewer, J. and Plumb, J.H., *The Birth of a Consumer Society* (London, 1983).

McKeon, M., *The Origins of the English Novel 1600–1740* (Baltimore, 1987).

Mackinnon, C.A., *Towards a Feminist Theory of the State* (Cambridge, 1989).

Maclean, I., *The Renaissance Notion of Woman: A Study in the Fortunes of Scholasticism and Medical Science in European Intellectual Life* (Cambridge, 1980).

McLuskie, K., *Renaissance Dramatists* (London, 1989).

Malcolmson, R.W., *Popular Recreations in English Society 1700–1850* (Cambridge, 1973).

Manning, R.B., *Hunters and Poachers: A Social and Cultural History of Unlawful Hunting in England* (Oxford, 1993).

Marius, R., *Thomas More* (London, 1985).

Mason, P., *The English Gentleman: The Rise and Fall of an Ideal* (London, 1982).

Mercer, E., *English Art 1553–1625* (Oxford, 1962).

Merchant, C., *The Death of Nature: Women, Ecology and the Scientific Revolution* (San Francisco, 1980).

Millet, K., *Sexual Politics* (London, 1977).

Minchinton, W.E., ed., *Wage Regulation in Pre-Industrial England* (Newton Abbot, 1972).

Morgan, J., *Godly Learning: Puritan Attitudes towards Reason, Learning and Education* (Cambridge, 1986).

Moscucci, O., *The Science of Woman: Gynaecology and Gender in England 1800–1929* (Cambridge, 1990).

Munsche, P.B., *Gentlemen and Poachers: The English Game Laws 1672–1831* (Cambridge, 1981).

Nagy, D.E., *Popular Medicine in Seventeenth-Century England* (Bowling Green, Ohio, 1988).

Nead, L., *Myths of Sexuality* (Oxford, 1988).

Norton, R., *Mother Clap's Molly House: The Gay Subculture in England 1700–1830* (London, 1992).

Oakley, A., *Subject Women* (Oxford, 1981).

O'Day, R., *Education and Society 1500–1800: The Social Foundations of Education in Early Modern Britain* (London, 1982).

Ollard, R., *An English Education: A Perspective of Eton* (London, 1982).

Ortner, S.B. and Whitehead, H., eds, *Sexual Meanings: The Cultural Construction of Gender and Sexuality* (Cambridge, 1981).

Otten, C.F., ed., *English Women's Voices 1540–1700* (Miami, 1992).

Partridge, E., *Shakespeare's Bawdy* (London, 1968).

Pateman, C., *The Sexual Contract* (Oxford, 1988).

Peck, L.L., *Court Patronage and Corruption in Early Stuart England* (London, 1990).

Pevsner, N., *Cumberland and Westmoreland* (London, 1967).

Phillips, R., *Untying the Knot: A Short History of Divorce* (Cambridge, 1991).

Phythian-Adams, C., *Desolation of a City: Coventry and the Urban Crisis of the Late Middle Ages* (Cambridge, 1979).

Pinchbeck, I., *Women Workers and the Industrial Revolution 1750–1850* (London, 1969).

Pointon, M., *Hanging the Head* (New Haven, 1993).

Pollock, L.A., *Forgotten Children: Parent–Child Relations from 1500 to 1900* (Cambridge, 1983).

Pollock, L.A., *A Lasting Relationship: Parents and their Children over Three Centuries* (London, 1987).

Pollock, L.A., *With Faith and Physic: The Life of a Tudor Gentlewoman Lady Grace Mildmay 1552–1620* (London, 1993).

Porter, R. and Hall, L., *The Facts of Life: The Creation of Sexual Knowledge in Britain* (London, 1995).

Powell, C.L., *English Domestic Relations, 1487–1653* (New York, 1917).

Prest, W.R., *The Inns of Court under Elizabeth I and the Early Stuarts 1590–1640* (London, 1972).

Quaife, G.R., *Wanton Wenches and Wayward Wives* (London, 1979).

Radford Reuther, R., *Sexism and God-talk* (Boston, Massachusetts, 1983).

Rappaport, S., *Worlds within Worlds: Structures of Life in Sixteenth-Century London* (Cambridge, 1989).

Rendall, J., *The Origins of Modern Feminism: Women in Britain, France and the United States, 1780–1860* (London, 1985).

Robson, K., *Some Aspects of Education in Cheshire in the Eighteenth Century* (Chetham Society, 1966).

Rogers, K., *The Troublesome Helpmate* (Seattle, 1966).

Roper, L., *The Holy Household: Women and Morals in Reformation Augsburg* (Oxford, 1989).

Roper, L., *Oedipus and the Devil: Witchcraft, Sexuality and Religion in Early Modern Europe* (London, 1994).

Roper, M. and Tosh, J., eds, *Manful Assertions: Masculinities in Britain since 1800* (London, 1991).

Rowland, B., ed., *Medieval Woman's Guide to Health: The First English Gynaecological Handbook* (Kent, Ohio, 1981).

Rule, J., *The Experience of Labour in Eighteenth-Century Industry* (London, 1981).

Rumbold, V., *Woman's Place in Pope's World* (Cambridge, 1989).

Schiebinger, L., *The Mind has no Sex?* (Cambridge, Massachusetts, 1989).

Schochet, G.J., *Patriarchalism in Political Thought* (London, 1975).

Schwarz, L.D., *London in the Age of Industrialisation: Entrepreneurs, Labour Force and Living Conditions 1700–1851* (Cambridge, 1992).

Seaver, P.S., *Wallington's World* (London, 1985).

Segal, L., *Is the Future Female? Troubled Thoughts on Contemporary Feminism* (London, 1987).

Segal, L., *Slow Motion: Changing Masculinities, Changing Men* (London, 1990).

Shahan, S., *Childhood in the Middle Ages* (London, 1990).

Shapiro, B.J., *Probability and Certainty in Seventeenth-Century England: A Study of the Relationships between Natural Science, Religion, History, Law and Literature* (Princeton, 1983).

Sharpe, J.A., *Defamation and Sexual Slander in Early Modern England: The Church Courts at York* (Borthwick Papers, St Anthony's Hall, no. 58, York, 1981).

Sharpe, J., *Early Modern England: A Social History 1550–1760* (London, 1987).

Shepherd, A., *Gender and Authority in Sixteenth-Century England* (Keele, 1994).

Shevelow, K., *Women and Print Culture: The Construction of Femininity in the Early Periodical* (London, 1989).

Shorter, E., *The Making of the Modern Family* (London, 1975).

Simmons, J., ed., *English County Historians* (Wakefield, 1978).

Slater, M., *Family Life in the Seventeenth Century: The Verneys of Claydon House* (London, 1984).

Smith, H.L., *Reason's Disciples* (Urbana, 1982).

Snell, K.D.M., *Annals of the Labouring Poor: Social Change and Agrarian England 1600–1900* (Cambridge, 1985).

Summerville, J.P., *Thomas Hobbes: Political Ideas in Historical Context* (London, 1992).

Spargo, J.W., *Juridical Folklore in England* (Durham, North Carolina, 1944).

Spencer, J., *The Rise of the Woman Novelist: from Aphra Behn to Jane Austen* (Oxford, 1987).

Spufford, M., *Contrasting Communities: English Villagers in the Sixteenth and Seventeenth Centuries* (Cambridge, 1974).

Spufford, M., *Small-Books and Pleasant Histories: Popular Fiction and its Readership in Seventeenth-Century England* (London, 1981).

Stephens, J.E., ed., *Aubrey on Education* (London, 1972).

Stoltenberg, J., *Refusing to be Man* (London, 1990).

Stone, L., *The Crisis of the Aristocracy* (Oxford, 1965).

Stone, L., ed., *The University in Society* (Princeton, 1975).

Stone, L., *The Family, Sex and Marriage in England 1500–1800* (London, 1977).

Stone, L., *Road to Divorce: England 1530–1989* (Oxford, 1990).

Stone, L., *Broken Lives: Separation and Divorce in England 1660–1857* (Oxford, 1993).

Strong, R., *Gloriana: Portraits of Queen Elizabeth I* (London, 1987).

Sulloway, A.G., *Jane Austen and the Province of Womanhood* (Philadelphia, 1989).

Thomas, K.V., *Religion and the Decline of Magic* (London, 1971).

Thomas, K.V., *Rule and Misrule in the Schools of Early Modern England* (University of Reading, 1976).

Thomas, K.V., *Man and the Natural World* (London, 1983).

Thompson, E.P., *Whigs and Hunters* (London, 1975).

Thompson, E.P., *Customs in Common* (London, 1991).

Tilley, M.P., *A Dictionary of Proverbs in England in the Sixteenth and Seventeenth Centuries* (Ann Arbor, 1950).

Tillyard, E.M.W., *The Elizabethan World Picture* (London, 1943).

Todd, M., *Christian Humanism and the Puritan Social Order* (Cambridge, 1987).

Tompson, R.S., *Classics or Charity? The Dilemma of the Eighteenth Century Grammar School* (Manchester, 1971).

Trumbach, R., *The Rise of the Egalitarian Family* (London, 1978).

Underdown, D.E., *Revel, Riot and Rebellion* (Oxford, 1985).

Underdown, D.E., *Fire Under Heaven: The Life of an English Town in the Seventeenth Century* (London, 1992).

Vale, M., *The Gentleman's Recreations: Accomplishments and Pastimes of the English Gentleman 1580–1630* (Cambridge, 1977).

Vincent, W.A.L., *The Grammar Schools: Their Continuing Tradition 1660–1714* (London, 1969).

Wagner, P., *Eros Revised: Erotica of the Enlightenment in England and America* (London, 1988).

Walker Bynum, C., Hassell, S., and Richman, P., eds, *Gender and Religion: On the Complexity of Symbols* (Boston, 1986).

Watson, F., *The English Grammar Schools to 1660* (London, 1968).

Watt, I., *The Rise of the Novel* (London, 1957).

Watt, T., *Cheap Print and Popular Piety 1550–1640* (Cambridge, 1991).

Webster, C., *From Paracelsus to Newton: Magic and the Making of Modern Science* (Cambridge, 1982).

Weeks, J., *Sexuality and its Discontents* (London, 1985).

Weiner, M.E., *Women and Gender in Early Modern Europe* (Cambridge, 1993).

Whitfield, C., ed., *Robert Dover and the Cotswold Games* (London, 1962).

Wilson, A., ed., *Rethinking Social History: English Society 1570–1920 and its Interpretation* (Manchester, 1993).

Wilson, D., *Signs and Portents: Monstrous Births from the Middle Ages to the Enlightenment* (London, 1993).

Wilson, J.H., *The Private Life of Mr Pepys* (London, 1959).

Woodbridge, L., *Women and the English Renaissance: Literature and the Nature of Womankind, 1540–1620* (Urbana, 1986).

Wrightson, K., *English Society 1580–1680* (London, 1982).

Wurzbach, N., *The Rise of the English Street Ballad 1550–1650* (Cambridge, 1990).

Yates, F.A., *Astraea: The Imperial Theme in the Sixteenth Century* (London, 1977).

Zohar, D., *The Quantum Self* (London, 1990).

Zohar, D. and Marshall, I., *The Quantum Society* (London, 1993).

ARTICLES

Andrew, D.T., 'The Code of Honour and its Critics: the Opposition to Duelling in England 1700–1850', *Social History* 5 (1980).

Ashton, M., 'Segregation in Church', in W.J. Sheils and D. Wood, eds, 'Women in the Church', *Studies in Church History* 27 (1990).

Atkinson, C. and J.B., 'Subordinating Women: Thomas Bentley's use of Biblical Women in "The Monument of Matrons" (1582)', *Church History* 60 (1991).

Barker, J., '"Stolen Goods": The Sexual Harrassment of Female Servants in West Wales during the Nineteenth Century', *Rural History: Economy, Society, Culture* 4 (1993).

Baron, C., 'The "Golden Age" of Women in Medieval London', in *Medieval Women in Southern England*, (Reading Medieval Studies, 15, 1989).

Bean, J.C., 'Comic Structure and the Humanising of Kate in *The Taming of the Shrew*', in C. Lenz, G. Greene, and C. Needy, eds, *The Woman's Part: Feminist Criticism of Shakespeare* (Urbana, 1980).

Beattie, J.M., 'The Criminality of Women in Eighteenth-Century England', *Journal of Social History* VIII (1974–5).

Belsey, A. and C., 'Icons of Divinity: Portraits of Elizabeth I', in L. Gent and N. Llewellyn, eds, *Renaissance Bodies: The Human Figure in English Culture c. 1540–1660* (London, 1990).

Belsey, C., 'Disrupting Sexual Difference: Meaning and Gender in the Comedies', in J. Drakakis, ed., *Alternative Shakespeares* (London, 1985).

Ben-Amos, I., 'Service and Coming of Age of Young Men in Seventeenth-Century England', *Continuity and Change* 3 (1988).

Bennett, J.M., 'Feminism and History', *Gender and History* 1 (1989).

Bennett, J.M., 'Misogyny, Popular Culture and Women's Work', *History Workshop Journal* 31 (1991).

Bennett, J.M., 'Conviviality and Charity in Medieval and Early Modern England', *Past and Present* 134 (1992).

Bennett, J.M., 'Medieval Women, Modern Women: Across the Great Divide', in D. Aers, ed., *Culture and History 1350–1600: Essays in English Communities, Identities and Writing* (London, 1992).

Black, J.M., 'Going up to Oxford: Charles Weston's Account in 1748', *Oxoniensia* LIV (1989).

Black, J.M., 'Anglo-Dutch Relations 1728–1732: The Chesterfield–Waldegrave Correspondence', *Nederlandse Historische Brounen* 10 (1992).

Bray, A., 'Homosexuality and the Signs of Male Friendship in Elizabethan England', *History Workshop Journal* 29 (1990).

Brooks, C.W., 'Apprenticeship', in J. Barry and C.W. Brooks, eds, *The Middling Sort* (London, 1984(a)).

Brooks, C.W., 'Professions, Ideology and the Middling Sort in the Late Sixteenth and Seventeenth Centuries', in J. Barry and C.W. Brooks, eds, *The Middling Sort* (London, 1984(b)).

Bryson, A., 'The Rhetoric of Status: Gesture, Demeanour and the Image of the Gentleman in Sixteenth and Seventeenth-Century England', in L. Gent and N. Llewellyn, eds, *Renaissance Bodies: The Human Figure in English Culture c. 1540–1660* (London, 1990).

Bullough, V.L., 'Medieval Medical Views of Woman', *Viator* 4 (1973).

Castle, T., 'Matters Not Fit to be Mentioned: Fielding's *The Female Husband*', *English Literary History*, 49 (1982).

Clark, A., 'Whores and Gossips: Sexual Reputation in London 1770–1825', in A. Angerman, ed., *Current Issues in Women's History* (London, 1989).

Clark, J.C.D., 'England's Ancien Regime as a Confessional Stage', *Albion* XXI (1989).

Cody, L., 'The Doctor's in Labour: or a New Whim Wham from Guildford', *Gender and History* 4 (1992).

Cohen, M., 'The Grand Tour: Constructing the English Gentleman in Eighteenth-Century France', *History of Education* 21 (1992).

Coleman, D.C., 'Labour in the English Economy of the Seventeenth Century' *Economic History Review* 8 (1955–6).

Collinson, P., '"A magazine of Religious Patterns": An Erasmian Topic Transposed in English Protestantism', in D. Baker ed., *Renaissance and Renewal in Christian History* (Oxford, 1977).

Crawford, P., 'Attitudes to Menstruation in Seventeenth-Century England', *Past and Present* 91 (1981)

Crawford, P., 'Katharine and Philip Henry and their Children: A Case Study in Family Ideology', *Transactions of the Historic Society of Lancashire and Cheshire* 134 (1984).

Crawford, P., 'The Sucking Child: Adult Attitudes to Child Care in the First Year of Life in Seventeenth-Century England', *Continuity and Change* 1 (1986).

Crawford, P., 'The Construction and Experience of Maternity in Seventeenth-Century England', in V. Fildes, ed., *Women as Mothers in Pre-Industrial England* (London, 1990).

Crawford, P., 'The Challenges to Patriarchism: How did the Revolution affect Women?', in J.S. Morrill, ed., *Revolution and Restoration: England in the 1650s* (London, 1992).

Cressy, D., 'Purification, Thanksgiving and the Churching of Women in Post-Reformation England', *Past and Present* 141 (1993).

Cust, R. and Lake, P.G., 'Sir Richard Grosvenor and the Rhetoric of Magistracy', *Bulletin of the Institute of Historical Research* LIV (1981).

Davies, K.M., 'Continuity and Change in Literary Advice on Marriage', in R.B. Outhwaithe, ed., *Marriage and Society* (London, 1981).

Davis, N.Z., 'What is Women's History?', in J. Gardiner, ed., *What is History Today?* (London, 1988).

D'Cruze, S., 'To Acquaint the Ladies: Women Traders in Colchester c. 1750–1800', *Local Historian* 17 (1986).

Dymond, D., 'A Lost Social Institution: The Camping Close', *Rural History: Economy, Society, Culture* I (1990).

Eales, J.S., 'Sir Robert Harley KB (1579–1656) and the "Character" of a Puritan', *British Library Journal* XV (1989).

Eales, J., 'Samuel Clarke and the "Lives" of Godly Women in Seventeenth Century England', in W. Sheils, ed., *Women in the Church* (Studies in Church History, 27, 1990).

Earle, P., 'The Female Labour Market in London in the Late Seventeenth and Early Eighteenth Centuries', *Economic History Review* 42 (1989).

Eaton, S., 'Beatrice-Joanna and the Rhetoric of Love', in D.S. Kastan and P. Stallybrass, eds, *Staging the Renaissance: Reinterpretations of Elizabethan and Jacobean Drama* (London, 1991).

Erickson, A.L., 'Common Law versus Common Practice: The Use of Marriage Settlements in Early Modern England', *Economic History Review* XLIII (1990).

Esdaile, K.A., 'The monument of the First Lord Rich at Felsted', *Essex Archaeological Society Transactions* XXII (1940).

Esdaile, K.A., 'The Gorges Monument in Salisbury Cathedral', *Wiltshire Archaeological Magazine* L (1942–4).

Ezell, M.J.M., 'John Locke's Images of Childhood', *Eighteenth Century Studies* 17 (1983–4).

Fisell, M.E., 'Readers, Texts and Contexts: Vernacular Medical Works in Early Modern England', in R. Porter, ed., *The Popularisation of Medicine 1650–1850* (London, 1992).

Fisher, F.J., 'The Development of London as a Centre for Conspicuous Consumption in the Sixteenth and Seventeenth Centuries', *TRHS*, XXX (1948).

Fletcher, A.J., 'The Expansion of Education in Berkshire and Oxfordshire 1500–1700', *British Journal of Educational Studies* XV (1967).

Fletcher, A.J., 'Honour, Reputation and Local Officeholding in Elizabethan and Stuart England', in A.J. Fletcher and J. Stevenson, eds, *Order and Disorder in Early Modern England* (Cambridge, 1985).

Fletcher, A.J., 'Men's Dilemma: The Future of Patriarchy in England 1560–1660', *TRHS* IV (1994).

Fletcher, A.J., 'The Protestant Idea of Marriage in Early Modern England', in A.J. Fletcher and P.R. Roberts, eds, *Religion, Culture and Society in Early Modern Britain* (Cambridge, 1994).

Fletcher, A.J., 'Prescription and Practice: Protestantism and the Upbringing of Children 1560–1700', in D. Wood, ed., *The Church and Childhood* (Studies in Church History, XXXI, Oxford, 1994).

Forster, G.C.F., 'Faction and County Government in Stuart Yorkshire', *Northern History* XI (1975).

Foyster, E.A., 'A Laughing Matter? Marital Discord and Gender Control in Seventeenth-Century England', *Rural History: Economy, Society, Culture*, vol. 4, no. 1 (1993).

Garber, M., 'The Logic of the Transvestite', in D.S. Kastan and P. Stallybrass, eds, *Staging the Renaissance: Reinterpretations of Elizabethan and Jacobean Drama* (London, 1991).

Gaskill, M., 'Witchcraft and Power in Early Modern England: the Case of Margaret Moore', in J. Kermode and G. Walker, eds, *Women, Crime and the Courts in Early Modern England* (London, 1994).

Goreau, A., 'Two English Women in the Seventeenth Century: Notes for an Anatomy of Feminine Desire', in P. Aries and A. Bejin, eds, *Western Sexuality* (Oxford, 1985).

Gowing, L., 'Gender and the Language of Insult in Early Modern London', *History Workshop Journal* 35 (1993).

Gowing, L., 'Language, Power and the Law: Women's Slander Litigation in Early Modern London', in J. Kermode and G. Walker, eds, *Women, Crime and the Courts in Early Modern England* (London, 1994).

Hanawalt, B.A., 'Peasant Women's Contribution to the Home Economy in Late Medieval England', in B.A. Hanawalt, ed., *Women and Work in Pre-Industrial Europe* (Bloomington, Indiana, 1986).

Harris, B.J., 'Property, Power and Personal Relations: Elite Mothers and Sons in Yorkist and Early Tudor England', *Signs* XV (1990).

Hassell Smith, A., 'Labourers in Late Sixteenth-Century England: A Case Study from North Norfolk', *Continuity and Change* 4 (1989).

Hattaway, M., 'Fleshing his Will in the Spoil of her Honour: Desire, Misogyny and the Perils of Chivalry', *Shakespeare Survey* (1993).

Heal, F., 'The Crown, the Gentry and London: The Enforcement of Proclamation 1596–1640', in C. Cross, D. Loades and J.J. Scarisbrick, eds, *Law and Government under the Tudors* (Cambridge, 1988).

Hodgkin, K., 'The Diary of Lady Anne Clifford: A Study of Class and Gender in the Seventeenth Century', *History Workshop Journal* 19 (1985).

Hodgkin, K., 'Thomas Whythorne and the Problems of Mastery', *History Workshop Journal* 29 (1990).

Holmes, C., 'Women: Witnesses and Witches', *Past and Present* 140 (1993).

Houlbrooke, R.A., 'Women's Social Life and Common Action in England from the Fifteenth Century to the Eve of the Civil War', *Continuity and Change* 1 (1986).

Howard, J.E., 'Crossdressing, the Theatre and Gender Struggle in Early Modern England', *Shakespeare Quarterly* 39 (1988).

Hufton, O., 'Women in History: Early Modern Europe', *Past and Present* 101 (1983).

Hunt, M., 'Wife Beating, Domesticity and Women's Independence in Eighteenth-Century London', *Gender and History* 4 (1992).

Ingram, M., 'Ridings, Rough Music and "the Reform of Popular Culture" in Early Modern England', *Past and Present* 105 (1984).

Ingram, M., 'Ridings, Rough Music and Mocking Rhymes in Early Modern England', in B. Reay, ed., *Popular Culture in Seventeenth-Century England* (London, 1985).

Ingram, M., '"Scolding Women Cucked or Washed": A Crisis of Gender Relations in Early Modern England', in J. Kermode and G. Walker, eds, *Women, Crime and the Courts in Early Modern England* (London, 1994).

Jardine, L., '"Why should he call her whore?": Defamation and Desdemona's Case', in M. Tudeau-Clayton and M. Warner, eds, *Addressing Frank Kermode* (Urbana, 1991).

Jardine, L., 'Twins and Tranvestites: Gender, Dependency and Sexual Availability in *Twelfth Night*', in S. Zimmerman, ed., *Erotic Politics: Desire on the Renaissance Stage* (London, 1992).

Jardine, L. and Grafton, A., '"Studied for Action": How Gabriel Harvey read his Livy', *Past and Present* 129 (1990).

Jones, A.R. and Stallybrass, P., 'Fetishizing Gender: Constructing the Hermaphrodite in Renaissance Europe', in J. Epstein and K. Straub, eds, *Bodyguards: The Cultural Politics of Gender Ambiguity* (London, 1991).

Kent, F., 'Folk Justice and Royal Justice in Early Seventeenth-Century England: a Charivari in the Midlands', *Midland History* VIII (1983).

Kent, J.R., 'Attitudes of Members of the House of Commons to the Regulation of Personal Conduct in Late Elizabethan and Early Stuart England', *BIHR* XLV (1972).

Kinnaird, J.K., 'Mary Astell and the Conservative Contribution to English Feminism',

Journal of British Studies 19 (1979).

Lacey, K.E., 'Women and Work in Fourteenth and Fifteenth Century London', in L. Charles and L. Duffin, eds, *Women and Work in Pre-Industrial Europe* (London, 1985).

Lake, P., 'Feminine Piety and Personal Potency: the Emancipation of Mrs Jane Ratcliffe', *The Seventeenth Century* II (1987).

Lamb, M.E., 'The Agency of the Split Subject: Lady Anne Clifford and the Uses of Reading', *English Literary Renaissance* 22 (1992).

Larminie, V., 'The Undergraduate Account Book of John and Richard Newdigate', *Camden Miscellany* XXX (Camden Society, 39, 1990).

Laurence, A., 'Women's Psychological Disorders in Seventeenth-Century Britain', in A. Angerman, ed., *Current Issues in Women's History* (London, 1989).

Lewis, P.M., 'Mummy, Matron and the Maids: Feminine Presence and Absence in Male Institutions 1934–63', in M. Roper and J. Tosh, eds, *Manful Assertions: Masculinities in Britain since 1800* (London, 1991).

Lilley, K. 'True State Within: Women's Elegy 1640–1700', in I. Grundy and S. Wiseman, eds, *Women, Writing, History 1640–1740* (London, 1992).

Llewellyn, N., 'Claims to Status through Visual Coles: Heraldry in post-Reformation Funeral Monuments', in S. Anglo, ed., *Chivalry in the Renaissance* (London, 1990).

Looney, J., 'Undergraduate Education at Early Stuart Cambridge', *History of Education* 10 (1981).

Loudon, I., 'The Disease called Chlorosis', *Psychological Medicine* 14 (1984).

Loux, F., 'Popular Culture and Knowledge of the Body: Infancy and the Medical Anthropologist', in R. Porter and A. Wear, eds, *Problems and Methods in the History of Medicine* (London, 1987).

Macdonald, M., 'Madness, Suicide and the Computer', in R. Porter and A. Wear, eds, *Problems and Methods in the History of Medicine* (London, 1987).

Mack, P., 'Women as Prophets during the English Civil War', *Feminist Studies* 8 (1982).

McLaren, D., 'Marital Fertility and Lactation 1570–1720', in M. Prior, ed., *Women in English Society* (London, 1985).

McLuskie, K., 'The Patriarchal Bard: Feminist Criticism and Shakespeare: *King Lear* and *Measure for Measure*', in J. Dollimore and A. Sinfield, eds, *Political Shakespeare* (Manchester, 1985).

McMullen, N., 'The Education of English Gentlewomen 1540–1640', *History of Education* 6 (1977).

McPelling, 'Child Health as a Social Value in Early Modern England', *Journal of the Society for the Social History of Medicine* (1988).

Markland, H., 'Instructions by Henry Percy touching the Management of his Estate', *Archaeologia* 27 (1838).

Meldrum, T., 'A Women's Court in London: Defamation at the Bishop of London's Consistory Court, 1700–1745', *London Journal* 19 (1994).

Mendelson, S.H., 'Stuart Women's Diaries and Occasional Memoirs', in M. Prior, ed., *Women in English Society 1500–1800* (London, 1985).

Michel, R.H., 'English Attitudes towards Women 1640–1700', *Canadian Journal of History* 8 (1978).

Middleton, C., 'Women's Labour and the Transition to Pre-Industrial Capitalism', in L. Charles and L. Duffin, eds, *Women and Work in Pre-Industrial Europe* (London, 1985).

Morgan, V.H.M., 'Cambridge University and "The Country" 1560–1640', in L. Stone, ed., *The University in Society* (Princeton, 1975).

Nadelhaft, J., 'The Englishwoman's Sexual Civil War: Feminist Attitudes towards Men, Women and Marriage 1650–1740', *Journal of the History of Ideas* 43 (1982).

Okin, S.M., 'Women and the Making of the Sentimental Family', *Philosophy and Public Affairs* 11 (1982).

Orgel, S., 'The Subtexts of *The Roaring Girl*', in S. Zimmerman, ed., *Erotic Politics: Desire on the Renaissance Stage* (London, 1992).

Phythian-Adams, C., 'Ceremony and the Citizen: The Communal Year at Coventry 1450–1550', in P. Clark and P. Slack, eds, *Crisis and Order in English Towns 1500–1700* (London, 1972).

Phythian-Adams, C., 'Rural Culture', in G.E., Mingay, ed., *The Victorian Countryside* (London, 1981).

Phythian-Adams, C., 'Milk and Soot: The Changing Vocabulary of a Popular Ritual in Stuart and Hanoverian London', in D. Fraser and A. Sutcliffe, eds, *The Pursuit of Urban History* (London, 1983).

Pollock, L.A., 'Teach her to Live under Obedience: The Making of Women in the Upper Ranks of Early Modern England', *Continuity and Change* 4 (1989).

Pollock, L.A., 'Embarking on a Rough Passage: The Experience of Pregnancy in Early Modern Society', in V. Fildes, ed., *Women as Mothers in Pre-Industrial England* (London, 1990).

Pollock, L.A., 'Living on the Stage of the World: The Concept of Privacy among the Elite of Early Modern England', in A. Wilson, ed., *Rethinking Social History: English Society 1570–1920 and its Interpretation* (Manchester, 1993).

Porter, R., 'Mixed Feelings: the Enlightenment and Sexuality in Eighteenth-Century Britain', in P.G. Bouce', ed., *Sexuality in Eighteenth Century Britain* (Manchester, 1982).

Porter, R., '"The Secrets of Generation Display'd": *Aristotle's* Masterpiece in Eighteenth Century England', in R.P. Maccubbin, ed. *'Tis Nature's Fault: Unauthorised Sexuality during the Enlightenment* (Cambridge, 1987).

Prest, W.R., 'Law and Women's Rights in Early Modern England', *The Seventeenth Century* VI (1991).

Prior, M., 'Women and the Urban Economy: Oxford 1500–1800', in M. Prior, ed., *Women in English Society 1500–1800* (London, 1985).

Prior, M., 'Conjugal Love and the Flight from Marriage: Poetry as a Source for the History of Women and the Family', in V. Fildes, ed., *Women as Mothers in Pre-Industrial England* (London, 1990).

Purkiss, D., 'Material Girls: The Seventeenth-century Woman Debate', in C. Brant and D. Purkiss, eds, *Women, Texts and Histories 1575–1760* (London, 1992).

Quilligan, M., 'Staging Gender: William Shakespeare and Elizabeth Cary', in J.G. Turner, ed., *Sexuality and Gender in Early Modern Europe: Institutions, Texts, Images* (Cambridge, 1993).

Radford Reuther, R., 'The Liberation of Christology from Patriarchy', in A. Loades, ed., *Feminist Theology: A Reader* (London, 1990).

Roberts, M., 'Sickles and Scythes: Women's Work and Men's Work at Harvest Time', *History Workshop Journal* 7 (1979).

Roberts, M., 'Words they are Women and Deeds they are Men: Images of Work and Gender in Early Modern England', in L. Charles and L. Duffin, eds, *Women and Work in Pre-Industrial England* (London, 1985).

Roberts, M., 'Women and Work in Sixteenth-century English Towns', in P.J. Corfield and D. Keene, eds, *Work in Towns 850–1850* (Leicester, 1990).

Roper, L., '"Going to Church and Street": Weddings in Reformation Augsburg', *Past and Present* 106 (1985).

Rushton, P., 'Women, Witchcraft and Slander in Early Modern England: Cases from the Church Courts of Durham 1560–1675', *Northern History* 18 (1982).

Rushton, P., 'Property, Power and Family Networks in the Problem of Disputed Marriages in Early Modern England', *Journal of Family History* 11 (1986).

Russell, C.S.R., 'Divine Rights in the Early Seventeenth Century', in J.S. Morrill, P. Slack and D. Woolf, eds, *Public Duty and Private Conscience in the Senventeenth Century* (Oxford, 1993).

Scott, J., 'Gender: A Useful Category of Historical Analysis', *American Historical Review* 91 (1980).

Seaver, P.J., 'Declining Status in an Aspiring Age: The Problems of the Gentle Apprentice in Seventeenth-Century London', in B.Y. Kunze and D.D. Brautigam, eds, *Court, Country and Culture* (Rochester, New York, 1992).

Shammas, C., 'The World Women Knew: Women Workers in the North of England during the Late Seventeenth Century', in R.S. Dunn and M.M. Dunn, eds, *The World of William Penn* (Philadelphia, 1986).

Shapiro, S.C., 'Feminists in Elizabethan England', *History Today* (1977).

Sharpe, J.A., 'Domestic Homicide in Early Modern England', *Historical Journal* 24 (1981).

Sharpe, J.A., 'Witchcraft and Women in Seventeenth-century England: Some Northern Evidence', *Continuity and Change* 6 (1991).

Sharpe, J.A., 'Women, Witchcraft and the Legal Process', in J. Kermode and G. Walker, eds, *Women, Crime and the Courts in Early Modern England* (London, 1994).

Shepherd, A., 'Henry Howard and the Lawful Regiment of Women', *History of Political Thought* XII (1991).

Slack, P., 'Mirrors of Health and Treasures of Poor Men: The Uses of the Vernacular Medical Literature of Tudor England', in C. Webster, ed., *Health Medicine and Mortality in the Sixteenth Century* (Cambridge, 1979).

Slater, M., 'The Weightiest Business: Marriage in an Upper-Class Gentry Family in Seventeenth-Century England', *Past and Present* 72 (1976).

Smith, H., 'Gynaecology and Ideology in Seventeenth-Century England', in B.A. Carroll, ed., *Liberating Women's History* (Urbana, 1976).

Smith, H.L., '"All Men and Both Sexes": Concepts of Men's Development, Women's Education and Feminism in the Seventeenth Century', in D.C. Mall, ed., *Man, God and Nature in the Enlightenment* (London, 1989).

Smith, S.R., 'The London Apprentices as Seventeenth-Century Adolescents', *Past and Present* 61 (1973).

Snell, K.D.M., 'Agricultural Seasonal Unemployment, the Standard of Living, and Women's Work in the South and East 1690–1860', *Economic History Review* 34 (1981).

Snucker, R.V., 'Puritan Attitudes towards Childhood Discipline 1560–1634', in V. Fildes, ed., *Women as Mothers in Pre-Industrial England* (London, 1990).

Spacks, P., 'Every Woman is at Heart a Rake', *Eighteenth Century Studies* VIII (1974–5).

Stallybrass, P., 'Patriarchal Territories: the Body Enclosed', in M.W. Ferguson, M. Quilligan and N.J. Vickers, eds, *Rewriting the Renaissance* (Chicago, 1986).

Stone, L., 'The Verney Tomb at Middle Claydon' *Records of Bucks* XVI (1948).

Stretton, T., 'Women, History and Equity in the Court of Requests', in J. Kermode and G. Walker, eds, *Women, Crime and the Courts in Early Modern England* (London, 1994).

Thomas, K.V., 'The Double Standard', *Journal of the History of Ideas* XX (1959).

Thomas, K.V., 'Age and Authority in Early Modern England', *Proceedings of the British Academy* LXII (1976).

Thompson, E.P., 'Patrician Society, Plebeian Culture', *Journal of Social History* VII (1974).

Thompson, E.P., 'Eighteenth-Century English Society: Class Struggle without Class?', *Social History* III (1978).

Thwaites, W., 'Women in the Market Place: Oxfordshire c. 1690–1800', *Midland History* IX (1984).

Tosh, J., 'What Should Historians do with Masculinity?', *History Workshop Journal* 33 (1994).

Trumbach, R., 'London's Sapphists: From Three Sexes to Four Genders in the Making of Modern Culture', in J. Epstein and K. Straub, eds, *Bodyguards: The Cultural Politics of Gender Ambiguity* (London, 1991).

Underdown, D.E., 'The Taming of the Scold: The Enforcement of Partriarchal Authority in Early Modern England', in A.J. Fletcher and A. Stevenson, eds, *Order and Disorder in Early Modern England* (Cambridge, 1985).

Valenze, D., 'The Art of Women and the Business of Men: Women's Work and the Dairy Industry c. 1740–1840', *Past and Present* 130 (1991).

Vickery, A., 'Women and the World of Goods: A Lancashire Consumer and her Possessions 1751–81', in J. Brewer and R. Porter, eds, *Consumption and the World of Goods* (London, 1993).

Walker, G., 'Women, Theft and the World of Stolen Goods', in J. Kermode and G. Walker, eds, *Women, Crime and the Courts in Early Modern England* (London, 1994).

Walker, J., 'Grain Riots and Popular Attitudes to the Law: Maldon and the Crisis of 1629', in J. Brewer and J. Styles, eds, *An Ungovernable People* (London, 1980).

Wall, A.D., 'Elizabethan Precept and Feminine Practice: The Thynne Family of Longleat', *History* LXXV (1990).

Wallbank, M.V., 'Eighteenth-century Public Schools and the Education of the Governing Elite', *History of Education* 8 (1979).

Walters, J., '"No More than a Boy": The Shifting Construction of Masculinity from Ancient Greece to the Middle Ages', *Gender and History* 5 (1993).

Wear, A., 'The Popularisation of Medicine in Early Modern England', in R. Porter, ed., *The Popularisation of Medicine 1650–1850* (London, 1992).

Weiner, C.Z., 'Sex Roles and Crime in Late Elizabethan Hertfordshire', *Journal of Social History* VIII (1974–5).

Wilson, A., 'Participant or Patient? Seventeenth Century Childbirth from the Mother's Point of View', in R. Porter, ed., *Patients or Practitioners: Lay Perceptions of Medicine in Pre-Industrial Society* (Cambridge, 1985).

Wilson, A., 'The Ceremony of Childbirth and its Interpretation', in V. Fildes, ed., *Women as Mothers in Pre-Industrial England* (London, 1990).

Wright, S., '"Churmaids, Huswyfes and Hucksters": The Employment of Women in Tudor and Stuart Salisbury', in L. Charles and L. Duffin, eds, *Women and Work in Pre-Industrial England* (London, 1985).

Wrightson, K., 'Infanticide in Earlier Seventeenth Century England', *Local Population Studies*, 15 (1975).

Wrightson, K., 'The Social Order of Early Modern England: Three Approaches', in C. Bonfield, R.M. Smith, and K. Wrightson, eds, *The World We Have Gained* (Oxford, 1986).

Wrightson, K., 'Death in Whickham', in J. Walter and R.S. Schofield, eds, *Famine, Disease and Social Order in Early Modern England* (Cambridge, 1989).

Wrightson, K., 'Estates, Degrees and Sorts: Changing Perceptions of Society in Tudor and Stuart England', in P.J. Corfield, ed., *Language, History and Class* (Oxford, 1991).

Wyman, A.L., 'The Surgeoness: The Female Practitioner of Surgery 1400–1800', *Medical History* 28 (1984).

THESES

Adams, S., 'Some Observations of the Religious Life of Family Members within the Seventeenth-Century Protestant Household' (BA dissertation, Durham University, 1992).

Chaytor, S., 'Family Life in the Seventeenth Century: Sir William Chaytor 1639–1721' (MA dissertation, Durham University, 1992).

Childs, F.A., 'Prescriptions for Manners in English Courtesy Literature 1690–1760 and their Social Implications' (DPhil thesis, Oxford University, 1984).

Chynoweth, J., 'The Gentry of Tudor Cornwall' (PhD thesis, Exeter University, 1994).

Duffin, A., 'The Political Allegiance of the Cornish Gentry c. 1600–c. 1642' (PhD thesis, Exeter University, 1989).

Fielding, A.J., 'Conformists, Puritans and Church Courts: The Diocese of Peterborough 1603–1642' (PhD thesis, Birmingham University, 1989).

Gibbons, B., 'Gender in the British Behmenist Thought' (PhD thesis, Durham University, 1993).

Gowing, L., 'Women, Sex and Honour: The London Church Courts 1572–1640' (PhD thesis, London University, 1993).

Kugler, A., 'Prescription, Culture and Shaping Identity: Lady Sarah Cowper 1644–1720' (PhD thesis, University of Michigan, 1994).

McClendon, M., 'The Quiet Reformation: Norwich Magistrates and the Coming of Protestantism' (PhD thesis, Stanford University, 1990).

Maltby, J., 'Approaches to the Study of Religious Conformity in Late Elizabethan and Early Stuart England' (PhD thesis, Cambridge University, 1991).

Sawyer, R.W., 'Patients, Healers and Disease in the South-east Midlands 1597–1634' (PhD thesis, University of Wisconsin, Madison, 1986).

Stretton, T., 'Women and Litigation in the Elizabethan Court of Requests' (PhD thesis, Cambridge University, 1993).

Turner, D., 'Rakes, Libertines and Sexual Honour in Restoration England 1660–1700' (MA thesis, Durham University, 1994).

Wheeler, P., 'The Significance of Social and Religious Change in the Development of Funerary Monument Sculpture: Hampshire Parish Churches 1500–1800' (BA dissertation, Durham University, 1991).

Wolfe, M., 'The County Government of Devon 1625–1640' (PhD thesis, Exeter University, 1993).

Index